A Non-Random Walk Down Wall Street

A Non-Random Walk Down Wall Street

Andrew W. Lo

A. Craig MacKinlay

Princeton University Press
Princeton, New Jersey

Copyright © 1999 by Princeton University Press
Published by Princeton University Press, 41 William Street,
Princeton, New Jersey 08540
In the United Kingdom: Princeton University Press, Chichester,
West Sussex

Library of Congress Cataloging-in-Publication Data

Lo, Andrew W. (Andrew Wen-Chuan)
    A non-random walk down Wall Street / Andrew W. Lo and
A. Craig MacKinlay.
        p.   cm.
    Includes bibliographical references and index.
    ISBN 0-691-05774-5 (alk. paper)
    1. Stocks—Prices—Mathematical models. 2. Random walks
    (Mathematics)   I. MacKinlay, Archie Craig, 1955– .   II. Title.
HG4915.L6   1999
332.63'222—dc21   98–31390
                                                                              CIP

This book was composed in ITC New Baskerville with LaTeX by Archetype Publishing Inc.,
15 Turtle Pointe Road, Monticello, IL 61856

The paper used in this publication meets
the minimum requirements of
ANSI/NISO Z39.48-1992 (R1997)
(*Permanence of Paper*)

http://pup.princeton.edu

Printed in the United States of America

10 9 8 7 6 5 4 3 2 1

To my mother
AWL

To my parents
ACM

Contents

List of Figures   xiii

List of Tables   xv

Preface   xxi

1   Introduction   **3**
- 1.1   The Random Walk and Efficient Markets   4
- 1.2   The Current State of Efficient Markets   6
- 1.3   Practical Implications   8

Part I   **13**

2   Stock Market Prices Do Not Follow Random Walks: Evidence from a Simple Specification Test   **17**
- 2.1   The Specification Test   19
  - 2.1.1   Homoskedastic Increments   20
  - 2.1.2   Heteroskedastic Increments   24
- 2.2   The Random Walk Hypothesis for Weekly Returns   26
  - 2.2.1   Results for Market Indexes   27
  - 2.2.2   Results for Size-Based Portfolios   30
  - 2.2.3   Results for Individual Securities   32
- 2.3   Spurious Autocorrelation Induced by Nontrading   34
- 2.4   The Mean-Reverting Alternative to the Random Walk . . .   38
- 2.5   Conclusion   39

Appendix A2: Proof of Theorems   41

3 **The Size and Power of the Variance Ratio Test in Finite Samples:**
   A Monte Carlo Investigation   **47**
   3.1 Introduction   47
   3.2 The Variance Ratio Test   49
        3.2.1 The IID Gaussian Null Hypothesis   49
        3.2.2 The Heteroskedastic Null Hypothesis   52
        3.2.3 Variance Ratios and Autocorrelations   54
   3.3 Properties of the Test Statistic under the Null Hypotheses .   55
        3.3.1 The Gaussian IID Null Hypothesis   55
        3.3.2 A Heteroskedastic Null Hypothesis   61
   3.4 Power   68
        3.4.1 The Variance Ratio Test for Large q   69
        3.4.2 Power against a Stationary AR(1) Alternative   70
        3.4.3 Two Unit Root Alternatives to the Random Walk . .   73
   3.5 Conclusion   81

4 **An Econometric Analysis of Nonsynchronous Trading**   **85**
   4.1 Introduction   85
   4.2 A Model of Nonsynchronous Trading   88
        4.2.1 Implications for Individual Returns   90
        4.2.2 Implications for Portfolio Returns   93
   4.3 Time Aggregation   95
   4.4 An Empirical Analysis of Nontrading   99
        4.4.1 Daily Nontrading Probabilities Implicit in Auto-
               correlations 101
        4.4.2 Nontrading and Index Autocorrelations 104
   4.5 Extensions and Generalizations 105

   Appendix A4: Proof of Propositions   108

5 **When Are Contrarian Profits Due to Stock Market Overreaction?** **115**
   5.1 Introduction 115
   5.2 A Summary of Recent Findings 118
   5.3 Analysis of Contrarian Profitability 121
        5.3.1 The Independently and Identically Distributed Bench-
               mark 124
        5.3.2 Stock Market Overreaction and Fads 124
        5.3.3 Trading on White Noise and Lead–Lag Relations . 126
        5.3.4 Lead–Lag Effects and Nonsynchronous Trading . . 127
        5.3.5 A Positively Dependent Common Factor and the
               Bid–Ask Spread 130
   5.4 An Empirical Appraisal of Overreaction 132

5.5   Long Horizons Versus Short Horizons 140
5.6   Conclusion 142

Appendix A5   143

6 Long-Term Memory in Stock Market Prices   147
6.1   Introduction 147
6.2   Long-Range Versus Short-Range Dependence 149
      6.2.1 The Null Hypothesis 149
      6.2.2 Long-Range Dependent Alternatives 152
6.3   The Rescaled Range Statistic 155
      6.3.1 The Modified R/S Statistic 158
      6.3.2 The Asymptotic Distribution of Q_n 160
      6.3.3 The Relation Between Q_n and $\tilde{Q}_n$ 161
      6.3.4 The Behavior of Q_n Under Long Memory
            Alternatives 163
6.4 R/S Analysis for Stock Market Returns 165
      6.4.1 The Evidence for Weekly and Monthly Returns . . . 166
6.5   Size and Power 171
      6.5.1 The Size of the R/S Test 171
      6.5.2 Power Against Fractionally-Differenced Alternatives 174
6.6   Conclusion 179

Appendix A6: Proof of Theorems   181

Part II   185

7 Multifactor Models Do Not Explain Deviations from the CAPM   189
7.1   Introduction 189
7.2   Linear Pricing Models, Mean-Variance Analysis,
      and the Optimal Orthogonal Portfolio 192
7.3   Squared Sharpe Measures 195
7.4   Implications for Risk-Based Versus Nonrisk-Based
      Alternatives 196
      7.4.1 Zero Intercept F-Test 197
      7.4.2 Testing Approach 198
      7.4.3 Estimation Approach 206
7.5   Asymptotic Arbitrage in Finite Economies 208
7.6   Conclusion 212

8 Data-Snooping Biases in Tests of Financial Asset Pricing Models 213
8.1   Quantifying Data-Snooping Biases With Induced Order
      Statistics 215
      8.1.1 Asymptotic Properties of Induced Order Statistics . 216
      8.1.2 Biases of Tests Based on Individual Securities 219

		8.1.3	Biases of Tests Based on Portfolios of Securities	. .	224
		8.1.4	Interpreting Data-Snooping Bias as Power	. . . . .	228
	8.2	Monte Carlo Results			230
		8.2.1	Simulation Results for $\tilde{\theta}_p$		231
		8.2.2	Effects of Induced Ordering on F-Tests		231
		8.2.3	F-Tests With Cross-Sectional Dependence		236
	8.3	Two Empirical Examples			238
		8.3.1	Sorting By Beta		238
		8.3.2	Sorting By Size		240
	8.4	How the Data Get Snooped			243
	8.5	Conclusion			246

9 Maximizing Predictability in the Stock and Bond Markets — **249**

	9.1	Introduction			249
	9.2	Motivation			252
		9.2.1	Predicting Factors vs. Predicting Returns		252
		9.2.2	Numerical Illustration		254
		9.2.3	Empirical Illustration		256
	9.3	Maximizing Predictability			257
		9.3.1	Maximally Predictable Portfolio		258
		9.3.2	Example: One-Factor Model		259
	9.4	An Empirical Implementation			260
		9.4.1	The Conditional Factors		261
		9.4.2	Estimating the Conditional-Factor Model		262
		9.4.3	Maximizing Predictability		269
		9.4.4	The Maximally Predictable Portfolios		271
	9.5	Statistical Inference for the Maximal R^2			273
		9.5.1	Monte Carlo Analysis		273
	9.6	Three Out-of-Sample Measures of Predictability			276
		9.6.1	Naive vs. Conditional Forecasts		276
		9.6.2	Merton's Measure of Market Timing		279
		9.6.3	The Profitability of Predictability		281
	9.7	Conclusion			283

Part III — **285**

10 An Ordered Probit Analysis of Transaction Stock Prices — **287**

	10.1	Introduction			287
	10.2	The Ordered Probit Model			290
		10.2.1 Other Models of Discreteness			294
		10.2.2 The Likelihood Function			294
	10.3	The Data			295
		10.3.1 Sample Statistics			297
	10.4	The Empirical Specification			307

10.5 The Maximum Likelihood Estimates 310
    10.5.1 Diagnostics 316
    10.5.2 Endogeneity of Δt_k and IBS_k 318
10.6 Applications 320
    10.6.1 Order-Flow Dependence 321
    10.6.2 Measuring Price Impact Per Unit Volume of Trade . 322
    10.6.3 Does Discreteness Matter? 331
10.7 A Larger Sample 338
10.8 Conclusion 344

11 Index-Futures Arbitrage and the Behavior of Stock Index Futures Prices   **347**
11.1 Arbitrage Strategies and the Behavior of Stock Index Futures Prices 348
    11.1.1 Forward Contracts on Stock Indexes (No Transaction Costs) 349
    11.1.2 The Impact of Transaction Costs 350
11.2 Empirical Evidence 352
    11.2.1 Data 353
    11.2.2 Behavior of Futures and Index Series 354
    11.2.3 The Behavior of the Mispricing Series 360
    11.2.4 Path Dependence of Mispricing 364
11.3 Conclusion 367

12 Order Imbalances and Stock Price Movements on October 19 and 20, 1987   **369**
12.1 Some Preliminaries 370
    12.1.1 The Source of the Data 371
    12.1.2 The Published Standard and Poor's Index 372
12.2 The Constructed Indexes 373
12.3 Buying and Selling Pressure 378
    12.3.1 A Measure of Order Imbalance 378
    12.3.2 Time-Series Results 380
    12.3.3 Cross-Sectional Results 381
    12.3.4 Return Reversals 385
12.4 Conclusion 387
Appendix A12   389
A12.1 Index Levels 389
A12.2 Fifteen-Minute Index Returns 393

References   **395**

Index   **417**

List of Figures

4.1 First-order autocorrelation of temporally aggregated observed individual and portfolio returns as a function of the per period nontrading probability p, where q is the aggregation value and $\xi = \mu/\sigma$ 97

5.1 Loci of nontrading probability pairs (p_a, p_b) that imply a constant cross-autocorrelation $\rho_{ab}^q(k)$, for $\rho_{ab}^q(k) = .05, .10, .15, .20, .25, k = 1, q = 5$ 138

5.2 Cross-autocorrelation $\rho_{ab}^q(k)$ as a function of p_a and p_b, for $q = 5, k = 1$ 139

6.1 Distribution and density function of the range V of a Brownian bridge 162

6.2 Autocorrelograms of equally-weighted CRSP daily and monthly stock returns indexes and fractionally-differenced process with $d = 1/4$ 170

7.1 Distributions for the CAPM zero-intercept test statistic for four alternatives with monthly data 203

7.2 Distributions for the CAPM zero-intercept test statistic for four alternatives with weekly data 206

10.1 Illustration of ordered probit probabilities p_i of observing a price change of s_i ticks, which are determined by where the unobservable "virtual" price change Z_k^* falls 293

10.2 Histograms of price changes, time-between-trades, and dollar volume for the period from January 4, 1988, to December 30, 1988 301

10.3 Comparison of estimated ordered probit probabilities of price change, conditioned on a sequence of increasing prices $(1/1/1)$ versus a sequence of constant prices $(0/0/0)$ 327

10.4   Percentage price impact as a function of dollar volume com-
       puted from ordered probit probabilities, conditional on the
       three most recent trades being buyer-initiated, and the three
       most recent price changes being +1 tick each for the period
       from January 4, 1988, to December 30, 1988   330
10.5   Discreteness matters   332

11.1   Mispricing (percent of index value) for (a) December 1984
       and (b) March 1987 S&P 500 futures contracts   361
11.2   Boundary of mean absolute mispricing as a function of time
       to maturity   364

12.1   Comparison of price indexes for NYSE stocks included in
       the S&P 500 Index and not included for October 19 and 20,
       1987   375
12.2   Plot of dollar volume in each fifteen-minute interval on Oc-
       tober 19 and 20, 1987 as a percent of the market value of the
       stocks outstanding separately for S&P and non-S&P stocks . .   376
12.3   Plot of fifteen-minute returns on S&P stocks versus the or-
       der imbalance in S&P stocks in the same fifteen minutes for
       October 19, 1987   381
12.4   Plot of fifteen-minute returns on S&P stocks versus the order
       imbalance in the same fifteen minutes for October 20, 1987 .   382
12.5   Plot of fifteen-minute returns on non-S&P stocks versus the
       order imbalance in the same fifteen minutes for October 19,
       1987   383
12.6   Plot of fifteen-minute returns on non-S&P stocks versus the
       order imbalance in the same fifteen minutes for October 20,
       1987   385

12A.1 Comparison of various constructed indexes measuring the
       S&P Composite Index with the published S&P Index on Oc-
       tober 19, 1987   391

List of Tables

2.1a Variance-ratio test of the random walk hypothesis for CRSP equal- and value-weighted indexes 28

2.1b Market index results for a four-week base observation period 29

2.2 Variance-ratio test of the random walk hypothesis for size-sorted portfolios 31

2.3 Means of variance ratios over all individual securities with complete return histories from September 2, 1962, to December 26, 1985 (625 stocks) 33

2.4 Spuriously induced autocorrelations are reported for nontrading probabilities $1 - p$ of 10 to 50 percent 37

3.1 Empirical sizes of nominal 1, 5, and 10 percent two-sided variance ratio tests of the random walk null hypothesis with homoskedastic disturbances 56

3.2 Empirical quantiles of the (Dickey-Fuller) t-statistic 61

3.3 Empirical sizes of nominal 1, 5, and 10 percent two-sided variance ratio tests of the random walk null hypothesis with homoskedastic disturbances 63

3.4 Empirical quantiles of the (asymptotically) $\mathcal{N}(0, 1)$ variance ratio test statistic $z_1(q)$ under simulated IID Gaussian random walk increments 71

3.5 Power of the two-sided variance ratio test 74

4.1 Sample first-order autocorrelation matrix $\hat{\Gamma}_1$ for the 5×1 subvector $[R_1^o, R_5^o, R_{10}^o, R_{15}^o, R_{20}^o]'$ of observed returns to twenty equally-weighted size-sorted portfolios 102

4.2 Estimates of daily nontrading probabilities implicit in 20 weekly and monthly size-sorted portfolio return autocorrelations 103

4.3   Estimates of the first-order autocorrelation ρ_m of weekly returns of an equal-weighted portfolio of twenty size-sorted portfolios   105

5.1   Sample statistics   119
5.2   Averages of autocorrelation coefficients for weekly returns on individual securities, for the period July 6, 1962, to December 31, 1987   120
5.3   Analysis of the profitability of the return-reversal strategy applied to weekly returns, for the sample of 551 CRSP NYSE–AMEX stocks with nonmissing weekly returns from July 6, 1962, to 31 December 1987 (1330 weeks)   133
5.4   Autocorrelation matrices   136

6.1   Comparison of autocorrelation functions   154
6.2   Fractiles of the distribution $F_V(v)$ 157
6.3 R/S analysis of daily equal- and value-weighted CRSP stock returns indexes from July 3, 1962, to December 31, 1987 . . .   168
6.4 R/S analysis of monthly equal- and value-weighted CRSP stock returns indexes from January 30, 1926, to December 31, 1987   169
6.5   Finite sample distribution of the modified R/S statistic under an IID null hypothesis   173
6.6   Power of the modified R/S statistic under a Gaussian fractionally differenced alternative with differencing parameter $d = 1/3$ 177

7.1   Historical Sharpe measures for selected stock indices, where the Sharpe measure is defined as the ratio of the mean excess return to the standard deviation of the excess return   201
7.2   A comparison of the maximum squared Sharpe measure for two economies denoted A and B   211

8.1   Theoretical sizes of nominal 5 percent χ_n^2-tests of H: $\alpha_i = 0$ $(i = 1, \ldots, n)$ for individual securities   223
8.2   Theoretical sizes of nominal 5 percent χ_q^2-tests of H: $\alpha_i = 0$ $(i = 1, \ldots, n)$ for portfolios   226
8.3   Critical values $C_{.05}$ for 5 percent χ^2-tests of H: $\alpha_i = 0$ $(i = 1, \ldots, n)$ 227
8.4   Empirical sizes of nominal 5 percent χ_q^2-tests of H: $\alpha_i = 0$ $(i = 1, \ldots, n)$ 232
8.5   Empirical size of $F_{q,T-q}$ tests based on q portfolios sorted by a random characteristic whose squared correlation with $\hat{\alpha}_i$ is R^2   235

8.6   Empirical size of $F_{q,T-q}$ tests based on q portfolios sorted by
       a random characteristic whose squared correlation with $\hat{\alpha}_i$ is
       approximately 0.05 237
8.7   Theoretical sizes of nominal 5 percent χ_q^2-tests under the
       null hypothesis of the Sharpe-Lintner CAPM 240
8.8   Comparison of p-values 242
8.9   Theoretical sizes of nominal 5 percent χ_q^2-tests of H: $\alpha_i = 0$
       $(i = 1,\dots, n)$ 246

9.1   Comparison of predictability of PC1 portfolio and MPP for
       a universe of two assets, A and B 256
9.2   Ordinary least squares regression results for individual asset
       returns in SBU asset group from 1947:1 to 1993:12 263
9.3   Ordinary least squares regression results for individual asset
       returns in the SIZE asset group from 1947:1 to 1993:12 265
9.4   Ordinary least squares regression results for individual asset
       returns in the SECTOR asset group from 1947:1 to 1993:12 . 267
9.5   Conditional expected return of MPP for the three asset
       groups from 1947:1 to 1993:12 270
9.6   Portfolio weights of MPP for three asset groups from 1947:1
       to 1993:12 272
9.7   Simulated finite-sample distribution of maximum R^2 of MPP
       of N assets under null hypothesis of no predictability, using
       six variables as predictors 274
9.8   Finite-sample distribution of R^2 of a given portfolio under
       null hypothesis of no predictability, using six variables as pre-
       dictors 275
9.9   Out-of-sample evaluation of conditional one-step-ahead fore-
       casts of MPP using a regression model with six predictors . . . 278
9.10 Out-of-sample evaluation of conditional one-step-ahead fore-
       casts of MPP using Merton's measure of market timing 280
9.11 Out-of-sample evaluation of conditional one-step-ahead fore-
       casts of MPP using a comparison of passive and active invest-
       ment strategies in the portfolio 282

10.1 Summary statistics for transaction prices and corresponding
       ordered probit explanatory variables for the period from
       January 4, 1988, to December 30, 1988 299
10.2a Maximum likelihood estimates 312
10.2b Cross-autocorrelation coefficients $\hat{v}_j$, $j = 1,\dots, 12$, of gen-
       eralized residuals $\{\hat{\epsilon}_k\}$ 314
10.2c Score test statistics $\hat{\xi}_j$, $j = 1,\dots, 12$, where $\hat{\xi}_j \overset{a}{\sim} \chi_1^2$ 315

10.3   Price impact of trades as measured by the change in condi-
        tional mean of Z_k, or $\Delta E[Z_k]$, when trade sizes are increased
        incrementally above the base case of a \$5,000 trade   324

10.4   Discreteness cannot be completely captured by simple
        rounding   329

10.5   Names, ticker symbols, market values, and sample sizes over
        the period from January 4, 1988, to December 30, 1988 for
        100 randomly selected stocks   336

10.6   Summary statistics for the sample of 100 randomly chosen
        securities for the period from January 4, 1988, to December
        30, 1988   339

10.7   Price impact measures, defined as the increase in conditional
        expected price change given by the ordered probit model as
        the volume of the most recent trade is increased from a base
        case of \$1,000 to either the median level of volume for each
        security or a level of \$100,000   342

10.8   Summary of the cross-sectional dispersion in price impact
        measures and the nonlinearity of the price-change/volume
        relation (as measured by the Box-Cox parameters, $\hat{\lambda}_i$)   343

10.9   Robust measure of the cross-sectional dispersion in price im-
        pact measures and the nonlinearity of the price-change/
        volume relation (as measured by the Box-Cox parameters
        $\hat{\lambda}_i$)   344

11.1   Autocorrelations for changes of the logarithm of price in the
        S&P 500 futures and index by contract, September 1983 to
        June 1987   356

11.2   Summary statistics for the changes of the logarithm of price
        in the S&P 500 futures and Index by contract, September
        1983 to June 1987   358

11.3   Aggregate variance-ratio results (based on 16 contracts,
        September 1983 to June 1987)   360

11.4   Summary statistics on the levels and first differences in mis-
        pricing in the S&P 500 futures contracts, by expiration   362

11.5   Mispricing violations for S&P 500 index futures   365

12.1   Percentage returns on S&P and non-S&P stocks cross-classified
        by firm size quartiles for three time intervals on October 19
        and 20, 1987   377

12.2   Cross-sectional rank correlations of individual security re-
        turns and normalized order imbalance by half hour intervals   384

12A.1 Realized returns from Friday close cross-classified by opening
time and trading interval for S&P stocks during the first hour
and a half of trading on October 19, 1987 392
12A.2 Percentage of S&P stocks traded by firm size quartile in each
fifteen-minute interval during the opening hour of October
19, 1987 393

Preface

A volume of collected works is almost always a bad sign for one's research trajectory, an indication of declining productivity as much as professional recognition. We hope to be the exception that proves this rule because neither of us is willing to concede that we have reached the apex of our careers. However, we do think that the papers collected in this volume form a coherent and exciting story, one that bears retelling now that we have the luxury of seeing the forest for the trees. When we began our collaboration over a decade ago, we certainly had no intention of embarking on as ambitious a research agenda as this volume might imply. And although we are still actively engaged in exploring these issues, when we were presented with the opportunity to bring together a group of our papers, we simply could not resist. Whether by design or by coincidence, here we are with eleven papers and an introduction, the running total of our research on the Random Walk Hypothesis and predictability in financial markets.

Although we were sorely tempted to revise our papers to incorporate the benefits of hindsight, we have resisted that temptation so as to keep our contributions in their proper context. However, we do provide general introductions to each of the three parts that comprise this collection of papers, which we hope will clarify and sharpen some of the issues that we only touched upon when we were in the midst of the research. Also, we have updated all our references, hence on occasion there may be a few temporal inconsistencies, e.g., citations of papers published several years after ours.

We hope that this volume will add fuel to the fires of debate and controversy, and expand the arena to include a broader set of participants, particularly those who may have more practical wisdom regarding the business of predicting financial markets. Although Paul Samuelson once chided economists for predicting "five out of the past three recessions", our research has given us a deeper appreciation for both the challenges and the successes of quantitative investment management. As for whether or not this little book contains the secrets to greater wealth, we are reminded of the streetwise aphorism that the first principle of making money is learning how not to lose it. Indeed, although there are probably still only a few ways to make money reliably, the growing complexity of financial markets has created many more ways to lose it and lose it quickly. We have argued that our research has not uncovered tremendous untapped profit opportunities, but on the other hand, our research does provide some guidance on how not to lose money. What more can one expect?

During the course of our research we have accumulated a number of intellectual debts—fortunately, they bear no interest otherwise we would have become insolvent years ago. First and foremost, we thank our advisors— Andy Abel and Jerry Hausman (AWL), and Gene Fama and Arnold Zellner (ACM)—who gave us the training and guidance that launched our careers and continue to sustain us.

We are also grateful to our many friends and colleagues who provided us with support and stimulus from our graduate-student days to the present— Marshall Blume, John Cox, Richard Caves, Bruce Grundy, Chi-fu Huang, Dale Jorgenson, Nobu Kiyotaki, Bob Merton, Krishna Ramaswamy, Robert Stambaugh, and Phil Vasan.

Our families have been an enormous and continuing source of inspiration throughout our careers, and we thank Mom, Martin, Cecilia, Nancy, and Derek (AWL), and Tina, Andrew, and Catie (ACM) for their love and patience during this and other projects that may have taken our attention away from them on occasion.

We thank our editor, Peter Dougherty, and Princeton University Press for their unflagging enthusiasm for our work, and Stephanie Hogue, Lori Pickert, and the staff at Archetype for their skills and patience in producing this book. We were also blessed with the very able assistance of Stephanie Hogue, Li Jin, Fiona Wang, and Wesley Chan in proofreading the final version of the manuscript.

We wish to acknowledge the financial support of several organizations— the Alfred P. Sloan Foundation, Batterymarch Financial Management, the Geewax-Terker Research Program at the Rodney White Center, the MIT Laboratory for Financial Engineering, the National Bureau of Economic Research, the National Science Foundation, and the John M. Olin Foundation. Without their combined support over the years, the research contained in this volume would not have been possible.

Finally, we thank the following sources and co-authors for allowing us to reprint our articles as chapters in this book:

Chapter 2:   *Review of Financial Studies*, Volume 1, 1988.

Chapter 3:   *Journal of Econometrics*, Volume 40, 1989.

Chapter 4:   *Journal of Econometrics*, Volume 45, 1990.

Chapter 5:   *Review of Financial Studies*, Volume 3, 1990.

Chapter 6:   *Econometrica*, Volume 59, 1991.

Chapter 7:   *Journal of Financial Economics*, Volume 38, 1995.

Chapter 8:   *Review of Financial Studies*, Volume 3, 1990.

Chapter 9:   *Macroeconomic Dynamics*, Volume 1, 1997.

Chapter 10:   *Journal of Financial Economics*, Volume 31, 1992 (coauthored with Jerry Hausman)

Chapter 11:   *Review of Financial Studies*, Volume 1, 1988 (co-authored with Krishna Ramaswamy).

Chapter 12:   *Journal of Finance*, Volume 44, 1989 (co-authored with Marshall Blume and Bruce Terker).

A Non-Random Walk Down Wall Street

1
Introduction[1]

ONE OF THE EARLIEST and most enduring models of the behavior of security prices is the Random Walk Hypothesis, an idea that was conceived in the sixteenth century as a model of games of chance.[2] Closely tied to the birth of probability theory, the Random Walk Hypothesis has had an illustrious history, with remarkable intellectual forbears such as Bachelier, Einstein, Lévy, Kolmogorov, and Wiener.

More recently, and as with so many of the ideas of modern economics, the first serious application of the Random Walk Hypothesis to financial markets can be traced back to Paul Samuelson (1965), whose contribution is neatly summarized by the title of his article: "Proof that Properly Anticipated Prices Fluctuate Randomly." In an informationally efficient market—not to be confused with an allocationally or Pareto-efficient market—price changes must be unforecastable if they are properly anticipated, i.e., if they fully incorporate the expectations and information of all market participants. Fama (1970) encapsulated this idea in his pithy dictum that "prices fully reflect all available information."

Unlike the many applications of the Random Walk Hypothesis in the natural and physical sciences in which randomness is assumed almost by default, because of the absence of any natural alternatives, Samuelson argues that randomness is achieved through the active participation of many investors seeking greater wealth. Unable to curtail their greed, an army of investors aggressively pounce on even the smallest informational advantages at their disposal, and in doing so, they incorporate their information into market prices and quickly eliminate the profit opportunities that gave rise to their aggression. If this occurs instantaneously, which it must in an idealized world of "frictionless" markets and costless trading, then prices must always fully reflect all available information and no profits can be gar-

---

[1] Parts of this introduction are adapted from Lo (1997a,b) and Lo and MacKinlay (1998).
[2] See, for example, Hald (1990, Chapter 4).

nered from information-based trading (because such profits have already been captured). This has a wonderfully counter-intuitive and seemingly contradictory flavor to it: the more efficient the market, the more random the sequence of price changes generated by such a market, and the most efficient market of all is one in which price changes are completely random and unpredictable.

For these reasons, the Random Walk Hypothesis and its close relative, the Efficient Markets Hypothesis, have become icons of modern financial economics that continue to fire the imagination of academics and investment professionals alike. The papers collected in this volume comprise our own foray into this rich literature, spanning a decade of research that we initiated in 1988 with our rejection of the Random Walk Hypothesis for US stock market prices, and then following a course that seemed, at times, to be self-propelled, the seeds of our next study planted by the results of the previous one.

If there is one central theme that organizes the papers contained in this volume, it is this: financial markets *are* predictable to some degree, but far from being a symptom of inefficiency or irrationality, predictability is the oil that lubricates the gears of capitalism. Indeed, quite by accident and rather indirectly, we have come face to face with an insight that Ronald Coase hit upon as an undergraduate over half a century ago: price discovery is neither instantaneous nor costless, and frictions play a major role in determining the nature of competition and the function of markets.

1.1 The Random Walk and Efficient Markets

One of the most common reactions to our early research was surprise and disbelief. Indeed, when we first presented our rejection of the Random Walk Hypothesis at an academic conference in 1986, our discussant—a distinguished economist and senior member of the profession—asserted with great confidence that we had made a programming error, for if our results were correct, this would imply tremendous profit opportunities in the stock market. Being too timid (and too junior) at the time, we responded weakly that our programming was quite solid thank you, and the ensuing debate quickly degenerated thereafter. Fortunately, others were able to replicate our findings exactly, and our wounded pride has healed quite nicely with the passage of time (though we still bristle at the thought of being prosecuted for programming errors without "probable cause"). Nevertheless, this experience has left an indelible impression on us, forcing us to confront the fact that the Random Walk Hypothesis was so fully ingrained into the canon of our profession that it was easier to attribute our empirical results to programming errors than to accept them at face value.

Is it possible for stock market prices to be predictable to some degree in an efficient market?

This question hints at the source of disbelief among our early critics: an implicit—and incorrect—link between the Random Walk Hypothesis and the Efficient Markets Hypothesis. It is not difficult to see how the two ideas might be confused. Under very special circumstances, e.g., risk neutrality, the two are equivalent. However, LeRoy (1973), Lucas (1978), and many others have shown in many ways and in many contexts that the Random Walk Hypothesis is neither a necessary nor a sufficient condition for rationally determined security prices. In other words, unforecastable prices need not imply a well-functioning financial market with rational investors, and forecastable prices need not imply the opposite.

These conclusions seem sharply at odds with Samuelson's "proof" that properly anticipated prices fluctuate randomly, an argument so compelling that it is reminiscent of the role that uncertainty plays in quantum mechanics. Just as Heisenberg's uncertainty principle places a limit on what we can know about an electron's position and momentum if quantum mechanics holds, Samuelson's version of the Efficient Markets Hypothesis places a limit on what we can know about future price changes if the forces of economic self-interest hold.

Nevertheless, one of the central insights of modern financial economics is the necessity of some trade-off between risk and expected return, and although Samuelson's version of the Efficient Markets Hypothesis places a restriction on expected returns, it does not account for risk in any way. In particular, if a security's expected price change is positive, it may be just the reward needed to attract investors to hold the asset and bear the associated risks. Indeed, if an investor is sufficiently risk averse, he might gladly *pay* to avoid holding a security that has unforecastable returns.

In such a world, the Random Walk Hypothesis—a purely statistical model of returns—need not be satisfied even if prices do fully reflect all available information. This was demonstrated conclusively by LeRoy (1973) and Lucas (1978), who construct explicit examples of informationally efficient markets in which the Efficient Markets Hypothesis holds but where prices do not follow random walks.

Grossman (1976) and Grossman and Stiglitz (1980) go even further. They argue that perfectly informationally efficient markets are an *impossibility*, for if markets are perfectly efficient, the return to gathering information is nil, in which case there would be little reason to trade and markets would eventually collapse. Alternatively, the degree of market *inefficiency* determines the effort investors are willing to expend to gather and trade on information, hence a non-degenerate market equilibrium will arise only when there are sufficient profit opportunities, i.e., inefficiencies, to compensate investors for the costs of trading and information-gathering. The profits earned by these industrious investors may be viewed as economic rents that accrue to those willing to engage in such activities. Who are the providers of these rents? Black (1986) gives us a provocative answer: noise traders, individuals who trade on what they think is information but is in fact merely noise. More generally, at any time there are always investors who trade for reasons other than information—for example, those with unexpected liquidity needs—and these investors are willing to "pay up" for the privilege of executing their trades immediately.

These investors may well be losing money on average when they trade with information-motivated investors, but there is nothing irrational or inefficient about either group's behavior. In fact, an investor may be trading for liquidity reasons one day and for information reasons the next, and losing or earning money depending on the circumstances surrounding the trade.

1.2 The Current State of Efficient Markets

There is an old joke, widely told among economists, about an economist strolling down the street with a companion when they come upon a $100 bill lying on the ground. As the companion reaches down to pick it up, the economist says "Don't bother—if it were a real $100 bill, someone would have already picked it up."

This humorous example of economic logic gone awry strikes dangerously close to home for students of the Efficient Markets Hypothesis, one of the most important controversial and well-studied propositions in all the social sciences. It is disarmingly simple to state, has far-reaching consequences for academic pursuits and business practice, and yet is surprisingly resilient to empirical proof or refutation. Even after three decades of research and literally thousands of journal articles, economists have not yet reached a consensus about whether markets—particularly financial markets—are efficient or not.

What can we conclude about the Efficient Markets Hypothesis? Amazingly, there is still no consensus among financial economists. Despite the many advances in the statistical analysis, databases, and theoretical models surrounding the Efficient Markets Hypothesis, the main effect that the large number of empirical studies have had on this debate is to harden the resolve of the proponents on each side.

One of the reasons for this state of affairs is the fact that the Efficient Markets Hypothesis, by itself, is not a well-defined and empirically refutable hypothesis. To make it operational, one must specify additional structure, e.g., investors' preferences, information structure, business conditions, etc. But then a test of the Efficient Markets Hypothesis becomes a test of several auxiliary hypotheses as well, and a rejection of such a joint hypothesis tells us little about which aspect of the joint hypothesis is inconsistent with the data. Are stock prices too volatile because markets are inefficient, or is it due to risk aversion, or dividend smoothing? All three inferences are consistent with the data. Moreover, new statistical tests designed to distinguish among them will no doubt require auxiliary hypotheses of their own which, in turn, may be questioned.

More importantly, tests of the Efficient Markets Hypothesis may not be the most informative means of gauging the efficiency of a given market. What is often of more consequence is the *relative* efficiency of a particular market, relative to other markets, e.g., futures vs. spot markets, auction vs. dealer markets, etc. The advantages of the concept of relative efficiency, as opposed to the all-or-nothing notion of absolute efficiency, are easy to spot by way of an analogy. Physical systems are often given an efficiency rating based on the relative proportion of energy or fuel converted to useful work. Therefore, a piston engine may be rated at 60% efficiency, meaning that on average 60% of the energy contained in the engine's fuel is used to turn the crankshaft, with the remaining 40% lost to other forms of work, e.g., heat, light, noise, etc.

Few engineers would ever consider performing a statistical test to determine whether or not a given engine is perfectly efficient—such an engine exists only in the idealized frictionless world of the imagination. But measuring relative efficiency—relative to a frictionless ideal—is commonplace. Indeed, we have come to expect such measurements for many household products: air conditioners, hot water heaters, refrigerators, etc. Therefore, from a practical point of view, and in light of Grossman and Stiglitz (1980), the Efficient Markets Hypothesis is an idealization that is economically unrealizable, but which serves as a useful benchmark for measuring relative efficiency.

A more practical version of the Efficient Markets Hypothesis is suggested by another analogy, one involving the notion of thermal equilibrium in statistical mechanics. Despite the occasional "excess" profit opportunity, on average and over time, it is not possible to earn such profits consistently without some type of competitive advantage, e.g., superior information, superior technology, financial innovation, etc. Alternatively, in an efficient market, the only way to earn positive profits *consistently* is to develop a competitive advantage, in which case the profits may be viewed as the economic rents that accrue to this competitive advantage. The consistency of such profits is an important qualification—in this version of the Efficient Markets Hypothesis, an occasional free lunch is permitted, but free lunch plans are ruled out.

To see why such an interpretation of the Efficient Markets Hypothesis is a more practical one, consider for a moment applying the classical version of the Efficient Markets Hypothesis to a non-financial market, say the market for biotechnology. Consider, for example, the goal of developing a vaccine for the AIDS virus. If the market for biotechnology is efficient in the classical sense, such a vaccine can *never* be developed—if it could, someone would have already done it! This is clearly a ludicrous presumption since it ignores the difficulty and gestation lags of research and development in biotechnology. Moreover, if a pharmaceutical company does succeed in developing such a vaccine, the profits earned would be measured in the billions of dollars. Would this be considered "excess" profits, or economic rents that accrue to biotechnology patents?

Financial markets are no different in principle, only in degrees. Consequently, the profits that accrue to an investment professional need not be a market *inefficiency*, but may simply be the fair reward to breakthroughs in financial technology. After all, few analysts would regard the hefty profits of Amgen over the past few years as evidence of an inefficient market for pharmaceuticals—Amgen's recent profitability is readily identified with the development of several new drugs (Epogen, for example, a drug that stimulates the production of red blood cells), some considered breakthroughs in biotechnology. Similarly, even in efficient financial markets there are very handsome returns to breakthroughs in financial technology.

Of course, barriers to entry are typically lower, the degree of competition is much higher, and most financial technologies are not patentable (though this may soon change) hence the "half life" of the profitability of financial innovation is considerably smaller. These features imply that financial markets should be relatively more efficient, and indeed they are. The market for "used securities" is considerably more efficient than the market for used cars. But to argue that financial markets must be perfectly efficient is tantamount to the claim that an AIDS vaccine cannot be found. In an efficient market, it is difficult to earn a good living, but not impossible.

1.3 Practical Implications

Our research findings have several implications for financial economists and investors. The fact that the Random Walk Hypothesis hypothesis can be rejected for recent US equity returns suggests the presence of predictable components in the stock market. This opens the door to superior long-term investment returns through disciplined active investment management. In much the same way that innovations in biotechnology can garner superior returns for venture capitalists, innovations in financial technology can garner equally superior returns for investors.

However, several qualifications must be kept in mind when assessing which of the many active strategies currently being touted is appropriate for an particular investor. First, the riskiness of active strategies can be very different from passive strategies, and such risks do not necessarily "average out" over time. In particular, an investor's risk tolerance must be taken into account in selecting the long-term investment strategy that will best match the investor's goals. This is no simple task since many investors have little understanding of their own risk preferences, hence consumer education is perhaps the most pressing need in the near term. Fortunately, computer technology can play a major role in this challenge, providing scenario analyses, graphical displays of potential losses and gains, and realistic simulations of long-term investment performance that are user-friendly and easily incorporated into an investor's world view. Nevertheless, a good understanding of the investor's understanding of the nature of financial risks and rewards is the natural starting point for the investment process.

Second, there are a plethora of active managers vying for the privilege of managing institutional and pension assets, but they cannot all outperform the market every year (nor should we necessarily expect them to). Though often judged against a common benchmark, e.g., the S&P 500, active strategies can have very diverse risk characteristics and these must be weighed in assessing their performance. An active strategy involving high-risk venture-capital investments will tend to outperform the S&P 500 more often than a less aggressive "enhanced indexing" strategy, yet one is not necessarily better than the other.

In particular, past returns should not be the *sole* or even the *major* criterion by which investment managers are judged. This statement often surprises investors and finance professionals—after all, isn't this the bottom line? Put another way, "If it works, who cares why?". Selecting an investment manager this way is one of the surest paths to financial disaster. Unlike the experimental sciences such as physics and biology, financial economics (and most other social sciences) relies primarily on statistical inference to test its theories. Therefore, we can never know with perfect certainty that a particular investment strategy is successful since even the most successful strategy can always be explained by pure luck (see Chapter 8 for some concrete illustrations).

Of course, some kinds of success are easier to attribute to luck than others, and it is precisely this kind of attribution that must be performed in deciding on a particular active investment style. Is it luck, or is it genuine?

While statistical inference can be very helpful in tackling this question, in the final analysis the question is not about statistics, but rather about economics and financial innovation. Under the practical version of the Efficient Markets Hypothesis, it is difficult—but not impossible—to provide investors with consistently superior investment returns. So what are the sources of superior performance promised by an active manager and why have other competing managers not recognized these opportunities? Is it better mathematical models of financial markets? Or more accurate statistical methods for identifying investment opportunities? Or more timely data in a market where minute delays can mean the difference between profits and losses? Without a compelling argument for *where* an active manager's value-added is coming from, one must be very skeptical about the prospects for future performance. In particular, the concept of a "black box"—a device that performs a known function reliably but obscurely—may make sense in engineering applications where repeated experiments can validate the reliability of the box's performance, but has no counterpart in investment management where performance attribution is considerably more difficult. For analyzing investment strategies, it matters a great deal *why* a strategy is supposed to work.

Finally, despite the caveats concerning performance attribution and proper motivation, we *can* make some educated guesses about where the likely sources of value-added might be for active investment management in the near future.

- The revolution in computing technology and datafeeds suggest that highly computation-intensive strategies—ones that could not have been implemented five years ago—that exploit certain regularities in securities prices, e.g., clientele biases, tax opportunities, information lags, can add value.

- Many studies have demonstrated the enormous impact that transactions costs can have on long-term investment performance. More sophisticated methods for measuring and controlling transactions costs—methods which employ high-frequency data, economic models of price impact, and advanced optimization techniques—can add value. Also, the introduction of financial instruments that reduce transactions costs, e.g., swaps, options, and other derivative securities, can add value.

- Recent research in psychological biases inherent in human cognition suggest that investment strategies exploiting these biases can add value. However, contrary to the recently popular "behavioral" approach to investments which proposes to take advantage of individual "irrationality," I suggest that value-added comes from creating investments with more attractive risk-sharing characteristics suggested by psychological models. Though the difference may seem academic, it has far-reaching consequences for the long-run performance of such strategies: taking advantage of individual irrationality cannot be a recipe for long-term success, but providing a better set of opportunities that more closely matches what investors desire seems more promising.

Of course, forecasting the sources of future innovations in financial technology is a treacherous business, fraught with many half-baked successes and some embarrassing failures. Perhaps the only reliable prediction is that the innovations of future are likely to come from unexpected and underappreciated sources. No one has illustrated this principal so well as Harry Markowitz, the father of modern portfolio theory and a winner of the 1990 Nobel Prize in economics. In describing his experience as a Ph.D. student on the eve of his graduation in the following way, he wrote in his Nobel address:

> ... [W]hen I defended my dissertation as a student in the Economics Department of the University of Chicago, Professor Milton Friedman argued that portfolio theory was not Economics, and that they could not award me a Ph.D. degree in Economics for a dissertation which was not Economics. I assume that he was only half serious, since they did award me the degree without long debate. As to the merits of his arguments, at this point I am quite willing to concede: at the time I defended my dissertation, portfolio theory was not part of Economics. But now it is.

It is our hope and conceit that the research contained in this volume will be worthy of the tradition that Markowitz and others have so firmly established.

Power of The text.

Part I

THE FIVE CHAPTERS IN THIS FIRST PART focus squarely on whether the Random Walk Hypothesis is a plausible description of recent US stock market prices. At the time we started our investigations—in 1985, just a year after we arrived at the Wharton School—the Random Walk Hypothesis was taken for granted as gospel truth. A number of well-known empirical studies had long since established the fact that markets were "weak-form efficient" in Roberts's (1967) terminology, implying that past prices could not be used to forecast future prices changes (see, for example, Cowles and Jones (1973), Kendall (1953), Osborne (1959, 1962), Roberts (1959, 1967), Larson (1960), Cowles (1960), Working (1960), Alexander (1961, 1964), Granger and Morgenstern (1963), Mandelbrot (1963), Fama (1965), and Fama and Blume (1966)). And although some of these studies did find evidence against the random walk, e.g., Cowles and Jones (1973), they were largely dismissed as statistical anomalies or not economically meaningful after accounting for transactions costs, e.g., Cowles (1960). For example, after conducting an extensive empirical analysis of the "runs' of US stock returns from 1956 to 1962, Fama (1965) concludes that, "... there is no evidence of important dependence from either an investment or a statistical point of view."

It was in this milieu that we decided to revisit the Random Walk Hypothesis. Previous studies had been unable to reject the random walk, hence we surmised that perhaps a more sensitive statistical test was needed, one capable of detecting small but significant departures from pure randomness. In the jargon of statistical inference, we hoped to develop a more "powerful" test, a test that has a higher probability of rejecting the Random Walk Hypothesis if it is indeed false. Motivated partly by an insight of Merton's (1980), that variances can be estimated more accurately than means when data is sampled at finer intervals, we proposed a test of the random walk based on a comparison of variances at different sampling intervals. And

13

Compare Variances

by casting the comparison as a Hausman (1978) specification test, we were able to obtain an asymptotic sampling theory for the variance ratio statistic almost immediately, which we later generalized and extended in many ways. These results and their empirical implementation are described in Chapter 2.

In retrospect, our motivation for the variance ratio test was completely unnecessary.

Although Merton's (1980) observation holds quite generally, the overwhelming rejections of the Random Walk Hypothesis that we obtained for weekly US stock returns from 1962 to 1985 implied that a more powerful test was not needed—the random walk could have been rejected on the basis of the simple first-order autocorrelation coefficient, which we estimated to be 30 percent for the equal-weighted weekly returns index! We were taken completely by surprise (and carefully re-checked our programs several times for coding errors before debuting these results in a November 1986 conference). How could such compelling evidence against the random walk be overlooked by the vast literature we were fed as graduate students?

At first, we attributed this to our using weekly returns—prior studies used either daily or monthly. We chose a weekly sampling interval to balance the desire for a large sample size against the problems associated with high-frequency financial data, e.g., nonsynchronous prices, bid/ask "bounce," etc. But we soon discovered that the case against the random walk was equally compelling with daily returns.

This puzzling state of affairs sparked the series of studies contained in Chapters 3 to 6, studies that attempted to reconcile what we, and many others, viewed as a sharp contradiction between our statistical inferences and the voluminous literature that came before us. We checked the accuracy of our statistical methods (Chapter 3), we quantified the potential biases introduced by nonsynchronous prices (Chapter 4), we investigated the sources of the rejections of the random walk and traced them to large positive cross-autocorrelations and lead/lag effects (Chapter 5), and we considered statistical fractals as an alternative to the random walk (Chapter 6). Despite our best efforts, we were unable to explain away the evidence against the Random Walk Hypothesis.

With the benefit of hindsight and a more thorough review of the literature, we have come to the conclusion that the apparent inconsistency between the broad support for the Random Walk Hypothesis and our empirical findings is largely due to the common misconception that the Random Walk Hypothesis is equivalent to the Efficient Markets Hypothesis, and the near religious devotion of economists to the latter (see Chapter 1). Once we saw that we, and our colleagues, had been trained to study the data through the filtered lenses of classical market efficiency, it became clear that the problem lay not with our empirical analysis, but with the economic implications that others incorrected attributed to our results—unbounded profit opportunities, irrational investors, and the like.

We also discovered that ours was not the first study to reject the random walk, and that the departures from the random walk uncovered by Osborne (1962), Larson (1960), Cootner (1962), Steiger (1964), Niederhoffer and Osborne (1966), and Schwartz and Whitcomb (1977), to name just a few examples, were largely ignored by the academic community and unknown to us until after our own papers were published.[3] We were all in a collective fog regarding the validity of the Random Walk Hypothesis, but as we confronted the empirical evidence from every angle and began to rule out other explanations, slowly the fog lifted for us.

In Niederhoffer's (1997) entertaining and irreverent autobiography, he sheds some light on the kind of forces at work in creating this fog. In describing the Random Walk Hypothesis as it developed at the University of Chicago in the 1960's, he writes:

> This theory and the attitude of its adherents found classic expression in one incident I personally observed that deserves memorialization. A team of four of the most respected graduate students in finance had joined forces with two professors, now considered venerable enough to have won or to have been considered for a Nobel prize, but at that time feisty as Hades and insecure as a kid on his first date. This elite group was studying the possible impact of volume on stock price movements, a subject I had researched. As I was coming down the steps from the library on the third floor of Haskell Hall, the main business building, I could see this Group of Six gathered together on a stairway landing, examining some computer output. Their voices wafted up to me, echoing off the stone walls of the building. One of the students was pointing to some output while querying the professors, "Well, what if we really do find something? We'll be up the creek. It won't be consistent with the random walk model." The younger professor replied, "Don't worry, we'll cross that bridge in the unlikely event we come to it."
>
> I could hardly believe my ears—here were six scientists openly hoping to find no departures from ignorance. I couldn't hold my tongue, and blurted out, "I sure am glad you are all keeping an open mind about your research." I could hardly refrain from grinning as I walked past them. I heard muttered imprecations in response.

---

[3]In fact, both Alexander (1961) and Schwartz and Whitcomb (1977) use variance ratios to test the Random Walk Hypothesis, and although they do not employ the kind of rigorous statistical inference that we derived in our study, nevertheless it was our mistake to have overlooked their contributions. Our only defense is that none of our colleagues were aware of these studies either, for no one pointed out these references to us either before or after our papers were published.

From this, Niederhoffer (1997) concludes that "As usual, academicians are way behind the form" and with respect to the Random Walk Hypothesis, we are forced to agree.

But beyond the interesting implications that this cognitive dissonance provides for the sociology of science, we think there is an even more important insight to be gleaned from all of this. In a recent update of our original variance ratio test for weekly US stock market indexes, we discovered that the most current data (1986–1996) conforms more closely to the random walk than our original 1962–1985 sample period. Moreover, upon further investigation, we learned that over the past decade several investment firms—most notably, Morgan Stanley and D.E. Shaw—have been engaged in high-frequency equity trading strategies specifically designed to take advantage of the kind of patterns we uncovered in 1988. Previously known as "pairs trading" and now called "statistical arbitrage," these strategies have fared reasonably well until recently, and are now regarded as a very competitive and thin-margin business because of the proliferation of hedge funds engaged in these activities. This provides a plausible explanation for the trend towards randomness in the recent data, one that harkens back to Samuelson's "Proof that Properly Anticipated Prices Fluctuate Randomly."

But if Morgan Stanley and D.E. Shaw were profiting in the 1980's from the predictability in stock returns that is now waning because of competition, can we conclude that markets were inefficient in the 1980's? Not without additional information about the cost and risk of their trading operations, and the novelty of their trading strategies relative to their competitors'.

In particular, the profits earned by the early statistical arbitrageurs may be viewed as economic rents that accrued to their innovation, creativity, perseverance, and appetite for risk. Now that others have begun to reverse engineer and mimick their technologies, profit margins are declining. Therefore, neither the evidence against the random walk, nor the more recent trend towards the random walk, are inconsistent with the practical version of the Efficient Markets Hypothesis. Market opportunities need not be market inefficiencies.

2
Stock Market Prices Do Not Follow Random Walks: Evidence from a Simple Specification Test

SINCE KEYNES' (1936) NOW FAMOUS PRONOUNCEMENT that most investors' decisions "can only be taken as a result of animal spirits—of a spontaneous urge to action rather than inaction, and not as the outcome of a weighted average of benefits multiplied by quantitative probabilities," a great deal of research has been devoted to examining the efficiency of stock market price formation. In Fama's (1970) survey, the vast majority of those studies were unable to reject the "efficient markets" hypothesis for common stocks. Although several seemingly anomalous departures from market efficiency have been well documented,[1] many financial economists would agree with Jensen's (1978a) belief that "there is no other proposition in economics which has more solid empirical evidence supporting it than the Efficient Markets Hypothesis."

Although a precise formulation of an empirically refutable efficient markets hypothesis must obviously be model-specific, historically the majority of such tests have focused on the forecastability of common stock returns. Within this paradigm, which has been broadly categorized as the "random walk" theory of stock prices, few studies have been able to reject the random walk model statistically. However, several recent papers have uncovered empirical evidence which suggests that stock returns contain predictable components. For example, Keim and Stambaugh (1986) find statistically significant predictability in stock prices by using forecasts based on certain predetermined variables. In addition, Fama and French (1988) show that

---

[1] See, for example, the studies in Jensen's (1978b) volume on anomalous evidence regarding market efficiency.

17

long holding-period returns are significantly negatively serially correlated, implying that 25 to 40 percent of the variation of longer-horizon returns is predictable from past returns.

In this chapter we provide further evidence that stock prices do not follow random walks by using a simple specification test based on variance estimators. Our empirical results indicate that the random walk model is generally not consistent with the stochastic behavior of weekly returns, especially for the smaller capitalization stocks. However, in contrast to the negative serial correlation that Fama and French (1988) found for longer-horizon returns, we find significant positive serial correlation for weekly and monthly holding-period returns. For example, using 1216 weekly observations from September 6, 1962, to December 26, 1985, we compute the weekly first-order autocorrelation coefficient of the equal-weighted Center for Research in Security Prices (CRSP) returns index to be 30 percent! The statistical significance of our results is robust to heteroskedasticity. We also develop a simple model which indicates that these large autocorrelations cannot be attributed solely to the effects of infrequent trading. This empirical puzzle becomes even more striking when we show that autocorrelations of individual securities are generally negative.

Of course, these results do not necessarily imply that the stock market is inefficient or that prices are not rational assessments of "fundamental" values. As Leroy (1973) and Lucas (1978) have shown, rational expectations equilibrium prices need not even form a martingale sequence, of which the random walk is a special case. Therefore, without a more explicit economic model of the price-generating mechanism, a rejection of the random walk hypothesis has few implications for the efficiency of market price formation. Although our test results may be interpreted as a rejection of *some* economic model of efficient price formation, there may exist other plausible models that are consistent with the empirical findings. Our more modest goal in this study is to employ a test that is capable of distinguishing among several interesting alternative stochastic price processes. Our test exploits the fact that the variance of the increments of a random walk is linear in the sampling interval. If stock prices are generated by a random walk (possibly with drift), then, for example, the variance of monthly sampled log-price relatives must be 4 times as large as the variance of a weekly sample. Comparing the (per unit time) variance estimates obtained from weekly and monthly prices may then indicate the plausibility of the random walk theory.[2] Such a comparison

---

[2]The use of variance ratios is, of course, not new. Most recently, Campbell and Mankiw (1987), Cochrane (1987b, 1987c), Fama and French (1988), French and Roll (1986), and Huizinga (1987) have all computed variance ratios in a variety of contexts; however, these studies do not provide any formal sampling theory for our statistics. Specifically, Cochrane (1988), Fama and French (1988), and French and Roll (1986) all rely on Monte Carlo simulations to obtain standard errors for their variance ratios under the null. Campbell and Mankiw (1987)

is formed quantitatively along the lines of the Hausman (1978) specification test and is particularly simple to implement.

In Section 2.1 we derive our specification test for both homoskedastic and heteroskedastic random walks. Our main results are given in Section 2.2, where rejections of the random walk are extensively documented for weekly returns indexes, size-sorted portfolios, and individual securities. Section 2.3 contains a simple model which demonstrates that infrequent trading cannot fully account for the magnitude of the estimated autocorrelations of weekly stock returns. In Section 2.4 we discuss the consistency of our empirical rejections with a mean-reverting alternative to the random walk model. We summarize briefly and conclude in Section 2.5.

$\ln P_t = \mu + \ln P_{t-1} + \epsilon$

2.1 The Specification Test

a check of relative variances

Denote by P_t the stock price at time t and define $X_t \equiv \ln P_t$ as the log-price process. Our maintained hypothesis is given by the recursive relation

$$X_t = \mu + X_{t-1} + \epsilon_t \qquad (2.1.1)$$

where μ is an arbitrary drift parameter and ϵ_t is the random disturbance term. We assume throughout that for all t, $E[\epsilon_t] = 0$, where $E[\cdot]$ denotes the

and Cochrane (1987c) do derive the asymptotic variance of the variance ratio but only under the assumption that the aggregation value q grows with (but more slowly than) the sample size T. Specifically, they use Priestley's (1981, page 463) expression for the asymptotic variance of the estimator of the spectral density of ΔX_t at frequency 0 (with a Bartlett window) as the appropriate asymptotic variance of the variance ratio. But Priestley's result requires (among other things) that $q \to \infty$, $T \to \infty$, and $q/T \to 0$. In this chapter we develop the formal sampling theory of the variance-ratio statistics for the more general case.

Our variance ratio may, however, be related to the spectral-density estimates in the following way. Letting $f(0)$ denote the spectral density of the increments ΔX_t at frequency 0, we have the following relation:

$$\pi f(0) = \gamma(0) + 2 \sum_{k=1}^{\infty} \gamma(k)$$

where $\gamma(k)$ is the autocovariance function. Dividing both sides by the variance $\gamma(0)$ then yields

$$\pi f^*(0) = 1 + 2 \sum_{k=1}^{\infty} \rho(k)$$

where f^* is the normalized spectral density and $\rho(k)$ is the autocorrelation function. Now in order to estimate the quantity $\pi f^*(0)$, the infinite sum on the right-hand side of the preceding equation must obviously be truncated. If, in addition to truncation, the autocorrelations are weighted using Newey and West's (1987) procedure, then the resulting estimator is formally equivalent to our $M_r(q)$-statistic. Although he does not explicitly use this variance ratio, Huizinga (1987) does employ the Newey and West (1987) estimator of the normalized spectral density.

expectations operator. Although the traditional random walk hypothesis restricts the ϵ_t's to be independently and identically distributed (IID) Gaussian random variables, there is mounting evidence that financial time series often possess time-varying volatilities and deviate from normality. Since it is the unforecastability, or uncorrelatedness, of price changes that is of interest, a rejection of the IID Gaussian random walk because of heteroskedasticity or nonnormality would be of less import than a rejection that is robust to these two aspects of the data. In Section 2.1.2 we develop a test statistic which is sensitive to correlated price changes but which is otherwise robust to many forms of heteroskedasticity and nonnormality. Although our empirical results rely solely on this statistic, for purposes of clarity we also present in Section 2.1.1 the sampling theory for the more restrictive IID Gaussian random walk.

2.1.1 Homoskedastic Increments

We begin with the null hypothesis H that the disturbances ϵ_t are independently and identically distributed normal random variables with variance σ_o^2; thus,

$$\text{H:} \quad \epsilon_t \ \text{IID} \ \mathcal{N}(0, \sigma_o^2). \tag{2.1.2}$$

In addition to homoskedasticity, we have made the assumption of independent Gaussian increments. An example of such a specification is the exact discrete-time process X_t obtained by sampling the following well-known continuous-time process at equally spaced intervals:

$$dX(t) = \mu \, dt + \sigma_o \, dW(t) \tag{2.1.3}$$

where $dW(t)$ denotes the standard Wiener differential. The solution to this stochastic differential equation corresponds to the popular lognormal diffusion price process.

One important property of the random walk X_t is that the variance of its increments is linear in the observation interval. That is, the variance of $X_t - X_{t-2}$ is twice the variance of $X_t - X_{t-1}$. Therefore, the plausibility of the random walk model may be checked by comparing the variance estimate of $X_t - X_{t-1}$ to, say, one-half the variance estimate of $X_t - X_{t-2}$. This is the essence of our specification test; the remainder of this section is devoted to developing the sampling theory required to compare the variances quantitatively.

Suppose that we obtain $2n + 1$ observations $X_0, X_1, \ldots, X_{2n}$ of X_t at equally spaced intervals and consider the following estimators for the unknown parameters μ and σ_o^2:

$$\hat{\mu} \equiv \frac{1}{2n} \sum_{k=1}^{2n} (X_k - X_{k-1}) = \frac{1}{2n} (X_{2n} - X_0) \tag{2.1.4a}$$

$$\hat{\sigma}_a^2 \equiv \frac{1}{2n} \sum_{k=1}^{2n} (X_k - X_{k-1} - \hat{\mu})^2 \qquad (2.1.4b)$$

$$\hat{\sigma}_b^2 \equiv \frac{1}{2n} \sum_{k=1}^{n} (X_{2k} - X_{2k-2} - 2\hat{\mu})^2. \qquad (2.1.4c)$$

The estimators $\hat{\mu}$ and $\hat{\sigma}_a^2$ correspond to the maximum-likelihood estimators of the μ and σ_o^2 parameters; $\hat{\sigma}_b^2$ is also an estimator of σ_o^2 but uses only the subset of $n+1$ observations X_0, X_2, X_4, ..., X_{2n} and corresponds formally to $\frac{1}{2}$ times the variance estimator for increments of even-numbered observations. Under standard asymptotic theory, all three estimators are strongly consistent; that is, holding all other parameters constant, as the total number of observations $2n$ increases without bound the estimators converge almost surely to their population values. In addition, it is well known that both $\hat{\sigma}_a^2$ and $\hat{\sigma}_b^2$ possess the following Gaussian limiting distributions:

$$\sqrt{2n}\,(\hat{\sigma}_a^2 - \sigma_o^2) \overset{a}{\sim} \mathcal{N}(0, 2\sigma_o^4) \qquad (2.1.5a)$$

$$\sqrt{2n}\,(\hat{\sigma}_b^2 - \sigma_o^2) \overset{a}{\sim} \mathcal{N}(0, 4\sigma_o^4) \qquad (2.1.5b)$$

where $\overset{a}{\sim}$ indicates that the distributional equivalence is asymptotic. Of course, it is the limiting distribution of the *difference* of the variances that interests us. Although it may readily be shown that such a difference is also asymptotically Gaussian with zero mean, the variance of the limiting distribution is not apparent since the two variance estimators are clearly not asymptotically uncorrelated. However, since the estimator $\hat{\sigma}_a^2$ is asymptotically efficient under the null hypothesis H, we may apply Hausman's (1978) result, which shows that the asymptotic variance of the difference is simply the difference of the asymptotic variances.[3] If we define $J_d \equiv \hat{\sigma}_b^2 - \hat{\sigma}_a^2$, then we have the result

$$\sqrt{2n}\,J_d \overset{a}{\sim} \mathcal{N}(0, 2\sigma_o^4). \qquad (2.1.6)$$

Using any consistent estimator of the asymptotic variance of J_d, a standard significance test may then be performed. A more convenient alternative

---

[3]Briefly, Hausman (1978) exploits the fact that any asymptotically efficient estimator of a parameter θ, say $\hat{\theta}_e$, must possess the property that it is asymptotically uncorrelated with the difference $\hat{\theta}_a - \hat{\theta}_e$, where $\hat{\theta}_a$ is any other estimator of θ. If not, then there exists a linear combination of $\hat{\theta}_e$ and $\hat{\theta}_a - \hat{\theta}_e$ that is more efficient than $\hat{\theta}_e$, contradicting the assumed efficiency of $\hat{\theta}_e$. The result follows directly, then, since

$$\text{aVar}(\hat{\theta}_a) = \text{aVar}(\hat{\theta}_e + \hat{\theta}_a - \hat{\theta}_e) = \text{aVar}(\hat{\theta}_e) + \text{aVar}(\hat{\theta}_a - \hat{\theta}_e)$$
$$\Rightarrow \text{aVar}(\hat{\theta}_a - \hat{\theta}_e) = \text{aVar}(\hat{\theta}_a) - \text{aVar}(\hat{\theta}_e)$$

where $\text{aVar}(\cdot)$ denotes the asymptotic variance operator.

test statistic is given by the ratio of the variances, J_r:[4]

$$J_r \equiv \frac{\hat{\sigma}_b^2}{\hat{\sigma}_a^2} - 1 \qquad \sqrt{2n}\, J_r \overset{a}{\sim} \mathcal{N}(0, 2). \tag{2.1.7}$$

Although the variance estimator $\hat{\sigma}_b^2$ is based on the differences of every other observation, alternative variance estimators may be obtained by using the differences of every qth observation. Suppose that we obtain $nq + 1$ observations $X_0, X_1, \ldots, X_{nq}$, where q is any integer greater than 1. Define the estimators:

$$\hat{\mu} \equiv \frac{1}{nq} \sum_{k=1}^{nq} (X_k - X_{k-1}) = \frac{1}{nq}(X_{nq} - X_0) \tag{2.1.8a}$$

$$\hat{\sigma}_a^2 \equiv \frac{1}{nq} \sum_{k=1}^{nq} (X_k - X_{k-1} - \hat{\mu})^2 \tag{2.1.8b}$$

$$\hat{\sigma}_b^2(q) \equiv \frac{1}{nq} \sum_{k=1}^{n} (X_{qk} - X_{qk-q} - q\hat{\mu})^2 \tag{2.1.8c}$$

$$J_d(q) \equiv \hat{\sigma}_b^2(q) - \hat{\sigma}_a^2, \qquad J_r(q) \equiv \frac{\hat{\sigma}_b^2(q)}{\hat{\sigma}_a^2} - 1. \tag{2.1.8d}$$

The specification test may then be performed using Theorem 2.1.[5]

Theorem 2.1. *Under the null hypothesis* H, *the asymptotic distributions of* $J_d(q)$ *and* $J_r(q)$ *are given by*

$$\sqrt{nq}\, J_d(q) \overset{a}{\sim} \mathcal{N}(0, 2(q-1)\sigma_o^4) \tag{2.1.9a}$$

$$\sqrt{nq}\, J_r(q) \overset{a}{\sim} \mathcal{N}(0, 2(q-1)). \tag{2.1.9b}$$

Two further refinements of the statistics J_d and J_r result in more desirable finite-sample properties. The first is to use *overlapping* qth differences of X_t in estimating the variances by defining the following estimator of σ_o^2:

$$\hat{\sigma}_c^2(q) = \frac{1}{nq^2} \sum_{k=q}^{nq} (X_k - X_{k-q} - q\hat{\mu})^2. \tag{2.1.10}$$

---

[4]Note that if $(\hat{\sigma}_a^2)^2$ is used to estimate σ_o^4, then the standard t-test of $J_d = 0$ will yield inferences identical to those obtained from the corresponding test of $J_r = 0$ for the ratio, since

$$\frac{J_d}{\sqrt{2\hat{\sigma}_a^4}} = \frac{\hat{\sigma}_b^2 - \hat{\sigma}_a^2}{\sqrt{2}\,\hat{\sigma}_a^2} = \frac{J_r}{\sqrt{2}} \sim \mathcal{N}(0, 1).$$

[5]Proofs of all the theorems are given in the Appendices.

This differs from the estimator $\hat{\sigma}_b^2(q)$ since this sum contains $nq - q + 1$ terms, whereas the estimator $\hat{\sigma}_b^2(q)$ contains only n terms. By using overlapping qth increments, we obtain a more efficient estimator and hence a more powerful test. Using $\hat{\sigma}_c^2(q)$ in our variance-ratio test, we define the corresponding test statistics for the difference and the ratio as

$$M_d(q) \equiv \hat{\sigma}_c^2(q) - \hat{\sigma}_a^2 \qquad M_r(q) \equiv \frac{\hat{\sigma}_c^2(q)}{\hat{\sigma}_a^2} - 1. \qquad (2.1.11)$$

The second refinement involves using unbiased variance estimators in the calculation of the M-statistics. Denote the unbiased estimators as $\bar{\sigma}_a^2$ and $\bar{\sigma}_c^2(q)$, where

$$\bar{\sigma}_a^2 = \frac{1}{nq - 1} \sum_{k=1}^{nq} (X_k - X_{k-1} - \hat{\mu})^2 \qquad (2.1.12a)$$

$$\bar{\sigma}_c^2 = \frac{1}{m} \sum_{k=q}^{nq} (X_k - X_{k-q} - q\hat{\mu})^2$$

$$m = q(nq - q + 1)\left(1 - \frac{q}{nq}\right) \qquad (2.1.12b)$$

and define the statistics:

$$\bar{M}_d(q) \equiv \bar{\sigma}_c^2(q) - \bar{\sigma}_a^2, \qquad \bar{M}_r(q) \equiv \frac{\bar{\sigma}_c^2(q)}{\bar{\sigma}_a^2} - 1. \qquad (2.1.13)$$

Although this does not yield an unbiased variance ratio, simulation experiments show that the finite-sample properties of the test statistics are closer to their asymptotic counterparts when this bias adjustment is made.[6] Inference for the overlapping variance differences and ratios may then be performed using Theorem 2.2.

Theorem 2.2. *Under the null hypothesis* H, *the asymptotic distributions of the statistics* $M_d(q)$, $M_r(q)$, $\bar{M}_d(q)$, *and* $\bar{M}_r(q)$ *are given by*

$$\sqrt{nq}\, M_d(q) \overset{a}{\sim} \sqrt{nq}\, \bar{M}_d(q) \overset{a}{\sim} \mathcal{N}\left(0, \frac{2(2q-1)(q-1)}{3q}\sigma_o^4\right) \qquad (2.1.14a)$$

$$\sqrt{nq}\, M_r(q) \overset{a}{\sim} \sqrt{nq}\, \bar{M}_r(q) \overset{a}{\sim} \mathcal{N}\left(0, \frac{2(2q-1)(q-1)}{3q}\right). \qquad (2.1.14b)$$

---

[6]According to the results of Monte Carlo experiments in Lo and MacKinlay (1989a), the behavior of the bias-adjusted M-statistics (which we denote as $\bar{M}_d(q)$ and $\bar{M}_r(q)$) does not depart significantly from that of their asymptotic limits even for small sample sizes. Therefore, all our empirical results are based on the $\bar{M}_r(q)$-statistic.

In practice, the statistics in Equations (2.1.14) may be standardized in the usual manner (e.g., define the (asymptotically) standard normal test statistic $z(q) \equiv \sqrt{nq} \, \bar{M}_r(q)(2(2q-1)(q-1)/3q)^{-1/2} \stackrel{a}{\sim} \mathcal{N}(0,1)$).

To develop some intuition for these variance ratios, observe that for an aggregation value q of 2, the $M_r(q)$-statistic may be reexpressed as

$$M_r(2) = \hat{\rho}(1) - \frac{1}{4n\hat{\sigma}_a^2} \left[(X_1 - X_0 - \hat{\mu})^2 + (X_{2n} - X_{2n-1} - \hat{\mu})^2 \right] \simeq \hat{\rho}(1).$$

$$(2.1.15)$$

Hence, for $q = 2$ the $M_r(q)$-statistic is approximately the first-order autocorrelation coefficient estimator $\hat{\rho}(1)$ of the differences. More generally, it may be shown that

$$M_r(q) \simeq \frac{2(q-1)}{q} \hat{\rho}(1) + \frac{2(q-2)}{q} \hat{\rho}(2) + \cdots + \frac{2}{q} \hat{\rho}(q-1) \qquad (2.1.16)$$

where $\hat{\rho}(k)$ denotes the kth-order autocorrelation coefficient estimator of the first differences of X_t.[7] Equation (2.1.16) provides a simple interpretation for the variance ratios computed with an aggregation value q: They are (approximately) linear combinations of the first $q - 1$ autocorrelation coefficient estimators of the first differences with arithmetically declining weights.[8]

2.1.2 Heteroskedastic Increments

Since there is already a growing consensus among financial economists that volatilities do change over time,[9] a rejection of the random walk hypothesis because of heteroskedasticity would not be of much interest. We therefore wish to derive a version of our specification test of the random walk model that is robust to changing variances. As long as the increments are uncorrelated, even in the presence of heteroskedasticity the variance ratio must still approach unity as the number of observations increase without bound, for the variance of the sum of uncorrelated increments must still equal the sum of the variances. However, the asymptotic variance of the variance ratios will clearly depend on the type and degree of heteroskedasticity present. One possible approach is to assume some specific form of heteroskedasticity and then to calculate the asymptotic variance of $\bar{M}_r(q)$ under this null

---

[7]See Equation (A.1.6a) in the Appendix.

[8]Note the similarity between these variance ratios and the Box-Pierce Q-statistic, which is a linear combination of *squared* autocorrelations with all the weights set identically equal to unity. Although we may expect the finite-sample behavior of the variance ratios to be comparable to that of the Q-statistic under the null hypothesis, they can have very different power properties under various alternatives. See Lo and MacKinlay (1989a) for further details.

[9]See, for example, Merton (1980), Poterba and Summers (1986), and French, Schwert, and Stambaugh (1987).

hypothesis. However, to allow for more general forms of heteroskedasticity, we employ an approach developed by White (1980) and by White and Domowitz (1984). This approach also allows us to relax the requirement of Gaussian increments, an especially important extension in view of stock returns' well-documented empirical departures from normality.[10] Specifically, we consider the null hypothesis H*:[11]

(A1) For all t, $E(\epsilon_t) = 0$, and $E(\epsilon_t \epsilon_{t-\tau}) = 0$ for any $\tau \neq 0$.

(A2) $\{\epsilon_t\}$ is ϕ-mixing with coefficients $\phi(m)$ of size $r/(2r-1)$ or is α-mixing with coefficients $\alpha(m)$ of size $r/(r-1)$, where $r > 1$, such that for all t and for any $\tau \geq 0$, there exists some $\delta > 0$ for which

$$E|\epsilon_t \epsilon_{t-\tau}|^{2(r+\delta)} < \Delta < \infty. \tag{2.1.17}$$

(A3) $\lim_{nq\to\infty} \dfrac{1}{nq} \sum_{t=1}^{nq} E(\epsilon_t^2) = \sigma_o^2 < \infty.$

(A4) For all t, $E(\epsilon_t \epsilon_{t-j} \epsilon_t \epsilon_{t-k}) = 0$ for any nonzero j and k where $j \neq k$.

This null hypothesis assumes that X_t possesses uncorrelated increments but allows for quite general forms of heteroskedasticity, including deterministic changes in the variance (due, for example, to seasonal factors) and Engle's (1982) ARCH processes (in which the conditional variance depends on past information).

Since $\bar{M}_r(q)$ still approaches zero under H*, we need only compute its asymptotic variance (call it $\theta(q)$) to perform the standard inferences. We do this in two steps. First, recall that the following equality obtains asymptotically:

$$\bar{M}_r(q) \overset{a}{=} \sum_{j=1}^{q-1} \frac{2(q-j)}{q} \hat{\rho}(j). \tag{2.1.18}$$

Second, note that under H* (condition 2.1.2) the autocorrelation coefficient estimators $\hat{\rho}(j)$ are asymptotically uncorrelated.[12] If we can obtain

[10]Of course, second moments are still assumed to finite; otherwise, the variance ratio is no longer well defined. This rules out distributions with infinite variance, such as those in the stable Pareto-Levy family (with characteristic exponents that are less than 2) proposed by Mandelbrot (1963) and Fama (1965). We do, however, allow for many other forms of leptokurtosis, such as that generated by Engle's (1982) autoregressive conditionally heteroskedastic (ARCH) process.

[11]Condition 2.1.2 is the essential property of the random walk that we wish to test. Conditions 2.1.2 and 2.1.2 are restrictions on the maximum degree of dependence and heterogeneity allowable while still permitting some form of the law of large numbers and the central limit theorem to obtain. See White (1984) for the precise definitions of ϕ- and α-mixing random sequences. Condition 2.1.2 implies that the sample autocorrelations of ϵ_t are asymptotically uncorrelated; this condition may be weakened considerably at the expense of computational simplicity (see note 12).

[12]Although this restriction on the fourth cross-moments of ϵ_t may seem somewhat unintuitive, it is satisfied for any process with independent increments (regardless of heterogeneity)

asymptotic variances $\delta(j)$ for each of the $\hat{\rho}(j)$ under H*, we may readily calculate the asymptotic variance $\theta(q)$ of $\bar{M}_r(q)$ as the weighted sum of the $\delta(j)$,
where the weights are simply the weights in relation (2.1.18) squared. More
formally, we have:

Theorem 2.3. *Denote by $\delta(j)$ and $\theta(q)$ the asymptotic variances of $\hat{\rho}(j)$ and $\bar{M}_r(q)$,
respectively. Then under the null hypothesis H*:*

1. *The statistics $J_d(q)$, $J_r(q)$, $M_d(q)$, $M_r(q)$, $\bar{M}_d(q)$, and $\bar{M}_r(q)$ all converge
   almost surely to zero for all q as n increases without bound.*
2. *The following is a heteroskedasticity-consistent estimator of $\delta(j)$:*

$$\hat{\delta}(j) = \frac{nq \sum_{k=j+1}^{nq} (X_k - X_{k-1} - \hat{\mu})^2 (X_{k-j} - X_{k-j-1} - \hat{\mu})^2}{\left[\sum_{k=1}^{nq} (X_k - X_{k-1} - \hat{\mu})^2 \right]^2}. \tag{2.1.19}$$

3. *The following is a heteroskedasticity-consistent estimator of $\theta(q)$:*

$$\hat{\theta}(q) \equiv \sum_{j=1}^{q-1} \left[\frac{2(q-j)}{q} \right]^2 \hat{\delta}(j). \tag{2.1.20}$$

Despite the presence of general heteroskedasticity, the standardized test
statistic $z^*(q) \equiv \sqrt{nq}\, \bar{M}_r(q)/\sqrt{\hat{\theta}}$ is still asymptotically standard normal. In
Section 2.2 we use the $z^*(q)$ statistic to test empirically for random walks in
weekly stock returns data.

2.2 The Random Walk Hypothesis for Weekly Returns

To test for random walks in stock market prices, we focus on the 1216-week
time span from September 6, 1962, to December 26, 1985. Our choice of a
weekly observation interval was determined by several considerations. Since
our sampling theory is based wholly on asymptotic approximations, a large
number of observations is appropriate. While daily sampling yields many

---

and also for linear Gaussian ARCH processes. This assumption may be relaxed entirely, requiring the estimation of the asymptotic covariances of the autocorrelation estimators in order to
estimate the limiting variance θ of $\bar{M}_r(q)$ via relation (2.1.18). Although the resulting estimator of θ would be more complicated than Equation (2.1.20), it is conceptually straightforward
and may readily be formed along the lines of Newey and West (1987). An even more general
(and possibly more exact) sampling theory for the variance ratios may be obtained using the
results of Dufour (1981) and Dufour and Roy (1985). Again, this would sacrifice much of the
simplicity of our asymptotic results.

observations, the biases associated with nontrading, the bid-ask spread, asynchronous prices, etc., are troublesome. Weekly sampling is the ideal compromise, yielding a large number of observations while minimizing the biases inherent in daily data.

The weekly stock returns are derived from the CRSP daily returns file. The weekly return of each security is computed as the return from Wednesday's closing price to the following Wednesday's close. If the following Wednesday's price is missing, then Thursday's price (or Tuesday's if Thursday's is missing) is used. If both Tuesday's and Thursday's prices are missing, the return for that week is reported as missing.[13]

In Section 2.2.1 we perform our test on both equal- and value-weighted CRSP indexes for the entire 1216-week period, as well as for 608-week subperiods, using aggregation values q ranging from 2 to 16.[14] Section 2.2.2 reports corresponding test results for size-sorted portfolios, and Section 2.2.3 presents results for individual securities.

2.2.1 Results for Market Indexes

Tables 2.1a and 2.1b report the variance ratios and the test statistics $z^*(q)$ for CRSP NYSE-AMEX market-returns indexes. Table 2.1a presents the results for a one-week base observation period, and Table 2.1b reports similar results for a four-week base observation period. The values reported in the main rows are the actual variance ratios $[\bar{M}_r(q) + 1]$, and the entries enclosed in parentheses are the $z^*(q)$ statistics.[15]

Panel A of Table 2.1a displays the results for the CRSP equal-weighted index. The first row presents the variance ratios and test statistics for the entire 1216-week sample period, and the next two rows give the results for the two 608-week subperiods. The random walk null hypothesis may be rejected at all the usual significance levels for the entire time period and all subperiods. Moreover, the rejections are not due to changing variances since the $z^*(q)$ statistics are robust to heteroskedasticity. The estimates of the variance ratio are *larger* than 1 for all cases. For example, the entries in the first column of panel A correspond to variance ratios with an aggregation value q of 2. In view of Equation (2.1.15), ratios with $q = 2$ are approximately equal to 1 plus the first-order autocorrelation coefficient estimator of weekly returns; hence, the entry in the first row, 1.30, implies that the

---

[13]The average fraction (over all securities) of the entire sample where this occurs is less than 0.5 percent of the time for the 1216-week sample period.

[14]Additional empirical results (304-week subperiods, larger q values, etc.) are reported in Lo and MacKinlay (1987b).

[15]Since the values of $z^*(q)$ are always smaller than the values of $z(q)$ in our empirical results, to conserve space we report only the more conservative statistics. Both statistics are reported in Lo and MacKinlay (1987b).

Table 2.1a.   *Variance-ratio test of the random walk hypothesis for CRSP equal- and value-weighted indexes, for the sample period from September 6, 1962, to December 26, 1985, and subperiods. The variance ratios $1 + \bar{M}_r(q)$ are reported in the main rows, with the heteroskedasticity-robust test statistics $z^*(q)$ given in parentheses immediately below each main row. Under the random walk null hypothesis, the value of the variance ratio is 1 and the test statistics have a standard normal distribution (asymptotically). Test statistics marked with asterisks indicate that the corresponding variance ratios are statistically different from 1 at the 5 percent level of significance.*

Time period	Number nq of base observations	Number q of base observations aggregated to form variance ratio			
		2	4	8	16
A. Equal-weighted CRSP NYSE-AMEX index					
620906–851226	1216	1.30	1.64	1.94	2.05
		(7.51)*	(8.87)*	(8.48)*	(6.59)*
620906–740501	608	1.31	1.62	1.92	2.09
		(5.38)*	(6.03)*	(5.76)*	(4.77)*
740502–851226	608	1.28	1.65	1.93	1.91
		(5.32)*	(6.52)*	(6.13)*	(4.17)*
B. Value-weighted CRSP NYSE-AMEX index					
620906–851226	1216	1.08	1.16	1.22	1.22
		(2.33)*	(2.31)*	(2.07)*	(1.38)
620906–740501	608	1.15	1.22	1.27	1.32
		(2.89)*	(2.28)*	(1.79)	(1.46)
740502–851226	608	1.05	1.12	1.18	1.10
		(0.92)	(1.28)	(1.24)	(0.46)

first-order autocorrelation for weekly returns is approximately 30 percent. The random walk hypothesis is easily rejected at common levels of significance. The variance ratios increase with q, but the magnitudes of the $z^*(q)$ statistics do not. Indeed, the test statistics seem to decline with q; hence, the significance of the rejections becomes weaker as coarser-sample variances are compared to weekly variances. Our finding of *positive* autocorrelation for weekly holding-period returns differs from Fama and French's (1988) finding of negative serial correlation for long holding-period returns. This positive correlation is significant not only for our entire sample period but also for all subperiods.

The rejection of the random walk hypothesis is much weaker for the value-weighted index, as panel B indicates; nevertheless, the general patterns persist: the variance ratios exceed 1, and the $z^*(q)$ statistics decline as

Table 2.1b. *Market index results for a four-week base observation period*

Time period	Number nq of base observations	Number q of base observations aggregated to form variance ratio			
		2	4	8	16
A. Equal-weighted CRSP NYSE-AMEX index					
620906–851226	304	1.15	1.19	1.30	1.30
		$(2.26)^*$	(1.54)	(1.52)	(1.07)
620906–740501	152	1.13	1.23	1.40	
		(1.39)	(1.32)	(1.46)	
740502–851226	152	1.15	1.11	1.02	
		(1.68)	(0.64)	(0.09)	
B. Value-weighted CRSP NYSE-AMEX index					
620906–851226	304	1.05	1.00	1.11	1.07
		(0.75)	(0.00)	(0.57)	(0.26)
620906–740501	152	1.02	1.04	1.12	
		(0.26)	(0.26)	(0.46)	
740502–851226	152	1.05	0.95	0.89	
		(0.63)	(−0.31)	(−0.42)	

Variance-ratio test of the random walk hypothesis for CRSP equal- and value-weighted indexes, for the sample period from September 6, 1962, to December 26, 1985, and subperiods. The variance ratios $1 + \bar{M}_r(q)$ are reported in the main rows, with the heteroskedasticity-robust test statistics $z^*(q)$ given in parentheses immediately below each main row. Under the random walk null hypothesis, the value of the variance ratio is 1 and the test statistics have a standard normal distribution (asymptotically). Test statistics marked with asterisks indicate that the corresponding variance ratios are statistically different from 1 at the 5 percent level of significance.

q increases. The rejections for the value-weighted index are due primarily to the first 608 weeks of the sample period.

Table 2.1b presents the variance ratios using a base observation period of four weeks; hence, the first entry of the first row, 1.15, is the variance ratio of eight-week returns to four-week returns. With a base interval of four weeks, we generally do not reject the random walk model even for the equal-weighted index. This is consistent with the relatively weak evidence against the random walk that previous studies have found when using monthly data.

Although the test statistics in Tables 2.1a and 2.1b are based on nominal stock returns, it is apparent that virtually the same results would obtain with real or excess returns. Since the volatility of weekly nominal returns is so much larger than that of the inflation and Treasury-bill rates, the use of nominal, real, or excess returns in a volatility-based test will yield practically identical inferences.

2.2.2 Results for Size-Based Portfolios

An implication of the work of Keim and Stambaugh (1986) is that, conditional on stock and bond market variables, the logarithms of wealth relatives of portfolios of smaller stocks do not follow random walks. For portfolios of larger stocks, Keim and Stambaugh's results are less conclusive. Consequently, it is of interest to explore what evidence our tests provide for the random walk hypothesis for the logarithm of size-based portfolio wealth relatives.

We compute weekly returns for five size-based portfolios from the NYSE-AMEX universe on the CRSP daily returns file. Stocks with returns for any given week are assigned to portfolios based on which quintile their market value of equity is in. The portfolios are equal-weighted and have a continually changing composition.[16] The number of stocks included in the portfolios varies from 2036 to 2720.

Table 2.2 reports the $\bar{M}_r(q)$ test results for the size-based portfolios, using a base observation period of one week. Panel A reports the results for the portfolio of small firms (first quintile), panel B reports the results for the portfolio of medium-size firms (third quintile), and panel C reports the results for the portfolio of large firms (fifth quintile). Evidence against the random walk hypothesis for small firms is strong for all time periods considered; in panel A all the $z^*(q)$ statistics are well above 2.0, ranging from 6.12 to 11.92. As we proceed through the panels to the results for the portfolio of large firms, the $z^*(q)$ statistics become smaller, but even for the large-firms portfolio the evidence against the null hypothesis is strong. As in the case of the returns indexes, we may obtain estimates of the first-order autocorrelation coefficient for returns on these size-sorted portfolios simply by subtracting 1 from the entries in the $q = 2$ column. The values in Table 2.2 indicate that the portfolio returns for the smallest quintile have a 42 percent weekly autocorrelation over the entire sample period! Moreover, this autocorrelation reaches 49 percent in subperiod 2 (May 2, 1974, to December 26, 1985). Although the serial correlation for the portfolio returns of the largest quintile is much smaller (14 percent for the entire sample period), it is statistically significant.

---

[16]We also performed our tests using value-weighted portfolios and obtained essentially the same results. The only difference appeared in the largest quintile of the value-weighted portfolio, for which the random walk hypothesis was generally not rejected. This, of course, is not surprising, given that the largest value-weighted quintile is quite similar to the value-weighted market index.

Table 2.2. *Variance-ratio test of the random walk hypothesis for size-sorted portfolios, for the sample period from September 6, 1962, to December 26, 1985, and subperiods. The variance ratios $1 + \bar{M}_r(q)$ are reported in the main rows, with the heteroskedasticity-robust test statistics $z^*(q)$ given in parentheses immediately below each main row. Under the random walk null hypothesis, the value of the variance ratio is 1 and the test statistics have a standard normal distribution (asymptotically). Test statistics marked with asterisks indicate that the corresponding variance ratios are statistically different from 1 at the 5 percent level of significance.*

Time period	Number nq of base observations	Number q of base observations aggregated to form variance ratio			
		2	4	8	16
A. Portfolio of firms with market values in smallest NYSE-AMEX quintile					
620906–851226	1216	1.42	1.97	2.49	2.68
		(8.81)*	(11.58)*	(11.92)*	(9.65)*
620906–740501	608	1.37	1.83	2.27	2.52
		(6.12)*	(7.83)*	(7.94)*	(6.68)*
740502–851226	608	1.49	2.14	2.76	2.87
		(6.44)*	(8.66)*	(9.06)*	(7.06)*
B. Portfolio of firms with market values in central NYSE-AMEX quintile					
620906–851226	1216	1.28	1.60	1.84	1.91
		(7.38)*	(8.37)*	(7.70)*	(5.78)*
620906–740501	608	1.30	1.59	1.85	2.01
		(5.31)*	(5.73)*	(5.33)*	(4.42)*
740502–851226	608	1.27	1.59	1.80	1.69
		(5.31)*	(5.73)*	(5.33)*	(4.42)*
C. Portfolio of firms with market values in largest NYSE-AMEX quintile					
620906–851226	1216	1.14	1.27	1.36	1.34
		(3.82)*	(3.99)*	(3.45)*	(2.22)*
620906–740501	608	1.21	1.36	1.45	1.44
		(4.04)*	(3.70)*	(2.96)*	(2.02)*
740502–851226	608	1.09	1.20	1.27	1.18
		(1.80)	(2.18)*	(1.95)	(0.87)

Using a base observation interval of four weeks, much of the evidence against the random walk for size-sorted portfolios disappears. Although the smallest-quintile portfolio still exhibits a serial correlation of 23 percent with a $z^*(2)$ statistic of 3.09, none of the variance ratios for the largest-quintile portfolio is significantly different from 1. In the interest of brevity, we do not report those results here but refer interested readers to Lo and MacKinlay (1987b).

The results for size-based portfolios are generally consistent with those for the market indexes. The patterns of (1) the variance ratios increasing in q and (2) the significance of rejections decreasing in q that we observed for the indexes also obtain for these portfolios. The evidence against the random walk hypothesis for the logarithm of wealth relatives of small-firms portfolios is strong in all cases considered. For larger firms and a one-week base observation interval, the evidence is also inconsistent with the random walk; however, as the base observation interval is increased to four weeks, our test does not reject the random walk model for larger firms.

2.2.3 Results for Individual Securities

For completeness, we performed the variance-ratio test on all individual stocks that have complete return histories in the CRSP database for our entire 1216-week sample period, yielding a sample of 625 securities. Owing to space limitations, we report only a brief summary of these results in Table 2.3. Panel A contains the cross-sectional means of variance ratios for the entire sample as well as for the 100 smallest, 100 intermediate, and 100 largest stocks. Cross-sectional standard deviations are given in parentheses below the main rows. Since the variance ratios are clearly not cross-sectionally independent, these standard deviations cannot be used to form the usual tests of significance; they are reported only to provide some indication of the cross-sectional dispersion of the variance ratios.

The average variance ratio for individual securities is less than unity when $q = 2$, implying that there is negative serial correlation on average. For all stocks, the average serial correlation is -3 percent, and -6 percent for the smallest 100 stocks. However, the serial correlation is both statistically and economically insignificant and provides little evidence against the random walk hypothesis. For example, the largest average $z^*(q)$ statistic over all stocks occurs for $q = 4$ and is -0.90 (with a cross-sectional standard deviation of 1.19); the largest average $z^*(q)$ for the 100 smallest stocks is -1.67 (for $q = 2$, with a cross-sectional standard deviation of 1.75). These results complement French and Roll's (1986) finding that daily returns of individual securities are slightly negatively autocorrelated.

For comparison, panel B reports the variance ratios of equal- and value-weighted portfolios of the 625 securities. The results are consistent with those in Tables 2.1 and 2.2; significant positive autocorrelation for the equal-weighted portfolio, and less significant positive autocorrelation for the value-weighted portfolio.

That the returns of individual securities have statistically insignificant autocorrelation is not surprising. Individual returns contain much company-

Table 2.3. *Means of variance ratios over all individual securities with complete return histories from September 2, 1962, to December 26, 1985 (625 stocks). Means of variance ratios for the smallest 100 stocks, the intermediate 100 stocks, and the largest 100 stocks are also reported. For purposes of comparison, panel B reports the variance ratios for equal- and value-weighted portfolios, respectively, of the 625 stocks. Parenthetical entries for averages of individual securities (panel A) are standard deviations of the cross-section of variance ratios. Because the variance ratios are not cross-sectionally independent, the standard deviation cannot be used to perform the usual significance tests; they are reported only to provide an indication of the variance ratios' cross-sectional dispersion. Parenthetical entries for portfolio variance ratios (panel B) are the heteroskedasticity-robust $z^*(q)$ statistics. Asterisks indicate variance ratios that are statistically different from 1 at the 5 percent level of significance.*

Sample	Number nq of base observations	Number q of base observations aggregated to form variance ratio			
		2	4	8	16
A. Averages of variance ratios over individual securities					
All stocks	1216	0.97	0.94	0.92	0.89
(625 stocks)		(0.05)*	(0.08)	(0.11)	(0.15)
Small stocks	1216	0.94	0.91	0.90	0.88
(100 stocks)		(0.06)	(0.10)	(0.13)	(0.18)
Medium stocks	1216	0.98	0.97	0.96	0.93
(100 stocks)		(0.05)	(0.09)	(0.12)	(0.15)
Large stocks	1216	0.97	0.94	0.86	0.86
(100 stocks)		(0.04)	(0.07)	(0.11)	(0.17)
B. Variance ratios of equal- and value-weighted portfolios of all stocks					
Equal-weighted portfolio	1216	1.21	1.64	1.65	1.76
(625 stocks)		(5.94)*	(6.71)*	(6.06)*	(4.25)*
Value-weighted portfolio	1216	1.04	1.08	1.12	1.12
(625 stocks)		(1.30)	(1.24)	(1.16)	(0.76)

specific, or "idiosyncratic," noise that makes it difficult to detect the presence of predictable components. Since the idiosyncratic noise is largely attenuated by forming portfolios, we would expect to uncover the predictable "systematic" component more readily when securities are combined. Nevertheless, the negativity of the individual securities' autocorrelations is an interesting contrast to the positive autocorrelation of the portfolio returns. Since this is a well-known symptom of infrequent trading, we consider such an explanation in Section 2.3.

2.3 Spurious Autocorrelation Induced by Nontrading

Although we have based our empirical results on weekly data to minimize the biases associated with market microstructure issues, this alone does not ensure against the biases' possibly substantial influences. In this section we explicitly consider the conjecture that infrequent or nonsynchronous trading may induce significant spurious correlation in stock returns.[17] The common intuition for the source of such artificial serial correlation is that small capitalization stocks trade less frequently than larger stocks. Therefore, new information is impounded first into large-capitalization stock prices and then into smaller-stock prices with a lag. This lag induces a positive serial correlation in, for example, an equal-weighted index of stock returns. Of course, this induced positive serial correlation would be less pronounced in a value-weighted index. Since our rejections of the random walk hypothesis are most resounding for the equal-weighted index, they may very well be the result of this nontrading phenomenon. To investigate this possibility, we consider the following simple model of nontrading.[18]

Suppose that our universe of stocks consists of N securities indexed by i, each with the return-generating process

$$R_{it} = R_{Mt} + \epsilon_{it} \qquad i = 1, \ldots, N \qquad (2.3.1)$$

where R_{Mt} represents a factor common to all returns (e.g., the market) and is assumed to be an independently and identically distributed (IID) random variable with mean μ_M and variance σ_M^2. The ϵ_{it} term represents the idiosyncratic component of security i's return and is also assumed to be IID (over *both* i and t), with mean 0 and variance σ_M^2. The return-generating process may thus be identified with N securities each with a unit beta such that the theoretical R^2 of a market-model regression for each security is 0.50.

Suppose that in each period t there is some chance that security i does not trade. One simple approach to modeling this phenomenon is to distinguish between the observed returns process and the virtual returns process. For example, suppose that security i has traded in period $t - 1$; consider its behavior in period t. If security i does not trade in period t, we define its vir-

---

[17]See, for example, Scholes and Williams (1977) and Cohen, Hawawini, Maier, Schwartz, and Whitcomb (1983a).

[18]Although our model is formulated in discrete time for simplicity, it is in fact slightly more general than the Scholes and Williams (1977) continuous-time model of nontrading. Specifically, Scholes and Williams implicitly assume that each security trades at least once within a given time interval by "ignoring periods over which no trades occur" (page 311), whereas our model requires no such restriction. As a consequence, it may be shown that, ceteris paribus, the magnitude of spuriously induced autocorrelation is lower in Scholes and Williams (1977) than in our framework. However, the qualitative predictions of the two models of nontrading are essentially the same. For example, both models imply that returns for individual securities will exhibit negative serial correlation but that portfolio returns will be positively autocorrelated.

tual return as R_{it} (which is given by Equation (2.3.1)), whereas its observed return R_{it}^o is zero. If security i then trades at $t+1$, its observed return R_{it+1}^o is defined to be the sum of its virtual returns R_{it} and R_{it+1}; hence, nontrading is assumed to cause returns to cumulate. The cumulation of returns over periods of nontrading captures the essence of spuriously induced correlations due to the nontrading lag.

To calculate the magnitude of the positive serial correlation induced by nontrading, we must specify the probability law governing the nontrading event. For simplicity, we assume that whether or not a serucity trades may be modeled by a Bernoulli trial, so that in each period and for each security there is a probability p that it trades and a probability $1 - p$ that is does not. It is assumed that these Bernoulli trials are IID across securities and, for each security, are IID over time. Now consider the observed return R_t^o at time t of an equal-weighted portfolio:

$$R_t^o \equiv \frac{1}{N} \sum_i^N R_{it}^o. \tag{2.3.2}$$

The observed return R_{it}^o for security i may be expressed as

$$R_{it}^o = X_{it}(0)R_{it} + X_{it}(1)R_{it-1} + X_{it}(2)R_{it-2} + \cdots \tag{2.3.3}$$

where $X_{it}(j)$, $j = 1, 2, 3, \ldots$ are random variables defined as

$$X_{it}(0) \equiv \begin{cases} 1 & \text{if } i \text{ trades at } t \\ 0 & \text{otherwise} \end{cases} \tag{2.3.4a}$$

$$X_{it}(1) \equiv \begin{cases} 1 & \text{if } i \text{ does not trade at } t-1 \text{ and } i \text{ trades at } t \\ 0 & \text{otherwise} \end{cases} \tag{2.3.4b}$$

$$X_{it}(2) \equiv \begin{cases} 1 & \text{if } i \text{ trades at } t \text{ and does not trade at } t-1 \text{ and } t-2 \\ 0 & \text{otherwise} \end{cases} \tag{2.3.4c}$$

$$\vdots$$

The $X_{it}(j)$ variables are merely indicators of the number of *consecutive* periods before t in which security j has not traded. Using this relation, we have

$$R_t^o = \frac{1}{N} \sum_i^N X_{it}(0)R_{it} + \frac{1}{N} \sum_i^N X_{it}(1)R_{it-1} + \frac{1}{N} \sum_i^N X_{it}(2)R_{it-2} + \cdots \tag{2.3.5}$$

For large N, it may readily be shown that because the ϵ_{it} component of each security's return is idiosyncratic and has zero expectation, the following approximation obtains:

$$R_t^o \simeq \frac{1}{N}\sum_i^N X_{it}(0)R_{Mt} + \frac{1}{N}\sum_i^N X_{it}(1)R_{Mt-1} + \frac{1}{N}\sum_i^N X_{it}(2)R_{Mt-2} + \cdots$$
(2.3.6)

It is also apparent that the averages $(1/N)\sum_i^N X_{it}(j)$ become arbitrarily close, again for large N, to the probability of j consecutive no-trades followed by a trade; that is,

$$\text{plim}_{N\to\infty}\frac{1}{N}\sum_i^N X_{it}(j) = p(1-p)^j.$$
(2.3.7)

The observed equal-weighted return is then given by the approximation

$$R_t^o \simeq pR_{Mt} + p(1-p)R_{Mt-1} + p(1-p)^2R_{Mt-2} + \cdots$$
(2.3.8)

Using this expression, the general jth-order autocorrelation coefficient $\rho(j)$ may be readily computed as

$$\rho(j) \equiv \frac{\text{Cov}(R_t^o, R_{t-j}^o)}{\text{Var}(R_t^o)} = (1-p)^j.$$
(2.3.9)

Assuming that the implicit time interval corresponding to our single period is one trading day, we may also compute the weekly (five-day) first-order autocorrelation coefficient of R_t^o as

$$\rho^W(1) = \frac{\rho(1) + 2\rho(2) + \cdots + 5\rho(5) + 4\rho(6) + \cdots + \rho(9)}{5 + 8\rho(1) + 6\rho(2) + 4\rho(3) + 2\rho(4)}.$$
(2.3.10)

By specifying reasonable values for the probability of nontrading, we may calculate the induced autocorrelation using Equation (2.3.10). To develop some intuition for the parameter p, observe that the total number of securities that trade in any given period t is given by the sum $\sum_i^N X_{it}(0)$. Under our assumptions, this random variable has a binomial distribution with parameters (N, p); hence, its expected value and variance are given by Np and $Np(1-p)$, respectively. Therefore, the probability p may be interpreted as the fraction of the total number of N securities that trades on average in any given period. A value of .90 implies that, on average, 10 percent of the securities do not trade in a single period.

Table 2.4 presents the theoretical daily and weekly autocorrelations induced by nontrading for nontrading probabilities of 10 to 50 percent. The first row shows that when (on average) 10 percent of the stocks do not trade each day, this induces a weekly autocorrelation of only 2.1 percent! Even when the probability of nontrading is increased to 50 percent (which is quite

Table 2.4. *Spuriously induced autocorrelations are reported for nontrading probabilities* $1 - p$ *of 10 to 50 percent. In the absence of the nontrading phenomenon, the theoretical values of daily jth-order autocorrelations* $\rho(j)$ *and the weekly first-order autocorrelation* $\rho^W(1)$ *are all zero.*

$1 - p$	$\rho(1)$	$\rho(2)$	$\rho(3)$	$\rho(4)$	$\rho(5)$	$\rho^W(1)$
.10	.1000	.0100	.0010	.0001	.0000	.0211
.20	.2000	.0400	.0080	.0016	.0003	.0454
.30	.3000	.0900	.0270	.0081	.0024	.0756
.40	.4000	.1600	.0640	.0256	.0102	.1150
.50	.5000	.2500	.1250	.0625	.0312	.1687

unrealistic), the induced weekly autocorrelation is 17 percent.[19] We conclude that our rejection of the random walk hypothesis cannot be attributed solely to infrequent trading.

The positive autocorrelation of portfolio returns and the negative autocorrelation of individual securities is puzzling. Although our stylized model suggests that infrequent trading cannot fully account for the 30 percent autocorrelation of the equal-weighted index, the combination of infrequent

---

[19] Several other factors imply that the actual sizes of the spurious autocorrelations induced by infrequent trading are lower than those given in Table 2.4. For example, in calculating the induced correlations using Equation (2.3.9), we have ignored the idiosyncratic components in returns because diversification makes these components trivial in the limit; in practice, perfect diversification is never achieved. But any residual risk increases the denominator of Equation (2.3.9) and does not necessarily increase the numerator (since the ϵ_{it}'s are cross-sectionally uncorrelated). To see this explicitly, we simulated the returns for 1000 stocks over 5120 days, calculated the weekly autocorrelations for the virtual returns and for the observed returns, computed the difference of those autocorrelations, repeated this procedure 20 times, and then averaged the differences. With a (daily) nontrading probability of 10 percent, the simulations yield a difference in *weekly* autocorrelations of 2.1 percent, of 4.3 percent for a nontrading probability of 20 percent, and of 7.6 percent for a nontrading probability of 30 percent.

Another factor that may reduce the spurious positive autocorrelation empirically is that, within the CRSP files, if a security does not trade, its price is reported as the average of the bid-ask spread. As long as the specialist adjusts the apread to reflect the new information, even if no trade occurs the reported CRSP price will reflect the new information. Although there may still be some delay before the bid-ask spread is adjusted, it is presumably less than the lag between trades.

Also, if it is assumed that the probability of no-trades depends upon whether or not the security has traded recently, it is natural to suppose that the likelihood of a no-trade tomorrow is lower if there is a no-trade today. In this case, it may readily be shown that the induced autocorrelation is even lower than that computed in our IID framework.

trading and Roll's (1984a) bid-ask effect may explain a large part of the small negative autocorrelation in individual returns.

One possible stochastic model that is loosely consistent with these observations is to let returns be the sum of a positively autocorrelated common component and an idiosyncratic white-noise component. The common component induces significant positive autocorrelation in portfolios since the idiosyncratic component is trivialized by diversification. The white-noise component reduces the positive autocorrelation of individual stock returns, and the combination of infrequent trading and the bid-ask spread effects drives the autocorrelation negative. Of course, explicit statistical estimation is required in order to formalize such heuristics and, ultimately, what we seek is an economic model of asset prices that might give rise to such empirical findings. This is beyond the scope of this chapter, but it is the focus of current investigation.

2.4 The Mean-Reverting Alternative to the Random Walk

Although the variance-ratio test has shown weekly stock returns to be incompatible with the random walk model, the rejections do not offer any explicit guidance toward a more plausible model for the data. However, the *patterns* of the test's rejections over different base observation intervals and aggregation values q do shed considerable light on the relative merits of competing alternatives to the random walk. For example, one currently popular hypothesis is that the stock-returns process may be described by the sum of a random walk and a stationary mean-reverting component, as in Summers (1986) and in Fama and French (1988).[20] One implication of this alternative is that returns are negatively serially correlated for all holding periods. Another implication is that, up to a certain holding period, the serial correlation becomes more negative as the holding period increases.[21] If returns are in fact generated by such a process, then their variance ratios

[20]Shiller and Perron (1985) propose only a mean-reverting process (the Ornstein-Uhlenbeck process), whereas Poterba and Summers (1988) propose the sum of a random walk and a stationary mean-reverting process. Although neither study offers any theoretical justification for its proposal, both studies motivate their alternatives as models of investors' fads.
[21]If returns are generated by the sum of a random walk and a stationary mean-reverting process, their serial correlation will be a U-shaped function of the holding period; the first-order autocorrelation becomes more negative as shorter holding periods lengthen, but it graudally returns to zero for longer holding periods because the random walk component dominates. The curvature of this U-shaped function depends on the relative variability of the random walk and mean-reverting components. Fama and French's (1988) parameter estimates imply that the autocorrelation coefficient is monotonically decreasing for holding periods up to three years; that is, the minimum of the U-shaped curve occurs at a holding period greater than or equal to three years.

should be less than unity when $q = 2$ (since negative serial correlation is implied by this process). Also, the rejection of the random walk should be stronger as q increases (larger $z^*(q)$ values for larger q).[22] But Tables 2.1 and 2.2 and those in Lo and MacKinlay (1987b) show that both these implications are contradicted by the empirical evidence.[23] Weekly returns do not follow a random walk, but they do not fit a stationary mean-reverting alternative any better.

Of course, the negative serial correlation in Fama and French's (1988) study for long (three- to five-year) holding-period returns is, on purely theoretical grounds, not necessarily inconsistent with positive serial correlation for shorter holding-period returns. However, our results do indicate that the sum of a random walk and a mean-reverting process cannot be a complete description of stock-price behavior.

2.5 Conclusion

We have rejected the random walk hypothesis for weekly stock market returns by using a simple volatility-based specification test. These rejections cannot be explained completely by infrequent trading or time-varying volatilities. The patterns of rejections indicate that the stationary mean-reverting models of Shiller and Perron (1985), Summers (1986), Poterba and Summers (1988), and Fama and French (1988) cannot account for the departures of weekly returns from the random walk.

As we stated in the introduction, the rejection of the random walk model does not necessarily imply the inefficiency of stock-price formation. Our results do, however, impose restrictions upon the set of plausible economic models for asset pricing; any structural paradigm of rational price formation must now be able to explain this pattern of serial correlation present in weekly data. As a purely descriptive tool for examining the stochastic evolution of prices through time, our specification test also serves a useful purpose, especially when an empirically plausible statistical model of the price process is more important than a detailed economic paradigm of equilibrium. For example, the pricing of complex financial claims often depends critically upon the specific stochastic process driving underlying asset returns. Since such models are usually based on arbitrage considerations, the particular economic equilibrium that generates prices is of less consequence. One specific implication of our empirical findings is that

[22]This pattern of stronger rejections with larger q is also only true up to a certain value of q. In view of Fama and French's (1988) results, this upper limit for q is much greater than 16 when the base observation interval is one week. See note 21.

[23]See Lo and MacKinlay (1989a) for explicit power calculations against this alternative and against a more empirically relevant model of stock prices.

the standard Black-Scholes pricing formula for stock index options is mis-specified.

Although our variance-based test may be used as a diagnostic check for the random walk specification, it is a more difficult task to determine precisely which stochastic process best fits the data. The results of French and Roll (1986) for return variances when markets are open versus when they are closed add yet another dimension to this challenge. The construction of a single stochastic process that fits both short and long holding-period returns data is one important direction for further investigation. However, perhaps the more pressing problem is to specify an economic model that might give rise to such a process for asset prices, and this will be pursued in subsequent research.

Appendix A2
Proof of Theorems

Proof of Theorem 2.1

Under the IID Gaussian distributional assumption of the null hypothesis H, $\hat{\sigma}_a^2$ and $\hat{\sigma}_b^2$ are maximum-likelihood estimators of σ_o^2 with respect to data sets consisting of every observation and of every qth observation, respectively (the dependence of $\hat{\sigma}_b^2$ on q is suppressed for notational simplicity). Therefore, it is well known that

$$\sqrt{nq}\,(\hat{\sigma}_a^2 - \hat{\sigma}_0^2) \overset{a}{\sim} \mathcal{N}(0, 2\sigma_o^4) \tag{A2.1}$$

$$\sqrt{nq}\,(\hat{\sigma}_b^2 - \hat{\sigma}_0^2) \overset{a}{\sim} \mathcal{N}(0, 2\sigma_o^4)\,. \tag{A2.2}$$

Since, under the null hypothesis H, $\hat{\sigma}_a^2$ is the maximum-likelihood estimator of σ_o^2 using *every* observation, it is asymptotically efficient. Therefore, following Hausman's (1978) approach, we conclude that the asymptotic variance of $\sqrt{nq}(\hat{\sigma}_b^2 - \hat{\sigma}_a^2)$ is simply the difference of the asymptotic variances of $\sqrt{nq}(\hat{\sigma}_b^2 - \sigma_o^2)$ and $\sqrt{nq}(\hat{\sigma}_a^2 - \sigma_o^2)$. Thus, we have

$$\sqrt{nq}\,J_d(r) \equiv \sqrt{nq}(\hat{\sigma}_b^2 - \hat{\sigma}_a^2) \overset{a}{\sim} \mathcal{N}(0, 2(q-1)\sigma_o^4)\,. \tag{A2.3}$$

The asymptotic distribution of the ratio then follows by applying the "delta method" to the quantity $\sqrt{nq}(g(\hat{\sigma}_a^2, \hat{\sigma}_b^2) - g(\sigma_o^2, \sigma_o^2))$, where the bivariate function g is defined as $g(u, v) \equiv v/u$; hence,

$$\sqrt{nq}\,J_r(q) = \sqrt{nq}\left(\frac{\hat{\sigma}_b^2}{\hat{\sigma}_a^2} - 1 \right) \overset{a}{\sim} \mathcal{N}(0, 2(q-1))\,. \tag{A2.4}$$

Q.E.D.

Proof of Theorem 2.2

To derive the limiting distributions of $\sqrt{nq}\,M_d$ and $\sqrt{nq}\,M_r$, we require the asymptotic distribution of $\sqrt{nq}(\hat{\sigma}_c^2 - \sigma_o^2)$ (the dependence of $\hat{\sigma}_c^2$ on q is suppressed for notational convenience). Our approach is to reexpress this variance estimator as a function of the autocovariances of the $(X_k - X_{k-q})$ terms and then employ well-known limit theorems for autocovariances. Consider the quantity

$$
\hat{\sigma}_c^2 = \frac{1}{nq^2} \sum_{k=q}^{nq} (X_k - X_{k-q} - q\hat{\mu})^2
$$

$$
= \frac{1}{nq^2} \sum_{k=q}^{nq} \left[\sum_{j=1}^{q} (X_{k-j+1} - X_{k-j} - \hat{\mu}) \right]^2 \tag{A2.5a}
$$

$$
= \frac{1}{nq^2} \sum_{k=q}^{nq} \left(\sum_{j=1}^{q} \hat{\epsilon}_{k-j+1} \right)^2 \tag{A2.5b}
$$

where $\hat{\epsilon}_{k-j+1} \equiv X_{k-j+1} - X_{k-j} - \hat{\mu}$. But then we have

$$
\hat{\sigma}_c^2 = \frac{1}{nq^2} \sum_{k=q}^{nq} \left(\sum_{j=1}^{q} \hat{\epsilon}_{k-j+1}^2 + 2\sum_{j=1}^{q-1} \hat{\epsilon}_{k-j+1}\,\hat{\epsilon}_{k-j} \right.
$$
$$
\left. + 2\sum_{j=1}^{q-2} \hat{\epsilon}_{k-j+1}\,\hat{\epsilon}_{k-j-1} + \cdots + 2\hat{\epsilon}_k\,\hat{\epsilon}_{k-q+1} \right) \tag{A2.6a}
$$

$$
= \frac{1}{nq^2} \left\{ q\sum_{k=1}^{nq} \hat{\epsilon}_k^2 - \sum_{k=1}^{q-1} [(q-k)\hat{\epsilon}_k^2 + k\hat{\epsilon}_{nq-q+k+1}^2] \right.
$$
$$
+ 2(q-1)\sum_{k=2}^{nq} \hat{\epsilon}_k\,\hat{\epsilon}_{k-1} - 2\sum_{k=2}^{q-1}[(q-k)\hat{\epsilon}_k\,\hat{\epsilon}_{k-1}
$$
$$
+ (k-1)\hat{\epsilon}_{nq-q+k+1}\,\hat{\epsilon}_{nq-q+k}]
$$
$$
+ 2(q-2)\sum_{k=3}^{nq} \hat{\epsilon}_k\,\hat{\epsilon}_{k-2} - 2\sum_{k=3}^{q-1}[(q-k)\hat{\epsilon}_k\,\hat{\epsilon}_{k-2}
$$
$$
+ (k-2)\hat{\epsilon}_{nq-q+k+1}\,\hat{\epsilon}_{nq-q+k-1}]
$$
$$
\left. + \cdots + 2\sum_{k=q}^{nq} \hat{\epsilon}_k\,\hat{\epsilon}_{k-q+1} \right\} \tag{A2.6b}
$$

$$= \hat{\gamma}(0) - o_p(n^{-1/2}) + \frac{2(q-1)}{q}\,\hat{\gamma}(1) - o_p(n^{-1/2})$$

$$+ \frac{2(q-2)}{q}\,\hat{\gamma}(2) - o_p(n^{-1/2}) + \cdots + \frac{2}{q}\hat{\gamma}(q-1) \qquad \text{(A2.6c)}$$

where $\hat{\gamma}(j) \equiv (1/nq)\sum_{k=j+1}^{nq} \hat{\epsilon}_k \hat{\epsilon}_{k-j}$ and $o_p(n^{-1/2})$ denotes a quantity that is of an order smaller than $n^{-1/2}$ in probability. Now define the $(q \times 1)$ vector $\hat{\gamma} \equiv [\hat{\gamma}(0)\,\hat{\gamma}(1)\ldots\hat{\gamma}(q-1)]'$. A standard limit theorem for sample autocovariances $\hat{\gamma}$ of a stationary time series with independent Gaussian increments is (see, for example, Fuller, 1976, chap. 6.3)

$$\sqrt{nq}(\hat{\gamma} - \sigma_o^2 e_1) \overset{a}{\sim} \mathcal{N}[0, \sigma_o^4(I_q + e_1 e_1')] \qquad \text{(A2.7)}$$

where e_1 is the $(q \times 1)$ vector $[1\,0\ldots0]'$ and I_q is the identity matrix of order q. Returning to the quantity $\sqrt{nq}(\hat{\sigma}_c^2 - \sigma_o^2)$, we have

$$\sqrt{nq}(\hat{\sigma}_c^2 - \sigma_o^2) = \sqrt{nq}\Big[(\hat{\gamma}(0) - \sigma_o^2) + \frac{2(q-1)}{q}\,\hat{\gamma}(1) + \cdots$$

$$+ \frac{2}{q}\hat{\gamma}(q-1)\Big] - \sqrt{nq}\,o_p(n^{-1/2}) . \qquad \text{(A2.8)}$$

Combining Equations (A2.7) and (A2.8) then yields the following result:

$$\sqrt{nq}(\hat{\sigma}_c^2 - \sigma_o^2) \overset{a}{\sim} \mathcal{N}(0,\, V_c) \qquad \text{(A2.9a)}$$

where

$$V_c \equiv 2\sigma_o^4 + \left(\frac{2(q-1)}{q}\right)^2 \sigma_o^4 + \cdots + \left(\frac{2}{q}\right)^2 \sigma_o^4 = 2\sigma_o^4 \left(\frac{2q}{3} + \frac{1}{3q}\right). \qquad \text{(A2.9b)}$$

Given the asymptotic distributions (A2.1) and (A2.5), Hausman's (1978) method may be applied in precisely the same manner as in Theorem 2.1 to yield the desired result:

$$\sqrt{nq}\,M_d(q) \overset{a}{\sim} \mathcal{N}\left(0,\, \frac{2(2q-1)(q-1)}{3q}\sigma_o^4\right)$$

$$\sqrt{nq}\,M_r(q) \overset{a}{\sim} \mathcal{N}\left(0,\, \frac{2(2q-1)(q-1)}{3q}\right).$$

The distributional results for $\overline{M}_d(q)$ and $\overline{M}_r(q)$ follow immediately since asymptotically these statistics are equivalent to $M_d(q)$ and $M_r(q)$, respectively.

Q.E.D.

Proof of Theorem 2.3

1. We prove the result for $\overline{M}_r(q)$; the proofs for the other statistics follow almost immediately from this case. Define the increments process as $Y_t \equiv X_t - X_{t-1}$ and define $\hat{\rho}(\tau)$ as

$$\hat{\rho}(\tau) \equiv \frac{\frac{1}{nq}\sum_{t=\tau}^{nq}(Y_t - \hat{\mu})(Y_{t-\tau} - \hat{\mu})}{\frac{1}{T}\sum_{t=1}^{T}(Y_t - \hat{\mu})^2} \equiv \frac{A(\tau)}{B(\tau)}. \tag{A2.10}$$

Consider first the numerator $A(\tau)$ of $\hat{\rho}(\tau)$:

$$A(\tau) \equiv \frac{1}{nq}\sum_{t=\tau}^{nq}(Y_t - \hat{\mu})(Y_{t-\tau} - \hat{\mu})$$

$$= \frac{1}{nq}\sum_{t=\tau}^{nq}(\mu - \hat{\mu} + \epsilon_t)(\mu - \hat{\mu} + \epsilon_{t-\tau}) \tag{A2.11a}$$

$$= \frac{nq - \tau + 1}{nq}(\mu - \hat{\mu})^2 + (\mu - \hat{\mu})\frac{1}{nq}\sum_{t=\tau}^{nq}\epsilon_t$$

$$+(\mu - \hat{\mu})\frac{1}{nq}\sum_{t=\tau}^{nq}\epsilon_{t-\tau} + \frac{1}{nq}\sum_{t=\tau}^{nq}\epsilon_t\epsilon_{t-\tau}. \tag{A2.11b}$$

Since $\hat{\mu}$ converges almost surely (a.s.) to μ, the first term of Equation (A2.11b) converges a.s. to zero as $nq \to \infty$. Moreover, under condition 2.1.2 it is apparent that $\{\epsilon_t\}$ satisfies the conditions of White's (1984) corollary 3.48; hence, H*'s condition 2.1.2 implies that the second and third terms of (A2.11b) also vanish a.s. Finally, because $\epsilon_t\epsilon_{t-\tau}$ is clearly a measurable function of the ϵ_t's, $\{\epsilon_t\epsilon_{t-\tau}\}$, is also mixing with coefficients of the same size as $\{\epsilon_t\}$. Therefore, under condition 2.1.2, corollary 3.48 of White (1984) may also be applied to $\{\epsilon_t\epsilon_{t-\tau}\}$, for which condition 2.1.2 implies that the fourth term of Equation (A2.11b) converges a.s. to zero as well. By similar arguments, it may also be shown that

$$B(\tau) \equiv \frac{1}{nq}\sum_{t=1}^{nq}(Y_t - \hat{\mu})^2 \overset{a.s.}{\to} \sigma_o^2. \tag{A2.12}$$

Therefore, we have $\hat{\rho}(\tau) \overset{a.s.}{\to} 0$ for all $\tau \neq 0$; hence, we conclude that

$$\overline{M}_r(q) \overset{a.s.}{\to} 0 \quad \text{as} \quad nq \to \infty.$$

2. By considering the regression of increments ΔX_t on a constant term and lagged increments ΔX_{t-j}, this follows directly from White and Domowitz

(1984). Taylor (1984) also obtains this result under the assumption that the multivariate distribution of the sequence of disturbances is symmetric.

3. This result follows trivially from Equation (2.1.14a) and condition 2.1.2.

Q.E.D.

3

The Size and Power of the
Variance Ratio Test in Finite Samples:
A Monte Carlo Investigation

3.1 Introduction

WHETHER OR NOT an economic time series follows a random walk has long
been a question of great interest to economists. Although its origins lie in
the modelling of games of chance, the random walk hypothesis is also an
implication of many diverse models of rational economic behavior.[1] Several
recent studies have tested the random walk theory of exploiting the fact that
the variance of random walk increments is linear in the sampling interval.[2]
Therefore the variance of, for example, quarterly increments must be three
times as large as the variance of monthly differences. Comparing the (per
unit time) variance estimates from quarterly to monthly data will then yield
an indication of the random walk's plausibility. Such a comparison may be
formed quantitatively along the lines of the Hausman (1978) specification
test and is developed in Lo and MacKinlay (1988b). Due to intractable non-
linearities, the sampling theory of Lo and MacKinlay is based on standard
asymptotic approximations.

In this chapter, we investigate the quality of those approximations under
the two most commonly advanced null hypotheses: the random walk with
independently and identically distributed Gaussian increments, and with
uncorrelated but heteroskedastic increments. Under both null hypotheses,
the variance ratio test is shown to yield reliable inferences even for moderate
sample sizes. Indeed, under a specific heteroskedastic null the variance ratio

---

[1]See, for example, Gould and Nelson (1974), Hall (1978), Lucas (1978), Shiller (1981),
Kleidon (1986), and Marsh and Merton (1986).
[2]See, for example, Campbell and Mankiw (1987), Cochrane (1987b, 1987c), Huizinga
(1987), Lo and MacKinlay (1988b), and Poterba and Summers (1988).

test is somewhat more reliable than both the Dickey-Fuller t and Box-Pierce portmanteau tests.

We also compare the power of these tests against three empirically interesting alternative hypotheses: a stationary AR(1) which has been advanced as a model of stock market fads, the sum of this AR(1) and a pure random walk, and an ARIMA(1, 1, 0) which is more consistent with stock market data. Although the Dickey-Fuller t-test is more powerful than the Box-Pierce Q-test against the first alternative and vice versa against the second, the variance ratio test is comparable to the most powerful of the two tests against the first alternative, and more powerful against the second two alternatives when the variance ratio's sampling intervals are chosen appropriately.

Since the random walk is closely related to what has come to be known as a 'unit root' process, a few comments concerning the variance ratio test's place in the unit root literature are appropriate. It is obvious that the random walk possesses a unit root. In addition, random walk increments are required to be uncorrelated. Although earlier studies of unit root tests (e.g., Dickey and Fuller, 1979, 1981) also assumed uncorrelated increments, Phillips (1986, 1987), Phillips and Perron (1988), and Perron (1986) show that much of those results obtain asymptotically even when increments are weakly dependent.[3] Therefore, the random walk model is a proper subset of the unit root null hypothesis. This implies that the power of a consistent unit root test against the random walk hypothesis will converge to the size of the test asymptotically.

The focus of random walk tests also differs from that of the unit root tests. This is best illustrated in the context of Beveridge and Nelson's (1981) decomposition of a unit root process into the sum of a random walk and a stationary process.[4] Recent applications of unit root tests propose the null hypothesis that the random walk component does not exist, whereas tests of the random walk have as their null hypothesis that the stationary component does not exist.[5]

Since there are some important departures from the random walk that unit root tests cannot detect, the variance ratio test is preferred when the attribute of interest is the uncorrelatedness of increments. Moreover, in contrast to the dependence of the unit root test statistics' distributions on nuisance parameters, the variance ratio's limiting distribution is Gaussian and independent of any nuisance parameters.[6] Although we report simula-

---

[3]Dickey and Fuller (1979, 1981) make the stronger assumption of independently and identically distributed Gaussian disturbances.

[4]Also, see Cochrane (1987c) who uses this fact to show that trend-stationarity and difference-stationarity cannot be distinguished with a finite amount of data.

[5]We are grateful to one of the two referees for this insight.

[6]The usual regression t-statistic's limiting distribution depends discontinuously on the presence or absence of a nonzero drift (see Nankervis and Savin, 1985; Perron, 1986). This

tion results for the Dickey-Fuller t and the Box-Pierce Q-tests for comparison with the performance of the variance ratio test, we emphasize that these three tests are not direct competitors since they have been designed with different null hypotheses in mind.

The chapter is organized as follows. In Section 3.2 we define the variance ratio statistic, summarize its asymptotic sampling theory, and define the Dickey-Fuller and Box-Pierce tests. Section 3.3 presents Monte Carlo results for the three tests under two null hypotheses, and Section 3.4 contains the power results for the three alternative hypotheses. We summarize and conclude in Section 3.5.

3.2 The Variance Ratio Test

Since the asymptotic sampling theory for the variance ratio statistic is fully developed in Lo and MacKinlay (1988b), we present only a brief summary here. Let X_t denote a stochastic process satisfying the following recursive relation:

$$X_t = \mu + X_{t-1} + \epsilon_t, \quad \mathrm{E}[\epsilon_t] = 0, \quad \text{for all } t, \quad (3.2.1a)$$

or

$$\Delta X_t = \mu + \epsilon_t, \quad \Delta X_t \equiv X_t - X_{t-1}, \quad (3.2.1b)$$

where the drift μ is an arbitrary parameter. The essence of the random walk hypothesis is the restriction that the disturbances ϵ_t are serially uncorrelated or that innovations are unforecastable from past innovations. We develop our test under two null hypotheses which capture this aspect of the random walk: independently and identically distributed Gaussian increments, and the more general case of uncorrelated but weakly dependent and possibly heteroskedastic increments.

3.2.1 The IID Gaussian Null Hypothesis

Let the null hypothesis H_1 denote the case where the ϵ_t's are IID normal random variables with variance σ^2. Hence

$$\mathrm{H}_1: \epsilon_t \text{ IID } \mathcal{N}(0, \sigma^2). \quad (3.2.2)$$

In addition to homoskedasticity, we have made the assumption of independent *Gaussian* increments as in Dickey and Fuller (1979, 1981) and Evans

---

dependence on the drift may be eliminated by the inclusion of a time trend in the regression, but requires the estimation of an additional parameter and may affect the power of the resulting test. Section 3.4 reports power comparisons.

and Savin (1981a, 1981b, 1984).[7] Suppose we obtain $nq + 1$ observations $X_0, X_1, \ldots, X_{nq}$ of X_t, where both n and q are arbitrary integers greater than one. Consider the following estimators for the unknown parameters μ and σ^2:

$$\hat{\mu} \equiv \frac{1}{nq} \sum_{k=1}^{nq} [X_k - X_{k-1}] \equiv \frac{1}{nq} [X_{nq} - X_0], \qquad (3.2.3)$$

$$\hat{\sigma}_a^2 \equiv \frac{1}{nq} \sum_{k=1}^{nq} [X_k - X_{k-1} - \hat{\mu}]^2. \qquad (3.2.4)$$

The estimator $\hat{\sigma}_a^2$ is simply the sample variance of the first-difference of X_t; it corresponds to the maximum likelihood estimator of the parameter σ^2 and therefore possesses the usual consistency, asymptotic normality and efficiency properties.

Consider the variance of qth differences of X_t which, under H_1, is q times the variance of first-differences. By dividing by q, we obtain the estimator $\hat{\sigma}_b^2(q)$ which also converges to σ^2 under H_1, where

$$\hat{\sigma}_b^2(q) \equiv \frac{1}{nq^2} \sum_{k=q}^{nq} [X_k - X_{k-q} - q\hat{\mu}]^2. \qquad (3.2.5)$$

We have written $\hat{\sigma}_b^2(q)$ as a function of q (which we term the *aggregation value*) to emphasize the fact that a distinct alternative estimator of σ^2 may be formed for *each* q.[8] Under the null hypothesis of a Gaussian random walk, the two estimators $\hat{\sigma}_a^2$ and $\hat{\sigma}_b^2(q)$ should be 'close'; therefore a test of the random walk may be constructed by computing the difference $M_d(q) = \hat{\sigma}_b^2(q) - \hat{\sigma}_a^2$ and checking its proximity to zero. Alternatively, a test may also be based upon the dimensionless centered variance ratio $M_r(q) \equiv \hat{\sigma}_b^2(q)/\hat{\sigma}_a^2 - 1$, which converges in probability to zero as well.[9] It is shown in Lo and MacKinlay (1988b) that $M_d(q)$ and $M_r(q)$ possess the following limiting distributions

[7]The Gaussian assumption may, of course, be weakened considerably. We present results for this simple case only for purposes of comparison to other results in the literature that are derived under identical conditions. In Section 3.2.2 we relax both the independent and the identically distributed assumptions.

[8]Although we have defined the total number of observations $T \equiv nq$ to be divisible by the aggregation value q, this is only for expositional convenience and may be easily generalized.

[9]The use of variance ratios is, of course, not new. Most recently, Campbell and Mankiw (1987), Cochrane (1987b, 1987c), French and Roll (1986) and Huizinga (1987) have all computed variance ratios in a variety of contexts. However, those studies do not provide any formal sampling theory for our statistics. Specifically, Cochrane (1988) and French and Roll (1986) rely upon Monte Carlo simulations to obtain standard errors for their variance ratios under the null. Campbell and Mankiw (1987) and Cochrane (1987c) do derive the asymptotic variance of the variance ratio, but only under the assumption that the aggregation value q grows with (but more slowly than) the sample size T. Specifically, they use Priestley's (1981, p. 463) expression for the asymptotic variance of the estimator of the spectral density of ΔX_t at frequency

under the null hypothesis H_1:

$$\sqrt{nq}\, M_d(q) \overset{a}{\sim} \mathcal{N}\left(0, \frac{2(2q-1)(q-1)}{3q}\sigma^4\right), \qquad (3.2.6a)$$

$$\sqrt{nq}\, M_r(q) \overset{a}{\sim} \mathcal{N}\left(0, \frac{2(2q-1)(q-1)}{3q}\right). \qquad (3.2.6b)$$

An additional adjustment that may improve the finite-sample behavior of the test statistics is to use unbiased estimators $\bar{\sigma}_a^2$ and $\bar{\sigma}_b^2(q)$ in computing $M_d(q)$ and $M_r(q)$, where

$$\bar{\sigma}_a^2 \equiv \frac{1}{(nq-1)} \sum_{k=1}^{nq} (X_k - X_{k-1} - \hat{\mu})^2, \qquad (3.2.7a)$$

$$\bar{\sigma}_b^2(q) \equiv \frac{1}{m} \sum_{k=q}^{nq} (X_k - X_{k-q} - q\hat{\mu})^2, \qquad (3.2.7b)$$

with

$$m \equiv q(nq - q + 1)\left(1 - \frac{q}{nq}\right).$$

We denote the resulting adjusted specification test statistics $\overline{M}_d(q)$ and $\overline{M}_r(q)$. Of course, although the variance estimators $\bar{\sigma}_a^2$ and $\bar{\sigma}_b^2(q)$ are unbiased, only $\overline{M}_d(q)$ is unbiased; $\overline{M}_r(q)$ is not.

zero with a Bartlett window as the appropriate asymptotic variance of the variance ratio. But Priestley's result requires (among other things) that $q \to \infty$, $T \to \infty$, and $q/T \to 0$. In this chapter, we develop the formal sampling theory of the variance ratio statistics for the more general case.

Our variance ratio may, however, be related to the spectral density estimates in the following way. Letting $f(0)$ denote the spectral density of the increments ΔX_t at frequency zero, we have the following relation:

$$\pi f(0) = \gamma(0) + 2 \cdot \sum_{k=1}^{\infty} \gamma(k),$$

where $\gamma(k)$ is the autocovariance function. Dividing both sides by the variance $\gamma(0)$ then yields

$$\pi f^*(0) = 1 + 2 \cdot \sum_{k=1}^{\infty} \rho(k),$$

where f^* is the normalized spectral density and $\rho(k)$ is the autocorrelation function. Now in order to estimate the quantity $\pi f^*(0)$, the infinite sum on the right-hand side of the preceding equation must obviously be truncated. If, in addition to truncation, the autocorrelations are weighted using Newey and West's (1987) procedure, then the resulting estimator is formally equivalent to our $\overline{M}_r(q)$ statistic. Although he does not explicitly use this variance ratio, Huizinga (1987) does employ the Newey and West (1987) estimator of the normalized spectral density.

3.2.2 The Heteroskedastic Null Hypothesis

Since there is already a growing consensus that many economic time series possess time-varying volatilities, we derive a version of our specification test of the random walk model that is robust to heteroskedasticity. As long as the increments are uncorrelated, the variance ratio must still converge to one in probability even with heteroskedastic disturbances. Heuristically, this is simply because the variance of the sum of uncorrelated increments must still equal the sum of the variances. Of course, the asymptotic variance of the variance ratios will depend on the type and degree of heteroskedasticity present. By controlling the degree of heterogeneity and dependence of the process, it is possible to obtain consistent estimators of this asymptotic variance. To relax the IID Gaussian restriction of the ϵ_t's, we follow White's (1980) and White and Domowitz's (1984) use of mixing and moment conditions to derive heteroskedasticity-consistent estimators of our variance ratio's asymptotic variance. We require the following assumptions on $\{\epsilon_t\}$, which form our second null hypothesis:

H_2:

(A1) For all t, $E[\epsilon_t] = 0$, $E[\epsilon_t \epsilon_{t-\tau}] = 0$ for any $\tau \neq 0$.

(A2) $\{\epsilon_t\}$ is ψ-mixing with coefficients $\psi(m)$ of size $r/(2r - 1)$ or is α-mixing with coefficients $\alpha(m)$ of size $r/(r - 1)$, $r > 1$, such that for all t and for any $\tau \geq 0$, there exists some $\delta > 0$ for which

$$E|\epsilon_t \epsilon_{t-\tau}|^{2(r+\delta)} < \Delta < \infty. \qquad (3.2.8)$$

(A3) $\displaystyle \lim_{T \to \infty} \frac{1}{T} \sum_{t=1}^{T} E[\epsilon_t^2] = \sigma_0^2 < \infty.$

(A4) For all t, $E[\epsilon_t \epsilon_{t-j} \epsilon_t \epsilon_{t-k}] = 0$ for any nonzero j, k where $j \neq k$.

Assumption (A1) is the essential property of the random walk that we wish to test. Assumptions (A2) and (A3) are restrictions on the degree of dependence and heterogeneity which are allowed and yet still permit some form of law of large numbers and central limit theorem to obtain. This allows for a variety of forms of heteroskedasticity including deterministic changes in the variance (due, for example, to seasonal components) as well as Engle's (1982) ARCH processes (in which the conditional variance depends upon past information).[10] Assumption (A4) implies that the sample autocorrela-

---

[10]In addition to admitting heteroskedasticity, it should be emphasized that assumptions (A2) and (A3) also follow for more general heterogeneity and weak dependence. Our reason for focusing on heteroskedasticity is merely its intuitiveness: it is more difficult to produce an interesting example of, for example, an uncorrelated homoskedastic time series which is weakly dependent and heterogeneously distributed.

tions of ϵ_t are asymptotically uncorrelated.[11] Under the null hypothesis H_2, we may obtain heteroskedasticity-consistent estimators $\hat{\delta}(j)$ of the asymptotic variance $\delta(j)$ of the autocorrelations $\hat{\rho}(j)$ of ΔX_t. Using the fact that the variance ratio may be written as an approximate linear combination of autocorrelations (see (3.2.12) below) yields the following limiting distribution for $\overline{M}_r(q)$:[12]

$$\overline{M}_r(q) \overset{a}{\sim} \mathcal{N}[0, V(q)], \tag{3.2.9a}$$

where

$$V(q) = \sum_{j=1}^{q-1} \left[\frac{2(q-j)}{q} \right]^2 \cdot \delta(j), \quad \widehat{V}(q) = \sum_{j=1}^{q-1} \left[\frac{2(q-j)}{q} \right]^2 \cdot \hat{\delta}(j), \tag{3.2.9b}$$

$$\hat{\delta}(j) = \frac{nq \sum_{k=j+1}^{nq} (X_k - X_{k-1} - \hat{\mu})^2 \cdot (X_{k-j} - X_{k-j-1} - \hat{\mu})^2}{\left[\sum_{k=1}^{nq} (X_k - X_{k-1} - \hat{\mu})^2 \right]^2}. \tag{3.2.9c}$$

Tests of H_1 and H_2 may then be based on the normalized variance ratios $z_1(q)$ and $z_2(q)$, respectively, where

$$z_1(q) \equiv \sqrt{nq}\, \overline{M}_r(q) \cdot \left(\frac{2(2q-1)(q-1)}{3q} \right)^{-1/2} \overset{a}{\sim} \mathcal{N}(0, 1), \tag{3.2.10a}$$

$$z_2(q) \equiv \sqrt{nq}\, \overline{M}_r(q) \cdot \widehat{V}^{-1/2}(q) \overset{a}{\sim} \mathcal{N}(0, 1). \tag{3.2.10b}$$

---

[11]Although this assumption may be weakened considerably, it would be at the expense of computational simplicity since in that case the asymptotic covariances of the autocorrelations must be estimated. Specifically, since the variance ratio statistic is asymptotically equivalent to a linear combination of autocorrelations, its asymptotic variance is simply the asymptotic variance of the linear combination of autocorrelations. If (A4) obtains, this variance is equal to the weighted sum of the individual autocorrelation variances. If (A4) is violated, then the autocovariances of the autocorrelations must also be estimated. This is readily accomplished using, for example, the approach in Newey and West (1987). Note that an even more general (and possibly more exact) sampling theory for the variance ratios may be obtained using the results of Dufour and Roy (1985). Again, this would sacrifice much of the simplicity of our asymptotic results.

[12]An equivalent and somewhat more intuitive method of arriving at (3.2.9c) is to consider the regression of the increments ΔX_t on a constant and the jth lagged increment ΔX_{t-j}. The estimated slope coefficient is then simply the jth autocorrelation coefficient and the estimator $\delta(j)$ of its variance is numerically identical to White's (1980) heteroskedasticity-consistent covariance matrix estimator. Note that White (1980) requires independent disturbances, whereas White and Domowitz (1984) allow for weak dependence (of which uncorrelated errors is, under suitable regularity conditions, a special case). Taylor (1984) also obtains this result under the assumption that the multivariate distribution of the sequence of disturbances is symmetric.

3.2.3 Variance Ratios and Autocorrelations

To develop some intuition for the variance ratio, observe that for an aggregation value q of 2, the $M_r(q)$ statistic may be re-expressed as

$$M_r(2) = \hat{\rho}(1) - \frac{1}{4n\hat{\sigma}_a^2}\left[(X_1 - X_0 - \hat{\mu})^2 + (X_{2n} - X_{2n-1} - \hat{\mu})^2\right]. \quad (3.2.11)$$

Hence for $q = 2$ the $M_r(q)$ statistic is approximately the first-order autocorrelation coefficient estimator $\hat{\rho}(1)$ of the differences of X. More generally, we have the following relation for $q \geq 2$:

$$M_r(q) = \frac{2(q-1)}{q}\,\hat{\rho}(1) + \frac{2(q-2)}{q}\,\hat{\rho}(2)$$

$$+ \cdots + \frac{2}{q}\,\hat{\rho}(q-1) + o_p(n^{-1/2}), \quad (3.2.12)$$

where $o_p(n^{-1/2})$ denotes terms which are of order smaller than $n^{-1/2}$ in probability. Equation (3.2.12) provides a simple interpretation for the variance ratio computed with an aggregation value q: it is (approximately) a linear combination of the first $q - 1$ autocorrelation coefficient estimators of the first differences with arithmetically declining weights. Note the similarity between this and the Box-Pierce (1970) Q statistic of order $q - 1$,

$$Q_1(q-1) = T\sum_{k=1}^{q-1}\hat{\rho}^2(k), \quad (3.2.13)$$

which is asymptotically distributed as χ^2 with $q - 1$ degrees of freedom.[13] Using (3.2.9c) we can also construct a heteroskedasticity-robust Box-Pierce statistic in the obvious way, which we denote by $Q_2(q - 1)$. Since the Box-Pierce Q-statistics give equal weighting to the autocorrelations and are computed by squaring the autocorrelations, their properties will differ from those of the variance ratio test statistics.

For comparison, we also employ the Dickey-Fuller t-test. This involves computing the usual t-statistic under the hypothesis $\beta = 1$ in the regression

$$X_t = \mu + \omega t + \beta X_{t-1} + v_t, \quad (3.2.14)$$

and using the exact finite-sample distribution tabulated by Fuller (1976), Dickey and Fuller (1979, 1981), and Nankervis and Savin (1985).[14,15]

---

[13]Since we include the Box-Pierce test only as an illustrative comparison to the variance ratio test, we have not made any effort to correct for finite-sample biases as in Ljung and Box (1978).

[14]Due to the dependence of the t-statistic's distribution on the drift μ, a time trend t must be included in the regression to yield a sampling theory for the t-statistic which is independent of the nuisance parameter.

[15]Yet another recent test of the random walk hypothesis is the regression test proposed by

3.3 Properties of the Test Statistic under the Null Hypotheses

To gauge the quality of the asymptotic approximations in Section 3.2, we perform simulation experiments for the $\overline{M}_r(q)$ statistic under both the Gaussian IID null hypothesis and a simple heteroskedastic null. More extensive simulation experiments indicate that tests based upon the unadjusted statistic $M_r(q)$ generally yield less reliable inferences, hence, in the interest of brevity, we only report the results for $\overline{M}_r(q)$. For comparison, we also report the results of Monte Carlo experiments performed for the Box-Pierce Q-statistics and the Dickey-Fuller t-statistic. All simulations are based on 20,000 replications.[16]

3.3.1 The Gaussian IID Null Hypothesis

Tables 3.1a and 3.1b report the results of simulation experiments conducted under the independent and identically distributed Gaussian random walk null H_1. The results show that the empirical sizes of two-sided 5 percent variance ratio tests based on either the $z_1(q)$- or $z_2(q)$-statistics are close to their nominal values for sample sizes greater than 32. Not surprisingly, for an aggregation value q of 2 the behavior of the variance ratio is comparable to that of the Box-Pierce Q-statistic since $\overline{M}_r(2)$ is approximately equal to the first-order serial correlation coefficient. However, for larger aggregation values the behavior of the two statistics differs.

Table 3.1a shows that as the aggregation value q increases to one-half the sample size, the empirical size of the Box-Pierce Q_1-test generally declines well below its nominal value, whereas the size of the variance ratio's z_1-test seems to first increase slightly above and then fall back to its nominal value. For example, with a sample size of 1024, the size of the 5 percent Q_1-test falls monotonically from 5.1 to 0.0 percent as q goes from 2 to 512; the size of the 5 percent z_1-test starts at 5.2 percent when $q = 2$, increases to 6.2 percent at $q = 256$, and settles at 5.1 percent when $q = 512$.

Although the size of the variance ratio test is closer to its nominal value for larger q, this does not necessarily imply that large values of q are generally more desirable. To examine this issue, Table 3.1a separates the size of the variance ratio test into rejection rates of the lower and upper tails of the 1, 5, and 10 percent tests. When q becomes large relative to the sample size, the

Fama and French (1988). Since Monte Carlo experiments by Poterba and Summers (1988) indicate that the variance ratio is more powerful than this regression test against several interesting alternatives, we do not explore its finite-sample properties here.

[16]Null simulations were performed in single-precision FORTRAN on a DEC VAX 8700 using the random number generator GGNML of the IMSL subroutine library. Power simulations were performed on an IBM 3081 and a VAX 8700 also in single-precision FORTRAN using GGNML.

Table 3.1a. *Empirical sizes of nominal 1, 5, and 10 percent two-sided variance ratio tests of the random walk null hypothesis with homoskedastic disturbances. The statistic $z_1(q)$ is asymptotically $N(0,1)$ under the IID random walk. The rejection rates for each of the 1, 5, and 10 percent tests are broken down into upper and lower tail rejections to display the skewness of the z_1-statistic's empirical distribution. For comparison, the empirical sizes of the one-sided Box-Pierce Q-test (Q_1) using $q-1$ autocorrelations are also reported. Each set of rows with a given sample size forms a separate and independent simulation experiment based on 20,000 replications.*

Sample Size	q	Size of 1 Percent Test				Size of 5 Percent Test				Size of 10 Percent Test			
		Lower Tail $z_1(q)$	Upper Tail $z_1(q)$	Size $z_1(q)$	Size Q_1	Lower Tail $z_1(q)$	Upper Tail $z_1(q)$	Size $z_1(q)$	Size Q_1	Lower Tail $z_1(q)$	Upper Tail $z_1(q)$	Size $z_1(q)$	Size Q_1
32	2	0.005	0.006	0.011	0.006	0.027	0.030	0.057	0.044	0.057	0.058	0.115	0.093
32	4	0.000	0.020	0.020	0.007	0.005	0.049	0.054	0.035	0.028	0.078	0.106	0.073
32	8	0.000	0.035	0.035	0.007	0.000	0.065	0.065	0.028	0.000	0.088	0.088	0.056
32	16	0.000	0.027	0.027	0.004	0.000	0.050	0.050	0.016	0.000	0.073	0.073	0.030
64	2	0.005	0.005	0.010	0.008	0.026	0.027	0.053	0.047	0.051	0.053	0.104	0.094
64	4	0.000	0.014	0.014	0.008	0.013	0.039	0.052	0.040	0.037	0.067	0.104	0.084
64	8	0.000	0.023	0.023	0.010	0.002	0.052	0.053	0.039	0.019	0.077	0.096	0.073
64	16	0.000	0.034	0.034	0.011	0.000	0.062	0.062	0.034	0.000	0.084	0.084	0.057
64	32	0.000	0.027	0.027	0.006	0.000	0.050	0.050	0.015	0.000	0.068	0.068	0.025
128	2	0.006	0.005	0.011	0.010	0.028	0.027	0.055	0.051	0.053	0.051	0.104	0.099
128	4	0.001	0.009	0.011	0.009	0.017	0.035	0.052	0.046	0.041	0.061	0.102	0.092
128	8	0.000	0.016	0.016	0.011	0.008	0.044	0.052	0.044	0.032	0.070	0.102	0.087
128	16	0.000	0.025	0.025	0.011	0.001	0.055	0.056	0.041	0.014	0.081	0.095	0.076
128	32	0.000	0.037	0.037	0.011	0.000	0.066	0.066	0.031	0.000	0.087	0.087	0.054
128	64	0.000	0.029	0.029	0.004	0.000	0.054	0.054	0.010	0.000	0.072	0.072	0.017
256	2	0.005	0.004	0.009	0.009	0.026	0.025	0.051	0.049	0.050	0.051	0.101	0.099
256	4	0.002	0.008	0.010	0.010	0.021	0.031	0.052	0.049	0.045	0.056	0.100	0.095

(continued)

Table 3.1a. (*continued*)

Sample Size	q	Size of 1 Percent Test				Size of 5 Percent Test				Size of 10 Percent Test			
		Lower Tail $z_1(q)$	Upper Tail $z_1(q)$	Size $z_1(q)$	Size Q	Lower Tail $z_1(q)$	Upper Tail $z_1(q)$	Size $z_1(q)$	Size Q	Lower Tail $z_1(q)$	Upper Tail $z_1(q)$	Size $z_1(q)$	Size Q
256	8	0.001	0.013	0.014	0.011	0.013	0.038	0.051	0.047	0.036	0.064	0.100	0.092
256	16	0.000	0.016	0.016	0.012	0.006	0.045	0.051	0.048	0.028	0.072	0.099	0.092
256	32	0.000	0.026	0.026	0.011	0.000	0.055	0.055	0.042	0.013	0.080	0.093	0.077
256	64	0.000	0.037	0.037	0.007	0.000	0.065	0.065	0.023	0.000	0.088	0.088	0.043
256	128	0.000	0.029	0.029	0.001	0.000	0.052	0.052	0.004	0.000	0.072	0.072	0.007
512	2	0.005	0.005	0.010	0.010	0.025	0.026	0.051	0.050	0.050	0.051	0.101	0.100
512	4	0.003	0.008	0.011	0.009	0.022	0.030	0.052	0.046	0.046	0.055	0.102	0.093
512	8	0.002	0.010	0.012	0.009	0.018	0.035	0.052	0.046	0.042	0.060	0.102	0.092
512	16	0.001	0.013	0.013	0.010	0.013	0.039	0.052	0.045	0.035	0.063	0.099	0.090
512	32	0.000	0.019	0.019	0.010	0.005	0.047	0.052	0.043	0.027	0.072	0.099	0.083
512	64	0.000	0.028	0.028	0.008	0.000	0.056	0.057	0.032	0.012	0.080	0.092	0.062
512	128	0.000	0.036	0.036	0.004	0.000	0.064	0.064	0.013	0.000	0.086	0.086	0.025
512	256	0.000	0.029	0.029	0.000	0.000	0.052	0.052	0.001	0.000	0.072	0.072	0.001
1024	2	0.004	0.006	0.010	0.010	0.024	0.028	0.052	0.051	0.049	0.052	0.100	0.099
1024	4	0.003	0.007	0.010	0.010	0.020	0.030	0.050	0.050	0.046	0.055	0.101	0.096
1024	8	0.002	0.010	0.012	0.010	0.016	0.032	0.048	0.048	0.041	0.058	0.098	0.096
1024	16	0.001	0.011	0.012	0.010	0.014	0.036	0.051	0.046	0.038	0.062	0.100	0.092
1024	32	0.000	0.015	0.016	0.010	0.010	0.041	0.051	0.045	0.033	0.067	0.100	0.089
1024	64	0.000	0.019	0.019	0.010	0.004	0.045	0.050	0.043	0.026	0.070	0.095	0.081
1024	128	0.000	0.025	0.025	0.006	0.000	0.054	0.055	0.028	0.011	0.078	0.090	0.053
1024	256	0.000	0.034	0.034	0.001	0.000	0.062	0.062	0.006	0.000	0.082	0.082	0.013
1024	512	0.000	0.028	0.028	0.000	0.000	0.051	0.051	0.000	0.000	0.069	0.069	0.000

Table 3.1b. *Empirical sizes of nominal 1, 5, and 10 percent two-sided variance ratio tests of the random walk null hypothesis with homoskedastic disturbances. The statistic $z_2(q)$ is asymptotically $N(0,1)$ under the more general conditions of heteroskedastic and weakly dependent (but uncorrelated) random walk increments. The rejection rates for each of the 1, 5, and 10 percent tests are broken down into upper and lower tail rejections to display the skewness of the z_2-statistic's empirical distribution. For comparison, the empirical sizes of the heteroskedasticity-robust one-sided Box-Pierce Q-test (Q_2) using $q-1$ autocorrelations are also reported. Each set of rows with a given sample size forms a separate and independent simulation experiment based on 20,000 replications.*

Sample Size	q	Size of 1 Percent Test				Size of 5 Percent Test				Size of 10 Percent Test			
		Lower Tail $z_2(q)$	Upper Tail $z_2(q)$	Size $z_2(q)$	Size Q_2	Lower Tail $z_2(q)$	Upper Tail $z_2(q)$	Size $z_2(q)$	Size Q_2	Lower Tail $z_2(q)$	Upper Tail $z_2(q)$	Size $z_2(q)$	Size Q_2
32	2	0.005	0.007	0.012	0.006	0.033	0.038	0.071	0.049	0.064	0.070	0.134	0.107
32	4	0.000	0.024	0.025	0.009	0.011	0.061	0.072	0.044	0.038	0.090	0.128	0.097
32	8	0.000	0.042	0.042	0.014	0.000	0.075	0.075	0.054	0.007	0.098	0.105	0.104
32	16	0.000	0.035	0.035	0.025	0.000	0.065	0.065	0.071	0.000	0.087	0.087	0.123
64	2	0.004	0.006	0.010	0.007	0.027	0.030	0.057	0.048	0.056	0.058	0.114	0.102
64	4	0.001	0.014	0.015	0.009	0.016	0.044	0.060	0.046	0.041	0.073	0.114	0.096
64	8	0.000	0.027	0.027	0.013	0.004	0.058	0.061	0.053	0.025	0.084	0.109	0.100
64	16	0.000	0.038	0.038	0.021	0.000	0.069	0.069	0.066	0.001	0.090	0.092	0.116
64	32	0.000	0.034	0.034	0.032	0.000	0.059	0.059	0.084	0.000	0.079	0.079	0.134
128	2	0.006	0.005	0.011	0.009	0.029	0.028	0.057	0.052	0.055	0.054	0.109	0.103
128	4	0.001	0.010	0.012	0.010	0.018	0.038	0.056	0.049	0.043	0.064	0.107	0.101
128	8	0.000	0.017	0.017	0.012	0.010	0.046	0.056	0.053	0.035	0.073	0.109	0.103
128	16	0.000	0.027	0.027	0.017	0.001	0.059	0.060	0.060	0.017	0.085	0.103	0.110
128	32	0.000	0.040	0.040	0.027	0.000	0.071	0.071	0.075	0.000	0.092	0.093	0.124
128	64	0.000	0.036	0.036	0.041	0.000	0.063	0.063	0.095	0.000	0.082	0.082	0.143
256	2	0.005	0.004	0.010	0.009	0.026	0.026	0.052	0.050	0.051	0.052	0.103	0.100
256	4	0.002	0.008	0.010	0.011	0.022	0.032	0.054	0.050	0.045	0.057	0.103	0.098

(continued)

Table 3.1b. (*continued*)

Sample Size	q	Size of 1 Percent Test				Size of 5 Percent Test				Size of 10 Percent Test			
		Lower Tail $z_2(q)$	Upper Tail $z_2(q)$	Size $z_2(q)$	Size Q_2	Lower Tail $z_2(q)$	Upper Tail $z_2(q)$	Size $z_2(q)$	Size Q_2	Lower Tail $z_2(q)$	Upper Tail $z_2(q)$	Size $z_2(q)$	Size Q_2
256	8	0.001	0.014	0.015	0.012	0.014	0.039	0.053	0.050	0.038	0.065	0.104	0.101
256	16	0.000	0.018	0.018	0.015	0.007	0.047	0.054	0.059	0.030	0.074	0.104	0.110
256	32	0.000	0.027	0.027	0.019	0.001	0.057	0.058	0.068	0.016	0.083	0.099	0.119
256	64	0.000	0.040	0.040	0.029	0.000	0.070	0.070	0.083	0.000	0.093	0.093	0.137
256	128	0.000	0.035	0.035	0.047	0.000	0.060	0.060	0.108	0.000	0.081	0.081	0.161
512	2	0.005	0.005	0.010	0.010	0.025	0.026	0.051	0.050	0.050	0.052	0.101	0.100
512	4	0.003	0.008	0.011	0.009	0.022	0.031	0.052	0.047	0.047	0.056	0.103	0.095
512	8	0.001	0.010	0.012	0.011	0.018	0.035	0.053	0.047	0.043	0.061	0.104	0.095
512	16	0.001	0.013	0.014	0.011	0.013	0.039	0.052	0.050	0.037	0.065	0.101	0.100
512	32	0.000	0.020	0.020	0.014	0.006	0.048	0.054	0.056	0.029	0.073	0.103	0.107
512	64	0.000	0.030	0.030	0.018	0.001	0.059	0.059	0.066	0.014	0.083	0.097	0.118
512	128	0.000	0.039	0.039	0.030	0.000	0.068	0.068	0.085	0.000	0.090	0.090	0.138
512	256	0.000	0.034	0.034	0.048	0.000	0.060	0.060	0.110	0.000	0.080	0.080	0.164
1024	2	0.004	0.006	0.010	0.010	0.024	0.028	0.052	0.051	0.049	0.052	0.101	0.100
1024	4	0.003	0.007	0.010	0.010	0.020	0.030	0.050	0.050	0.046	0.056	0.102	0.097
1024	8	0.002	0.010	0.012	0.010	0.017	0.032	0.050	0.049	0.041	0.058	0.099	0.098
1024	16	0.001	0.011	0.012	0.010	0.015	0.036	0.051	0.050	0.038	0.063	0.101	0.098
1024	32	0.001	0.016	0.016	0.012	0.010	0.041	0.052	0.052	0.034	0.067	0.101	0.103
1024	64	0.000	0.020	0.020	0.016	0.005	0.046	0.051	0.062	0.027	0.071	0.099	0.114
1024	128	0.000	0.026	0.026	0.021	0.001	0.056	0.057	0.071	0.014	0.081	0.094	0.123
1024	256	0.000	0.036	0.036	0.032	0.000	0.066	0.066	0.091	0.000	0.087	0.087	0.146
1024	512	0.000	0.033	0.033	0.047	0.000	0.058	0.058	0.113	0.000	0.076	0.076	0.170

rejections of the variance ratio test are almost wholly due to the upper tail. One reason for this positive skewness of the $z_1(q)$-statistic is that the variance ratio is bounded below by zero, hence a related lower bound obtains for the test statistic.[17] Although this is of less consequence for the size of the variance ratio test, it has serious power implications and will be discussed more fully in Section 3.4.1.

Table 3.1b reports similar results for the heteroskedasticity-robust test statistics $z_2(q)$ and Q_2. For sample sizes greater than 32, the size of the variance ratio test is close to its nominal value when q is small relative to the sample size. As q increases for a given sample, the size increases and then declines, as in Table 3.1a. Again, the variance ratio rejections are primarily due to its upper tail as q increases relative to the sample size. In contrast to the Q_1-test, the heteroskedasticity-robust Box-Pierce test Q_2 increases in size as more autocorrelations are used. For example, in samples of 1024 observations the size of the 5 percent Q_2-test increases from 5.1 to 11.3 percent as q ranges from 2 to 512. In contrast, the size of the variance ratio test starts at 5.2 percent when $q = 2$, increases to 6.6 percent at $q = 256$, and falls to 5.8 percent at $q = 512$.

Tables 3.1a and 3.1b indicate that the empirical size of the variance ratio tests is reasonable even for moderate sample sizes, and is closer to its nominal value than the Box-Pierce tests when the aggregation value becomes large relative to the sample size. However, in such cases most of the variance ratio's rejections are from its upper tail; power considerations will need to be weighed against the variance ratio test's reliability under the null.

Since the sampling theory for the Q- and z-statistics obtain only asymptotically, the actual size of any test based on these statistics will of course differ from their nominal values in finite samples. Although Tables 3.1a and 3.1b indicate that such differences may not be large for reasonable aggregation values, it may nevertheless seem more desirable to base tests upon the regression t-statistic for which Fuller (1976), Dickey and Fuller (1979, 1981), and Nankervis and Savin (1985) have tabulated the exact finite-sample distribution. Due to the dependence of the t-statistic's distribution on the drift μ, an additional nuisance parameter (a time-trend coefficient) must be estimated to yield a sampling distribution that is independent of the drift. Although it has been demonstrated that the t-statistic from such a regression converges in distribution to that of Dickey and Fuller, there may be some discrepancies in finite samples. Table 3.2 presents the empirical quantiles of the distribution of the t-statistic associated with the hypothesis $\beta = 1$ in the regression (3.2.14). A comparison of these quantiles with those given in Fuller (1976, Table 8.5.2) suggests that there may be some significant

---

[17]More direct evidence of this skewness is presented in Table 3.4, in which the fractiles of the variance ratio test statistic are reported. See also the discussion in Section 3.4.1.

Table 3.2. *Empirical quantiles of the (Dickey-Fuller) t-statistic associated with the hypothesis $\beta = 1$ in the regression $X_t = \mu + \omega t + \beta X_{t-1} + \epsilon_t$, where ϵ_t is IID $\mathcal{N}(0, 1)$. Each row corresponds to a separate and independent simulation experiment based upon 20,000 replications.*

Sample Size	0.005	0.010	0.025	0.050	0.100
32	−4.767	−4.456	−4.043	−3.731	−3.361
64	−4.449	−4.188	−3.860	−3.570	−3.243
128	−4.324	−4.087	−3.777	−3.492	−3.186
256	−4.235	−3.990	−3.684	−3.424	−3.135
512	−4.173	−3.973	−3.676	−3.424	−3.131
1024	−4.160	−3.959	−3.663	−3.425	−3.130

Sample Size	0.900	0.950	0.975	0.990	0.995
32	−1.222	−0.887	−0.598	−0.246	−0.013
64	−1.230	−0.906	−0.620	−0.279	−0.019
128	−1.241	−0.918	−0.635	−0.273	−0.040
256	−1.241	−0.910	−0.649	−0.276	−0.049
512	−1.233	−0.903	−0.611	−0.299	−0.032
1024	−1.252	−0.951	−0.673	−0.319	−0.054

differences for small samples, but for sample sizes of 500 or greater the quantiles in Table 3.2 are almost identical to those of Dickey and Fuller.

3.3.2 A Heteroskedastic Null Hypothesis

To assess the reliability of the heteroskedasticity-robust statistic $z_2(q)$, we perform simulation experiments under the null hypothesis that the disturbance ϵ_t in (3.1) is serially uncorrelated but heteroskedastic in the following manner. Let the random walk disturbance ϵ_t satisfy the relation $\epsilon_t \equiv \sigma_t \lambda_t$, where λ_t is IID $\mathcal{N}(0, 1)$ and σ_t satisfies

$$\ln \sigma_t^2 = \psi \cdot \ln \sigma_{t-1}^2 + \zeta_t, \quad \zeta_t \sim \mathcal{N}(0, 1). \tag{3.3.1}$$

λ_t and ζ_t are assumed to be independent. The empirical studies of French, Schwert, and Stambaugh (1987) and Poterba and Summers (1986) posit such a process for the variance. Note that σ_t^2 cannot be interpreted as the unconditional variance of the random walk disturbance ϵ_t since σ_t^2 is itself stochastic and does not correspond to the unconditional expectation of any random variable. Rather, *conditional upon* σ_t^2, ϵ_t is normally distributed with expectation 0 and variance σ_t^2. If, in place of (3.3.1), the variance σ_t^2 were reparameterized to depend only upon exogenous variables in the time $t-1$ information set, this would correspond exactly to Engle's (1982) ARCH process.

The unconditional moments of ϵ_t may be readily deduced by expressing the process explicitly as a function of all the disturbances:

$$\epsilon_t = \lambda_t \sigma_0^{\psi^t} \cdot \prod_{k=1}^{t} \exp[\tfrac{1}{2}\psi^{t-k}\zeta_k]. \tag{3.3.2}$$

Since σ_0, λ_t and ζ_k are assumed to be mutually independent, it is apparent that ϵ_t is serially uncorrelated at all leads and lags (hence assumption (A1) is satisfied) but is nonstationary and temporally dependent. Moreover, it is evident that $\mathrm{E}[\epsilon_t^2 \epsilon_{t-j} \epsilon_{t-k}] = 0$ for all t and for $j \neq k$. Hence assumption (A4) is also satisfied. A straightforward calculation yields the moments of ϵ_t:

$$\mathrm{E}[\epsilon_t^{2p}] = \mathrm{E}\left[\sigma_0^{2p\psi^t}\right] \cdot \frac{(2p)!}{p!2^p} \exp\left[\frac{p}{2} \frac{1-\psi^{2t}}{1-\psi^2}\right], \tag{3.3.3a}$$

$$\mathrm{E}[\epsilon_t^{2p+1}] = 0, \quad p = 0, 1, 2, \ldots. \tag{3.3.3b}$$

From these expressions it is apparent that, for $\psi \in (0,1)$, ϵ_t possesses bounded moments of any order and is unconditionally heteroskedastic; similar calculations for the cross-moments verify assumption (A2). Finally, the following inequality is easily deduced:

$$\frac{1}{n}\sum_{k=1}^{n} \mathrm{E}[\epsilon_t^2] < \exp\left[\frac{5}{2(1-\psi^2)}\right] < \infty. \tag{3.3.4}$$

Thus assumption (A3) is verified. Note that the kurtosis of ϵ_t is

$$\frac{\mathrm{E}[\epsilon_t^4]}{\left(\mathrm{E}[\epsilon_t^2]\right)^2} = 3 \cdot \frac{\mathrm{E}\left[\sigma_0^{4\psi^t}\right]}{\left(\mathrm{E}\left[\sigma_0^{2\psi^t}\right]\right)^2} \geq 3, \tag{3.3.5}$$

by Jensen's inequality. This implies that, as for Engle's (1982) stationary ARCH process, the distribution of ϵ_t is more peaked and possesses fatter tails than that of a normal random variate. However, when $\psi = 0$ or as t increases without bound, the kurtosis of ϵ_t is equal to that of a Gaussian process.

Table 3.3a. Empirical sizes of nominal 1, 5, and 10 percent two-sided variance ratio tests of the random walk null hypothesis with heteroskedastic disturbances. The statistic $z_1(q)$ is asymptotically $\mathcal{N}(0,1)$ under the IID random walk; the $z_2(q)$-statistic is asymptotically $\mathcal{N}(0,1)$ under the more general conditions of heteroskedastic and weakly dependent (but uncorrelated) increments. For comparison, the empirical sizes of the two-sided Dickey-Fuller t-test (D-F), the one-sided Box-Pierce Q-test (Q_1) and its heteroskedasticity-consistent counterpart (Q_2) (both using $q-1$ autocorrelations) are also reported. The specific form of heteroskedasticity is given by $\ln \sigma_t^2 = \psi \ln \sigma_{t-1}^2 + \zeta_t$, ζ_t IID $\mathcal{N}(0,1)$ and $\psi = 0.50$. Each set of rows with a given sample size forms a separate and independent simulation experiment based on 20,000 replications.

Sample Size	q	1 Percent Test				5 Percent Test				10 Percent Test			
		$z_1(q)$	Q_1	$z_2(q)$	Q_2	$z_1(q)$	Q_1	$z_2(q)$	Q_2	$z_1(q)$	Q_1	$z_2(q)$	Q_2
32	2	0.024	0.014	0.015	0.003	0.093	0.069	0.071	0.036	0.161	0.133	0.141	0.098
32	4	0.028	0.010	0.030	0.005	0.071	0.047	0.076	0.035	0.132	0.094	0.133	0.080
32	8	0.032	0.008	0.039	0.009	0.064	0.028	0.075	0.042	0.088	0.054	0.112	0.087
32	16	0.023	0.003	0.036	0.017	0.047	0.011	0.065	0.054	0.070	0.020	0.089	0.100
32	D-F			0.023				0.073				0.124	
64	2	0.037	0.029	0.008	0.004	0.107	0.094	0.055	0.039	0.175	0.158	0.118	0.098
64	4	0.029	0.023	0.016	0.006	0.088	0.078	0.061	0.037	0.155	0.134	0.116	0.087
64	8	0.030	0.016	0.028	0.009	0.066	0.053	0.063	0.045	0.119	0.099	0.108	0.092
64	16	0.035	0.012	0.038	0.016	0.065	0.036	0.068	0.056	0.090	0.061	0.097	0.101
64	32	0.026	0.003	0.034	0.025	0.049	0.012	0.061	0.071	0.071	0.020	0.082	0.118
64	D-F			0.019				0.066				0.116	
128	2	0.043	0.039	0.007	0.005	0.123	0.115	0.051	0.043	0.195	0.184	0.109	0.098
128	4	0.033	0.032	0.013	0.007	0.104	0.103	0.053	0.039	0.174	0.169	0.106	0.087
128	8	0.028	0.025	0.018	0.008	0.077	0.080	0.053	0.045	0.138	0.134	0.102	0.090
128	16	0.030	0.020	0.027	0.013	0.063	0.055	0.059	0.052	0.106	0.095	0.097	0.096
128	32	0.036	0.012	0.038	0.021	0.065	0.033	0.067	0.064	0.086	0.056	0.091	0.112
128	64	0.026	0.003	0.032	0.030	0.050	0.008	0.059	0.082	0.070	0.014	0.081	0.132

(continued)

Table 3.3a. (continued)

Sample Size	q	1 Percent Test $z_1(q)$	Q_1	$z_2(q)$	Q_2	5 Percent Test $z_1(q)$	Q_1	$z_2(q)$	Q_2	10 Percent Test $z_1(q)$	Q_1	$z_2(q)$	Q_2
128	D-F		0.016				0.061				0.111		
256	2	0.053	0.050	0.008	0.007	0.134	0.129	0.047	0.045	0.207	0.200	0.102	0.096
256	4	0.041	0.043	0.010	0.007	0.112	0.122	0.049	0.042	0.183	0.192	0.101	0.089
256	8	0.029	0.033	0.014	0.009	0.087	0.096	0.050	0.044	0.152	0.161	0.099	0.093
256	16	0.025	0.023	0.020	0.010	0.067	0.073	0.052	0.050	0.122	0.127	0.098	0.097
256	32	0.029	0.018	0.027	0.016	0.057	0.053	0.055	0.057	0.096	0.091	0.092	0.106
256	64	0.035	0.010	0.037	0.023	0.063	0.027	0.065	0.073	0.083	0.049	0.087	0.126
256	128	0.027	0.001	0.032	0.035	0.050	0.003	0.058	0.091	0.070	0.005	0.079	0.145
256	D-F		0.012				0.058				0.111		
512	2	0.058	0.056	0.008	0.007	0.147	0.146	0.049	0.047	0.223	0.220	0.105	0.102
512	4	0.046	0.051	0.011	0.008	0.125	0.138	0.053	0.045	0.201	0.218	0.104	0.094
512	8	0.033	0.038	0.013	0.009	0.101	0.113	0.052	0.047	0.169	0.183	0.105	0.097
512	16	0.026	0.029	0.016	0.010	0.076	0.086	0.054	0.050	0.136	0.146	0.103	0.098
512	32	0.024	0.020	0.020	0.012	0.064	0.065	0.056	0.054	0.115	0.116	0.101	0.104
512	64	0.027	0.013	0.026	0.016	0.058	0.044	0.057	0.060	0.097	0.077	0.096	0.111
512	128	0.035	0.005	0.037	0.024	0.062	0.017	0.065	0.075	0.085	0.030	0.089	0.128
512	256	0.027	0.000	0.032	0.036	0.052	0.001	0.059	0.095	0.071	0.002	0.079	0.149
512	D-F		0.010				0.049				0.099		
1024	2	0.059	0.058	0.008	0.008	0.148	0.148	0.046	0.046	0.222	0.222	0.097	0.096
1024	4	0.047	0.057	0.009	0.009	0.128	0.148	0.050	0.049	0.197	0.226	0.100	0.100

(continued)

Table 3.3a. *(continued)*

Sample Size	q	1 Percent Test				5 Percent Test				10 Percent Test			
		$z_1(q)$	Q_1	$z_2(q)$	Q_2	$z_1(q)$	Q_1	$z_2(q)$	Q_2	$z_1(q)$	Q_1	$z_2(q)$	Q_2
1024	8	0.031	0.039	0.010	0.008	0.101	0.116	0.050	0.046	0.167	0.193	0.100	0.095
1024	16	0.021	0.029	0.011	0.010	0.079	0.095	0.050	0.051	0.139	0.160	0.101	0.100
1024	32	0.020	0.022	0.015	0.012	0.063	0.073	0.051	0.053	0.119	0.130	0.100	0.102
1024	64	0.023	0.016	0.021	0.014	0.057	0.058	0.054	0.057	0.106	0.100	0.099	0.107
1024	128	0.030	0.009	0.030	0.019	0.061	0.033	0.061	0.068	0.096	0.061	0.097	0.119
1024	256	0.037	0.002	0.039	0.027	0.064	0.008	0.068	0.083	0.088	0.015	0.093	0.137
1024	512	0.028	0.000	0.034	0.041	0.052	0.000	0.059	0.104	0.070	0.000	0.080	0.161
1024	D-F	0.012				0.054				0.105			

Table 3.3b. *Empirical sizes of nominal 1, 5, and 10 percent two-sided variance ratio tests of the random walk null hypothesis with heteroskedastic disturbances. The statistic $z_1(q)$ is asymptotically $N(0,1)$ under the IID random walk; the $z_2(q)$-statistic is asymptotically $N(0,1)$ under the more general conditions of heteroskedastic and weakly dependent (but uncorrelated) increments. For comparison, the empirical sizes of the two-sided Dickey-Fuller t-test (D-F), the one-sided Box-Pierce Q-test (Q_1) and its heteroskedasticity-consistent counterpart (Q_2) (both using $q - 1$ autocorrelations) are also reported. The specific form of heteroskedasticity is given by $\ln \sigma_t^2 = \psi \ln \sigma_{t-1}^2 + \zeta_t$, ζ_t IID $N(0,1)$ and $\psi = 0.95$. Each set of rows with a given sample size forms a separate and independent simulation experiment based on 20,000 replications.*

Sample Size	q	1 Percent Test				5 Percent Test				10 Percent Test			
		$z_1(q)$	Q_1	$z_2(q)$	Q_2	$z_1(q)$	Q_1	$z_2(q)$	Q_2	$z_1(q)$	Q_1	$z_2(q)$	Q_2
32	2	0.087	0.054	0.024	0.002	0.196	0.151	0.080	0.028	0.279	0.231	0.157	0.084
32	4	0.052	0.054	0.033	0.005	0.140	0.142	0.080	0.031	0.229	0.225	0.130	0.068
32	8	0.046	0.031	0.037	0.008	0.077	0.083	0.070	0.037	0.104	0.134	0.097	0.076
32	16	0.028	0.006	0.032	0.012	0.055	0.019	0.060	0.040	0.078	0.032	0.084	0.074
32	D-F	0.088				0.159				0.216			

(continued)

Table 3.3b. (continued)

Sample Size	q	1 Percent Test				5 Percent Test				10 Percent Test			
		$z_1(q)$	Q_1	$z_2(q)$	Q_2	$z_1(q)$	Q_1	$z_2(q)$	Q_2	$z_1(q)$	Q_1	$z_2(q)$	Q_2
64	2	0.166	0.142	0.014	0.002	0.288	0.261	0.059	0.031	0.377	0.347	0.126	0.088
64	4	0.127	0.193	0.022	0.005	0.258	0.341	0.068	0.032	0.353	0.439	0.117	0.076
64	8	0.072	0.173	0.032	0.008	0.158	0.312	0.066	0.039	0.262	0.406	0.099	0.081
64	16	0.057	0.084	0.035	0.011	0.089	0.167	0.062	0.045	0.115	0.231	0.085	0.086
64	32	0.037	0.013	0.032	0.016	0.066	0.029	0.059	0.044	0.089	0.044	0.081	0.077
64	D-F		0.106				0.186				0.252		
128	2	0.265	0.252	0.008	0.002	0.391	0.377	0.043	0.031	0.467	0.458	0.106	0.088
128	4	0.231	0.398	0.016	0.005	0.366	0.554	0.055	0.034	0.450	0.638	0.103	0.078
128	8	0.150	0.447	0.026	0.009	0.302	0.596	0.057	0.040	0.400	0.677	0.087	0.084
128	16	0.085	0.361	0.030	0.012	0.176	0.505	0.058	0.044	0.289	0.585	0.083	0.087
128	32	0.060	0.169	0.031	0.014	0.093	0.267	0.056	0.046	0.120	0.329	0.076	0.090
128	64	0.039	0.023	0.029	0.018	0.067	0.041	0.053	0.048	0.088	0.055	0.073	0.083
128	D-F		0.124				0.206				0.273		
256	2	0.367	0.359	0.005	0.003	0.493	0.487	0.036	0.031	0.564	0.557	0.095	0.087
256	4	0.343	0.592	0.013	0.006	0.472	0.717	0.048	0.033	0.544	0.778	0.091	0.076
256	8	0.284	0.691	0.022	0.009	0.429	0.802	0.054	0.040	0.513	0.852	0.087	0.081
256	16	0.177	0.662	0.028	0.011	0.340	0.771	0.058	0.043	0.443	0.824	0.082	0.082
256	32	0.096	0.513	0.031	0.014	0.193	0.623	0.060	0.047	0.314	0.678	0.081	0.088
256	64	0.071	0.241	0.035	0.019	0.102	0.329	0.060	0.053	0.127	0.383	0.079	0.094
256	128	0.043	0.030	0.031	0.022	0.072	0.047	0.055	0.055	0.094	0.060	0.074	0.092
256	D-F		0.134				0.223				0.289		

(continued)

Table 3.3b. *(continued)*

Sample Size	q	1 Percent Test					5 Percent Test					10 Percent Test			
		$z_1(q)$	Q_1	$z_2(q)$	Q_2	$z_1(q)$	Q_1	$z_2(q)$	Q_2	$z_1(q)$	Q_1	$z_2(q)$	Q_2
512	2	0.476	0.474	0.003	0.003	0.582	0.581	0.036	0.034	0.645	0.640	0.093	0.090
512	4	0.453	0.740	0.011	0.005	0.565	0.830	0.045	0.035	0.631	0.873	0.090	0.082
512	8	0.401	0.858	0.021	0.008	0.528	0.921	0.051	0.038	0.600	0.945	0.083	0.083
512	16	0.317	0.868	0.024	0.011	0.461	0.925	0.054	0.045	0.541	0.946	0.080	0.089
512	32	0.188	0.786	0.029	0.011	0.356	0.858	0.056	0.045	0.456	0.890	0.079	0.090
512	64	0.099	0.594	0.033	0.014	0.196	0.678	0.060	0.051	0.315	0.721	0.081	0.094
512	128	0.073	0.301	0.037	0.019	0.104	0.374	0.063	0.058	0.129	0.414	0.081	0.100
512	256	0.044	0.031	0.032	0.024	0.072	0.047	0.055	0.057	0.094	0.060	0.075	0.097
512	D-F		0.134				0.216				0.282		
1024	2	0.576	0.575	0.003	0.003	0.667	0.666	0.035	0.033	0.719	0.718	0.091	0.089
1024	4	0.559	0.851	0.010	0.006	0.651	0.908	0.045	0.036	0.702	0.931	0.096	0.083
1024	8	0.513	0.944	0.019	0.009	0.620	0.971	0.049	0.040	0.680	0.982	0.086	0.084
1024	16	0.445	0.959	0.024	0.010	0.565	0.981	0.053	0.043	0.631	0.988	0.080	0.088
1024	32	0.336	0.931	0.026	0.010	0.483	0.960	0.056	0.042	0.563	0.971	0.081	0.083
1024	64	0.198	0.830	0.029	0.012	0.364	0.885	0.058	0.046	0.464	0.907	0.080	0.089
1024	128	0.100	0.621	0.031	0.015	0.197	0.689	0.060	0.053	0.316	0.724	0.084	0.094
1024	256	0.072	0.320	0.036	0.021	0.103	0.376	0.063	0.059	0.130	0.409	0.085	0.101
1024	512	0.043	0.033	0.031	0.024	0.070	0.045	0.055	0.060	0.090	0.052	0.075	0.101
1024	D-F		0.127				0.214				0.281		

Table 3.3a reports simulation results for the z-, Q-, and Dickey-Fuller t-statistics under the heteroskedastic null hypothesis with parameter $\psi = 0.50$. It is apparent that both the z_1- and Q_1-statistics are unreliable in the presence of heteroskedasticity. Even in samples of 512 observations, the empirical size of the 5 percent variance ratio test with $q = 2$ is 14.7 percent; the corresponding Box-Pierce 5 percent test has an empirical size of 14.6 percent. In contrast, the Dickey-Fuller t-test's empirical size of 4.9 percent is much closer to its nominal value. This is not surprising since Phillips (1987) and Phillips and Perron (1988) have shown that the Dickey-Fuller t-test is robust to heteroskedasticity (and weak dependence) whereas the z_1- and Q_1-statistics are not. However, once the heteroskedasticity-robust z_2- and Q_2-statistics are used, both tests compare favorably with the Dickey-Fuller t-test. In fact, for the more severe case of heterscedasticity considered in Table 3.3b (where $\psi = 0.95$), the variance ratio and Box-Pierce tests using z_2 and Q_2 are both considerably more reliable than the Dickey-Fuller test.[18] For example, when q/T is $\frac{1}{2}$ in sample sizes of 512 observations, the sizes of 5 percent tests using z_2 and Q_2 are 4.7 and 5.7 percent, respectively; the size of the 5 percent Dickey-Fuller test is 21.6 percent.

3.4 Power

Since a frequent application of the random walk has been in modelling stock market returns, it is natural to examine the power of the variance ratio test against alternative models of asset price behavior. We consider three specific alternative hypotheses. The first two are specifications of the stock price process that have received the most recent attention: the stationary AR(1) process (as in Shiller, 1981; Shiller and Perron, 1985) and the sum of this process and a random walk (as in Fama and French, 1988; Poterba and Summers, 1988).[19] The third alternative is an integrated AR(1) process which is suggested by the empirical evidence in Lo and MacKinlay (1988b).

Before presenting the simulation results, we consider an important limitation of the variance ratio test in Section 3.4.1. In Section 3.4.2 we compare the power of the variance ratio test with that of the Dickey-Fuller and Box-Pierce tests against the stationary AR(1) alternative. Section 3.4.3 reports similar power comparisons for the remaining two alternatives.

---

[18]This provides further support for Schwert's (1987b) finding that, although the Dickey-Fuller distribution is still valid asymptotically for a variety of non-IID disturbances, the t-statistic's rate of convergence may be quite slow.

[19]The latter specification is, of course, not original to the financial economics literature but has its roots in Muth (1960) and, more recently, Beveridge and Nelson (1981).

3.4.1 The Variance Ratio Test for Large q

Although it will become apparent in Sections 3.4.2 and 3.4.3 that choosing an appropriate aggregation value q for the variance ratio test depends intimately on the alternative hypothesis of interest, several authors have suggested using large values of q generally.[20] But because the variance ratio test statistic is bounded below, when q is large relative to T the test may have little power. To see this, let the (asymptotic) variance of the test statistic $\overline{M}_r(q)$ be denoted by V, where we have from (3.2.6b)

$$V \equiv \frac{2(2q-1)(q-1)}{3nq^2} = \frac{4}{3n} \cdot \left[\frac{q^2 - \frac{3}{2}q + 1}{q^2} \right]. \qquad (3.4.1)$$

Note that for all natural numbers q, the bracketed function in (3.4.1) is bounded between $\frac{1}{2}$ and 1 and is monotonically increasing in q. Therefore, for fixed n, this implies upper and lower bounds $V_U \equiv 4/3n$ and $V_L \equiv 2/3n$ for the variance V. Since variances must be nonnegative, the lower bound for $\overline{M}_r(q)$ is -1 (since we have defined $\overline{M}_r(q)$ to be the variance ratio minus 1). Using these two facts, we have the following lower bound on the (asymptotically) standard normal test statistic $z_1(q) \equiv \overline{M}_r(q)/\sqrt{V}$:

$$\inf[z_1(q)] = \frac{-1}{\inf[\sqrt{V}]} = -\frac{1}{\sqrt{V_L}} = -\left[\frac{3n}{2} \right]^{1/2}. \qquad (3.4.2)$$

Note that n is *not* the sample size (which is given by nq), but is the number of nonoverlapping *coarse* increments (increments of aggregation value q) available in the sample and is given by T/q.

If q is large relative to the sample size T, this implies a small value for n. For example, if $q/T = \frac{1}{2}$, then the lower bound on the standard normal test statistic $z_1(q)$ is -1.73; the test will never reject draws from the left tail at the 95 percent level of significance!

Of course, there is no corresponding upper bound on the test statistic so in principle it may still reject via draws in the right tail of the distribution. However, for many alternative hypotheses of interest the population values of their variance ratios are less than unity,[21] implying that for those alternatives rejections are more likely to come from large negative rather than large positive draws of $z_1(q)$. For this reason and because of the unreliability of large-sample theory under the null when q/T is large, we have chosen q to be no more than one-half the total sample size throughout this study.

[20] For example, Campbell and Mankiw's (1987) asymptotic sampling theory requires that q goes to infinity as the sample size T goes to infinity (although q must grow at a slower rate than T). Also, for a sample size of T Huizinga (1987) sets q to $T - 1$.

[21] For example, as q increases without bound the variance ratio (population value) of increments any stationary process will converge to 0. For the sum of a random walk and an independent stationary process, the variance ratio of its increments will also converge to a quantity less than unity as q approaches infinity.

3.4.2 Power against a Stationary AR(1) Alternative

As a model of stock market fads, Shiller (1981) has suggested the following AR(1) specification for the log-price process X_t:

$$X_t = \alpha + \phi \cdot [X_{t-1} - \alpha] + \epsilon_t, \quad \epsilon_t \sim \mathcal{N}(0, \sigma_\epsilon^2), \qquad (3.4.3)$$

where ϕ is positive and less than unity. To determine the power of the variance ratio test against this alternative, we choose values of the parameters $(\phi, \sigma_\epsilon^2, \sigma_\gamma^2)$ that yield an interesting range of power across sample sizes and aggregation values. Since the power does not depend on α, we set it to zero without loss of generality. Table 3.5a reports the power of the variance ratio, Dickey-Fuller t- and Box-Pierce Q-tests at the 1, 5 and 10 percent levels against the AR(1) alternative with parameters $(\phi, \sigma_\epsilon^2) = (0.96, 1)$. The critical values of all three test statistics were empirically determined by simulation under the IID Gaussian null. In the interest of brevity, we report the empirical critical values in Table 3.4 for the variance ratio test only.[22]

For a fixed number of observations, the power of the variance ratio test first increases and then declines with the aggregation value q. The increase can be considerable; as the case of 1024 observations demonstrates, the power is 9.2 percent when $q = 2$ but jumps to 98.3 percent when $q = 256$. The explanation for the increase in power lies in the behavior of the AR(1) alternative over different sampling intervals: the first-order autocorrelation coefficient of AR(1) increments grows in absolute value (becomes more negative) as the increment interval increases. This implies that, although X_t may have a root close to unity (0.96), its first-differences behave less like random walk increments as the time interval of the increments grows. It is therefore easier to detect an AR(1) departure from the random walk by comparing longer first-difference variances to shorter ones, which is precisely what the variance ratio does for larger q. However, as q is increased further the power declines. This may be attributed to the imprecision with which the higher-order autocorrelations are estimated for a fixed sample size. Since the variance ratio with aggregation value q is approximately a linear combination of the first $q - 1$ autocorrelations, a larger value of q/T entails estimating higher-order autocorrelations with a fixed sample size.

---

[22]Diebold (1987) tabulates the finite sample distributions of actual variance ratios under many other null hypotheses of interest. Although we have not compared each of our empirical quantiles with his, we have spot-checked several for consistency and have found discrepancies only in the extreme tail areas. For example, with a sample size of 1024 and $q = 2$, Diebold's implied value for the upper 0.5 percent quantile of our test statistic z_1 is 2.48 (using his Table 16), whereas our value in Table 3.4 is 2.63. There are at least two possible causes for this discrepancy. First, Diebold's results are based on 10,000 replications whereas ours use 20,000. Second, we simulated the bias-corrected statistic whereas Diebold employed the unadjusted variance ratio. For larger tail areas, this discrepancy vanishes.

Table 3.4. *Empirical quantiles of the (asymptotically) $N(0,1)$ variance ratio test statistic $z_1(q)$ under simulated IID Gaussian random walk increments, where q is the aggregation value. Each set of rows with a given sample size forms a separate and independent simulation experiment based on 20,000 replications.*

T	q	0.005	0.010	0.025	0.050	0.100	0.900	0.950	0.975	0.990	0.995
32	2	-2.56	-2.33	-1.99	-1.70	-1.35	1.33	1.72	2.04	2.41	2.65
32	4	-1.96	-1.86	-1.67	-1.49	-1.25	1.45	1.95	2.43	3.02	3.34
32	8	-1.52	-1.47	-1.38	-1.28	-1.14	1.50	2.22	2.87	3.72	4.28
32	16	-1.13	-1.11	-1.06	-1.01	-0.92	1.34	1.96	2.63	3.39	3.99
64	2	-2.56	-2.35	-1.97	-1.66	-1.29	1.31	1.67	1.99	2.38	2.61
64	4	-2.16	-2.01	-1.79	-1.54	-1.26	1.37	1.83	2.22	2.72	3.10
64	8	-1.85	-1.75	-1.59	-1.42	-1.21	1.43	1.99	2.51	3.17	3.67
64	16	-1.47	-1.43	-1.35	-1.26	-1.12	1.46	2.18	2.86	3.82	4.48
64	32	-1.10	-1.08	-1.04	-0.99	-0.92	1.29	1.96	2.63	3.50	4.10
128	2	-2.63	-2.36	-2.01	-1.68	-1.29	1.30	1.66	1.98	2.35	2.56
128	4	-2.30	-2.11	-1.81	-1.57	-1.27	1.33	1.76	2.15	2.56	2.85
128	8	-2.05	-1.92	-1.71	-1.50	-1.24	1.39	1.86	2.32	2.88	3.24
128	16	-1.77	-1.69	-1.54	-1.40	-1.20	1.46	2.04	2.59	3.28	3.86
128	32	-1.45	-1.41	-1.33	-1.23	-1.11	1.50	2.25	2.95	3.84	4.60
128	64	-1.10	-1.08	-1.04	-0.99	-0.91	1.33	2.07	2.76	3.67	4.36

(continued)

Table 3.4. (continued)

T	q	0.005	0.010	0.025	0.050	0.100	0.900	0.950	0.975	0.990	0.995
256	2	-2.59	-2.34	-1.97	-1.65	-1.29	1.30	1.66	1.96	2.31	2.54
256	4	-2.33	-2.18	-1.89	-1.60	-1.26	1.31	1.70	2.08	2.49	2.81
256	8	-2.20	-2.03	-1.77	-1.53	-1.25	1.34	1.78	2.19	2.72	3.04
256	16	-2.00	-1.87	-1.67	-1.47	-1.22	1.40	1.88	2.33	2.91	3.39
256	32	-1.77	-1.67	-1.53	-1.38	-1.18	1.45	2.03	2.62	3.29	3.76
256	64	-1.45	-1.40	-1.32	-1.23	-1.10	1.51	2.24	2.99	3.91	4.57
256	128	-1.09	-1.07	-1.03	-0.98	-0.91	1.33	2.02	2.72	3.63	4.22
512	2	-2.57	-2.31	-1.96	-1.65	-1.29	1.28	1.65	1.98	2.33	2.58
512	4	-2.46	-2.24	-1.90	-1.61	-1.28	1.32	1.70	2.05	2.46	2.76
512	8	-2.34	-2.13	-1.83	-1.58	-1.26	1.33	1.75	2.11	2.58	2.91
512	16	-2.17	-2.02	-1.76	-1.52	-1.23	1.35	1.79	2.18	2.70	3.09
512	32	-1.97	-1.86	-1.66	-1.47	-1.22	1.39	1.92	2.39	2.93	3.39
512	64	-1.74	-1.67	-1.53	-1.38	-1.19	1.44	2.06	2.68	3.41	3.83
512	128	-1.43	-1.39	-1.31	-1.22	-1.10	1.48	2.22	2.95	3.91	4.64
512	256	-1.09	-1.07	-1.03	-0.98	-0.91	1.30	2.00	2.70	3.58	4.27
1024	2	-2.52	-2.28	-1.94	-1.63	-1.27	1.30	1.66	2.00	2.36	2.63
1024	4	-2.45	-2.19	-1.88	-1.60	-1.27	1.33	1.71	2.04	2.43	2.71
1024	8	-2.35	-2.14	-1.81	-1.56	-1.24	1.33	1.72	2.09	2.55	2.85
1024	16	-2.22	-2.05	-1.80	-1.54	-1.25	1.35	1.77	2.18	2.62	2.97
1024	32	-2.10	-1.96	-1.73	-1.51	-1.23	1.36	1.83	2.27	2.76	3.10
1024	64	-1.94	-1.84	-1.65	-1.46	-1.23	1.40	1.89	2.41	2.95	3.33
1024	128	-1.76	-1.66	-1.53	-1.38	-1.18	1.43	2.02	2.58	3.35	3.93
1024	256	-1.43	-1.39	-1.31	-1.23	-1.10	1.45	2.21	2.92	3.82	4.70
1024	512	-1.09	-1.07	-1.03	-0.98	-0.91	1.27	1.97	2.68	3.56	4.36

The increased sampling variation of these additional autocorrelations leads to the decline in power.[23]

Although the most powerful variance ratio test is more powerful than the Dickey-Fuller t-test, the difference is generally not large. However, the variance ratio test clearly dominates the Box-Pierce Q-test. With a sample of 512 observations the power of a 5 percent variance ratio test is 51.4 percent ($q = 128$) whereas the power of the corresponding Q-test is only 7.1 percent. However, with an aggregation value of $q = 2$ the variance ratio has comparable power to the Box-Pierce test. Again, this is as expected since they are quite similar statistics when $q = 2$ (the variance ratio is approximately one plus the first-order autocorrelation coefficient and the Box-Pierce statistic is the first-order autocorrelation squared).

We conclude that, against the stationary AR(1) alternative, the variance ratio test is comparable to the Dickey-Fuller t-test in power and both are considerably more powerful than the Box-Pierce test.

3.4.3 Two Unit Root Alternatives to the Random Walk

Several recent studies have suggested the following specification for the log-price process X_t:

$$X_t = Y_t + Z_t, \tag{3.4.4}$$

where Y_t is a stationary process and Z_t is a Gaussian random walk independent of Y_t.[24] To be specific, let Y_t be an AR(1); thus:

$$Y_t = \alpha + \phi \cdot [Y_{t-1} - \alpha] + \epsilon_t, \qquad \epsilon_t \text{ IID } \mathcal{N}(0, \sigma_\epsilon^2), \tag{3.4.5a}$$
$$Z_t = Z_{t-1} + \gamma_t, \qquad \gamma_t \text{ IID } \mathcal{N}(0, \sigma_\gamma^2). \tag{3.4.5b}$$

Again, without loss of generality we set α to 0; ρ is set to 0.96; σ_ϵ^2 is normalized to unity; and σ_γ^2 takes on the values 0.50, 1.00 and 2.00 so that the conditional variability of the random walk relative to the stationary component is two, one, and one-half, respectively. Tables 3.5b–3.5d report the power of the variance ratio, Dickey-Fuller t and Box-Pierce Q-tests against this alternative.

---

[23]If the variance ratio test were performed using asymptotic critical values against the AR(1) alternative, there is another cause of the power to decline as q increases. Under the AR(1) model, it is apparent that the theoretical values of the variance ratios are all less than unity, implying that the expectations of the z_1-statistics are negative. But it is shown in Section 3.4.1 that the z_1-statistic is bounded below when the asymptotic variance is used to form z_1, and that the lower bound is an increasing function of the ratio of q to the sample size. Therefore, when the deviation of the alternative from the random walk is in the form of negative draws of z_1 (as in the AR(1) case), the variance ratio test cannot reject the null hypothesis when q is large relative to the number of observations. This is yet another reason we choose q to be less than or equal to one-half the sample size.

[24]See, for example, Summers (1986), Fama and French (1988), and Poterba and Summers (1988).

Table 3.5a. *Power of the two-sided variance ratio test (using the $z_1(q)$ statistic) against the stationary AR(1) alternative $X_t = \phi X_{t-1} + \epsilon_t$, ϵ_t IID $\mathcal{N}(0, 1)$ and $\phi = 0.96$. For comparison, the power of the one-sided Box-Pierce Q-test (Q_1) and the two-sided Dickey-Fuller t-test (D-F) are also reported. Each set of rows with a given sample size forms a separate and independent simulation experiment based on 20,000 replications.*

Sample Size	q	1 Percent Test		5 Percent Test		10 Percent Test	
		$z_1(q)$	Q_1	$z_1(q)$	Q_1	$z_1(q)$	Q_1
32	2	0.008	0.009	0.047	0.047	0.093	0.097
32	4	0.009	0.009	0.049	0.045	0.101	0.096
32	8	0.009	0.010	0.048	0.048	0.096	0.098
32	16	0.009	0.010	0.049	0.050	0.101	0.099
32	D-F	0.010		0.050		0.098	
64	2	0.009	0.008	0.048	0.048	0.097	0.100
64	4	0.009	0.009	0.046	0.050	0.093	0.099
64	8	0.008	0.010	0.044	0.051	0.093	0.107
64	16	0.008	0.010	0.043	0.050	0.086	0.101
64	32	0.009	0.010	0.044	0.051	0.088	0.104
64	D-F	0.009		0.042		0.084	
128	2	0.010	0.010	0.047	0.050	0.100	0.106
128	4	0.010	0.011	0.051	0.053	0.102	0.106
128	8	0.011	0.011	0.050	0.054	0.102	0.104
128	16	0.012	0.009	0.053	0.056	0.102	0.112
128	32	0.010	0.009	0.053	0.054	0.103	0.112
128	64	0.010	0.009	0.046	0.053	0.088	0.108
128	D-F	0.008		0.047		0.095	
256	2	0.011	0.012	0.057	0.062	0.111	0.115
256	4	0.017	0.013	0.061	0.062	0.121	0.120
256	8	0.021	0.013	0.079	0.066	0.146	0.123
256	16	0.028	0.013	0.101	0.060	0.180	0.121
256	32	0.030	0.012	0.123	0.059	0.217	0.118
256	64	0.031	0.012	0.130	0.060	0.227	0.114
256	128	0.026	0.011	0.103	0.054	0.189	0.110
256	D-F	0.025		0.118		0.207	
512	2	0.016	0.017	0.066	0.070	0.125	0.131
512	4	0.023	0.019	0.090	0.082	0.165	0.150
512	8	0.038	0.020	0.140	0.087	0.227	0.162
512	16	0.075	0.020	0.225	0.088	0.341	0.161
512	32	0.144	0.019	0.341	0.083	0.491	0.158
512	64	0.203	0.017	0.469	0.079	0.640	0.140

(continued)

Table 3.5a. *(continued)*

Sample Size	q	1 Percent Test		5 Percent Test		10 Percent Test	
		$z_1(q)$	Q_1	$z_1(q)$	Q_1	$z_1(q)$	Q_1
512	128	0.196	0.016	0.514	0.071	0.686	0.130
512	256	0.097	0.014	0.345	0.064	0.517	0.124
512	D-F	0.189		0.478		0.654	
1024	2	0.026	0.025	0.092	0.091	0.159	0.162
1024	4	0.053	0.033	0.165	0.114	0.257	0.206
1024	8	0.124	0.034	0.304	0.136	0.413	0.238
1024	16	0.272	0.038	0.497	0.146	0.632	0.254
1024	32	0.510	0.034	0.755	0.134	0.853	0.235
1024	64	0.769	0.025	0.928	0.107	0.970	0.197
1024	128	0.859	0.023	0.981	0.092	0.995	0.170
1024	256	0.855	0.019	0.983	0.080	0.997	0.155
1024	512	0.530	0.018	0.844	0.075	0.934	0.147
1024	D-F	0.915		0.993		0.999	

Note that this specification contains a unit root (it is an ARIMA(1, 1, 1)), and hence, asymptotically, the power of the Dickey-Fuller t-test should equal its size.[25] However, since Schwert (1987a,b) has shown the finite-sample behavior of the Dickey-Fuller test to be quite erratic, we report its power for comparison.

Table 3.5b gives the power results for the z_1-, Q_1-, and t-statistics against this ARIMA(1, 1, 1) alternative where the variance of the random walk innovation is twice the variance of the AR(1) disturbance. Although none of the tests are especially powerful under these parameter values, the variance ratio test seems to dominate the other two. For a sample size of 1024, the power of the variance ratio test is 24.1 percent for $q = 32$ whereas the corresponding power of the Dickey-Fuller and Box-Pierce tests are 10.4 and 7.9 percent, respectively.

---

[25]To see this, observe that (3.4.4) has the following ARIMA(1, 1, 1) representation:

$$(1 - \rho L)(1 - L)X_t = (1 - \lambda L)v_t,$$

where

$$\lambda \equiv \rho\sigma_\epsilon^2 + \sigma_\gamma^2 \quad \text{and} \quad \sigma_v^2 \equiv \frac{\left[(1 + \rho^2)\sigma_\epsilon^2 + 2\sigma_\gamma^2\right]}{(1 + \lambda^2)}.$$

Table 3.5b. *Power of the two-sided variance ratio test (using the $z_1(q)$-statistic) against the ARIMA(1, 1, 1) alternative $X_t = Y_t + Z_t$, where $Y_t = 0.96\, Y_{t-1} + \epsilon_t$, ϵ_t IID $\mathcal{N}(0, 1)$ and $Z_t = Z_{t-1} + \gamma_t$, γ_t IID $\mathcal{N}(0, \frac{1}{2})$. For comparison, the power of the one-sided Box-Pierce Q-test (Q_1) and the two-sided Dickey-Fuller t-test (D-F) are also reported. Each set of rows with a given sample size forms a separate and independent simulation experiment based on 20,000 replications.*

Sample Size	q	1 Percent Test		5 Percent Test		10 Percent Test	
		$z_1(q)$	Q_1	$z_1(q)$	Q_1	$z_1(q)$	Q_1
32	2	0.008	0.010	0.045	0.048	0.095	0.098
32	4	0.010	0.010	0.045	0.047	0.098	0.096
32	8	0.010	0.011	0.047	0.049	0.094	0.101
32	16	0.009	0.010	0.046	0.051	0.094	0.100
32	D-F	0.010		0.049		0.094	
64	2	0.009	0.010	0.048	0.048	0.096	0.100
64	4	0.010	0.010	0.046	0.050	0.094	0.102
64	8	0.009	0.009	0.045	0.050	0.092	0.104
64	16	0.009	0.009	0.044	0.052	0.089	0.101
64	32	0.010	0.010	0.047	0.051	0.091	0.104
64	D-F	0.009		0.046		0.094	
128	2	0.009	0.010	0.046	0.051	0.098	0.104
128	4	0.011	0.011	0.052	0.053	0.099	0.104
128	8	0.012	0.011	0.053	0.052	0.104	0.102
128	16	0.011	0.011	0.052	0.054	0.103	0.107
128	32	0.009	0.009	0.047	0.053	0.102	0.105
128	64	0.010	0.009	0.045	0.053	0.087	0.106
128	D-F	0.009		0.048		0.101	
256	2	0.010	0.012	0.054	0.059	0.106	0.111
256	4	0.015	0.012	0.055	0.057	0.113	0.115
256	8	0.015	0.011	0.068	0.059	0.126	0.118
256	16	0.018	0.012	0.075	0.054	0.138	0.106
256	32	0.016	0.013	0.072	0.054	0.131	0.109
256	64	0.014	0.012	0.063	0.056	0.117	0.106
256	128	0.014	0.010	0.055	0.052	0.107	0.104
256	D-F	0.015		0.069		0.129	
512	2	0.014	0.014	0.061	0.065	0.119	0.123
512	4	0.018	0.017	0.077	0.074	0.141	0.139
512	8	0.025	0.016	0.101	0.072	0.178	0.140
512	16	0.034	0.014	0.124	0.071	0.210	0.133
512	32	0.036	0.014	0.120	0.064	0.206	0.129
512	64	0.027	0.014	0.095	0.065	0.170	0.119

(continued)

Table 3.5b.   *(continued)*

Sample Size	q	1 Percent Test		5 Percent Test		10 Percent Test	
		$z_1(q)$	Q_1	$z_1(q)$	Q_1	$z_1(q)$	Q_1
512	128	0.020	0.013	0.079	0.064	0.138	0.112
512	256	0.015	0.012	0.063	0.059	0.120	0.115
512	D-F	0.021		0.081		0.147	
1024	2	0.024	0.023	0.085	0.085	0.150	0.153
1024	4	0.040	0.024	0.132	0.091	0.207	0.169
1024	8	0.065	0.023	0.196	0.097	0.290	0.177
1024	16	0.096	0.021	0.236	0.092	0.355	0.163
1024	32	0.094	0.017	0.241	0.079	0.355	0.144
1024	64	0.064	0.014	0.178	0.067	0.277	0.129
1024	128	0.030	0.013	0.118	0.061	0.197	0.120
1024	256	0.025	0.011	0.085	0.057	0.148	0.117
1024	512	0.021	0.012	0.074	0.057	0.132	0.112
1024	D-F	0.032		0.104		0.173	

As in the case of the stationary AR(1) alternative, the power of the variance ratio test also rises and falls with q against the ARIMA(1, 1, 1) alternative. In addition to the factors discussed in Section 3.4.2, there is an added explanation for this pattern of power. For small to medium differencing intervals the increments of X_t behave much like increments of an AR(1), hence power increases with q in this range. For longer differencing intervals the random walk component dominates. Hence the power declines beyond some aggregation value q.

As the variance of the random walk's disturbance declines relative to the variance of the stationary component's, the power of the variance ratio test increases. Table 3.5c reports power results for the case where the variances of the two components' innovations are equal, and in Table 3.5d the variance of the random walk innovation is half the variance of the AR(1) innovation. In the latter case, the 5 percent variance ratio test has 89.8 percent power for $q = 32$ and $T = 1024$ compared to 41.7 percent and 18.4 percent power for the Dickey-Fuller and Box-Pierce tests, respectively. Although the qualitative behavior of the three tests are the same in Tables 3.5b–3.5d, the variance ratio test is considerably more powerful than the other two when the variance of the stationary component is larger than that of the random

Table 3.5c. *Power of the two-sided variance ratio test (using the $z_1(q)$-statistic) against the ARIMA(1, 1, 1) alternative $X_t = Y_t + Z_t$, where $Y_t = 0.96\,Y_{t-1} + \epsilon_t$, ϵ_t IID $\mathcal{N}(0, 1)$ and $Z_t = Z_{t-1} + \gamma_t$, γ_t IID $\mathcal{N}(0, 1)$. For comparison, the power of the one-sided Box-Pierce Q-test (Q_1) and the two-sided Dickey-Fuller t-test (D-F) are also reported. Each set of rows with a given sample size forms a separate and independent simulation experiment based on 20,000 replications.*

Sample Size	q	1 Percent Test		5 Percent Test		10 Percent Test	
		$z_1(q)$	Q_1	$z_1(q)$	Q_1	$z_1(q)$	Q_1
32	2	0.008	0.010	0.049	0.049	0.095	0.099
32	4	0.010	0.010	0.046	0.051	0.093	0.102
32	8	0.009	0.012	0.045	0.052	0.092	0.106
32	16	0.008	0.012	0.045	0.053	0.094	0.102
32	D-F	0.009		0.049		0.096	
64	2	0.010	0.010	0.048	0.049	0.096	0.102
64	4	0.008	0.009	0.048	0.054	0.100	0.105
64	8	0.009	0.009	0.047	0.054	0.099	0.111
64	16	0.010	0.009	0.048	0.054	0.095	0.105
64	32	0.010	0.009	0.047	0.052	0.093	0.107
64	D-F	0.009		0.045		0.092	
128	2	0.010	0.012	0.049	0.056	0.102	0.113
128	4	0.012	0.013	0.062	0.058	0.115	0.113
128	8	0.014	0.013	0.062	0.061	0.122	0.115
128	16	0.016	0.012	0.068	0.060	0.125	0.118
128	32	0.013	0.012	0.060	0.059	0.117	0.115
128	64	0.012	0.012	0.053	0.058	0.098	0.112
128	D-F	0.012		0.056		0.114	
256	2	0.013	0.015	0.060	0.065	0.114	0.122
256	4	0.021	0.015	0.073	0.071	0.142	0.136
256	8	0.027	0.015	0.103	0.072	0.178	0.137
256	16	0.034	0.013	0.120	0.062	0.212	0.122
256	32	0.026	0.013	0.120	0.058	0.207	0.117
256	64	0.023	0.014	0.092	0.062	0.165	0.118
256	128	0.019	0.012	0.072	0.056	0.133	0.112
256	D-F	0.024		0.098		0.175	
512	2	0.022	0.023	0.087	0.092	0.151	0.159
512	4	0.036	0.026	0.129	0.106	0.209	0.188
512	8	0.058	0.024	0.191	0.100	0.294	0.186
512	16	0.088	0.021	0.251	0.093	0.377	0.169
512	32	0.095	0.019	0.257	0.081	0.387	0.153
512	64	0.067	0.018	0.194	0.076	0.311	0.136

(continued)

Table 3.5c.   (continued)

Sample Size	q	1 Percent Test		5 Percent Test		10 Percent Test	
		$z_1(q)$	Q_1	$z_1(q)$	Q_1	$z_1(q)$	Q_1
512	128	0.044	0.017	0.146	0.070	0.224	0.129
512	256	0.028	0.014	0.106	0.064	0.171	0.124
512	D-F	0.053		0.155		0.241	
1024	2	0.038	0.036	0.122	0.123	0.201	0.206
1024	4	0.085	0.046	0.230	0.156	0.337	0.261
1024	8	0.173	0.043	0.393	0.162	0.513	0.272
1024	16	0.285	0.035	0.513	0.142	0.654	0.245
1024	32	0.305	0.028	0.552	0.116	0.686	0.203
1024	64	0.213	0.021	0.426	0.091	0.571	0.169
1024	128	0.093	0.019	0.259	0.078	0.381	0.148
1024	256	0.062	0.014	0.169	0.068	0.262	0.134
1024	512	0.040	0.013	0.126	0.065	0.200	0.131
1024	D-F	0.078		0.200		0.292	

walk. Moreover, the pattern of power as a function of q clearly demonstrates that against this alternative, it is not optimal to set q as large as possible.[26]

Since both the stationary AR(1) and the AR(1) plus random walk are not empirically supported by Lo and MacKinlay's (1988b) results for weekly stock returns, we consider the power of the variance ratio test against a more relevant alternative hypothesis suggested by their empirical findings: an integrated AR(1), i.e., an ARIMA(1, 1, 0). Specifically, if X_t is the log-price process, then we assume

$$(X_t - X_{t-1}) \; = \; \kappa \cdot (X_{t-1} - X_{t-2}) + \zeta_t, \quad \zeta_t \text{ IID } \mathcal{N}(0, \sigma_\zeta^2), \qquad (3.4.6)$$

where $|\kappa| < 1$. Since this alternative obviously possesses a unit root, we expect the standard unit root tests to have poor power against it. Nevertheless for comparison we report the power of the Dickey-Fuller t-test along with the power of the variance ratio and Box-Pierce tests. The parameters (κ, σ_ζ^2) are set to $(0.20, 1)$ for all the simulations in Table 3.5e. Unlike its behavior under the stationary AR(1) alternative, against this integrated process the variance ratio's power declines as q increases. With a sample size of 1024, the power of a 5 percent test is 100 percent when $q = 2$, but falls to 9.3 per-

---

[26]In fact, the q for which the variance test has the most power for a given sample size will depend on the ratio of the stationary component's innovation variance to the variance of the random walk's disturbance. Unfortunately, this fact cannot be observed in our tables because we have set q to be powers of 2 for computational convenience. If the variance ratio test's power were tabulated for $q = 2, 3, 4, \ldots, T - 1$, it would be apparent that against this ARIMA(1, 1, 1) alternative the optimal q changes with the ratio of the innovation invariances of the two components.

Table 3.5d. *Power of the two-sided variance ratio test (using the $z_1(q)$-statistic) against the ARIMA(1, 1, 1) alternative $X_t = Y_t + Z_t$, where $Y_t = 0.96\, Y_{t-1} + \epsilon_t$, ϵ_t IID $\mathcal{N}(0, 1)$ and $Z_t = Z_{t-1} + \gamma_t$, γ_t IID $\mathcal{N}(0, 2)$. For comparison, the power of the one-sided Box-Pierce Q-test (Q_1) and the two-sided Dickey-Fuller t-test (D-F) are also reported. Each set of rows with a given sample size forms a separate and independent simulation experiment based on 20,000 replications.*

Sample Size	q	1 Percent Test		5 Percent Test		10 Percent Test	
		$z_1(q)$	Q_1	$z_1(q)$	Q_1	$z_1(q)$	Q_1
32	2	0.008	0.010	0.045	0.048	0.091	0.097
32	4	0.010	0.010	0.048	0.050	0.093	0.103
32	8	0.009	0.012	0.046	0.054	0.096	0.110
32	16	0.008	0.012	0.044	0.054	0.093	0.102
32	D-F	0.009		0.048		0.093	
64	2	0.011	0.012	0.050	0.054	0.103	0.112
64	4	0.013	0.012	0.050	0.061	0.104	0.115
64	8	0.011	0.013	0.052	0.059	0.104	0.119
64	16	0.011	0.013	0.047	0.062	0.095	0.116
64	32	0.010	0.013	0.044	0.060	0.089	0.115
64	D-F	0.010		0.047		0.094	
128	2	0.011	0.014	0.054	0.061	0.106	0.117
128	4	0.014	0.014	0.070	0.065	0.127	0.128
128	8	0.019	0.014	0.080	0.068	0.149	0.127
128	16	0.023	0.012	0.089	0.065	0.156	0.124
128	32	0.016	0.011	0.084	0.062	0.155	0.120
128	64	0.014	0.012	0.063	0.057	0.120	0.113
128	D-F	0.015		0.072		0.139	
256	2	0.018	0.021	0.075	0.084	0.139	0.146
256	4	0.035	0.020	0.102	0.088	0.182	0.167
256	8	0.047	0.019	0.155	0.088	0.255	0.166
256	16	0.067	0.016	0.205	0.081	0.324	0.151
256	32	0.060	0.016	0.207	0.072	0.331	0.139
256	64	0.043	0.015	0.160	0.069	0.268	0.128
256	128	0.032	0.012	0.108	0.063	0.196	0.123
256	D-F	0.050		0.170		0.273	
512	2	0.032	0.035	0.113	0.119	0.187	0.196
512	4	0.063	0.040	0.193	0.149	0.299	0.249
512	8	0.121	0.039	0.322	0.145	0.448	0.251
512	16	0.210	0.031	0.463	0.124	0.607	0.220
512	32	0.255	0.025	0.516	0.104	0.669	0.192

(continued)

Table 3.5d.   *(continued)*

Sample Size	q	1 Percent Test		5 Percent Test		10 Percent Test	
		$z_1(q)$	Q_1	$z_1(q)$	Q_1	$z_1(q)$	Q_1
512	64	0.178	0.021	0.406	0.091	0.567	0.165
512	128	0.103	0.018	0.280	0.082	0.399	0.150
512	256	0.059	0.017	0.186	0.073	0.283	0.142
512	D-F	0.132		0.306		0.427	
1024	2	0.068	0.065	0.187	0.187	0.282	0.287
1024	4	0.170	0.095	0.374	0.256	0.496	0.391
1024	8	0.371	0.092	0.638	0.292	0.745	0.440
1024	16	0.613	0.074	0.825	0.249	0.904	0.396
1024	32	0.711	0.053	0.898	0.184	0.951	0.304
1024	64	0.576	0.035	0.811	0.134	0.899	0.230
1024	128	0.281	0.028	0.559	0.110	0.699	0.192
1024	256	0.163	0.022	0.344	0.090	0.471	0.169
1024	512	0.100	0.021	0.239	0.086	0.339	0.159
1024	D-F	0.227		0.417		0.525	

cent when $q = 512$. In contrast to the AR(1), the behavior of the integrated process's increments is farthest from a random walk for short differencing intervals (since the increments follow a stationary AR(1) by construction). As the differencing interval increases, the autocorrelation of the increments decreases and it becomes more difficult to distinguish between this process and the random walk.

Observe that for smaller aggregation values the variance ratio test is more powerful than the Q-test, but the Q-test dominates when q is large. This result is due to the fact that the Box-Pierce Q does not distinguish between the upper and lower tails of the null distribution (since Q is the sum of *squared* autocorrelations) whereas the variance ratio test does.

3.5 Conclusion

Our simulations indicate that the variance ratio test of the random walk hypothesis generally yields reliable inferences under both the IID Gaussian and the heteroskedastic null hypotheses. By selecting the aggregation value q appropriately, the power of the variance ratio test is comparable to that of the Box-Pierce and Dickey-Fuller tests against the stationary AR(1) alternative and is more powerful than either of the two tests against the two unit root alternatives. However, because of the variance ratio's skewed empirical

Table 3.5e. *Power of the two-sided variance ratio test (using the statistic $z_1(q)$) against the ARIMA(1, 1, 0) alternative $\Delta X_t = \kappa \Delta X_{t-1} + v_t$, v_t IID $\mathcal{N}(0, 1)$, $\kappa = 0.20$. For comparison, the power of the one-sided Box-Pierce Q-test (Q_1) and the two-sided Dickey-Fuller t-test (D-F) are also reported. Each set of rows with a given sample size forms a separate and independent simulation experiment based on 20,000 replications.*

Sample Size	q	1 Percent Test		5 Percent Test		10 Percent Test	
		$z_1(q)$	Q_1	$z_1(q)$	Q_1	$z_1(q)$	Q_1
32	2	0.057	0.037	0.176	0.128	0.270	0.213
32	4	0.046	0.021	0.141	0.094	0.226	0.167
32	8	0.029	0.022	0.098	0.086	0.168	0.157
32	16	0.026	0.023	0.095	0.085	0.166	0.147
32	D-F	0.143		0.240		0.301	
64	2	0.148	0.119	0.342	0.292	0.463	0.417
64	4	0.104	0.071	0.263	0.195	0.368	0.298
64	8	0.059	0.050	0.168	0.156	0.254	0.248
64	16	0.035	0.040	0.114	0.135	0.181	0.218
64	32	0.032	0.036	0.097	0.123	0.164	0.209
64	D-F	0.143		0.240		0.308	
128	2	0.377	0.323	0.600	0.564	0.719	0.687
128	4	0.257	0.197	0.455	0.413	0.576	0.542
128	8	0.122	0.126	0.280	0.305	0.388	0.422
128	16	0.059	0.082	0.167	0.231	0.254	0.344
128	32	0.034	0.058	0.108	0.184	0.175	0.290
128	64	0.029	0.050	0.093	0.166	0.153	0.268
128	D-F	0.138		0.235		0.302	
256	2	0.741	0.709	0.887	0.876	0.934	0.928
256	4	0.526	0.529	0.744	0.749	0.836	0.836
256	8	0.276	0.361	0.498	0.612	0.614	0.726
256	16	0.125	0.229	0.298	0.454	0.401	0.588
256	32	0.069	0.160	0.172	0.348	0.261	0.479
256	64	0.036	0.115	0.105	0.285	0.177	0.400
256	128	0.032	0.088	0.095	0.241	0.158	0.362
256	D-F	0.138		0.238		0.299	
512	2	0.972	0.969	0.993	0.993	0.997	0.997
512	4	0.871	0.918	0.957	0.976	0.978	0.988
512	8	0.571	0.813	0.779	0.931	0.855	0.965
512	16	0.290	0.652	0.523	0.845	0.633	0.909
512	32	0.139	0.481	0.300	0.706	0.407	0.809

(continued)

Table 3.5e.   *(continued)*

Sample Size	q	1 Percent Test		5 Percent Test		10 Percent Test	
		$z_1(q)$	Q_1	$z_1(q)$	Q_1	$z_1(q)$	Q_1
512	64	0.069	0.320	0.168	0.571	0.263	0.688
512	128	0.035	0.227	0.112	0.455	0.181	0.580
512	256	0.032	0.182	0.097	0.380	0.159	0.519
512	D-F	0.136		0.236		0.304	
1024	2	1.000	1.000	1.000	1.000	1.000	1.000
1024	4	0.996	0.999	0.999	1.000	1.000	1.000
1024	8	0.893	0.995	0.969	0.999	0.985	1.000
1024	16	0.585	0.978	0.783	0.996	0.862	0.998
1024	32	0.301	0.918	0.509	0.976	0.629	0.989
1024	64	0.144	0.767	0.295	0.911	0.411	0.952
1024	128	0.061	0.581	0.176	0.792	0.265	0.874
1024	256	0.035	0.411	0.110	0.663	0.174	0.780
1024	512	0.028	0.334	0.093	0.586	0.157	0.170
1024	D-F	0.142		0.248		0.314	

distribution, caution must be exercised when q is large relative to the sample size.

These results emphasize dramatically the obvious fact that the power of any test may differ substantially across alternatives. A sensible testing strategy must consider not only the null hypothesis but also the most relevant alternative. Although the variance ratio test has advantages over other tests under some null and alternative hypotheses, there are of course other situations in which those tests may possess more desirable properties. Nevertheless, the Monte Carlo evidence suggests that the variance ratio test has reasonable power against a wide range of alternatives.[27] The simplicity, reliability, and flexibility of the variance ratio test make it a valuable tool for inference.

---

[27]See Hausman (1988) for further evidence of this.

4

An Econometric Analysis of Nonsynchronous Trading

4.1 Introduction

IT HAS LONG BEEN RECOGNIZED that the sampling of economic time series plays a subtle but critical role in determining their stochastic properties. Perhaps the best example of this is the growing literature on temporal aggregation biases which are created by confusing stock and flow variables. This is the essence of Working's (1960) now classic result in which time-averages are mistaken for point-sampled data. More generally, econometric problems are bound to arise when we ignore the fact that the statistical behavior of sampled data may be quite different from the behavior of the underlying stochastic process from which the sample was obtained. Yet another manifestation of this general principle is what may be called the "nonsynchronicity" problem, which results from the assumption that multiple time series are sampled simultaneously when in fact the sampling is nonsynchronous. For example the daily prices of financial securities quoted in the *Wall Street Journal* are usually "closing" prices, prices at which the last transaction in each of those securities occurred on the previous business day. It is apparent that closing prices of distinct securities need not be set simultaneously, yet few empirical studies employing daily data take this into account.

Less apparent is the fact that ignoring this seemingly trivial nonsynchronicity can result in substantially biased inferences for the temporal behavior of asset returns. To see how, suppose that the returns to stocks i and j are temporally independent but i trades less frequently than j. If news affecting the aggregate stock market arrives near the close of the market on one day, it is more likely that j's end-of-day price will reflect this information than i's simply because i may not trade after the news arrives. Of course, i will respond to this information eventually but the fact that it responds with a lag induces spurious cross-autocorrelation between the *closing* prices of

i and j. As a result, a portfolio consisting of securities i and j will exhibit serial dependence even though the underlying data-generating process was assumed to be temporally independent. Spurious own-autocorrelation is created in a similar manner. These effects have obvious implications for the recent tests of the random walk and efficient markets hypotheses.

In this chapter we propose a simple stochastic model for this phenomenon, known to financial economists as the "nonsynchronous trading" or "nontrading" problem. Our specification captures the essence of nontrading but is tractable enough to permit explicit calculation of all the relevant time series properties of sampled data. Since most empirical investigations of stock price behavior focus on returns or price changes, we take as primitive the (unobservable) return-generating process of a collection of securities. The nontrading mechanism is modeled as a random censoring of returns where censored observations are cumulated, so that observed returns are the sum of all prior returns that were consecutively censored. For example, consider a sequence of five consecutive days for which returns are censored only on days 3 and 4; the observed return on day 2 is assumed to be the true or "virtual" return, determined by the primitive return-generating process. Observed returns on day 3 and 4 are zero, and the observed return on day 5 is the sum of virtual returns from days 3 to 5.[1] Each period's virtual return is random and captures movements caused by information arrival as well as idiosyncratic noise. The particular censoring (and cumulation) process we employ models the lag with which news and noise is incorporated into security prices due to infrequent trading. By allowing cross-sectional differences in the random censoring processes, we are able to capture the effects of nontrading on portfolio returns when only a subset of securities suffers from infrequent trading. Although the dynamics of our stylized model are surprisingly rich, they yield several important empirical implications. Using these results we estimate the probabilities of nontrading to quantify the effects of nonsynchronicity on returns-based inferences, such as the rejection of the random walk hypothesis in Lo and MacKinlay (1988b)).

Perhaps the first to recognize the importance of nonsynchronous price quotes was Fisher (1966)). Since then more explicit models of nontrading have been developed by Scholes and Williams (1977)), Cohen et al. (1978, 1986), and Dimson (1979)). Whereas earlier studies considered the effects of nontrading on empirical applications of the Capital Asset Pricing Model and the Arbitrage Pricing Theory,[2] more recent attention has been focused

---

[1] Day 1's return obviously depends on how many consecutive days prior to 1 that the security did not trade. If it traded on day 0, then the day 1 return is simply equal to its virtual return; if it did not trade at 0 but did trade at -1, then day 1's return is the sum of day 0 and day 1's virtual returns; etc.

[2] See, for example, Cohen et al. (1983a,b), Dimson (1979)), Scholes and Williams (1977)), and Shanken (1987a)).

on spurious autocorrelations induced by nonsynchronous trading.[3] Our emphasis also lies in the autocorrelation and cross-autocorrelation properties of nonsynchronously sampled data and the model we propose extends and generalizes existing results in several directions. First, previous formulations of nontrading require that each security trades within some *fixed* time interval whereas in our approach the time between trades is stochastic.[4] Second, our framework allows us to derive closed-form expressions for the means, variances, and covariances of observed returns as functions of the nontrading process. These expressions yield simple estimators for the probabilities of nontrading. For example we show that the relative likelihood of security i trading more frequently than security j is given by the ratio of the (i, j)th autocovariance with the (j, i)th autocovariance. With this result, specification tests for nonsynchronous trading may be constructed based on the degree of asymmetry in the autocovariance matrix of the returns process. Third, we present results for portfolios of securities grouped by their probabilities of nontrading; in contrast to the spurious autocorrelation induced in individual security returns which is proportional to the square of its expected return, we show that nontrading induced autocorrelation in portfolio returns does not depend on the mean. This implies that the effects of nontrading may not be detectable in the returns of individual securities (since the expected daily return is usually quite small), but will be more pronounced in portfolio returns. Fourth, we quantify the impact of time aggregation on nontrading effects by deriving closed-form expressions for the moments of time-aggregated observed returns. Allowing for random censoring at intervals arbitrarily finer than the finest sampling interval for which we have data lets us uncover aspects of infrequent trading previously invisible to econometric scrutiny. This also yields testable restrictions on the time series properties of coarser-sampled data once a sampling interval has been selected. Finally, we apply these results to daily, weekly, and monthly stock returns to gauge the empirical relevance of nontrading for recent findings of predictability in asset returns.

In Section 4.2 we present our model of nontrading and derive its implications for the time series properties of observed returns. Section 4.3 reports corresponding results for time-aggregated returns and we apply these results in Section 4.4 to daily, weekly, and monthly data. We discuss extensions and generalizations and conclude in Section 4.5.

---

[3]See Atchison, Butler, and Simonds (1987)), Cohen et al. (1979, 1986), Lo and MacKinlay (1988b)), and Muthuswamy (1988)).

[4]For example, Scholes and Williams (1977, fn. 4) assume: "All information about returns over days in which no trades occur is ignored." This is equivalent to forcing the security to trade at least once within the day. Muthuswamy (1988)) imposes a similar requirement. Assumption A1 of Cohen et al. (1986, ch. 6.1) requires that each security trades at least once in the last N periods, where N is fixed and exogenous.

4.2 A Model of Nonsynchronous Trading

Consider a collection of N securities with unobservable "virtual" continuously-compounded returns R_{it} at time t, where $i = 1, \ldots, N$. We assume
they are generated by the following stochastic model:

$$R_{it} = \mu_i + \beta_i \Lambda_t + \epsilon_{it}, \qquad i = 1, \ldots, N, \qquad (4.2.1)$$

where Λ_t is some zero-mean common factor and ϵ_{it} is zero-mean idiosyncratic noise that is temporally and cross-sectionally independent at all leads
and lags. Since we wish to focus on nontrading as the *sole* source of autocorrelation, we also assume that the common factor Λ_t is independently and
identically distributed and is independent of ϵ_{it-k} for all i, t, and k.[5]

In each period t, there is some chance that security i does not trade, say
with probability p_i. If it does not trade, its observed return for period t is
simply 0, although its true or "virtual" return R_{it} is still given by (4.2.1). In
the next period $t+1$ there is again some chance that security i does not trade,
also with probability p_i. We assume that whether or not the security traded
in period t does not influence the likelihood of its trading in period $t+1$ or
any other future period, hence our nontrading mechanism is independent
and identically distributed for each security i.[6] If security i does trade in
period $t + 1$ and did not trade in period t, we assume that its observed
return R^o_{it+1} at $t + 1$ is the sum of its virtual returns R_{it+1}, R_{it}, and virtual
returns for all past *consecutive* periods in which i has not traded. In fact,
the observed return in any period is simply the sum of its virtual returns for
all past consecutive periods in which it did not trade. That is, if security i
trades at time $t + 1$, has not traded from time $t - k$ to t, and has traded at
time $t - k - 1$, then its observed time $t + 1$ return is simply equal to the sum
of its virtual returns from $t - k$ to $t + 1$. This captures the essential feature
of nontrading as a source of spurious autocorrelation: news affects those
stocks that trade more frequently first and influences the returns of thinly
traded securities with a lag. In our framework the impact of news on returns
is captured by the virtual returns process (4.2.1), and the lag induced by thin
or nonsynchronous trading is modeled by the observed returns process R^o_{it}.

To derive an explicit expression for the observed returns process and
to deduce its time series properties we introduce two related stochastic processes:

---

[5] These strong assumptions are made primarily for expositional convenience and may be
relaxed considerably. See Section 4.5 for further discussion.

[6] This assumption may be relaxed to allow for state-dependent probabilities, i.e., autocorrelated nontrading; see the discussion in Section 4.5.

Definition 4.2.1. *Let δ_{it} and $X_{it}(k)$ be the following Bernoulli random variables:*

$$\delta_{it} = \begin{cases} 1 & \text{with probability } p_i, \\ 0 & \text{with probability } 1 - p_i, \end{cases} \tag{4.2.2}$$

$$X_{it}(k) \equiv (1 - \delta_{it})\delta_{it-1}\,\delta_{it-2}\cdots\delta_{it-k}, \qquad k > 0,$$

$$= \begin{cases} 1 & \text{with probability } (1 - p_i)p_i^k, \\ 0 & \text{with probability } 1 - (1 - p_i)p_i^k, \end{cases} \tag{4.2.3}$$

$$X_{it}(0) \equiv 1 - \delta_{it}, \tag{4.2.4}$$

where it has been implicitly assumed that $\{\delta_{it}\}$ is an independently and identically distributed random sequence for $i = 1, 2, \ldots, N$.

The indicator variable δ_{it} is unity when security i does not trade at time t and zero otherwise. $X_{it}(k)$ is also an indicator variable and takes on the value 1 when security i trades at time t but has not traded in any of the k previous periods, and is 0 otherwise. Since p_i is within the unit interval, for large k the variable $X_{it}(k)$ will be 0 with high probability. This is not surprising since it is highly unlikely that security i should trade today but never in the past.

Having defined the $X_{it}(k)$'s, it is now a simple matter to derive an expression for observed returns:

Definition 4.2.2. *The observed returns process R_{it}^o is given by the following stochastic process:*

$$R_{it}^o = \sum_{k=0}^{\infty} X_{it}(k)\,R_{it-k}, \qquad i = 1, \ldots, N. \tag{4.2.5}$$

If security i does not trade at time t, then $\delta_{it} = 1$ which implies that $X_{it}(k) = 0$ for all k, thus $R_{it}^o = 0$. If i does trade at time t, then its observed return is equal to the sum of today's virtual return R_{it} and its past $\tilde{k}_t$ virtual returns, where the random variable $\tilde{k}_t$ is the number of past *consecutive* periods that i has not traded. We call this the *duration* of nontrading and it may be expressed as:

$$\tilde{k}_{it} \equiv \sum_{k=1}^{\infty} \left\{ \prod_{j=1}^{k} \delta_{it-j} \right\}. \tag{4.2.6}$$

Although Definition 4.2.2 will prove to be more convenient for subsequent calculations, $\tilde{k}_{it}$ may be used to give a more intuitive definition of the observed returns process:

Definition 4.2.3. *The observed returns process R_{it}^o is given by the following stochastic process:*

$$R_{it}^o = \sum_{k=0}^{\tilde{k}_t} R_{it-k}, \qquad i = 1, \ldots, N. \tag{4.2.7}$$

Whereas expression (4.2.5) shows that in the presence of nontrading the observed returns process is a (stochastic) function of *all* past returns, the equivalent relation (4.2.7) reveals that R_{it}^o may also be viewed as a random sum with a random number of terms.[7] To see how the probability p_i is related to the duration of nontrading, consider the mean and variance of $\tilde{k}_{it}$:

$$E[\tilde{k}_{it}] = \frac{p_i}{1 - p_i}, \qquad (4.2.8)$$

$$\text{Var}[\tilde{k}_{it}] = \frac{p_i}{(1 - p_i)^2}. \qquad (4.2.9)$$

If $p_i = \frac{1}{2}$, then security i goes without trading for one period at a time on average; if $p_i = \frac{3}{4}$, then the average number of consecutive periods of nontrading is 3. As expected, if the security trades every period so that $p_i = 0$, both the mean and variance of $\tilde{k}_{it}$ are identically zero.

In Section 4.2.1, we derive the implications of our simple nontrading model for the time series properties of individual security returns and consider corresponding results for portfolio returns in Section 4.2.2.

4.2.1 Implications for Individual Returns

To see how nontrading affects the time series properties of individual returns, we require the moments of R_{it}^o which in turn depend on the moments of $X_{it}(k)$. To conserve space we summarize the results here and relegate their derivation to the appendix:

Proposition 4.2.1. *Under Definition 4.2.2 the observed returns processes $\{R_{it}^o\}$ ($i = 1, \ldots, N$) are covariance-stationary with the following first and second moments:*

$$E[R_{it}^o] = \mu_i, \qquad (4.2.10)$$

$$\text{Var}[R_{it}^o] = \sigma_i^2 + \frac{2p_i}{1 - p_i}\mu_i^2, \qquad (4.2.11)$$

---

[7]This is similar in spirit to the Scholes and Williams (1977)) subordinated stochastic process representation of observed returns, although we do not restrict the trading times to take values in a fixed finite interval. With suitable normalizations it may be shown that our nontrading model converges weakly to the continuous-time Poisson process of Scholes and Williams (1976)). From (4.2.5) the observed returns process may also be considered an infinite-order moving average of virtual returns where the MA coefficients are stochastic. This is in contrast to Cohen et al. (1986, ch. 6) in which observed returns are assumed to be a finite-order MA process with nonstochastic coefficients. Although our nontrading process is more general, their observed returns process includes a bid-ask spread component; ours does not.

$$\text{Cov}[R^o_{it}, R^o_{jt+n}] = \begin{cases} -\mu^2_i p^n_i & \text{for } i = j, \, n > 0, \\ \dfrac{(1 - p_i)(1 - p_j)}{1 - p_i p_j} \beta_i \beta_j \sigma^2_\lambda \, p^n_j & \text{for } i \neq j, \, n \geq 0, \end{cases} \tag{4.2.12}$$

$$\text{Corr}[R^o_{it}, R^o_{it+n}] = \frac{-\mu^2_i p^n_i}{\sigma^2_i + \dfrac{2p_i}{1 - p_i} \mu^2_i}, \qquad n > 0 \tag{4.2.13}$$

where $\sigma^2_i \equiv \text{Var}[R_{it}]$ *and* $\sigma^2_\lambda \equiv \text{Var}[\Lambda_t]$.

From (4.2.10) and (4.2.11) it is clear that nontrading does not affect the mean of observed returns but does increase their variance if the security has a nonzero expected return. Moreover, (4.2.13) shows that having a nonzero expected return induces negative serial correlation in individual security returns at all leads and lags which decays geometrically. That the autocorrelation vanishes if the security's mean return μ_i is zero is an implication of nonsynchronous trading that does not extend to the observed returns of portfolios.

Proposition 4.2.1 also allows us to calculate the maximal negative autocorrelation for individual security returns that is attributable to nontrading. Since the autocorrelation of observed returns (4.2.13) is a nonpositive continuous function of p_i, is zero at $p_i = 0$, and approaches zero as p_i approaches unity, it must attain a minimum for some $p_i \in [0, 1)$. Determining this lower bound is a straightforward exercise in calculus hence we calculate it only for the first-order autocorrelation and leave the higher-order cases to the reader.

Corollary 4.2.1. *Under Definition 4.2.2 the minimum first-order autocorrelation of the observed returns process* $\{R^o_{it}\}$ *with respect to nontrading probabilities* p_i *exists, is given by*

$$\min_{\{p_i\}} \text{Corr}[R^o_{it}, R^o_{it+1}] = -\left(\frac{|\xi_i|}{1 + \sqrt{2} \, |\xi_i|} \right)^2, \tag{4.2.14}$$

and is attained at

$$p_i = \frac{1}{1 + \sqrt{2} \, |\xi_i|}, \tag{4.2.15}$$

where $\xi_i \equiv \mu_i / \sigma_i$. *Over all values of* $p_i \in [0, 1)$ *and* $\xi_i \in (-\infty, +\infty)$, *we have*

$$\inf_{\{p_i, \xi_i\}} \text{Corr}[R^o_{it}, R^o_{it+1}] = -\tfrac{1}{2}, \tag{4.2.16}$$

which is the limit of (4.2.14) as $|\xi_i|$ *increases without bound, but is never attained by finite* ξ_i.

The maximal negative autocorrelation induced by nontrading is small for individual securities with small mean returns and large return variances.

For securities with small mean returns the nontrading probability required to attain (4.2.14) must be very close to unity. Corollary 4.2.1 also implies that nontrading induced autocorrelation is magnified by taking longer sampling intervals since under the hypothesized virtual returns process doubling the holding period doubles μ_i but only multiplies σ_i by a factor of $\sqrt{2}$. Therefore more extreme negative autocorrelations are feasible for longer-horizon individual returns. However, this is not of direct empirical relevance since the effects of time aggregation have been ignored. To see how, observe that the nontrading process of Definition 4.2.1 is not independent of the sampling interval but changes in a nonlinear fashion. For example, if a "period" is taken to be one week, the possibility of *daily* nontrading and all its concomitant effects on weekly observed returns is eliminated by assumption. A proper comparison of observed returns across distinct sampling intervals must allow for nontrading at the finest time increment, after which the implications for coarser-sampled returns may be developed. We shall postpone further discussion until Section 4.3 where we address this and other issues of time aggregation explicitly.

Other important empirical implications of our nontrading model are captured by (4.2.12) of Proposition 4.2.1. For example, the sign of the cross-autocovariances is determined by the sign of $\beta_i \beta_j$. Also, the expression is not symmetric with respect to i and j: if security i always trades so that $p_i = 0$, there is still spurious cross-autocovariance between R_{it}^o and R_{jt+n}^o, whereas this cross-autocovariance vanishes if $p_j = 0$ irrespective of the value of p_i. The intuition for this result is simple: when security j exhibits nontrading the returns to a constantly trading security i can forecast j due to the common factor Λ_t present in both returns. That j exhibits nontrading implies that future observed returns R_{jt+n}^o will be a weighted average of all past virtual returns R_{jt+n-k} (with the $X_{jt+n}(k)$'s as random weights), of which one term will be the current virtual return R_{jt}. Since the contemporaneous virtual returns R_{it} and R_{jt} are correlated (because of the common factor), R_{it} can forecast R_{jt+n}^o. The reverse however is not true. If security i exhibits nontrading but security j does not (so that $p_j = 0$), the covariance between R_{it}^o and R_{jt+n} is clearly zero since R_{it}^o is a weighted average of past virtual returns R_{it-k} which is independent of R_{jt+n} by assumption.[8]

The asymmetry of (4.2.12) yields an empirically testable restriction on the cross-autocovariances of returns. Since the only source of asymmetry in (4.2.12) is the probability of nontrading, information regarding these

---

[8]An alternative interpretation of this asymmetry may be found in the causality literature, in which R_{it}^o is said to "cause" R_{jt}^o if the return to i predicts the return to j. In the above example, security i "causes" security j when j is subject to nontrading but i is not. Since our nontrading process may be viewed as a form of measurement error, the fact that the returns to one security may be "exogenous" with respect to the returns of another has been proposed under a different guise in Sims (1974, 1977).

probabilities may be extracted from sample moments. Specifically, denote by R_t^o the vector $[R_{1t}^o \, R_{2t}^o \cdots R_{Nt}^o]'$ of observed returns of the N securities and define the autocovariance matrix Γ_n as

$$\Gamma_n = \mathrm{E}\left[(R_t^o - \mu)(R_{t+n}^o - \mu)'\right], \qquad \mu \equiv \mathrm{E}[R_t^o]. \qquad (4.2.17)$$

Denoting the (i, j)th element of Γ_n by $\gamma_{ij}(n)$, we have by definition

$$\gamma_{ij}(n) = \frac{(1 - p_i)(1 - p_j)}{1 - p_i p_j} \, \beta_i \, \beta_j \, \sigma_\lambda^2 \, p_j^n. \qquad (4.2.18)$$

If the nontrading probabilities p_i differ across securities, Γ_n is asymmetric. From (4.2.18) it is evident that:

$$\frac{\gamma_{ij}(n)}{\gamma_{ji}(n)} = \left(\frac{p_j}{p_i}\right)^n. \qquad (4.2.19)$$

Therefore relative nontrading probabilities may be estimated directly using sample autocovariances $\hat{\Gamma}_n$. To derive estimates of the probabilities p_i themselves we need only estimate one such probability, say p_1, and the remaining probabilities may be obtained from the ratios (4.2.19). A consistent estimator of p_1 is readily constructed with sample means and autocovariances via (4.2.12).

4.2.2 Implications for Portfolio Returns

Suppose we group securities by their nontrading probabilities and form equally-weighted portfolios based on this grouping so that portfolio A contains N_a securities with identical nontrading probability p_a, and similarly for portfolio B. Denote by R_{at}^o and R_{bt}^o the observed time-t returns on these two portfolios respectively, thus:

$$R_{\kappa t}^o \equiv \frac{1}{N_\kappa} \sum_{i \in I_\kappa} R_{it}^o, \qquad \kappa = a, b, \qquad (4.2.20)$$

where I_κ is the set of indices of securities in portfolio κ. Since individual returns are assumed to be continuously-compounded, $R_{\kappa t}$ is the return to a portfolio whose value is calculated as an unweighted geometric average of the included securities' prices.[9] The time series properties of (4.2.20) may

---

[9]The expected return of such a portfolio will be lower than that of an equally-weighted portfolio whose returns are calculated as the arithmetic means of the simple returns of the included securities. This issue is examined in greater detail by Modest and Sundaresan (1983)) and Eytan and Harpaz (1986)) in the context of the Value Line Index which until recently was an unweighted geometric average.

be derived from a simple asymptotic approximation that exploits the cross-sectional independence of the disturbances ϵ_{it}. Since similar asymptotic arguments can be found in the Arbitrage Pricing Theory literature, our assumption of independence may be relaxed to the same extent that it is relaxed in studies of the APT in which portfolios are required to be "well-diversified."[10] In such cases, we have:

Proposition 4.2.2. *As the number of securities in portfolios A and B (denoted by N_a and N_b, respectively) increases without bound, the following equalities obtain almost surely:*

$$R_\kappa^o \overset{\text{a.s.}}{=} \mu_\kappa + (1 - p_\kappa)\beta_\kappa \sum_{k=0}^{\infty} p_\kappa^k \Lambda_{t-k}, \tag{4.2.21}$$

where

$$\mu_\kappa \equiv \frac{1}{N_\kappa} \sum_{i \in I_\kappa} \mu_i, \qquad \beta_\kappa \equiv \frac{1}{N_\kappa} \sum_{i \in I_\kappa} \beta_i, \tag{4.2.22}$$

for $\kappa = a, b$. The first and second moments of the portfolios' returns are given by

$$\mathrm{E}[R_{\kappa t}^o] \overset{\text{a}}{=} \mu_\kappa = \mathrm{E}[R_{\kappa t}], \tag{4.2.23}$$

$$\mathrm{Var}[R_{\kappa t}^o] \overset{\text{a}}{=} \beta_\kappa^2 \left(\frac{1 - p_\kappa}{1 + p_\kappa}\right) \sigma_\lambda^2, \tag{4.2.24}$$

$$\mathrm{Cov}[R_{\kappa t}^o, R_{\kappa t+n}^o] \overset{\text{a}}{=} \beta_\kappa^2 \left(\frac{1 - p_\kappa}{1 + p_\kappa}\right) p_\kappa^n \sigma_\lambda^2, \qquad n \geq 0, \tag{4.2.25}$$

$$\mathrm{Corr}[R_{\kappa t}^o, R_{\kappa t+n}^o] \overset{\text{a}}{=} p_\kappa^n, \qquad n \geq 0, \tag{4.2.26}$$

$$\mathrm{Cov}[R_{at}^o, R_{bt+n}^o] \overset{\text{a}}{=} \frac{(1 - p_a)(1 - p_b)}{1 - p_a p_b} \beta_a \beta_b \sigma_\lambda^2 p_b^n, \tag{4.2.27}$$

where the symbol "$\overset{\text{a}}{=}$" indicates that the equality obtains only asymptotically.

From (4.2.23) we see that observed portfolio returns have the same mean as that of its virtual returns. In contrast to observed individual returns, R_{at}^o has a lower variance asymptotically than that of its virtual counterpart R_{at} since:

$$R_{at} = \frac{1}{N_a} \sum_{i \in I_a} R_{it} = \mu_a + \beta_a \Lambda_t + \frac{1}{N_a} \sum_{i \in I_a} \epsilon_{it}, \tag{4.2.28}$$

$$\overset{\text{a}}{=} \mu_a + \beta_a \Lambda_t, \tag{4.2.29}$$

---

[10]See, for example, Chamberlain (1983)), Chamberlain and Rothschild (1983)), and Wang (1988)). The essence of these weaker conditions is simply to allow a Law of Large Numbers to be applied to the average of the disturbances, so that "idiosyncratic risk" vanishes almost surely as the cross-section grows.

where (4.2.29) follows from the Law of Large Numbers applied to the last term in (4.2.28). Thus $\text{Var}[R_{at}] \stackrel{a}{=} \beta_a^2 \sigma_\lambda^2$, which is greater than or equal to $\text{Var}[R_{at}^o]$.

Since the nontrading-induced autocorrelation (4.2.26) declines geometrically, observed portfolio returns follow a first-order autoregressive process with autoregressive coefficient equal to the nontrading probability. In contrast to expression (4.2.12) for individual securities, the autocorrelations of observed portfolio returns do not depend explicitly on the expected return of the portfolio, yielding a much simpler estimator for p_κ: the nth root of the nth order autocorrelation coefficient. Therefore, we may easily estimate all nontrading probabilities by using only the sample first-order own-autocorrelation coefficients for the portfolio returns. Comparing (4.2.27) to (4.2.12) shows that the cross-autocovariance between observed portfolio returns takes the same form as that of observed individual returns. If there are differences across portfolios in the nontrading probabilities, the autocovariance matrix for observed portfolio returns will be asymmetric. This may give rise to the types of lead-lag relations empirically documented by Lo and MacKinlay (1990b)) in size-sorted portfolios. Ratios of the cross-autocovariances may be formed to estimate relative nontrading probabilities for portfolios since

$$\frac{\text{Cov}[R_{at}^o, R_{bt+n}^o]}{\text{Cov}[R_{bt}^o, R_{at+n}^o]} \stackrel{a}{=} \left(\frac{p_b}{p_a}\right)^n. \tag{4.2.30}$$

Moreover, for purposes of specification testing these ratios give rise to many "over-identifying" restrictions since

$$\frac{\gamma_{a\kappa_1}(n)\, \gamma_{\kappa_1\kappa_2}(n)\, \gamma_{\kappa_2\kappa_3}(n) \cdots \gamma_{\kappa_{r-1}\kappa_r}(n)\, \gamma_{\kappa_r b}(n)}{\gamma_{\kappa_1 a}(n)\, \gamma_{\kappa_2\kappa_1}(n)\, \gamma_{\kappa_3\kappa_2}(n) \cdots \gamma_{\kappa_r\kappa_{r-1}}(n)\, \gamma_{b\kappa_r}(n)} = \left(\frac{p_b}{p_a}\right)^n, \tag{4.2.31}$$

for any arbitrary sequence of distinct indices $\kappa_1, \kappa_2, \ldots, \kappa_r$, $a \neq b$, $r \leq N_p$, where N_p is the number of distinct portfolios and $\gamma_{\kappa_i\kappa_j}(n) \equiv \text{Cov}[R_{\kappa_i t}^o, R_{\kappa_j t+n}^o]$. Therefore, although there are N_p^2 distinct autocovariances in Γ_n, the restrictions implied by the nontrading process allow only $N_p(N_p + 1)/2$ of the autocovariances to be arbitrary.

4.3 Time Aggregation

The discrete-time framework we have so far adopted does not require the specification of the calendar length of a "period." This generality is more apparent than real since any empirical implementation of Propositions 4.2.1 and 4.2.2 must either implicitly or explicitly define a period to be a particular fixed calendar time interval. Once the calendar time interval has been chosen, the stochastic behavior of coarser-sampled data is restricted by the parameters of the most-finely-sampled process. For example, if the length of a period is taken to be one day then the moments of observed monthly returns may be expressed as functions of the parameters of the daily observed returns process. We derive such restrictions in this section. Towards this goal we require the following definition:

Definition 4.3.1. *Denote by $R_{i\tau}^o(q)$ the observed return of security i at time τ where one unit of τ time is equivalent to q units of t time, thus:*

$$R_{i\tau}^o(q) \equiv \sum_{t=(\tau-1)q+1}^{\tau q} R_{it}^o. \qquad (4.3.1)$$

The change of time scale implicit in (4.3.1) captures the essence of time aggregation. We then have the following result:

Proposition 4.3.1. *Under the assumptions of Definitions 4.2.1–4.2.3, the observed returns processes $\{R_{i\tau}^o(q)\}$ $(i = 1, \ldots, N)$ are covariance-stationary with the following first and second moments:*

$$\mathrm{E}[R_{i\tau}^o(q)] = q\mu_i, \qquad (4.3.2)$$

$$\mathrm{Var}[R_{i\tau}^o(q)] = q\sigma_i^2 + \frac{2p_i(1 - p_i^q)}{(1 - p_i)^2}\,\mu_i^2, \qquad (4.3.3)$$

$$\mathrm{Cov}\left[R_{i\tau}^o(q), R_{i\tau+n}^o(q)\right] = -\mu_i^2 p_i^{(n-1)q+1}\left(\frac{1 - p_i^q}{1 - p_i}\right)^2, \quad n > 0, \qquad (4.3.4)$$

$$\mathrm{Corr}\left[R_{i\tau}^o(q), R_{i\tau+n}^o(q)\right] = -\frac{\xi_i^2(1 - p_i^q)^2 p_i^{nq-q+1}}{q(1 - p_i)^2 + 2p_i(1 - p_i^q)\xi_i^2}, \quad n > 0, \qquad (4.3.5)$$

$$\mathrm{Cov}\left[R_{i\tau}^o(q), R_{j\tau+n}^o(q)\right] = \frac{(1 - p_i)(1 - p_j)}{1 - p_i p_j}\,\beta_i\beta_j\sigma_\lambda^2\,p_j^{(n-1)q+1}\left(\frac{1 - p_j^q}{1 - p_i}\right)^2,$$
$$i \neq j, \quad n \geq 0, \qquad (4.3.6)$$

where $\xi_i \equiv \mu_i/\sigma_i$.

Although expected returns time-aggregate linearly, (4.3.3) shows that variances do not. As a result of the negative serial correlation in R_{it}^o, the variance of a sum of these will be less than the sum of the variances. Time aggregation does not affect the sign of the autocorrelations in (4.3.5), although their magnitudes do decline with the aggregation value q. As in

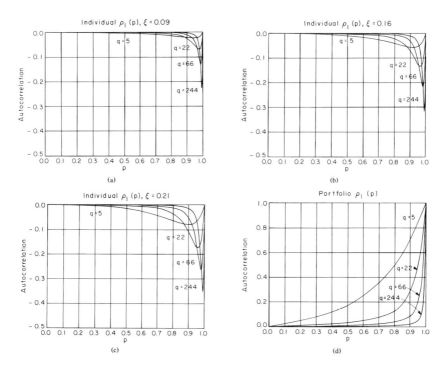

Figure 4.1. *First-order autocorrelation of temporally aggregated observed individual and portfolio returns as a function of the per period nontrading probability p, where q is the aggregation value and $\xi = \mu/\sigma$.*

Proposition 4.2.1, the autocorrelation of time-aggregated returns is a non-positive continuous function of p_i on $[0, 1)$ which is zero at $p_i = 0$ and approaches zero as p_i approaches unity, hence it attains a minimum. To explore the behavior of the first-order autocorrelation, we plot it as a function of p_i in Figure 4.1 for a variety of values of q and ξ. As a guide to an empirically plausible range of values for ξ, consider that the ratio of the sample mean to the sample standard deviation for daily, weekly, and monthly equally-weighted stock returns indexes are 0.09, 0.16, and 0.21 respectively for the sample period from 1962 to 1987.[11] The values of q are chosen to be 5, 22, 66, and 244 to correspond to weekly, monthly, quarterly, and annual returns since $q = 1$ is taken to be one day. Figure 4.1a plots the first-order autocorrelation $\rho_1(p)$ for the four values of q with $\xi = 0.09$. The curve marked "$q = 5$" shows that the weekly first-order autocorrelation induced by nontrading never exceeds −5 percent and only attains that value

---

[11]These are obtained from Lo and MacKinlay (1988b, Tables 1a, b, c).

with a daily nontrading probability in excess of 90 percent. Although the autocorrelation of coarser-sampled returns such as monthly or quarterly have more extreme minima, they are attained only at higher nontrading probabilities. Also, time aggregation need not always yield a more negative autocorrelation as is apparent from the portion of the graphs to the left of, say, $p = 0.80$; in that region, an increase in the aggregation value q leads to an autocorrelation closer to zero. Indeed as q increases without bound the autocorrelation (4.3.5) approaches zero for fixed p_i, hence nontrading has little impact on longer-horizon returns. The effects of increasing ξ are traced out in Figures 4.1b and c. Even if we assume $\xi = 0.21$ for daily data, a most extreme value, the nontrading-induced autocorrelation in weekly returns is at most -8 percent and requires a daily nontrading probability of over 90 percent. From (4.2.8) we see that when $p_i = 0.90$ the average duration of nontrading is 9 days! Since no security listed on the New York or American Stock Exchanges is inactive for two weeks (unless it has been delisted), we infer from Figure 4.1 that the impact of nontrading for individual short-horizon stock returns is negligible.

To see the effects of time aggregation on observed portfolio returns, we define the following:

Definition 4.3.2. Denote by $R_{a\tau}^o(q)$ the observed return of portfolio A at time τ where one unit of τ time is equivalent to q units of t time, thus:

$$R_{a\tau}^o(q) \equiv \sum_{t=(\tau-1)q+1}^{\tau q} R_{at}^o, \tag{4.3.7}$$

where R_{at}^o is given by (4.2.20).

Applying the asymptotic approximation of Proposition 4.2.2 then yields:

Proposition 4.3.2. Under the assumptions of Definitions 4.2.1–4.2.3, the observed portfolio returns processes $\{R_{a\tau}^o(q)\}$ and $\{R_{b\tau}^o(q)\}$ are covariance-stationary with the following first and second moments as N_a and N_b increase without bound:

$$E[R_{\kappa\tau}^o(q)] \overset{a}{=} q\mu_\kappa, \tag{4.3.8}$$

$$\text{Var}[R_{\kappa\tau}^o(q)] \overset{a}{=} \left[q - 2p_\kappa \frac{1-p_\kappa^q}{1-p_\kappa} \right] \beta_\kappa^2 \sigma_\lambda^2, \tag{4.3.9}$$

$$\text{Cov}\left[R_{\kappa\tau}^o(q), R_{\kappa\tau+n}^o(q) \right] \overset{a}{=} \left[\frac{1-p_\kappa}{1+p_\kappa} \right] \left[\frac{1-p_\kappa^q}{1-p_\kappa} \right]^2 p_\kappa^{nq-q+1} \beta_\kappa^2 \sigma_\lambda^2, \tag{4.3.10}$$

$$n > 0,$$

$$\text{Corr}\left[R_{\kappa\tau}^o(q), R_{\kappa\tau+n}^o(q) \right] \overset{a}{=} \frac{(1-p_\kappa^q)^2 p_\kappa^{nq-q+1}}{q(1-p_\kappa^2) - 2p_\kappa(1-p_\kappa^q)}, \quad n > 0, \tag{4.3.11}$$

$\text{Cov}\left[R_{a\tau}^o(q), R_{b\tau+n}^o(q)\right]$

$$\stackrel{a}{=} \begin{cases} \left[q - \dfrac{p_a(1 - p_a^q)(1 - p_b)^2 + p_b(1 - p_b^q)(1 - p_a)^2}{(1 - p_a)(1 - p_b)}\right] \dfrac{\beta_a \beta_b \sigma_\lambda^2}{1 - p_a p_b} \\ \qquad\qquad\qquad\qquad\qquad\qquad\qquad\qquad\qquad\qquad\qquad\qquad \text{for } n = 0, \\[2mm] \dfrac{(1 - p_a)(1 - p_b)}{1 - p_a p_b}\left[\dfrac{1 - p_b^q}{1 - p_b}\right]^2 p_b^{nq - q + 1} \beta_a \beta_b \sigma_\lambda^2 \\ \qquad\qquad\qquad\qquad\qquad\qquad\qquad\qquad\qquad\qquad\qquad\qquad \text{for } n > 0, \end{cases} \qquad (4.3.12)$$

for $\kappa = a, b, q > 1$, and arbitrary portfolios a, b, and time τ.

Equation (4.3.11) shows that time aggregation also affects the autocorrelation of observed portfolio returns in a highly nonlinear fashion. In contrast to the autocorrelation for time-aggregated individual securities, (4.3.11) approaches unity for any fixed q as p_κ approaches unity, hence the maximal autocorrelation is 1.0.[12] To investigate the behavior of the portfolio autocorrelation we plot it as a function of the portfolio nontrading probability p in Figure 4.1d for $q = 5, 22, 66$, and 55. Besides differing in sign, portfolio and individual autocorrelations also differ in absolute magnitude, the former being much larger than the latter for a given nontrading probability. If the nontrading phenomenon is extant, it will be most evident in portfolio returns. Also, portfolio autocorrelations are monotonically decreasing in q so that time aggregation always decreases nontrading induced serial dependence in portfolio returns. This implies that we are most likely to find evidence of nontrading in short-horizon returns. We exploit both these implications in Section 4.4.

4.4 An Empirical Analysis of Nontrading

Before considering the empirical evidence for nontrading effects we summarize the qualitative implications of the previous sections' propositions and corollaries. Although virtually all of these implications are consistent with earlier models of nonsynchronous trading, the sharp comparative static results are unique to our framework. The presence of nonsynchronous trading:

1. Does not affect the mean of either individual or portfolio returns.
2. Increases the variance of individual security returns (with nonzero mean). The smaller the mean, the smaller is the increase in the variance of observed returns.

---

[12]Muthuswamy (1988)) reports a maximal portfolio autocorrelation of only 50 percent because of his assumption that each stock trades at least once every T periods, where T is some fixed number.

3. Decreases the variance of observed portfolio returns when portfolios are well diversified and consist of securities with common nontrading probability.

4. Induces geometrically declining *negative* serial correlation in individual security returns (with nonzero mean). The smaller the mean (in absolute value), the closer the autocorrelation is to zero.

5. Induces geometrically declining *positive* serial correlation in observed portfolio returns when portfolios are well-diversified and consist of securities with a common nontrading probability, yielding an AR(1) for the observed returns process.

6. Induces geometrically declining cross-autocorrelation between observed returns of securities i and j which is of the same sign as $\beta_i \beta_j$. This cross-autocorrelation is *asymmetric*: the covariance of current observed returns to i with future observed returns to j is generally not the same as the covariance of current observed returns to j with future observed returns to i. This asymmetry is due solely to the assumption that different securities have different probabilities of nontrading.

7. Induces geometrically declining *positive* cross-autocorrelation between observed returns of portfolios A and B when portfolios are well-diversified and consist of securities with common nontrading probabilities. This cross-autocorrelation is also asymmetric and is due solely to the assumption that securities in different portfolios have different probabilities of nontrading.

8. Induces *positive* serial dependence in an equally-weighted index if the betas of the securities are generally of the same sign, and if individual returns have small means.

9. And time aggregation increases the maximal nontrading induced negative autocorrelation in observed individual security returns, but this maximal negative autocorrelation is attained at nontrading probabilities increasingly closer to unity as the degree of aggregation increases.

10. And time aggregation decreases the nontrading induced autocorrelation in observed portfolio returns for all nontrading probabilities.

Since the effects of nonsynchronous trading are more apparent in securities grouped by nontrading probabilities than in individual stocks, our empirical application uses the returns of twenty size-sorted portfolios for daily, weekly, and monthly data from 1962 to 1987. We use size to group securities because the relative thinness of the market for any given stock has long been known to be highly correlated with the stock's total market value, hence stocks with similar market values are likely to have similar non-trading probabilities.[13] We choose to form twenty portfolios to maximize

---

[13] This is confirmed by the entries of Table 4.3's second column and by Foerster and Keim (1989)).

the homogeneity of nontrading probabilities within each portfolio while still maintaining reasonable diversification so that the asymptotic approximations of Proposition 4.2.2 might still obtain.[14] In Section 4.4.1 we derive estimates of daily nontrading probabilities using daily, weekly, and monthly autocorrelations, and in Section 4.4.2 we consider the impact of nontrading on the autocorrelation of the equally-weighted market index.

4.4.1 Daily Nontrading Probabilities Implicit in Autocorrelations

Table 4.1 reports first-order autocorrelation matrices Γ_1 for the vector of five of the twenty size-sorted portfolio returns using daily, weekly, and monthly data taken from the Center for Research in Security Prices (CRSP) database. Portfolio 1 contains stocks with the smallest market values and portfolio 20 contains those with the largest.[15] From casual inspection it is apparent that these autocorrelation matrices are not symmetric. The second column of matrices are the autocorrelation matrices minus their transposes and it is evident that elements below the diagonal dominate those above it. This confirms the lead-lag pattern reported in Lo and MacKinlay (1990b)). That the returns of large stocks tend to lead those of smaller stocks does support the hypothesis that nonsynchronous trading is a source of correlation. However, the magnitudes of the autocorrelations for weekly and monthly returns imply an implausible level of nontrading. This is most evident in Table 4.2, which reports estimates of daily nontrading probabilities implicit in the weekly and monthly own-autocorrelations of Table 4.1. For example, using (4.3.11) of Proposition 4.3.2 the daily nontrading probability implied by an estimated weekly autocorrelation of 46 percent for portfolio 1 is estimated to be 77.9 percent.[16] Using (4.2.8) we estimate the average time between trades to be 3.5 days! The corresponding daily nontrading probability is 86.2 percent using monthly returns implying an average nontrading duration of 6.2 days.

---

[14]The returns to these portfolios are continuously-compounded returns of individual simple returns arithmetically averaged. We have repeated the correlation analysis for continuously-compounded returns of portfolios whose values are calculated as unweighted geometric averages of included securities' prices. The results for these portfolio returns are practically identical to those for the continuously-compounded returns of equally-weighted portfolios.

[15]We report only a subset of five portfolios for the sake of brevity; the complete set of autocorrelations may be obtained from the authors on request.

[16]Standard errors for autocorrelation-based probability and nontrading duration estimates are obtained by applying the "delta" method to (4.2.8) and (4.3.11) using heteroskedasticity- and autocorrelation-consistent standard errors for daily, weekly, and monthly first-order autocorrelation coefficients. These latter standard errors are computed by regressing returns on a constant and lagged returns, and using Newey and West's (1987) procedure to calculate heteroskedasticity- and autocorrelation consistent standard errors for the slope coefficient (which is simply the first-order autocorrelation coefficient of returns).

Table 4.1. *Sample first-order autocorrelation matrix $\hat{\Gamma}_1$ for the 5×1 subvector $[R_1^o \, R_5^o \, R_{10}^o \, R_{15}^o \, R_{20}^o]'$ of observed returns to twenty equally-weighted size-sorted portfolios using daily, weekly, and monthly stock returns data from the CRSP files for the period 31 December 1962 to 31 December 1987, where portfolios are rebalanced monthly. Only securities with complete daily return histories within each month were included in the daily and monthly returns calculations. R_1^o is the return to the portfolio containing securities with the smallest market values and R_{20}^o is the return to the portfolio of securities with the largest. There are approximately equal numbers of securities in each portfolio. The entry in the ith row and jth column is the correlation between R_{it}^o and R_{jt+1}^o. To gauge the degree of asymmetry in these autocorrelation matrices, the difference $\hat{\Gamma}_1 - \hat{\Gamma}_1'$ is also reported.*

		$\hat{\Gamma}_1$						$\hat{\Gamma}_1 - \hat{\Gamma}_1'$			
		1	5	10	15	20	1	5	10	15	20
Daily	1	.35	.28	.21	.15	.02	.00	−.13	−.18	−.23	−.31
	5	.41	.33	.28	.22	.06	.13	.00	−.08	−.16	−.30
	10	.39	.36	.31	.27	.09	.18	.08	.00	−.08	−.27
	15	.38	.38	.35	.31	.12	.23	.16	.08	.00	−.21
	20	.33	.36	.36	.33	.17	.31	.30	.27	.21	.00

		$\hat{\Gamma}_1$						$\hat{\Gamma}_1 - \hat{\Gamma}_1'$			
		1	5	10	15	20	1	5	10	15	20
Weekly	1	.46	.32	.22	.16	.01	.00	−.13	−.20	−.22	−.28
	5	.45	.35	.25	.19	.01	.13	.00	−.11	−.16	−.28
	10	.42	.36	.27	.21	.03	.20	.11	.00	−.06	−.20
	15	.38	.35	.27	.22	.04	.22	.16	.06	.00	−.16
	20	.29	.29	.23	.20	.04	.28	.28	.20	.16	.00

		$\hat{\Gamma}_1$						$\hat{\Gamma}_1 - \hat{\Gamma}_1'$			
		1	5	10	15	20	1	5	10	15	20
Monthly	1	.20	.07	.04	.01	.00	.00	−.20	−.25	−.29	−.23
	5	.27	.15	.10	.07	.03	.20	.00	−.09	−.14	−.14
	10	.29	.19	.13	.10	.05	.25	.09	.00	−.05	−.05
	15	.30	.21	.15	.13	.06	.29	.14	.05	.00	−.02
	20	.23	.17	.10	.08	.01	.23	.14	.05	.02	.00

For comparison Table 4.2 also reports estimates of the nontrading probabilities using daily data and using trade information from the CRSP files. In the absence of time aggregation, own-autocorrelations of portfolio returns are consistent estimators of nontrading probabilities, hence the entries in the column of Table 4.2 labelled "$\hat{p}_\kappa (q = 1)$" are simply taken from the diagonal of the autocovariance matrix in Table 4.1. For the smaller securities, the point estimates yield plausible nontrading durations, but the estimated

Table 4.2. *Estimates of daily nontrading probabilities implicit in 20 weekly and monthly size-sorted portfolio return autocorrelations. Entries in the column labelled "$\hat{p}_\kappa$" are averages of the fraction of securities in portfolio κ that did not trade on the last trading day of the month, where the average is computed over month-end trading days in 1963 and from 1973 to 1987 (the trading-status data from 1964 to 1972 were not used due to errors uncovered by Foerster and Keim (1989))). Entries in the "$\hat{p}_\kappa (q = 1)$" column are the first-order autocorrelation coefficients of daily portfolio returns, which are consistent estimators of daily nontrading probabilities. Entries in the "$\hat{p}_\kappa (q = 5)$" and "$\hat{p}_\kappa (q = 22)$" columns are estimates of daily nontrading probabilities obtained from first-order weekly and monthly portfolio return autocorrelation coefficients, using the time aggregation relations of Section 3 ($q = 5$ for weekly returns and $q = 22$ for monthly returns since there are 5 and 22 trading days in a week and a month, respectively). Entries in columns labelled "$\hat{E}[\tilde{k}]$" are estimates of the expected number of consecutive days without trading implied by the probability estimates in column to the immediate left. Standard errors are reported in parentheses; all are heteroskedasticity- and autocorrelation-consistent except for those in the second column.*

κ	$\hat{p}_\kappa$	$\hat{p}_\kappa(q=1)$	$\hat{E}[\tilde{k}]$	$\hat{p}_\kappa(q=5)$	$\hat{E}[\tilde{k}]$	$\hat{p}_\kappa(q=22)$	$\hat{E}[\tilde{k}]$
1	.291	.351	0.54	.779	3.51	.862	6.23
	(0.003)	(0.025)	(0.06)	(0.019)	(0.38)	(0.033)	(1.72)
5	.090	.332	0.50	.701	2.35	.828	4.83
	(0.002)	(0.021)	(0.05)	(0.026)	(0.29)	(0.055)	(1.85)
10	.025	.315	0.46	.626	1.68	.802	4.05
	(0.001)	(0.015)	(0.03)	(0.031)	(0.22)	(0.054)	(1.38)
15	.011	.306	0.44	.569	1.32	.806	4.14
	(0.001)	(0.016)	(0.03)	(0.037)	(0.20)	(0.055)	(1.45)
20	.008	.165	0.20	.193	0.24	.165	0.20
	(0.001)	(0.024)	(0.03)	(0.129)	(0.20)	(1.205)	(1.73)

durations decline only marginally for larger-size portfolios. A duration of even only a third of a day is much too large for securities in the second largest portfolio. More direct evidence is provided in the column labelled $\hat{p}_\kappa$, which reports the average fraction of securities in a given portfolio that do not trade during the last trading day of the month.[17] This average is computed over all month-end trading days in 1963 and from 1973 to 1987.

---

[17]This information is provided in the CRSP daily files in which the closing price of a security is reported to be the negative of the average of the bid and ask prices on days when that security did not trade. See Foerster and Keim (1989) for a more detailed account. Standard errors for probability estimates based on the fraction of no-trades reported by CRSP are derived under the assumption of a temporally IID nontrading process $\{\delta_{it}\}$; the usual binomial approximation yields $\sqrt{\hat{p}_\kappa(1 - \hat{p}_\kappa)/N_\kappa T}$ as the standard error for the estimate $\hat{p}_\kappa$, where N_κ is the number of securities in portfolio κ and T is the number of daily observations with which the nontrading probability p_κ is estimated. For our sample and portfolios, $N_\kappa T$ fluctuates about 20,000 (192 daily observations, 105 securities per portfolio on average).

The period between 1963 and 1973 is omitted due to trading-status reporting errors uncovered by Foerster and Keim (1989)). Comparing the entries
in this column with those in the others shows the limitations of nontrading
as an explanation for the autocorrelations in the data. Nontrading may
be responsible for some of the time series properties of stock returns but
cannot be the only source of autocorrelation.

4.4.2 Nontrading and Index Autocorrelations

Denote by R_{mt}^o the observed return in period t to an equal-weighted portfolio
of all N securities. Its autocovariance and autocorrelation are readily shown
to be

$$\text{Cov}\left[R_{mt}^o, R_{mt+n}^o\right] = \frac{\iota' \Gamma_n \iota}{N^2}, \tag{4.4.1}$$

$$\text{Corr}\left[R_{mt}^o, R_{mt+n}^o\right] = \frac{\iota' \Gamma_n \iota}{\iota' \Gamma_o \iota}, \tag{4.4.2}$$

where Γ_o is the contemporaneous covariance matrix of R_t^o and ι is an $N \times 1$-
vector of ones. If the betas of the securities are generally of the same sign and
if the mean returns to each security is small, then R_{mt}^o is likely to be positively
autocorrelated. Alternatively, if the cross-autocovariances are positive and
dominate the negative own-autocovariances the equal-weighted index will
exhibit positive serial dependence.

　　With little loss in generality we let $N = 20$ and consider the equal-
weighted portfolio of the twenty size-sorted portfolios, which is an approximately equal-weighted portfolio of all securities. Using (4.3.6) of Proposition 4.3.1 we may calculate the *weekly* autocorrelation of R_{mt}^o induced by particular *daily* nontrading probabilities p_i and beta coefficients β_i. To do this,
we need to select empirically plausible values for p_i and β_i, $i = 1, 2, \ldots, 20$.
This is done in Table 4.3 using four different ways of estimating the p_i's and
two different assumptions for the β_i's. The first row corresponds to weekly
autocorrelations computed with the nontrading probabilities obtained from
the fractions of negative share prices reported by CRSP. The first entry, 0.014,
is the first-order autocorrelation of the weekly equal-weighted index assuming that all twenty portfolio betas are 1.0, and the second entry, 0.018, is
computed under the alternative assumption that the betas decline linearly
from $\beta_1 = 1.5$ for the portfolio of smallest stocks to $\beta_{20} = 0.5$ for the
portfolio of the largest. The next three rows report similar autocorrelations implied by nontrading probabilities estimated from daily, weekly, and
monthly autocorrelations using (4.3.11).

　　The largest first-order autocorrelation for the weekly equal-weighted
returns index reported in Table 4.3 is only 7.5 percent. Using direct estimates of nontrading via negative share prices yields an autocorrelation of

Table 4.3. *Estimates of the first-order autocorrelation ρ_m of weekly returns of an equal-weighted portfolio of twenty size-sorted portfolios (which approximates an equal-weighted portfolio of all securities), using four different estimators of daily nontrading probabilities: the average fraction of negative share prices reported by CRSP, and daily nontrading probabilities implied by first-order autocorrelations of daily, weekly, and monthly returns to an equal-weighted index. Since the index autocorrelation depends on the betas of the twenty portfolios it is computed for two sets of betas, one in which all betas are set to 1.0, and another in which the betas decline linearly from $\beta_1 = 1.5$ to $\beta_{20} = 0.5$.*

Estimator of p_i	ρ_m $(\beta_1 = 1, \beta_{20} = 1)$	ρ_m $(\beta_1 = 1.5, \beta_{20} = 0.5)$
Negative Share Price	0.014	0.018
Daily Implied	0.072	0.075
Weekly Implied	0.067	0.074
Monthly Implied	0.029	0.031

less than 2 percent! These magnitudes are still considerably smaller than the 30 percent autocorrelation reported by Lo and MacKinlay (1988b)). Taken together, the evidence in Sections 4.4.1 and 4.4.2 provide little support for nonsynchronous trading as an important source of spurious correlation in the returns of common stock.

4.5 Extensions and Generalizations

Despite the simplicity of our model of nonsynchronous trading, we hope to have shown the richness of its implications for observed time series. Although its immediate application is to the behavior of asset returns, the stochastic model of random censoring may be of more general relevance to situations involving randomly cumulative measurement errors. Moreover, this framework may be extended and generalized in many directions with little difficulty, and we conclude by discussing some of these here. We mention them only in passing since a more complete analysis is beyond the scope of the present study, but we hope to encourage further research along these lines.

It is a simple matter to relax the assumption that individual virtual returns are independently and identically distributed by allowing the common factor to be autocorrelated and the disturbances to be cross-sectionally correlated. For example, assuming that Λ_t is a stationary AR(1) is conceptually straightforward although the computations of the Appendix become somewhat more involved. This specification will yield a decomposition of observed autocorrelations into two components: one due to the common factor and another due to nontrading. Allowing cross-sectional dependence in the disturbances also complicates the moment calculations but does not create any intractabilities.[18] Indeed, generalizations to multiple factors, time series dependence of the disturbances, and correlation between factors and disturbances are only limited by the patience and perseverance of the reader; the necessary moment calculations are not incalculable, but merely tedious.

We may also build dependence into the nontrading process itself by assuming that the δ_{it}'s are Markov chains, so that the conditional probability of trading tomorrow depends on whether or not a trade occurs today. Although this specification admits compact and elegant expressions for the moments of the observed returns process space limitations will not permit a complete exposition here. However, a brief summary of its implications for the time series properties of observed returns may suffice: (1) Individual security returns may be positively autocorrelated, portfolio returns may be negatively autocorrelated (but these possibilities are unlikely given empirically relevant parameter values), (2) it is possible (but unlikely) for autocorrelation matrices to be symmetric, and (3) spurious index autocorrelation induced by nontrading is higher (lower) when there is positive (negative) persistence in nontrading. Our initial hope was that property (3) might be sufficient to explain the magnitude of index autocorrelations in recent stock market data. However, several calibration experiments indicate the degree of persistence in nontrading required to yield weekly autocorrelations of 30 percent is empirically implausible.

One final direction for further investigation is the possibility of dependence between the nontrading and virtual returns processes. If virtual returns are taken to be new information then the extent to which traders exploit this information in determining when (and what) to trade will show itself as correlation between R_{it} and δ_{jt}. Many strategic considerations are involved in models of information-based trading, and an empirical analysis of such issues promises to be as challenging as it is exciting. However, if it is indeed the case that autocorrelation in returns is induced by information-based nontrading, in what sense is this autocorrelation spurious? Our premise is that nontrading is a symptom of institutional features such as lagged adjustments and nonsynchronously reported prices, and our empirical results show that this is of little practical relevance. But if nonsyn-

---

[18]As we discussed earlier, some form of cross-sectional weak dependence must be imposed so that the asymptotic arguments of the portfolio results still obtain. Of course, such an assumption may not always be appropriate as, for example, in the case of companies within the same industry, whose residual risks we might expect to be positively correlated. Therefore, the asymptotic approximation will be most accurate for well-diversified portfolios.

chronicity is purposeful and informationally motivated then the subsequent serial dependence in asset returns may well be considered genuine, since it is the result of economic forces rather than mismeasurement. Although this is beyond the purview of the current framework, it is nevertheless a fascinating avenue for future research and may explain several currently puzzling empirical findings.

Appendix A4
Proof of Propositions

Proof of Proposition 4.2.1

To derive (4.2.10)–(4.2.13), we require the corresponding moments and co-moments of the Bernoulli variables $X_{it}(k)$. From Definition 4.2.1 it follows that

$$E[X_{it}(k)] = (1 - p_i)p_i^k, \tag{A4.1}$$

$$E[X_{it}^2(k)] = (1 - p_i)p_i^k, \tag{A4.2}$$

for arbitrary i, t, and k. To compute $E[X_{it}(k) X_{it+n}(l)]$, recall from Definition 4.2.1 that

$$X_{it}(k)X_{it+n}(l) = (1 - \delta_{it})\delta_{it-1} \cdots \delta_{it-k} \cdot (1 - \delta_{it+n})\delta_{it+n-1} \cdots \delta_{it+n-l}. \tag{A4.3}$$

If $l \geq n$, then $E[X_{it}(k) X_{it+n}(l)] = 0$ since both δ_{it} and $1 - \delta_{it}$ are included in the product (A4.3), hence the product is zero with probability one. If $l < n$, it may readily be shown that the expectation reduces to $(1 - p_i)^2 p_i^{k+l}$, hence we have

$$E[X_{it}(k) X_{it+n}(l)] = \begin{cases} (1 - p_i)^2 p_i^{k+l} & \text{if } l < n, \\ 0 & \text{if } l \geq n. \end{cases} \tag{A4.4}$$

From Definition 4.2.2, we have

$$E[R_{it}^o] = \sum_{k=0}^{\infty} E[X_{it}(k) R_{it-k}] = \sum_{k=0}^{\infty} E[X_{it}(k)]E[R_{it-k}], \tag{A4.5a}$$

$$= \mu_i \sum_{k=0}^{\infty} (1 - p_i)p_i^k = \mu_i, \tag{A4.5b}$$

where the second equality in (A4.5a) follows from the mutual independence of $X_{it}(k)$ and R_{it-k}. This establishes (4.2.10). To derive (4.2.11) we first obtain an expression for the second uncentered moment of R_{it}^o:

$$E[R_{it}^{o\,2}] = E\left[\sum_{k=0}^{\infty} X_{it}(k)\,R_{it-k} \cdot \sum_{l=0}^{\infty} X_{it}(l)\,R_{it-l}\right], \tag{A4.6a}$$

$$= \sum_{k=0}^{\infty} E[X_{it}^2(k)\,R_{it-k}^2]$$
$$+ 2\sum\sum_{k<l} E[X_{it}(k)\,X_{it}(l)\,R_{it-k}\,R_{it-l}], \tag{A4.6b}$$

$$= (\mu_i^2 + \sigma_i^2)\sum_{k=0}^{\infty}(1 - p_i)p_i^k$$
$$+ 2\sum\sum_{k<l} E[X_{it}(k)\,X_{it}(l)] \cdot E[R_{it-k}\,R_{it-l}], \tag{A4.6c}$$

$$= \mu_i^2 + \sigma_i^2 + 2\sum\sum_{k<l}(1 - p_i)p_i^l\left[\mu_i^2 + \sigma_i^2\theta(k - l)\right], \tag{A4.6d}$$
$$\text{where}\quad \theta(x) \equiv \begin{cases} 0 & \text{if}\quad x \neq 0, \\ 1 & \text{if}\quad x = 0, \end{cases}$$

$$= \mu_i^2 + \sigma_i^2 + 2\sum_{k=0}^{\infty}\sum_{l=k+1}^{\infty}(1 - p_i)p_i^l\left[\mu_i^2 + \sigma_i^2\theta(k - l)\right], \tag{A4.6e}$$

$$= \mu_i^2 + \sigma_i^2 + 2(1 - p_i)\sum_{k=0}^{\infty}\left(p_i^{k+1}\sum_{l=0}^{\infty}\mu_i^2 p_i^l\right), \tag{A4.6f}$$

$$= \mu_i^2 + \sigma_i^2 + 2\mu_i^2\frac{p_i}{1 - p_i}. \tag{A4.6g}$$

This yields (4.2.11) since

$$\text{Var}[R_{it}^o] = E[R_{it}^{o\,2}] - E^2[R_{it}^o] = \sigma_i^2 + 2\mu_i^2\frac{p_i}{1 - p_i}. \tag{A4.7}$$

The autocovariance of R_{it}^o may be obtained similarly by first calculating the uncentered moment:

$$E[R_{it}^o\,R_{it+n}^o] = E\left[\sum_{k=0}^{\infty} X_{it}(k)\,R_{it-k} \cdot \sum_{l=0}^{\infty} X_{it+n}(l)\,R_{it+n-l}\right], \tag{A4.8a}$$

$$= \sum_{k=0}^{\infty}\sum_{l=0}^{\infty} E[X_{it}(k)\,X_{it+n}(l)\,R_{it-k}\,R_{it+n-l}], \tag{A4.8b}$$

$$= \sum_{k=0}^{\infty}\sum_{l=0}^{\infty} E[X_{it}(k)\,X_{it+n}(l)] \cdot E[R_{it-k}\,R_{it+n-l}], \tag{A4.8c}$$

$$= \sum_{k=0}^{\infty} \sum_{l=0}^{n-1} (1 - p_i)^2 p_i^{k+l} \mathrm{E}[R_{it-k} R_{it+n-l}], \qquad (A4.8d)$$

$$= \sum_{k=0}^{\infty} \sum_{l=0}^{n-1} (1 - p_i)^2 p_i^{k+l} \mu_i^2 = \mu_i^2 (1 - p_i^n). \qquad (A4.8e)$$

Note that the upper limit of the l-summation in (A4.8d) is finite, which follows from (A4.4). Also, (A4.8e) follows from the fact that $\{R_{it}\}$ is an IID sequence and the only combinations of indices k and l that appear in (A4.8d) are those for which R_{it-k} and R_{it+n-l} are not contemporaneous, hence the expectation of the product in the summands of (A4.8d) reduces to μ_i^2 in (A4.8e). The autocovariance (4.2.12) then follows since

$$\mathrm{Cov}[R_{it}^o, R_{it+n}^o] = \mathrm{E}[R_{it}^o R_{it+n}^o] - \mathrm{E}[R_{it}^o]\mathrm{E}[R_{it+n}^o] = -\mu_i^2 p_i^n. \qquad (A4.9)$$

The calculation for the cross-autocovariance between R_{it}^o and R_{jt+n}^o differs only in that the common factor induces contemporaneous cross-sectional correlation between the virtual returns of securities i and j. Using the fact that

$$\mathrm{E}[R_{it-k} R_{jt+n-l}] = \mu_i \mu_j + \beta_i \beta_j \sigma_\lambda^2 \theta(l - k - n), \qquad (A4.10)$$

then yields the following:

$$\mathrm{E}[R_{it}^o R_{jt+n}^o] = \mathrm{E}\left[\sum_{k=0}^{\infty} X_{it}(k) R_{it-k} \cdot \sum_{l=0}^{\infty} X_{jt+n}(l) R_{jt+n-l} \right], \qquad (A4.11a)$$

$$= \sum_{k=0}^{\infty} \sum_{l=0}^{\infty} \mathrm{E}[X_{it}(k) X_{jt+n}(l) R_{it-k} R_{jt+n-l}], \qquad (A4.11b)$$

$$= \sum_{k=0}^{\infty} \sum_{l=0}^{\infty} \mathrm{E}[X_{it}(k)] \cdot \mathrm{E}[X_{jt+n}(l)] \cdot \mathrm{E}[R_{it-k} R_{jt+n-l}], \qquad (A4.11c)$$

$$= \sum_{k=0}^{\infty} \sum_{l=0}^{\infty} (1 - p_i) p_i^k (1 - p_j) p_j^l \times [\mu_i \mu_j + \beta_i \beta_j \sigma_\lambda^2 \theta(l - k - n)], \qquad (A4.11d)$$

$$= \sum_{k=0}^{\infty} \sum_{l=0}^{\infty} (1 - p_i) p_i^k (1 - p_j) p_j^l \mu_i \mu_j + \sum_{k=0}^{\infty} \sum_{l=0}^{\infty} (1 - p_i) p_i^k (1 - p_j) p_j^l \beta_i \beta_j \sigma_\lambda^2 \theta(l - k - n), \qquad (A4.11e)$$

$$= \mu_i \mu_j + \sum_{k=0}^{\infty} (1 - p_i)(1 - p_j) \beta_i \beta_j \sigma_\lambda^2 p_i^k p_j^{k+n}, \qquad (A4.11f)$$

$$= \mu_i \mu_j + (1 - p_i)(1 - p_j) \beta_i \beta_j \sigma_\lambda^2 \, p_j^n \sum_{k=0}^{\infty} (p_i p_j)^k, \qquad \text{(A4.11g)}$$

$$= \mu_i \mu_j + \frac{(1 - p_i)(1 - p_j)}{1 - p_i p_j} \beta_i \beta_j \sigma_\lambda^2 \, p_j^n, \qquad \text{(A4.11h)}$$

where the cross-sectional independence of the nontrading processes has been used to derive (A4.11c). This yields (4.2.12) since

$$\mathrm{Cov}[R_{it}^o, R_{jt+n}^o] = \mathrm{E}[R_{it}^o R_{jt+n}^o] - \mathrm{E}[R_{it}^o]\mathrm{E}[R_{jt+n}^o], \qquad \text{(A4.12a)}$$

$$= \frac{(1 - p_i)(1 - p_j)}{1 - p_i p_j} \beta_i \beta_j \sigma_\lambda^2 \, p_j^n. \qquad \text{(A4.12b)}$$

Proof of Proposition 4.2.2

By definition of R^o_{at}, we have

$$R^o_{at} = \frac{1}{N_a} \sum_{i \in I_a} R^o_{it} = \frac{1}{N_a} \sum_{i \in I_a} \sum_{k=0}^{\infty} X_{it}(k) \, R_{it-k}, \qquad \text{(A4.13a)}$$

$$= \sum_{k=0}^{\infty} \left(\frac{1}{N_a} \sum_{i \in I_a} X_{it}(k) \, R_{it-k} \right), \qquad \text{(A4.13b)}$$

$$= \sum_{k=0}^{\infty} \left[\frac{1}{N_a} \sum_{i \in I_a} \mu_i X_{it}(k) + \frac{\Lambda_{t-k}}{N_a} \sum_{i \in I_a} \beta_i X_{it}(k) \right.$$
$$\left. + \frac{1}{N_a} \sum_{i \in I_a} \epsilon_{it-k} X_{it}(k) \right]. \qquad \text{(A4.13c)}$$

The three terms in (A4.13c) may be simplified by verifying that the summands satisfy the hypotheses of Kolmogorov's strong law of large numbers, hence:

$$\frac{1}{N_a} \sum_{i \in I_a} \mu_i X_{it}(k) - \mathrm{E}\left[\frac{1}{N_a} \sum_{i \in I_a} \mu_i X_{it}(k) \right] \xrightarrow{\text{a.s.}} 0, \qquad \text{(A4.14a)}$$

$$\frac{1}{N_a} \sum_{i \in I_a} \beta_i X_{it}(k) - \mathrm{E}\left[\frac{1}{N_a} \sum_{i \in I_a} \beta_i X_{it}(k) \right] \xrightarrow{\text{a.s.}} 0, \qquad \text{(A4.14b)}$$

$$\frac{1}{N_a} \sum_{i \in I_a} \epsilon_{it-k} X_{it}(k) - \mathrm{E}\left[\frac{1}{N_a} \sum_{i \in I_a} \epsilon_{it-k} X_{it}(k) \right] \xrightarrow{\text{a.s.}} 0. \qquad \text{(A4.14c)}$$

From Definition 4.2.1 we have

$$\mathrm{E}\left[\frac{1}{N_a} \sum_{i \in I_a} \mu_i X_{it}(k) \right] = (1 - p_a) p_a^k \mu_a, \quad \mu_a \equiv \frac{1}{N_a} \sum_{i \in I_a} \mu_i, \qquad \text{(A4.15a)}$$

$$\mathrm{E}\left[\frac{1}{N_a} \sum_{i \in I_a} \beta_i X_{it}(k) \right] = (1 - p_a) p_a^k \beta_a, \quad \beta_a \equiv \frac{1}{N_a} \sum_{i \in I_a} \beta_i, \qquad \text{(A4.15b)}$$

$$\mathrm{E}\left[\frac{1}{N_a} \sum_{i \in I_a} \epsilon_{it-k} X_{it}(k) \right] = 0. \qquad \text{(A4.15c)}$$

Substituting these expressions into (A4.13c) then yields (4.2.21):

$$R^o_{at} \overset{\text{a.s.}}{=} \mu_a + (1 - p_a)\beta_a \sum_{k=0}^{\infty} \Lambda_{t-k} \, p_a^k. \qquad \text{(A4.16)}$$

To compute the cross-autocovariance between the two portfolio returns, we use (A4.16):

$$\text{Cov}[R^o_{at}, R^o_{bt+n}]$$

$$\stackrel{a}{=} (1 - p_a)(1 - p_b)\beta_a\beta_b\text{Cov}\left[\sum_{k=0}^{\infty}\Lambda_{t-k}p_a^k, \sum_{l=0}^{\infty}\Lambda_{t+n-l}p_b^l\right], \quad \text{(A4.17a)}$$

$$= (1 - p_a)(1 - p_b)\beta_a\beta_b\sum_{k=0}^{\infty}\sum_{l=0}^{\infty}\text{Cov}[\Lambda_{t-k}, \Lambda_{t+n-l}]p_a^k p_b^l, \quad \text{(A4.17b)}$$

$$= (1 - p_a)(1 - p_b)\beta_a\beta_b\sum_{k=0}^{\infty}\sum_{l=0}^{\infty}\sigma_\lambda^2 p_a^k p_b^l\theta(l - k - n), \quad \text{(A4.17c)}$$

$$= (1 - p_a)(1 - p_b)\beta_a\beta_b\sigma_\lambda^2 p_b^n\sum_{k=0}^{\infty}\sum_{l=0}^{\infty}(p_a p_b)^k, \quad \text{(A4.17d)}$$

$$\stackrel{a}{=} \frac{(1 - p_a)(1 - p_b)\beta_a\beta_b}{1 - p_a p_b}\sigma_\lambda^2 p_b^n, \quad \text{(A4.17e)}$$

where the symbol $\stackrel{a}{=}$ indicates that the equality obtains only asymptotically.

Proofs of Propositions 4.3.1 and 4.3.2

Since the proofs consist of computations virtually identical to those of Propositions 4.2.1 and 4.2.2, we leave them to the reader for the sake of brevity.

5

When Are Contrarian Profits
Due to Stock Market Overreaction?

5.1 Introduction

SINCE THE PUBLICATION of Louis Bachelier's thesis *Theory of Speculation* in 1900, the theoretical and empirical implications of the random walk hypothesis as a model for speculative prices have been subjects of considerable interest to financial economists. First developed by Bachelier from rudimentary economic considerations of "fair games," the random walk has received broader support from the many early empirical studies confirming the unpredictability of stock-price changes.[1] Of course, as Leroy (1973) and Lucas (1978) have shown, the unforecastability of asset returns is neither a necessary nor a sufficient condition of economic equilibrium. And, in view of the empirical evidence in Lo and MacKinlay (1988b), it is also apparent that historical stock market prices do not follow random walks.

This fact surprises many economists because the defining property of the random walk is the uncorrelatedness of its increments, and deviations from this hypothesis necessarily imply price changes that are forecastable to some degree. But our surprise must be tempered by the observation that forecasts of stock returns are still imperfect and may be subject to considerable forecast errors, so that "excess" profit opportunities and market inefficiencies are not necessarily consequences of forecastability. Nevertheless, several recent studies maintain the possibility of significant profits and market inefficiencies, even after controlling for risk in one way or another.

---

[1] See, for example, the papers in Cootner (1964), and Fama (1965,Fama (1970). Our usage of the term "random walk" differs slightly from the classical definition of a process with independently and identically distributed increments. Since historically the property of primary economic interest has been the uncorrelatedness of increments, we also consider processes with uncorrelated but heterogeneously distributed dependent increments to be random walks.

Some of these studies have attributed this forecastability to what has come to be known as the "stock market overreaction" hypothesis, the notion that investors are subject to waves of optimism and pessimism and therefore create a kind of "momentum" that causes prices to temporarily swing away from their fundamental values. (See, e.g., DeBondt and Thaler, 1985, 1987; DeLong, Shleifer, Summers, and Waldmann, 1989; Lehmann, 1988; Poterba and Summers, 1988; and Shefrin and Statman, 1985.) Although such a hypothesis does imply predictability, since what goes down must come up and vice versa, a well-articulated equilibrium theory of overreaction with sharp empirical implications has yet to be developed.

But common to virtually all existing theories of overreaction is one very specific empirical implication: Price changes must be *negatively* autocorrelated for some holding period. For example, DeBondt and Thaler (1985) write: "If stock prices systematically overshoot, then their reversal should be predictable from past return data alone." Therefore, the extent to which the data are consistent with stock market overreaction, broadly defined, may be distilled into an empirically decidable question: are return reversals responsible for the predictability in stock returns?

A more specific consequence of overreaction is the profitability of a contrarian portfolio strategy, a strategy that exploits negative serial dependence in asset returns in particular. The defining characteristic of a contrarian strategy is the purchase of securities that have performed poorly in the past and the sale of securities that have performed well.[2] Selling the "winners" and buying the "losers" will earn positive expected profits in the presence of negative serial correlation because current losers are likely to become future winners and current winners are likely to become future losers. Therefore, one implication of stock market overreaction is positive expected profits from a contrarian investment rule. It is the apparent profitability of several contrarian strategies that has led many to conclude that stock markets do indeed overreact.

In this chapter, we question this reverse implication, namely that the profitability of contrarian investment strategies necessarily implies stock market overreaction. As an illustrative example, we construct a simple return-generating process in which each security's return is serially independent and yet will still yield positive expected profits for a portfolio strategy that buys losers and sells winners.

This counterintuitive result is a consequence of positive *cross-autocovariances* across securities, from which contrarian portfolio strategies benefit. If, for example, a high return for security A today implies that security B's return will probably be high tomorrow, then a contrarian investment

---

[2]Decisions about how performance is defined and for what length of time generates as many different kinds of contrarian strategies as there are theories of overreaction.

strategy will be profitable even if each security's returns are unforecastable using past returns of that security alone. To see how, suppose the market consists of only the two stocks, A and B; if A's return is higher than the market today, a contrarian sells it and buys B. But if A and B are positively cross-autocorrelated, a higher return for A today implies a higher return for B tomorrow on average, thus the contrarian will have profited from his long position in B on average. Nowhere is it required that the stock market overreacts, that is, that individual returns are negatively autocorrelated. Therefore, the fact that some contrarian strategies have positive expected profits need not imply stock market overreaction. In fact, for the particular contrarian strategy we examine, over half of the expected profits are due to cross effects and not to negative autocorrelation in individual security returns.

Perhaps the most striking aspect of our empirical findings is that these cross effects are generally positive in sign and have a pronounced lead–lag structure: The returns of large-capitalization stocks almost always lead those of smaller stocks. This result, coupled with the observation that individual security returns are generally weakly negatively autocorrelated, indicates that the recently documented positive autocorrelation in weekly returns indexes is *completely* attributable to cross effects. This provides important guidance for theoretical models of equilibrium asset prices attempting to explain positive index autocorrelation via time-varying conditional expected returns. Such theories must be capable of generating lead–lag patterns, since it is the cross-autocorrelations that are the source of positive dependence in stock returns.

Of course, positive index autocorrelation and lead–lag effects are also a symptom of the so-called "nonsynchronous trading" or "thin trading" problem, in which the prices of distinct securities are mistakenly assumed to be sampled simultaneously. Perhaps the first to show that nonsynchronous sampling of prices induces autocorrelated portfolio returns was Fisher (1966), hence the nonsynchronous trading problem is also known as the "Fisher effect."[3] Lead–lag effects are also a natural consequence of thin trading, as the models of Cohen et al. (1986) and Lo and MacKinlay (1990c) show. To resolve this issue, we examine the magnitudes of index autocorrelation and cross-autocorrelations generated by a simple but general model of thin trading. We find that although some of correlation observed in the data may be due to this problem, to attribute all of it to thin trading would require unrealistically thin markets.

Because we focus only on the expected profits of the contrarian investment rule and not on its risk, our results have implications for stock market

---

[3]We refrain from this usage since the more common usage of the "Fisher effect" is the one-for-one change in nominal interest rates with changes in expected inflation, due to Irving Fisher.

efficiency only insofar as they provide restrictions on economic models that might be consistent with the empirical results. In particular, we do not assert or deny the existence of "excessive" contrarian profits. Such an issue cannot be addressed without specifying an economic paradigm within which asset prices are rationally determined in equilibrium. Nevertheless, we show that the contrarian investment strategy is still a convenient tool for exploring the autocorrelation properties of stock returns.

In Section 5.2 we provide a summary of the autocorrelation properties of weekly returns, documenting the positive autocorrelation in portfolio returns and the negative autocorrelations of individual returns. Section 5.3 presents a formal analysis of the expected profits from a specific contrarian investment strategy under several different return-generating mechanisms and shows that positive expected profits need not be related to overreaction. We also develop our model of nonsynchronous trading and calculate the impact on the time-series properties of the observed data, to be used later in our empirical analysis. In Section 5.4, we attempt to quantify empirically the proportion of contrarian profits that can be attributed to overreaction, and find that a substantial portion cannot be. We show that a systematic lead–lag relationship among returns of size-sorted portfolios is an important source of contrarian profits, and is the *sole* source of positive index autocorrelation. Using the nontrading model of Section 5.3, we also conclude that the lead–lag patterns cannot be completely attributed to nonsynchronous prices. In Section 5.5 we provide some discussion of our use of weekly returns in contrast to the much longer-horizon returns used in previous studies of stock market overreaction, and we conclude in Section 5.6.

5.2 A Summary of Recent Findings

In Table 5.1 we report the first four autocorrelations of weekly equal-weighted and value-weighted returns indexes for the sample period from July 6, 1962, to December 31, 1987, where the indexes are constructed from the Center for Research in Security Prices (CRSP) daily returns files.[4] During this period, the equal-weighted index has a first-order autocorrelation $\hat{\rho}_1$ of approximately 30 percent. Since its heteroskedasticity-consistent standard

---

[4]Unless stated otherwise, we take returns to be simple returns and not continuously-compounded. The weekly return of each security is computed as the return from Wednesday's closing price to the following Wednesday's closing price. If the following Wednesday's price is missing, then Thursday's price (or Tuesday's if Thursday's is also missing) is used. If both Tuesday's and Thursday's prices are missing, the return for that week is reported as missing; this occurs only rarely. To compute weekly returns on size-sorted portfolios, for each week all stocks with nonmissing returns that week are assigned to portfolios based on which quintile their market value of equity lies in. The sorting is done only once, using mid-sample equity values, hence the compositions of the portfolios do not change over time.

Table 5.1. *Sample statistics for the weekly equal-weighted and value-weighted CRSP NYSE-AMEX stock returns indexes, for the period from July 6, 1962, to December 31, 1987 and subperiods. Heteroskedasticity-consistent standard errors for autocorrelation coefficients are given in parentheses.*

Time Period	Sample Size	Mean Return $\% \times 100$	Std. Dev. of Return $\% \times 100$	$\hat{\rho}_1$ (SE)	$\hat{\rho}_2$ (SE)	$\hat{\rho}_3$ (SE)	$\hat{\rho}_4$ (SE)
Equal-Weighted:							
620706–871231	1330	0.359	2.277	0.296 (0.046)	0.116 (0.037)	0.081 (0.034)	0.045 (0.035)
620706–750403	665	0.264	2.326	0.338 (0.053)	0.157 (0.048)	0.082 (0.052)	0.044 (0.053)
750404–871231	665	0.455	2.225	0.248 (0.076)	0.071 (0.058)	0.078 (0.042)	0.040 (0.045)
Value-Weighted:							
620706–871231	1330	0.210	2.058	0.074 (0.040)	0.007 (0.037)	0.021 (0.036)	−0.005 (0.037)
620706–750403	665	0.135	1.972	0.055 (0.058)	0.020 (0.055)	0.058 (0.060)	−0.021 (0.058)
750404–871231	665	0.285	2.139	0.091 (0.055)	−0.003 (0.049)	−0.014 (0.042)	0.007 (0.046)

error is 0.046, this autocorrelation is statistically different from zero at all conventional significance levels. The subperiod autocorrelations show that this significance is not an artifact of any particularly influential subsample; equal-weighted returns are strongly positively autocorrelated throughout the sample. Higher-order autocorrelations are also positive although generally smaller in magnitude, and decay at a somewhat slower rate than the geometric rate of an autoregressive process of order 1 [AR(1)] (for example, $\hat{\rho}_1^2$ is 8.8 percent whereas $\hat{\rho}_2$ is 11.6 percent).

To develop a sense of the economic importance of the autocorrelations, observe that the R^2 of a regression of returns on a constant and its first lag is the square of the slope coefficient, which is simply the first-order autocorrelation. Therefore, an autocorrelation of 30 percent implies that 9 percent of weekly return variation is predictable using only the preceding week's returns. In fact, the autocorrelation coefficients implicit in Lo and MacKinlay's (1988) variance ratios are as high as 49 percent for a subsample of the portfolio of stocks in the smallest-size quintile, implying an R^2 of about 25 percent.

It may, therefore, come as some surprise that individual returns are generally weakly negatively autocorrelated. Table 5.2 shows the cross-sectional

Table 5.2.   *Averages of autocorrelation coefficients for weekly returns on individual securities, for the period July 6, 1962, to December 31, 1987. The statistic $\overline{\hat{\rho}}_j$ is the average of jth-order autocorrelation coefficients of returns on individual stocks that have at least 52 nonmissing returns. The population standard deviation (SD) is given in parentheses. Since the autocorrelation coefficients are not cross-sectionally independent, the reported standard deviations cannot be used to draw the usual inferences; they are presented merely as a measure of cross-sectional variation in the autocorrelation coefficients.*

Sample	Number of Securities	$\overline{\hat{\rho}}_1$ (SD)	$\overline{\hat{\rho}}_2$ (SD)	$\overline{\hat{\rho}}_3$ (SD)	$\overline{\hat{\rho}}_4$ (SD)
All Stocks	4786	−0.034 (0.084)	−0.015 (0.065)	−0.003 (0.062)	−0.003 (0.061)
Smallest Quintile	957	−0.079 (0.095)	−0.017 (0.077)	−0.007 (0.068)	−0.004 (0.071)
Central Quintile	958	−0.027 (0.082)	−0.015 (0.068)	−0.003 (0.067)	−0.000 (0.065)
Largest Quintile	957	−0.013 (0.054)	−0.014 (0.050)	−0.002 (0.050)	−0.005 (0.047)

average of autocorrelation coefficients across all stocks that have at least 52 nonmissing weekly returns during the sample period. For the entire cross section of the 4786 such stocks, the average first-order autocorrelation coefficient, denoted by $\overline{\hat{\rho}}_1$, is −3.4 percent with a cross-sectional standard deviation of 8.4 percent. Therefore, most of the individual first-order autocorrelations fall between −20 percent and 13 percent. This implies that most R^2's of regressions of individual security returns on their return last week fall between 0 and 4 percent, considerably less than the predictability of equal-weighted index returns. Average higher-order autocorrelations are also negative, though smaller in magnitude. The negativity of autocorrelations may be an indication of stock market overreaction for individual stocks, but it is also consistent with the existence of a bid–ask spread. We discuss this further in Section 5.3.

Table 5.2 also shows average autocorrelations within size-sorted quintiles.[5] The negative autocorrelations are stronger in the smallest quintile, but even the largest quintile has a negative average autocorrelation. Compared to the 30 percent autocorrelation of the equal-weighted index, the magnitudes of the individual autocorrelations indicated by the means (and standard deviations) in Table 5.2 are generally much smaller.

[5]Securities are allocated to quintiles by sorting only once (using market values of their sample periods); hence, their composition of quintiles does not change over time.

To conserve space, we omit corresponding tables for daily and monthly returns, in which similar patterns are observed. Autocorrelations are strongly positive for index returns (35.5 and 14.8 percent $\hat{\rho}_1$'s for the equal-weighted daily and monthly indexes, respectively), and weakly negative for individual securities (-1.4 and -2.9 percent $\overline{\hat{\rho}_1}$'s for daily and monthly returns, respectively).

The importance of cross-autocorrelations is foreshadowed by the general tendency for individual security returns to be negatively autocorrelated and for portfolio returns, such as those of the equal- and value-weighted market index, to be positively autocorrelated. To see this, observe that the first-order autocovariance of an equal-weighted index may be written as the sum of the first-order own-autocovariances and *cross-autocovariances* of the component securities. If the own-autocovariances are generally negative, and the index autocovariance is positive, then the cross-autocovariances must be positive. Moreover, the cross-autocovariances must be large, so large as to exceed the sum of the negative own-autocovariances. Whereas virtually all contrarian strategies have focused on exploiting the negative own-autocorrelations of individual securities (see, e.g., DeBondt and Thaler, 1985, 1987, and Lehmann 1988), primarily attributed to overreaction, we show below that forecastability *across* securities is at least as important a source of contrarian profits both in principle and in fact.

5.3 Analysis of Contrarian Profitability

To show the relationship between contrarian profits and the cross effects that are apparent in the data, we examine the expected profits of one such strategy under various return-generating processes. Consider a collection of N securities and denote by R_t the $N \times 1$ vector of their period t returns $[R_{1t} \cdots R_{Nt}]'$. For convenience, we maintain the following assumption throughout this section:

(A1) R_t is a jointly covariance-stationary stochastic process with expectation $\mathrm{E}[R_t] = \mu \equiv [\mu_1 \, \mu_2 \, \cdots \, \mu_N]'$ and autocovariance matrices $\mathrm{E}[(R_{t-k} - \mu)(R_t - \mu)'] = \Gamma_k$ where, with no loss of generality, we take $k \geq 0$ since $\Gamma_k = \Gamma'_{-k}$.[6]

---

[6]Assumption (A1) is made for notational simplicity, since joint covariance-stationarity allows us to eliminate time-indexes from population moments such as μ and Γ_k; the qualitative features of our results will not change under the weaker assumptions of weakly dependent heterogeneously distributed vectors R_t. This would merely require replacing expectations with corresponding probability limits of suitably defined time-averages. The empirical results of Section 5.4 are based on these weaker assumptions; interested readers may refer to conditions 1–3 in Appendix A.

In the spirit of virtually all contrarian investment strategies, consider buying stocks at time t that were losers at time $t - k$ and selling stocks at time t that were winners at time $t - k$, where winning and losing is determined with respect to the equal-weighted return on the market. More formally, if $\omega_{it}(k)$ denotes the fraction of the portfolio devoted to security i at time t, let

$$\omega_{it}(k) = -(1/N)(R_{it-k} - R_{mt-k}) \qquad i = 1, \ldots, N, \qquad (5.3.1)$$

where $R_{mt-k} \equiv \sum_{i=1}^{N} R_{it-k}/N$ is the equal-weighted market index.[7] If, for example, $k = 1$, then the portfolio strategy in period t is to short the winners and buy the losers of the previous period, $t - 1$. By construction, $\omega_t(k) \equiv [\omega_{1t}(k)\,\omega_{2t}(k)\cdots\omega_{Nt}(k)]'$ is an arbitrage portfolio since the weights sum to zero. Therefore, the total investment long (or short) at time t is given by $I_t(k)$ where

$$I_t(k) \equiv \frac{1}{2} \sum_{i=1}^{N} |\omega_{it}(k)|. \qquad (5.3.2)$$

Since the portfolio weights are proportional to the differences between the market index and the returns, securities that deviate more positively from the market at time $t - k$ will have greater negative weight in the time t portfolio, and vice versa. Such a strategy is designed to take advantage of stock market overreactions as characterized, for example, by DeBondt and Thaler (1985): "(1) Extreme movements in stock prices will be followed by extreme movements in the opposite direction. (2) The more extreme the initial price movement, the greater will be the subsequent adjustment." The profit $\pi_t(k)$ from such a strategy is simply

$$\pi_t(k) = \sum_{i=1}^{N} \omega_{it}(k) R_{it}. \qquad (5.3.3)$$

Rearranging Equation (5.3.3) and taking expectations yields the following:

$$\mathrm{E}[\pi_t(k)] = \frac{\iota'\Gamma_k\iota}{N^2} - \frac{1}{N}\mathrm{tr}(\Gamma_k) - \frac{1}{N}\sum_{i=1}^{N}(\mu_i - \mu_m)^2, \qquad (5.3.4)$$

where $\mu_m \equiv \mathrm{E}[R_{mt}] = \mu'\iota/N$ and $\mathrm{tr}(\cdot)$ denotes the trace operator.[8] The first term of (5.3.4) is simply the kth-order autocovariance of the equal-weighted market index. The second term is the cross-sectional average of

---

[7]This is perhaps the simplest portfolio strategy that captures the essence of the contrarian principle. Lehmann (1990) also considers this strategy, although he employs a more complicated strategy in his empirical analysis in which the portfolio weights (Equation (5.3.1)) are re-normalized each period by a random factor of proportionality, so that the investment is always $1 long and short. This portfolio strategy is also similar to that of DeBondt and Thaler (1985, 1987), although in contrast to our use of weekly returns, they consider holding periods of three years. See Section 5.5 for further discussion.

[8]The derivation of (5.3.4) is included in Appendix A for completeness. This is the population counterpart of Lehmann's (1988) sample moment equation (5) divided by N.

the kth-order autocovariances of the individual securities, and the third term is the cross-sectional variance of the mean returns. Since this last term is independent of the autocovariances Γ_k and does not vary with k, we define the *profitability index* $L_k \equiv L(\Gamma_k)$ and the constant $\sigma^2(\mu)$ as

$$L_k \equiv \frac{\iota' \Gamma_k \iota}{N^2} - \frac{1}{N} \text{tr}(\Gamma_k) \qquad \sigma^2(\mu) \equiv \frac{1}{N} \sum_{i=1}^{N} (\mu_i - \mu_m)^2. \qquad (5.3.5)$$

Thus,

$$\text{E}[\pi_t(k)] = L_k - \sigma^2(\mu). \qquad (5.3.6)$$

For purposes that will become evident below, we re-write L_k as

$$L_k = C_k + O_k, \qquad (5.3.7)$$

where

$$C_k \equiv \frac{1}{N^2} [\iota' \Gamma_k \iota - \text{tr}(\Gamma_k)], \qquad O_k \equiv -\left(\frac{N-1}{N^2}\right) \text{tr}(\Gamma_k). \qquad (5.3.8)$$

Hence,

$$\text{E}[\pi_t(k)] = C_k + O_k - \sigma^2(\mu). \qquad (5.3.9)$$

Written this way, it is apparent that expected profits may be decomposed into three terms: one (C_k) depending on only the off-diagonals of the auto-covariance matrix Γ_k, the second (O_k) depending on only the diagonals, and a third ($\sigma^2(\mu)$) that is independent of the autocovariances. This allows us to separate the fraction of expected profits due to the cross-autocovariances C_k versus the own-autocovariances O_k of returns.

Equation (5.3.9) shows that the profitability of the contrarian strategy (5.3.1) may be perfectly consistent with a positively autocorrelated market index and negatively autocorrelated individual security returns. Positive cross-autocovariances imply that the term C_k is positive, and negative autocovariances for individual securities imply that O_k is also positive. Conversely, the empirical finding that equal-weighted indexes are strongly positively autocorrelated while individual security returns are weakly negatively autocorrelated implies that there must be significant positive cross-autocorrelations across securities. To see this, observe that the first-order autocorrelation of the equal-weighted index R_{mt} is simply

$$\frac{\text{Cov}[R_{mt-1}, R_{mt}]}{\text{Var}[R_{mt}]} = \frac{\iota' \Gamma_1 \iota}{\iota' \Gamma_0 \iota} = \frac{\iota' \Gamma_1 \iota - \text{tr}(\Gamma_1)}{\iota' \Gamma_0 \iota} + \frac{\text{tr}(\Gamma_1)}{\iota' \Gamma_0 \iota}. \qquad (5.3.10)$$

The numerator of the second term on the right-hand side of (5.3.10) is simply the sum of the first-order autocovariances of individual securities; if this is negative, then the first term must be positive in order for the sum to be positive. Therefore, the positive autocorrelation in weekly returns may be attributed solely to the positive cross-autocorrelations across securities.

The expression for L_k also suggests that stock market overreaction need not be the reason that contrarian investment strategies are profitable. To anticipate the examples below, if returns are positively cross-autocorrelated, then a return-reversal strategy will yield positive profits on average, even if individual security returns are *serially independent!* The presence of stock market overreaction, that is, negatively autocorrelated individual returns, enhances the profitability of the return-reversal strategy, but it is not required for such a strategy to earn positive expected returns.

To organize our understanding of the sources and nature of contrarian profits, we provide five illustrative examples below. Although simplistic, they provide a useful taxonomy of conditions necessary for the profitability of the portfolio strategy (5.3.1).

5.3.1 The Independently and Identically Distributed Benchmark

Let returns R_t be both cross-sectionally and serially independent. In this case $\Gamma_k = 0$ for all nonzero k, hence,

$$L_k \;=\; C_k \;=\; O_k \;=\; 0, \qquad \mathrm{E}[\pi_t(k)] \;=\; -\sigma^2(\mu) \;\leq\; 0. \qquad (5.3.11)$$

Although returns are both serially and cross-sectionally unforecastable, the expected profits are negative as long as there is some cross-sectional variation in expected returns. In this case, our strategy reduces to shorting the higher and buying the lower mean return securities, respectively, a losing proposition even when stock market prices do follow random walks. Since $\sigma^2(\mu)$ is generally of small magnitude and does not depend on the auto-covariance structure of R_t, we will focus on L_k and ignore $\sigma^2(\mu)$ for the remainder of Section 5.3.

5.3.2 Stock Market Overreaction and Fads

Almost any operational definition of stock market overreaction implies that individual security returns are negatively autocorrelated over some holding period, so that "what goes up must come down," and vice versa. If we denote by $\gamma_{ij}(k)$ the (i, j)th element of the autocovariance matrix Γ_k, the overreaction hypothesis implies that the diagonal elements of Γ_k are negative, that is, $\gamma_{ii}(k) < 0$, at least for $k = 1$ when the span of one period corresponds to a complete cycle of overreaction.[9] Since the overreaction hypothesis generally does not restrict the cross-autocovariances, for simplicity we set them

---

[9]See Section 5.5 for further discussion of the importance of the return horizon.

to zero, that is, $\gamma_{ij}(k) = 0$, $i \neq j$. Hence, we have

$$
\Gamma_k = \begin{pmatrix} \gamma_{11}(k) & 0 & \cdots & 0 \\ 0 & \gamma_{22}(k) & \cdots & 0 \\ \vdots & \vdots & \ddots & \vdots \\ 0 & 0 & \cdots & \gamma_{NN}(k) \end{pmatrix}. \tag{5.3.12}
$$

The profitability index under these assumptions for R_t is then

$$
L_k = O_k = -\left(\frac{N-1}{N^2}\right)\operatorname{tr}(\Gamma_k)
$$

$$
= -\left(\frac{N-1}{N^2}\right)\sum_{i=1}^{N}\gamma_{ii}(k) > 0, \tag{5.3.13}
$$

where the cross-autocovariance term C_k is zero. The positivity of L_k follows from the negativity of the own-autocovariances, assuming $N > 1$. Not surprisingly, if stock markets do overreact, the contrarian investment strategy is profitable on average.

Another price process for which the return-reversal strategy will yield positive expected profits is the sum of a random walk and an AR(1), which has been recently proposed, by Summers (1986), for example, as a model of "fads" or "animal spirits." Specifically, let the dynamics for the log-price X_{it} of each security i be given by

$$
X_{it} = Y_{it} + Z_{it} \tag{5.3.14}
$$

where

$$
\begin{aligned} Y_{it} &= \mu_i + Y_{it-1} + \epsilon_{it}, \\ Z_{it} &= \rho_i Z_{it-1} + \nu_{it}, \qquad 0 < \rho < 1 \end{aligned} \tag{5.3.15}
$$

and the disturbances $\{\epsilon_{it}\}$ and $\{\nu_{it}\}$ are serially, mutually, and cross-sectionally independent at all *nonzero* leads and lags.[10] The kth-order autocovariance for the return vector R_t is then given by the following diagonal matrix:

$$
\Gamma_k = \operatorname{diag}\left[-\rho_1^{k-1}\frac{1-\rho_1}{1+\rho_1}\sigma_{\nu_1}^2, \ldots, -\rho_N^{k-1}\left(\frac{1-\rho_N}{1+\rho_N}\right)\sigma_{\nu_N}^2\right] \tag{5.3.16}
$$

and the profitability index follows immediately as

$$
L_k = O_k = -\left(\frac{N-1}{N^2}\right)\operatorname{tr}(\Gamma_k)
$$

$$
= \frac{N-1}{N^2}\sum_{i=1}^{N}\rho_i^{k-1}\left(\frac{1-\rho_i}{1+\rho_i}\right)\sigma_{\nu_i}^2 > 0. \tag{5.3.17}
$$

[10]This last assumption requires only that ϵ_{it-k} is independent of ϵ_{jt} for $k \neq 0$; hence, the disturbances may be contemporaneously cross-sectionally dependent without loss of generality.

Since the own-autocovariances in Equation (5.3.16) are all negative, this is a special case of Equation (5.3.12) and therefore may be interpreted as an example of stock market overreaction. However, the fact that returns are negatively autocorrelated at all lags is an artifact of the first-order autoregressive process and need not be true for the sum of a random walk and a general stationary process, a model that has been proposed for both stock market fads and time-varying expected returns (e.g., see Fama and French (1988) and Summers (1986)). For example, let the "temporary" component of Equation (5.3.14) be given by the following stationary AR(2) process:

$$ Z_{it} = \frac{9}{7}Z_{it-1} - \frac{5}{7}Z_{it-2} + v_{it}. \tag{5.3.18} $$

It is easily verified that the first difference of Z_{it} is positively autocorrelated at lag 1 implying that $L_1 < 0$. Therefore, stock market overreaction necessarily implies the profitability of the portfolio strategy (5.3.1) (in the absence of cross-autocorrelation), but stock market fads do not.

5.3.3 Trading on White Noise and Lead–Lag Relations

Let the return-generating process for R_t be given by

$$ R_{it} = \mu_i + \beta_i \Lambda_{t-i} + \epsilon_{it}, \qquad \beta_i > 0, \qquad i = 1, \ldots, N, \tag{5.3.19} $$

where Λ_t is a serially independent common factor with zero mean and variance σ_λ^2, and the ϵ_{it}'s are assumed to be both cross-sectionally and serially independent. These assumptions imply that for each security i, its returns are white noise (with drift) so that future returns to i are not forecastable from its past returns. This serial independence is *not* consistent with either the spirit or form of the stock market overreaction hypothesis. And yet it *is* possible to predict i's returns using past returns of security j, where $j < i$. This is an artifact of the dependence of the ith security's return on a lagged common factor, where the lag is determined by the security's index. Consequently, the return to security 1 leads that of securities 2, 3, etc.; the return to security 2 leads that of securities 3, 4, etc.; and so on. However, the current return to security 2 provides no information for future returns to security 1, and so on. To see that such a lead–lag relation will induce positive expected profits for the contrarian strategy (5.3.1), observe that when $k < N$, the autocovariance matrix Γ_k has zeros in all entries except along the kth superdiagonal, for which $\gamma_{ii+k} = \sigma_\lambda^2 \beta_i \beta_{i+k}$. Also, observe that this lead–lag model yields an *asymmetric* autocovariance matrix Γ_k. The profitability index is then

$$ L_k = C_k = \frac{\sigma_\lambda^2}{N^2} \sum_{i=1}^{N-k} \beta_i \beta_{i+k} > 0. \tag{5.3.20} $$

This example highlights the importance of the cross effects—although each security is individually unpredictable, a contrarian strategy may still profit if securities are positively cross-correlated at various leads and lags. Less contrived return-generating processes will also yield positive expected profits to contrarian strategies, as long as the cross-autocovariances are sufficiently large.

5.3.4 Lead–Lag Effects and Nonsynchronous Trading

One possible source of such cross effects is what has come to be known as the "nonsynchronous trading" or "nontrading" problem, in which the prices of distinct securities are mistakenly assumed to be sampled simultaneously. Treating nonsynchronous prices as if they were observed at the same time can create spurious autocorrelation and cross-autocorrelation, as Fisher (1966), Scholes and Williams (1977), and Cohen et al. (1986) have demonstrated. To gauge the importance of nonsynchronous trading for contrarian profits, we derive the magnitude of the spurious cross-autocorrelations using the nontrading model of Lo and MacKinlay (1990c).[11]

Consider a collection of N securities with *unobservable* "virtual" continuously compounded returns R_{it} at time t, where $i = 1, \ldots, N$, and assume that they are generated by the following stochastic model:

$$R_{it} = \mu_i + \beta_i \Lambda_t + \epsilon_{it} \qquad i = 1, \ldots, N \qquad (5.3.21)$$

where Λ_t is some zero-mean common factor and ϵ_{it} is zero-mean idiosyncratic noise that is temporally and cross-sectionally independent at all leads and lags. Since we wish to focus on nontrading as the *sole* source of autocorrelation, we also assume that the common factor Λ_t is independently and identically distributed and is independent of ϵ_{it-k} for all i, t, and k.

In each period t there is some chance that security i does not trade, say with probability p_i. If it does not trade, its observed return for period t is simply 0, although its true or virtual return R_{it} is still given by Equation (5.3.21). In the next period $t + 1$ there is again some chance that security i does not trade, also with probability p_i. We assume that whether or not the security traded in period t does not influence the likelihood of its trading in period $t + 1$ or any other future period; hence, our nontrading mechanism is independent and identically distributed for each security i.[12] If security i does trade in period $t + 1$ and did not trade in period t, we assume that its observed return R^o_{it+1} at $t + 1$ is the sum of its virtual returns

---

[11] The empirical relevance of other nontrading effects, such as the negative autocorrelation of individual returns, is beyond the scope of this study and is explored in depth by Atkinson et al. (1987) and Lo and MacKinlay (1990c).

[12] This assumption may be relaxed to allow for state-dependent probabilities, that is, autocorrelated nontrading (see Lo and MacKinlay (1990c) for further details).

R_{it+1}, R_{it}, and virtual returns for all past *consecutive* periods in which i has not traded. In fact, the observed return in any period is simply the sum of its virtual returns for all past consecutive periods in which it did not trade. This captures the essential feature of nontrading as a source of spurious autocorrelation: News affects those stocks that trade more frequently first and influences the returns of thinly traded securities with a lag. In this framework, the effect of news is captured by the virtual returns process (5.3.21), and the lag induced by nonsynchronous trading is therefore built into the observed returns process R_{it}^o.

More formally, the observed returns process may be written as the following weighted average of past virtual returns:

$$R_{it}^o = \sum_{k=0}^{\infty} X_{it}(k)R_{it-k} \qquad i = 1, \ldots, N. \tag{5.3.22}$$

Here the (random) weights $X_{it}(k)$ are defined as products of no-trade indicators:

$$
\begin{aligned}
X_{it}(k) &\equiv (1 - \delta_{it})\delta_{it-1}\delta_{it-2}\cdots\delta_{it-k} \\
&= \begin{cases} 1 & \text{with probability } (1 - p_i)p_i^k \\ 0 & \text{with probability } 1 - (1 - p_i)p_i^k \end{cases}
\end{aligned} \tag{5.3.23}
$$

for $k > 0$, $X_{it}(0) \equiv 1 - \delta_{it}$, and where the δ_{it}'s are independently and identically distributed Bernoulli random variables that take on the value 1 when security i does not trade at time t, and zero otherwise. The variable $X_{it}(k)$ is also an indicator variable, and takes on the value 1 if security i trades at time t but not in any of the k previous periods, and takes on the value 0 otherwise. If security i does not trade at time t, then $\delta_{it} = 1$, which implies that $X_{it}(k) = 0$ for all k, thus, $R_{it}^o = 0$. If i does trade at time t, then its observed return is equal to the sum of today's virtual return R_{it} and its past $\tilde{k}_{it}$ virtual returns, where the random variable $\tilde{k}_{it}$ is the number of past *consecutive* periods that i has not traded. We call this the *duration* of nontrading, and it may be expressed as

$$\tilde{k}_{i,t} \equiv \sum_{k=1}^{\infty}\left(\prod_{j=1}^{k}\delta_{it-j}\right). \tag{5.3.24}$$

To develop some intuition for the nontrading probabilities p_i, observe that

$$E[\tilde{k}_{i,t}] = p_i/(1 - p_i). \tag{5.3.25}$$

If $p_i = \frac{1}{2}$, then the average duration of nontrading for security i is one period. However, if $p_i = \frac{3}{4}$, then the average duration of nontrading increases to three periods. As expected if the security trades every period so that $p_i = 0$, the mean (and variance) of $\tilde{k}_{i,t}$ is zero.

Further simplification results from grouping securities with common nontrading probabilities into portfolios. If, for example, an equal-weighted portfolio contains securities with common nontrading probability p_κ, then the observed return to portfolio κ may be approximated as

$$R^o_{\kappa t} \stackrel{a}{=} \mu_\kappa + (1 - p_\kappa)\beta_\kappa \sum_{k=0}^{\infty} p^k_\kappa \Lambda_{t-k} \qquad (5.3.26)$$

where the approximation becomes exact as the number of securities in the portfolio approaches infinity, and where β_κ is the average beta of the securities in the portfolio.

Now define $R^o_{\kappa \tau}(q)$ as the observed return of portfolio κ over q periods, that is, $R^o_{\kappa \tau}(q) \equiv \sum_{l=(\tau-1)q+1}^{\tau q} R^o_{\kappa l}$. We wish to work with time-aggregated returns $R^o_{\kappa t}(q)$ to allow nontrading to take place at intervals finer than the sampling interval.[13] Using Equation (5.3.26), we have the following moments and co-moments of observed portfolio returns:[14]

$$E[R^o_{\kappa \tau}](q) \stackrel{a}{=} q\mu_\kappa = E[R_{\kappa \tau}(q)] \qquad (5.3.27)$$

$$\text{Var}[R^o_{\kappa \tau}(q)] \stackrel{a}{=} \left[q - 2p_\kappa \frac{1 - p^q_\kappa}{1 - p^2_\kappa}\right]\beta^2_\kappa \sigma^2_\lambda \qquad (5.3.28)$$

$$\text{Cov}\left[R^o_{\kappa \tau - k}(q), R^o_{\kappa \tau}(q)\right] \stackrel{a}{=} \left[\frac{1 - p_\kappa}{1 + p_\kappa}\right]\left[\frac{1 - p^q_\kappa}{1 - p_\kappa}\right]^2 p^{kq - q + 1}_\kappa \beta^2_\kappa \sigma^2_\lambda \quad k > 0 \;\; (5.3.29)$$

$$\text{Corr}\left[R^o_{a\tau - k}(q), R^o_{br}(q)\right] \stackrel{a}{=} \frac{(1 - p^q_\kappa)^2 p^{kq - q + 1}_\kappa}{q(1 - p^2_\kappa) - 2p_\kappa(1 - p^q_\kappa)} \quad n > 0 \qquad (5.3.30)$$

$$\text{Cov}[R^o_{a\tau - k}(q), R^o_{br}(q)] \stackrel{a}{=} \frac{(1 - p_a)(1 - p_b)}{1 - p_a p_b}\left[\frac{1 - p^q}{1 - p_b}\right]^2 p^{kq - q + 1}_b \beta_a \beta_b \sigma^2_\lambda \;\; (5.3.31)$$

$$\text{Corr}[R^o_{a\tau - k}(q), R^o_{br}(q)] \equiv \rho^q_{ab}(k)$$

$$\stackrel{a}{=} \left[\frac{(1 - p_a)(1 - p_b)}{1 - p_a p_b}\left(\frac{1 - p^q}{1 - p_b}\right)^2 p^{kq - q + 1}_b\right]$$

$$\times \left(\sqrt{q - 2p_a \frac{1 - p^q_a}{1 - p^2_a}}\sqrt{q - 2p_b \frac{1 - p^q}{1 - p^2_b}}\right)^{-1} \qquad (5.3.32)$$

---

[13]So, for example, although we use weekly returns in our empirical analysis below, the implications of nontrading that we are about to derive still obtain for securities that may not trade on some days within the week.

[14]See Lo and MacKinlay (1990c) for the derivations.

where $R_{a\tau}^o(q)$ and $R_{b\tau}^o(q)$ are the observed q-period returns of two arbitrary portfolios a and b. Using (5.3.29) and (5.3.32), the effects of nontrading on contrarian profits may be quantified explicitly. A lead–lag structure may also be deduced from (5.3.32). To see this, consider the ratio of the cross-autocorrelation coefficients:

$$\frac{\rho_{ab}^q(k)}{\rho_{ba}^q(k)} = \left(\frac{1 - p_b^q}{1 - p_a^q} \cdot \frac{1 - p_b}{1 - p_a} \right)^2 \left(\frac{p_b}{p_a} \right)^{kq-q+1} \qquad (5.3.33)$$

$$\gtreqless 1 \quad \text{as} \quad p_b \gtreqless p_a$$

which shows that portfolios with higher nontrading probabilities tend to lag those with lower nontrading probabilities. For example, if $p_b > p_a$ so that securities in portfolio b trade less frequently than those in portfolio a, then the correlation between today's return on a and tomorrow's return on b exceeds the correlation between today's return on b and tomorrow's return on a.

To check the magnitude of the cross-correlations that can result from nonsynchronous prices, consider two portfolios a and b with daily non-trading probabilities $p_a = .10$ and $p_b = .25$. Using (5.3.32), with $q = 5$ for weekly returns and $k = 1$ for the first-order cross-autocorrelation, yields $\text{Corr}[R_{a\tau-1}^o(q), R_{b\tau}^o(q)] = .066$ and $\text{Corr}[R_{b\tau-1}^o(q), R_{a\tau}^o(q)] = .019$. Although there is a pronounced lead–lag effect, the cross-autocorrelations are small. We shall return to these cross-autocorrelations in our empirical analysis below, where we show that values of .10 and .25 for nontrading probabilities are considerably larger than the data suggest. Even if we eliminate nontrading in portfolio a so that $p_a = 0$, this yields $\text{Corr}[R_{a\tau-1}^o(q), R_{b\tau}^o(q)] = .070$ and $\text{Corr}[R_{b\tau-1}^o(q), R_{a\tau}^o(q)] = .000$. Therefore, the magnitude of weekly cross-autocorrelations cannot be completely attributed to the effects of non-synchronous trading.

5.3.5 A Positively Dependent Common Factor and the Bid–Ask Spread

A plausible return-generating mechanism consistent with positive index au-tocorrelation and negative serial dependence in individual returns is to let each R_{it} be the sum of three components: a positively autocorrelated com-mon factor, idiosyncratic white noise, and a bid–ask spread process.[15] More formally, let

$$R_{it} = \mu_i + \beta_i \Lambda_t + \eta_{it} + \epsilon_{it} \qquad (5.3.34)$$

where

$$\text{E}[\Lambda_t] = 0, \qquad \text{E}[\Lambda_{t-k}\Lambda_t] \equiv \gamma_\lambda(k) > 0 \qquad (5.3.35)$$

---

[15]This is suggested in Lo and MacKinlay (1988b). Conrad, Kaul, and Nimalendran (1988) investigate a similar specification.

$$\mathrm{E}[\epsilon_{it}] = \mathrm{E}[\eta_{it}] = 0 \qquad \forall i, t \tag{5.3.36}$$

$$\mathrm{E}[\epsilon_{it-k}\,\epsilon_{jt}] = \begin{cases} \sigma_i^2 & \text{if } k = 0 \text{ and } i = j \\ 0 & \text{otherwise.} \end{cases} \tag{5.3.37}$$

$$\mathrm{E}[\eta_{it-k}\,\eta_{jt}] = \begin{cases} -\frac{s_i^2}{4} & \text{if } k = 1 \text{ and } i = j \\ 0 & \text{otherwise.} \end{cases} \tag{5.3.38}$$

Implicit in Equation (5.3.38) is Roll's (1984a) model of the bid–ask spread, in which the first-order autocorrelation of η_{it} is the negative of one-fourth the square of the percentage bid–ask spread s_i, and all higher-order auto-correlations and all cross-correlations are zero. Such a return-generating process will yield a positively autocorrelated market index since averaging the white-noise and bid–ask components will trivialize them, leaving the common factor Λ_t. Yet if the bid–ask spread is large enough, it may dominate the common factor for each security, yielding negatively autocorrelated individual security returns.

The autocovariance matrices for Equation (5.3.34) are given by

$$\Gamma_1 = \gamma_\lambda(1)\beta\beta' - \tfrac{1}{4}\mathrm{diag}[s_1^2, s_2^2, \dots, s_N^2] \tag{5.3.39}$$

$$\Gamma_k = \gamma_\lambda(k)\beta\beta' \qquad k > 1 \tag{5.3.40}$$

where $\beta \equiv [\beta_1\,\beta_2\cdots\beta_N]'$. In contrast to the lead–lag model of Section 5.3.4, the autocovariance matrices for this return-generating process are all symmetric. This is an important empirical implication that distinguishes the common factor model from the lead–lag process, and will be exploited in our empirical appraisal of overreaction.

Denote by β_m the cross-sectional average $\sum_{i=1}^{N} \beta_i/N$. Then the profitability index is given by

$$L_1 = -\frac{\gamma_\lambda(1)}{N}\sum_{i=1}^{N}(\beta_i - \beta_m)^2 + \frac{N-1}{N^2}\sum_{i=1}^{N}\frac{s_i^2}{4} \tag{5.3.41}$$

$$L_k = -\frac{\gamma_\lambda(k)}{N}\sum_{i=1}^{N}(\beta_i - \beta_m)^2 \qquad k > 1. \tag{5.3.42}$$

Equation (5.3.41) shows that if the bid–ask spreads are large enough and the cross-sectional variation of the β_k's is small enough, the contrarian strategy (5.3.1) may yield positive expected profits when using only one lag ($k = 1$) in computing portfolio weights. However, the positivity of the profitability index is due solely to the negative autocorrelations of individual security returns induced by the bid–ask spread. Once this effect is removed, for example, when portfolio weights are computed using lags 2 or higher, relation

(5.3.42) shows that the profitability index is of the opposite sign of the index autocorrelation coefficient $\gamma_\lambda(k)$. Since $\gamma_\lambda(k) > 0$ by assumption, expected profits are negative for lags higher than 1. In view of the empirical results to be reported in Section 5.4, in which L_k is shown to be positive for $k > 1$, it seems unlikely that the return-generating process (5.3.34) can account for the weekly autocorrelation patterns in the data.

5.4 An Empirical Appraisal of Overreaction

To see how much of contrarian profits is due to stock market overreaction, we estimate the expected profits from the return-reversal strategy of Section 5.3 for a sample of CRSP NYSE-AMEX securities. Recall that $E[\pi_t(k)] = C_k + O_k - \sigma^2(\mu)$ where C_k depends only on the cross-autocovariances of returns and O_k depends only on the own-autocovariances. Table 5.4 shows estimates of $E[\pi_t(k)]$, C_k, O_k, and $\sigma^2(\mu)$ for the 551 stocks that have no missing weekly returns during the entire sample period from July 6, 1962, to December 31, 1987. Estimates are computed for the sample of all stocks and for three size-sorted quintiles. All size-sorted portfolios are constructed by sorting only once (using market values of equity at the middle of the sample period); hence, their composition does not change over time. We develop the appropriate sampling theory in Appendix A, in which the covariance-stationarity assumption (A1) is replaced with weaker assumptions allowing for serial dependence and heterogeneity.

Consider the last three columns of Table 5.4, which show the magnitudes of the three terms $\hat{C}_k$, $\hat{O}_k$, and $\sigma^2(\hat{\mu})$ as percentages of expected profits. At lag 1, half the expected profits from the contrarian strategy are due to positive cross autocovariances. In the central quintile, about 67 percent of the expected profits is attributable to these cross-effects. The results at lag 2 are similar: Positive cross-autocovariances account for about 50 percent of the expected profits, 66 percent for the smallest quintile.

The positive expected profits at lags 2 and higher provide direct evidence against the common component/bid–ask spread model of Section 5.3.5. If returns contained a positively autocorrelated common factor and exhibited negative autocorrelation due to "bid–ask bounce," expected profits can be positive only at lag 1; higher lags must exhibit negative expected profits as Equation (5.3.42) shows. Table 5.4 shows that estimated expected profits are significantly positive for lags 2 through 4 in all portfolios except one.

The z-statistics for $\hat{C}_k$, $\hat{O}_k$, and $\hat{E}[\pi_t(k)]$ are asymptotically standard normal under the null hypothesis that the population values corresponding to the three estimators are zero. At lag 1, they are almost all significantly different from zero at the 1 percent level. At higher lags, the own- and

Table 5.3. *Analysis of the profitability of the return-reversal strategy applied to weekly returns, for the sample of 551 CRSP NYSE–AMEX stocks with nonmissing weekly returns from July 6, 1962, to 31 December 1987 (1330 weeks). Expected profits is given by $E[\pi_t(k)] = C_k + O_k - \sigma^2(\mu)$, where C_k depends only on cross-autocovariances and O_k depends only on own-autocovariances. All z-statistics are asymptotically $N(0,1)$ under the null hypothesis that the relevant population value is zero, and are robust to heteroskedasticity and autocorrelation. The average long position $\bar{I}_t(k)$ is also reported, with its sample standard deviation in parentheses underneath. The analysis is conducted for all stocks as well as for the five size-sorted quintiles; to conserve space, results for the second and fourth quintiles have been omitted.*

Portfolio	Lag k	$\hat{C}_k^a$ (z-stat)	$\hat{O}_k^a$ (z-stat)	$\sigma^2(\hat{\mu})^a$	$\hat{E}[\pi_t(k)]^a$ (z-stat)	$\bar{I}_t(k)^a$ (SD^a)	%-$\hat{C}_k$	%-$\hat{O}_k$	%-$\sigma^2(\hat{\mu})$
All Stocks	1	0.841 (4.95)	0.862 (4.54)	0.009	1.694 (20.81)	151.9 (31.0)	49.6	50.9	−0.5
Smallest	1	2.048 (6.36)	2.493 (7.12)	0.009	4.532 (18.81)	208.8 (47.3)	45.2	55.0	−0.2
Central	1	0.703 (4.67)	0.366 (2.03)	0.011	1.058 (13.84)	138.4 (32.2)	66.5	34.6	−1.0
Largest	1	0.188 (1.18)	0.433 (2.61)	0.005	0.617 (11.22)	117.0 (28.1)	30.5	70.3	−0.8
All Stocks	2	0.253 (1.64)	0.298 (1.67)	0.009	0.542 (10.63)	151.8 (31.0)	46.7	54.9	−1.6
Smallest	2	0.803 (3.29)	0.421 (1.49)	0.009	1.216 (8.86)	208.8 (47.3)	66.1	34.7	−0.7
Central	2	0.184 (1.20)	0.308 (1.64)	0.011	0.481 (7.70)	138.3 (32.2)	38.3	64.0	−2.3
Largest	2	−0.053 (−0.39)	0.366 (2.28)	0.005	0.308 (5.89)	116.9 (28.1)	−17.3	118.9	−1.6

(continued)

Table 5.3. (continued)

Portfolio	Lag k	$\hat{C}_k^a$ (z-stat)	$\hat{O}_k^a$ (z-stat)	$\sigma^2(\hat{\mu})^a$	$\hat{E}[\pi_t(k)]^a$ (z-stat)	$\bar{I}_t(k)^a$ (SD)^a	%-$\hat{C}_k$	%-$\hat{O}_k$	%-$\sigma^2(\hat{\mu})$
All Stocks	3	0.223 (1.60)	−0.066 (−0.39)	0.009	0.149 (3.01)	151.7 (30.9)	149.9	−44.0	−5.9
Smallest	3	0.552 (2.73)	0.038 (0.14)	0.009	0.582 (3.96)	208.7 (47.3)	94.9	6.6	−1.5
Central	3	0.237 (1.66)	−0.192 (−1.07)	0.011	0.035 (0.50)	138.2 (32.1)	677.6	−546.7	−30.9
Largest	3	0.064 (0.39)	−0.003 (−0.02)	0.005	0.056 (1.23)	116.9 (28.1)	114.0	−5.3	−8.8
All Stocks	4	0.056 (0.43)	0.083 (0.51)	0.009	0.130 (2.40)	151.7 (30.9)	43.3	63.5	−6.7
Smallest	4	0.305 (1.53)	0.159 (0.59)	0.009	0.455 (3.27)	208.7 (47.3)	67.0	34.9	−1.9
Central	4	0.023 (0.18)	−0.045 (−0.26)	0.011	−0.033 (−0.44)	138.2 (32.0)	—^{b}	—^{b}	—^{b}
Largest	4	−0.097 (−0.65)	0.128 (0.77)	0.005	0.026 (0.52)	116.8 (28.0)	−374.6	493.4	−18.8

^{a}Multiplied by 10,000.
^{b}Not computed when expected profits are negative.

cross-autocovariance terms are generally insignificant. However, estimated expected profits retains its significance even at lag 4, largely due to the behavior of small stocks. The curious fact that $\hat{E}[\pi_t(k)]$ is statistically different from zero whereas $\hat{C}_k$ and $\hat{O}_k$ are not suggests that there is important negative correlation between the two estimators $\hat{C}_k$ and $\hat{O}_k$.[16] That is, although they are both noisy estimates, the variance of their sum is less than each of their variances because they co-vary negatively. Since $\hat{C}_k$ and $\hat{O}_k$ are both functions of second moments and co-moments, significant correlation of the two estimators implies the importance of fourth co-moments, perhaps as a result of co-skewness or kurtosis. This is beyond the scope of this chapter, but bears further investigation.

Table 5.4 also reports the average long (and hence short) positions generated by the return-reversal strategy over the 1330-week sample period. For all stocks, the average weekly long-short position is $152 and the average weekly profit is $1.69. In contrast, applying the same strategy to a portfolio of small stocks yields an expected profit of $4.53 per week, but requires only $209 long and short each week on average. The ratio of expected profits to average long investment is 1.1 percent for all stocks, and 2.2 percent for stocks in the smallest quintile. Of course, in the absence of market frictions such comparisons are irrelevant, since an arbitrage portfolio strategy may be scaled arbitrarily. However, if the size of one's long-short position is constrained, as is sometimes the case in practice, then the average investment figures reported in Table 5.4 suggest that applying the contrarian strategy to small firms would be more profitable on average.

Using stocks with continuous listing for over 20 years obviously induces a survivorship bias that is difficult to evaluate. To reduce this bias we have performed similar analyses for two subsamples: stocks with continuous listing for the first and second halves of the 1330-week sample respectively. In both subperiods positive cross effects account for at least 50 percent of expected profits at lag 1, and generally more at higher lags. Since the patterns are virtually identical to those in Table 5.4, to conserve space we omit these additional tables.

To develop further intuition for the pattern of these cross effects, we report in Table 5.4 cross-autocorrelation matrices $\hat{\Upsilon}_k$ for the vector of returns on the five size-sorted quintiles and the equal-weighted index using the sample of 551 stocks. Let Z_t denote the vector $[R_{1t}\ R_{2t}\ R_{3t}\ R_{4t}\ R_{5t}\ R_{mt}]'$, where R_{it} is the return on the equal-weighted portfolio of stocks in the ith quintile, and R_{mt} is the return on the equal-weighted portfolio of all stocks. Then the kth-order autocorrelation *matrix* of Z_t is given by $\Upsilon_k \equiv D^{-1/2}E[(Z_{t-k} - \mu)(Z_t - \mu)'] = D^{-1/2}$, where $D \equiv \text{diag}[\sigma_1^2, \ldots, \sigma_5^2, \sigma_m^2]$ and $\mu \equiv E[Z_t]$. By

---

[16]We have investigated the unlikely possibility that $\sigma^2(\hat{\mu})$ is responsible for this anomaly; it is not.

Table 5.4. *Autocorrelation matrices of the vector $Z_t \equiv [R_{1t}\, R_{2t}\, R_{3t}\, R_{4t}\, R_{5t}\, R_{mt}]'$ where R_{it} is the return on the portfolio of stocks in the ith quintile, $i = 1, \ldots, 5$ (quintile 1 contains the smallest stocks) and R_{mt} is the return on the equal-weighted index, for the sample of 551 stocks with nonmissing weekly returns from July 6, 1962, to December 31, 1987 (1330 observations). Note that $\Upsilon_k \equiv D^{-1/2}\mathrm{E}[(Z_{t-k}-\mu)(Z_t - \mu)']D^{-1/2}$ where $D \equiv \mathrm{diag}[\sigma_1^2, \ldots, \sigma_5^2, \sigma_m^2]$, thus the (i, j)th element is the correlation between R_{it-k} and R_{jt}. Asymptotic standard errors for the autocorrelations under an IID null hypothesis are given by $1/\sqrt{T} = 0.027$.*

	R_{1t}	R_{2t}	R_{3t}	R_{4t}	R_{5t}	R_{mt}
R_{1t}	1.000	0.919	0.857	0.830	0.747	0.918
R_{2t}	0.919	1.000	0.943	0.929	0.865	0.976
$\hat{\Upsilon}_0 = \quad R_{3t}$	0.857	0.943	1.000	0.964	0.925	0.979
R_{4t}	0.830	0.929	0.964	1.000	0.946	0.974
R_{5t}	0.747	0.865	0.925	0.946	1.000	0.933
R_{mt}	0.918	0.976	0.979	0.974	0.933	1.000

	R_{1t}	R_{2t}	R_{3t}	R_{4t}	R_{5t}	R_{mt}
R_{1t-1}	0.333	0.244	0.143	0.101	0.020	0.184
R_{2t-1}	0.334	0.252	0.157	0.122	0.033	0.195
$\hat{\Upsilon}_1 = \quad R_{3t-1}$	0.325	0.265	0.175	0.140	0.051	0.207
R_{4t-1}	0.316	0.262	0.177	0.139	0.050	0.204
R_{5t-1}	0.276	0.230	0.154	0.122	0.044	0.178
R_{mt-1}	0.333	0.262	0.168	0.130	0.041	0.202

	R_{1t}	R_{2t}	R_{3t}	R_{4t}	R_{5t}	R_{mt}
R_{1t-2}	0.130	0.087	0.044	0.022	0.005	0.064
R_{2t-2}	0.133	0.101	0.058	0.039	0.017	0.076
$\hat{\Upsilon}_2 = \quad R_{3t-2}$	0.114	0.088	0.046	0.027	0.002	0.061
R_{4t-2}	0.101	0.085	0.048	0.029	0.008	0.059
R_{5t-2}	0.067	0.055	0.020	0.008	−0.012	0.031
R_{mt-2}	0.115	0.087	0.045	0.026	0.004	0.061

	R_{1t}	R_{2t}	R_{3t}	R_{4t}	R_{5t}	R_{mt}
R_{1t-3}	0.089	0.047	0.015	0.013	−0.005	0.036
R_{2t-3}	0.094	0.066	0.038	0.041	0.018	0.056
$\hat{\Upsilon}_3 = \quad R_{3t-3}$	0.096	0.079	0.059	0.061	0.041	0.072
R_{4t-3}	0.084	0.067	0.047	0.049	0.031	0.059
R_{5t-3}	0.053	0.044	0.031	0.034	0.015	0.038
R_{mt-3}	0.087	0.063	0.038	0.040	0.020	0.054

(continued)

Table 5.4. (continued)

		R_{1t}	R_{2t}	R_{3t}	R_{4t}	R_{5t}	R_{mt}
	R_{1t-4}	0.050	0.001	−0.014	−0.029	−0.030	−0.002
	R_{2t-4}	0.064	0.023	−0.002	−0.012	−0.020	0.014
$\hat{\Upsilon}_4 =$	R_{3t-4}	0.065	0.029	0.006	−0.002	−0.017	0.019
	R_{4t-4}	0.072	0.042	0.017	0.005	−0.008	0.029
	R_{5t-4}	0.048	0.023	0.002	−0.007	−0.022	0.011
	R_{mt-4}	0.062	0.024	0.001	−0.010	−0.021	0.014

this convention, the (i, j)th element of Υ_k is the correlation of R_{it-k} with R_{jt}. The estimator $\hat{\Upsilon}_k$ is the usual sample autocorrelation matrix. Note that it is only the upper left 5×5 submatrix of Υ_k that is related to Γ_k, since the full matrix Υ_k also contains autocorrelations between portfolio returns and the equal-weighted market index R_{mt}.[17]

An interesting pattern emerges from Table 5.4: The entries below the diagonals of $\hat{\Upsilon}_k$ are almost always larger than those above the diagonals (excluding the last row and column, which are the autocovariances between portfolio returns and the market). This implies that current returns of smaller stocks are correlated with past returns of larger stocks, but not vice versa, a distinct lead–lag relation based on size. For example, the first-order autocorrelation between last week's return on large stocks (R_{5t-1}) with this week's return on small stocks (R_{1t}) is 27.6 percent, whereas the first-order autocorrelation between last week's return on small stocks (R_{1t-1}) with this week's return on large stocks (R_{5t}) is only 2.0 percent! Similar patterns may be seen in the higher-order autocorrelation matrices, although the magnitudes are smaller since the higher-order cross-autocorrelations decay. The asymmetry of the $\hat{\Upsilon}_k$ matrices implies that the autocovariance matrix estimators $\hat{\Gamma}_k$ are also asymmetric. This provides further evidence against the sum of the positively autocorrelated factor and the bid–ask spread as the true return-generating process, since Equation (5.3.34) implies symmetric autocovariance (and hence autocorrelation) matrices.

Of course, the nontrading model of Section 5.3.4 also yields an asymmetric autocorrelation matrix. However, it is easy to see that unrealistically high probabilities of nontrading are required to generate cross-autocorrelations of the magnitude reported in Table 5.4. For example, consider the first-order cross-autocorrelation between R_{2t-1} (the return of the second-smallest quintile portfolio) and R_{1t} (the return of the smallest quintile portfolio) which is 33.4 percent. Using Equation (5.3.28) and (5.3.32) with $k = 1$

---

[17]We include the market return in our autocovariance matrices so that those who wish to may compute portfolio betas and market volatilities from our tables.

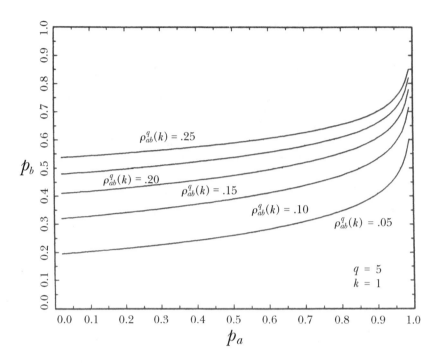

Figure 5.1. *Loci of nontrading probability pairs* (p_a, p_b) *that imply a constant cross-autocorrelation* $\rho^q_{ab}(k)$, *for* $\rho^q_{ab}(k) = .05, .10, .15, .20, .25, k = 1, q = 5$. *If the probabilities are interpreted as* daily *probabilities of nontrading, then* $p^q_{ab}(k)$ *represents the first-order weekly cross-autocorrelation between this week's return to portfolio a and next week's return to portfolio b when* $q = 5$ *and* $k = 1$.

and $q = 5$ days, we may compute the set of daily nontrading probabilities (p_1, p_2) of portfolios 1 and 2, respectively, that yield such a weekly cross-autocorrelation. For example, the combinations (.010, .616), (.100, .622), (.500, .659), (.750, .700), and (.990, .887) all yield a cross-autocorrelation of 33.4 percent. But none of these combinations are empirically plausible nontrading probabilities—the first pair implies an average duration of non-trading of 1.6 days for securities in the second smallest quintile, and the implications of the other pairs are even more extreme! Figure 5.1 plots the iso-autocorrelation loci for various levels of cross-autocorrelations, from which it is apparent that nontrading cannot be the sole source of cross-autocorrelation in stock market returns.[18]

[18]Moreover, the implications for nontrading probabilities are even more extreme if we consider *hourly* instead of daily nontrading, that is, if we set $q = 35$ hours (roughly the number of trading hours in a week). Also, relaxing the restrictive assumptions of the nontrading model

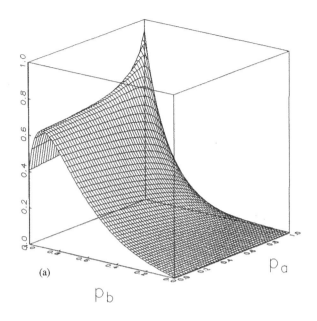

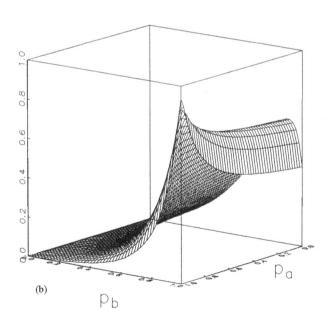

Figure 5.2. *Cross-autocorrelation* $\rho_{ab}^{q}(k)$ *as a function of* p_a *and* p_b, *for* $q = 5$, $k = 1$. *(a) Front view; (b) rear view.*

Further evidence against nontrading comes from the pattern of cross-autocorrelations within each column of the first-order autocorrelation matrix $\hat{\Upsilon}_1$.[19] For example, consider the first column of $\hat{\Upsilon}_1$ whose first element is .333 and fifth element is .276. These values show that the correlation between the returns of portolio a this week and those of portfolio b next week do not change significantly as portfolio a varies from the smallest firms to the largest. However, if cross-autocorrelations on the order of 30 percent are truly due to nontrading effects, Equation (5.3.32) implies an inverted U-shaped pattern for the cross-autocorrelation as portfolio a is varied. This is most easily seen in Figure 5.2a and b, in which an inverted U-shape is obtained by considering the intersection of the cross-autocorrelation surface with a vertical plane parallel to the p_a axis and perpendicular to the p_b axis, where the intersection occurs in the region where the surface rises to a level around 30 percent. The resulting curve is the nontrading-induced cross-autocorrelation for various values of p_a, holding p_b fixed at some value. These figures show that the empirical cross-autocorrelations are simply not consistent with nontrading, either in pattern or in the implied nontrading probabilities.

The results in Tables 5.3 and 5.4 point to the complex patterns of cross effects among securities as significant sources of positive index autocorrelation, as well as expected profits for contrarian investment rules. The presence of these cross effects has important implications, irrespective of the nature of contrarian profits. For example, if such profits are genuine, the fact that at least half may be attributed to cross-autocovariances suggests further investigation of mechanisms by which aggregate shocks to the economy are transmitted from large capitalization companies to small ones.

5.5 Long Horizons Versus Short Horizons

Since several recent studies have employed longer-horizon returns in examining contrarian strategies and the predictability of stock returns, we provide some discussion here of our decision to focus on weekly returns. Distinguishing between short- and long-return horizons is important, as it is now well known that weekly fluctuations in stock returns differ in many ways from movements in three- to five-year returns. Therefore, inferences concerning the performance of the long-horizon strategies cannot be drawn directly from results such as ours. Because our analysis of the contrarian investment strategy (5.3.1) uses only weekly returns, we have little to say

---

of Section 5.3.4 does not affect the order of magnitude of the above calculations. See Lo and MacKinlay (1990c) for further details.

[19]We are grateful to Michael Brennan for suggesting this analysis.

about the behavior of long-horizon returns. Nevertheless, some suggestive comparisons are possible.

Statistically, the predictability of short-horizon returns, especially weekly and monthly, is stronger and more consistent through time. For example, Blume and Friend (1978) have estimated a time series of cross-sectional correlation coefficients of returns in adjacent months using monthly NYSE data from 1926 to 1975, and found that in 422 of the 598 months the sample correlation was negative. This proportion of negative correlations is considerably higher than expected if returns are unforecastable. But in their framework, a negative correlation coefficient implies positive expected profits in our Equation (5.3.4) with $k = 1$. Jegadeesh (1990) provides further analysis of monthly data and reaches similar conclusions. The results are even more striking for weekly stock returns, as we have seen. For example, Lo and MacKinlay (1988b) show evidence of strong predictability for portfolio returns using New York and American Stock Exchange data from 1962 to 1985. Using the same data, Lehmann (1990) shows that a contrarian strategy similar to (5.3.1) is almost always profitable.[20] Together these two observations imply the importance of cross-effects, a fact we established directly in Section 5.4.

Evidence regarding the predictability of long-horizon returns is more mixed. Perhaps the most well-known studies of a contrarian strategy using long-horizon returns are those of DeBondt and Thaler (1985, 1987) in which winners are sold and losers are purchased, but where the holding period over which winning and losing is determined is three years. Based on data from 1926 through 1981 they conclude that the market overreacts since the losers outperform the winners. However, since the difference in performance is due largely to the January seasonal in small firms, it seems inappropriate to attribute this to long-run overreaction.[21]

Fama and French (1988) and Poterba and Summers (1988) have also examined the predictability of long-horizon portfolio returns and find negative serial correlation, a result consistent with those of DeBondt and Thaler. However, this negative serial dependence is quite sensitive to the sample period employed, and may be largely due to the first 10 years of the 1926 to 1987 sample (see Kim, Nelson, and Startz, 1991). Furthermore, the

---

[20]Since such profits are sensitive to the size of the transactions costs (for some cases a one-way transactions cost of 0.40 percent is sufficient to render them positive half the time and negative the other half), the importance of Lehmann's findings hinges on the relevant costs of turning over securities frequently. The fact that our Table 5.4 shows the smallest firms to be the most profitable on average (as measured by the ratio of expected profits to the dollar amount long) may indicate that a round-trip transaction cost of 0.80 percent is low. In addition to the bid–ask spread, which is generally $0.125 or larger and will be a larger percentage of the price for smaller stocks, the price effect of trades on these relatively thinly traded securities may become significant.

[21]See Zarowin (1990) for further discussion.

statistical inference on which the long-horizon predictability is based has been questioned by Richardson (1993), who shows that properly adjusting for the fact that multiple time horizons (and test statistics) are considered simultaneously yields serial correlation estimates that are statistically indistinguishable from zero.

These considerations point to short-horizon returns as the more immediate source from which evidence of predictability and stock market overreaction might be culled. This is not to say that a careful investigation of returns over longer time spans will be uninformative. Indeed, it may be only at these lower frequencies that the effect of economic factors, such as the business cycle, is detectable. Moreover, to the extent that transaction costs are greater for strategies exploiting short-horizon predictability, long-horizon predictability may be a more genuine form of unexploited profit opportunity.

5.6 Conclusion

Traditional tests of the random walk hypothesis for stock market prices have generally focused on the returns either to individual securities or to portfolios of securities. In this chapter, we show that the cross-sectional interaction of security returns over time is an important aspect of stock-price dynamics. We document the fact that stock returns are often positively cross-autocorrelated, which reconciles the negative serial dependence in individual security returns with the positive autocorrelation in market indexes. This also implies that stock market overreaction need not be the sole explanation for the profitability in contrarian portfolio strategies. Indeed, the empirical evidence suggests that less than 50 percent of the expected profits from a contrarian investment rule may be attributed to overreaction; the majority of such profits is due to the cross effects among the securities. We have also shown that these cross effects have a very specific pattern for size-sorted portfolios: They display a lead–lag relation, with the returns of larger stocks generally leading those of smaller ones. But a tantalizing question remains to be investigated: What are the economic sources of positive cross-autocorrelations across securities?

Appendix A5

Derivation of Equation (5.3.4)

$$\pi_t(k) \;=\; \sum_{i=1}^{N} \omega_{it}(k) R_{it} = -\frac{1}{N} \sum_{i=1}^{N} (R_{it-k} - R_{mt-k}) R_{it} \tag{A5.1}$$

$$=\; -\frac{1}{N} \sum_{i=1}^{N} R_{it-k} R_{it} + \frac{1}{N} \sum_{i=1}^{N} R_{mt-k} R_{it} \tag{A5.2}$$

$$=\; -\frac{1}{N} \sum_{i=1}^{N} R_{it-k} R_{it} + R_{mt-k} R_{mt} \tag{A5.3}$$

$$\mathrm{E}[\pi_t(k)] \;=\; -\frac{1}{N} \sum_{i=1}^{N} \mathrm{E}[R_{it-k} R_{it}] + \mathrm{E}[R_{mt-k} R_{mt}] \tag{A5.4}$$

$$=\; -\frac{1}{N} \sum_{i=1}^{N} \big(\mathrm{Cov}[R_{it-k}, R_{it}] + \mu_i^2 \big)$$
$$+ \big(\mathrm{Cov}[R_{mt-k}, R_{mt}] + \mu_m^2 \big) \tag{A5.5}$$

$$=\; -\frac{1}{N} \mathrm{tr}(\Gamma_k) - \frac{1}{N} \sum_{i=1}^{N} \mu_i^2 + \frac{\iota' \Gamma_k \iota}{N^2} + \mu_m^2 \tag{A5.6}$$

$$\mathrm{E}[\pi_t(k)] \;=\; \frac{\iota' \Gamma_k \iota}{N^2} - \frac{1}{N} \mathrm{tr}(\Gamma_k) - \frac{1}{N} \sum_{i=1}^{N} (\mu_i - \mu_m)^2.$$

Sampling Theory for $\hat{C}_k$, $\hat{O}_k$, and $\hat{E}[\pi_t(k)]$

To derive the sampling theory for the estimators $\hat{C}_k$, $\hat{O}_k$, and $\hat{E}[\pi_t(k)]$, we reexpress them as averages of artificial time series and then apply standard asymptotic theory to those averages. We require the following assumptions:

(A1) For all t, i, j, and k the following condition is satisfied for finite constants $K > 0$, $\delta > 0$, and $r \geq 0$:

$$E[|R_{it-k}R_{jt}|^{4(r+\delta)}] < K < \infty. \tag{A5.7}$$

(A2) The vector of returns R_t is either α-mixing with coefficients of size $2r/(r-1)$ or ϕ-mixing with coefficients of size $2r/(2r-1)$.

These assumptions specify the trade-off between dependence and heterogeneity in R_t that is admissible while still permitting some form of the central limit theorem to obtain. The weaker is the moment condition (Assumption (A2)), the quicker the dependence in R_t must decay, and vice versa.[22] Observe that the covariance-stationarity of R_t is *not* required. Denote by C_{kt} and O_{kt} the following two time series:

$$C_{kt} \equiv R_{mt-k}R_{mt} - \hat{\mu}_m^2 - \frac{1}{N^2}\sum_{i=1}^{N}(R_{it-k}R_{it} - \hat{\mu}_i^2) \tag{A5.8}$$

$$O_{kt} \equiv -\frac{N-1}{N^2}\sum_{i=1}^{N}(R_{it-k}R_{it} - \hat{\mu}_i^2) \tag{A5.9}$$

where $\hat{\mu}_i$ and $\hat{\mu}_m$ are the usual sample means of the returns to security i and the equal-weighted market index, respectively. Then the estimators $\hat{C}_k$, $\hat{O}_k$, and $\sigma^2(\hat{\mu})$ are given by

$$\hat{C}_k = \frac{1}{T-k}\sum_{t=k+1}^{T} C_{kt} \tag{A5.10}$$

$$\hat{O}_k = \frac{1}{T-k}\sum_{t=k+1}^{T} O_{kt} \tag{A5.11}$$

$$\sigma^2(\hat{\mu}) = \frac{1}{N}\sum_{i=1}^{N}(\hat{\mu}_i - \hat{\mu}_m)^2. \tag{A5.12}$$

Because we have not assumed covariance-stationarity, the population quantities C_k and O_k obviously need not be interpretable according to Equation

---

[22]See Phillips (1987) and White (1984) for further discussion of this trade-off.

(5.3.8) since the autocovariance matrix of R_t may now be time dependent. However, we do wish to interpret C_k and O_k as some fixed quantities that are time independent; thus, we require:

(A3) The following limits exist and are finite:

$$\lim_{T \to \infty} \frac{1}{T-k} \sum_{t=k+1}^{T} \mathrm{E}[C_{kt}] = C_k \qquad (A5.13)$$

$$\lim_{T \to \infty} \frac{1}{T-k} \sum_{t=k+1}^{T} \mathrm{E}[O_{kt}] = O_k. \qquad (A5.14)$$

Although the expectations $\mathrm{E}(C_{kt})$ and $\mathrm{E}(O_{kt})$ may be time dependent, Assumption (A3) asserts that their averages converge to well-defined limits; hence, the quantities C_k and O_k may be viewed as "average" cross- and own-autocovariance contributions to expected profits. Consistent estimators of the asymptotic variance of the estimators $\hat{C}_k$ and $\hat{O}_k$ may then be obtained along the lines of Newey and West (1987), and are given by $\hat{\sigma}_c^2$ and $\hat{\sigma}_o^2$, respectively, where

$$\hat{\sigma}_c^2 = \frac{1}{T-k}\left[\hat{\gamma}_{c_k}(0) + 2\sum_{j=1}^{q} \alpha_j(q)\, \hat{\gamma}_{c_k}(j) \right] \qquad (A5.15)$$

$$\hat{\sigma}_o^2 = \frac{1}{T-k}\left[\hat{\gamma}_{o_k}(0) + 2\sum_{j=1}^{q} \alpha_j(q)\, \hat{\gamma}_{o_k}(j) \right] \qquad (A5.16)$$

$$\alpha_j(q) \equiv 1 - \frac{j}{q+1} \qquad q < T \qquad (A5.17)$$

and $\hat{\gamma}_{c_k}(j)$ and $\hat{\gamma}_{o_k}(j)$ are the sample jth order autocovariances of the time series C_{kt} and O_{kt}, respectively, that is,

$$\hat{\gamma}_{c_k}(j) = \frac{1}{T-k} \sum_{t=k+j+1}^{T} (C_{kt-j} - \hat{C}_k)(C_{kt} - \hat{C}_k) \qquad (A5.18)$$

$$\hat{\gamma}_{o_k}(j) = \frac{1}{T-k} \sum_{t=k+j+1}^{T} (O_{kt-j} - \hat{O}_k)(O_{kt} - \hat{O}_k). \qquad (A5.19)$$

Assuming that $q \sim o(T^{1/4})$, Newey and West (1987) show the consistency (A1)–(A3).[23] Observe that these asymptotic variance estimators are robust to general forms of heteroskedasticity and autocorrelation in the C_{kt} and O_{kt}

---

[23] In our empirical work we choose $q = 8$.

time series. Since the derivation of heteroskedasticity- and autocorrelation-consistent standard errors for the estimated expected profits $\hat{E}[\pi_t(k)]$ is virtually identical, we leave this to the reader.

6

Long-Term Memory
in Stock Market Prices

6.1 Introduction

THAT ECONOMIC TIME SERIES can exhibit long-range dependence has been a hypothesis of many early theories of the trade and business cycles. Such theories were often motivated by the distinct but nonperiodic cyclical patterns that typified plots of economic aggregates over time, cycles of many periods, some that seem nearly as long as the entire span of the sample. In the frequency domain such time series are said to have power at low frequencies. So common was this particular feature of the data that Granger (1966) considered it the "typical spectral shape of an economic variable." It has also been called the "Joseph Effect" by Mandelbrot and Wallis (1968), a playful but not inappropriate biblical reference to the Old Testament prophet who foretold of the seven years of plenty followed by the seven years of famine that Egypt was to experience. Indeed, Nature's predilection towards long-range dependence has been well-documented in hydrology, meteorology, and geophysics, and to the extent that the ultimate sources of uncertainty in economics are natural phenomena like rainfall or earthquakes, we might also expect to find long-term memory in economic time series.[1]

The presence of long-memory components in asset returns has important implications for many of the paradigms used in modern financial economics. For example, optimal consumption/savings and portfolio decisions may become extremely sensitive to the investment horizon if stock returns were long-range dependent. Problems also arise in the pricing of derivative securities (such as options and futures) with martingale methods, since the continuous time stochastic processes most commonly employed are incon-

---

[1] Haubrich (1993) and Haubrich and Lo (1989) provide a less fanciful theory of long-range dependence in economic aggregates.

sistent with long-term memory (see Maheswaran, 1990; Maheswaran and Sims, 1990; Sims, 1984, for example). Traditional tests of the capital asset pricing model and the arbitrage pricing theory are no longer valid since the usual forms of statistical inference do not apply to time series exhibiting such persistence. And the conclusions of more recent tests of "efficient" markets hypotheses or stock market rationality also hang precariously on the presence or absence of long-term memory.[2]

Among the first to have considered the possibility and implications of persistent statistical dependence in asset returns was Mandelbrot (1971). Since then, several empirical studies have lent further support to Mandelbrot's findings. For example, Greene and Fielitz (1977) claim to have found long-range dependence in the daily returns of many securities listed on the New York Stock Exchange. More recent investigations have uncovered anomalous behavior in long-horizon stock returns;[3] alternately attributed to speculative fads and to time-varying conditional expected returns, these long-run swings may be further evidence of the Joseph effect.

In this chapter we develop a test for such forms of long-range dependence using a simple generalization of a statistic first proposed by the English hydrologist Harold Edwin Hurst (1951). This statistic, called the "rescaled range" or "range over standard deviation" or "R/S" statistic, has been refined by Mandelbrot (1972, 1975) and others in several important ways (see, for example, Mandelbrot and Taqqu, 1979, and Mandelbrot and Wallis, 1968, 1969a–c). However, such refinements were not designed to distinguish between short-range and long-range dependence (in a sense to be made precise below), a severe shortcoming in applications of R/S analysis to recent stock returns data since Lo and MacKinlay (1988b, 1990b) show that such data display substantial short-range dependence. Therefore, to be of current interest, any empirical investigation of long-term memory in stock returns must first account for the presence of higher frequency autocorrelation.

By modifying the rescaled range appropriately, we construct a test statistic that is robust to short-range dependence, and derive its limiting distribution under both short-range and long-range dependence. Contrary to the findings of Greene and Fielitz (1977) and others, when this statistic is applied to daily and monthly stock return indexes over several different sample periods and sub-periods, there is no evidence of long-range dependence once the effects of short-range dependence are accounted for. Monte Carlo experiments indicate that the modified R/S test has reasonable power against at least two particular models of long-range dependence, suggesting

---

[2]See LeRoy (1989) and Merton (1987) for excellent surveys of this recent literature.

[3]See, for example, Fama and French (1988), Jegadeesh (1989, 1990), and Poterba and Summers (1988).

that the time series behavior of stock returns may be adequately captured by more conventional models of short-range dependence.

The particular notions of short-term and long-term memory are defined in Section 6.2 and some illustrative examples are given. The test statistic is presented in Section 6.3 and its limiting distributions under the null and alternative hypotheses are derived via functional central limit theory. In Section 6.4 the empirical results are reported, and Monte Carlo simulations that illustrate the size and power of the test in finite samples are presented in Section 6.5. We conclude in Section 6.6.

6.2 Long-Range Versus Short-Range Dependence

To develop a method for detecting long-term memory, the distinction between long-range and short-range statistical dependence must be made precise. One of the most widely used concepts of short-range dependence is the notion of "strong-mixing" due to Rosenblatt (1956), a measure of the decline in statistical dependence between events separated by successively longer spans of time. Heuristically, a time series is strong-mixing if the maximal dependence between events at any two dates becomes trivially small as the time span between those two dates increases. By controlling the rate at which the dependence between past and future events declines, it is possible to extend the usual laws of large numbers and central limit theorems to dependent sequences of random variables. We adopt strong-mixing as an operational definition of short-range dependence in the null hypothesis of Section 6.2.1. In Section 6.2.2, we give examples of alternatives to short-range dependence such as the class of fractionally-differenced processes proposed by Granger and Joyeux (1980), Hosking (1981), and Mandelbrot and Van Ness (1968).

6.2.1 The Null Hypothesis

Let P_t denote the price of an asset at time t and define $X_t \equiv \log P_t - \log P_{t-1}$ to be the continuously compounded single-period return of that asset from $t-1$ to t. With little loss in generality, let all dividend payments be reinvested in the asset so that X_t is indeed the total return of the asset between $t-1$ and t.[4] It is assumed throughout that

$$X_t = \mu + \epsilon_t, \tag{6.2.1}$$

where μ is an arbitrary but fixed parameter and ϵ_t is a zero mean random variable. Let this stochastic process $\{X_t(\omega)\}$ be defined on the probability

---

[4]This is in fact how the stock returns data are constructed.

space $(\Omega, \mathcal{F}, P)$ and define

$$\alpha(\mathcal{A}, \mathcal{B}) \equiv \sup_{\{A \in \mathcal{A}, B \in \mathcal{B}\}} |P(A \cap B) - P(A)P(B)|, \quad \mathcal{A} \subset \mathcal{F}, \mathcal{B} \subset \mathcal{F}. \quad (6.2.2)$$

The quantity $\alpha(\mathcal{A}, \mathcal{B})$ is a measure of the dependence between the two σ-fields $\mathcal{A}$ and $\mathcal{B}$ in $\mathcal{F}$. Denote by $\mathcal{B}_s^t$ the Borel σ-field generated by $\{X_s(\omega), \ldots, X_t(\omega)\}$, i.e., $\mathcal{B}_s^t \equiv \sigma(X_s(\omega), \ldots, X_t(\omega)) \subset \mathcal{F}$. Define the coefficients α_k as

$$\alpha_k \equiv \sup_j \alpha(\mathcal{B}_{-\infty}^j, \mathcal{B}_{j+k}^\infty). \quad (6.2.3)$$

Then $\{X_t(\omega)\}$ is said to be *strong-mixing* if $\lim_{k \to \infty} \alpha_k = 0.$[5] Such mixing conditions have been used extensively in the recent literature to relax the assumptions that ensure the consistency and asymptotic normality of various econometric estimators (see, for example, Chan and Wei, 1988; Phillips, 1987; White, 1980; White and Domowitz, 1984). As Phillips (1987) observes, these conditions are satisfied by a great many stochastic processes, including all Gaussian finite-order stationary ARMA models. Moreover, the inclusion of a moment condition also allows for heterogeneously distributed sequences, an especially important extension in view of the apparent instabilities of financial time series.

In addition to strong mixing, several other conditions are required as part of the null hypothesis in order to develop a sampling theory for the test statistic proposed in Section 6.3. In particular, the null hypothesis is composed of the following four conditions on ϵ_t:

(A1) $E[\epsilon_t] = 0$ for all t;

(A2) $\sup_t E[|\epsilon_t|^\beta] < \infty$ for some $\beta > 2$;

(A3) $0 < \sigma^2 = \lim_{n \to \infty} E\left[\frac{1}{n} \left(\sum_{j=1}^n \epsilon_j \right)^2 \right] < \infty$;

(A4) $\{\epsilon_t\}$ is strong-mixing with mixing coefficients α_k that satisfy

$$\sum_{j=1}^\infty \alpha_j^{1 - \frac{2}{\beta}} < \infty.$$

Condition (A1) is standard. Conditions (A2) through (A4) are restrictions on the maximal degree of dependence and heterogeneity allowable while

---

[5]There are several other ways of measuring the degree statistical dependence, giving rise to other notions of "mixing." For further details, see Eberlein and Taqqu (1986), Rosenblatt (1956), and White (1984).

still permitting some form of the law of large numbers and the (functional) central limit theorem to obtain. Although (A2) rules out infinite variance marginal distributions of ϵ_t such as those in the stable family with characteristic exponent less than 2, the disturbances may still exhibit unconditional leptokurtosis via time-varying conditional moments (e.g., conditional heteroskedasticity). Moreover, since there is a trade-off between (A2) and (A4), the uniform bound on the moments can be relaxed if the mixing coefficients decline faster than (A4) requires.[6] For example, if ϵ_t is required to have finite absolute moments of all orders (corresponding to $\beta \rightarrow \infty$), then α_k must decline faster than $1/k$. However, if ϵ_t is restricted to have finite moments only up to order 4, then α_k must decline faster than $1/k^2$. These conditions are discussed at greater length by Phillips (1987).

Of course, it is too much to hope that *all* forms of short-memory processes are captured by (A1)–(A4). For example, if ϵ_t were the first difference of a stationary process, its spectral density at frequency zero vanishes, violating (A3). Yet such a process certainly need not be long-range dependent. A more subtle example is given by Ibragimov and Rozanov (1978)—a stationary Gaussian process with spectral density function

$$f(\omega) = \exp\left\{\sum_{k=1}^{\infty} \frac{\cos k\omega}{k \log k + 1}\right\}, \qquad (6.2.4)$$

which is strong-mixing but has unbounded spectral density at the origin. The stochastic process with $1/f(\omega)$ for its spectral density is also strong-mixing, but $1/f(\omega)$ vanishes at the origin. Although neither process is long-range dependent, they both violate (A3). Unfortunately, a general characterization of the implications of such processes for the behavior of the test statistic proposed in Section 6.3 is currently unavailable. Therefore, a rejection of the null hypothesis does not necessarily imply that long-range dependence is present but merely that, if the rejection is not a type I error, the stochastic process does not satisfy all four conditions simultaneously. Whether or not the composite null (A1)–(A4) is a useful one must therefore depend on the particular application at hand.

In particular, although mixing conditions have been widely used in the recent literature, several other sets of assumptions might have served equally well as our short-range dependent null hypothesis. For example, if $\{\epsilon_t\}$ is assumed to be stationary and ergodic, the moment condition (A2) can be relaxed and more temporal dependence than (A4) is allowable (see Hall and Heyde, 1980). Whether or not the assumption of stationarity is a

---

[6]See Herrndorf (1985). One of Mandelbrot's (1972) arguments in favor of R/S analysis is that finite second moments are not required. This is indeed the case if we are interested only in the almost sure convergence of the statistic. But since for purposes of inference the *limiting distribution* is required, a stronger moment condition is needed here.

restrictive one for financial time series is still an open question. There is ample evidence of changing variances in stock returns over periods longer than five years, but unstable volatilities can be a symptom of *conditional* heteroskedasticity which can manifest itself in stationary time series. Since the empirical evidence regarding changing conditional moments in asset returns is mixed, allowing for nonstationarities in our null hypothesis may still have value. Moreover, (A1)–(A4) may be weakened further, allowing for still more temporal dependence and heterogeneity, hence widening the class of processes contained in our null hypothesis.[7]

Note, however, that conditions (A1)–(A4) are satisfied by many of the recently proposed stochastic models of persistence, such as those of Campbell and Mankiw (1987), Fama and French (1988), and Poterba and Summers (1988). Therefore, since such models of longer-term correlations are contained in our null, the kind of long-range dependence that (A1)–(A4) were designed to exclude are quite different. Although the distinction between dependence in the short run and the long run may appear to be a matter of degree, strongly dependent processes behave so differently from weakly dependent time series that the dichotomy proposed in our null seems most natural. For example, the spectral densities at frequency zero of strongly dependent processes are either unbounded or zero whereas they are nonzero and finite for processes in our null. The partial sums of strongly dependent processes do not converge in distribution at the same rate as weakly dependent series. And graphically, their behavior is marked by cyclical patterns of all kinds, some that are virtually indistinguishable from trends.

6.2.2 Long-Range Dependent Alternatives

In contrast to the short-term memory of "weakly dependent" (i.e., mixing) processes, natural phenomena often display long-term memory in the form of nonperiodic cycles. This has lead several authors to develop stochastic models that exhibit dependence even over very long time spans, such as the fractionally-integrated time series models of Granger (1980), Granger and Joyeux (1980), Hosking (1981), and Mandelbrot and Van Ness (1968). These stochastic processes are not strong-mixing, and have autocorrelation functions that decay at much slower rates than those of weakly dependent processes. For example, let X_t satisfy the following difference equation:

$$(1 - L)^d X_t = \epsilon_t, \qquad \epsilon_t \sim \text{WN}(0, \sigma_\epsilon^2), \qquad (6.2.5)$$

where L is the lag operator and ϵ_t is white noise. Granger and Joyeux (1980) and Hosking (1981) show that when the quantity $(1 - L)^d$ is extended to

---

[7]Specifically, that the sequence $\{\epsilon_t\}$ is strong-mixing may be replaced by the weaker assumption that it is a near-epoch dependent function of a strong-mixing process. See McLeish (1977) and Wooldridge and White (1988) for further details.

noninteger powers of d in the mathematically natural way, the result is a well-defined time series that is said to be "fractionally-differenced" of order d (or, equivalently, "fractionally-integrated" of order $-d$). Briefly, this involves expanding the expression $(1 - L)^d$ via the binomial theorem for noninteger powers:

$$(1 - L)^d = \sum_{k=0}^{\infty} (-1)^k \binom{d}{k} L^k,$$

$$\binom{d}{k} \equiv \frac{d(d-1)(d-2)\cdots(d-k+1)}{k!}, \qquad (6.2.6)$$

and then applying the expansion to X_t:

$$(1 - L)^d X_t = \sum_{k=0}^{\infty} (-1)^k \binom{d}{k} L^k X_t = \sum_{k=0}^{\infty} A_k X_{t-k} = \epsilon_t \qquad (6.2.7)$$

where the autoregressive coefficients A_k are often re-expressed in terms of the gamma function:

$$A_k = (-1)^k \binom{d}{k} = \frac{\Gamma(k-d)}{\Gamma(-d)\,\Gamma(k+1)}. \qquad (6.2.8)$$

X_t may also be viewed mechanically as an infinite-order MA process since

$$X_t = (1 - L)^{-d}\epsilon_t = B(L)\epsilon_t, \qquad B_k = \frac{\Gamma(k+d)}{\Gamma(d)\,\Gamma(k+1)}. \qquad (6.2.9)$$

It is not obvious that such a definition of fractional-differencing might yield a useful stochastic process, but Granger (1980), Granger and Joyeux (1980), and Hosking (1981) show that the characteristics of fractionally-differenced time series are interesting indeed. For example, it may be shown that X_t is stationary and invertible for $d \in (-\frac{1}{2}, \frac{1}{2})$ (see Hosking, 1981), and exhibits a unique kind of dependence that is positive or negative depending on whether d is positive or negative, i.e., the autocorrelation coefficients of X_t are of the same sign as d. So slowly do the autocorrelations decay that when d is positive their sum diverges to infinity, and collapses to zero when d is negative.[8] To develop a sense of this long-range dependence, compare the autocorrelations of a fractionally-differenced X_t with those of a stationary AR(1) in Table 6.1. Although both the AR(1) and the fractionally-differenced ($d = \frac{1}{3}$) series have first-order autocorrelations of 0.500, at lag 25

---

[8]Mandelbrot and others have called the $d < 0$ case "anti-persistence," reserving the term "long-range dependence" for the $d > 0$ case. However, since both cases involve autocorrelations that decay much more slowly than those of more conventional time series, we call both long-range dependent.

Table 6.1. *Comparison of autocorrelation functions of fractionally differenced time series* $(1 - L)^d X_t = \epsilon_t$ *for* $d = \frac{1}{3}$, $-\frac{1}{3}$ *with that of an* AR(1) $X_t = \rho X_{t-1} + \epsilon_t$, $\rho = .5$. *The variance of* ϵ_t *was chosen to yield a unit variance for* X_t *in all three cases.*

Lag k	$\rho(k)$ $[d = \frac{1}{3}]$	$\rho(k)$ $[d = -\frac{1}{3}]$	$\rho(k)$ [AR(1), $\rho = .5$]
1	0.500	−0.250	0.500
2	0.400	−0.071	0.250
3	0.350	−0.036	0.125
4	0.318	−0.022	0.063
5	0.295	−0.015	0.031
10	0.235	−0.005	0.001
25	0.173	−0.001	2.98×10^{-8}
50	0.137	-3.24×10^{-4}	8.88×10^{-16}
100	0.109	-1.02×10^{-4}	7.89×10^{-31}

the AR(1) autocorrelation is 2.98×10^{-8} whereas the fractionally-differenced series has autocorrelation 0.173, declining only to 0.109 at lag 100.

In fact, the defining characteristic of long-range dependent processes has been taken by many to be this slow decay of the autocovariance function. Therefore, more generally, long-range dependent processes may be defined to be those processes with autocovariance functions γ_k such that

$$\gamma_k \sim \begin{cases} k^\nu L(k) & \text{for } \nu \in (-1, 0) \text{ or} \\ -k^\nu L(k) & \text{for } \nu \in (-2, -1), \end{cases} \quad \text{as} \quad k \to \infty, \qquad (6.2.10)$$

where $L(k)$ is any slowly varying function at infinity.[9] This is the definition we shall adopt in the analysis to follow. As an example, the autocovariance function of the fractionally-differenced process (6.2.5) is

$$\gamma_k = \frac{\sigma_\epsilon^2 \Gamma(1 - 2d) \Gamma(k + d)}{\Gamma(d) \Gamma(1 - d) \Gamma(k + 1 - d)} \sim c k^{2d-1} \quad \text{as} \quad k \to \infty, \qquad (6.2.11)$$

where $d \in (-\frac{1}{2}, \frac{1}{2})$ and c is some constant. Depending on whether d is

---

[9] A function $f(x)$ is said to be *regularly varying at infinity with index* ρ if $\lim_{t \to \infty} f(tx)/f(t) = x^\rho$ for all $x > 0$; hence regularly varying functions are functions that behave like power functions asymptotically. When $\rho = 0$, the function is said to be *slowly varying at infinity*, since it behaves like a constant for large x. An example of a function that is slowly varying at infinity is log x. See Resnick (1987) for further properties of regularly varying functions.

negative or positive, the spectral density of (6.2.5) at frequency zero, given by

$$f(\lambda) \cong (1 - e^{-i\lambda})^{-d}(1 - e^{i\lambda})^{-d}\sigma_\epsilon^2 \sim \sigma_\epsilon^2 \lambda^{-2d} \quad \text{as} \quad \lambda \to 0, \quad (6.2.12)$$

will either be zero or infinite; thus such processes violate condition (A3).[10] Furthermore, the results of Helson and Sarason (1967) show that these processes are not strong-mixing; hence they also violate condition (A4) of our null hypothesis.[11]

6.3 The Rescaled Range Statistic

To detect long-range or "strong" dependence, Mandelbrot has suggested using the range over standard deviation or R/S statistic, also called the "rescaled range," which was developed by Hurst (1951) in his studies of river discharges. The R/S statistic is the range of partial sums of deviations of a time series from its mean, rescaled by its standard deviation. Specifically, consider a sample of returns $X_1, X_2, \ldots, X_n$ and let $\overline{X}_n$ denote the sample mean $(1/n)\sum_j X_j$. Then the classical rescaled range statistic, denoted by $\tilde{Q}_n$, is defined as

$$\tilde{Q}_n \equiv \frac{1}{s_n} \left[\underset{1 \leq k \leq n}{\text{Max}} \sum_{j=1}^{k} (X_j - \overline{X}_n) - \underset{1 \leq k \leq n}{\text{Min}} \sum_{j=1}^{k} (X_j - \overline{X}_n) \right], \quad (6.3.1)$$

where s_n is the usual (maximum likelihood) standard deviation estimator:

$$s_n \equiv \left[\frac{1}{n} \sum_j (X_j - \overline{X}_n)^2 \right]^{1/2}. \quad (6.3.2)$$

The first term in brackets in (6.3.1) is the maximum (over k) of the partial sums of the first k deviations of X_j from the sample mean. Since the sum of all n deviations of X_j's from their mean is zero, this maximum is always nonnegative. The second term in (6.3.1) is the minimum (over k) of this same sequence of partial sums; hence it is always nonpositive. The difference of the two quantities, called the "range" for obvious reasons, is always nonnegative, hence $\tilde{Q}_n \geq 0$.[12]

---

[10]This has also been advanced as a definition of long-range dependence—see, for example, Mandelbrot (1972).

[11]Note, Helson and Sarason (1967) only consider the case of linear dependence; hence their conditions are sufficient to rule out strong-mixing but not necessary. For example, white noise may be approximated by a nonlinear deterministic time series (e.g. the tent map) and will have constant spectral density, but will be strongly dependent. We are grateful to Lars Hansen for pointing this out.

[12]The behavior of $\tilde{Q}_n$ may be better understood by considering its origins in hydrological studies of reservoir design. To accommodate seasonalities in riverflow, a reservoir's capacity

In several seminal papers Mandelbrot, Taqqu, and Wallis demonstrate
the superiority of R/S analysis to more conventional methods of determining long-range dependence, such as analyzing autocorrelations, variance
ratios, and spectral decompositions. For example, Mandelbrot and Wallis
(1969a) show by Monte Carlo simulation that the R/S statistic can detect
long-range dependence in highly non-Gaussian time series with large skewness and kurtosis. In fact, Mandelbrot (1972, 1975) reports the almost-sure
convergence of the R/S statistic for stochastic processes with infinite variances, a distinct advantage over autocorrelations and variance ratios which
need not be well-defined for such processes. Further aspects of the R/S
statistic's robustness are derived in Mandelbrot and Taqqu (1979). Mandelbrot (1972) also argues that, unlike spectral analysis which detects periodic
cycles, R/S analysis can detect *nonperiodic* cycles, cycles with periods equal
to or greater than the sample period.

Although these claims may all be contested to some degree, it is a well-
established fact that long-range dependence can indeed be detected by the
"classical" R/S statistic. However, perhaps the most important shortcoming
of the rescaled range is its sensitivity to short-range dependence, implying
that any incompatibility between the data and the predicted behavior of
the R/S statistic under the null hypothesis need not come from long-term
memory, but may merely be a symptom of short-term memory.

To see this, first observe that under a simple IID null hypothesis, it
is well-known (and is a special case of Theorem 6.3.1 below) that as n increases without bound, the rescaled range converges in distribution to a
well-defined random variable V when properly normalized, i.e.,

$$\frac{1}{\sqrt{n}} \tilde{Q}_n \Rightarrow V \qquad (6.3.3)$$

must be chosen to allow for fluctuations in the supply of water above the dam while still
maintaining a relatively constant flow of water below the dam. Since dam construction costs
are immense, the importance of estimating the reservoir capacity necessary to meet long term
storage needs is apparent. The range is an estimate of this quantity. If X_j is the riverflow
(per unit time) above the dam and $\overline{X}_n$ is the desired riverflow below the dam, the bracketed
quantity in (6.3.1) is the capacity of the reservoir needed to ensure this smooth flow given the
pattern of flows in periods 1 through n. For example, suppose annual riverflows are assumed
to be 100, 50, 100, and 50 in years 1 through 4. If a constant annual flow of 75 below the dam
is desired each year, a reservoir must have a minimum total capacity of 25 since it must store 25
units in years 1 and 3 to provide for the relatively dry years 2 and 4. Now suppose instead that
the natural pattern of riverflow is 100, 100, 50, 50 in years 1 through 4. To ensure a flow of 75
below the dam in this case, the minimum capacity must increase to 50 so as to accommodate
the excess storage needed in years 1 and 2 to supply water during the "dry spell" in years 3
and 4. Seen in this context, it is clear that an increase in persistence will increase the required
storage capacity as measured by the range. Indeed, it was the apparent persistence of "dry
spells" in Egypt that sparked Hurst's life-long fascination with the Nile, leading eventually to
his interest in the rescaled range.

Table 6.2. *Fractiles of the distribution $F_V(v)$.*

$P(V < v)$	.005	.025	.050	.100	.200	.300	.400	.500
v	0.721	0.809	0.861	0.927	1.018	1.090	1.157	1.223

$P(V < v)$	.543	.600	.700	.800	.900	.950	.975	.995
v	$\sqrt{\dfrac{\pi}{2}}$	1.294	1.374	1.473	1.620	1.747	1.862	2.098

where "$\Rightarrow$" denotes weak convergence and V is the range of a Brownian bridge on the unit interval.[13]

Now suppose, instead, that $\{X_j\}$ were short-range dependent—for example, let X_j be a stationary AR(1):[14]

$$\epsilon_t = \rho\epsilon_{t-1} + \eta_t, \quad \eta_t \sim \mathrm{WN}(0, \sigma_\eta^2), \quad |\rho| \in (0, 1). \tag{6.3.4}$$

Although $\{\epsilon_t\}$ is short-range dependent, it yields a $\widetilde{Q}_n$ that does not satisfy (6.3.3). In fact, it may readily be shown that for (6.3.4) the limiting distribution of $\widetilde{Q}_n/\sqrt{n}$ is ξV where $\xi \equiv \sqrt{(1+\rho)/(1-\rho)}$ (see Proposition 6.3.1 below). For some portfolios of common stock, $\hat{\rho}$ is as large as 50 percent, implying that the mean of $\widetilde{Q}_n/\sqrt{n}$ may be biased upward by 73 percent! Since the mean of V is $\sqrt{\pi/2} \approx 1.25$, the mean of the classical rescaled range would be 2.16 for such an AR(1) process. Using the critical values of V reported in Table 6.2, it is evident that a value of 2.16 would yield a rejection of the null hypothesis at any conventional significance level.

This should come as no surprise since the values in Table 6.2 correspond to the distribution of V, not ξV. Now by taking into account the "short-term" autocorrelations of the X_j's—by dividing Q_n by ξ for example—convergence to V may be restored. But this requires knowledge of ξ which, in turn, requires knowledge of ρ. Moreover, if X_j follows a short-range dependent process other than an AR(1), the expression for ξ will change, as Proposition 6.3.1 below shows. Therefore, correcting for short-range dependence on a case-by-case basis is impractical. Ideally, we would like to correct for short-term memory without taking too strong a position on what form it takes. This is precisely what the modified rescaled range of Section 6.3.1 does—its limiting distribution is invariant to many forms of short-range dependence, and yet it is still sensitive to the presence of long-range dependence.

---

[13]See Billingsley (1968) for the definition of weak convergence. We discuss the Brownian bridge and V more formally below.

[14]It is implicitly assumed throughout that white noise has a Lebesgue-integrable characteristic function to avoid the pathologies of Andrews (1984).

Although aware of the effects of short-range dependence on the rescaled range, Mandelbrot (1972, 1975) did not correct for this bias since his focus was the relation of the R/S statistic's logarithm to the logarithm of the sample size as the sample size increases without bound. For short-range dependent time series such as strong-mixing processes the ratio $\log \widetilde{Q}_n / \log n$ approaches $\frac{1}{2}$ in the limit, but converges to quantities greater or less than $\frac{1}{2}$ according to whether there is positive or negative long-range dependence. The limit of this ratio is often denoted by H and is called the "Hurst" coefficient. For example, the fractionally-differenced process (6.2.1) satisfies the simple relation: $H = d + \frac{1}{2}$.

Mandelbrot and Wallis (1969a) suggest estimating the Hurst coefficient by plotting the logarithm of $\widetilde{Q}_n$ against the logarithm of the sample size n. Beyond some large n, the slope of such a plot should settle down to H. However, although $H = \frac{1}{2}$ across general classes of short-range dependent processes, the finite-sample properties of the *estimated* Hurst coefficient are not invariant to the form of short-range dependence. In particular, Davies and Harte (1987) show that even though the Hurst coefficient of a stationary Gaussian AR(1) is precisely $\frac{1}{2}$, the 5 percent Mandelbrot regression test rejects this null hypothesis 47 percent of the time for an autoregressive parameter of 0.3. Additional Monte Carlo evidence is reported in Section 6.5.

6.3.1 The Modified R/S Statistic

To distinguish between long-range and short-range dependence, the R/S statistic must be modified so that its statistical behavior is invariant over a general class of short memory processes, but deviates for long memory processes. This is accomplished by the following statistic Q_n:

$$Q_n \equiv \frac{1}{\hat{\sigma}_n(q)} \left[\underset{1 \le k \le n}{\text{Max}} \sum_{j=1}^{k} (X_j - \overline{X}_n) - \underset{1 \le k \le n}{\text{Min}} \sum_{j=1}^{k} (X_j - \overline{X}_n) \right] \qquad (6.3.5)$$

where

$$\hat{\sigma}_n^2(q) \equiv \frac{1}{n} \sum_{j=1}^{n} (X_j - \overline{X}_n)^2$$

$$+ \frac{2}{n} \sum_{j=1}^{q} \omega_j(q) \left\{ \sum_{i=j+1}^{n} (X_i - \overline{X}_n)(X_{i-j} - \overline{X}_n) \right\} \qquad (6.3.6)$$

$$= \hat{\sigma}_x^2 + 2 \sum_{j=1}^{q} \omega_j(q)\, \hat{\gamma}_j, \qquad \omega_j(q) \equiv 1 - \frac{j}{q+1}, \qquad q < n, \qquad (6.3.7)$$

and $\hat{\sigma}_x^2$ and $\hat{\gamma}_j$ are the usual sample variance and autocovariance estimators of X.

Q_n differs from $\tilde{Q}_n$ only in its denominator, which is the square root of a consistent estimator of the partial sum's variance. If $\{X_t\}$ is subject to short-range dependence, the variance of the partial sum is not simply the sum of the variances of the individual terms, but also includes the autocovariances. Therefore, the estimator $\hat{\sigma}_n(q)$ involves not only sums of squared deviations of X_j, but also its weighted autocovariances up to lag q. The weights $\omega_j(q)$ are those suggested by Newey and West (1987) and always yield a positive $\hat{\sigma}_n^2(q)$, an estimator of 2π times the (unnormalized) spectral density function of X_t at frequency zero using a Bartlett window. Theorem 4.2 of Phillips (1987) demonstrates the consistency of $\hat{\sigma}_n(q)$ under the following conditions:[15]

(A2′) $\sup\limits_{t} E[|\epsilon_t|^{2\beta}] < \infty$ for some $\beta > 2$.

(A5) As n increases without bound, q also increases without bound such that $q \sim o(n^{1/4})$.

By allowing q to increase with (but at a slower rate than) the number of observations n, the denominator of Q_n adjusts appropriately for general forms of short-range dependence. Of course, although the conditions (A2′) and (A5) ensure the consistency of $\hat{\sigma}^2(q)$, they provide little guidance in selecting a truncation lag q. Monte Carlo studies such as Andrews (1991) and Lo and MacKinlay (1989a) have shown that when q becomes large relative to the sample size n, the finite-sample distribution of the estimator can be radically different from its asymptotic limit. However q cannot be chosen too small since the autocovariances beyond lag q may be substantial and should be included in the weighted sum. Therefore, the truncation lag must be chosen with some consideration of the data at hand. Andrews (1991) does provide a data-dependent rule for choosing q, however its minimax optimality is still based on an asymptotic mean-squared error criterion—little is known about how best to pick q in finite samples. Some Monte Carlo evidence is reported in Section 6.5.

Since there are several other consistent estimators of the spectral density function at frequency zero, conditions (A2′) and (A5) can be replaced with weaker assumptions if conditions (A1), (A3), and (A4) are suitably modified. If, for example, X_t is m-dependent (so that observations spaced greater than m periods apart are independent), it is well-known that the spectral density at frequency zero may be estimated consistently with a finite number of unweighted autocovariances (see, for example, Hansen, 1982, Lemma 3.2). Other weighting functions may be found in Hannan (1970, Chapter V.4) and may yield better finite-sample properties for Q_n than the Bartlett

---

[15]Andrews (1991) has improved the rate restriction in (A5) to $o(n^{1/2})$, and it has been conjectured that $o(n)$ is sufficient.

window without altering the limiting null distribution derived in the next section.[16]

6.3.2 The Asymptotic Distribution of Q_n

To derive the limiting distribution of the modified rescaled range Q_n under our null hypothesis, consider the behavior of the following standardized partial sum:

$$W_n(\tau) \equiv \frac{1}{\sigma \sqrt{n}} S_{[n\tau]}, \qquad \tau \in [0, 1], \tag{6.3.8}$$

where S_k denotes the partial sum $\sum_{j=1}^{k} \epsilon_j$ and $[n\tau]$ is the greatest integer less than or equal to $n\tau$. The sample paths of $W_n(\tau)$ are elements of the function space $\mathcal{D}[0, 1]$, the space of all real-valued functions on $[0, 1]$ that are right-continuous and possess finite left limits. Under certain conditions it may be shown that $W_n(\tau)$ converges weakly to a Brownian motion $W(\tau)$ on the unit interval, and that well-behaved functionals of $W_n(\tau)$ converge weakly to the same functionals of Brownian motion (see Billingsley, 1968, for further details). Armed with these results, the limiting distribution of the modified rescaled range may be derived in three easy steps, summarized in the following theorem.[17]

Theorem 6.3.1.[18] *If $\{\epsilon_t\}$ satisfies assumptions (A1), (A2), (A3)–(A5), then as n increases without bound:*

(a) $\displaystyle \operatorname*{Max}_{1 \le k \le n} \frac{1}{\hat{\sigma}_n(q)\sqrt{n}} \sum_{j=1}^{k} (X_j - \overline{X}_n) \Rightarrow \operatorname*{Max}_{0 \le \tau \le 1} W^\circ(\tau) \equiv M^\circ,$

(b) $\displaystyle \operatorname*{Min}_{1 \le k \le n} \frac{1}{\hat{\sigma}_n(q)\sqrt{n}} \sum_{j=1}^{k} (X_j - \overline{X}_n) \Rightarrow \operatorname*{Min}_{0 \le \tau \le 1} W^\circ(\tau) \equiv m^\circ,$

(c) $\displaystyle \frac{1}{\sqrt{n}} Q_n \Rightarrow M^\circ - m^\circ \equiv V.$

Parts (a) and (b) of Theorem 6.3.1 follow from Lemmas A.1 and A.2 of the Appendix, and Theorem 4.2 of Phillips (1987), and show that the maximum and minimum of the partial sum of deviations of X_j from its mean converge respectively to the maximum and minimum of the celebrated Brownian bridge $W^\circ(\tau)$ on the unit interval, also called "pinned" or "tied-down" Brownian motion because $W^\circ(0) = W^\circ(1) = 0$. That the limit of

---

[16]For example, Andrews (1991) and Gallant (1987) both advocate the use of Parzen weights, which also yields a positive semi-definite estimator of the spectral density at frequency zero but is optimal in an asymptotic mean-squared error sense.

[17]Mandelbrot (1975) derives similar limit theorems for the statistic $\widetilde{Q}_n$ under the more restrictive IID assumption, in which case the limiting distribution will coincide with that of Q_n. Since our null hypothesis includes weakly dependent disturbances, we extend his results via the more general functional central limit theorem of Herrndorf (1984, 1985).

[18]Proofs of theorems are given in the Appendix.

the partial sums is a Brownian bridge is not surprising since the summands are deviations from the mean and must therefore sum to zero at $k = n$. Part (6.3.1) of the theorem follows immediately from Lemma A.2 and is the key result, allowing us to perform large sample statistical inference once the distribution function for the range of the Brownian bridge is obtained. This distribution function is implicitly contained in Feller (1951), and is given explicitly by Kennedy (1976) and Siddiqui (1976) as[19]

$$F_V(v) = 1 + 2\sum_{k=1}^{\infty}(1 - 4k^2v^2)e^{-2(kv)^2}. \qquad (6.3.9)$$

Critical values for tests of any significance level are easily obtained from this simple expression (6.3.9) for F_V. The values most commonly used are reported in Table 6.2. The moments of V may also be readily computed from (6.3.9); a simple calculation shows that $E[V] = \sqrt{\pi/2}$ and $E[V^2] = \pi^2/6$, thus the mean and standard deviation of V are approximately 1.25 and 0.27 respectively. Plots of F_V and f_V are given in Figure 6.1, along with Gaussian distribution and density functions (with the same mean and variance as V) for comparison. The distribution of V is positively skewed and most of its mass falls between $\frac{3}{4}$ and 2.

6.3.3 The Relation Between Q_n and $\tilde{Q}_n$

Since Q_n and $\tilde{Q}_n$ differ solely in how the range is normalized, the limiting behavior of our modified R/S statistic and Mandelbrot's original will only coincide when $\hat{\sigma}_n(q)$ and s_n are asymptotically equivalent. From the definitions of $\hat{\sigma}_n(q)$ and s_n, it is apparent that the two will generally converge in probability to different limits in the presence of autocorrelation. Therefore, under the weakly dependent null hypothesis the statistic $\tilde{Q}_n/\sqrt{n}$ will converge to the range V of a Brownian bridge multiplied by some constant. More formally, we have the almost trivial result:

Proposition 6.3.1. *If* $\lim_{n\to\infty} E[\sum_{j=1}^{n} \epsilon_j^2/n]$ *is finite and positive, then under assumptions (A1)–(A4),* $\tilde{Q}_n/\sqrt{n} \Rightarrow \xi V$ *where*

$$\xi^2 \equiv \frac{\lim_{n\to\infty} E\left[\frac{1}{n}\left(\sum_{j=1}^{n}\epsilon_j\right)^2\right]}{\lim_{n\to\infty} E\left[\frac{1}{n}\sum_{j=1}^{n}\epsilon_j^2\right]}. \qquad (6.3.10)$$

Therefore, normalizing the range by s_n in place of $\hat{\sigma}_n(q)$ changes the limiting distribution of the rescaled range by the multiplicative constant

---

[19]We are grateful to David Aldous and Yin-Wong Cheung for these last two references.

$F_v(v)$ and $f_v(v)$

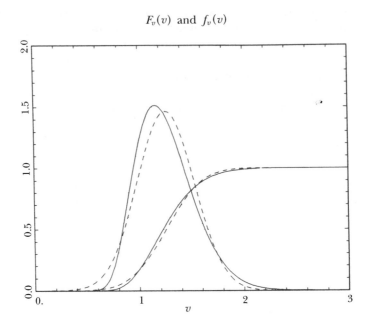

Figure 6.1.   *Distribution and density function of the range V of a Brownian bridge. Dashed curves are the normal distribution and density functions with mean and variance equal to those of V ($\sqrt{\pi/2}$ and $\pi^2/6$ respectively).*

ξ. This result was used above to derive the limiting distribution of $\widetilde{Q}_n$ in the AR(1) case, and closed-form expressions for ξ for general stationary ARMA(p, q) processes may readily be obtained using (6.3.10).

Since it is robust to many forms of heterogeneity and weak dependence, tests based on the modified R/S statistic Q_n cover a broader set of null hypotheses than those using $\widetilde{Q}_n$. More to the point, the modified rescaled range is able to distinguish between short-range and long-range dependence—the classical rescaled range cannot. Whereas an extreme value for Q_n indicates the likelihood of long-range dependence, a rejection based on the $\widetilde{Q}_n$ statistic is also consistent with short-range dependence in the data. Of course, it is always possible to tabulate the limiting distribution of the classical R/S statistic under a particular model of short-range dependence, but this obviously suffers from the drawback of specificity. The modified rescaled range converges weakly to the range of a Brownian bridge under *general* forms of weak dependence.

Despite its sensitivity to short-range dependence, the classical R/S statistic may still be used to test for independently and identically distributed X_t's. Indeed, the AR(1) example of Section 6.3 and the results of Davies and

Harte (1987) suggest that such a test may have considerable power against non-IID alternatives. However, since there is already a growing consensus among financial economists that stock market prices are not independently and identically distributed, this null hypothesis is of less immediate interest. For example, it is now well-known that aggregate stock market returns exhibit significant serial dependence for short-horizon holding periods and are therefore not independently distributed.

6.3.4 The Behavior of Q_n Under Long Memory Alternatives

To complete the analysis of the modified rescaled range, its behavior under long-range dependent alternatives remains to be investigated. Although this depends of course on the specific alternative at hand, surprisingly general results are available based on the following result from Taqqu (1975).

Theorem 6.3.2 (Taqqu). *Let $\{\epsilon_t\}$ be a zero-mean stationary Gaussian stochastic process such that:*

$$\sigma_n^2 \equiv \text{Var}[S_n] \sim n^{2H} L(n) \tag{6.3.11}$$

where S_n is the partial sum $\sum_{j=1}^{n} \epsilon_j$, $H \in (0, 1)$, and $L(n)$ is a slowly varying function at infinity. Define the following function on $\mathcal{D}[0, 1]$:

$$W_n(\tau) \equiv \frac{1}{\sigma_n} S_{[n\tau]}, \qquad \tau \in (0, 1). \tag{6.3.12}$$

Then $W_n(\tau) \Rightarrow W_H(\tau)$, where $W_H(\tau)$ is a fractional Brownian motion of order H on $[0, 1]$.

Theorem 6.3.2 is a functional central limit theorem for strongly dependent processes, and is only a special case of Taqqu's (1975) considerably more general results. In contrast to the usual functional central limit theorem in which properly normalized partial sums converge to a standard Brownian motion, Theorem 6.3.2 states that long-range dependent partial sums converge weakly to a *fractional* Brownian motion, first defined by Mandelbrot and Van Ness (1968) as the following stochastic integral:

$$W_H(\tau) \equiv \frac{1}{\Gamma\left(H + \frac{1}{2}\right)} \int_0^\tau (\tau - x)^{H - \frac{1}{2}} \, dW(x). \tag{6.3.13}$$

Observe that when $H = \frac{1}{2}$, $W_H(\tau)$ reduces to a standard Brownian motion. In that case, there is no long-range dependence, the variance of the partial sums grows at rate n, and the spectral density at frequency zero is finite and positive. If $H \in (\frac{1}{2}, 1)$ ($H \in (0, \frac{1}{2})$), there is positive (negative) long-range dependence, the variance grows faster (slower) than n, hence the spectral density at frequency zero is infinite (zero).

In a fashion analogous to Theorem 6.3.1, the behavior of Q_n under long-range dependent alternatives may now be derived in several steps using Lemmas A.2, A.3, and Theorem 6.3.2:

Theorem 6.3.3. *Let $\{\epsilon_t\}$ be a zero-mean stationary Gaussian stochastic process with autocovariance function γ_k such that*

$$\gamma_k \sim \begin{cases} k^{2H-2}L(k) & \text{for } H \in (\tfrac{1}{2}, 1) \text{ or,} \\ -k^{2H-2}L(k) & \text{for } H \in (0, \tfrac{1}{2}) \end{cases} \qquad as \qquad k \to \infty \qquad (6.3.14)$$

where $L(k)$ is a slowly varying function at infinity. Then as n and q increase without bound such that $(q/n) \to 0$, we have:

(a)
$$\underset{1\leq k\leq n}{\text{Max}} \; \frac{1}{\sigma_n} \sum_{j=1}^{k}(X_j - \overline{X}_n) \;\Rightarrow\; \underset{0\leq\tau\leq1}{\text{Max}} \; W_H^\circ(\tau) \equiv M_H^\circ,$$

(b)
$$\underset{1\leq k\leq n}{\text{Min}} \; \frac{1}{\sigma_n} \sum_{j=1}^{k}(X_j - \overline{X}_n) \;\Rightarrow\; \underset{0\leq\tau\leq1}{\text{Min}} \; W_H^\circ(\tau) \equiv m_H^\circ,$$

(c)
$$R_n \equiv \frac{\hat{\sigma}_n(q)\sqrt{n}}{\sigma_n} \cdot \frac{1}{\sqrt{n}} Q_n \;\Rightarrow\; M_H^\circ - m_H^\circ \equiv V_H,$$

(d)
$$a_n \equiv \frac{\sigma_n}{\hat{\sigma}_n(q)\sqrt{n}} \;\overset{p}{\to}\; \begin{cases} \infty & \text{for } H \in (\tfrac{1}{2}, 1), \\ 0 & \text{for } H \in (0, \tfrac{1}{2}), \end{cases}$$

(e)
$$\frac{1}{\sqrt{n}} Q_n = a_n R_n \;\overset{p}{\to}\; \begin{cases} \infty & \text{for } H \in (\tfrac{1}{2}, 1), \\ 0 & \text{for } H \in (0, \tfrac{1}{2}), \end{cases}$$

where $\hat{\sigma}_n(q)$ is defined in (6.3.6), σ_n is defined in Theorem 6.3.2, and $W_H^\circ(\tau) \equiv W_H(\tau) - \tau W_H(1)$.[20]

Theorem 6.3.3 shows that the modified rescaled range test is consistent against a class of long-range dependent stationary Gaussian alternatives. In the presence of positive strong dependence, the R/S statistic diverges in probability to infinity; in the presence of negative strong dependence, it converges in probability to zero. In either case, the probability of rejecting the null hypothesis approaches unity for all stationary Gaussian stochastic processes satisfying (6.3.14), a broad set of alternatives that includes all fractionally-differenced Gaussian ARIMA(p, d, q) models with $d \in (-\tfrac{1}{2}, \tfrac{1}{2})$.

From (a) and (b) of Theorem 6.3.3 it is apparent that the normalized *population* rescaled, $R_n/\sqrt{n}$, converges to zero in probability. Therefore,

---

[20]Although it is tempting to call $W_H^\circ(\tau)$ a "fractional Brownian bridge," this is not the most natural definition despite the fact that it is "tied down." See Jonas (1983, Chapter 3.3) for a discussion.

whether or not $Q_n/\sqrt{n}$ approaches zero or infinity in the limit depends entirely on the limiting behavior of the ratio $\sigma_n/\hat{\sigma}_n(q)$. That is,

$$\frac{Q_n}{\sqrt{n}} = \frac{\sigma_n}{\hat{\sigma}_n(q)} \frac{R_n}{\sqrt{n}} \qquad (6.3.15)$$

so that if the ratio $\sigma_n/\hat{\sigma}_n(q)$ diverges fast enough to overcompensate for the convergence of $R_n/\sqrt{n}$ to zero, then the test will reject in the upper tail, otherwise it will reject in the lower tail. This is determined by whether d lies in the interval $(0, \frac{1}{2})$ or $(-\frac{1}{2}, 0)$. When $d = 0$, the ratio $\sigma_n/\hat{\sigma}_n(q)$ converges to unity in probability and, as expected, the normalized R/S statistic converges in distribution to the range of the standard Brownian bridge.

Of course, if one is interested exclusively in fractionally-differenced alternatives, a more efficient means of detecting long-range dependence might be to estimate the fractional differencing parameter directly. In such cases, the approaches taken by Geweke and Porter-Hudak (1983), Sowell (1990), and Yajima (1985, 1988) may be preferable. The modified R/S test is perhaps most useful for detecting departures into a broader class of alternative hypotheses, a kind of "portmanteau" test statistic that may complement a comprehensive analysis of long-range dependence.

6.4 *R/S* Analysis for Stock Market Returns

The importance of long-range dependence in asset markets was first considered by Mandelbrot (1971). More recently, the evidence uncovered by Fama and French (1988), Lo and MacKinlay (1988b), and Poterba and Summers (1988) may be symptomatic of a long-range dependent component in stock market prices. In particular, Lo and MacKinlay (1988b) show that the ratios of k-week stock return variances to k times the variance of one-week returns generally exceed unity when k is small (2 to 32). In contrast, Poterba and Summers (1988) find that this same variance ratio falls below one when k is much larger (96 and greater).

To see that such a phenomenon can easily be generated by long-range dependence, denote by X_t the time-t return on a stock and let it be the sum of two components X_{at} and X_{bt} where

$$(1 - L)^d X_{at} = \epsilon_t, \qquad (1 - \rho L) X_{bt} = \eta_t, \qquad (6.4.1)$$

and assign the values $(-0.2, 0.25, 1, 1.1)$ to the parameters $(d, \rho, \sigma_\epsilon^2, \sigma_\eta^2)$. Let the ratio of the k-period return variance to k times the variance of X_t

be denoted by $VR(k)$. Then a simple calculation will show that for the parameter values chosen:

$VR(2) = 1.04,$	$VR(10) = 10.4,$
$VR(3) = 1.06,$	$VR(50) = 0.97,$
$VR(4) = 1.07,$	$VR(100) = 0.95,$
$VR(5) = 1.06,$	$VR(250) = 0.92.$

The intuition for this pattern of variance ratios comes from observing that $VR(k)$ is a weighted sum of the first $k-1$ autocorrelation coefficients of X_t with linearly declining weights (see Lo and MacKinlay, 1988b). When k is small the autocorrelation of X_t is dominated by the positively autocorrelated AR(1) component X_{bt}. But since the autocorrelations of X_{bt} decay rapidly relative to those of X_{at}, as k grows the influence of the long-memory component eventually outweighs that of the AR(1), ultimately driving the variance ratio below unity.

6.4.1 The Evidence for Weekly and Monthly Returns

Greene and Fielitz (1977) were perhaps the first to apply R/S analysis to common stock returns. More recent applications include Booth and Kaen (1979) (gold prices), Booth, Kaen, and Koveos (1982) (foreign exchange rates), and Helms, Kaen, and Rosenman (1984) (futures contracts). These and earlier applications of R/S analysis by Mandelbrot and Wallis (1969a) have three features in common: (1) They provide no sampling theory with which to judge the statistical significance of their empirical results; (2) they use the Q_n statistic which is not robust to short-range dependence; and (3) they do not focus on the R/S statistic itself, but rather on the regression of its logarithm on (sub)sample sizes. The shortcomings of (1) and (2) are apparent from the discussion in the preceding sections. As for (3), Davies and Harte (1987) show such regression tests to be significantly biased toward rejection even for a stationary AR(1) process with an autoregressive parameter of 0.3.

To test for long-term memory in stock returns, we use data from the Center for Research in Security Prices (CRSP) monthly and daily returns files. Tests are performed for the value- and equal-weighted CRSP indexes. Daily observations for the returns indexes are available from July 3, 1962, to December 31, 1987 yielding a sample size of 6,409 observations. Monthly indexes are each composed of 744 observations from January 30, 1926, to December 31, 1987. The following statistic is computed for the various returns indexes:

$$V_n(q) \equiv \frac{1}{\sqrt{n}} Q_n \overset{a}{\sim} V, \qquad\qquad (6.4.2)$$

where the distribution F_V of V is given in (6.3.9). Using the values in Table 6.2 a test of the null hypothesis may be performed at the 95 percent level of confidence by accepting or rejecting according to whether V_n is or is not contained in the interval [0.809, 1.862] which assigns equal probability to each tail.

$V_n(q)$ is written as a function of q to emphasize the dependence of the modified rescaled range on the truncation lag. To check the sensitivity of the statistic to the lag length, $V_n(q)$ is computed for several different values of q. The normalized classical Hurst-Mandelbrot rescaled range $\widetilde{V}_n$ is also computed for comparison, where

$$\widetilde{V}_n \equiv \frac{1}{\sqrt{n}} \widetilde{Q}_n \overset{a}{\sim} \xi V. \tag{6.4.3}$$

Table 6.3 reports results for the daily equal- and value-weighted returns indexes. The panel labelled "Equal-Weighted" contains the $V_n(q)$ and $\widetilde{V}_n$ statistics for the equal-weighted index for the entire sample period (the first row), two equally-partitioned sub-samples (the next two rows), and four equally-partitioned sub-samples (the next four rows). The modified rescaled range is computed with q-values of 90, 180, 270, and 360 days. The columns labelled "%-Bias" report the estimated bias of the original rescaled range $\widetilde{V}_n$, and is $100 \cdot (\hat{\xi} - 1)$ where $\hat{\xi} = \hat{\sigma}_n(q)/s_n = \widetilde{V}_n/V_n$.

Although Table 6.3 shows that the classical R/S statistic $\widetilde{V}_n$ is statistically significant at the 5 percent level for the daily equal-weighted CRSP returns index, the modified R/S statistic V_n is not. While $\widetilde{V}_n$ is 2.63 for the entire sample period the modified R/S statistic is 1.46 with a truncation lag of 90 days, and 1.50 with a truncation lag of 360 days. The importance of normalizing by $\hat{\sigma}_n(q)$ is clear—dividing by s_n imparts a potential upward bias of 80 percent!

The statistical insignificance of the modified R/S statistics indicates that the data are consistent with the short-memory null hypothesis. The stability of the $V_n(q)$ across truncation lags q also supports the hypothesis that there is little dependence in daily stock returns beyond one or two months. For example, using 90 lags yields a V_n of 1.46 whereas 270 and 360 lags both yield 1.50, virtually the same point estimate. The results are robust to the sample period—none of the sub-period $V_n(q)$'s are significant. The classical rescaled range is significant only in the first half of the sample for the value-weighted index, and is insignificant when the entire sample is used.

Table 6.4 reports similar results for monthly returns indexes with four values of q employed: 3, 6, 9, and 12 months. None of the modified R/S statistics are statistically significant at the 5 percent level in any sample period or sub-period for either index. The percentage bias is generally lower for monthly data, although it still ranges from -0.2 to 25.3 percent.

To develop further intuition for these results, Figure 6.2 contains the autocorrelograms of the daily and monthly equal-weighted returns indexes, where the maximum lag is 360 for daily returns and 12 for monthly. For both

Table 6.3. R/S analysis of daily equal- and value-weighted CRSP stock returns indexes from July 3, 1962, to December 31, 1987 using the classical rescaled range $\tilde{V}_n$ and the modified rescaled range $V_n(q)$. Entries in the %-bias columns are computed as $[(\tilde{V}_n/V_n(q)) - 1] \cdot 100$, and are estimates of the bias of the classical R/S statistic in the presence of short-term dependence. Asterisks indicate significance at the 5 percent level.

Time Period	Sample Size	$\tilde{V}_n$	$V_n(90)$	%-Bias	$V_n(180)$	%-Bias	$V_n(270)$	%-Bias	$V_n(360)$	%-Bias
Equal-Weighted:										
620703–871231	6409	2.63*	1.46	79.9	1.45	81.1	1.50	75.2	1.50	75.4
620703–750428	3204	3.18*	1.61	97.0	1.57	102.0	1.63	95.2	1.62	96.8
750429–871231	3205	1.45	0.92	57.2	0.97	49.0	1.05	38.5	1.14	27.3
620703–681217	1602	2.40*	1.39	72.2	1.46	64.7	1.72	39.7	1.78	34.8
681219–750428	1602	2.03*	1.07	90.7	1.10	84.9	1.19	70.6	1.23	65.3
750428–810828	1602	1.35	0.89	51.6	1.23	9.5	1.49	-9.2	1.71	-21.0
810831–871231	1603	1.79	1.15	55.8	1.10	62.4	1.18	51.6	1.27	41.4
Value-Weighted:										
620703–871231	6409	1.55	1.29	20.8	1.26	22.9	1.30	19.1	1.33	16.8
620703–750428	3204	1.97*	1.43	37.3	1.39	41.4	1.43	37.5	1.45	35.5
750429–871231	3205	1.29	1.22	5.8	1.24	4.1	1.32	-2.3	1.42	-9.4
620703–681217	1602	1.67	1.43	16.8	1.45	15.3	1.62	3.4	1.69	-1.3
681219–750428	1602	1.85	1.34	38.2	1.34	38.2	1.40	31.7	1.45	27.1
750428–810828	1602	1.08	1.12	-3.7	1.26	-14.7	1.34	-19.4	1.42	-24.2
810831–871231	1603	1.50	1.38	8.8	1.37	9.2	1.50	-0.3	1.63	-8.0

Table 6.4. *R/S analysis of monthly equal- and value-weighted CRSP stock returns indexes from January 30, 1926, to December 31, 1987, using the classical rescaled range V_n and the modified rescaled range $\tilde{V}_n$, and the %-bias columns are computed as $[(V_n/V_n(q)) - 1] \cdot 100$, and are estimates of the bias of the classical R/S statistic in the presence of short-term dependence. Asterisks indicate significance at the 5 percent level.*

Time Period	Sample Size	$\tilde{V}_n$	$V_n(3)$	%-Bias	$V_n(6)$	%-Bias	$V_n(9)$	%-Bias	$V_n(12)$	%-Bias
Equal-Weighted:										
260130–871231	744	1.17	1.07	9.1	1.10	6.6	1.09	7.2	1.06	10.4
260130–561231	372	1.32	1.21	9.4	1.26	5.1	1.24	7.1	1.18	12.1
570131–871231	372	1.37	1.26	8.4	1.23	11.1	1.27	7.6	1.30	5.2
260130–410630	186	1.42	1.31	8.3	1.40	1.6	1.39	2.6	1.32	8.0
410731–561231	186	1.60	1.42	13.1	1.34	20.0	1.28	25.3	1.28	25.1
570131–720630	186	1.20	1.04	15.9	0.99	21.9	1.03	17.4	1.07	12.3
720731–871231	186	1.57	1.51	3.8	1.51	4.3	1.55	1.2	1.57	−0.2
Value-Weighted:										
260130–871231	744	1.33	1.27	4.5	1.26	5.5	1.22	8.4	1.19	11.1
260130–561231	372	1.57	1.51	4.5	1.51	4.3	1.44	9.5	1.38	14.5
570131–871231	372	1.28	1.22	4.4	1.18	7.9	1.21	5.6	1.24	2.7
260130–410630	186	1.57	1.52	3.2	1.55	1.0	1.49	5.5	1.42	10.6
410731–561231	186	1.26	1.18	6.4	1.11	12.9	1.07	17.1	1.08	16.1
570131–720630	186	1.05	0.96	9.3	0.92	14.7	0.95	10.9	1.01	4.7
720731–871231	186	1.51	1.48	1.6	1.45	4.0	1.47	2.4	1.49	1.1

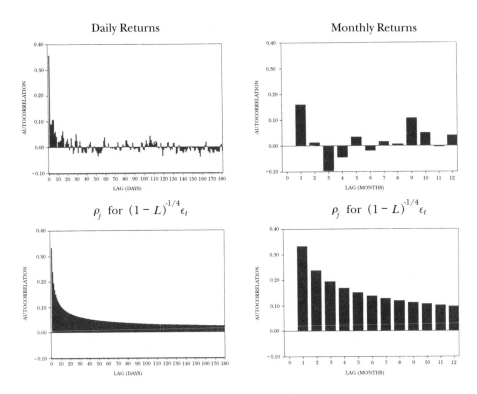

Figure 6.2. *Autocorrelograms of equally-weighted CRSP daily and monthly stock returns indexes and fractionally-differenced process with $d = 1/4$. The sample period for the daily index is July 1962 to December 1987, and is January 1926 to December 1987 for the monthly index.*

indexes only the lowest order autocorrelation coefficients are statistically significant. For comparison, alongside each of the index's autocorrelogram is the autocorrelogram of the fractionally-differenced process (6.2.1) with $d = .25$ and the variance of the disturbance chosen to yield a first-order autocorrelation of $\frac{1}{3}$. Although the general shapes of the fractionally-differenced autocorrelograms seem consistent with the data, closer inspection reveals that the index autocorrelations decay much more rapidly. Therefore, although short-term correlations are large enough to drive $\tilde{Q}_n$ and Q_n apart, there is little evidence of long-range dependence in Q_n itself.

Additional results are available for weekly and annual stock returns data but since they are so similar to those reported here, we have omitted them to conserve space. Although the annual data spans 115 years (1872 to 1986), neither the classical nor the modified R/S statistics are statistically significant over this time span.

The evidence in Tables 6.3 and 6.4 shows that the null hypothesis of short-range dependence cannot be rejected by the data—there is little support for long-term memory in U.S. stock returns. With adjustments for autocorrelation at lags up to one calendar year, estimates of the modified rescaled range are consistent with the null hypothesis of weak dependence. This reinforces Kandel and Stambaugh's (1989) contention that the long-run predictability of stock returns uncovered by Fama and French (1988) and Poterba and Summers (1988) may not be "long-run" in the time series sense, but may be the result of more conventional models of short-range dependence.[21] Of course, since our inferences rely solely on asymptotic distribution theory, we must check our approximations before dismissing the possibility of long-range dependence altogether. The finite-sample size and power of the modified rescaled range test are considered in the next sections.

6.5 Size and Power

To explore the possibility that the inability to reject the null hypothesis of short-range dependence is merely a symptom of low power, and to check the quality of Section 6.3's asymptotic approximations for various sample sizes, we perform several illustrative Monte Carlo experiments. Section 6.5.1 reports the empirical size of the test statistic under two Gaussian null hypotheses: IID and AR(1) disturbances. Section 6.5.2 presents power results against the fractionally-differenced process (6.2.1) for $d = \frac{1}{3}$ and $-\frac{1}{3}$.

6.5.1 The Size of the R/S Test

Table 6.5a contains simulation results for the modified R/S statistic with sample sizes of 100, 250, 500, 750, and 1,000 under the null hypothesis of independently and identically distributed Gaussian errors. All simulations were performed on an IBM 4381 in double precision using the random generator G05DDF from the Numerical Algorithms Group Fortran Library Mark 12. For each sample size the statistic $V_n(q)$ is computed with $q = 0, 5, 10, 25, 50$, and with q chosen by Andrews' (1991) data-dependent formula:

$$q = [k_n], \qquad k_n \equiv \left(\frac{3n}{2}\right)^{\frac{1}{3}} \cdot \left(\frac{2\hat{\rho}}{1 - \hat{\rho}^2}\right)^{\frac{2}{3}}, \qquad (6.5.1)$$

---

[21]Moreover, several papers have suggested that these long-run results may be spurious. See, for example, Kim, Nelson, and Startz (1991), Richardson (1993), and Richardson and Stock (1990).

where $[k_n]$ denotes the greatest integer less than or equal to k_n, and $\hat{\rho}$ is the estimated first-order autocorrelation coefficient of the data.[22] (Note that this is an optimal truncation lag only for an AR(1) data-generating process—a different expression obtains if, for example, the data-generating process were assumed to be an ARMA(1,1). See Andrews (1991) for further details.) In this case, the entry reported in the column labelled "q" is the mean of the q's chosen, with the population standard deviation reported in parentheses below the mean. When $q = 0$, $V_n(q)$ is identical to Mandelbrot's classical R/S statistic $\widetilde{V}_n$.

The entries in the last three columns of Table 6.5a show that the classical R/S statistic tends to reject too frequently—even for sample sizes of 1,000 the empirical size of a 5 percent test based on $\widetilde{V}_n$ is 5.9 percent. The modified R/S statistic tends to be conservative for values of q that are not too large relative to the sample size. For example, with 100 observations and 5 lags the empirical size of the 5 percent test using $V_n(q)$ is 2.1 percent. However, with 50 lags this test has a rejection rate of 31 percent! That the sampling properties worsen with the number of lags is not surprising—the imprecision with which the higher-order autocovariances are estimated can introduce considerable noise into the statistic (see, for example, Lo and MacKinlay, 1989b). But for 1,000 observations and 5 lags, the size of a 5 percent test based on $V_n(q)$ is 5.1 percent. Andrews' procedure yields intermediate results, with sizes in between those of the classical R/S statistic and the closest of the modified R/S statistics.

Table 6.5b reports the results of simulations under the null hypothesis of a Gaussian AR(1) with autoregressive coefficient 0.5 (recall that such a process is weakly dependent). The last three columns confirm the example of Section 6.3 and accord well with the results of Davies and Harte (1987): tests based on the classical R/S statistic have considerable power against an AR(1) null. In samples of only 100 observations the empirical size of the 5 percent test based on $\widetilde{V}_n$ is 38 percent and increases to 62 percent for sample sizes of 1,000. In contrast, the empirical sizes of tests based on $V_n(q)$ are much closer to their nominal values since the geometrically declining autocorrelations are taken into account by the denominator $\hat{\sigma}_n(q)$ of $V_n(q)$. When q is chosen via Andrews' procedure, this yields conservative test sizes, ranging from 2.8 percent for a sample of 100, to 4.3 percent for a sample of 1,000.

---

[22]For this procedure, the Newey-West autocorrelation weights (6.3.7) are replaced by those suggested by Andrews (1991):

$$\omega_j = 1 - \left| \frac{j}{k_n} \right|.$$

Table 6.5a. *Finite sample distribution of the modified R/S statistic under an IID null hypothesis. Each set of rows of a given sample size n corresponds to a separate and independent Monte Carlo experiment based on 10,000 replications. A lag q of 0 corresponds to Mandelbrot's classical R/S statistic, and a noninteger lag value indicates the mean lag (standard deviation given in parentheses) chosen via Andrews' (1991) data-dependent procedure assuming an AR(1) data-generating process. Standard errors for the empirical size may be computed using the usual normal approximation: they are 9.95×10^{-4}, 2.18×10^{-3}, and 3.00×10^{-3} for the 1%, 5%, and 10% tests respectively.*

n	q	Min	Max	Mean	S.D.	Size 1%-Test	Size 5%-Test	Size 10%-Test
100	0	0.534	2.284	1.144	0.263	0.029	0.095	0.153
100	5	0.649	1.913	1.179	0.207	0.002	0.021	0.050
100	10	0.710	1.877	1.223	0.175	0.000	0.003	0.012
100	25	0.858	2.296	1.383	0.186	0.001	0.014	0.039
100	50	0.918	3.119	1.694	0.360	0.137	0.313	0.414
100	0.97 (0.83)	0.557	2.164	1.150	0.247	0.019	0.070	0.127
250	0	0.496	2.527	1.183	0.270	0.021	0.075	0.133
250	5	0.580	2.283	1.196	0.243	0.008	0.041	0.089
250	10	0.654	2.048	1.211	0.221	0.003	0.021	0.054
250	25	0.757	1.905	1.264	0.176	0.000	0.001	0.006
250	50	0.877	2.206	1.372	0.169	0.000	0.005	0.020
250	0.97 (0.83)	0.497	2.442	1.185	0.263	0.017	0.064	0.120
500	0	0.518	2.510	1.201	0.267	0.015	0.061	0.117
500	5	0.589	2.357	1.207	0.252	0.008	0.047	0.094
500	10	0.630	2.227	1.215	0.240	0.004	0.032	0.073
500	25	0.677	2.051	1.240	0.210	0.000	0.008	0.029
500	50	0.709	1.922	1.285	0.176	0.000	0.001	0.005
500	0.96 (0.82)	0.549	2.510	1.202	0.263	0.014	0.057	0.112
750	0	0.558	2.699	1.207	0.270	0.014	0.061	0.120
750	5	0.597	2.711	1.212	0.260	0.009	0.049	0.101
750	10	0.615	2.553	1.217	0.251	0.006	0.039	0.087
750	25	0.677	2.279	1.235	0.228	0.001	0.017	0.052
750	50	0.758	1.971	1.266	0.198	0.000	0.002	0.015
750	0.96 (0.83)	0.558	2.670	1.208	0.268	00.013	0.058	0.117

(continued)

Table 6.5a.   *(continued)*

n	q	Min	Max	Mean	S.D.	Size 1%-Test	Size 5%-Test	Size 10%-Test
1000	0	0.542	2.577	1.211	0.270	0.014	0.059	0.113
1000	5	0.566	2.477	1.214	0.262	0.011	0.051	0.103
1000	10	0.570	2.405	1.218	0.256	0.008	0.045	0.089
1000	25	0.616	2.203	1.231	0.237	0.003	0.025	0.061
1000	50	0.716	2.036	1.253	0.211	0.000	0.007	0.029
1000	0.96 (0.81)	0.549	2.546	1.212	0.268	0.012	0.056	0.111

6.5.2 Power Against Fractionally-Differenced Alternatives

Tables 6.6a and b report the power of the R/S tests against the Gaussian fractionally-differenced alternative:

$$(1 - L)^d \epsilon_t = \eta_t, \qquad \eta_t \text{ IID } \mathcal{N}(0, \sigma_\eta^2), \qquad (6.5.2)$$

with $d = \frac{1}{3}$ and $-\frac{1}{3}$, and $\sigma_\eta^2 = \Gamma^2(1-d)/\Gamma(1-2d)$ so as to yield a unit variance for ϵ_t. For sample sizes of 100, tests based on $V_n(q)$ have very little power, but when the sample size reaches 250 the power increases dramatically. According to Table 6.6a, the power of the 5 percent test with $q = 5$ against the $d = \frac{1}{3}$ alternative is 33.5 percent with 250 observations, 62.8 percent with 500 observations, and 84.6 percent with 1,000 observations. Although Andrews' automatic truncation lag procedure is generally less powerful, its power is still 63.0 percent for a sample size of 1,000. Also, the rejections are generally in the right tail of the distribution, as the entries in the "Max" column indicate. This is not surprising in light of Theorem 6.3.3, which shows that under this alternative the modified R/S statistic diverges in probability to infinity.

For a fixed sample size, the power of the $V_n(q)$-based test declines as the number of lags is increased. This is due to the denominator $\hat{\sigma}_n(q)$, which generally increases with q since there is positive dependence when $d = \frac{1}{3}$. The increase in the denominator decreases the mean and variance of the statistic, shifting the distribution towards the left and pulling probability mass from both tails, thereby reducing the frequency of draws in the right tail's critical region, where virtually all the power is coming from.

Against the $d = -\frac{1}{3}$ alternative, Table 6.6b shows that the test seems to have somewhat higher power. However, in contrast to Table 6.6a the rejections are now coming from the left tail of the distribution, as Theorem 6.3.3 predicts. Although less powerful, tests based on Andrews' procedure

Table 6.5b. *Finite sample distribution of the modified R/S statistic under an AR(1) null hypothesis with autoregressive coefficient 0.5. Each set of rows of a given sample size n corresponds to a separate and independent Monte Carlo experiment based on 10,000 replications. A lag q of 0 corresponds to Mandelbrot's classical R/S statistic, and a noninteger lag value indicates the mean lag (standard deviation given in parentheses) chosen via Andrews' (1991) data-dependent procedure, assuming an AR(1) data-generating process. Standard errors for the empirical size may be computed using the usual normal approximation; they are 9.95×10^{-4}, 2.18×10^{-3}, and 3.00×10^{-3} for the 1%, 5%, and 10% tests respectively.*

n	q	Min	Max	Mean	S.D.	Size 1%-Test	Size 5%-Test	Size 10%-Test
100	0	0.764	3.418	1.764	0.402	0.203	0.382	0.486
100	5	0.634	1.862	1.201	0.220	0.003	0.027	0.059
100	10	0.693	1.805	1.178	0.176	0.000	0.010	0.030
100	25	0.779	2.111	1.290	0.175	0.000	0.005	0.015
100	50	0.879	3.013	1.571	0.341	0.074	0.198	0.284
100	5.61 (1.25)	0.636	1.974	1.195	0.219	0.004	0.028	0.063
250	0	0.865	3.720	1.913	0.432	0.309	0.505	0.614
250	5	0.597	2.478	1.268	0.262	0.005	0.038	0.086
250	10	0.615	2.137	1.212	0.228	0.003	0.023	0.063
250	25	0.734	1.811	1.218	0.177	0.000	0.004	0.015
250	50	0.809	2.119	1.304	0.166	0.000	0.003	0.010
250	8.07 (1.07)	0.603	2.357	1.227	0.242	0.004	0.030	0.071
500	0	0.836	4.392	1.980	0.456	0.363	0.559	0.665
500	5	0.622	2.557	1.302	0.285	0.012	0.055	0.109
500	10	0.579	2.297	1.236	0.256	0.007	0.039	0.085
500	25	0.627	1.980	1.214	0.215	0.001	0.015	0.041
500	50	0.734	1.894	1.243	0.178	0.000	0.002	0.009
500	10.40 (0.99)	0.577	2.353	1.236	0.256	0.007	0.039	0.085
750	0	0.839	4.211	2.017	0.459	0.389	0.592	0.696
750	5	0.567	2.637	1.323	0.291	0.011	0.062	0.118
750	10	0.557	2.429	1.253	0.265	0.007	0.043	0.091
750	25	0.614	2.114	1.222	0.232	0.003	0.022	0.058
750	50	0.702	1.891	1.235	0.200	0.000	0.005	0.022
750	12.03 (0.93)	0.556	2.324	1.244	0.260	0.007	0.041	0.088

(continued)

Table 6.5b.   (continued)

n	q	Min	Max	Mean	S.D.	Size 1%-Test	Size 5%-Test	Size 10%-Test
1000	0	0.926	4.327	2.045	0.465	0.414	0.617	0.716
1000	5	0.625	2.768	1.340	0.296	0.014	0.065	0.125
1000	10	0.592	2.622	1.268	0.272	0.009	0.047	0.096
1000	25	0.608	2.350	1.231	0.244	0.004	0.030	0.072
1000	50	0.636	1.997	1.236	0.217	0.001	0.011	0.038
1000	13.30 (0.89)	0.590	2.548	1.252	0.265	0.008	0.043	0.090

still exhibit reasonable power, ranging from 33.1 percent in samples of 100 observations to 94.5 percent in samples of 1,000.

For the larger sample sizes the power again declines as the number of lags increases, due to the denominator $\hat{\sigma}_n(q)$, which declines as q increases because the population autocorrelations are all negative when $d = -\frac{1}{3}$. The resulting increase in the mean of $V_n(q)$'s sampling distribution overwhelms the increase in its variability, leading to a lower rejection rate from the left tail.

Table 6.6a and b shows that the modified R/S statistic has reasonable power against at least two specific models of long-term memory. However, these simulations are merely illustrative—a more conclusive study would include further simulations with several other values for d, and perhaps with short-range dependence as well.[23] Moreover, since our empirical work has

---

[23] The very fact that the modified R/S statistic yields few rejections under the null simulations of Section 6.5.1 shows that the test may have low power against *some* long-range dependent alternatives, since the pseudo-random number generator used in those simulations is, after all, a long-range dependent process. A more striking example is the "tent" map, a particularly simple nonlinear deterministic map (it has a correlation dimension of 1) which yields sequences that are virtually uncorrelated but long-range dependent. In particular, the tent map is given by the following recursion:

$$X_t = \begin{cases} 2X_{t-1} & \text{if } X_{t-1} < \frac{1}{2} \\ 2(1 - X_{t-1}) & \text{if } X_{t-1} \geq \frac{1}{2}, \end{cases} \qquad t = 1, \ldots, T, \qquad X_0 \in (0, 1).$$

As an illustration, we performed two Monte Carlo experiments using the tent map to generate samples of 500 and 1,000 observations (each with 10,000 replications) with an independent uniform $(0,1)$ starting value for each replication. Neither the Mandelbrot rescaled range, nor its modification with fixed or automatic truncation lags have any power against the tent map. In fact, the finite sample distributions are quite close to the null distribution. Of course, one could argue that if the dynamics and the initial condition were unknown, then even if a deterministic system *were* generating the data, the resulting time series would be short-range dependent "for all practical purposes" and *should* be part of our null. We are grateful to Lars Hansen for suggesting this analysis.

Table 6.6a. *Power of the modified R/S statistic under a Gaussian fractionally differenced alternative with differencing parameter d = 1/3. The variance of the process has been normalized to unity. Each set of rows of a given sample size n corresponds to a separate and independent Monte Carlo experiment based on 10,000 replications. A lag q of 0 corresponds to Mandelbrot's classical R/S statistic, and a noninteger lag value indicates the mean lag (standard deviation given in parentheses) chosen via Andrews' (1991) data-dependent procedure assuming an AR(1) data-generating process.*

n	q	Min	Max	Mean	S.D.	Power 1%-Test	Power 5%-Test	Power 10%-Test
100	0	0.729	4.047	2.025	0.513	0.429	0.600	0.680
100	5	0.635	2.089	1.361	0.242	0.001	0.014	0.065
100	10	0.686	1.746	1.237	0.171	0.000	0.005	0.015
100	25	0.723	2.148	1.208	0.156	0.000	0.002	0.008
100	50	0.823	2.803	1.399	0.328	0.035	0.096	0.154
100	4.27 (1.43)	0.650	2.330	1.411	0.257	0.003	0.040	0.104
250	0	0.938	5.563	2.678	0.709	0.774	0.878	0.918
250	5	0.713	2.924	1.699	0.364	0.153	0.335	0.442
250	10	0.705	2.304	1.475	0.277	0.006	0.091	0.186
250	25	0.681	1.852	1.264	0.175	0.000	0.003	0.012
250	50	0.756	1.971	1.208	0.140	0.000	0.002	0.007
250	6.63 (1.36)	0.711	2.596	1.619	0.317	0.067	0.240	0.360
500	0	1.061	7.243	3.336	0.929	0.924	0.967	0.980
500	5	0.731	3.726	2.055	0.491	0.450	0.628	0.709
500	10	0.692	2.944	1.750	0.384	0.197	0.385	0.494
500	25	0.623	2.164	1.429	0.258	0.001	0.045	0.123
500	50	0.687	1.763	1.271	0.178	0.000	0.003	0.009
500	8.96 (1.37)	0.709	3.201	1.809	0.384	0.242	0.447	0.557
750	0	1.228	8.059	3.799	1.052	0.972	0.990	0.995
750	5	0.838	4.280	2.313	0.565	0.620	0.766	0.830
750	10	0.769	3.421	1.955	0.447	0.370	0.557	0.655
750	25	0.734	2.478	1.569	0.310	0.042	0.195	0.304
750	50	0.722	1.925	1.359	0.223	0.000	0.005	0.036
750	10.58 (1.33)	0.798	3.324	1.942	0.421	0.363	0.559	0.657
1000	0	1.398	8.615	4.174	1.174	0.985	0.996	0.998
1000	5	0.898	4.672	2.521	0.635	0.720	0.846	0.892
1000	10	0.779	3.766	2.121	0.504	0.494	0.669	0.747

(continued)

Table 6.6a.   *(continued)*

n	q	Min	Max	Mean	S.D.	Power 1%-Test	Power 5%-Test	Power 10%-Test
1000	25	0.641	2.734	1.686	0.354	0.135	0.322	0.431
1000	50	0.628	2.118	1.441	0.259	0.001	0.052	0.138
1000	11.87 (1.31)	0.766	3.613	2.044	0.454	0.446	0.630	0.718

Table 6.6b.   *Power of the modified R/S statistic under a Gaussian fractionally differenced alternative with differencing parameter $d = -1/3$. The variance of the process has been normalized to unity. Each set of rows of a given sample size n corresponds to a separate and independent Monte Carlo experiment based on 10,000 replications. A lag q of 0 corresponds to Mandelbrot's classical R/S statistic, and a noninteger lag value indicates the mean lag (standard deviation given in parentheses) chosen via Andrews' (1991) data-dependent procedure assuming an AR(1) data-generating process.*

n	q	Min	Max	Mean	S.D.	Power 1%-Test	Power 5%-Test	Power 10%-Test
100	0	0.367	1.239	0.678	0.120	0.670	0.858	0.923
100	5	0.637	1.710	1.027	0.153	0.006	0.054	0.134
100	10	0.762	2.030	1.217	0.161	0.000	0.001	0.005
100	25	0.953	2.638	1.587	0.207	0.014	0.095	0.211
100	50	1.052	3.478	2.033	0.354	0.425	0.679	0.785
100	2.94 (0.99)	0.478	1.621	0.889	0.155	0.131	0.331	0.466
250	0	0.303	1.014	0.561	0.089	0.951	0.991	0.997
250	5	0.549	1.479	0.851	0.128	0.146	0.409	0.571
250	10	0.632	1.752	1.005	0.143	0.007	0.065	0.152
250	25	0.833	1.936	1.292	0.157	0.000	0.001	0.004
250	50	0.977	2.357	1.594	0.186	0.007	0.078	0.198
250	4.20 (0.86)	0.448	1.437	0.796	0.129	0.301	0.578	0.716
500	0	0.292	0.819	0.479	0.071	0.997	1.000	1.000
500	5	0.458	1.244	0.728	0.105	0.517	0.794	0.888
500	10	0.555	1.489	0.861	0.121	0.111	0.366	0.543
500	25	0.706	1.735	1.105	0.143	0.000	0.004	0.022
500	50	0.881	2.089	1.356	0.157	0.000	0.002	0.011
500	5.45 (0.77)	0.443	1.318	0.725	0.108	0.529	0.793	0.887

(continued)

Table 6.6b. *(continued)*

n	q	Min	Max	Mean	S.D.	Power 1%-Test	Power 5%-Test	Power 10%-Test
750	0	0.276	0.700	0.433	0.063	1.000	1.000	1.000
750	5	0.422	1.070	0.659	0.094	0.764	0.932	0.973
750	10	0.499	1.262	0.779	0.109	0.325	0.641	0.789
750	25	0.689	1.570	1.001	0.132	0.003	0.049	0.138
750	50	0.837	1.802	1.227	0.148	0.000	0.000	0.002
750	6.34 (0.73)	0.424	1.133	0.682	0.099	0.679	0.892	0.951
1000	0	0.257	0.775	0.403	0.057	1.000	1.000	1.000
1000	5	0.401	1.149	0.613	0.085	0.895	0.978	0.993
1000	10	0.487	1.376	0.725	0.099	0.525	0.809	0.907
1000	25	0.633	1.596	0.930	0.121	0.020	0.154	0.306
1000	50	0.778	1.820	1.139	0.139	0.000	0.000	0.006
1000	7.01 (0.70)	0.412	1.235	0.651	0.092	0.789	0.945	0.978

employed data sampled at different frequencies (implying different values of d for different sample sizes), the trade-off between the time span of the data and the frequency of observation for the test's power may be an important issue. Nevertheless, the simulation results suggest that short-range dependence may be the more significant feature of recent stock market returns.

6.6 Conclusion

Using a simple modification of the Hurst-Mandelbrot rescaled range that accounts for short-term dependence, and contrary to previous studies, we find little evidence of long-term memory in historical U.S. stock market returns. If the source of serial correlation is lagged adjustment to new information, the absence of strong dependence in stock returns should not be surprising from an economic standpoint, given the frequency with which financial asset markets clear. Surely financial security prices must be immune to persistent informational asymmetries, especially over longer time spans. Perhaps the fluctuations of aggregate economic output are more likely to display such long-run tendencies, as Kondratiev and Kuznets have suggested, and this long-memory in output may eventually manifest itself in the return to equity. But if some form of long-range dependence is indeed present in stock returns, it will not be easily detected by any of our current statistical tools, especially in view of the optimality of the R/S statistic in the Mandelbrot and Wallis (1969b) sense. Direct estimation of particular parametric models may provide more positive evidence of long-term memory and is currently being pursued by several investigators.[24]

---

[24]See, for example, Boes et al. (1989), Diebold and Rudebusch (1989), Fox and Taqqu (1986), Geweke and Porter-Hudak (1983), Porter-Hudak (1990), Sowell (1989, 1990), and Yajima (1985, 1988).

Appendix A6
Proof of Theorems

Proofs of the theorems rely on the following three lemmas:

Lemma A.1 (Herrndorf (1984)). *If $\{\epsilon_t\}$ satisfies assumptions (A1)–(A4) then as n increases without bound, $W_n(\tau) \Rightarrow W(\tau)$.*

Lemma A.2 (Extended Continuous Mapping Theorem).[25] *Let h_n and h be measurable mappings from $\mathcal{D}[0, 1]$ to itself and denote by E the set of $x \in \mathcal{D}[0, 1]$ such that $h_n(x_n) \to h(x)$ fails to hold for some sequence x_n converging to x. If $W_n(\tau) \Rightarrow W(\tau)$ and E is of Wiener-measure zero, i.e., $P(W \in E) = 0$, then $h_n(W_n) \Rightarrow h(W)$.*

Lemma A.3. *Let $R_n \Rightarrow R$ where both R_n and R have nonnegative support, and let $P(R = 0) = P(R = \infty) = 0$. If $a_n \xrightarrow{p} \infty$, then $a_n R_n \xrightarrow{p} \infty$. If $a_n \xrightarrow{p} 0$, then $a_n R_n \xrightarrow{p} 0$.*

Proof of Theorem 6.3.1

Let $S_n = \sum_{j=1}^{n} \epsilon_j$ and define the following function $Y_n(\tau)$ on $\mathcal{D}[0, 1]$:

$$Y_n(\tau) = \frac{1}{\sigma \sqrt{n}} S_{[n\tau]}, \qquad \tau \in [0, 1], \qquad (A6.1)$$

where $[n\tau]$ denotes the greatest integer less than or equal to $n\tau$, and σ is defined in condition (A3) of the null hypothesis. By convention, set $Y_n(0) \equiv 0$. Under conditions (A1), (A2′), (A3), and (A4) Herrndorf (1984)

---

[25] See Billingsley (1968) for a proof.

has shown that $Y_n(\tau) \Rightarrow W(\tau)$. But consider:

$$\underset{1 \le k \le n}{\text{Max}} \frac{1}{\hat{\sigma}_n(q)\sqrt{n}} \sum_{j=1}^{k}(X_j - \bar{X}_n)$$

$$= \underset{1 \le k \le n}{\text{Max}} \frac{1}{\hat{\sigma}_n(q)\sqrt{n}} \left(S_k - \frac{k}{n}S_n \right) \qquad \text{(A6.2a)}$$

$$= \underset{0 \le \tau \le 1}{\text{Max}} Z_n(\tau) \qquad \text{(A6.2b)}$$

where

$$Z_n(\tau) \equiv Y_n(\tau) - \frac{[n\tau]}{n} Y_n(1). \qquad \text{(A6.2c)}$$

Since the sequence of functions h_n that map $Y_n(\tau)$ to $Z_n(\tau)$ satisfies the conditions of Lemma A.2, where the limiting mapping h takes $Y_n(\tau)$ to $Y_n(\tau) - \tau Y_n(1)$, it may be concluded that

$$h_n\big(Y_n(\tau)\big) = Z_n(\tau) \Rightarrow h\big(W(\tau)\big) = W(\tau) - \tau W(1) = W^0(\tau). \quad \text{(A6.3)}$$

If the estimator $\hat{\sigma}_n(q)$ is substituted in place of σ in the construction of $Z_n(\tau)$, then under conditions (A2′) and (A5), Theorem 4.2 of Phillips (1987) shows that (A3) still obtains. The rest of the theorem follows directly from repeated application of Lemma A.2.   **Q.E.D.**

Proof of Theorem 6.3.2

See Davydov (1970) and Taqqu (1975).

Proof of Theorem 6.3.3

Parts (6.3.3)–(6.3.3) follow directly from Theorem 6.3.2 and Lemma A.2, and part (6.3.3) follows immediately from Lemma A.3. Therefore, we need only prove (6.3.3). Let $H \in (\frac{1}{2}, 1)$ so that $\gamma(k) \sim k^{2H-2}L(k)$. This implies that

$$\text{Var}[S_n] \sim n^{2H}L(n). \qquad \text{(A6.4)}$$

Therefore, to show that $a_n \overset{p}{\to} \infty$, it suffices to show that

$$\frac{\hat{\sigma}^2(q)}{n^{2H-1}L(n)} \overset{p}{\to} 0. \qquad \text{(A6.5)}$$

Consider the population counterpart to (A6.5):

$$\frac{\sigma^2(q)}{n^{2H-1}L(n)} = \frac{1}{n^{2H-1}L(n)} \left(\sigma_\epsilon^2 + 2\sum_{j=1}^{q} \omega_j \gamma_j \right) \qquad \text{(A6.6)}$$

where $\omega_j = 1 - j/(q+1)$. Since by assumption $\gamma_j \sim j^{2H-2}L(j)$, there exists some integer q_a and $M > 0$ such that for $j > q_a$, $\gamma_j < Mj^{2H-2}L(j)$. Now it is well known that a slowly-varying function satisfies the inequality $j^{-\epsilon} < L(j) < j^\epsilon$ for any $\epsilon > 0$ and $j > q_b$, for some $q_b(\epsilon)$. Choose $\epsilon < 2 - 2H$, and observe that

$$\gamma_j < Mj^{2H-2}j^\epsilon, \qquad j > q_0 \equiv \max(q_a, q_b) \qquad \text{(A6.7)}$$

which implies:

$$2\sum_{j=1}^{q} \omega_j \gamma_j < 2\sum_{j=1}^{q_0} \omega_j \gamma_j + 2M \sum_{j=q_0+1}^{q} \omega_j j^{2H-2+\epsilon} \qquad \text{(A6.8)}$$

where, without loss of generality, we have assumed that $q > q_0$. As q increases without bound, the first sum of the right-side of (A6.8) remains finite, and the second sum may be bounded by observing that its summands are positive and decreasing, hence (see, for example, Buck, 1978, Chapter 5.5):

$$2M \sum_{j=q_0+1}^{q} \omega_j j^{2H-2+\epsilon} \leq 2M \int_{q_0}^{q} \left(1 - \frac{x}{q+1}\right) x^{2H-2+\epsilon} \, dx \qquad \text{(A6.9a)}$$

$$\sim O(q^{2H-1+\epsilon}) \qquad \text{(A6.9b)}$$

where the asymptotic equivalence follows by direct integration. If $q \sim O(n^\delta)$ where $\delta \in (0, 1)$, a weaker condition than required by our null hypothesis, then the ratio $\sigma^2(q)/(n^{2H-1}L(n))$ is at most of order $O(n^{(2H-1+\epsilon)(\delta-1)})$, which converges to zero. If we can now show that (A6.6) and its sample counterpart are equal in probability, then we are done. This is accomplished by the following sequence of inequalities:

$$E\left|\frac{\hat{\sigma}^2(q)}{n^{2H-1}} - \frac{\sigma^2(q)}{n^{2H-1}}\right| = \frac{1}{n^{2H-1}} E\left|(\hat{\sigma}_\epsilon^2 - \sigma_\epsilon^2) + 2\sum_{j=1}^{q} \omega_j(\hat{\gamma}_j - \gamma_j)\right| \qquad \text{(A6.10a)}$$

$$\leq \frac{E|\hat{\sigma}_\epsilon^2 - \sigma_\epsilon^2|}{n^{2H-1}}$$

$$+ \frac{2}{n^{2H-1}} \sum_{j=1}^{q} \omega_j E|\hat{\gamma}_j - \gamma_j| \qquad \text{(A6.10b)}$$

$$\leq \frac{E|\hat{\sigma}_\epsilon^2 - \sigma_\epsilon^2|}{n^{2H-1}}$$

$$+ \frac{2}{n^{2H-1}} \sum_{j=1}^{q} \omega_j \sqrt{E(\hat{\gamma}_j - \gamma_j)^2}. \tag{A6.10c}$$

But since Hosking (1984, Theorem 2) provides rates of convergence for sample auto-covariances of stationary Gaussian processes satisfying (6.3.14), an integral evaluation similar to that in (A6.9a) shows that the sum in (A6.10c) vanishes asymptotically when $q \sim o(n)$. This completes the proof. Since the proof for $H \in (0, \frac{1}{2})$ is similar, it is left to the reader.   **Q.E.D.**

Part II

THE FOCUS OF THE FIVE CHAPTERS in Part I has been the Random Walk Hypothesis and the forecastability of asset returns through time. In the three chapters of Part II, we shift our focus to questions of the predictability of relative returns for a given time period. On average, is the return to one stock or portfolio higher than the return to another stock or portfolio? If the answer to this age-old question is yes, can we explain the difference, perhaps through differences in risk?

These questions are central to financial economics since they bear directly on the trade-off between risk and expected return, one of the founding pillars of modern financial theory. This theory suggests that lower risk investments such as bonds or utility stocks will yield lower returns on average than riskier investments such airline or technology stocks, which accords well with common business sense: investors require a greater incentive to bear more risk, and this incentive manifests itself in higher expected returns. The issue, then, is whether the profits of successful investment strategies can be attributed to the presence of higher risks—if so, then the profits are compensation for risk-bearing capacity and nothing unusual; if not, then further investigation is warranted.

Over the past three decades, a number of studies have reported so-called anomalies, strategies that, when applied to historical data, lead to return differences that are not easily explained by risk differences. For example, one of the most enduring anomalies is the "size effect," the apparent excess expected returns that accrue to stocks of small-capitalization companies–in excess of their risks—which was first discovered by Banz (1981). Rozeff and Kinney (1976), Keim (1983), and Roll (1983) document a related anomaly: small capitalization stocks tend to outperform large capitalization stocks by a wide margin over the turn of the calendar year. Other well-known anomalies include: the Value Line enigma (Copeland and Mayers, 1982); the profitability of return-reversal strategies (DeBondt and Thaler, 1985; Rosenberg, Reid, and Lanstein, 1985; Lehmann, 1990; Chopra, Lakonishok, and Ritter, 1992); the underreaction to earnings announcements or "post-earnings announcement drift" (Ball and Brown, 1968; Bernard and Thomas, 1990); the relation between price/earnings ratios and expected returns (Basu, 1977); the relation between book-value/market-value ratios and expected returns (Fama and French, 1992); the volatility of orange juice futures prices (Roll, 1984b); and calendar effects such as holiday, weekend, and turn-of-the-month seasonalities (Lakonishok and Smidt, 1988).

In light of these anomalies, it is clear that we need a risk/reward benchmark to tell us how much risk is required for a given level of expected return. In the academic jargon, we require an equilibrium asset-pricing model. The workhorse asset-pricing model that virtually all anomaly studies use to make risk adjustments is the Capital Asset Pricing Model (CAPM) of Sharpe (1964) and Lintner (1965). In the CAPM framework, an asset's "beta" is the relevant measure of risk—stocks with higher betas should earn higher returns on average. And in many of the recent anomaly studies, the authors argue forcefully that differences in beta cannot fully explain the magnitudes of return differences, hence the term "anomaly."

There are many possible explanations for these anomalies, but most of them fall neatly into two general categories: risk-based alternatives and non-risk-based alternatives. Risk-based alternatives include the CAPM and multifactor generalizations such as Ross's (1976) Arbitrage Pricing Theory and Merton's (1973) Intertemporal CAPM, all developed under the assumptions of investor rationality and well-functioning capital markets. Among these alternatives, the source of deviations from the CAPM is omitted risk factors, i.e., the CAPM is an incomplete model of the risk/reward relation, hence average return differences cannot be explained solely by the standard CAPM betas.

Non-risk-based alternatives include statistical biases that might afflict the empirical methods, the existence of market frictions and institutional rigidities not captured by standard asset-pricing models, and explanations based on investor irrationality and market inefficiency.

The heated debate among academics concerning the explanation for the anomalies motivated our studies in chapters 7 and 8. Chapter 7 provides a general statistical framework to distinguish between the risk-based and non-risk-based alternatives. The idea is to consider the overall risk/reward trade-off implied by the anomaly and ask if it can be plausibly explained by risk differences. We conclude that the magnitude of the expected return differences is too large to be explained purley by differences in risk.

In Chapter 8 we turn to non-risk-based alternatives and focus specifically on statistical biases that arise from searching through the data until something "interesting" is discovered. Anomalies obtained in this way are hardly anomalous—they are merely manifestations of *data-snooping biases*, spurious statistical artifacts that are due to random chance. For example, a typical adult individual in the United States is unlikely to be taller than 6'5", hence the average height in a random sample of individuals is probably less than 6'5". However, if we construct our sample by searching for the tallest individuals in a given population—by focusing our attention only on professional basketball players, for example—then the average height in this biased sample may well exceed 6'5". This comes as no surprise because we searched over the population for "tallness," and the fact that the average height in this sample is greater than 6'5" does not imply that heights are increasing in the general population.

In much the same way, searching through historical data for superior investment performance may well yield superior performance, but this need not be evidence of genuine performance ability. Even in the absence of superior performance abilities, with a large enough dataset and a sufficiently diligent search process, spurious superior performance can almost always be found. While such biases are unavoidable in non-experimental disciplines such as financial economics, acknowledging this possibility and understanding the statistical properties of these biases can go a long way towards reducing their effects.

In Chapter 8, we provide a formal analysis of this phenomenon in the context of linear factor models, and show that even small amounts of data-snooping can lead to very large spurious differences in return performance. Because with hindsight one can almost always "discover" return differences that appear large, it is critical to account for this effect by modifying the standard statistical procedures appropriately and we propose one method for doing so.

Having explored the "downside" of data-snooping—finding superior performance when none exists—we consider the "upside" in Chapter 9, in which we maximize predictability directly by constructing portfolios of stocks and bonds in a very particular manner. Many financial economists and investment professionals have undertaken the search for predictability in earnest and with great vigor. But as important as it is, predictability is rarely maximized systematically in empirical investigations, even though it may dictate the course of the investigation at many critical junctures and, as a consequence, is maximized *implicitly* over time and over sequences of investigations.

In Chapter 9, we maximize the predictability in asset returns *explicitly* by constructing portfolios of assets that are the most predictable in a time-series context. Such explicit maximization can add several new insights to findings based on less formal methods. Perhaps the most obvious is that it yields an upper bound to what even the most industrious investigator will achieve in his search for predictability among portfolios (how large can data-snooping biases be?). As such, it provides an informal yardstick against which other findings may be measured. For example, the results in Part I imply that approximately 10% of the variation in the CRSP equal-weighted weekly return index from 1962 to 1985 can be explained by the previous week's returns—is this large or small? The answer will depend on whether the maximum predictability for weekly portfolio returns is 15% or 75%.

The maximization of predictability can also direct us towards more disaggregated sources of persistence and time-variation in asset returns, in the form of portfolio weights of the most predictable portfolio, and sensitivities of those weights to specific predictors, e.g., industrial production, dividend yield, etc. A primitive example of this kind of disaggregation is the lead/lag relation among size-sorted portfolios we documented in Chapter 5, in which the predictability of weekly stock index returns is traced to the tendency for the returns of larger capitalization stocks to lead those of smaller stocks. The more general framework of Chapter 9 includes lead/lag effects as a special case, but captures predictability explicitly as a function of time-varying economic risk premia rather than as a function of past returns only.

More importantly, maximizing predictability may be a better alternative than the current two-step procedure for exploiting predictabilities in asset returns: (1) construct a linear factor model of returns based on cross-sectional explanatory power, e.g., factor analysis, principal components decomposition, etc.; and (2) analyze the predictability of these factors. This two-step approach is motivated by the risk-based alternatives literature we alluded to earlier: the CAPM and ICAPM, the APT, and their many variants in which expected returns are linearly related to contemporaneous "systematic" risk factors.

While the two-step approach can shed considerable light on the nature of asset-return predictability—especially when the risk factors are known—it may not be as informative when the factors are unknown. For example, it is possible that the set of factors which best explain the cross-sectional variation in expected returns are relatively unpredictable through time, whereas other factors that *can* be used to predict expected returns are not nearly as useful contemporaneously in capturing the cross-sectional variation of expected returns. Therefore, focusing on the predictability of factors which are important contemporaneously may yield a very misleading picture of the true nature of predictability in asset returns. The approach in Chapter 9 offers an alternative in which predictability is maximized directly.

Taken together, the chapters in Part II present a more detailed analysis of the sources and nature of predictability in the stock and bond markets, providing the statistical machinery to differentiate between risk-based and non-risk-based explanations of asset-pricing anomalies, to quantify and control for the impact of data-snooping biases, and to exploit more fully the genuine predictabilities that might be present in the data.

7

Multifactor Models Do Not Explain Deviations from the CAPM

7.1 Introduction

ONE OF THE IMPORTANT PROBLEMS of modern financial economics is the quantification of the tradeoff between risk and expected return. Although common sense suggests that investments free of risk will generally yield lower returns than riskier investments such as the stock market, it was only with the development of the Sharpe-Lintner capital asset pricing model (CAPM) that economists were able to quantify these differences in returns. In particular, the CAPM shows that the cross-section of expected excess returns of financial assets must be linearly related to the market betas, with an intercept of zero. Because of the practical importance of this risk–return relation, it has been empirically examined in numerous studies. Over the past fifteen years, a number of studies have presented evidence that contradict the CAPM, statistically rejecting the hypothesis that the intercept of a regression of excess returns on the excess return of the market is zero.

The apparent violations of the CAPM have spawned research into possible explanations. In this chapter, the explanations will be divided into two categories: risk-based alternatives and nonrisk-based alternatives. The risk-based category includes multifactor asset pricing models developed under the assumptions of investor rationality and perfect capital markets. For this category, the source of deviations from the CAPM is either missing risk factors or the misidentification of the market portfolio as in Roll (1977).

The nonrisk-based category includes biases introduced in the empirical methodology, the existence of market frictions, or explanations arising from the presence of irrational investors. Examples are data-snooping biases, biases in computing returns, transaction costs and liquidity effects, and market inefficiencies. Although some of these explanations contain elements of risk, the elements of risk are different than those associated with perfect capital markets.

The empirical finding that the intercepts of the CAPM deviate statistically from zero has naturally led to the empirical examination of multifactor asset pricing models motivated by the arbitrage pricing theory (APT) developed by Ross (1976) and the intertemporal capital asset pricing model (ICAPM) developed by Merton (1973) (see Fama, 1993, for a detailed discussion of these multifactor model theories). The basic approach has been to introduce additional factors in the form of excess returns on traded portfolios and then reexamine the zero-intercept hypothesis. Fama and French (1993) use this approach and document that the estimates of the CAPM intercepts deviate from zero for portfolios formed on the basis of the ratio of book value to market value of equity as well as for portfolios formed based on market capitalization.[1] On finding that the intercepts for these portfolios with a three-factor model are closer to zero, they conclude that missing risk factors in the CAPM are the source of the deviations. They go on to advocate the use of a multifactor model, stating that, with respect to the use of the Sharpe-Lintner CAPM, their results "should help to break this common habit" (p. 44).

However, the conclusion that additional risk factors are required may be premature. One of several explanations consistent with the presence of deviations is data-snooping, as presented in Lo and MacKinlay (1990). The argument is that on an *ex post* basis one will always be able to find deviations from the CAPM. Such deviations considered in a group will appear statistically significant. However, they are merely a result of grouping assets with common disturbance terms. Since in financial economics our empirical analysis is *ex post* in nature, this problem is difficult to control. Direct adjustments for potential snooping are difficult to implement and, when implemented, make it very difficult to find real deviations.

While it is generally difficult to quantify and adjust for the effects of data-snooping biases, there are some related biases that can be examined. One such case pursued by Kothari, Shanken, and Sloan (1995) is sample selection bias. The authors show that significant biases can arise in academic research when the analysis is conditioned on the assets appearing in both the Center for Research in Security Prices (CRSP) database and the Compustat database. Their analysis suggests that deviations from the CAPM such as those documented by Fama and French (1993) can be explained by sample selection biases. Breen and Korajczyk (1993) provide further evidence on selection biases that supports the Kothari, Shanken, and Sloan conclusion.

---

[1]Fama and French are also concerned with the observation that the relation between average returns and market betas is weak. Although not addressed here, this point has been addressed in a number of recent papers, including Chan and Lakonishok (1993), Kandel and Stambaugh (1995), Kothari, Shanken, and Sloan (1995), and Roll and Ross (1994).

Other researchers interpret the deviations from the CAPM as indications of the presence of irrational behavior by market participants (e.g., DeBondt and Thaler, 1985). A number of theories have been developed that are consistent with this line of thought. A recent example is the work of Lakonishok, Shleifer, and Vishny (1994) who argue that the deviations arise from investors following naive strategies, such as extrapolating past growth rates too far into the future, assuming a trend in stock prices, overreacting to good or bad news, or preferring to invest in firms with a high level of profitability. With this alternative the possibility of nonzero intercepts arises not only from missing risk factors but also from specific firm characteristics.

Conrad and Kaul (1993) consider the possibility that biases in computed returns explain the deviations. They find that the implicit portfolio rebalancing in most analyses biases measured returns upwards, leading to overstated returns and CAPM deviations. This problem will be most severe for tests using frequently rebalanced portfolios and short observation intervals.

Finally, market frictions and liquidity effects could induce a nonzero intercept in the CAPM tests. Since the model is developed in a perfect market, such effects are not accommodated. Amihud and Mendelson (1986) present some evidence of returns containing effects from market frictions and demands for liquidity.

The controversy over whether or not the CAPM deviations are due to missing risk factors flourishes because empirically it is hard to distinguish between the various hypotheses. On an *ex post* basis, one can always find a set of risk factors that will make the asset pricing model intercept zero. Without a specific theory identifying the risk factors, one will always be able to explain the cross-section of expected returns with a multifactor asset pricing model, even if the real explanation lies in one of the nonrisk-based categories.

Although it is difficult to distinguish between the risk-based and nonrisk-based categories, the practical implications of the distinction are important. For example, if the risk-based explanation is correct, then cost of capital calculations using the CAPM can be badly misspecified. A better approach would be to use a multifactor model that captures the missing risk factors. On the other hand, if the deviations are a result of the nonrisk-based explanations, then disposing of the CAPM in favor of a multifactor model may lead to serious errors. The cost of capital estimate from a multifactor model can be very different than the estimate from the CAPM.

In this chapter, we discriminate between the risk-based and the nonrisk-based explanations using *ex ante* analysis. The objective is to evaluate the plausibility of the argument that the deviations from the CAPM can be explained by additional risk factors. We argue that one should expect *ex ante* that CAPM deviations due to missing risk factors will be very difficult to detect because the deviation in expected return is also accompanied by increased variance. We formally analyze the issue using mean-variance efficient set mathematics in conjunction with the zero-intercept F-test presented in Gibbons, Ross, and Shanken (1989) and MacKinlay (1987). The difficulty exists because when deviations from the CAPM or other multifactor pricing models are the result of omitted risk factors, there is an upper limit on the distance between the null distribution of the test statistic and the alternative distribution. With the nonrisk-based alternatives, for which the source of the deviations is something other than missing factors, no such limit exists because the deviations need not be linked to the variances and covariances.

The chapter also draws on a related distinction between the two categories, namely the difference in the behavior of the maximum squared Sharpe measure as the cross-section of securities is increased. (The Sharpe measure is the ratio of the mean excess return to the standard deviation of the excess return.) For the risk-based alternatives the maximum squared Sharpe measure is bounded, and for the nonrisk-based alternatives the maximum squared Sharpe measure is a less useful construct and can, in principle, be unbounded.

The results of the chapter underscore the important role that economic analysis plays in distinguishing among different pricing models for the relation between risk and return. In the absence of specific alternative theories, and without very long time series of data, one is limited in what can be said about risk–return relations among financial securities.

The chapter proceeds as follows. In Section 2 the framework for the analysis is presented and the *optimal orthogonal portfolio* is defined. This portfolio will play a key role in the arguments of the chapter. Many of the results in the chapter can be related to the values of the squared Sharpe measure for relevant portfolios. In Section 3 the relations between the parameters of the returns and the Sharpe measures are presented. Section 4 develops the implications relating to the controversy over missing risk factors. Theoretically, the framework used to distinguish between risk-based and nonrisk-based explanations assumes a large number of assets. Section 5 illustrates that the usefulness of the framework does not depend on this assumption. The chapter concludes with Section 6.

7.2 Linear Pricing Models, Mean-Variance Analysis, and the Optimal Orthogonal Portfolio

We begin by specifying the distributional properties of excess returns for $\overline{N}$ primary assets in the economy. Let z_t represent the $\overline{N} \times 1$ vector of excess returns for period t. Assume z_t is stationary and ergodic with mean μ and a covariance matrix V that is full rank. Given these assumptions for any set of factor portfolios, a linear relation between the excess returns and the portfolios' excess returns results. The relation can be expressed as

$$z_t = \alpha + B z_{pt} + \epsilon_t, \tag{7.2.1}$$

$$\mathrm{E}[\epsilon_t] = 0, \tag{7.2.2}$$

$$\mathrm{E}[\epsilon_t \epsilon_t'] = \Sigma, \tag{7.2.3}$$

$$\mathrm{E}[z_{pt}] = \mu_p, \quad \mathrm{E}[(z_{pt} - \mu_p)(z_{pt} - \mu_p)'] = \Omega_p, \tag{7.2.4}$$

$$\mathrm{Cov}[z_{pt}, \epsilon_t] = 0. \tag{7.2.5}$$

B is the $\overline{N} \times K$ matrix of factor loadings, z_{pt} is the $K \times 1$ vector of time-t factor portfolio excess returns, and α and ϵ_t are $\overline{N} \times 1$ vectors of asset return intercepts and disturbances, respectively. The values of α, B, and Σ will depend on the factor portfolios. This dependence is suppressed for notational convenience.

It is well-known that all of the elements of the vector α will be zero if a linear combination of the factor portfolios forms the tangency portfolio (i.e., the mean-variance efficient portfolio of risky assets given the presence of a risk-free asset). Let z_{qt} be the excess return of the (*ex ante*) tangency portfolio and let x_q be the $\overline{N} \times 1$ vector of portfolio weights. Here, and throughout the chapter, let ι represent a conforming vector of ones. From mean-variance analysis:

$$x_q = (\iota' V^{-1} \mu)^{-1} V^{-1} \mu. \tag{7.2.6}$$

In the context of our previous discussion, the asset pricing model will be considered well-specified when the tangency portfolio can be formed from a linear combination of the K-factor portfolios.

Our interest is in formally developing the relation between the deviations from the asset pricing model, α, and the residual covariance matrix Σ when a linear combination of the factor portfolios does not form the tangency portfolio. To facilitate this we define the *optimal orthogonal portfolio*,[2] which is the unique portfolio given $\overline{N}$ assets that can be combined with the factor portfolios to form the tangency portfolio and is orthogonal to the factor portfolios.

Take as given K-factor portfolios which cannot be combined to form the tangency portfolio or the global minimum variance portfolio. A portfolio

---

[2]See Roll (1980) for properties of orthogonal portfolios in a general context and Lehmann (1987, 1988, 1992) for discussions of the role of orthogonal portfolios in asset pricing tests. Also related is the orthogonal factor employed in MacKinlay (1987), the active portfolio considered by Gibbons, Ross, and Shanken (1989), and the modifying payoff used in Hansen and Jagannathan (1997).

h will be defined as the optimal orthogonal portfolio with respect to these K-factor portfolios if

$$x_q = X_p \omega + x_h (1 - \iota' \omega), \tag{7.2.7}$$

$$x_h' V X_p = 0, \tag{7.2.8}$$

for a $K \times 1$ vector ω, where X_p is the $\overline{N} \times K$ matrix of asset weights for the factor portfolios, x_h is the $\overline{N} \times 1$ vector of asset weights for the optimal orthogonal portfolio, and x_q is the $\overline{N} \times 1$ vector of asset weights for the tangency portfolio. If one considers a model without any factor portfolios ($K = 0$), then the optimal orthogonal portfolio will be the tangency portfolio.

The weights of portfolio h can be expressed in terms of the parameters of the K-factor model. For the vector of weights,

$$x_h = (\iota' V^{-1} \alpha)^{-1} V^{-1} \alpha = (\iota' \Sigma^\dagger \alpha)^{-1} \Sigma^\dagger \alpha, \tag{7.2.9}$$

where the $\dagger$ superscript indicates the generalized inverse. The usefulness of this portfolio comes from the fact that when added to (7.2.1) the intercept will vanish and the factor-loading matrix B will not be altered. The optimality restriction in (7.2.7) leads to the intercept vanishing, and the orthogonality condition in (7.2.8) leads to B being unchanged. Adding in z_{ht}:

$$z_t = B z_{pt} + \beta_h z_{ht} + u_t, \tag{7.2.10}$$

$$E[u_t] = 0, \tag{7.2.11}$$

$$E[u_t u_t'] = \Phi, \tag{7.2.12}$$

$$E[z_{ht}] = \mu_h, \quad E[(z_{ht} - \mu_h)^2] = \sigma_h^2, \tag{7.2.13}$$

$$Cov[z_{pt}, u_t] = 0, \tag{7.2.14}$$

$$Cov[z_{ht}, u_t] = 0. \tag{7.2.15}$$

The link results from comparing (7.2.1) and (7.2.10). Taking the unconditional expectations of both sides,

$$\alpha = \beta_h \mu_h, \tag{7.2.16}$$

and by equating the variance of ϵ_t with the variance of $\beta_h z_{ht} + u_t$:

$$\Sigma = \beta_h \beta_h' \sigma_h^2 + \Phi = \alpha \alpha' \frac{\sigma_h^2}{\mu_h^2} + \Phi. \tag{7.2.17}$$

The key link between the model deviations and the residual variances and covariances emerges from (7.2.17). The intuition for the link is straightforward. Deviations from the model must be accompanied by a common component in the residual variance to prevent the formation of a portfolio with a positive deviation and a residual variance that decreases to zero as the number of securities in the portfolio grows. When the link is not present (i.e., the link is undone by Φ), asymptotic arbitrage opportunities will exist.

7.3 Squared Sharpe Measures

The squared Sharpe measure is a useful construct for interpreting much of the ensuing analysis. The Sharpe measure for a given portfolio is calculated by dividing the mean excess return by the standard deviation of return. It is well-known that the tangency portfolio q will have the maximum squared Sharpe measure of all portfolios.[3] The squared Sharpe measure of q, s_q^2, is

$$s_q^2 = \mu' V^{-1} \mu. \tag{7.3.1}$$

Since the K-factor portfolios p and the optimal orthogonal portfolio h can be combined to form the tangency portfolio, it follows that the maximum squared Sharpe measure of these $K + 1$ portfolios will be s_q^2. Since h is orthogonal to the portfolios p, one can express s_q^2 as the sum of the squared Sharpe measure of the orthogonal portfolio and the squared maximum Sharpe measure of the factor portfolios,

$$s_q^2 = s_h^2 + s_p^2, \tag{7.3.2}$$

where $s_h^2 = \mu_h^2/\sigma_h^2$ and $s_p^2 = \mu_p'\Omega_p^{-1}\mu_p$.

In applications we will be employing subsets of the $\overline{N}$ assets. The factor portfolios need not be linear combinations of the subset of assets. Results similar to those above will hold within a subset of N assets. For the subset analysis when considering the tangency portfolio (of the subset), the maximum squared Sharpe measure of the assets and factor portfolios, and the optimal orthogonal portfolio for the subset, it is necessary to augment the N assets with the factor portfolios p. Defining z_t^* as the $N + K \times 1$ vector $[z_t'\ z_{pt}']'$ with mean $\mu_s^{*'}$ and covariance matrix V_s^*, for the tangency portfolio of these $N + K$ assets:

$$s_{q_s}^2 = \mu_s^{*'} V_s^{*-1} \mu_s^*. \tag{7.3.3}$$

The subscript s indicates that a subset of the assets is being considered. If any combination of the factor portfolios is a linear combination of the N assets, it will be necessary to use the generalized inverse in (7.3.3).

As we shall see, the analysis (with a subset of assets) will involve the quadratic $\alpha'\Sigma^{-1}\alpha$ computed using the parameters for the N assets. Gibbons, Ross, and Shanken (1989) and Lehmann (1988, 1992) provide interpretations of this quadratic term in terms of Sharpe measures. Assuming Σ

---

[3]See Jobson and Korkie (1982) for a development of this point and a performance measurement application. The existence of a maximum Sharpe measure as the number of assets becomes large is central to the arbitrage pricing theory. For further discussion see Chamberlain and Rothschild (1983) and Ingersoll (1984).

is of full rank (if Σ is singular then one must use the generalized inverse), they show

$$\alpha_s' \Sigma_s^{-1} \alpha_s = s_{q_s}^2 - s_p^2. \tag{7.3.4}$$

Consistent with (7.3.2), for the subset of assets $\alpha' \Sigma^{-1} \alpha$ will be the squared Sharpe measure of the subset's optimal orthogonal portfolio h_s. Therefore, for a given subset of assets:

$$s_{h_s}^2 = \alpha_s' \Sigma_s^{-1} \alpha_s, \tag{7.3.5}$$

$$s_{q_s}^2 = s_{h_s}^2 + s_p^2. \tag{7.3.6}$$

Also note that the squared Sharpe measure of the subset's optimal orthogonal portfolio is less than or equal to that of the population optimal orthogonal portfolio:

$$s_{h_s}^2 \leq s_h^2. \tag{7.3.7}$$

Next we use the optimal orthogonal portfolio and the Sharpe measure results together with the model deviation residual variance link to develop implications for distinguishing among asset pricing models. Hereafter we will suppress the s subscript. No ambiguity will result since, in the subsequent analysis, we will be working only with subsets of the assets.

7.4 Implications for Risk-Based Versus Nonrisk-Based Alternatives

Many asset pricing model tests involve testing the null hypothesis that the model intercept is zero using tests in the spirit of the zero-intercept F-test.[4] A common conclusion is that rejection of this hypothesis using one or more factor portfolios shows that more risk factors are required to explain the risk–return relation, leading to the inclusion of additional factors so that the null hypothesis will be accepted (Fama and French, 1993, adopt this approach). A shortcoming of this approach is that there are multiple potential interpretations of why the hypothesis is accepted. One view is that genuine progress in terms of identifying the "right" asset pricing model has been made. However, the apparent success in identifying a better model may also have come from finding a good within-sample fit through data-snooping. The likelihood of this possibility is increased by the fact that the additional factors lack theoretical motivation.

---

[4]Examples of tests of this type include Campbell (1987), Connor and Korajczyk (1988), Fama and French (1993), Gibbons, Ross, and Shanken (1989), Huberman, Kandel, and Stambaugh (1987), Kandel and Stambaugh (1990), Lehmann and Modest (1988), and MacKinlay (1987). The arguments in the chapter can also be related to the zero-beta CAPM tests in Gibbons (1982), Shanken (1985), and Stambaugh (1982).

This section integrates the link between the pricing model intercept and the residual covariance matrix of (7.2.17) and the squared Sharpe measure results with the distribution theory for the zero-intercept F-test to discriminate between the two interpretations. We consider two approaches. The first approach is a testing approach that compares the null hypothesis test statistic distribution with the distribution under each of the alternatives. The second approach is estimation-based, drawing on the squared Sharpe measure analysis to develop estimators for the squared Sharpe measure of the optimal orthgonal portfolio. Before presenting the two approaches, the zero-intercept F-test is summarized.

7.4.1 Zero Intercept F-Test

To implement the F-test, the additional assumption that excess asset returns are jointly normal and temporally independently and identically distributed is added. This assumption, though restrictive, buys us exact finite sample distributional results, thereby simplifying the analysis. However, it is important to note that this assumption is not central to the point; similar results will hold under much weaker assumptions. Using a generalized method of moments approach, MacKinlay and Richardson (1991) present a more general test statistic that has asymptotically a chi-square distribution. Analysis similar to that presented for the F-test holds for this general statistic.

We begin with a summary of the zero-intercept F-test of the null hypothesis that the intercept vector α from (7.2.1) is zero. Let H_0 be the null hypothesis and H_a be the alternative:

$$H_0: \quad \alpha = 0 \tag{7.4.1}$$

$$H_a: \quad \alpha \neq 0. \tag{7.4.2}$$

H_0 can be tested using the following test statistic:

$$\theta_1 = [(T - N - K)/N][1 + \hat{\mu}_p' \hat{\Omega}_p^{-1} \hat{\mu}_p]^{-1} \hat{\alpha}' \hat{\Sigma}^{-1} \hat{\alpha}, \tag{7.4.3}$$

where T is the number of time series observations, N is the number of assets or portfolios of assets included, and K is the number of factor portfolios. The hat superscripts indicate the maximum likelihood estimators. Under the null hypothesis, θ_1 is unconditionally distributed central F with N degrees of freedom in the numerator and $T - N - K$ degrees of freedom in the denominator.

The distribution of θ_1 can also be characterized in general. Conditional on the factor portfolio excess returns, the distribution of θ_1 is

$$\theta_1 \sim F_{N,T-N-K}(\lambda), \tag{7.4.4}$$

$$\lambda = T[1 + \hat{\mu}_p' \hat{\Omega}_p^{-1} \hat{\mu}_p]^{-1} \alpha' \Sigma^{-1} \alpha, \tag{7.4.5}$$

where λ is the noncentrality parameter of the F distribution. If $K = 0$, then the term $[1 + \hat{\mu}_p' \hat{\Omega}_p^{-1} \hat{\mu}_p]^{-1}$ will not appear in (7.4.3) or in (7.4.5) and θ_1 will be unconditionally distributed noncentral F.

7.4.2 Testing Approach

In this approach we consider the distribution of θ_1 under two different alternatives. The alternatives can be separated by their implications for the maximum value of the squared Sharpe measure. With the risk-based multifactor alternative there will be an upper bound on the squared Sharpe measure, whereas with the nonrisk-based alternatives the maximum squared Sharpe measure can be unbounded (as the number of assets increases).

First we consider the distribution of θ_1 under the alternative hypothesis when deviations are due to missing factors. Drawing on the results for the squared Sharpe measures, the noncentrality parameter of the F distribution is

$$\lambda = T [1 + \hat{\mu}_p' \hat{\Omega}_p^{-1} \hat{\mu}_p]^{-1} s_{h_s}^2. \qquad (7.4.6)$$

From (7.3.7), the third term in (7.4.6) is positive and bounded above by s_h^2. The second term is bounded between zero and one. Thus there is an upper bound for λ,

$$\lambda < T s_h^2 \leq T s_q^2. \qquad (7.4.7)$$

The second inequality follows from the fact that the tangency portfolio q has the maximum Sharpe measure of any asset or portfolio.[5]

Given a maximum value for the squared Sharpe measure, the upper bound on the noncentrality parameter can be important. With this bound, independent of how one arranges the assets to be included as dependent variables in the pricing model regression and for any value of N, there is a limit on the distance between the null distribution and the distribution when the alternative is missing factors. (In practice, when using the F-test it will be necessary for N to be less than $T - K$ so that $\hat{\Sigma}$ will be of full rank.) All the assets can be mispriced and yet the bound will still apply. As a consequence, one should be cautious in interpreting rejections of the zero intercept as evidence in favor of a model with more risk factors.

In contrast, when the source of nonzero intercepts is nonrisk-based, such as data-snooping, market frictions, or market irrationalities, the notion of a maximum squared Sharpe measure is not useful. The squared Sharpe measure (and the noncentrality parameter) are in principle unbounded because the argument linking the deviations and the residual variances and

---

[5]The first half of this bound appears in MacKinlay (1987) for the case of the Sharpe-Lintner CAPM. Related results appear in Kandel and Stambaugh (1987), Shanken (1987b), and Hansen and Jagannathan (1991).

covariances does not apply. When comparing alternatives with the intercepts of about the same magnitude, in general, one would expect to see larger test statistics in this nonrisk-based case.

One can examine the potential usefulness of the above analysis by considering alternatives with realistic parameter values. We construct the distribution of the test statistic for three cases: the null hypothesis, the missing risk factors alternative, and the nonrisk-based alternative. For the risk-based alternative, we draw on a framework designed to be similar to that in Fama and French (1993). For the nonrisk-based alternative we use a setup that is consistent with the analysis of Lo and MacKinlay (1990) and the work of Lakonishok, Shleifer, and Vishny (1994).

Consider a one-factor asset pricing model using a time series of the excess returns for 32 portfolios for the dependent variable. The one factor (independent variable) is the excess return of the market so that the zero-intercept null hypothesis is the CAPM. The length of the time series is 342 months. This setup corresponds to that of Fama and French (1993, Table 9, regression ii). The null distribution of the test statistic θ_1 is

$$\theta_1 \sim F_{32,309}(0). \tag{7.4.8}$$

To define the distribution of θ_1 under the risk-based and nonrisk-based alternatives one needs to specify the parameters necessary to calculate the noncentrality parameter. For the risk-based alternative, given a value for the squared Sharpe measure of the optimal orthogonal portfolio, the distribution corresponding to the upper bound of the noncentrality parameter from (7.4.7) can be considered. The Sharpe measure of the optimal orthogonal portfolio can be obtained using (7.3.2) given the squared Sharpe measures of the tangency portfolio and of the included factor portfolio. Our view is that in a perfect capital markets setting, a reasonable value for the squared Sharpe measure of the tangency portfolio for an observation interval of one month is 0.031 (or approximately 0.6 for the Sharpe measure on an annualized basis). This value, for example, corresponds to a portfolio with an annual expected excess return of 10% and a standard deviation of 16%. If the maximum squared Sharpe measure of the included factor portfolios is the *ex post* squared Sharpe measure of the CRSP value-weighted index, the implied maximum squared Sharpe measure for the optimal orthogonal portfolio is 0.021. This monthly value of 0.021 would be consistent with a portfolio which has an annualized mean excess return of 8% and annualized standard deviation of 16%.

The selection of the above Sharpe measure can be rationalized both theoretically and empirically. For theoretical justification we consider Sharpe measures of equity returns in the literature examining the equity risk premium puzzle (see Mehra and Prescott, 1985). While the focus of this research does not concern the Sharpe measure, that measure can be calculated from the analysis provided by Cecchetti and Mark (1990) and Kandel and Stambaugh (1991). Both papers are informative for the question at hand since they do not assume any imperfections in the asset markets. If their models, with reasonable parameters, imply Sharpe measures that are higher than the value selected for use in this chapter, the value selected here should perhaps be reconsidered. However, one should not completely rely on the measures from these papers for justification. In the presented models the aggregate equity portfolio generally will not be mean-variance efficient and therefore need not have the highest Sharpe measure of all equity portfolios.

Common to the papers is the use of a representative agent framework and a Markov switching model for the consumption process. The parameters of the consumption process are chosen to match estimates from the data. Cecchetti and Mark, using the standard time-separable constant relative risk aversion utility function, specify a range of values for the time preference parameter and the risk aversion coefficient. For each pair of values they generate the implied theoretical unconditional mean and standard deviation of the equity risk premium from which the Sharpe measures can be calculated. The annualized Sharpe measures range from 0.08 to 0.16, substantially below the value of 0.60 suggested above.

Kandel and Stambaugh allow for more general preferences. For the representative agent, a class is used that allows separation of the effects of risk aversion and intertemporal substitution. The standard time-separable model is a special case with the elasticity of intertemporal substitution equal to the inverse of the risk aversion coefficient. They set the monthly rate of time preference at 0.9978 and consider 16 pairs of the risk aversion coefficient and the intertemporal substitution parameter. The risk aversion coefficient varies from $\frac{1}{2}$ to 29 and the intertemporal substitution parameter varies from $\frac{1}{29}$ to 2. For thirteen of the sixteen cases the annual Sharpe measure of equity is less than 0.6. The three cases where the Sharpe measure is greater than 0.6 seem implausible since they imply the equity risk premium and the interest rate have almost the same variance, an impliciation which is strongly contradicted by historical data. These are the cases with high values for both the risk aversion parameter and the intertemporal substitution parameter. In aggregate, the results in these papers are consistent with the value specified for the maximum squared Sharpe measure in the context of frictionless asset markets.

One can also ask what Sharpe measure is empirically reasonable. To do this, we present historical Sharpe measures for a number of broad-based indices. These measures, some of which represent portfolios actually held, are reported in Table 7.1. For each index, the *ex post* measure (based on maximum likelihood estimates) and an unbiased squared Sharpe measure estimate are presented. For the July 1963 through December 1991 period the squared Sharpe measures are presented for the CRSP value-weighted

Table 7.1.   *Historical Sharpe measures for selected stock indices, where the Sharpe measure is defined as the ratio of the mean excess return to the standard deviation of the excess return. $\hat{s}_p^2$ is the monthly ex post squared Sharpe measure and $\hat{s}_p(ann)$ is the positive square root of this measure annualized. $\tilde{s}_p^2$ is an unbiased estimate of the monthly squared Sharpe measure and $\tilde{s}_p(ann)$ is the positive square root of this measure annualized. The CRSP value-weighted index is a value-weighted portfolio of all NYSE and Amex stocks. The CRSP small-stock portfolio is the value-weighted portfolio of stocks in the lowest joint NYSE-Amex market value decile. The portfolio of four indices is the portfolio with the maximum ex post squared Sharpe measure. The four indices are the CRSP value-weighted index, the CRSP small-stock decile, the CRSP long-term government bond index, and the CRSP corporate bond index. The bond indices are from the CRSP SBBI file. The S&P 500 index is a value-weighted index of 500 stocks. The S&P-Barra value index is an index of stocks within the S&P 500 universe with low ratios of price per share to book value per share. Every six months a breakpoint price-to-book-value ratio is determined so that approximately half the market capitalization of the S&P 500 is below the breakpoint and the other half is above. The value index is a value-weighted index of those stocks in the group of low price-to-book-value ratios. The S&P 500-Barra growth index is an index of stocks within the S&P 500 universe with high price-to-book-value ratios. The growth index is a value-weighted index of those S&P 500 stocks in the group of high price-to-book-value ratios.*

Time Period	Index	$\hat{s}_p^2$	$\hat{s}_p(ann)$	$\tilde{s}_p^2$	$\tilde{s}_p(ann)$
6307–9112	CRSP value-weighted index	0.0091	0.33	0.0061	0.27
6307–9112	CRSP small-stock portfolio	0.0142	0.40	0.0100	0.35
6307–9112	Portfolio of four indices	0.0145	0.41	0.0021	0.16
8101–9206	S&P 500 index	0.0161	0.44	0.0085	0.32
8101–9206	S&P-Barra value index	0.0208	0.50	0.0130	0.40
8101–9206	S&P-Barra growth index	0.0108	0.36	0.0033	0.20

index, the CRSP small-stock (10th decile) portfolio, and the *ex post* optimal portfolio of these two indices plus the long-term government index and the corporate bond index distributed by CRSP in the stock, bonds, bills, and inflation file. The small-stock portfolio has a monthly squared Sharpe measure of 0.014 (or 0.010 using the unbiased estimate), substantially below the value we use for the tangency portfolio. The *ex post* optimal four-index portfolio's measure is only slightly higher at 0.015.

Table 7.1 also contains results for the period from January 1981 through June 1992 for the S&P 500 Index, a value index, and a growth index. The value index contains the S&P 500 stocks with low price-to-book-value ratios and the growth index is constructed from stocks with high price-to-book-value ratios. The source of the index return statistics used to calculate the measures is Capaul, Rowley, and Sharpe (1993). These results provide a useful perspective on the maximum magnitudes of Sharpe measures since it is generally acknowledged that the 1980s was a period of strong stock market performance, especially for value-based investment strategies. Given this characterization, one would expect these results to provide a high estimate of possible Sharpe measures. The Sharpe measures from this period are in line with (and lower than) the value used in the analysis of the risk-based alternative. The highest *ex post* estimate is 0.021 for the value index. Generally, we interpret the evidence in this table as supporting the measure selected to calibrate the analysis for the risk-based alternative.

Proceeding using a squared Sharpe measure of 0.021 for the optimal orthogonal portfolio to calculate λ, the distribution of θ_1 is

$$\theta_1 \sim F_{32,309}(7.1). \tag{7.4.9}$$

This distribution will be used to characterize the risk-based alternative.

We specify the distribution for two nonrisk-based alternatives by specifying values of α, Σ, and $\hat{\mu}_p' \hat{\Omega}_p^{-1} \hat{\mu}_p$, and then calculating λ from (7.4.5). To specify the intercepts we assume that the elements of α are normally distributed with a mean of zero. We consider two values for the standard deviation, 0.0007 and 0.001. When the standard deviation of the elements of α is 0.001 about 95% of the alphas will lie between -0.002 and $+0.002$, an annualized spread of about 4.8%. A standard deviation of 0.0007 for the alphas would correspond to an annual spread of about 3.4%. These spreads are consistent with spreads that could arise from data-snooping[6] and are also plausible and even somewhat conservative given the contrarian strategy returns presented in Lakonishok, Shleifer, and Vishny. For Σ we use a sample estimate based on portfolios sorted by market capitalization for the period 1963 to 1991 (inclusive). The effect of $\hat{\mu}_p' \hat{\Omega}_p^{-1} \hat{\mu}_p$ on λ will typically be small, so we set it to zero. To get an idea of a reasonable value for the noncentrality parameter given this alternative, we calculate the expected value of λ given the distributional assumption for the elements of α conditional upon $\Sigma = \hat{\Sigma}$. The expected value of the noncentrality parameter is 39.4 for a standard deviation of 0.0007 and 80.3 for a standard deviation of 0.001. Using these values for the noncentrality parameter, the distribution of θ_1 is

$$\theta_1 \sim F_{32,309}(39.4) \quad \text{when} \quad \sigma_\alpha = 0.0007, \tag{7.4.10}$$

$$\theta_1 \sim F_{32,309}(80.3) \quad \text{when} \quad \sigma_\alpha = 0.001. \tag{7.4.11}$$

A plot of the four distributions from (7.4.8), (7.4.9), (7.4.10), and (7.4.11) is in Figure 7.1. The vertical bar on the plot represents the value

---

[6]With data-snooping the distribution of θ_1 is not exactly a noncentral F (see Lo and MacKinlay, 1990), but for the purposes of this chapter, the noncentral F will be a good approximation.

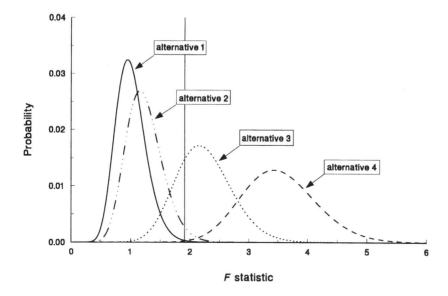

Figure 7.1. *Distributions for the CAPM zero-intercept test statistic for four alternatives. Alternative 1 is the CAPM (null hypothesis); alternative 2 is the risk-based alternative (deviations from the CAPM are from missing risk factors); alternatives 3 and 4 are the nonrisk-based alternative (deviations from the CAPM are unrelated to risk). The distributions are $F_{32,309}(0)$, $F_{32,309}(7.1)$, $F_{32,309}(39.4)$, and $F_{32,309}(80.3)$ for alternatives 1, 2, 3, and 4, respectively. The degrees of freedom are set to correspond to monthly observations from July 1963 to December 1992 (342 observations). Using 25 stock portfolios and 7 bond portfolios, and the CRSP value-weighted index as proxy for the market portfolio, the test statistic is 1.91, represented by the vertical line. The probability is calculated using an interval width of 0.02.*

1.91 which Fama and French calculate for the test statistic. From this figure notice that the null hypothesis distribution and the risk-based alternative distribution are quite close together, reflecting the impact of the upper bound on the noncentrality parameter (see MacKinlay, 1987, for detailed analysis of this alternative). In contrast, the nonrisk-based alternatives' distributions are far to the right of the other two distributions, consistent with the noncentrality parameter being unbounded for these alternatives.

What do we learn from this plot? First, if the objective is to distinguish among risk-based linear asset pricing models, the zero-intercept test is not particularly useful because the null distribution and the alternative distribution have substantial overlap. Second, if the goal is to compare a risk-based pricing model with a nonrisk-based alternative, the zero-intercept test can be very useful since the distributions of the test statistic for these alternatives have little overlap. Likelihood analysis provides another interpretation of the plot. Specifically, one can compare the values of the densities for the four alternatives at $\theta_1 = 1.91$. Such a comparison leads to the conclusion that the first nonrisk-based alternative is much more likely than the other three.

This analysis can be related to the Fama and French (1993) finding that a model with three factors does a good job in explaining the cross-section of expected returns. For a given finite cross-section under any alternative, the inclusion of the optimal orthogonal portfolio will lead to their result. As a consequence, their result on its own does not support the risk-based category. Indeed, the Fama and French approach to building the extra factors will tend to create a portfolio like the optimal orthogonal portfolio independent of the explanation for the CAPM deviations. Their extra factors essentially assign positive weights to the high positive alpha stocks and negative weights to the large negative alpha stocks. This procedure is likely to lead to a portfolio similar to the optimal orthogonal portfolio because the extreme alpha assets are likely to have the largest (in magnitude) weights in the optimal orthogonal portfolio (since its weights are proportional to $\Sigma^\dagger \alpha$; see (7.2.9)). Further, the fact that when Fama and French increase the number of factors to three the significance of the test statistic only decreases marginally is also consistent with the argument that missing risk factors are not the whole story.

More evidence of the potential importance of nonrisk explanations can be constructed using weekly data. To see why the analysis of weekly data can be informative, consider the biases introduced with market frictions such as the bid–ask spread. Blume and Stambaugh (1983) show that in the presence of the bid–ask bounce, there is an upward bias in observed returns. For asset i and time period t, Blume and Stambaugh show the following approximation for the relation between expected observed returns and expected true returns:

$$\mathrm{E}(R_{it}^{\mathrm{o}}) = \mathrm{E}(R_{it}) + \vartheta_i, \qquad (7.4.12)$$

where the superscript "o" distinguishes the returns observed with bid–ask bounce contamination from the true returns; ϑ_t is the bias which is equal to one-fourth of the proportional bid–ask spread squared. The bias will carry over into the intercept of any factor model. Consider a one-factor model in which the factor is *ex ante* the tangency portfolio. In this model the intercept for all true asset returns will be zero. However, the intercepts for the observed returns and the squared Sharpe measure of the optimal orthogonal portfolio will be nonzero. If the bias of the observed factor return is zero and if the factor return is uncorrelated with the bid–ask bounce process, then the intercept of the observed returns is

$$\alpha_i^{\mathrm{o}} = \vartheta_i, \qquad (7.4.13)$$

since α_i of the true return will be zero. Then, the squared Sharpe measure of the optimal orthogonal portfolio is

$$s_h^2 = \vartheta' \Sigma^{o(-1)} \vartheta, \qquad (7.4.14)$$

where Σ^o is the residual covariance matrix for the weekly observed returns and ϑ is the vector of biases for the included portfolios.[7] When the null hypothesis that the intercepts are zero is examined using observed returns, violations exist solely due to the presence of the bid–ask spread.

Bias of the type induced by the bid–ask spread is interesting because its magnitude does not depend on the length of the observation interval. As a consequence its effect will statistically be more pronounced with shorter observation intervals when the variance of the true returns is smaller. To examine the potential relevance of the above example, the F-test statistic is calculated using a sample of weekly returns for 32 portfolios. The data extends from July 1962 through December 1992 (1,591 weeks). NYSE and Amex stocks are allocated to the portfolios based on beginning-of-year market capitalization. Each portfolio is allocated an equal number of stocks and the portfolios are equal-weighted with rebalancing each week. For these portfolios, using the CRSP value-weighted index as the one factor, the F-test statistic is 2.82. Under the null hypothesis, this statistic has a central F distribution with 32 degrees of freedom in the numerator and 1,558 degrees of freedom in the denominator. (Diagnostics reveal some serial correlation in the residuals of the weekly one-factor model, in which case the null distribution will not be exactly central F.) This statistic can be cast in terms of the alternatives presented in Figure 7.1 since the noncentrality parameter of the F distribution will be approximately invariant to the observation interval and hence only the degrees of freedom need to be adjusted. Figure 7.2 presents the results that correspond to the weekly observation interval. Basically, these results reinforce the monthly observation results in that the observed statistic is most consistent with the nonrisk-based category.

In summary, the results suggest that the risk-based missing risk factors argument is not the whole story. Figures 7.1 and 7.2 show that the test statistic is still in the upper tail when the distribution of θ_1 in the presence of missing risk factors is tabulated. The p-value using this distribution is 0.03 for the monthly data and less than 0.001 for weekly data. Hence there is a lack of support for the view that missing factors completely explain the deviations.

On the other hand, given the parametrizations considered, there is some support for the nonrisk-based alternative views. The test statistic falls

---

[7]The bias of a portfolio will be a weighted average of the bias of the member assets if the weights are independent of the returns process, as when the portfolio is rebalanced period by period versus when the portfolio is weighted to represent a buy and hold strategy (as in a value-weighted portfolio). In the latter case the bias at the portfolio level will be minimal.

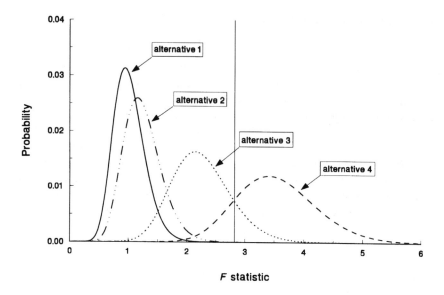

Figure 7.2. *Distributions for the CAPM zero-intercept test statistic for four alternatives. Alternative 1 is the CAPM (null hypothesis); alternative 2 is the risk-based alternative (deviations from the CAPM are from missing risk factors); alternatives 3 and 4 are the nonrisk-based alternative (deviations from the CAPM are unrelated to risk). The distributions are $F_{32,1558}(0)$, $F_{32,1558}(7.1)$, $F_{32,1558}(39.4)$, and $F_{32,1558}(80.3)$ for alternatives 1, 2, 3, and 4, respectively. The degrees of freedom are set to correspond to weekly observations from July 1962 to December 1992 (1,591 observations). Using 32 stock portfolios and the CRSP value-weighted index as a proxy for the market portfolio, the test statistic is 2.82, represented by the vertical line. The probability is calculated using an interval width of 0.02.*

almost in the middle of the nonrisk-based alternative with the lower standard deviation of the elements of alpha. Several of the nonrisk-based alternatives could equally well explain the results. Different nonrisk-based views can give the same noncentrality parameter and test statistic distribution. The results are consistent with the data-snooping alternative of Lo and MacKinlay (1990), the related sample selection biases discussed by Kothari, Shanken, and Sloan (1995) and Breen and Korajczyk (1993), and the presence of market inefficiencies. The analysis suggests that missing risk factors alone cannot explain the empirical results.

7.4.3 Estimation Approach

In this section we present an estimation approach to make inferences about possible values for Sharpe measures. An estimator for the squared Sharpe measure of the optimal orthogonal portfolio for a given subset of assets is employed. Using this estimator and its variance, confidence intervals for the squared Sharpe measure can be constructed, facilitating judgments on the question of the value implied by the data and reasonable alternatives given this value. An unbiased estimator of the squared Sharpe measure is presented. This estimator corrects for the bias that is introduced by searching over N assets to find the maximum and is derived using the fact that θ_1 from (7.4.4) is distributed as a noncentral F variate. Its moments follow from the moments of the noncentral F distribution. The estimator is

$$\tilde{s}_{h_s}^2 = \left[\theta_1 - \frac{(T-N-K)}{(T-N-K-2)} \right] \left[\frac{N(T-N-K-2)}{T(T-N-K)} \right] [1 + \hat{\mu}_p'\hat{\Omega}_p^{-1}\hat{\mu}_p],$$

(7.4.15)

$$\mathrm{Var}(\tilde{s}_{h_s}^2 \mid \hat{\mu}_p'\hat{\Omega}_p^{-1}\hat{\mu}_p)$$

$$= \left[\frac{2(1 + \hat{\mu}_p'\hat{\Omega}_p^{-1}\hat{\mu}_p)^2}{T^2} \right]$$

$$\times \left[\frac{(N+T[1+\hat{\mu}_p'\hat{\Omega}_p^{-1}\hat{\mu}_p]^{-1}s_{h_s}^2)^2+(N+2T[1+\hat{\mu}_p'\hat{\Omega}_p^{-1}\hat{\mu}_p]^{-1}s_{h_s}^2)(T-N-K-2)}{(T-N-K-4)} \right].$$

(7.4.16)

Conditional on the factor portfolio returns, the estimator of $s_{h_s}^2$ in (7.4.15) is unbiased, that is

$$\mathrm{E}[\tilde{s}_{h_s}^2 \mid \hat{\mu}_p'\hat{\Omega}_p^{-1}\hat{\mu}_p] = s_{h_s}^2.$$

(7.4.17)

Recall that when $K = 0$ the optimal orthogonal portfolio is the tangency portfolio and hence $s_{h_s}^2 = s_{q_s}^2$. The estimator can be applied when $K = 0$ by setting $\hat{\mu}_p'\hat{\Omega}_p^{-1}\hat{\mu}_p = 0$. Jobson and Korkie (1980) contains results for the $K = 0$ case.

The estimation approach is illustrated using the above estimator for the Fama and French (1993) portfolios. We consider the case of $K = 0$ and therefore the maximum squared Sharpe measure from 33 assets: the value-weighted CRSP index, 25 stock portfolios, and 7 bond portfolios are being estimated. (Recall that, with $K = 0$, $s_{h_s}^2 = s_{q_s}^2$.) The estimator of $s_{h_s}^2$ can be readily calculated, but the variance of $\tilde{s}_{h_s}^2$ cannot since it depends on $s_{h_s}^2$. To calculate the variance we use a consistent estimator, $\tilde{s}_{h_s}^2$, and then asymptotically (as T increases):

$$\tilde{s}_{h_s}^2 \sim N(s_{h_s}^2, \widehat{\mathrm{Var}}(\tilde{s}_{h_s}^2)).$$

(7.4.18)

Using monthly data from July 1963 through December 1991, the estimate of $s_{h_s}^2$ is 0.092 and the asymptotic standard error is 0.044. Using this data set, a two-sided centered 90% confidence interval is thus (0.020, 0.163) and a one-sided 90% confidence interval is (0.036, ∞). It is worth noting the upward bias of the *ex post* maximum squared Sharpe measure as an estimator. For the above case the *ex post* maximum is 0.209, substantially higher than the unbiased estimate of 0.092. The bias is particularly severe when N is large (relative to T).

In terms of an annualized Sharpe measure, the two-sided interval corresponds to a lower value of 0.49 and an upper value of 1.40, and the one-sided interval corresponds to a lower value of 0.65. Given that the tangency portfolio and the optimal orthogonal portfolio are the same, this interval can be used to provide an indication of the magnitude of the maximum Sharpe measure needed for a set of factor portfolios to explain the cross-section of excess returns of portfolios based on market-to-book-value ratios. Consistent with the CRSP value-weighted index being unable to explain the cross-section of returns, its *ex post* Sharpe measure lies well outside the intervals, with an annualized value of 0.33. In general, one can use the confidence intervals to decide on promising alternatives. For example, if one believes that *ex ante* Sharpe measures in the 90% confidence interval are unlikely in a risk-based world, then the nonrisk-based alternatives provide an attractive area for future study.

7.5 Asymptotic Arbitrage in Finite Economies

In the absence of the link between the model deviation and the residual variance expressed in (7.2.17), asymptotic arbitrage opportunities can exist. However, the analysis of this chapter is based on the importance of the link in a finite economy. To illustrate this importance we use a simple comparison of two economies, economy A in which the link is present and economy B in which the link is absent. The absence of the link is the only distinguishing feature of economy B. For each economy, the behavior of the maximum squared Sharpe measure as a function of the number of securities is examined.

Specification of the mean excess return vector and the covariance matrix is necessary. We draw on the previously introduced notation. In addition to the risk-free asset, assume there exist N risky assets with mean excess return μ and nonsingular covariance matrix V, and a risky factor portfolio with mean excess return μ_p and variance σ_p^2. The factor portfolio is not a linear combination of the N assets. If necessary this criterion can be met by eliminating one of the assets included in the factor portfolio. For both economies A and B,

$$\mu = \alpha + \beta_p \mu_p, \tag{7.5.1}$$

$$V = \beta_p \beta_p' \sigma_p^2 + \delta \delta' \sigma_h^2 + I \sigma_u^2. \tag{7.5.2}$$

Given the above mean and covariance matrix and the assumption that the factor portfolio p is a holdable asset, the maximum squared Sharpe measure for economy I is

$$s_I^2 = s_p^2 + \alpha'(\delta\delta'\sigma_h^2 + I\sigma_u^2)^{-1}\alpha. \tag{7.5.3}$$

Analytically inverting $(\delta\delta'\sigma_h^2 + I\sigma_\epsilon^2)$ and simplifying, (7.5.3) can be expressed as

$$s_I^2 = s_p^2 + \frac{1}{\sigma_u^2}\left[\alpha'\alpha + \frac{\sigma_h^2(\alpha'\delta)^2}{(\sigma_u^2 + \sigma_h^2\delta'\delta)}\right]. \tag{7.5.4}$$

To complete the specification, the cross-sectional properties of the elements of α and δ are required. We assume that the elements of α are cross-sectionally independent and identically distributed,

$$\alpha_i \sim \text{IID}(0, \sigma_\alpha^2), \qquad i = 1, \ldots, N. \tag{7.5.5}$$

The specification of the distribution of the elements of δ conditional on α differentiates economies A and B. For economy A,

$$\delta_i \mid \alpha \sim \text{IID}(\alpha_i, 0), \qquad i = 1, \ldots, N, \tag{7.5.6}$$

and for economy B,

$$\delta_i \mid \alpha \sim \text{IID}(0, \sigma_\alpha^2), \qquad i = 1, \ldots, N. \tag{7.5.7}$$

Unconditionally, the cross-sectional distribution of δ will be the same for both economies, but for economy A conditional on α, δ is fixed. This incorporates the link between the deviation and the residual variance. Because δ is independent of α in economy B, the link is absent.

Using (7.5.4) and the cross-sectional distributional properties of the elements of α and δ, an approximation for the maximum squared Sharpe measure for each economy can be derived. For both economies, $(1/N)\alpha'\alpha$ converges to σ_α^2, and $(1/N)\delta'\delta$ converges to σ_α^2. For economy A, $(1/N^2)(\alpha'\delta)^2$ converges to σ_α^4 and, for economy B, $(1/N)(\alpha'\delta)^2$ converges to σ_α^4. Substituting these limits into (7.5.4) gives approximations of the maximum squared Sharpe measures squared for each economy. Substitution into (7.5.4) gives

$$s_A^2 = s_p^2 + \frac{N\sigma_\alpha^2}{\sigma_u^2 + N\sigma_h^2\sigma_\alpha^2}, \tag{7.5.8}$$

$$s_B^2 = s_p^2 + N\frac{\sigma_\alpha^2}{\sigma_u^2}\left[1 - \frac{\sigma_h^2\sigma_\alpha^2}{\sigma_u^2 + N\sigma_h^2\sigma_\alpha^2}\right], \tag{7.5.9}$$

for economies A and B, respectively. The accuracy of these approximations for values of N equal to 100 and higher is examined. Simulations show that these approximations are very precise.

The importance of the link asymptotically can be confirmed by considering the values of s_q^2 in (7.5.8) and (7.5.9) for large N. For economy A and large N,

$$s_q^2 = s_p^2 + \frac{1}{\sigma_h^2}, \qquad (7.5.10)$$

and for economy B,

$$s_q^2 = s_p^2 + N\left[\frac{\sigma_\alpha^2}{\sigma_u^2}\right]. \qquad (7.5.11)$$

The maximum squared Sharpe measure is bounded as N increases for economy A and unbounded for economy B. Using the correspondence between boundedness of the maximum squared Sharpe measure and the absence of asymptotic opportunities (see Ingersoll, 1984, Theorem I) there will be asymptotic arbitrage opportunities only in economy B.

However, our interest here is to examine the importance of the link between the deviation and the residual variance given a finite number of assets. We do this by considering the value of the maximum Sharpe measures for various values of N. The values of N considered are 100, 500, 1,000, and 5,000. For completeness, we also report the maximum squared Sharpe measure for $N = \infty$. Shanken (1992) presents related results for an economy similar to B with δ restricted to be zero for $N = 3000$ and $N = 3,000,000$. He notes (p. 1574) that for $N = 3,000,000$ "something close to a 'pure' arbitrage is possible." Given (7.5.8) and (7.5.9), to complete the calculations, $s_p^2, \sigma_h^2, \sigma_u^2$, and σ_α^2 must be specified. The parameters are selected so that μ and V are realistic for stock returns measured at a monthly observation interval. The selected parameter values are $s_p^2 = 0.01$, $\sigma_h = 2.66$, and $\sigma_u = 0.05$. Two values are considered for σ_α, 0.001 and 0.002. The results are reported in Table 7.2. The difference in the behavior of the maximum squared Sharpe measures between economies A and B is dramatic. For economy A, the boundedness is apparent as the maximum squared Sharpe measure ranges from 0.023 to 0.030 as N increases from 100 to infinity. For economy A the impact of increasing the cross-sectional variation in the mean return is minimal. Comparing $\sigma_\alpha = 0.001$ to $\sigma_\alpha = 0.002$ reveals few differences, with the exception of differences for the $N = 100$ case. For economy B it is a different story. The maximum squared Sharpe measure is very sensitive to both increases in the number of securities and increases in the cross-sectional variation in the mean return. For $\sigma_\alpha = 0.002$, the maximum squared Sharpe measure increases from 0.169 to 1.608 as N increases from 100 to 1,000. When σ_α increases from 0.001 to 0.002 the maximum squared Sharpe measure increases from 0.21 to 0.80 for N equal to 500.

In addition to the maximum squared Sharpe measures, Table 7.2 reports the approximate probability that the annual excess return of the portfolio

Table 7.2. *A comparison of the maximum squared Sharpe measure for two economies denoted A and B, where the Sharpe measure is the ratio of the mean excess return to the standard deviation of the excess return. The excess return covariance matrix for the two economies is identical and the cross-sectional dispersion in mean excess returns is identical. The economies differ in that economy A displays stronger dependence between the mean excess returns and the covariance matrix of excess returns. The mean and covariance matrix parameters for the economies are calibrated to correspond roughly to monthly returns (see the text for details). N is the number of securities, s_I^2 is the maximum squared Sharpe measure for economy I, $I = A, B$, and $p(z_I < 0)$ is the approximate probability for economy I that the annual return of the portfolio with the maximum Sharpe measure squared will be less than the risk-free return assuming that monthly returns are jointly normally distributed and that the mean excess return is positive. σ_α is the cross-sectional standard deviation of the component of the mean return that is explained by a second factor in economy A and that is not explained by a common factor in economy B.*

N	s_A^2	$p(z_A < 0)$	s_B^2	$p(z_B < 0)$
$\sigma_\alpha = 0.001$				
100	0.023	0.298	0.050	0.220
500	0.028	0.280	0.210	0.056
1000	0.029	0.277	0.410	0.013
5000	0.030	0.275	2.010	**
∞	0.030	0.274	∞	**
$\sigma_\alpha = 0.002$				
100	0.028	0.282	0.169	0.077
500	0.030	0.276	0.808	**
1000	0.030	0.275	1.608	**
5000	0.030	0.274	8.008	**
∞	0.030	0.274	∞	**

** Less than 0.001.

with the maximum squared Sharpe measure is negative. For this probability calculation, it is assumed that returns are jointly normally distributed and that the mean excess return of the portfolio with the maximum squared Sharpe measure is nonnegative. The mean and variance are annualized by multiplying the monthly values by 12. This probability allows for an economic interpretation of the size of the Sharpe measure. Since the excess return represents a payoff on a zero investment position, if the probability of a negative outcome is zero then there is an arbitrage opportunity. For economy A this probability is about 28% and stable as N increases. However, for economy B the probability of a negative annual excess return quickly approaches zero. For example, for the case of σ_α equal to 0.002 and N equal to 500 the probability of a negative outcome is less than 0.001. (For the 67 years from 1926 through 1992 the excess return of the S&P index has been negative 37.3% of the years and the excess return of the CRSP small-stock index has been negative 34.3% of the years; over the 30-year period from 1963 through 1992 the S&P Index has been negative 36.7% of the time and the small-stock index has been negative 30.0% of the time.) Since negative outcomes can occur, the excess return distributions cannot be completely ruled out on economic grounds. However, in aggregate it appears that, given the above model for economy B, unrealistic investment opportunites can be constructed with a relatively small number of stocks. This is not the case for economy A. The bottom line is that in a perfect capital markets environment, the link between the model deviations and the residual variance is important even with a limited number of securities. Analysis which does not recognize this link is unlikely to shed light on the potential for omitted risk factors to explain the deviations.

7.6 Conclusion

Empirical work in economics in general and in finance in particular is *ex post* in nature, making it sometimes difficult to discriminate among various explanations for observed phenomena. A partial solution to this difficulty is to examine the alternatives and make judgments from an *ex ante* point of view. The current explanations of the empirical results on asset pricing are particularly well-suited to *ex ante* analysis. This chapter presents a framework based on the economics of mean-variance analysis to address and reinterpret prior empirical results.

Multifactor asset pricing models have been proposed as an alternative to the Sharpe-Lintner CAPM. However, the results in this chapter suggest that looking at other alternatives will be fruitful. The evidence against the CAPM can also be interpreted as evidence that multifactor models on their own cannot explain the deviations from the CAPM. Generally, the results suggest that more can be learned by considering the likelihood of various existing empirical results under differing specific economic models.

8

Data-Snooping Biases in Tests of Financial Asset Pricing Models

Introduction

THE RELIANCE OF ECONOMIC SCIENCE upon nonexperimental inference is, at once, one of the most challenging and most nettlesome aspects of the discipline. Because of the virtual impossibility of controlled experimentation in economics, the importance of statistical data analysis is now well-established. However, there is a growing concern that the procedures under which formal statistical inference have been developed may not correspond to those followed in practice.[1] For example, the classical statistical approach to selecting a method of estimation generally involves minimizing an expected loss function, irrespective of the actual data. Yet in practice the properties of the realized data almost always influence the choice of estimator.

Of course, ignoring obvious features of the data can lead to nonsensical inferences even when the estimation procedures are optimal in some metric. But the way we incorporate those features into our estimation and testing procedures can affect subsequent inferences considerably. Indeed, by the very nature of empirical innovation in economics, the axioms of classical statistical analysis are violated routinely: future research is often motivated by the successes and failures of past investigations. Consequently, few empirical studies are free of the kind of data-instigated pretest biases discussed in Leamer (1978). Moreover, we can expect the degree of such biases to increase with the number of published studies performed on any single data

---

[1] Perhaps the most complete analysis of such issues in economic applications is by Leamer (1978). Recent papers by Lakonishok and Smidt (1988), Merton (1987), and Ross (1987) address data snooping in financial economics. Of course, data snooping has been a concern among probabilists and statisticians for quite some time, and is at least as old as the controversy between Bayesian and classical statisticians. Interested readers should consult Berger and Wolpert (1984, Chapter 4.2) and Leamer (1978, Chapter 9) for further discussion.

set—the more scrutiny a collection of data is subjected to, the more likely will interesting (spurious) patterns emerge. Since stock market prices are perhaps the most studied economic quantities to date, tests of financial asset pricing models seem especially susceptible.

In this paper, we attempt to quantify the inferential biases associated with one particular method of testing financial asset pricing models such as the capital asset pricing model (CAPM) and the arbitrage pricing theory (APT). Because there are often many more securities than there are time series observations of stock returns, asset pricing tests are generally performed on the returns of *portfolios* of securities. Besides reducing the cross-sectional dimension of the joint distribution of returns, grouping into portfolios has also been advanced as a method of reducing the impact of measurement error. However, the selection of securities to be included in a given portfolio is almost never at random, but is often based on some of the stocks' empirical characteristics. The formation of size-sorted portfolios, portfolios based on the market value of the companies' equity, is but one example. Conducting classical statistical tests on portfolios formed this way creates potentially significant biases in the test statistics. These are examples of "data-snooping statistics," a term used by Aldous (1989, p. 252) to describe the situation "where you have a family of test statistics $T(a)$ whose null distribution is known for fixed a, but where you use the test statistic $T = T(a)$ for some a chosen using the data." In our application the quantity a may be viewed as a vector of zeros and ones that indicates which securities are to be included in or omitted from a given portfolio. If the choice of a is based on the data, then the sampling distribution of the resulting test statistic is generally not the same as the null distribution with a fixed a; hence, the actual size of the test may differ substantially from its nominal value under the null. Under plausible assumptions our calculations show that this kind of data snooping can lead to rejections of the null hypothesis with probability 1 even when the null hypothesis is true!

Although the term "data snooping" may have an unsavory connotation, our usage neither implies nor infers any sort of intentional misrepresentation or dishonesty. That prior empirical research may influence the way current investigations are conducted is often unavoidable, and this very fact results in what we have called data snooping. Moreover, it is not at all apparent that this phenomenon necessarily imparts a "bias" in the sense that it affects inferences in an undesirable way. After all, the primary reason for publishing scientific discoveries is to add to a store of common knowledge on which future research may build.

But when scientific discovery is statistical in nature, we must weigh the significance of newly discovered relations in view of past inferences. This is recognized implicitly in many formal statistical circumstances, as in the theory of sequential hypothesis testing. But it is considerably more difficult to correct for the effects of specification searches in practice since such searches often consist of *sequences* of empirical studies undertaken by many individuals over many years.[2] For example, as a consequence of the many investigations relating the behavior of stock returns to size, Chen, Roll, and Ross (1986, p. 394) write: "It has been facetiously noted that size may be the best theory we now have of expected returns. Unfortunately, this is less of a theory than an empirical observation." Then, as Merton (1987, p. 107) asks in a related context: "Is it reasonable to use the standard *t*-statistic as a valid measure of significance when the test is conducted on the same data used by many earlier studies whose results influenced the choice of theory to be tested?" We rephrase this question in the following way: Are standard tests of significance valid when the construction of the test statistics is influenced by empirical relations derived from the very same data to be used in the test? Our results show that using prior information only marginally correlated with statistics of interest can distort inferences dramatically.

In Section 8.1 we quantify the data-snooping biases associated with testing financial asset pricing models with portfolios formed by sorting on some empirically motivated characteristic. Using the theory of induced order statistics, we derive in closed form the asymptotic distribution of a commonly used test statistic before and after sorting. This not only yields a measure of the effect of data snooping, but also provides the appropriate sampling theory when snooping is unavoidable. In Section 8.2 we report the results of Monte Carlo experiments designed to gauge the accuracy of the asymptotic approximations used in Section 8.1. In Section 8.3 two empirical examples are provided that illustrate the potential importance of data-snooping biases in existing tests of asset pricing models, and in Section 8.4, we show how these biases can arise naturally from our tendency to focus on the unusual. We conclude in Section 8.5.

8.1 Quantifying Data-Snooping Biases With Induced Order Statistics

Many tests of the CAPM and APT have been conducted on returns of groups of securities rather than on individual security returns, where the grouping is often according to some empirical characteristic of the securities. Perhaps the most common attribute by which securities are grouped is market value of equity or "size." The prevalence of size-sorted portfolios in recent tests of asset pricing models has not been precipitated by any economic

---

[2]Statisticians have considered a closely related problem, known as the "file drawer problem," in which the overall significance of several published studies must be assessed while accounting for the possibility of unreported insignificant studies languishing in various investigators' file drawers. An excellent review of the file drawer problem and its remedies, which has come to be known as "meta-analysis," is provided by Iyengar and Greenhouse (1988).

theory linking size to asset prices. It is a consequence of a series of empirical studies demonstrating the statistical relation between size and the stochastic behavior of stock returns.[3] Therefore, we must allow for our foreknowledge of size-related phenomena in evaluating the actual significance of tests performed on size-sorted portfolios. More generally, grouping securities by some characteristic that is empirically motivated may affect the size of the usual significance tests,[4] particularly when the empirical motivation is derived from the very data set on which the test is based. We quantify these effects in the following sections by appealing to asymptotic results for induced order statistics, and show that even mild forms of data snooping can change inferences substantially. In Section 8.1.1, a brief summary of the asymptotic properties of induced order statistics, is provided. In Section 8.1.2, results for tests based on individual securities are presented, and in Section 8.1.3, corresponding results for portfolios are reported. We provide a more positive interpretation of data-snooping biases as power against deviations from the null hypothesis in Section 8.1.4.

8.1.1 Asymptotic Properties of Induced Order Statistics

Since the particular form of data snooping we are investigating is most common in empirical tests of financial asset pricing models, our exposition will lie in that context. Suppose for each of N securities we have some consistent estimator $\hat{\alpha}_i$ of a parameter α_i which is to be used in the construction of an aggregate test statistic. For example, in the Sharpe-Lintner CAPM, $\hat{\alpha}_i$ would be the estimated intercept from the following regression:

$$R_{it} - R_{ft} = \hat{\alpha}_i + (R_{mt} - R_{ft})\beta_i + \epsilon_{it} \qquad (8.1.1)$$

where R_{it}, R_{mt}, and R_{ft} are the period-t returns on security i, the market portfolio, and a risk-free asset, respectively. A test of the null hypothesis that $\alpha_i = 0$ would then be a proper test of the Sharpe-Lintner version of the CAPM; thus, $\hat{\alpha}_i$ may serve as a test statistic itself. However, more powerful tests may be obtained by combining the $\hat{\alpha}_i$'s for many securities. But how should we combine them?

Suppose for each security i we observe some characteristic X_i, such as its out-of-sample market value of equity or average annual earnings, and we learn that X_i is correlated empirically with $\hat{\alpha}_i$. By this we mean that the relation between X_i and $\hat{\alpha}_i$ is an empirical fact uncovered by "searching"

---

[3]See Banz (1978, 1981), Brown, Kleidon, and Marsh (1983), and Chan, Chen, and Hsieh (1985), for example. Although Banz's (1978) original investigation may have been motivated by theoretical considerations, virtually all subsequent empirical studies exploiting the size effect do so because of Banz's empirical findings, and not his theory.

[4]Unfortunately the use of "size" to mean both market value of equity and type I error is unavoidable. Readers beware.

through the data, and not motivated by any a priori theoretical considerations. This search need not be a systematic sifting of the data, but may be interpreted as any one of Leamer's (1978) six specification searches, which even the most meticulous of classical statisticians has conducted at some point. The key feature is that our interest in characteristic X_i is derived from a look at the data, the same data to be used in performing our test. Common intuition suggests that using information contained in the X_i's can yield a more powerful test of economic restrictions on the $\hat{\alpha}_i$'s. But if this characteristic is not a part of the original null hypothesis, and only catches our attention after a look at the data (or after a look at another's look at the data), using it to form our test statistics may lead us to reject those economic restrictions even when they obtain. More formally, if we write $\hat{\alpha}_i$ as

$$\hat{\alpha}_i = \alpha_i + \zeta_i, \tag{8.1.2}$$

then it is evident that under the null hypothesis where $\alpha_i = 0$, any correlation between X_i and $\hat{\alpha}_i$ must be due to correlation between the characteristic and estimation or measurement error ζ_i. Although measurement error is usually assumed to be independent of all other relevant economic variables, the very process by which the characteristic comes to our attention may induce spurious correlation between X_i and ζ_i. We formalize this intuition in Section 8.4 and proceed now to show that such spurious correlation has important implications for testing the null hypothesis.

This is most evident in the extreme case where the null hypothesis $\alpha_i = 0$ is tested by performing a standard t-test on the largest of the $\hat{\alpha}_i$'s. Clearly such a test is biased toward rejection unless we account for the fact that the largest $\hat{\alpha}_i$ has been drawn from the set $\{\hat{\alpha}_j\}$. Otherwise, extreme realizations of estimation error will be confused with a violation of the null hypothesis. If, instead of choosing $\hat{\alpha}_i$ by its value relative to other $\hat{\alpha}_j$'s, our choice is based on some characteristic X_i correlated with the estimation errors of $\hat{\alpha}_i$, a similar bias might arise, albeit to a lesser degree.

To formalize the preceding intuition, suppose that only a subset of n securities is used to form the test statistic and these n are chosen by sorting the X_i's. That is, let us reorder the bivariate vectors $[X_i \ \hat{\alpha}_i]'$ according to their first components, yielding the sequence

$$\begin{pmatrix} X_{1:N} \\ \hat{\alpha}_{[1:N]} \end{pmatrix}, \begin{pmatrix} X_{2:N} \\ \hat{\alpha}_{[2:N]} \end{pmatrix}, \ldots, \begin{pmatrix} X_{N:N} \\ \hat{\alpha}_{[N:N]} \end{pmatrix}, \tag{8.1.3}$$

where $X_{1:N} < X_{2:N} < \cdots < X_{N:N}$ and the notation $X_{i:N}$ follows that of the statistics literature in denoting the ith order statistic from the sample of N observations $\{X_i\}$.[5] The notation $\hat{\alpha}_{[i:N]}$ denotes the ith *induced order statistic*

---

[5]It is implicitly assumed throughout that both $\hat{\alpha}_i$ and X_i have continuous joint and marginal cumulative distribution functions; hence, strict inequalities suffice.

corresponding to $X_{i:N}$, or the *i*th *concomitant* of the order statistic $X_{i:N}$.[6] That is, if the bivariate vectors $[X_i \ \hat{\alpha}_i]'$ are ordered according to the X_i entries, $\hat{\alpha}_{[i:N]}$ is defined to be the second component of the *i*th ordered vector. The $\hat{\alpha}_{[i:N]}$'s are not themselves ordered but correspond to the ordering of the $X_{i:N}$'s.[7] For example, if X_i is firm size and $\hat{\alpha}_i$ is the intercept from a market-model regression of firm *i*'s excess return on the excess market return, then $\hat{\alpha}_{[j:N]}$ is the $\hat{\alpha}$ of the *j*th smallest of the N firms. We call this procedure *induced ordering* of the $\hat{\alpha}_i$'s.

It is apparent that if we construct a test statistic by choosing n securities according to the ordering (8.1.3), the sampling theory cannot be the same as that of n securities selected independently of the data. From the following remarkably simple result by Yang (1977), an asymptotic sampling theory for test statistics based on induced order statistics may be derived analytically:[8]

Theorem 8.1.1. *Let the vectors* $[X_i \ \hat{\alpha}_i]'$, $i = 1, \ldots, N$, *be independently and identically distributed and let* $1 < i_1 < i_2 < \cdots < i_n < N$ *be sequences of integers such that, as* $N \to \infty$, $i_k/N \to \xi_k \in (0, 1)$ $(k = 1, 2, \ldots, n)$. *Then*

$$\lim_{N \to \infty} \Pr(\hat{\alpha}_{[i_1:N]} < a_1, \ldots, \hat{\alpha}_{[i_n:N]} < a_n) = \prod_{k=1}^{n} \Pr(\hat{\alpha}_k < a_k \mid F_x(X_k) = \xi_k),$$

(8.1.4)

where $F_x(\cdot)$ *is the marginal cumulative distribution function of* X_i.

Proof. See Yang (1977).   **Q.E.D.**

This result gives the large-sample joint distribution of a finite subset of induced order statistics whose identities are determined solely by their relative rankings ξ_k (as ranked according to the order statistics $X_{i:N}$). From (8.1.4) it is evident that the $\hat{\alpha}_{[i:N]}$'s are mutually independent in large samples. If X_i were the market value of equity of the *i*th company, Theorem 8.1.1 shows that the $\hat{\alpha}_i$ of the security with size at, for example, the 27th percentile is asymptotically independent of the $\hat{\alpha}_j$ of the security with size at the 45th percentile.[9] If the characteristics $\{X_i\}$ and $\{\hat{\alpha}_i\}$ are statistically independent,

---

[6]The term *concomitant* of an order statistic was introduced by David (1973), who was perhaps the first to systematically investigate its properties and applications. The term *induced* order statistic was coined by Bhattacharya (1974) at about the same time. Although the former term seems to be more common usage, we use the latter in the interest of brevity. See Bhattacharya (1984) for an excellent review.

[7]If the vectors are independently and identically distributed and X_i is perfectly correlated with $\hat{\alpha}_i$, then $\hat{\alpha}_{[i:N]}$ are also order statistics. But as long as the correlation coefficient ρ is strictly between -1 and 1, then, for example, $\hat{\alpha}_{[N:N]}$ will generally not be the largest $\hat{\alpha}_i$.

[8]See also David and Galambos (1974) and Watterson (1959). In fact, Yang (1977) provides the exact finite-sample distribution of any finite collection of induced order statistics, but even assuming bivariate normality does not yield a tractable form for this distribution.

[9]This is a limiting result and implies that the identities of the stocks with 27th and 45th percentile sizes will generally change as N increases.

the joint distribution of the latter clearly cannot be influenced by ordering according to the former. It is tempting to conclude that as long as the correlation between X_i and $\hat{\alpha}_i$ is economically small, induced ordering cannot greatly affect inferences. Using Yang's result we show the fallacy of this argument in Sections 8.1.2 and 8.1.3.

8.1.2 Biases of Tests Based on Individual Securities

We evaluate the bias of induced ordering under the following assumption:

(A1) The vectors $[X_i \, \hat{\alpha}_i]'$ $(i = 1, 2, \ldots, N)$ are independently and identically distributed bivariate normal random vectors with mean $[\mu_x \, \alpha]'$, variance $[\sigma_x^2 \, \sigma_\alpha^2]'$, and correlation $\rho \in (-1, 1)$.

The null hypothesis H is then

$$\text{H: } \alpha \,=\, 0.$$

Examples of asset pricing models that yield restrictions of this form are the Sharpe-Lintner CAPM and the exact factor pricing version of Ross's APT.[10] Under this null hypothesis, the $\hat{\alpha}_i$'s deviate from zero solely through estimation error.

Since the sampling theory provided by Theorem 8.1.1 is asymptotic, we construct our test statistics using a finite subset of n securities where it is assumed that $n \ll N$. If these securities are selected without the prior use of data, then we have the following well-known result:

$$\theta \;\equiv\; \frac{1}{\hat{\sigma}_\alpha^2} \sum_{i=1}^{n} \hat{\alpha}_i^2 \;\overset{a}{\sim}\; \chi_n^2, \tag{8.1.5}$$

where $\hat{\sigma}_\alpha^2$ is any consistent estimator of σ_α^2.[11] Therefore, a 5 percent test of H may be performed by checking whether θ is greater or less than $C_{.05}^n$,

---

[10]See Chamberlain (1983), Huberman and Kandel (1987), Lehmann and Modest (1988), and Wang (1988) for further discussion of exact factor pricing models. Examples of tests that fit into the framework of H are those in Campbell (1987), Connor and Korajczyk (1988), Gibbons, Ross, and Shanken (1989), Huberman and Kandel (1987), Lehmann and Modest (1988), and MacKinlay (1987).

[11]In most contexts the consistency of $\hat{\sigma}_\alpha^2$ is with respect to the number of time series observations T. In that case something must be said of the relative rates at which T and N increase without bound so as to guarantee convergence of θ. However, under H the parameter σ_α^2 may be estimated cross-sectionally; hence, the relation $\overset{a}{\sim}$ in (8.1.5) need only represent N-asymptotics.

where $C_{.05}^n$ is defined by

$$F_{\chi_n^2}(C_{.05}^n) \;=\; .95 \tag{8.1.6}$$

and $F_{\chi_n^2}(\cdot)$ is the cumulative distribution function of a χ_n^2 variate.

Now suppose we construct θ from the induced order statistics $\hat{\alpha}_{[i_k:N]}$, $k = 1, \ldots n$, instead of the $\hat{\alpha}_i$'s. Specifically, define the following test statistic:

$$\tilde{\theta} \;\equiv\; \frac{1}{\hat{\sigma}_\alpha^2} \sum_{k=1}^{n} \hat{\alpha}_{[i_k:N]}^2. \tag{8.1.7}$$

Using Theorem 8.1.1, the following proposition is easily established:

Proposition 8.1.1. *Under the null hypothesis H and assumption (A1), as N increases without bound the induced order statistics $\hat{\alpha}_{[i_k:N]}$ ($k = 1, \ldots n$) converge in distribution to independent Gaussian random variables with mean μ_k and variance σ_k^2, where*

$$\mu_k \;\equiv\; \rho\,(\sigma_\alpha/\sigma_x)\left[F_x^{-1}(\xi_k) - \mu_x\right] = \rho\sigma_\alpha\Phi^{-1}(\xi_k), \tag{8.1.8}$$

$$\sigma_k^2 \;\equiv\; \sigma_\alpha^2(1 - \rho^2), \tag{8.1.9}$$

which implies

$$\tilde{\theta} \;\overset{a}{\sim}\; (1 - \rho^2) \cdot \chi_n^2(\lambda), \tag{8.1.10}$$

with noncentrality parameter

$$\lambda \;=\; \sum_{k=1}^{n}\left(\frac{\mu_k}{\sigma_k}\right)^2 = \frac{\rho^2}{1 - \rho^2} \sum_{k=1}^{n}\left[\Phi^{-1}(\xi_k)\right]^2, \tag{8.1.11}$$

where $\Phi(\cdot)$ is the standard normal cumulative distribution function.

Proof. This follows directly from the definition of a noncentral chi-squared variate. The second equality in (8.1.8) follows from the fact that $\Phi(\xi_k) = F_x(\xi_k\sigma_x + \mu_x)$. ∎

Proposition 8.1.1 shows that the null hypothesis H is violated by induced ordering since the means of the ordered $\hat{\alpha}_i$'s are no longer zero. Indeed, the mean of $\hat{\alpha}_{[i_k:N]}$ may be positive or negative depending on ρ and the (limiting) relative rank ξ_k. For example, if $\rho = 0.10$ and $\sigma_\alpha = 1$, the mean of the induced order statistic in the 95th percentile is 0.164.

The simplicity of $\tilde{\theta}$'s asymptotic distribution follows from the fact that the $\hat{\alpha}_{[i_k:N]}$'s become independent as N increases without bound. It follows from the fact that induced order statistics are conditionally independent when conditioned on the order statistics that determine the induced ordering. This seemingly counterintuitive result is easy to see when $[X_i\,\hat{\alpha}_i]$ is bivariate normal, since, in this case

$$\hat{\alpha}_i = \alpha + \rho\,(\sigma_\alpha/\sigma_x)[X_i - \mu_x] + Z_i,$$

$$Z_i \quad \text{IID} \quad \mathcal{N}(0, \sigma_\alpha^2(1 - \rho^2)), \tag{8.1.12}$$

where X_i and Z_i are independent. Therefore, the induced order statistics may be represented as

$$\hat{\alpha}_{[i_k:N]} = \alpha + \rho\,(\sigma_\alpha/\sigma_x)[X_{i_k:N} - \mu_x] + Z_{[i_k]},$$

$$Z_{[i_k]} \quad \text{IID} \quad \mathcal{N}(0, \sigma_\alpha^2(1 - \rho^2)), \qquad (8.1.13)$$

where the $Z_{[i_k]}$ are independent of the (order) statistics $X_{i_k:N}$. But since $X_{i_k:N}$ is an order statistic, and since the sequence i_k/N converges to ξ_k, $X_{i_k:N}$ converges to the ξ_kth quantile, $F^{-1}(\xi_k)$. Using (8.1.13) then shows that $\hat{\alpha}_{[i_k:N]}$ is Gaussian, with mean and variance given by (8.1.8) and (8.1.9), and independent of the other induced order statistics.[12]

To evaluate the size of a 5 percent test based on the statistic $\tilde{\theta}$, we need only evaluate the cumulative distribution function of the noncentral $\chi_n^2(\lambda)$ at the point $C_{.05}^n/(1 - \rho^2)$, where $C_{.05}^n$ is given in (8.1.6). Observe that the noncentrality parameter λ is an increasing function of ρ^2. If $\rho^2 = 0$ then the distribution of $\tilde{\theta}$ reduces to a central χ_n^2 which is identical to the distribution of θ in (8.1.5)—sorting on a characteristic that is statistically independent of the $\hat{\alpha}_i$'s cannot affect the null distribution of θ. As $\hat{\alpha}_i$ and X_i become more highly correlated, the noncentral χ^2 distribution shifts to the right. However, this does not imply that the actual size of a 5 percent test necessarily increases since the relevant critical value for $\tilde{\theta}$, $C_{.05}^n/(1 - \rho^2)$, also grows with ρ^2.[13]

Numerical values for the size of a 5 percent test based on $\tilde{\theta}$ may be obtained by first specifying choices for the relative ranks $\{\xi_k\}$ of the n secu-

---

[12]In fact, this shows how our parametric specification may be relaxed. If we replace normality by the assumption that $\hat{\alpha}_i$ and X_i satisfy the linear regression equation

$$\hat{\alpha}_i = \mu_\alpha + \beta_i(X_i - \mu_x) + Z_i,$$

where Z_i is independent of X_i, then our results remain unchanged. Moreover, this specification may allow us to relax the rather strong IID assumption since David (1981, Chapters 2.8 and 5.6) does present some results for order statistics in the nonidentically distributed and the dependent cases separately. However, combining and applying them to the above linear regression relation is a formidable task which we leave to the more industrious.

[13]In fact, if $\rho^2 = 1$, the limiting distribution of $\tilde{\theta}$ is degenerate since the test statistic converges in probability to the following limit:

$$\sum_{k=1}^{n} \left[\Phi^{-1}(\xi_k)\right]^2.$$

This limit may be greater or less than $C_{.05}^n$ depending on the values of ξ_k; hence, the size of the test in this case may be either zero or unity.

rities. We choose three sets of $\{\xi_k\}$, yielding three distinct test statistics $\tilde{\theta}_1$, $\tilde{\theta}_2$, and $\tilde{\theta}_3$:

$$\tilde{\theta}_1 \Leftrightarrow \xi_k = \frac{k}{n+1}, \qquad k = 1, 2, \ldots, n; \tag{8.1.14}$$

$$\tilde{\theta}_2 \Leftrightarrow \xi_k = \begin{cases} \dfrac{k}{(m+1)(n_o+1)}, & \text{for } k = 1, 2, \ldots, n_o, \\[3mm] \dfrac{k + m(n_o+1) - n_o}{(m+1)(n_o+1)}, & \text{for } k = n_o+1, \ldots, 2n_o; \end{cases} \tag{8.1.15}$$

$$\tilde{\theta}_3 \Leftrightarrow \xi_k = \begin{cases} \dfrac{k + n_o + 1}{(m+1)(n_o+1)}, & \text{for } k = 1, 2, \ldots, n_o, \\[3mm] \dfrac{k + (m-1)(n_o+1) - n_o}{(m+1)(n_o+1)}, & \text{for } k = n_o+1, \ldots, 2n_o; \end{cases} \tag{8.1.16}$$

where $n \equiv 2n_o$ and n_o is an arbitrary positive integer. The first method (8.1.14) simply sets the ξ_k's so that they divide the unit interval into n equally spaced increments. The second procedure (8.1.15) first divides the unit interval into $m+1$ equally spaced increments, sets the first half of the ξ_k's to divide the *first* such increment into equally spaced intervals each of width $1/(m+1)(n_o+1)$, and then sets the remaining half so as to divide the *last* increment into equally spaced intervals also of width $1/(m+1)(n_o+1)$ each. The third procedure is similar to the second, except that the ξ_k's are chosen to divide the second smallest and second largest $m+1$ increments into equally spaced intervals of width $1/(m+1)(n_o+1)$.

These three ways of choosing n securities allow us to see how an attempt to create (or remove) dispersion—as measured by the characteristic X_i— affects the null distribution of the statistics. The first choice for the relative ranks is the most dispersed, being evenly distributed on $(0, 1)$. The second yields the opposite extreme: the $\hat{\alpha}_{[i_k:N]}$'s selected are those with characteristics in the lowest and highest $100/(m+1)$-percentiles. As the parameter m is increased, more extreme outliers are used to compute $\tilde{\theta}_2$. This is also true for $\tilde{\theta}_3$, but to a lesser extent since the statistic is based on $\hat{\alpha}_{[i_k:N]}$'s in the second lowest and second highest $100/(m+1)$-percentiles.

Table 8.1 shows the size of the 5 percent test using $\tilde{\theta}_1$, $\tilde{\theta}_2$, and $\tilde{\theta}_3$ for various values of n, ρ^2, and m. For concreteness, observe that ρ^2 is simply the R^2 of the cross-sectional regression of $\hat{\alpha}_i$ on X_i, so that $\rho = \pm.10$ implies that only 1 percent of the variation in $\hat{\alpha}_i$ is explained by X_i. For this value of R^2, the entries in the second panel of Table 8.1 show that the size of a 5 percent test using $\tilde{\theta}_1$ is 4.9 percent for samples of 10 to 100 securities. However, using securities with extreme characteristics does affect the size, as the entries in the "$\tilde{\theta}_2$-test" and "$\tilde{\theta}_3$-test" columns indicate. Nevertheless the largest deviation is only 8.1 percent. As expected, the size is larger for

Table 8.1.   *Theoretical sizes of nominal 5 percent χ_n^2-tests of H: $\alpha_i = 0$ $(i = 1, \ldots, n)$ using the test statistics $\tilde{\theta}_j$, where $\tilde{\theta}_j \equiv \sum_{k=1}^{2n} \hat{\alpha}_{[i_k(j):N]}^2/\hat{\sigma}_\alpha^2$, $j = 1, 2, 3$, for various sample sizes n. The statistic $\tilde{\theta}_1$ is based on induced order statistics with relative ranks evenly spaced in $(0, 1)$; $\tilde{\theta}_2$ is constructed from induced order statistics ranked in the lowest and highest $100/(m+1)$-percent fractiles; and $\tilde{\theta}_3$ is constructed from those ranked in the second lowest and second highest $100/(m + 1)$-percent fractiles. The R^2 is the square of the correlation between $\hat{\alpha}_i$ and the sorting characteristic.*

n	$\tilde{\theta}_1$-Test	$\tilde{\theta}_2$-Test $(m = 4)$	$\tilde{\theta}_3$-Test $(m = 4)$	$\tilde{\theta}_2$-Test $(m = 9)$	$\tilde{\theta}_3$-Test $(m = 9)$	$\tilde{\theta}_2$-Test $(m = 19)$	$\tilde{\theta}_3$-Test $(m = 19)$
$R^2 = 0.005$							
10	0.049	0.051	0.049	0.053	0.050	0.054	0.052
20	0.050	0.052	0.049	0.054	0.050	0.056	0.052
50	0.050	0.053	0.048	0.056	0.050	0.060	0.053
100	0.050	0.054	0.047	0.059	0.050	0.064	0.054
$R^2 = 0.01$							
10	0.049	0.053	0.048	0.056	0.050	0.059	0.053
20	0.049	0.054	0.047	0.058	0.050	0.063	0.054
50	0.049	0.056	0.046	0.063	0.051	0.071	0.057
100	0.049	0.059	0.045	0.069	0.051	0.081	0.059
$R^2 = 0.05$							
10	0.045	0.063	0.041	0.080	0.051	0.101	0.066
20	0.045	0.070	0.038	0.096	0.052	0.130	0.073
50	0.046	0.086	0.033	0.135	0.053	0.201	0.087
100	0.047	0.107	0.028	0.190	0.054	0.304	0.106
$R^2 = 0.10$							
10	0.040	0.076	0.032	0.116	0.052	0.166	0.083
20	0.041	0.093	0.028	0.158	0.053	0.244	0.099
50	0.042	0.133	0.020	0.267	0.055	0.442	0.137
100	0.043	0.192	0.014	0.423	0.058	0.680	0.191
$R^2 = 0.20$							
10	0.030	0.104	0.019	0.202	0.052	0.330	0.121
20	0.032	0.146	0.013	0.318	0.054	0.528	0.163
50	0.034	0.262	0.006	0.599	0.059	0.862	0.272
100	0.036	0.432	0.002	0.857	0.064	0.987	0.429

the test based on $\tilde{\theta}_2$ than for that of $\tilde{\theta}_3$ since the former statistic is based on more extreme induced order statistics than the latter.

When the R^2 increases to 10 percent the bias becomes more important. Although tests based on a set of securities with evenly spaced characteristics still have sizes approximately equal to their nominal 5 percent value, the size deviates more substantially when securities with extreme characteristics are used. For example, the size of the $\tilde{\theta}_2$ test that uses the 100 securities in the lowest and highest characteristic decile is 42.3 percent! In comparison, the 5 percent test based on the second lowest and second highest deciles exhibits only a 5.8 percent rejection rate. These patterns become even more pronounced for R^2's higher than 10 percent.

The intuition for these results may be found in (8.1.8)—the more extreme induced order statistics have means farther away from zero; hence, a statistic based on evenly distributed $\hat{\alpha}_{[i_k:N]}$'s will not provide evidence against the null hypothesis $\alpha = 0$. If the relative ranks are extreme, as is the case for $\tilde{\theta}_2$ and $\tilde{\theta}_3$, the resulting $\hat{\alpha}_{[i_k:N]}$'s may appear to be statistically incompatible with the null.

8.1.3 Biases of Tests Based on Portfolios of Securities

The entries in Table 8.1 show that as long as the n securities chosen have characteristics evenly distributed in relative rankings, test statistics based on individual securities yield little inferential bias. However, in practice the ordering by characteristics such as market value of equity is used to group securities into *portfolios*, and the portfolio returns are used to construct test statistics. For example, let $n \equiv n_o q$, where n_o and q are arbitrary positive integers, and consider forming q portfolios with n_o securities in each portfolio, where the portfolios are formed randomly. Under the null hypothesis H we have the following:

$$\phi_k \equiv \frac{1}{n_o} \sum_{j=(k-1)n_o+1}^{kn_o} \hat{\alpha}_j \sim \mathcal{N}\left(0, \frac{\sigma_\alpha^2}{n_o}\right), \qquad k = 1, 2, \ldots, q, \qquad (8.1.17)$$

$$\theta_p \equiv \frac{n_o}{\hat{\sigma}_\alpha^2} \sum_{k=1}^{q} \phi_k^2 \overset{a}{\sim} \chi_q^2, \qquad (8.1.18)$$

where ϕ_k is the estimated alpha of portfolio k and θ_p is the aggregate test statistic for the q portfolios. To perform a 5 percent test of H using θ_p, we simply compare it with the critical value $C_{.05}^q$ defined by

$$F_{\chi_q^2}(C_{.05}^q) = 0.95. \qquad (8.1.19)$$

Suppose, however, we compute this test statistic using the induced order statistics $\{\hat{\alpha}_{[i_k:N]}\}$ instead of randomly chosen $\{\hat{\alpha}_i\}$. From Theorem 8.1.1 we have:

Proposition 8.1.2. *Under the null hypothesis H and assumption (A1), as N increases without bound, the statistics $\tilde{\phi}_k$ ($k = 1, 2, \ldots, q$) and $\tilde{\theta}_p$ converge in distribution* *to the following:*

$$\tilde{\phi}_k \equiv \frac{1}{n_o} \sum_{j=(k-1)n_o+1}^{kn_o} \hat{\alpha}_{[i_j:N]} \stackrel{a}{\sim} \mathcal{N}\left(\sum_{j=(k-1)n_o+1}^{kn_o} \frac{\mu_j}{n_o}, \frac{\sigma_\alpha^2(1-\rho^2)}{n_o} \right), \quad (8.1.20)$$

$$\tilde{\theta}_p \equiv \frac{n_o}{\hat{\sigma}_\alpha^2} \sum_{k=1}^{q} \tilde{\phi}_k^2 \stackrel{a}{\sim} (1-\rho^2) \cdot \chi_q^2(\lambda), \quad (8.1.21)$$

with noncentrality parameter

$$\lambda = \frac{n_o \rho^2}{1-\rho^2} \sum_{k=1}^{q} \left(\frac{1}{n_o} \sum_{j=(k-1)n_o+1}^{kn_o} \left[\Phi^{-1}(\xi_j) \right] \right)^2. \quad (8.1.22)$$

Proof.   Again, this follows directly from the definition of a noncentral chi-squared variate and the asymptotic independence of the induced order statistics. ∎

The noncentrality parameter (8.1.22) is similar to that of the statistic based on individual securities—it is increasing in ρ^2 and equals zero when $\rho = 0$. However, it differs in one respect: because of portfolio aggregation, each term of the outer sum (the sum with respect to k) is the average of $\Phi^{-1}(\xi_j)$ over all securities in the kth portfolio. To see the importance of this, consider the case where the relative ranks ξ_j are chosen to be evenly spaced in $(0, 1)$, that is,

$$\xi_j = j/(n_o q + 1). \quad (8.1.23)$$

Recall from Table 8.1 that for individual securities the size of 5 percent tests based on *evenly spaced* ξ_j's was not significantly biased. Table 8.2 reports the size of 5 percent tests based on the portfolio statistic $\tilde{\theta}_p$, also using evenly spaced relative rankings. The contrast is striking—even for as low an R^2 as 1 percent, which implies a correlation of only ± 10 percent between $\hat{\alpha}_i$ and X_i, a 5 percent test based on 50 portfolios with 50 securities in each rejects 67 percent of the time! We can also see how portfolio grouping affects the size of the test for a fixed number of securities by comparing the ($q = i$, $n_o = j$) entry with the ($q = j$, $n_o = i$) entry. For example, in a sample of 250 securities a test based on 5 portfolios of 50 securities has size 16.5 percent, whereas a test based on 50 portfolios of 5 securities has only a 7.5 percent rejection rate. Grouping securities into portfolios increases the size considerably. The entries in Table 8.2 are also monotonically increasing across rows and across columns, implying that the test size increases with the number of securities, regardless of whether the number of portfolios or the number of securities per portfolio is held fixed.

   To understand why forming portfolios yields much higher rejection rates than using individual securities, recall from (8.1.8) and (8.1.9) that the

Table 8.2.   *Theoretical sizes of nominal 5 percent χ_q^2-tests of H: $\alpha_i = 0$ $(i = 1, \ldots, n)$ using the test statistic $\tilde{\theta}_p$, where $\tilde{\theta}_p \equiv n_o \sum_{k=1}^{q} \tilde{\phi}_k^2 / \sigma_\alpha^2$, and $\tilde{\phi}_k \equiv (1/n_o) \sum_{j=(k-1)q+1}^{kq} \hat{\alpha}_{[ij:N]}$ is constructed from portfolio k, with portfolios formed by sorting on some characteristic correlated with estimates $\hat{\alpha}_i$. This induced ordering alters the null distribution of $\tilde{\theta}_p$ from χ_q^2 to $(1 - R^2)/\chi_q^2(\lambda)$ where the noncentrality parameter λ is a function of the number q of portfolios, the number n_o of securities in each portfolio, and the squared correlation coefficient R^2 between $\hat{\alpha}_i$ and the sorting characteristic.*

q	$n_o = 5$	$n_o = 10$	$n_o = 20$	$n_o = 25$	$n_o = 50$
$R^2 = 0.005$					
5	0.053	0.058	0.068	0.073	0.102
10	0.055	0.062	0.077	0.086	0.134
20	0.057	0.067	0.091	0.105	0.185
25	0.058	0.070	0.097	0.113	0.208
50	0.062	0.079	0.123	0.148	0.311
$R^2 = 0.01$					
5	0.056	0.066	0.087	0.099	0.165
10	0.060	0.075	0.110	0.130	0.247
20	0.065	0.088	0.146	0.179	0.382
25	0.067	0.093	0.161	0.202	0.440
50	0.075	0.117	0.232	0.302	0.669
$R^2 = 0.05$					
5	0.080	0.140	0.288	0.368	0.716
10	0.104	0.212	0.477	0.602	0.941
20	0.142	0.333	0.728	0.854	0.998
25	0.159	0.387	0.808	0.914	1.000
50	0.235	0.607	0.971	0.995	1.000
$R^2 = 0.10$					
5	0.114	0.255	0.568	0.697	0.971
10	0.174	0.434	0.847	0.935	1.000
20	0.276	0.688	0.985	0.998	1.000
25	0.323	0.773	0.996	1.000	1.000
50	0.523	0.960	1.000	1.000	1.000
$R^2 = 0.20$					
5	0.193	0.514	0.913	0.971	1.000
10	0.348	0.816	0.997	1.000	1.000
20	0.596	0.980	1.000	1.000	1.000
25	0.688	0.994	1.000	1.000	1.000
50	0.926	1.000	1.000	1.000	1.000

mean of $\hat{\alpha}_{[i_k:N]}$ is a function of its relative rank i_k/N (in the limit), whereas its variance $\sigma_\alpha^2(1 - \rho^2)$ is fixed. Forming a portfolio of the induced order statistics within a characteristic-fractile amounts to averaging a collection of n_o approximately independent random variables with similar means and identical variances. The result is a statistic $\tilde{\phi}_k$ with a comparable mean but

Table 8.3. *Critical values $C_{.05}$ for 5 percent χ^2-tests of $H: \alpha_i = 0$ $(i = 1, \ldots, n)$ using the test statistic $\tilde{\theta}_p$, where $\tilde{\theta}_p \equiv n_o \sum_{k=1}^{q} \tilde{\phi}_k^2 / \sigma_\alpha^2$, and $\tilde{\phi}_k \equiv (1/n_o) \sum_{j=(k-1)q+1}^{kq} \hat{\alpha}_{[ij:N]}$ is constructed from portfolio k, with portfolios formed by sorting on some characteristic correlated with estimates $\hat{\alpha}_i$. This induced ordering alters the null distribution of $\tilde{\theta}_p$ from χ_q^2 to $(1 - R^2)/\chi_q^2(\lambda)$, where the noncentrality parameter λ is a function of the number q of portfolios, the number n_o of securities in each portfolio, and the squared correlation coefficient R^2 between $\hat{\alpha}_i$ and the sorting characteristic. $C_{.05}$ is defined implicitly by the relation $\Pr(\tilde{\theta}_p > C_{.05}) = 1 - F_{\chi_q^2(\lambda)}\left(C_{.05}/(1 - R^2)\right) = 0.05$. For comparison, we also report the 5 percent critical value of the central χ_q^2 distribution in the second column.*

q	$C_{.05}$-χ_q^2	$C_{.05}$-$\chi_q^2(\lambda)$ $(n_o = 5)$	$C_{.05}$-$\chi_q^2(\lambda)$ $(n_o = 10)$	$C_{.05}$-$\chi_q^2(\lambda)$ $(n_o = 20)$	$C_{.05}$-$\chi_q^2(\lambda)$ $(n_o = 25)$	$C_{.05}$-$\chi_q^2(\lambda)$ $(n_o = 50)$
$R^2 = 0.005$						
5	11.07	11.22	11.45	11.93	12.16	13.29
10	18.31	18.60	19.03	19.87	20.28	22.31
20	31.41	31.97	32.72	34.22	34.96	38.58
25	37.65	38.33	39.24	41.05	41.94	46.33
50	67.50	68.78	70.44	73.72	75.35	83.39
$R^2 = 0.01$						
5	11.07	11.36	11.83	12.74	13.19	15.31
10	18.31	18.89	19.73	21.36	22.16	26.00
20	31.41	32.52	34.01	36.93	38.36	45.31
25	37.65	39.01	40.81	44.34	46.08	54.52
50	67.50	70.05	73.33	79.79	82.98	98.60
$R^2 = 0.05$						
5	11.07	12.45	14.53	18.39	20.21	28.68
10	18.31	21.09	24.88	32.00	35.41	51.54
20	31.41	36.72	43.62	56.75	63.09	93.59
25	37.65	44.18	52.56	68.59	76.35	113.82
50	67.50	79.85	95.41	125.47	140.16	211.67
$R^2 = 0.10$						
5	11.07	13.65	17.45	24.37	27.63	42.96
10	18.31	23.58	30.62	43.74	50.02	79.98
20	31.41	41.60	54.63	79.32	91.27	148.98
25	37.65	50.21	66.13	96.44	111.15	182.43
50	67.50	91.49	121.42	179.11	207.33	345.24
$R^2 = 0.20$						
5	11.07	15.70	22.44	34.82	40.71	68.73
10	18.31	27.98	40.86	65.01	76.65	132.76
20	31.41	50.51	74.89	121.32	143.91	253.93
25	37.65	61.32	91.29	148.61	176.58	313.10
50	67.50	113.43	170.67	281.43	335.83	603.10

with a variance n_o times smaller than each of the $\hat{\alpha}_{[i_k:N]}$'s. This variance reduction amplifies the importance of the deviation of the $\tilde{\phi}_k$ mean from zero, and is ultimately reflected in the entries of Table 8.2. A more dramatic illustration is provided in Table 8.3, which reports the appropriate 5 percent critical values for the tests in Table 8.2—when $R^2 = 0.05$, the 5 percent critical value for the χ^2 test with 50 securities in each of 50 portfolios is

211.67. If induced ordering is unavoidable, these critical values may serve as a method for bounding the effects of data snooping on inferences.

When the R^2 increases to 10 percent, implying a cross-sectional correlation of about ± 32 percent between $\hat{\alpha}_i$ and X_i, the size approaches unity for tests based on 20 or more portfolios with 20 or more securities in each portfolio. These results are especially surprising in view of the sizes reported in Table 8.1, since the portfolio test statistic is based on evenly spaced induced order statistics $\hat{\alpha}_{[i_k:N]}$. Using 100 securities, Table 8.1 shows a size of 4.3 percent with evenly spaced $\hat{\alpha}_{[i_k:N]}$'s; Table 8.2 shows that placing those 100 securities into 5 portfolios with 20 securities in each increases the size to 56.8 percent. Computing $\tilde{\theta}_p$ with extreme $\hat{\alpha}_{[i_k:N]}$ would presumably yield even higher rejection rates. The biases reported in Tables 8.2 and 8.3 are even more surprising in view of the limited use we have made of the data. The only data-related information impounded in the induced order statistics is the rankings of the characteristics $\{X_i\}$. Nowhere have we exploited the values of the X_i's, which contain considerably more precise information about the $\hat{\alpha}_i$'s.

8.1.4 Interpreting Data-Snooping Bias as Power

We have so far examined the effects of data snooping under the null hypothesis that $\alpha_i = 0$, for all i. Therefore, the degree to which induced ordering increases the probability of rejecting this null is implicitly assumed to be a bias, an increase in type I error. However, the results of the previous sections may be reinterpreted as describing the power of tests based on induced ordering against certain alternative hypotheses.

Recall from (8.1.2) that $\hat{\alpha}_i$ is the sum of α_i and estimation error ζ_i. Since all α_i's are zero under H, the induced ordering of the estimates $\hat{\alpha}_i$ creates a spurious incompatibility with the null arising solely from the sorting of the estimation errors ζ_i. But if the α_i's are nonzero and vary across i, then sorting by some characteristic X_i related to α_i and forming portfolios does yield a more powerful test. Forming portfolios reduces the estimation error through diversification (or the law of large numbers), and grouping by X_i maintains the dispersion of the α_i's across portfolios. Therefore what were called biases in Sections 8.1.1–8.1.3 may also be viewed as measures of the power of induced ordering against alternatives in which the α_i's differ from zero and vary cross-sectionally with X_i. The values in Table 8.2 show that grouping on a marginally correlated characteristic can increase the power substantially.[14]

---

[14]However, implicit in Table 8.2 is the assumption that the $\hat{\alpha}_i$'s are cross-sectionally independent, which may be too restrictive a requirement for interesting alternative hypotheses. For example, if the null hypothesis $\alpha_i = 0$ corresponds to the Sharpe-Lintner CAPM, then one natural alternative might be a two-factor APT. In that case, the $\hat{\alpha}_i$'s of assets with similar factor loadings would tend to be positively cross-sectionally correlated as a result of the omitted

To formalize the above intuition within our framework, suppose that the α_i's were IID random variables independent of ζ_i and have mean μ_α and variance σ_α^2. Then the $\hat{\alpha}_i$'s are still independently and identically distributed, but the null hypothesis that $\alpha_i = 0$ is now violated. Suppose the estimation error ζ_i were identically zero, so that all variation in $\hat{\alpha}_i$ was due to variations in α_i. Then the values in Table 8.2 would represent the *power* of our test against this alternative, where the squared correlation is now given by

$$\rho_p^2 = \frac{\text{Cov}^2[X_i, \alpha_i]}{\text{Var}[X_i] \cdot \text{Var}[\alpha_i]}. \tag{8.1.24}$$

If, as under our null hypothesis, all α_i's were identically zero, then the values in Table 8.2 must be interpreted as the *size* of our test, where the squared correlation reduces to

$$\rho_s^2 = \frac{\text{Cov}^2[X_i, \zeta_i]}{\text{Var}[X_i] \cdot \text{Var}[\zeta_i]}. \tag{8.1.25}$$

More generally, the squared correlation ρ^2 is related to ρ_s^2 and ρ_p^2 in the following way:

$$\rho^2 = \frac{\text{Cov}^2[X_i, \hat{\alpha}_i]}{\text{Var}[X_i] \cdot \text{Var}[\hat{\alpha}_i]} = \frac{(\text{Cov}[X_i, \alpha_i] + \text{Cov}[X_i, \zeta_i])^2}{\text{Var}[X_i] \cdot (\text{Var}[\alpha_i] + \text{Var}[\zeta_i])} \tag{8.1.26}$$

$$= \left(\rho_s \sqrt{\pi} + \rho_p \sqrt{1 - \pi} \right)^2, \qquad \pi \equiv \frac{\text{Var}[\zeta_i]}{\text{Var}[\hat{\alpha}_i]}. \tag{8.1.27}$$

Holding the correlations ρ_s and ρ_p fixed, the importance of the spurious portion of ρ^2, given by ρ_s, increases with π, the fraction of variability in $\hat{\alpha}_i$ due to estimation error. Conversely, if the variability of $\hat{\alpha}_i$ is largely due to fluctuations in α_i, then ρ^2 will reflect mostly ρ_p^2.

Of course, the essence of the problem lies in our inability to identify π except in very special cases. We observe an empirical relation between X_i and $\hat{\alpha}_i$, but we do not know whether the characteristic varies with α_i or with estimation error ζ_i. It is a type of identification problem that is unlikely to be settled by data analysis alone, but must be resolved by providing theoretical motivation for a relation, or no relation, between X_i and α_i. That is, economic considerations must play a dominant role in determining π. We shall return to this issue in the empirical examples of Section 8.3.

---

factor. This positive correlation reduces the benefits of grouping. Grouping by induced ordering does tend to cluster $\hat{\alpha}_i$'s with similar (nonzero) means together, but correlation works against the variance reduction that gives portfolio-based tests their power. The importance of cross-sectional dependence is evident in MacKinlay's (1987) power calculations. We provide further discussion in Section 8.2.3.

8.2 Monte Carlo Results

Although the values in Tables 8.1–8.3 quantify the magnitude of the biases associated with induced ordering, their practical relevance may be limited in at least three respects. First, the test statistics we have considered are similar in spirit to those used in empirical tests of asset pricing models, but implicitly use the assumption of cross-sectional independence. The more common practice is to estimate the covariance matrix of the N asset returns using a finite number T of time series observations, from which an F-distributed quadratic form may be constructed. Both sampling error from the covariance matrix estimator and cross-sectional dependence will affect the null distribution of $\tilde{\theta}$ in finite samples.

Second, the sampling theory of Section 8.1 is based on asymptotic approximations, and few results on rates of convergence for Theorem 8.1.1 are available.[15] How accurate are such approximations for empirically realistic sample sizes?

Finally, the form of the asymptotics does not correspond exactly to procedures followed in practice. Recall that the limiting result involves a finite number n of securities with relative ranks that converge to fixed constants ξ_i as the number of securities N increases without bound. This implies that as N increases, the number of securities in between any two of our chosen n must also grow without bound. However, in practice characteristic-sorted portfolios are constructed from *all* securities within a fractile, not just from those with particular relative ranks. Although intuition suggests that this may be less problematic when n is large (so that within any given fractile there will be many securities), it is surprisingly difficult to verify.[16]

In this section we report results from Monte Carlo experiments that show the asymptotic approximations of Section 8.1 to be quite accurate in practice despite these three reservations. In Section 8.2.1, we evaluate the quality of the asymptotic approximations for the $\tilde{\theta}_p$ test used in calculating Tables 8.2 and 8.3. In Section 8.2.2, we consider the effects of induced ordering on F-tests with fixed N and T when the covariance matrix is estimated and the data-generating process is cross-sectionally independent. In Section 8.2.3, we consider the effects of relaxing the independence assumption.

---

[15]However, see Bhattacharya (1984) and Sen (1981).

[16]When n is large relative to a finite N, the asymptotic approximation breaks down. In particular, the dependence between adjacent induced order statistics becomes important for nontrivial n/N. A few elegant asymptotic approximations for sums of induced order statistics are available using functional central limit theory and may allow us to generalize our results to the more empirically relevant case. See, for example, Bhattacharya (1974), Nagaraja (1982a, 1982b, 1984), Sandström (1987), Sen (1976, 1981), and Yang (1981a, 1981b). However, our Monte Carlo results suggest that this generalization may be unnecessary.

8.2.1 Simulation Results for $\tilde{\theta}_p$

The $\chi_q^2(\lambda)$ limiting distribution of $\tilde{\theta}_p$ obtains because any finite collection of induced order statistics, each with a fixed distinct limiting relative rank ξ_i in $(0, 1)$, becomes mutually independent as the total number N of securities increases without bound. This asymptotic approximation implies that between any two of the n chosen securities there will be an increasing number of securities omitted from all portfolios as N increases. In practice, all securities within a particular characteristic fractile are included in the sorted portfolios; hence, the theoretical sizes of Table 8.2 may not be an adequate approximation to this more empirically relevant situation. To explore this possibility we simulate bivariate normal vectors $(\hat{\alpha}_i, X_i)$ with squared correlation R^2, form portfolios using the induced ordering by the X_i's, compute $\tilde{\theta}_p$ using *all* the $\hat{\alpha}_{[i:N]}$'s (in contrast to the asymptotic experiment where only those induced order statistics of given relative ranks are used), and then repeat this procedure 5,000 times to obtain the finite sample distribution.

Table 8.4 reports the results of these simulations for the same values of R^2, n_o, and q as in Table 8.2. Except when both n_o and q are small, the empirical sizes of Table 8.4 match their asymptotic counterparts in Table 8.2 closely. Consider, for example, the $R^2 = 0.05$ panel; with 5 portfolios each with 5 securities, the difference between the theoretical and empirical size is 1.1 percentage points, whereas this difference is only 0.2 percentage points for 25 portfolios each with 25 securities. When n_o and q are both small, the theoretical and empirical sizes differ more for larger R^2, by as much as 7.4 percent when $R^2 = 0.20$. However, for the more relevant values of R^2, the empirical and theoretical sizes of the $\tilde{\theta}_p$ test are virtually identical.

8.2.2 Effects of Induced Ordering on F-Tests

Although the results of Section 8.2.1 support the accuracy of our asymptotic approximation to the sampling distribution of $\tilde{\theta}_p$, the closely related *F*-statistic is used more frequently in practice. In this section we consider the finite-sample distribution of the *F*-statistic after induced ordering. We perform Monte Carlo experiments under the now standard multivariate data-generating process common to virtually all static financial asset pricing models. Let r_{it} denote the return of asset i between dates $t-1$ and t, where $i = 1, 2, \ldots, N$ and $t = 1, 2, \ldots, T$. We assume that for all assets i and dates t the following obtains:

$$r_{it} = \alpha_i + \sum_{j=1}^{k} \beta_{ij} r_t^j + \epsilon_{it}, \qquad (8.2.1)$$

where α_i and β_{ij} are fixed parameters, r_t^j is the return on some portfolio j (systematic risk), and ϵ_{it} is mean-zero (idiosyncratic) noise. Depending on

Table 8.4.   *Empirical sizes of nominal 5 percent χ_q^2-tests of H: $\alpha_i = 0$ $(i = 1, \ldots, n)$ using the test statistic $\tilde{\theta}_p$, where $\tilde{\theta}_p \equiv n_o \sum_{k=1}^q \tilde{\phi}_k^2 / \sigma_\alpha^2$, and $\tilde{\phi}_k \equiv (1/n_o) \sum_{j=(k-1)q+1}^{kq} \hat{\alpha}_{[ij:N]}$ is constructed from portfolio k, with portfolios formed by sorting on some characteristic correlated with estimates $\hat{\alpha}_i$. This induced ordering alters the null distribution of $\tilde{\theta}_p$ from χ_q^2 to $(1 - R^2) \cdot \chi_q^2(\lambda)$, where the noncentrality parameter λ is a function of the number q of portfolios, the number n_o of securities in each portfolio, and the squared correlation coefficient R^2 between $\hat{\alpha}_i$ and the sorting characteristic. Each simulation is based on 5000 replications; asymptotic standard errors for the size estimates may be obtained from the usual binomial approximation, and is 3.08×10^{-3} for the 5 percent test.*

q	$n_o = 5$	$n_o = 10$	$n_o = 20$	$n_o = 25$	$n_o = 50$
$R^2 = 0.005$					
5	0.055	0.057	0.067	0.075	0.108
10	0.054	0.063	0.080	0.084	0.139
20	0.056	0.068	0.086	0.106	0.182
25	0.062	0.070	0.104	0.112	0.209
50	0.059	0.077	0.119	0.146	0.314
$R^2 = 0.01$					
5	0.058	0.064	0.093	0.105	0.174
10	0.059	0.076	0.119	0.130	0.257
20	0.057	0.083	0.140	0.188	0.385
25	0.069	0.100	0.170	0.206	0.445
50	0.083	0.118	0.244	0.300	0.679
$R^2 = 0.05$					
5	0.091	0.149	0.310	0.392	0.723
10	0.117	0.227	0.493	0.611	0.943
20	0.156	0.351	0.744	0.854	0.999
25	0.163	0.401	0.818	0.916	1.000
50	0.249	0.616	0.971	0.997	1.000
$R^2 = 0.10$					
5	0.141	0.285	0.601	0.721	0.973
10	0.197	0.473	0.854	0.937	1.000
20	0.308	0.709	0.985	0.998	1.000
25	0.338	0.789	0.995	1.000	1.000
50	0.545	0.961	1.000	1.000	1.000
$R^2 = 0.20$					
5	0.267	0.577	0.922	0.974	1.000
10	0.405	0.833	0.997	1.000	1.000
20	0.635	0.982	1.000	1.000	1.000
25	0.728	0.996	1.000	1.000	1.000
50	0.933	1.000	1.000	1.000	1.000

the particular application, r_{it} may be taken to be nominal, real, or excess asset returns. The process (8.2.1) may be viewed as a factor model where the factors correspond to particular portfolios of traded assets, often called the "mimicking portfolios" of an exact factor pricing model. In matrix notation, we have

$$r_t = \alpha + Br_t^p + \epsilon_t, \qquad \mathrm{E}[\epsilon_t \mid r_t^p] = 0, \qquad \mathrm{E}[r_t^p] = \mu_p; \qquad (8.2.2)$$

$$\mathrm{E}[\epsilon_s \epsilon_t'] = \begin{cases} \Sigma, & \text{for } s = t, \\ 0, & \text{otherwise;} \end{cases} \qquad (8.2.3)$$

$$\mathrm{E}[(r_s^p - \mu_p)(r_t^p - \mu_p)'] = \begin{cases} \Omega, & \text{for } s = t, \\ 0, & \text{otherwise.} \end{cases} \qquad (8.2.4)$$

Here, r_t is the $N \times 1$ vector of asset returns at time t, B is the $N \times k$ matrix of factor loadings, r_t^p is the $k \times 1$ vector of time-t spanning portfolio returns, and α and ϵ_t are $N \times 1$ vectors of asset return intercepts and disturbances, respectively.

This data-generating process is the starting point of the two most popular static models of asset pricing, the CAPM and the APT. Further restrictions are usually imposed by the specific model under consideration, often reducing to the following null hypothesis:

$$\mathrm{H}: g(\alpha, B) = 0,$$

where the function g is model dependent.[17] Many tests simply set $g(\alpha, B) = \alpha$ and define r_t as excess returns, such as those of the Sharpe-Lintner CAPM and the exact factor-pricing APT. With the added assumption that r_t and r_t^p are jointly normally distributed, the finite-sample distribution of the following test statistic is well known:

$$\psi = \kappa \cdot \frac{\hat{\alpha}'\hat{\Sigma}^{-1}\hat{\alpha}}{1 + \bar{r}^p\hat{\Omega}^{-1}\bar{r}^p} \sim F_{N, T-k-N}, \qquad \kappa \equiv \frac{T - k - N}{N}, \qquad (8.2.5)$$

where $\hat{\Sigma}$ and $\hat{\Omega}$ are the maximum likelihood estimators of the covariance matrices of the disturbances $\hat{\epsilon}_t$ and the spanning portfolio returns r_t^p, respectively, and $\bar{r}^p$ is the vector of sample means of r_t^p. If the number of available securities N is greater than the number of time series observations T less $k + 1$, the estimator $\hat{\Sigma}$ is singular and the test statistic (8.2.5) cannot

---

[17]Examples of tests that fit into this framework are those in Campbell (1987), Connor and Korajczyk (1988), Gibbons (1982), Gibbons and Ferson (1985), Gibbons, Ross, and Shanken (1989), Huberman and Kandel (1987), Lehmann and Modest (1988), MacKinlay (1987), Stambaugh (1982), and Shanken (1985).

be computed without additional structure. This problem is most often circumvented in practice by forming portfolios. That is, let r_t be a $q \times 1$ vector of returns of q portfolios of securities where $q \ll N$. Since the return-generating process is linear for each security i, a linear relation also obtains for portfolio returns. However, as the analysis of Section 8.1 foreshadows, if the portfolios are constructed by sorting on some characteristic correlated with $\hat{\alpha}$ then the null distribution of ψ is altered.

To evaluate the null distribution of ψ under characteristic-sorting data snooping, we design our simulation experiments in the following way. The number of time series observations T is set to 60 for all simulations. With little loss in generality, we set the number of spanning portfolios k to zero so that $\hat{\alpha}_i = \sum_{t=1}^{T} r_{it}/T$. To separate the effects of *estimating* the covariance matrix from the effects of cross-sectional dependence, we first assume that the covariance matrix $\sum$ of ϵ_t is equal to the identity matrix I—this assumption is relaxed in Section 8.2.3. We simulate T observations of the $N \times 1$ Gaussian vector r_t (where N takes the values 200, 500, and 1000), and compute $\hat{\alpha}$. We then form q portfolios (where q takes the values 10 and 20) by constructing a characteristic X_i that has correlation ρ with $\hat{\alpha}_i$ (where ρ^2 takes the values 0.005, 0.01, 0.05, 0.10, and 0.20), and then sorting the $\hat{\alpha}_i$'s by this characteristic. To do this, we define

$$X_i \equiv \hat{\alpha}_i + \eta_i, \qquad \eta_i \quad \text{IID} \quad \mathcal{N}(0, \sigma_\eta^2), \qquad \sigma_\eta^2 = \frac{1-\rho^2}{T\rho^2}. \qquad (8.2.6)$$

Having constructed the X_i's, we order $\{\hat{\alpha}_i\}$ to obtain $\{\hat{\alpha}_{[i:N]}\}$, construct portfolio intercept estimates that we call $\hat{\phi}_k$, $k = 1, \ldots, n$,

$$\hat{\phi}_k = \frac{1}{n_o} \sum_{i=(k-1)n_o+1}^{kn_o} \hat{\alpha}_{[i:N]}, \qquad N \equiv n_o q, \qquad (8.2.7)$$

from which we form the F-statistic,

$$\psi = \kappa \cdot \hat{\phi}' \hat{\Sigma}^{-1} \hat{\phi} \sim F_{q,T-q}, \qquad \kappa \equiv (T-q)/q, \qquad (8.2.8)$$

where $\hat{\phi}$ denotes the $q \times 1$ vector of $\hat{\phi}_k$'s, and $\hat{\Sigma}$ is the maximum likelihood estimator of the $q \times q$ covariance matrix of the q portfolio returns. This procedure is repeated 5000 times, and the mean and standard deviation of the resulting distribution for the statistic ψ are reported in Table 8.5, as well as the size of 1, 5, and 10 percent F-tests.

Even for as small an R^2 as 1 percent, the empirical size of the 5 percent F-test differs significantly from its nominal value for all values of q and n_o. For the sample of 1000 securities grouped into ten portfolios, the empirical rejection rate of 36.7 percent deviates substantially from 5 percent. When the 1000 securities are grouped into 20 portfolios, the size is somewhat

Table 8.5. *Empirical size of $F_{q,T-q}$ tests based on q portfolios sorted by a random characteristic whose squared correlation with $\hat{\alpha}_i$ is R^2. n_o is the number of securities in each portfolio and $n \equiv n_o q$ is the total number of securities. The number of time series observations T is set to 60. The mean and standard deviation of the test statistic over the 5000 replications are reported. The population mean and standard deviation of $F_{10,50}$ are 1.042 and 0.523, respectively; those of the $F_{20,40}$ are 1.053 and 0.423, respectively. Asymptotic standard errors for the size estimates may be obtained from the usual binomial approximation; they are 4.24×10^{-3}, 3.08×10^{-3}, and 1.41×10^{-3} for the 10, 5, and 1 percent tests, respectively.*

q	n_o	n	Mean	Std. Dev.	Size 10%	Size 5%	Size 1%
$R^2 = 0.005$							
10	20	200	1.111	0.542	0.124	0.041	0.014
20	10	200	1.081	0.424	0.107	0.054	0.009
10	50	500	1.238	0.611	0.177	0.070	0.026
20	25	500	1.147	0.462	0.152	0.079	0.018
10	100	1000	1.406	0.679	0.270	0.118	0.046
20	50	1000	1.240	0.500	0.194	0.114	0.033
$R^2 = 0.01$							
10	20	200	1.225	0.619	0.181	0.071	0.026
20	10	200	1.148	0.460	0.148	0.079	0.018
10	50	500	1.512	0.728	0.318	0.152	0.070
20	25	500	1.301	0.514	0.240	0.143	0.036
10	100	1000	2.030	0.908	0.576	0.367	0.203
20	50	1000	1.554	0.596	0.405	0.268	0.098
$R^2 = 0.05$							
10	20	200	1.980	0.883	0.549	0.342	0.189
20	10	200	1.505	0.582	0.369	0.241	0.082
10	50	500	3.501	1.335	0.945	0.846	0.700
20	25	500	2.264	0.801	0.798	0.670	0.382
10	100	1000	5.991	1.976	0.999	0.997	0.986
20	50	1000	3.587	1.169	0.992	0.972	0.879
$R^2 = 0.10$							
10	20	200	2.961	1.196	0.868	0.713	0.538
20	10	200	1.977	0.727	0.658	0.510	0.257
10	50	500	5.939	1.931	0.999	0.997	0.987
20	25	500	3.526	1.128	0.988	0.968	0.868
10	100	1000	10.888	3.050	1.000	1.000	1.000
20	50	1000	6.123	1.811	1.000	1.000	0.999
$R^2 = 0.20$							
10	20	200	4.831	1.657	0.997	0.982	0.937
20	10	200	2.895	0.992	0.948	0.882	0.667
10	50	500	10.796	3.022	1.000	1.000	1.000
20	25	500	6.005	1.758	1.000	1.000	0.998
10	100	1000	20.695	5.112	1.000	1.000	1.000
20	50	1000	11.194	2.988	1.000	1.000	1.000

lower—26.8 percent—matching the pattern in Table 8.2. Also similar is the monotonicity of the size with respect to the number of securities. For 200 securities the empirical size is only 7.1 percent with 10 portfolios, but it is more than quintupled with 1000 securities. When the squared correlation between $\hat{\alpha}_i$ and X_i increases to 10 percent, the size of the F-test is essentially unity for sample sizes of 500 or more. Thus even for finite sample sizes of practical relevance, the importance of data snooping via induced ordering cannot be overemphasized.

8.2.3 F-Tests With Cross-Sectional Dependence

The substantial bias that induced ordering imparts on the size of portfolio-based F-tests comes from the fact that the induced order statistics $\{\hat{\alpha}_{[i:N]}\}$ generally have nonzero means;[18] hence, the averages of these statistics within sorted portfolios also have nonzero means but reduced variances about those means. Alternatively, the bias from portfolio formation is a result of the fact that the $\hat{\alpha}_i$'s of the extreme portfolios do not approach zero as more securities are combined, whereas the residual variances of the portfolios (and consequently the variances of the portfolio $\hat{\alpha}_i$'s) do tend to zero. Of course, our assumption that the disturbances ϵ_t of (8.2.2) are cross-sectionally independent implies that the portfolio residual variance approaches zero rather quickly (at rate $1/n_o$). But in many applications (such as the CAPM), cross-sectional independence is counterfactual. Firm size and industry membership are but two factors that might induce cross-sectional correlation in return residuals. In particular, when the residuals are positively cross-sectionally correlated, the bias is likely to be smaller since there is less variance reduction in forming portfolios than in the cross-sectionally independent case.

To see how restrictive the independence assumption is, we simulate a data-generating process in which disturbances are cross-sectionally correlated. The design is identical to that of Section 8.2.2 except that the residual covariance matrix Σ is no longer diagonal. Instead, we set

$$\Sigma = \delta\delta' + I, \tag{8.2.9}$$

where δ is an $N \times 1$ vector of parameters and I is the identity matrix. Such a covariance matrix would arise, for example, from a single common factor model for the $N \times 1$ vector of disturbances ϵ_t:

$$\epsilon_t = \delta\Lambda_t + v_t, \tag{8.2.10}$$

where Λ_t is some IID zero-mean unit-variance common factor independent of v_t, and v_t is N-dimensional vector white noise with covariance matrix I.

---

[18]Only those $\hat{\alpha}_{[i:N]}$ for which $i/N \rightarrow \frac{1}{2}$ will have zero expectation under the null hypothesis H.

Table 8.6.   *Empirical size of $F_{q,T-q}$ tests based on q portfolios sorted by a random characteristic whose squared correlation with $\hat{\alpha}_i$ is approximately 0.05. n_o is the number of securities in each portfolio and $n \equiv n_o q$ is the total number of securities. The $\hat{\alpha}_i$'s of the portfolios are cross-sectionally correlated, where the source of correlation is an IID zero-mean common factor in the returns. The number of time series observations T is set to 60. The mean and standard deviation of the test statistic over the 5000 replications are reported. The population mean and standard deviation of $F_{10,50}$ are 1.042 and 0.523, respectively; those of the $F_{20,40}$ are 1.053 and 0.423, respectively. Asymptotic standard errors for the size estimates may be obtained from the usual binomial approximation; they are 4.24×10^{-3}, 3.08×10^{-3}, and 1.41×10^{-3} for the 10, 5, and 1 percent tests, respectively.*

q	n_o	n	Mean	Std. Dev.	Size 10%	Size 5%	Size 1%
$R^2 \approx 0.05$							
10	20	200	1.700	0.763	0.422	0.216	0.100
20	10	200	1.372	0.528	0.270	0.167	0.047
10	50	500	2.520	1.041	0.765	0.565	0.367
20	25	500	1.867	0.693	0.593	0.322	0.205
10	100	1000	3.624	1.605	0.925	0.820	0.682
20	50	1000	2.516	0.966	0.844	0.743	0.501

For our simulations, the parameters δ are chosen to be equally spaced in the interval $[-1, 1]$. With this design the cross-correlation of the disturbances will range from -0.5 to 0.5. The X_i's are constructed as in (8.2.6) with

$$\sigma_\eta^2 = \frac{(1 - \rho^2)\sigma^2(\alpha)}{\rho^2}, \qquad \sigma^2(\alpha) \equiv \frac{1}{NT} \sum_{i=1}^{N} (\delta_i^2 + 1), \qquad (8.2.11)$$

where ρ^2 is fixed at 0.05.

Under this design, the results of the simulation experiments may be compared to the third panel of Table 8.5, and are reported in Table 8.6.[19] Despite the presence of cross-sectional dependence, the impact of induced ordering on the size of the F-test is still significant. For example, with 20 portfolios each containing 25 securities the empirical size of the 5 percent test is 32.3 percent; with 10 portfolios of 50 securities each the empirical size increases to 82.0 percent. As in the cross-sectionally independent case, the bias increases with the number of securities given a fixed number of portfolios, and the bias decreases as the number of portfolios is increased given a fixed number of securities. Not surprisingly, for fixed n_o and q, cross-sectional dependence of the $\hat{\alpha}_i$'s lessens the bias. However, the en-

---

[19]The correspondence between the two tables is not exact because the dependency introduced in (8.2.9) induces cross-sectional heteroscedasticity in the $\hat{\alpha}_i$'s; hence, $\rho^2 = 0.05$ yields an R^2 of 0.05 only approximately.

tries in Table 8.6 demonstrate that the effects of data-snooping may still be substantial even in the presence of cross-sectional dependence.

8.3 Two Empirical Examples

To illustrate the potential relevance of data-snooping biases associated with induced ordering, we provide two examples drawn from the empirical literature. The first example is taken from the early tests of the Sharpe-Lintner CAPM, where portfolios were formed by sorting on out-of-sample betas. We show that such tests can be biased towards falsely rejecting the CAPM if in-sample betas are used instead, underscoring the importance of the elaborate sorting procedures used by Black, Jensen, and Scholes (1972) and Fama and MacBeth (1973). Our second example concerns tests of the APT that reject the zero-intercept null hypothesis when applied to portfolio returns sorted by market value of equity. We show that data-snooping biases can account for much the same results, and that only additional economic restrictions will determine the ultimate source of the rejections.

8.3.1 Sorting By Beta

Although tests of the Sharpe-Lintner CAPM may be conducted on individual securities, the potential benefits of using multiple securities are well known. One common approach for allocating securities to portfolios has been to rank them by their betas and then group the sorted securities. Beta-sorted portfolios will exhibit more risk dispersion than portfolios of randomly chosen securities, and may therefore yield more information about the CAPM's risk–return relation. Ideally, portfolios would be formed according to their true betas. However, since the population betas are unobservable, in practice portfolios have grouped securities by their estimated betas. For example, both Black, Jensen, and Scholes (1972) and Fama and MacBeth (1973) use portfolios formed by sorting on estimated betas, where the betas are estimated with a *prior* sample of stock returns. Their motivation for this more complicated procedure was to to avoid grouping common estimation or measurement error since, within the sample, securities with high estimated betas will tend to have positive realizations of estimation error, and vice versa for securities with low estimated betas.

Suppose, instead, that securities are grouped by betas estimated *in-sample*. Can grouping common estimation error change inferences substantially? To answer this question within our framework, suppose the Sharpe-Lintner CAPM obtains so that

$$r_{it} = \beta_i r_{mt} + \epsilon_{it}, \qquad E[\epsilon_t \mid r_{mt}] = 0, \qquad E[\epsilon_t \epsilon_t'] = \sigma_\epsilon^2 I, \qquad (8.3.1)$$

where r_{it} denotes the excess return of security i, r_{mt} is the excess market return, and ϵ_t is the $N \times 1$ vector of disturbances. To assess the impact of sorting on in-sample betas, we require the squared correlation of $\hat{\alpha}_i$ and $\hat{\beta}_i$. However, since our framework requires that both $\hat{\alpha}_i$ and $\hat{\beta}_i$ be independently and identically distributed, and since $\hat{\beta}_i$ is the sum of β_i and estimation error ζ_i, we assume β_i to be random to allow for cross-sectional variation in the betas. Therefore, let

$$\beta_i \text{ IID } \mathcal{N}(\mu_\beta, \sigma_\beta^2), \qquad i = 1, 2, \ldots, N,$$

where each β_i is independent of all ϵ_{jt} in (8.3.1). The squared correlation between $\hat{\alpha}_i$ and $\hat{\beta}_i$ may then be explicitly calculated as

$$\rho^2(\hat{\alpha}_i, \hat{\beta}_i) = \frac{\text{Cov}^2[\hat{\alpha}_i, \hat{\beta}_i]}{\text{Var}[\hat{\alpha}_i]\text{Var}[\hat{\beta}_i]} = \frac{\hat{S}_m^2}{1 + \hat{S}_m^2} \cdot \frac{1}{1 + (\sigma_\beta^2 \hat{\sigma}_m^2/\sigma_\epsilon^2)\, T}, \qquad (8.3.2)$$

where $\hat{\mu}_m$ and $\hat{\sigma}_m$ are the sample mean and standard deviation of the excess market return, respectively, $S_m \equiv \hat{\mu}_m/\hat{\sigma}_m$ is the ex post Sharpe measure, and T is the number of time series observations used to estimate the α_i's and β_i's.

The term $\sigma_\beta^2 \hat{\sigma}_m^2 T/\sigma_\epsilon^2$ in (8.3.2) captures the essence of the errors-in-variables problem for in-sample beta sorting. This is simply the ratio of the cross-sectional variance in betas, σ_β^2, to the variance of the beta estimation error, $\sigma_\epsilon^2/(\hat{\sigma}_m^2 T)$. When the cross-sectional dispersion of the betas is much larger than the variance of the estimation errors, this ratio is large, implying a small value for ρ^2 and little data-snooping bias. In fact, since the estimation error of the betas declines with the number of observations T, as the time period lengthens, in-sample beta sorting becomes less problematic. However, when the variance of the estimation error is large relative to the cross-sectional variance of the betas, then ρ^2 is large and grouping common estimation errors becomes a more serious problem.

To show just how serious this might be in practice, we report in Table 8.7 the estimated ρ^2 between $\hat{\alpha}_i$ and $\hat{\beta}_i$ for five-year subperiods from January 1954 to December 1988, where each estimate is based on the first 200 securities listed in the CRSP monthly returns files with complete return histories within the particular five-year subsample, and the CRSP equal-weighted index. Also reported is the probability of rejecting the null hypothesis $\alpha_i = 0$ when it is true using a 5 percent test, assuming a sample of 2500 securities, where the number of portfolios q is 10, 20, or 50 and the number of securities per portfolio n_o is defined accordingly.[20]

---

[20]Our analysis is limited by the counterfactual assumption that the market model disturbances are cross-sectionally uncorrelated. But the simulation results presented in Section 8.2.3 indicate that biases are still substantial even in the presence of cross-sectional dependence. A more involved application would require a deeper analysis of cross-sectional dependence in the ϵ_{it}'s.

Table 8.7. *Theoretical sizes of nominal 5 percent χ_q^2-tests under the null hypothesis of the Sharpe-Lintner CAPM using q in-sample beta-sorted portfolios with n_o securities per portfolio, where $\hat{R}^2$ is the estimated squared correlation between $\hat{\beta}_i$ and $\hat{\alpha}_i$ under the null hypothesis that $\alpha_i = 0$ and that the β_i's are IID normal random variables with mean and variance μ_β and σ_β^2, respectively. Within each subsample, the estimate $\hat{R}^2$ is based on the first 200 stocks in the CRSP monthly returns files with complete return histories over the five-year subperiod, and the CSRP equal-weighted index. For illustrative purposes, the theoretical size is computed under the assumption that the total number of securities $n \equiv n_o q$ is fixed at 2500.*

Sample Period	$\hat{R}^2$	$q = 10$ $n_o = 250$	$q = 20$ $n_o = 125$	$q = 50$ $n_o = 50$
January 1954–December 1958	0.044	1.000	1.000	1.000
January 1959–December 1963	0.007	0.790	0.656	0.435
January 1964–December 1968	0.048	1.000	1.000	1.000
January 1969–December 1973	0.008	0.869	0.756	0.529
January 1974–December 1978	0.001	0.183	0.139	0.100
January 1979–December 1983	0.023	1.000	1.000	0.991
January 1984–December 1988	0.002	0.248	0.183	0.123

The entries in Table 8.7 show that the null hypothesis is quite likely to be rejected even when it is true. For many of the subperiods, the probability of rejecting the null is unity, and when only 10 beta-sorted portfolios are used, the smallest size of a nominal 5 percent test is still 18.3 percent. We conclude, somewhat belatedly, that the elaborate out-of-sample sorting procedures used by Black, Jensen, and Scholes (1972) and Fama and MacBeth (1973) were indispensable to the original tests of the Sharpe-Lintner CAPM.

8.3.2 Sorting By Size

As a second example of the practical relevance of data-snooping biases, we consider Lehmann and Modest's (1988) multivariate test of a 15-factor APT model, in which they reject the zero-intercept null hypothesis using five portfolios formed by grouping securities ordered by market value of equity.[21] We focus on this particular study because of the large number of factors employed—our framework requires the disturbances ϵ_t of (8.2.2) to be cross-sectionally independent, and since 15 factors are included in Lehmann and Modest's cross-sectional regressions, a diagonal covariance matrix for ϵ_t is not implausible.

It is well-known that the estimated intercept $\hat{\alpha}_i$ from the single-period CAPM regression (excess individual security returns regressed on an inter-

---

[21] See Lehmann and Modest (1988, Table 1, last row). Connor and Korajczyk (1988) report similar findings.

cept and the market risk premium) is negatively cross-sectionally correlated with log size.[22] Since this $\hat{\alpha}_i$ will in general be correlated with the estimated intercept from a 15-factor APT regression, it is likely that the estimated APT-intercept and log size will also be empirically correlated.[23] Unfortunately, we do not have a direct measure of the correlation of the APT intercept and log size which is necessary to derive the appropriate null distribution after induced ordering.[24] As an alternative, we estimate the cross-sectional R^2 of the estimated CAPM alpha with the logarithm of size, and we use this R^2 as well as $\frac{1}{2}R^2$ and $\frac{1}{4}R^2$ to estimate the bias attributable to induced ordering.

Following Lehmann and Modest (1988), we consider four five-year time periods from January 1963 to December 1982. X_i is defined to be the logarithm of beginning-of-period market values of equity. The $\hat{\alpha}_i$'s are the intercepts from regressions of excess returns on the market risk premium as measured by the difference between an equal-weighted NYSE index and monthly Treasury bill returns, where the NYSE index is obtained from the Center for Research in Security Prices (CRSP) database. The R^2's of these regressions are reported in the second column of Table 8.8. One cross-sectional regression of $\hat{\alpha}_i$ on log size X_i is run for each five-year time period using monthly NYSE-AMEX data from CRSP. We run regressions only for those stocks having complete return histories within the relevant five-year period.

Table 8.8 contains the test statistics for a 15-factor APT framework using five size-sorted portfolios. The first four rows contain results for each of the four subperiods and the last row contains aggregate test statistics. To apply the results of Sections 8.1 and 8.2 we transform Lehmann and Modest's (1988) F-statistics into (asymptotic) χ^2 variates.[25] The total number of available securities ranges from a minimum of 1001 for the first five-year subperiod to a maximum of 1359 for the second subperiod. For each test statistic in Table 8.8 we report four different p-values: the first is with respect to the null distribution that ignores data snooping, and the next three are with respect to null distributions that account for induced ordering to various degrees.

The entries in Table 8.8 show that the potential biases from sorting by characteristics that have been empirically selected can be immense. The

---

[22]See, for example, Banz (1981) and Brown, Kleidon, and Marsh (1983).

[23]We recognize that correlation is not transitive, so if X is correlated with Y and Y with Z, X need not be correlated with Z. However, since the intercepts from the two regressions will be functions of some common random variables, situations in which they are independent are the exception rather than the rule.

[24]Nor did Lehmann and Modest prior to their extensive investigations. If they are subject to any data-snooping biases it is only from their awareness of size-related empirical results for the single-period CAPM, and of corresponding results for the APT as in Chan, Chen, and Hsieh (1985).

[25]Since Lehmann and Modest (1988) use weekly data, the null distribution of their test statistics is $F_{5,240}$. In practice the inferences are virtually identical using the χ^2_5 distribution after multiplying the test statistic by 5.

Table 8.8.   *Comparison of p-values for Lehmann and Modest's (1988) tests of the APT with and without correcting for the effects of induced ordering. In the absence of data snooping, the appropriate test statistics and their p-values (using the central χ^2 distribution) are given in Lehmann and Modest (1988, Table 1) and reported below in columns 4 and 5 (we transform their F-statistics into χ^2 variates for purposes of comparison). Corresponding p-values that account for induced ordering are calculated in columns labelled "$\chi^2(\lambda_i)$ p-value"($i = 1, 2, 3$) (using the noncentral χ^2 distribution), where λ_1, λ_2, and λ_3 are noncentrality parameters computed with $\hat{R}^2$, $\frac{1}{2}\hat{R}^2$, and $\frac{1}{4}\hat{R}^2$, respectively. In all cases, five portfolios are formed from the total number of securities; this yields five degrees of freedom for the χ^2 statistics in the first four rows, and 20 degrees of freedom for the aggregate χ^2 statistics.*

Sample	N	$\hat{R}^2$	$\tilde{\theta}_p$	χ^2 p-value	$\chi^2(\lambda_1)$ p-value	$\chi^2(\lambda_2)$ p-value	$\chi^2(\lambda_3)$ p-value
6301–6712	1001	0.015	13.70	0.018	0.687	0.315	0.131
6801–7212	1359	0.040	15.50	0.008	1.000	0.919	0.520
7301–7712	1346	0.033	10.20	0.070	1.000	0.963	0.720
7801–8212	1281	0.004	12.05	0.034	0.272	0.134	0.078
Aggregate	—	—	51.45	0.00014	1.000	0.917	0.298

p-values range from 0.008 to 0.070 in the four subperiods according to the standard theoretical null distribution, yielding an aggregate *p*-value of 0.00014, considerable evidence against the null. When we adjust for the fact that the sorting characteristic is selected empirically (using the $\hat{R}^2$ from the cross-sectional regression of $\hat{\alpha}_i$ on X_i), the *p*-values for these same four subperiods range from 0.272 to 1.000, yielding an aggregate *p*-value of 1.000! Therefore, whether or not induced ordering is allowed for can change inferences dramatically.

The appropriate R^2 in the preceding analysis is the squared correlation between log size and the intercept from a 15-factor APT regression, and not the one used in Table 8.8. To see how this may affect our conclusions, recall from (8.1.2) that the cross-sectional correlation between $\hat{\alpha}_i$ and log size can arise from two sources: the estimation error ζ_i in $\hat{\alpha}_i$, and the cross-sectional dispersion in the "true" CAPM α_i (which is zero under the null hypothesis). Correlation between X_i and ζ_i will be partially reflected in correlation between the estimated APT intercept and log size. The second source of correlation will not be relevant *under the APT null hypothesis* since under that scenario we assume that the 15-factor APT obtains and therefore the intercept vanishes for all securities. As a conservative estimate for the appropriate R^2 to be used in Table 8.8, we set the squared correlation equal to $\frac{1}{2}\hat{R}^2$ and $\frac{1}{4}\hat{R}^2$, yielding the *p*-values reported in the last two columns of Table 8.8. Even when the squared correlation is only $\frac{1}{4}\hat{R}^2$, the inferences change markedly after induced ordering, with p-values ranging from 0.078 to 0.720 in the four subperiods and 0.298 in the aggregate. This simple example illustrates the severity with which even a mild form of data snooping can bias our inferences in practice.

Nevertheless, it should not be inferred from Table 8.8 that all size-related phenomena are spurious. After all, the correlation between X_i and $\hat{\alpha}_i$ may be the result of cross-sectional variations in the population α_i's, and not estimation error. Even so, tests using size-sorted portfolios are still biased if based on the same data from which the size effect was previously observed. A procedure that is free from such biases is to decide today that size is an interesting characteristic, collect ten years of new data, and then perform tests on size-sorted portfolios from this fresh sample. Provided that the old and new samples are statistically independent, this will yield a perfectly valid test of the null hypothesis H, since the only possible source of correlation between the X_i's and the $\hat{\alpha}_i$'s in the new sample is from the α_i's (presumably the result of some underlying economic relation between the two), and not from the estimation errors. In such cases, induced ordering cannot affect the distribution of the test statistics under the null hypothesis, and will yield a considerably more powerful test against many alternatives.

8.4 How the Data Get Snooped

Whether the probabilities of rejection in Table 8.2 are to be interpreted as size or power depends, of course, on the particular null and alternative hypotheses at hand, the key distinction being the source of correlation between $\hat{\alpha}_i$ and the characteristic X_i. Since our starting point in Section 8.1 was the assertion that this correlation is "spurious," we view the values of Table 8.2 as probabilities of falsely rejecting the null hypothesis. We suggested in Section 8.1 that the source of this spurious correlation is correlation between the characteristic and the estimation errors in $\hat{\alpha}_i$, since such errors are the only source of variation in $\hat{\alpha}_i$ under the null. But how does this correlation arise? One possibility is the very mechanism by which characteristics are selected. Without any economic theories for motivation, a plausible behavioral model of how we determine characteristics to be particularly "interesting" is that we tend to focus on those that have unusually large squared sample correlations or R^2's with the $\hat{\alpha}_i$'s. In the spirit of Ross (1987), economists study "interesting" events, as well as events that are interesting from a theoretical perspective. If so, then even in a collection of K characteristics all of which are independent of the $\hat{\alpha}_i$'s, correlation between the $\hat{\alpha}_i$'s and the most "interesting" characteristic is artificially induced.

More formally, suppose for each of N securities we have a collection of K distinct and mutually independent characteristics Y_{ik}, $k = 1, 2, \ldots, K$, where Y_{ik} is the kth characteristic of the ith security. Let the null hypothesis obtain so that $\alpha_i = 0$, for all i, and assume that all characteristics are independent of $\{\hat{\alpha}_i\}$. This last assumption implies that the distribution of a test statistic based on grouped $\hat{\alpha}_i$'s is unaffected by sorting on any of the characteristics. For simplicity let each of the characteristics and the $\hat{\alpha}_i$'s be normally distributed with zero mean and unit variance, and consider the sample correlation coefficients:

$$\hat{\rho}_k = \frac{\sum_{i=1}^{N}(Y_{ik} - \bar{Y}_k)(\hat{\alpha}_i - \bar{\hat{\alpha}})}{\sqrt{\sum_{i=1}^{N}(Y_{ik} - \bar{Y}_k)^2} \cdot \sqrt{\sum_{i=1}^{N}(\hat{\alpha}_i - \bar{\hat{\alpha}})^2}}, \qquad k = 1, 2, \ldots, K, \quad (8.4.1)$$

where $\bar{Y}_k$ and $\bar{\hat{\alpha}}$ are the sample means of characteristic k and the $\hat{\alpha}_i$'s, respectively. Suppose we choose as our sorting characteristic the one that has the largest squared correlation with the $\hat{\alpha}_i$'s, and call this characteristic X_i. That is, $X_i \equiv Y_{ik^*}$, where the index k^* is defined by

$$\hat{\rho}_{k^*}^2 = \max_{1 \leq k \leq K} \hat{\rho}_k^2. \qquad (8.4.2)$$

This X_i is a new characteristic in the statistical sense, in that its distribution is no longer the same as that of the Y_{ik}'s.[26] It is apparent that X_i and $\hat{\alpha}_i$ are not mutually independent since the $\hat{\alpha}_i$'s were used in selecting this characteristic. By construction, extreme realizations of the random variables $\{X_i\}$ tend to occur when extreme realizations of $\{\hat{\alpha}_i\}$ occur.

To estimate the magnitude of correlation spuriously induced between X_i and $\hat{\alpha}_i$, first observe that although the correlation between Y_{ik} and $\hat{\alpha}_i$ is zero for all k, $E[\hat{\rho}_k^2] = 1/(N-1)$ under our normality assumption. Therefore, $1/(N-1)$ should be our benchmark in assessing the degree of spurious correlation between X_i and $\hat{\alpha}_i$. Since the $\hat{\rho}_k^2$'s are well-known to be independently and identically distributed $\text{Beta}(\frac{1}{2}, \frac{1}{2}(N-2))$ variates, the distribution and density functions of $\hat{\rho}_{k^*}^2$, denoted by $F_*(v)$ and $f_*(v)$, respectively, may be readily derived as[27]

$$F_*(v) = [F_\beta(v)]^K, \qquad v \in (0, 1), \qquad (8.4.3)$$

$$f_*(v) = K[F_\beta(v)]^{K-1} f_\beta(v), \qquad v \in (0, 1), \qquad (8.4.4)$$

---

[26]In fact, if we denote by Y_k the $N \times 1$ vector containing values of characteristic k for each of the N securities, then the vector most highly correlated with $\hat{\alpha}$ (which we have called X) may be viewed as the concomitant $Y_{[K:K]}$ of the Kth order statistic $\hat{\rho}_{[K:K]}^2 = \hat{\rho}_k^{2*}$. As in the scalar case, induced ordering does change the distribution of the vector concomitants.

[27]That the squared correlation coefficients are IID Beta random variables follows from our assumptions of normality and the mutual independence of the characteristics and the $\hat{\alpha}_i$'s [see Stuart and Ord (1987, Chapter 16.28) for example]. The distribution and density functions of the maximum follow directly from this.

where F_β and f_β are the cumulative distribution function and probability density function of the Beta distribution with parameters $\frac{1}{2}$ and $\frac{1}{2}(N-2)$. A measure of that portion of squared correlation between X_i with $\hat{\alpha}_i$ due to sorting on $\hat{\rho}_k^2$ is then given by

$$\gamma \equiv \mathrm{E}[\hat{\rho}_{k*}^2] - \mathrm{E}[\hat{\rho}_k^2] = \int_0^1 v f_*(v)\,dv - \frac{1}{N-1}. \qquad (8.4.5)$$

For 25 securities and 50 characteristics, γ is 20.5 percent![28] With 100 securities, γ is still 5.4 percent and only declines to 1.1 percent for 500 securities. With only 25 characteristics, the values of γ for 25, 100, and 500 securities fall to 16.4, 4.2, and 0.8 percent, respectively. However, these smaller values of γ can still yield misleading inferences for tests based on few portfolios, each containing many securities. This is seen in Table 8.9, in which the theoretical sizes of 5 percent tests with R^2's equal to the appropriate γ for each cell are displayed. For example, the first entry in the first row of Table 8.9, 0.163, is the size of the 5 percent portfolio-based test with five portfolios and five securities in each, where the R^2 used to perform the calculation is the γ corresponding to 25 securities and 25 characteristics, or 16.4 percent. As the number of securities per portfolio grows, γ declines but the bias worsens—with 50 securities in each of five portfolios, γ is only 1.7 percent but the actual size of a 5 percent test is 26.4 percent. Although there is in fact no statistical relation between any of the characteristics and the $\hat{\alpha}_i$'s, a procedure that focuses on the most striking characteristic can *create* spurious statistical dependence.

As the number of securities N increases, this particular source of dependence becomes less important since all the sample correlation coefficients $\hat{\rho}_k$ converge almost surely to zero, as does γ. However, recall from Table 8.2 that as the sample size grows the bias increases if the number of portfolios is held fixed; hence, as Table 8.9 illustrates, a larger N and thus a smaller γ need not imply a smaller bias. Moreover, since γ is increasing in the number of characteristics K, we cannot find refuge in the law of large numbers without weighing the number of securities against the number of characteristics and portfolios in some fashion. Table 8.9 provides one informal measure of this trade-off.

---

[28]Note that γ is only an approximation to the squared population correlation:

$$\left[\frac{\mathrm{E}(X_i - \mathrm{E}[X])(\hat{\alpha}_i - \mathrm{E}[\hat{\alpha}])}{\sqrt{\mathrm{E}(X_i - \mathrm{E}[X])^2} \cdot \sqrt{\mathrm{E}(\hat{\alpha}_i - \mathrm{E}[\hat{\alpha}])^2}} \right]^2.$$

However, Monte Carlo simulations with 10,000 replications show that this approximation is excellent even for small sample sizes. For example, fixing K at 50, the correlation from the simulations is 22.82 percent for $N = 25$, whereas (8.4.5) yields $\gamma = 20.47$ percent; for $N = 100$ the simulations yield a correlation of 6.25 percent, compared to a γ of 5.39 percent.

Table 8.9.   *Theoretical sizes of nominal 5 percent χ_q^2-tests of H: $\alpha_i = 0$ $(i = 1, \ldots, n)$ using the test statistic $\tilde{\theta}_p$, where $\tilde{\theta}_p \equiv n_o \sum_{k=1}^{q} \tilde{\phi}_k^2 / \sigma_\alpha^2$, and $\tilde{\phi}_k \equiv (1/n_o) \sum_{j=(k-1)q+1}^{kq} \hat{\alpha}_{[ij:N]}$ is constructed from portfolio k, with portfolios formed by sorting on some characteristic correlated with estimates $\hat{\alpha}_i$. This induced ordering alters the null distribution of $\hat{\theta}_p$ from χ_q^2 to $(1 - R^2) \cdot \chi_q^2(\lambda)$, where the noncentrality parameter λ is a function of the number q of portfolios, the number n_o of securities in each portfolio, and the squared correlation coefficient R^2 between $\hat{\alpha}_i$ and the sorting characteristic. The values of R^2 used for the size calculations vary with the total number of securities $n_o q$ and with K, the total number of independent characteristics from which the most "interesting" is selected.*

q	$n_o = 5$	$n_o = 10$	$n_o = 20$	$n_o = 25$	$n_o = 50$
K = 25					
5	0.163	0.216	0.246	0.253	0.264
10	0.150	0.182	0.200	0.202	0.210
20	0.125	0.144	0.153	0.155	0.159
25	0.117	0.132	0.140	0.142	0.145
50	0.096	0.104	0.109	0.110	0.112
K = 50					
5	0.197	0.270	0.311	0.319	0.337
10	0.183	0.228	0.254	0.259	0.270
20	0.151	0.178	0.192	0.195	0.201
25	0.141	0.163	0.175	0.177	0.182
50	0.112	0.125	0.131	0.133	0.136

Perhaps even the most unscrupulous investigator might hesitate at the kind of data snooping we have just considered. However, the very review process that published research undergoes can have much the same effect, since competition for limited journal space tilts the balance in favor of the most striking and dissonant of empirical results. Indeed, the "Anomalies" section of the *Journal of Economic Perspectives* is the most obvious example of our deliberate search for the unusual in economics. As a consequence, interest may be created in otherwise theoretically irrelevant characteristics. In the absence of an economic paradigm, such data-snooping biases are not easily distinguishable from violations of the null hypothesis. This inability to separate pretest bias from alternative hypotheses is the most compelling criticism of "measurement without theory."

8.5 Conclusion

Although the size effect may signal important differences between the economic structure of small and large corporations, how these differences are manifested in the stochastic properties of their equity returns cannot be reliably determined through data analysis alone. Much more convincing would be the empirical significance of size, or any other quantity, that is based on a model of economic equilibrium in which the characteristic is related to the behavior of asset returns endogenously. Our findings show that tests using securities grouped according to theoretically motivated correlations between X_i and $\hat{\alpha}_i$ can be powerful indeed—interestingly, tests of the APT with portfolios sorted by such characteristics (own-variance and dividend yield) no longer reject the null hypothesis (see Lehmann and Modest, 1988). Sorting on size yields rejections whereas sorting on theoretically relevant characteristics such as own-variance and dividend yield does not. This suggests that data-instigated grouping procedures should be employed cautiously.

It is widely acknowledged that incorrect conclusions may be drawn from procedures violating the assumptions of classical statistical inference, but the nature of these violations is often as subtle as it is profound. In observing that economists (as well as those in the natural sciences) tend to seek out anomalies, Merton (1987, p. 104) writes: "All this fits well with what the cognitive psychologists tell us is our natural individual predilection to focus, often disproportionately so, on the unusual.... This focus, both individually and institutionally, together with little control over the number of tests performed, creates a fertile environment for both unintended selection bias and for attaching greater significance to otherwise unbiased estimates than is justified." The recognition of this possibility is a first step in guarding against it. The results of our paper provide a more concrete remedy for such biases in the particular case of portfolio formation via induced ordering on data-instigated characteristics. However, nonexperimental inference may never be completely free from data-snooping biases since the attention given to empirical anomalies, incongruities, and unusual correlations is also the modus operandi for genuine discovery and progress in the social sciences. Formal statistical analyses such as ours may serve as primitive guides to a better understanding of economic phenomena, but the ability to distinguish between the spurious and the substantive is likely to remain a cherished art.

9

Maximizing Predictability in the Stock and Bond Markets

9.1 Introduction

THE SEARCH FOR PREDICTABILITY in asset returns has occupied the attention of investors and academics since the advent of organized financial markets. While investors have an obvious financial interest in predictability, its economic importance can be traced to at least three distinct sources: implications for how aggregate fluctuations in the economy are transmitted to and from financial markets, implications for optimal consumption and investment policies, and implications for market efficiency. For example, several recent papers claim that the apparent predictability in long-horizon stock return indexes is due to business cycle movements and changes in aggregate risk premia.[1] Others claim that such predictability is symptomatic of inefficient markets, markets populated with overreacting and irrational investors.[2] Following both explanations is a growing number of proponents of market timing or tactical asset allocation, in which predictability is exploited, ostensibly to improve investors' risk-return trade-offs.[3] Indeed, Roll (1988, p. 541) has suggested that "The maturity of a science is often gauged by its success in predicting important phenomena."

For these reasons, many economists have undertaken the search for predictability in earnest and with great vigor. Indeed, the very attempt to improve the goodness-of-fit of theories to observations—Leamer's (1978) so-called *specification searches*—can be viewed as a search for predictability.

---

[1] See Fama and French (1990) and Ferson and Harvey (1991b) for example.

[2] For example, see DeBondt and Thaler (1985), Lehmann (1990), and Chopra et al. (1992).

[3] A few of the most recent examples include Clarke et al. (1989), Droms (1989), Vandell and Stevens (1989), Hardy (1990), Kester (1990), Lee and Rahman (1990, 1991), Sy (1990), Weigel (1991), Shilling (1992), and Wagner et al. (1992). However, see Samuelson (1989, 1990) for a caution against such strategies.

249

But as important as it is, predictability is rarely maximized systematically in empirical investigations, even though it may dictate the course of the investigation at many critical junctures and, as a consequence, is maximized *implicitly* over time and over sequences of investigations.

In this chapter, we maximize the predictability in asset returns *explicitly* by constructing portfolios of assets that are the most predictable, in a sense to be made precise below. Such explicit maximization can add several new insights to findings based on less formal methods. Perhaps the most obvious is that it yields an upper bound to what even the most industrious investigator can achieve in his search for predictability among portfolios.[4] As such, it provides an informal yardstick against which other findings may be measured. For example, approximately 10% of the variation in the CRSP equal-weighted weekly return index from 1962 to 1992 can be explained by the previous week's returns—is this large or small? The answer will depend on whether the maximum predictability for weekly portfolio returns is 15 or 75%.

More importantly, the maximization of predictability can direct us toward more disaggregated sources of persistence and time variation in asset returns, in the form of portfolio weights of the most predictable portfolio, and sensitivities of those weights to specific predictors, e.g., industrial production, dividend yield. A primitive example of this kind of disaggregation is the lead/lag relation among size-sorted portfolios uncovered by Lo and MacKinlay (1990b), in which the predictability of weekly stock index returns is traced to the tendency for the returns of larger capitalization stocks to lead those of smaller stocks. The more general framework that we introduce below includes lead/lag effects as a special case, but captures predictability explicitly as a function of time-varying economic-risk premia rather than as a function of past returns only.

In fact, the evidence for time-varying expected returns in the stock and bond markets in the form of ex-ante economic variables that can forecast asset returns is now substantial.[5] Our results add to those of the existing literature in three ways: (1) We estimate the *maximally predictable portfolio* (MPP), given a specific model of time-varying risk premia; (2) we compute the sensitivities of this MPP with respect to ex-ante economic variables; and (3) we trace the sources of predictability, via the portfolio weights of the MPP, to spe-

---

[4]As will become apparent below, we maximize predictability across portfolios, holding fixed the set of regressors used to forecast asset returns. In a related paper, Foster et al. (1995) maximize predictability across subsets of regressors, holding fixed the asset return to be predicted. Therefore, our upper bound obtains over a fixed set of regressors, while Foster et al.'s obtains over a fixed set of assets.

[5]See, for example, Gibbons and Ferson (1985), Chen et al. (1986), Keim and Stambaugh (1986), Engle et al. (1987), Ferson et al. (1987), Lo and MacKinlay (1988b), Ferson (1989, 1990), Ferson and Harvey (1991), Fama and French (1990), Jegadeesh (1990), and Chen (1991).

cific industry sectors, market-capitalization classes, and stock/bond/utilities classes, over various holding periods.

Of course, both implicit and explicit maximization of predictability are forms of *data snooping* or *data mining* and may bias classical statistical inferences. But the biases from an explicit maximization are far easier to quantify and correct for—which we do below—than those from a series of informal and haphazard searches.[6] Moreover, we develop a procedure for maximizing predictability that does not impart any obvious data-snooping biases (although subtle biases may always arise), using an out-of-sample rolling estimation approach similar to that of Fama and MacBeth (1973). We use a subsample to estimate the optimal portfolio weights, form these portfolios with the returns from an adjacent subsample, and obtain estimates of predictability by rolling through the data.

When applied to monthly stock and bond returns from 1947 to 1993, we find that predictability can be increased considerably both by portfolio selection and by horizon selection. For example, if we consider as our universe of assets the 11 portfolios formed by industry or sector classification according to SIC codes, for an annual return horizon the MPP has an R^2 of 53%, whereas the largest R^2 of the 11 regressions of individual sector assets on the same predictors is 40 percent.

Moreover, the weights of the MPP change dramatically with the horizon, pointing to differences across market capitalization and sectors for forecasting purposes. For example, using the 11 sector assets as our universe and a monthly return horizon, the MPP has a long position in the trade sector (with a portfolio weight of 36%), and a substantial short position in the durables sector (with a portfolio weight of -138%). However, at an annual return horizon, the MPP is short in the trade sector (-70%), and long in durables (126%). Although the portfolio weights are much less volatile for the shortsales-constrained cases, they still vary considerably with the return horizon. Such findings suggest distinct forecasting horizons for the various sector assets, and may signal important differences in how such groups of securities respond to economic events.

In Section 9.2, we motivate our interest in the MPP by showing that the typical two-step approach of searching for predictability—fitting a contemporaneous linear multifactor model, and then predicting the factors—may significantly understate the true magnitude of predictability in asset returns and overstate the number of factors required to capture the predictability. In contrast, the MPP provides a more accurate assessment of the predictable

---

[6]For the biases of and possible corrections to such informal specification searches see Leamer (1978), Ross (1987), Iyengar and Greenhouse (1988), Lo and MacKinlay (1990a), and Foster et al. (1995).

variation. The MPP is developed more formally in Section 9.3 and an example of its economic relevance is provided. In Section 9.4, we apply these results to monthly stock and bond data from 1947 to 1993 and estimate the MPP for three distinct asset groups: a 5-asset group of stocks, bonds, and utilities; an 11-asset group of sector portfolios; and a 10-asset group of size-sorted portfolios. To correct for the obvious biases imparted by maximizing predictability, we report Monte Carlo results for the statistical inference of the maximal R^2's in Section 9.5. To gauge the economic significance of the MPP, in Section 9.6 we present three out-of-sample measures of the portfolio's predictability, measures that are not subject to the most obvious kinds of data-snooping biases associated with maximizing predictability. We conclude in Section 9.7.

9.2 Motivation

An increasingly popular approach to investigating predictability in asset returns is to follow a two-step procedure: (1) Construct a linear factor model of returns based on cross-sectional explanatory power, e.g., factor analysis, principal components decomposition, and (2) analyze the predictability of these factors. Such an approach is motivated by the substantial and still-growing literature on linear pricing models such as the CAPM, the APT, and its many variants in which expected returns are linearly related to contemporaneous "systematic" risk factors. Because time variation in expected returns can be a source of return predictability, several recent studies have followed this two-step procedure, e.g., Chen (1991), Ferson and Harvey (1991a, 1991b, 1993), and Ferson and Korajcyzk (1995).

While the two-step approach can shed considerable light on the nature of asset return predictability—especially when the risk factors are known—it may not be as informative when the factors are unknown. For example, it is possible that the set of factors that best explains the cross-sectional variation in expected returns is relatively unpredictable, whereas other factors that *can* be used to predict expected returns are not nearly as useful contemporaneously in capturing the cross-sectional variation of expected returns. Therefore, focusing on the predictability of factors that are important contemporaneously may yield a very misleading picture of the true nature of predictability in asset returns.

9.2.1 Predicting Factors vs. Predicting Returns

To formalize this intuition, consider a simple example consisting of two assets, A and B, which satisfy a linear two-factor model. In particular, let R_t

denote the (2×1) vector of de-meaned asset returns $[R_{at} \ R_{bt}]'$ and suppose that:

$$\boldsymbol{R}_t = \boldsymbol{\delta}_1 F_{1t} + \boldsymbol{\delta}_2 F_{2t} + \boldsymbol{\epsilon}_t, \tag{9.2.1}$$

where $\boldsymbol{\delta}_1 \equiv [\delta_{a1} \ \delta_{b1}]'$, $\boldsymbol{\delta}_2 \equiv [\delta_{a2} \ \delta_{b2}]'$, $\boldsymbol{\epsilon}_t \equiv [\epsilon_{at} \ \epsilon_{bt}]'$ is vector white noise with covariance matrix $\sigma_\epsilon^2 \boldsymbol{I}$, and F_{1t} and F_{2t} are the two factors that drive the expected returns of A and B. Without loss of generality, we assume that the two factors are mutually uncorrelated at all leads and lags, and have zero mean and unit variance; hence,

$$\mathrm{E}[F_{1t}] = \mathrm{E}[F_{2t}] = 0, \qquad \mathrm{Var}[F_{1t}] = \mathrm{Var}[F_{2t}] = 1, \tag{9.2.2}$$

$$\mathrm{Cov}[F_{1s}, F_{2t}] = 0 \quad \forall \, s, t. \tag{9.2.3}$$

Now suppose that F_{1t} is unpredictable through time, while F_{2t} is predictable. In particular, suppose that F_{1t} is a white-noise process, and that F_{2t} is an AR(1):

$$F_{1t} \sim \text{White Noise}, \qquad F_{2t} = \beta F_{2t-1} + \eta_t, \quad |\beta| \in [0, 1), \tag{9.2.4}$$

where $\{\eta_t\}$ is a white-noise process with variance $1 - \beta^2$ and independent of $\{\epsilon_t\}$ and $\{F_{1t}\}$. Under these assumptions, expected returns are explained by two contemporaneous factors, of which one is white noise and the other is predictable. For later reference, we observe that under this linear two-factor model the contemporaneous covariance matrix and the first-order autocovariance matrix of $\boldsymbol{R}_t$ are given by

$$\boldsymbol{\Gamma}_0 = \mathrm{Var}[\boldsymbol{R}_t] = \boldsymbol{\delta}_1 \boldsymbol{\delta}_1' + \boldsymbol{\delta}_2 \boldsymbol{\delta}_2' + \sigma_\epsilon^2 \boldsymbol{I} \tag{9.2.5}$$

$$\boldsymbol{\Gamma}_1 = \mathrm{Cov}[\boldsymbol{R}_t, \boldsymbol{R}_{t-1}] = \boldsymbol{\delta}_2 \boldsymbol{\delta}_2' \beta. \tag{9.2.6}$$

For the remainder of this section, we shall assume that while (9.2.1) is the true data-generating process, it is *unknown* to investors.

When the true factors F_{1t} and F_{2t} are unobserved, the most common approach to estimating (9.2.1) is to perform some kind of factor analysis or principal-components decomposition (see, e.g., Roll and Ross, 1980; Brown and Weinstein, 1983; Chamberlain, 1983; Chamberlain and Rothschild, 1983; Lehmann and Modest, 1985; Connor and Korajczyk, 1986, 1988). For this reason, a natural focus for the sources of predictability are the extracted factors or principal components. In our simple two-asset example, the first principal component is a portfolio ω_{PC1} which corresponds to the normalized eigenvector of the largest eigenvalue of the contemporaneous covariance matrix $\boldsymbol{\Gamma}_0$. This yields the portfolio return

$$R_{\mathrm{PC1},t} \equiv \omega_{\mathrm{PC1}}' \boldsymbol{R}_t, \tag{9.2.7}$$

which may be interpreted as the linear combination of the two assets that "explains" as much of the cross-sectional variation in returns as possible. In this sense, $R_{\text{PC1},t}$ may be viewed as the (cross-sectionally) "most important" factor. Therefore, this is a natural focus for the sources of predictability in expected returns.

How predictable is this most important factor? One measure is the theoretical or population R^2 of a regression of $R_{\text{PC1},t}$ on the lagged factors F_{1t-1} and F_{2t-1}. This is given by

$$R^2\,[R_{\text{PC1},t}] \;=\; \frac{(\omega'_{\text{PC1}}\delta_2\beta)^2}{\omega'_{\text{PC1}}\Gamma_0\omega_{\text{PC1}}}\,. \tag{9.2.8}$$

Observe that only the factor loading δ_2 of factor 2 appears in the numerator of (9.2.8). Since factor 1 is white noise, it contributes nothing to the predictability of $R_{\text{PC1},t}$; hence δ_1 plays no role in determining the R^2. However, δ_1 does appear implicitly in the denominator of (9.2.8) since it affects the variance of $R_{\text{PC1},t}$ (see (9.2.5)). Therefore, it is easy to see how an important cross-sectional factor may not have much predictability. By increasing the factor loading δ_1, the first factor becomes increasingly more important in the cross section, but holding other parameters constant, this will decrease the predictability of $R_{\text{PC1},t}$.

A second measure of predictability is the squared first-order autocorrelation coefficient of $R_{\text{PC1},t}$, which corresponds to the R^2 of the regression of $R_{\text{PC1},t}$ on $R_{\text{PC1},t-1}$. This is given by the expression

$$\rho_1^2\,[R_{\text{PC1},t}] \;=\; \frac{[(\omega'_{\text{PC1}}\delta_2)^2\beta]^2}{(\omega'_{\text{PC1}}\Gamma_0\omega_{\text{PC1}})^2}\,. \tag{9.2.9}$$

For similar reasons, it is apparent from (9.2.9) that an important cross-sectional factor need not reflect much predictability.

9.2.2 Numerical Illustration

For concreteness, consider the following numerical example:

$$R_t \;=\; \begin{bmatrix} 10.0 \\ 15.0 \end{bmatrix} F_{1t} \;+\; \begin{bmatrix} 0.5 \\ 1.0 \end{bmatrix} F_{2t} + \epsilon_t, \tag{9.2.10}$$

$$\mathrm{E}[\epsilon_t\epsilon_t'] \;=\; \sigma_\epsilon^2 I, \qquad \sigma_\epsilon^2 \;=\; 16, \qquad \beta \;=\; 0.90. \tag{9.2.11}$$

Under these parameter values, the first principal-component portfolio $R_{\text{PC1},t}$ accounts for 95.5% of the cross-sectional variation in returns, i.e., when the eigenvalues of Γ_0 are normalized to sum to one, the largest eigenvalue is

0.955. However, the predictability of $R_{\text{PC1},t}$ as measured by $R^2[R_{\text{PC1},t}]$ in (9.2.8) is a trivial 0.3%, and its squared own-autocorrelation is 0.0010%, despite the fact that factor 2 has an autocorrelation coefficient of 90%!

In Section 9.3, we shall propose an alternative to cross-sectional factors such as $R_{\text{PC1},t}$ for measuring predictability: the MPP. In contrast to $R_{\text{PC1},t}$ which is constructed by maximizing *variance*, the MPP is constructed by maximizing *predictability* or R^2. For this reason, it provides a more direct measure of the magnitude and sources of predictability in asset returns data. Although we develop the MPP more formally in the next section, it is instructive to anticipate those results by comparing the predictability of the MPP to that of $R_{\text{PC1},t}$ in this two-asset example.

As we shall see in Section 9.3, the MPP ω_{MPP} is defined to be the normalized eigenvector corresponding to the largest eigenvalue of the matrix $V^{-1}\tilde{\Gamma}_0$, where $\tilde{\Gamma}_0 = \delta_2\delta_2'\rho^2$ is the variance–covariance matrix of the one-step-ahead forecast of R_t using F_{1t-1} and F_{2t-1} (see Section 9.3 for further details and discussion). Substituting ω_{MPP} for ω_{PC1} in (9.2.7) and (9.2.8) then yields a comparable measure of predictability for the MPP: $R^2[R_{\text{MPP},t}]$.

By calibrating the parameter values of (9.2.1) to monthly data (measured in percent per month), we can compare the predictability of the MPP to the PC1 portfolio directly. In particular, if we let

$$R_t = \begin{bmatrix} 7.5 \\ 3.5 \end{bmatrix} F_{1t} + \begin{bmatrix} \delta_{a2} \\ 5.0 \end{bmatrix} F_{2t} + \epsilon_t, \tag{9.2.12}$$

$$\text{E}[\epsilon_t\epsilon_t'] = \sigma_\epsilon^2 I, \qquad \sigma_\epsilon^2 = 16, \qquad \beta = 0.90 \tag{9.2.13}$$

and let δ_{a2} vary, we can see how well the two portfolios ω_{PC1} and ω_{MPP} reflect the predictability inherent in the two assets.

Table 9.1 reports the R^2 measures for both portfolios under two different values for δ_{a2}. In panel (a), δ_{a2} is set to 0.50, in which case the stocks A and B have R^2's of 0.3 and 38.0%, respectively, and monthly standard deviations of 8.5 and 7.3%, respectively. In this case, observe that the PC1 portfolio has an R^2 of only 9.6% and a squared own-autocorrelation $\rho^2(1)$ of only 1.1%, and this despite the fact that the squared own-autocorrelation of stock B is 17.9%. In contrast, the MPP has an R^2 of 45.0% and a squared own-autocorrelation of 24.9%.

As δ_{a2} is increased to 7.5, factor 2 becomes more important in determining the expected return of stock A, and its monthly variance also increases to 11.3%. In this case, the PC1 portfolio more accurately reflects the predictability in A and B, with an R^2 and squared own-autocorrelation of 39.7 and 19.5%, respectively. Nevertheless, the MPP exhibits slightly more predictability, with an R^2 and squared own-autocorrelation of 41.6 and 21.4%, respectively.

Table 9.1.   *Comparison of predictability of PC1 portfolio and MPP for a universe of two assets, A and B[a]*

Asset	ω_a	ω_b	R^2[Asset]	ρ_1^2[Asset]
		(a) $\delta_{a2} = 0.50$		
Stock A	1.00	0.00	0.003	0.000
Stock B	0.00	1.00	0.380	0.179
PC1 portfolio	0.58	0.42	0.096	0.011
MPP	−0.51	1.51	0.450	0.249
		(b) $\delta_{a2} = 7.50$		
Stock A	1.00	0.00	0.355	0.155
Stock B	0.00	1.00	0.380	0.179
PC1 portfolio	0.64	0.36	0.397	0.195
MPP	0.33	0.67	0.416	0.214

[a]Returns satisfy a two-factor linear model where the first factor is white noise and the second factor is an AR(1) with autoregressive coefficient 0.90. Predictability is measured in two ways: the population R^2 of the regression of each asset on the first lag of both factors, and the population squared own-autocorrelation ρ_1^2 of each asset's returns. The return-generating processes for both assets are calibrated to correspond roughly to monthly returns (see the text for details).

9.2.3 Empirical Illustration

To illustrate the empirical relevance of the difference in the R^2 of the PC1 portfolio and the MPP in this simple context, we anticipate the more detailed empirical analysis of Section 9.4 by performing the following simple calculation here. Using a sample of 11 sector portfolio returns and 6 predetermined factors, we calculate the sample R^2 (see Section 9.4 for details about these portfolios and factors). Using monthly returns for the period 1947:1 to 1993:12, the sample R^2 of the MPP is 12.0%, whereas the sample R^2 of PC1 is only 7.2%. Similar results hold for annual returns. Using annual returns, the MPP R^2 is 52.5% and the PC1 R^2 is 35.5%. These results show that, empirically, the differences in the level of predictability of the returns on these two portfolios can be substantial.

This simple two-factor example illustrates the fact that while the PC1 portfolio may be interesting in studies of cross-sectional relations among asset returns, the MPP is more directly relevant when predictability is the object of interest. Furthermore, the sample R^2 results suggest that the difference can be empirically important. In the following sections, we shall define the MPP more precisely and examine its statistical and empirical properties at length.

9.3 Maximizing Predictability

To define the predictability of a portfolio, we require some notation. Consider a collection of n assets with returns $\mathbf{R}_t \equiv [R_{1t}\ R_{2t}\ \cdots\ R_{nt}]'$ and for convenience, assume the following throughout this section:[7]

(A1) R_t is a jointly stationary and ergodic stochastic process with finite expectation $\mathrm{E}[\mathbf{R}_t] = \boldsymbol{\mu} \equiv [\mu_1\ \mu_2\ \cdots\ \mu_n]'$ and finite autocovariance matrices $\mathrm{E}[(\mathbf{R}_{t-k} - \boldsymbol{\mu})(\mathbf{R}_t - \boldsymbol{\mu})'] = \boldsymbol{\Gamma}_k$, where, with no loss of generality, we take $k \geq 0$ since $\boldsymbol{\Gamma}_k = \boldsymbol{\Gamma}'_{-k}$.

For convenience, we shall refer to these n assets as *primary* assets, assets to be used to construct the MPP, but they can be portfolios too.

Denote by $\mathbf{Z}_t$ an $(n \times 1)$ vector of de-meaned primary asset returns, i.e., $\mathbf{Z}_t \equiv \mathbf{R}_t - \boldsymbol{\mu}$, and let $\tilde{\mathbf{Z}}_t$ denote some forecast of $\mathbf{Z}_t$ based on information available at time $t - 1$, which we denote by the information set Ω_{t-1}. For simplicity, we assume that $\tilde{\mathbf{Z}}_t$ is the conditional expectation of $\mathbf{Z}_t$ with respect to Ω_{t-1}, i.e.,

$$\tilde{\mathbf{Z}}_t = \mathrm{E}[\mathbf{Z}_t \mid \Omega_{t-1}], \tag{9.3.1}$$

which would be the optimal forecast under a quadratic loss function (although we are not assuming that such a loss function applies). We may then express $\mathbf{Z}_t$ as

$$\mathbf{Z}_t = \mathrm{E}[\mathbf{Z}_t \mid \Omega_{t-1}] + \boldsymbol{\epsilon}_t = \tilde{\mathbf{Z}}_t + \boldsymbol{\epsilon}_t, \tag{9.3.2}$$

$$\mathrm{E}[\boldsymbol{\epsilon}_t \mid \Omega_{t-1}] = 0, \qquad \mathrm{Var}[\boldsymbol{\epsilon}_t \mid \Omega_{t-1}] = \boldsymbol{\Sigma}. \tag{9.3.3}$$

Included in the information set Ω_{t-1} are ex-ante observable economic variables such as dividend yield, various interest-rate spreads, earnings announcements, and other leading economic indicators. Therefore, with a suitably defined intercept term, (9.3.2) and (9.3.3) contain conditional versions of the CAPM (see Merton, 1973; Constantinides, 1980; and Bossaerts and Green, 1989), a dynamic multifactor APT (Ohlson and Garman, 1980, and Connor and Korajczyk, 1989), and virtually all other *linear* asset pricing models as special cases.

---

[7]Assumption (A1) is made for notational simplicity, since stationarity allows us to eliminate time indexes from population moments such as $\boldsymbol{\mu}$ and $\boldsymbol{\Gamma}_k$. However, there are several alternatives to stationarity and ergodicity that permit time-varying unconditional moments and still satisfy a law of large numbers and central limit theorem, which is essentially all we require for our purposes. The qualitative features of our results will not change under such alternatives (e.g., weak dependence with moment conditions), but would merely require replacing expectations with corresponding probability limits of suitably defined time averages. See, for example, White (1984) and Lo and MacKinlay (1990b).

We also assume throughout that the ϵ_t's are conditionally homoskedastic and that the information structure $\{\Omega_t\}$ is well behaved enough to ensure that $\tilde{\mathbf{Z}}_t$ is also a stationary and ergodic stochastic process.[8]

9.3.1 Maximally Predictable Portfolio

Let γ denote a particular linear combination of the primary assets in $\mathbf{Z}_t$, and consider the predictability of this linear combination, as measured by the well-known coefficient of determination:

$$R^2(\gamma) \equiv 1 - \frac{\mathrm{Var}[\gamma'\epsilon_t]}{\mathrm{Var}[\gamma'\mathbf{Z}_t]} = \frac{\mathrm{Var}[\gamma'\tilde{\mathbf{Z}}_t]}{\mathrm{Var}[\gamma'\mathbf{Z}_t]} = \frac{\gamma'\tilde{\mathbf{\Gamma}}_0\gamma}{\gamma'\mathbf{\Gamma}_0\gamma}, \qquad (9.3.4)$$

where

$$\tilde{\mathbf{\Gamma}}_0 \equiv \mathrm{Var}[\tilde{\mathbf{Z}}_t] = \mathrm{E}[\tilde{\mathbf{Z}}_t\tilde{\mathbf{Z}}_t'], \qquad (9.3.5)$$

$$\mathbf{\Gamma}_0 \equiv \mathrm{Var}[\mathbf{Z}_t] = \mathrm{E}[\mathbf{Z}_t\mathbf{Z}_t']. \qquad (9.3.6)$$

$R^2(\gamma)$ is simply the fraction of the variability in the portfolio return $\gamma'\mathbf{Z}_t$ explained by its conditional expectation, $\gamma'\tilde{\mathbf{Z}}_t$. Maximizing the predictability of a portfolio of $\mathbf{Z}_t$ then amounts to maximizing $R^2(\gamma)$ subject to the constraint that γ is a portfolio, i.e., $\gamma'\iota = 1$. But since $R^2(\gamma) = R^2(c\gamma)$ for any constant c, the constrained maximization is formally equivalent to maximizing R^2 over *all* γ, and then rescaling this globally optimal γ so that its components sum to unity.

Such a maximization is straightforward and yields an explicit expression for the maximum R^2 and its maximizer, given by Gantmacher (1959) and Box and Tiao (1977).[9] Specifically, the maximum of $R^2(\gamma)$ with respect to γ is given by the largest eigenvalue λ^* of the matrix $\mathbf{B} \equiv \mathbf{\Gamma}_0^{-1}\tilde{\mathbf{\Gamma}}_0$, and is attained by the eigenvector γ^* associated with the largest eigenvalue of $\mathbf{B}$. Therefore, when properly normalized, γ^* is the MPP.[10]

Observe that the MPP has been derived from the unconditional covariance matrices (9.3.5) and (9.3.6) and, as a result, it is constant over time. A time-varying version of the MPP also can be constructed, simply by replacing (9.3.5) and (9.3.6) with their conditional counterparts. In that case, the MPP must be recalculated in each period since the matrix $\mathbf{B}_t$ will then be a function of the conditioning variables and will vary through time.

---

[8]Our analysis can easily be extended to conditionally heteroskedastic errors, but at the expense of notational and computational complexity. See Section 9.3.1 for further discussion.

[9]Two closely related techniques are the multivariate index model and the reduced rank regression model; see Reinsel (1983) and Velu, Reinsel, and Wichern (1986).

[10]Similarly, the minimum of $R^2(\gamma)$ with respect to γ is given by the smallest eigenvalue λ_* of $\mathbf{B}$ and is attained by the eigenvector γ_* associated with the smallest eigenvalue of $\mathbf{B}$. Therefore, γ_* is the *minimally predictable portfolio*, i.e., the portfolio that is closest to a random walk.

However, to do this we require a fully articulated model of the conditional covariances of both $\mathbf{Z}_t$ and $\tilde{\mathbf{Z}}_t$, which then must be estimated.[11] Although this is beyond the scope of this chapter, recent empirical evidence suggests that the conditional moments of asset returns do vary through time (see Bollerslev, Chou, and Kroner, 1992, for a review), hence the conditional MPP may be an important extension from an empirical standpoint.

9.3.2 Example: One-Factor Model

To develop some intuition for the economic relevance of the MPP, consider the following example. Suppose we forecast excess returns $\mathbf{Z}_t$ with only a single factor X_{t-1}, so that we hypothesize the relation

$$\mathbf{Z}_t = \beta X_{t-1} + \epsilon_t, \tag{9.3.7}$$

$$\mathrm{E}[\epsilon_t \mid X_{t-1}] = 0, \qquad \mathrm{Var}[\epsilon_t \mid X_{t-1}] = \Sigma, \tag{9.3.8}$$

where β is an $(n \times 1)$ vector of factor loadings, and Σ is any positive definite covariance matrix (not necessarily diagonal). Such a relation might arise from the CAPM, in which case X_{t-1} is the period $t-1$ forecast of the market risk premium at time t.[12] In this simple case, the relevant matrices may be calculated in closed form as

$$\tilde{\Gamma}_0 \equiv \mathrm{Var}[\tilde{\mathbf{Z}}_t] = \sigma_x^2 \beta \beta', \tag{9.3.9}$$

$$\Gamma_0 \equiv \mathrm{Var}[\mathbf{Z}_t] = \sigma_x^2 \beta \beta' + \Sigma, \tag{9.3.10}$$

where $\sigma_x^2 \equiv \mathrm{Var}[X_{t-1}]$. The MPP γ^* and its R^2 are then given by

$$\gamma^* = \frac{1}{\iota' \Sigma^{-1} \beta} \, \Sigma^{-1} \beta, \tag{9.3.11}$$

$$\lambda^* = R^2(\gamma^*) = \frac{\sigma_x^2 \beta' \Sigma^{-1} \beta}{1 + \sigma_x^2 \beta' \Sigma^{-1} \beta}. \tag{9.3.12}$$

---

[11] See, for example, Bollerslev, Engle, and Wooldridge (1988), Gallant and Tauchen (1989), and Hamilton (1994, Chapter 21).

[12] In particular, (9.3.8) may be viewed as a conditional version of a linear factor model where the factor $\mathbf{Z}_t$ is a linear function of economic variables observable at $t-1$ (namely, X_{t-1}). Examples of such a specification in the recent literature include Chen, Roll, and Ross (1986), Engle, Lilien, and Robbins (1987), Ferson (1989, 1990), Ferson and Harvey (1991b), and Harvey (1989). To underscore this factor-pricing interpretation, we have referred to β as the vector of *factor loadings* and will refer to the predictor X_{t-1} as a *conditional factor*. However, it should be emphasized that a structural factor-model for our return-generating process, one that links expected returns to *contemporaneous* risk premia (such as the security market line of the CAPM), is not required by our framework. But even if such a structural factor-model exists, the contemporaneous factors or risk premia are almost always written as linear functions of ex-ante economic variables, especially when applying them to time-series data. Therefore, the simple specification (9.3.8) is considerably more general than it may appear to be.

To develop further intuition for (9.3.11) and (9.3.12), suppose that $\Sigma = \sigma_\epsilon^2 I$, so that the MPP and its R^2 reduce to

$$\gamma^* = \frac{1}{\iota'\beta} \beta, \tag{9.3.13}$$

$$\lambda^* = R^2(\gamma^*) = \frac{\beta'\beta\sigma_x^2/\sigma_\epsilon^2}{1 + \beta'\beta\sigma_x^2/\sigma_\epsilon^2}. \tag{9.3.14}$$

Not surprisingly, with cross-sectionally uncorrelated errors, the MPP has weights directly proportional to the assets' betas. The larger the beta, the more predictable that asset's future return will be *ceteris paribus*; hence the MPP should place more weight on that asset. As expected, $R^2(\gamma^*)$ is an increasing function of the *signal-to-noise* ratio $\sigma_x^2/\sigma_\epsilon$. But interestingly, the MPP weights γ^* are not, and do not even depend on the σ_j^2's. This, of course, is an artifact of our extreme assumption that the assets' variances are identical. If, for example, we assumed that Σ were a diagonal matrix with elements σ_j^2, $j = 1, \ldots, n$, then the portfolio weights γ_j^* would be proportional to β_j/σ_j^2. The larger the β_j, the more weight asset j will have in the MPP, and the larger the σ_j^2, the less weight it will have.

Since the level of predictability of γ^* does depend on how important X_{t-1} is in determining the variability of Z_t, in the case where $\Sigma = \sigma_\epsilon^2 I$ as the signal-to-noise ratio increases the R^2 of the MPP also increases, eventually approaching unity as $\sigma_x^2/\sigma_\epsilon^2$ increases without bound. Also, from (9.3.14) it is apparent that $R^2(\gamma^*)$ increases with the number of assets *ceteris paribus*, since $\beta'\beta$ is simply the sum of squared betas. Of course, even in the most general case, $R^2(\gamma^*)$ must be a nondecreasing function of the number of assets because it is always possible to put zero weight on any newly introduced assets.

9.4 An Empirical Implementation

To implement the results of Section 9.3, we must first develop a suitable forecasting model for the vector of excess returns Z_t. Using monthly data from 1947:1 to 1993:12, we consider three sets of primary assets for our vector Z_t: (1) a five-asset group, consisting of the S&P 500, a small stock index, a government bond index, a corporate bond index, and a utilities index; (2) a 10-asset group consisting of deciles of size-sorted portfolios constructed from the CRSP monthly returns file; and (3) an 11-asset group of sector-sorted portfolios, also constructed from CRSP. The 11 sector portfolios are defined according to SIC code classifications: (1) wholesale and retail trade; (2) services; (3) nondurable goods; (4) construction; (5) capital goods; (6) durable goods; (7) finance, real estate, and insurance; (8) transportation; (9) basic industries; (10) utilities; and (11) coal and oil. Within each portfolio, the size-sorted portfolios and the sector-sorted portfolios are value weighted.

9.4.1 The Conditional Factors

In developing forecasting models for the three groups of assets, we draw on the substantial literature documenting the time variation in expected stock returns to select our conditional factors. From empirical studies by Rozeff (1984), Chen, Roll, and Ross (1986), Keim and Stambaugh (1986), Breen, Glosten, and Jagannathan (1989), Ferson (1990), Chen (1991), Estrella and Hardouvelis (1991), Ferson and Harvey (1991b), Kale, Hakansson, and Platt (1991), and many others, variables such as the growth in industrial production, dividend yield, and default and term spreads on fixed-income instruments have been shown to have forecast power. Also, the asymmetric lead/lag relations among size-sorted portfolios that Lo and MacKinlay (1990b) document suggest that lagged returns may have forecast power. Therefore, we were led to construct the following variables:

DY_t Dividend yield, defined as the aggregated dividends for the CRSP value-weighted index for the 12-month period ending at the end of month t divided by the index value at the end of month t.

DEF_t The default spread, defined as the average weekly yield for low-grade bonds in month t minus the average weekly yield for long-term government bonds (maturity greater than 10 years) in month t. The low grade bonds are rated Baa.

MAT_t The maturity spread, defined as the average weekly yield on long-term government bonds in month t minus the average weekly yield from the auctions of three-month Treasury bills in month t.

SPR_t The S&P 500 Index return, defined as the monthly return on a value-weighted portfolio of 500 common stocks.

IRT_t The interest-rate trend, defined as the monthly change of the average weekly yield on long-term government bonds.

$SPDY_t$ An interaction term to capture time variation in asset return betas, defined as the product $DY_t SPR_t$ of the dividend yield and the S&P 500 Index return variables.

Of course, there is a possible pre-test bias in our choosing these variables based on prior empirical studies. For example, Foster et al. (1995) show that choosing k out of m regressors ($k < m$) to maximize R^2 can yield seemingly significant R^2's even when no relation exists between the dependent variable and the regressors. They show that such a specification search may explain the findings of Keim and Stambaugh (1986), Campbell (1987), and Ferson and Harvey (1991a).[13]

---

[13]However, using similar conditional factors, Bessembinder and Chan (1992) find similar levels of predictability for various commodity and currency futures which are nearly uncorre-

Unfortunately, Foster et al.'s (1995) pre-test bias cannot be corrected easily in our application, for the simple reason that our selection procedure does not correspond precisely to choosing the "best" k regressors out of m. There is no doubt that prior empirical findings have influenced our choice of conditional factors, but in much subtler ways than this. In particular, theoretical considerations have also played a part in our choice, both in which variables to include and which to exclude. For example, even though a January indicator variable has been shown to have some predictive power, we have not included it as a conditional factor because we have no strong theoretical motivation for such a variable.

Because a combination of empirical and theoretical considerations has influenced our choice of conditional factors, Foster et al.'s (1995) corrections are not directly applicable. Moreover, if we apply their corrections *without* actually searching for the best k of m regressors, we will almost surely never find predictability even if it exists, i.e., tests for predictability will have no power against economically plausible alternative hypotheses of predictable returns. Therefore, other than alerting readers to the possibility of pre-test biases in our selection of conditional factors, there is little else that we can do to correct for this ubiquitous problem.

The final specification for the conditional factor model for $\mathbf{Z}_t$ is then given by

$$\mathbf{Z}_t = \alpha + \beta_1 \mathrm{DY}_{t-1} + \beta_2 \mathrm{DEF}_{t-1} + \beta_3 \mathrm{MAT}_{t-1} + \beta_4 \mathrm{IRT}_{t-1}$$
$$+ \beta_5 \mathrm{SPR}_{t-1} + \beta_6 \mathrm{SPDY}_{t-1} + \epsilon_t. \tag{9.4.1}$$

The interaction term SPDY_{t-1} allows the factor loading of the S&P 500 to vary through time as a linear function of the dividend yield DY_{t-1}.[14]

9.4.2 Estimating the Conditional-Factor Model

Tables 9.2–9.4 report ordinary least squares estimates of the conditional-factor model (9.4.1) for the three groups of assets, respectively: the (5×1) vector of stocks, bonds, and utilities (SBU); the (10×1) vector of size deciles (SIZE); and the (11×1) vector of sector portfolios (SECTOR). Panel (a) of

---

lated with equity returns. This is perhaps the most convincing empirical evidence to date for the genuine forecast power of dividend yields, short-term interest-rate yields, and the default premium.

[14]This interaction term is motivated by several recent empirical studies documenting time variation in asset-return betas, e.g., Ferson, Kandel, and Stambaugh (1987), Ferson (1989), Harvey (1989), and Ferson and Harvey (1991b). In principle, we can model all of the factor loadings as time-varying. However, the "curse of dimensionality" would arise, as well as the perils of overfitting. Moreover, the evidence in Ferson and Harvey (1991b, Table 8) suggests that the predictability in monthly size and sector portfolios is primarily due to changing risk premia, not changing betas. Therefore, our decision to leave β_1 through β_4 fixed through time is unlikely to be very restrictive.

Table 9.2. Ordinary least squares regression results for individual asset returns in SBU asset group from 1947:1 to 1993:12

Asset	Constant	DY	DEF	MAT	SPR	SPDY	IRT	D.W.[b]	R^2
					Regressors[a]				
				(a) Monthly results					
S&P 500	-2.27	0.70	-0.07	0.37	0.29	-0.09	-2.82	1.99	0.066
	(-2.79)	(3.86)	(-0.32)	(2.66)	(1.39)	(-1.72)	(-2.93)		
Small stocks	-2.67	0.71	0.24	0.26	0.73	-0.15	-2.52	1.89	0.055
	(-2.35)	(2.90)	(0.79)	(1.29)	(3.24)	(-2.66)	(-1.80)		
Gov't bonds	-1.08	0.16	0.15	0.31	-0.12	0.01	-0.26	1.94	0.044
	(-2.35)	(1.75)	(1.04)	(2.71)	(-1.07)	(0.31)	(-0.35)		
Corp. bonds	-1.28	0.19	0.22	0.32	-0.07	-0.01	-0.79	1.80	0.068
	(-2.85)	(2.14)	(1.54)	(3.02)	(-0.72)	(-0.22)	(-1.23)		
Utilities	-2.35	0.65	0.16	0.23	0.17	-0.05	-1.66	1.91	0.055
	(-3.25)	(4.22)	(0.82)	(1.91)	(1.12)	(-1.43)	(-2.15)		
				(b) Annual results					
S&P 500	-35.07	12.88	-4.34	2.68	6.04	-1.81	-28.18	2.12	0.426
	(-3.60)	(4.35)	(-1.72)	(1.81)	(2.01)	(-2.30)	(-2.44)		
Small stocks	-42.12	15.91	-3.06	0.83	10.46	-3.10	-58.59	1.87	0.341
	(-2.45)	(3.92)	(-0.84)	(0.39)	(2.82)	(-3.22)	(-2.63)		
Gov't bonds	-11.73	2.35	0.46	3.85	2.42	-0.74	1.42	2.21	0.345
	(-1.59)	(1.23)	(0.28)	(4.24)	(1.36)	(-1.48)	(0.13)		
Corp. bonds	-15.01	2.95	1.14	4.11	2.72	-0.83	3.53	2.15	0.425
	(-2.03)	(1.55)	(0.81)	(4.89)	(1.52)	(-1.70)	(0.37)		
Utilities	-38.65	12.58	-1.33	2.07	6.42	-1.88	-16.68	1.84	0.397
	(-4.36)	(5.06)	(-0.67)	(1.59)	(2.61)	(-2.86)	(-1.72)		

[a]DY = dividend yield; DEF = default premium; MAT = maturity premium; SPR = S&P 500 Index total return; SPDY = SPR × DY; IRT = interest-rate trend. The five assets in the SBU group are the S&P 500 Index, a small stock index, a government bond index, a corporate bond index, and a utilities index. Heteroskedasticity-consistent z-statistics are given in parentheses.

[b]Durbin-Watson test statistic for dependence in the regression residual.

Table 9.2 contains results for monthly SBU returns and Panel (b) contains annual results, and similarly for Tables 9.3 and 9.4.[15] We perform all multi-horizon return calculations with *nonoverlapping* returns since Monte Carlo and asymptotic calculations in Lo and MacKinlay (1989a) and Richardson and Stock (1990) show that overlapping returns can bias inferences substantially.

The performance of the conditional factors in the regressions of Tables 9.2–9.4 are largely consistent with findings in the recent empirical literature. Among the equity assets, the dividend yield is positively related to future returns and generally significant at the 5% level. The default premium generally has little incremental explanatory power for future returns. Additional analysis indicates that its usual explanatory power is captured by the interest-rate trend variable. The maturity premium has predictive power mostly for the utilities asset at the annual horizon. In contrast, the S&P 500 Index return and the interest-rate trend variables are strongest at the monthly horizon, the former affecting expected returns positively, and the latter negatively. For the bond assets, most of the forecastability is from the positive relation with the maturity spread.

From Tables 9.2–9.4, it is also apparent that the market betas for monthly equity returns exhibit substantial time variation since the SPDY regressor is significant at the 5% level for the small stocks in Panel (a) of Table 9.2, and for most of the assets in Panel (a) of Tables 9.3 and 9.4. In these cases, the estimated coefficient of SPDY is consistently negative, indicating that the sensitivity of equity assets to the lagged aggregate market return declines as the dividend yield rises. Note that in each of these cases DY has additional explanatory power as a separate regressor, as its estimated coefficient is also significant at conventional levels.

At the annual return-horizon, the market beta and the time variation in market beta's remains significant for the equity assets. In Panel (b) of Tables 9.2, 9.3, and 9.4, the coefficients for SPR and SPDY are statistically significant in many of the regressions. Also, DY is still significant, and in all cases the R^2 is larger for annual returns. In particular, whereas the R^2's for monthly asset returns reported in Panel (a) of Tables 9.2, 9.3, and 9.4 range from 3 to 9%, the R^2's for annual asset returns range from 16 to 44% in Panel (b) of Tables 9.2, 9.3, and 9.4.[16]

Of course, like any other statistic, the R^2 is a point estimate subject

[15]We have also analyzed quarterly and semi-annual returns, but do not report them here to conserve space. Although the variation in predictability across horizons exhibits some interesting features, the results generally fall in between the range of monthly and annual values.

[16]Note that the longer-horizon returns are *non*overlapping. In some unpublished Monte Carlo simulations, we have shown that overlapping returns can induce unusually high R^2's even when the conditional factors are statistically independent of the long-horizon returns. See also Richardson and Stock (1990).

Table 9.3. *Ordinary least squares regression results for individual asset returns in the SIZE asset group from 1947:1 to 1993:12*

Asset	Constant	DY	DEF	MAT	SPR	SPDY	IRT	D.W.[b]	R^2
				(a) Monthly results					
1	−2.90 (−1.90)	0.74 (2.38)	0.43 (0.95)	0.17 (0.65)	1.48 (4.22)	−0.28 (−3.40)	−2.69 (−1.67)	1.90	0.082
2	−2.74 (−2.03)	0.71 (2.59)	0.29 (0.73)	0.20 (0.93)	1.12 (4.25)	−0.21 (−3.32)	−2.69 (−1.77)	1.90	0.073
3	−3.33 (−2.63)	0.84 (3.22)	0.31 (0.90)	0.27 (1.30)	0.89 (3.64)	−0.18 (−3.00)	−2.61 (−1.76)	1.92	0.064
4	−3.01 (−2.49)	0.80 (3.22)	0.24 (0.72)	0.24 (1.20)	0.80 (3.52)	−0.16 (−2.91)	−2.54 (−1.81)	1.92	0.058
5	−3.15 (−2.72)	0.83 (3.46)	0.21 (0.68)	0.25 (1.27)	0.67 (3.11)	−0.14 (−2.63)	−2.89 (−2.04)	1.92	0.058
6	−3.16 (−2.81)	0.85 (3.56)	0.20 (0.67)	0.29 (1.53)	0.69 (3.34)	−0.15 (−2.89)	−3.07 (−2.28)	1.93	0.066
7	−2.83 (−2.74)	0.78 (3.60)	0.17 (0.64)	0.30 (1.70)	0.58 (2.98)	−0.13 (−2.77)	−3.24 (−2.54)	1.91	0.065
8	−2.89 (−2.96)	0.77 (3.71)	0.17 (0.67)	0.34 (2.01)	0.51 (2.69)	−0.12 (−2.65)	−3.12 (−2.61)	1.92	0.066
9	−2.65 (−2.81)	0.78 (3.85)	0.07 (0.28)	0.30 (1.86)	0.42 (2.19)	−0.11 (−2.35)	−3.09 (−2.76)	1.93	0.062
10	−2.15 (−2.67)	0.66 (3.72)	−0.09 (−0.44)	0.37 (2.67)	0.28 (1.34)	−0.08 (−1.67)	−2.68 (−2.79)	1.99	0.063

(continued)

Table 9.3.   *(continued)*

Asset	Constant	DY	DEF	MAT	SPR	SPDY	IRT	D.W.[b]	R^2
					(b) Annual results				
1	-41.45	18.20	-4.67	0.16	14.35	-4.21	-83.15	1.54	0.231
	(-1.33)	(3.01)	(-0.97)	(0.04)	(2.62)	(-3.03)	(-2.43)		
2	-40.67	16.77	-4.37	0.61	11.81	-3.55	-68.83	1.65	0.251
	(-1.61)	(3.14)	(-1.04)	(0.20)	(2.64)	(-3.18)	(-2.35)		
3	-48.33	17.66	-2.50	0.39	10.19	-3.11	-66.77	1.75	0.320
	(-2.28)	(3.79)	(-0.67)	(0.15)	(2.56)	(-3.10)	(-2.47)		
4	-46.98	17.63	-3.53	0.85	10.33	-3.18	-59.48	1.80	0.332
	(-2.40)	(4.02)	(-0.96)	(0.34)	(2.73)	(-3.35)	(-2.66)		
5	-48.08	17.32	-3.68	1.33	9.84	-3.00	-48.49	1.77	0.328
	(-2.68)	(4.04)	(-1.05)	(0.56)	(2.71)	(-3.28)	(-2.24)		
6	-46.88	16.72	-3.05	1.32	9.45	-2.81	-51.08	1.91	0.369
	(-2.92)	(4.27)	(-0.96)	(0.59)	(2.70)	(-3.13)	(-2.64)		
7	-44.42	16.04	-3.21	1.80	9.26	-2.77	-48.10	2.04	0.402
	(-3.06)	(4.38)	(-1.06)	(0.97)	(3.01)	(-3.45)	(-2.79)		
8	-44.36	15.64	-3.28	2.08	9.06	-2.73	-44.68	1.94	0.442
	(-3.40)	(4.48)	(-1.14)	(1.18)	(3.08)	(-3.44)	(-3.17)		
9	-36.50	13.75	-3.75	1.60	6.84	-2.07	-41.69	2.09	0.442
	(-3.23)	(4.52)	(-1.50)	(1.02)	(2.54)	(-2.90)	(-3.29)		
10	-33.18	12.08	-4.37	2.69	5.96	-1.75	-25.56	2.10	0.411
	(-3.48)	(4.20)	(-1.79)	(1.75)	(1.96)	(-2.24)	(-2.22)		

[a] DY = dividend yield; DEF = default premium; MAT = maturity premium; SPR = S&P 500 Index total return; SPDY = SPR × DY; IRT = interest-rate trend. The 10 SIZE assets are portfolios of stocks grouped according to their market value of equity. Heteroskedasticity-consistent z-statistics are given in parentheses.
[b] Durbin-Watson test statistic for dependence in the regression residual.

Table 9.4. *Ordinary least squares regression results for individual asset returns in the SECTOR asset group from 1947:1 to 1993:12*

Asset	Constant	DY	DEF	MAT	SPR	SPDY	IRT	D.W.[b]	R^2
				Regressors[a]					
				(a) Monthly results					
Trade	-3.46	0.74	0.52	0.35	0.80	-0.16	-2.84	1.82	0.077
	(-3.05)	(3.23)	(1.64)	(1.73)	(3.59)	(-2.93)	(-2.08)		
Services	-3.27	0.80	0.39	0.30	0.88	-0.17	-2.52	1.84	0.064
	(-2.56)	(3.09)	(1.12)	(1.41)	(3.68)	(-2.96)	(-1.80)		
Nondurables	-3.17	0.72	0.45	0.29	0.82	-0.17	-2.60	1.88	0.080
	(-3.16)	(3.41)	(1.58)	(1.69)	(4.12)	(-3.42)	(2.14)		
Construction	-3.77	0.95	0.28	0.22	0.99	-0.20	-4.69	1.89	0.092
	(-3.08)	(3.84)	(0.82)	(1.02)	(3.75)	(-3.21)	(-3.10)		
Capital goods	-2.96	0.80	0.16	0.23	0.87	-0.18	-2.78	1.87	0.061
	(-2.48)	(3.20)	(0.50)	(1.14)	(3.77)	(-3.17)	(-1.94)		
Durables	-3.44	0.88	0.25	0.35	0.89	-0.18	-2.61	1.88	0.060
	(-2.63)	(3.29)	(0.73)	(1.64)	(3.56)	(-3.04)	(-1.76)		
Fin, RE, Ins	-4.20	1.03	0.27	0.29	0.80	-0.16	-3.52	1.89	0.083
	(-3.43)	(4.30)	(0.77)	(1.46)	(3.28)	(-2.79)	(-2.63)		
Transportation	-3.21	0.87	0.13	0.29	0.81	-0.17	-3.47	1.87	0.058
	(-2.57)	(3.10)	(0.39)	(1.41)	(3.07)	(-2.60)	(-2.27)		
Basic industries	-2.21	0.71	0.02	0.16	0.61	-0.13	-3.26	1.96	0.055
	(-2.05)	(2.99)	(0.09)	(0.87)	(2.88)	(-2.46)	(-2.38)		
Utilities	-2.35	0.65	0.16	0.23	0.17	-0.05	-1.66	1.91	0.055
	(-3.25)	(4.22)	(0.82)	(1.91)	(1.12)	(-1.43)	(-2.15)		
Oil and coal	-1.25	0.73	-0.30	-0.17	0.67	-0.16	-3.12	1.90	0.034
	(-0.99)	(2.62)	(-0.92)	(-0.76)	(2.58)	(-2.38)	(-1.64)		

(continued)

Table 9.4. *(continued)*

| | | | | Regressors[a] | | | | | |
Asset	Constant	DY	DEF	MAT	SPR	SPDY	IRT	D.W.[b]	R^2
				(b) Annual results					
Trade	−57.42	18.09	0.34	1.95	12.86	−3.76	−51.01	1.62	0.324
	(−2.58)	(3.68)	(0.09)	(0.73)	(3.20)	(−3.70)	(−2.18)		
Services	−46.16	18.66	−3.87	0.09	12.92	−4.04	−74.54	1.69	0.335
	(−1.93)	(3.62)	(−0.99)	(0.03)	(3.31)	(−4.22)	(−2.85)		
Nondurables	−49.54	16.39	−0.31	0.77	10.97	−3.25	−57.55	1.92	0.383
	(−2.86)	(4.13)	(−0.09)	(0.35)	(3.37)	(−3.89)	(−3.24)		
Construction	−50.70	17.23	−2.52	1.75	9.11	−2.81	−57.43	1.83	0.345
	(−2.71)	(3.81)	(−0.67)	(0.69)	(2.52)	(−3.08)	(−3.10)		
Capital goods	−42.81	16.11	−3.73	0.17	9.20	−2.75	−58.77	1.89	0.291
	(−2.13)	(3.46)	(−0.93)	(0.06)	(2.24)	(−2.63)	(−2.51)		
Durables	−56.88	20.22	−3.55	0.67	13.29	−3.89	−63.26	1.83	0.345
	(−2.59)	(4.32)	(−0.83)	(0.26)	(3.23)	(−3.70)	(−2.61)		
Fin, RE, Ins	−57.06	18.49	−2.67	1.21	11.57	−3.21	−44.28	1.47	0.298
	(−2.85)	(4.28)	(−0.87)	(0.51)	(3.49)	(−4.02)	(−2.10)		
Transportation	−46.13	16.48	−3.53	2.19	7.57	−2.39	−63.51	1.90	0.324
	(−2.56)	(3.49)	(−0.73)	(0.97)	(1.42)	(−1.64)	(−3.22)		
Basic industries	−37.67	15.16	−5.06	1.02	7.66	−2.37	−48.11	2.09	0.342
	(−2.57)	(3.71)	(−1.45)	(0.52)	(1.97)	(−2.22)	(−2.82)		
Utilities	−38.65	12.58	−1.33	2.07	6.42	−1.88	−16.68	1.84	0.397
	(−4.36)	(5.06)	(−0.67)	(1.59)	(2.61)	(−2.86)	(−1.72)		
Oil and coal	−24.66	13.32	−7.56	−3.75	7.93	−1.91	−26.39	1.90	0.164
	(−1.05)	(1.99)	(−1.63)	(−0.94)	(1.32)	(−1.24)	(−0.82)		

[a]DY = dividend yield; DEF = default premium; MAT = maturity premium; SPR = S&P 500 Index total return; SPDY = SPR × DY; IRT = interest-rate trend. The eleven SECTOR assets are portfolios of stocks grouped according to their SIC codes. Heteroskedasticity-consistent z-statistics are given in parentheses.
[b]Durbin-Watson test statistic for dependence in the regression residual.

to sampling variation. Since longer-horizon returns yield fewer nonover-lapping observations, we might expect the R^2's from such regressions to exhibit larger fluctuations, with more extreme values than regressions for monthly data. We shall deal explicitly with the sampling theory of the R^2 in Section 9.5.

9.4.3 Maximizing Predictability

Given the estimated conditional-factor models in Tables 9.2–9.4, we can readily construct the (sample or estimated) MPP's. Given the estimate $\hat{\boldsymbol{B}} \equiv \hat{\boldsymbol{\Gamma}}_o^{-1} \hat{\boldsymbol{\Gamma}}_o$, the estimated MPP $\hat{\gamma}^*$ is simply the eigenvector corresponding to the largest eigenvalue of $\hat{\boldsymbol{B}}$.

We will also have occasion to consider the *constrained* MPP γ_c^*, constrained to have nonnegative portfolio weights. It will become apparent below that an unconstrained maximization of predictability yields considerably more extreme and unstable portfolio weights than a constrained maximization. Moreover, for many investors, the constrained case may be of more practical relevance. Although we do not have a closed-form expression for γ_c^*, it is a simple matter to calculate it numerically. Again, given $\hat{\boldsymbol{B}}$, we may obtain $\hat{\gamma}_c^*$ in a similar manner.

In Table 9.5, we report the conditional-factor model of the MPP for the SBU, SIZE, and SECTOR portfolios, constrained and unconstrained, for monthly and annual return-horizons using the factors of Section 9.4.1. In Panel (a) of Table 9.5, the patterns of the estimated coefficients are largely consistent with those of Table 9.2: The coefficient of the interaction variable SPDY is negative, though insignificant for monthly returns; the coefficient of dividend yield DY is positive and significant for all portfolios; and the maximal R^2 increases with the horizon.

As expected, the maximal R^2's are larger than the largest R^2's of the individual portfolio regressions. For example, the monthly constrained maximal R^2 is 9%, and the S&P 500 regression in Panel (a) of Table 9.2 has an R^2 of 7%. There is somewhat more improvement at an annual horizon. For example, the unconstrained maximal R^2 is 50% at an annual horizon, whereas the R^2's for the annual returns of the five individual assets in Panel (b) range from 34 to 43%.

Panels (a) and (b) of Table 9.5 exhibit similar findings for the SIZE and SECTOR assets. The R^2's of monthly size portfolios range from 6 to 8% in Panel (a) of Table 9.3, whereas Panel (b) of Table 9.5 reports the unconstrained maximal R^2 to be 12%, and the constrained to be 8%. But at an annual horizon, the R^2's for individual size portfolios range from 23 to 44%, while the maximal constrained and unconstrained R^2's from Table 9.5 are 45 and 61%, respectively.

Table 9.5. Conditional expected return of MPP for the three asset groups from 1947:1 to 1993:12

Asset	Constant	Regressors[a] DY	DEF	MAT	SPR	SPDY	IRT	D.W.[b]	R^2
				(a) SBU					
Monthly unconstrained	-1.50 (-2.78)	0.35 (3.01)	0.05 (0.29)	0.38 (3.83)	-0.11 (-0.72)	-0.01 (-0.36)	-1.76 (-2.87)	1.85	0.106
Monthly constrained	-1.61 (-3.43)	0.36 (3.64)	0.12 (0.86)	0.34 (3.59)	0.05 (0.50)	-0.03 (-1.19)	-1.48 (-2.41)	1.89	0.086
Annual unconstrained	-22.05 (-3.91)	6.53 (4.28)	-0.58 (-0.48)	3.34 (4.09)	4.36 (2.89)	-1.31 (-3.34)	-11.27 (-1.70)	2.06	0.497
Annual constrained	-22.05 (-3.91)	6.53 (4.28)	-0.58 (-0.48)	3.34 (4.09)	4.36 (2.89)	-1.31 (-3.34)	-11.27 (-1.70)	2.06	0.497
				(b) SIZE					
Unconstrained monthly	-0.08 (-0.01)	0.70 (-0.41)	2.58 (1.09)	-0.03 (-0.02)	9.47 (4.06)	-1.60 (-3.06)	-6.24 (-0.90)	1.96	0.116
Constrained monthly	-2.90 (-1.90)	0.74 (2.38)	0.43 (0.95)	0.17 (0.65)	1.48 (4.22)	-0.28 (-3.40)	-2.69 (-1.67)	1.90	0.082
Unconstrained annual	-112.73 (-4.78)	30.08 (5.02)	10.83 (1.95)	1.45 (0.49)	17.91 (3.03)	-5.23 (-3.29)	122.31 (-3.79)	1.46	0.615
Constrained annual	-39.68 (-3.41)	14.40 (4.54)	-3.62 (-1.38)	1.96 (1.21)	7.75 (2.78)	-2.33 (-3.13)	-40.94 (-3.21)	2.04	0.445
				(c) SECTOR					
Unconstrained monthly	-6.73 (-3.50)	1.15 (3.03)	1.27 (2.14)	0.41 (1.20)	1.92 (4.20)	-0.37 (-3.37)	-7.18 (-3.37)	1.72	0.120
Constrained monthly	-3.87 (3.21)	0.97 (4.01)	0.28 (0.82)	0.23 (1.13)	0.95 (3.73)	-0.20 (-3.19)	-4.42 (-3.03)	1.89	0.093
Unconstrained annual	-50.00 (-4.02)	18.82 (6.06)	-4.59 (-1.59)	1.74 (1.18)	11.47 (3.80)	-3.51 (-4.42)	-46.54 (-3.99)	1.87	0.525
Constrained annual	40.68 (-4.31)	13.99 (5.55)	-2.33 (-1.04)	1.76 (1.25)	7.35 (3.19)	-2.18 (-3.62)	-29.44 (-3.14)	1.87	0.455

[a] DY = dividend yield; DEF = default premium; MAT = maturity premium; SPR = maturity premium; SPR $\times$ DY; IRT = interest-rate trend. The asset groups are SBU, SIZE, and SECTOR. Heteroskedasticity-consistent z-statistics are given in parentheses.

[b] Durbin-Watson test statistic for dependence in the regression residual.

Table 9.5 also shows that the importance of the shortsales constraint for maximizing predictability depends critically on the particular set of assets over which predictability is being maximized. It is apparent that the shortsales constraint has little effect on the levels of the maximal R^2 for the five SBU assets. Indeed, the constraint is not binding for annual returns. However, this is not the case for either the 10 SIZE assets or the 11 SECTOR assets. When the shortsales constraint is imposed, maximal R^2's drop dramatically, from 62 to 45% for annual SIZE assets and from 53 to 46% for annual SECTOR assets.

9.4.4 The Maximally Predictable Portfolios

Whereas the coefficients of the regressions in Table 9.5 measure the sensitivity of the MPP to various factors, it is the portfolio weights of the MPPs that tell us which assets are the most important sources of predictability. Table 9.6 reports these portfolio weights for the three sets of assets, SBU, SIZE, and SECTOR.

Perhaps the most striking feature of Table 9.6 is how these portfolio weights change with the horizon. For example, the unconstrained maximally predictable SIZE portfolio has an extreme long position in decile 2 for monthly returns but an extreme short position for annual returns. The maximally predictable SECTOR and SBU portfolios exhibit similar patterns across the two horizons, but the weights are much less extreme. These changing weights are consistent with a changing covariance structure among the assets over horizons; as the structure changes, so must the portfolio weights to maximize predictability.

When the shortsales constraint is imposed, the portfolio weights vary less extremely—by construction, of course, since they are bounded between 0 and 1—but they still shift with the return horizon. For example, the constrained maximally predictable SBU portfolio is split between the S&P 500 and corporate bonds for monthly returns, but contains all assets for annual returns. More interestingly, the constrained maximally predictable SIZE portfolio is invested in decile 1 for monthly returns, but is concentrated in deciles 8, 9, and 10 for annual returns.

That the larger capitalization stocks should play so central a role in maximizing predictability among SIZE assets is quite unexpected, since it is the smaller stocks that are generally more highly autocorrelated. However, as the example in Section 9.3.2 illustrates, it is important to distinguish between the factors that predict returns and the assets that are most predictable. In the case of the SIZE assets, one explanation might be that over longer horizons, factors such as industrial production and dividend yield become more important for the larger companies since they track general business trends more closely than smaller companies (see Table 9.3).

Table 9.6. *Portfolio weights of MPP for three asset groups from 1947:1 to 1993:12*

Asset	Monthly unconstrained	Monthly constrained	Annual unconstrained	Annual constrained
		(a) SBU		
S&P 500	0.69	0.34	0.19	0.19
Small stocks	−0.38	0.00	0.13	0.13
Gov't bonds	−0.48	0.00	0.18	0.18
Corp. bonds	1.19	0.66	0.49	0.49
Utilities	−0.02	0.00	0.01	0.01
		(b) SIZE		
Decile 1	4.97	1.00	1.10	0.00
Decile 2	11.18	0.00	−4.68	0.00
Decile 3	−4.11	0.00	4.57	0.00
Decile 4	−7.13	0.00	−0.67	0.00
Decile 5	−13.97	0.00	−5.25	0.00
Decile 6	8.97	0.00	2.55	0.00
Decile 7	5.54	0.00	2.09	0.00
Decile 8	7.50	0.00	6.79	0.46
Decile 9	−12.01	0.00	−3.18	0.41
Decile 10	0.06	0.00	−2.32	0.13
		(c) SECTOR		
Trade	0.36	0.00	−0.70	0.00
Services	−0.13	0.00	0.49	0.00
Nondurables	2.15	0.00	0.27	0.00
Construction	1.93	0.77	0.19	0.00
Capital goods	−0.16	0.00	−1.70	0.00
Durables	−1.38	0.00	1.26	0.09
Fin, RE, Ins	0.32	0.23	−0.01	0.01
Transportation	0.22	0.00	0.01	0.06
Basic industries	−1.12	0.00	0.62	0.18
Utilities	−0.95	0.00	0.59	0.67
Oil and coal	−0.24	0.00	−0.03	0.00

Further insights concerning the sources of predictability are contained in the SECTOR portfolio weights. The constrained MPP for monthly SECTOR returns is invested in two assets: construction; and finance, real estate, and insurance. However, at an annual horizon, the composition of this portfolio changes dramatically, consisting mostly of two completely different assets: basic industries and utilities. This indicates that the sources of time variation in expected returns are sensitive to the return horizon. The sectors that are important for maximizing predictability for monthly returns may be quite different from those that maximize predictability for returns over longer horizons.

9.5 Statistical Inference for the Maximal R^2

Although the magnitudes of the sample R^2's of Section 9.4 suggest the presence of genuine predictability in stock returns, we must still consider data-snooping biases imparted by our *in-sample* maximization procedure. It is a well-known fact that the maximum of a collection of identically distributed random variables does not have the same distribution as the individual maximands. However, it is not always an easy task to deduce the distribution of the maximum, especially when the individual variables are not statistically independent as in our current application. Moreover, maximizing the R^2 over a continuum of portfolio weights cannot be easily recast into the maximum of a discrete set of random variables. Therefore, much of our inferences must be guided by Monte Carlo simulation experiments in which the sampling distribution of R^2 and related statistics are tabulated by generating pseudo-random data under the null hypothesis of no predictability.[17]

9.5.1 Monte Carlo Analysis

In particular, for the monthly return horizon, we simulate 564 observations of independently and identically distributed Gaussian stock returns, calculate the R^2 corresponding to the MPP of q-period returns using the conditional factors of Section 9.4.2, record this R^2, and repeat the same procedure 9,999 times, yielding 10,000 replications. For the annual horizon, we perform similar experiments: we simulate 10,000 independent samples at the annual horizon (a sample size of 47 observations), and record the maximum R^2 for each sample.

The simulations yield the finite-sample distribution for the maximal R^2 under the *null hypothesis* of no predictability. The features of that distribution are reported for various values of q in Panel (a) of Table 9.7 for the unconstrained MPP, and in Panel (b) for the constrained MPP. The rows with $q = 1$ correspond to a monthly return horizon and those with $q = 12$ correspond to an annual horizon. Within each panel, simulation results are reported for asset vectors with 5, 10, and 11 elements, corresponding to the number of SBU, SIZE, and SECTOR assets, respectively.

Table 9.7 shows that when predictability is maximized by combining assets into portfolios, spuriously large R^2's may be obtained. With a monthly horizon and 564 observations, the problem is not severe. For example, when $q = 1$ and $N = 11$, the mean maximal R^2 is 4.3%, a relatively small value. However, at an annual horizon, the problem becomes more serious. With 11

---

[17]We do have some analytical results for this problem, but they rely heavily on the assumption that returns are multivariate normal. Moreover, the exact sampling distribution of R^2 is given by the sum of zonal polynomials which is computationally tractable only for very simple special cases. See Lo and MacKinlay (1992) for further details.

Table 9.7. *Simulated finite-sample distribution of maximum R^2 of MPP of N assets under null hypothesis of no predictability, using six variables as predictors*[a]

q	Mean	S.D.	Min	Max	1%	5%	10%	50%	90%	95%	99%
				(a) Unconstrained portfolio weights							
$N = 5$											
1	0.027	0.008	0.007	0.071	0.012	0.016	0.018	0.026	0.038	0.042	0.050
12	0.317	0.078	0.084	0.669	0.164	0.199	0.221	0.312	0.422	0.452	0.517
$N = 10$											
1	0.043	0.010	0.017	0.095	0.024	0.028	0.031	0.042	0.055	0.060	0.069
12	0.473	0.077	0.232	0.758	0.308	0.350	0.374	0.470	0.573	0.606	0.664
$N = 11$											
1	0.045	0.010	0.020	0.109	0.026	0.031	0.033	0.044	0.058	0.063	0.073
12	0.500	0.075	0.241	0.769	0.332	0.378	0.404	0.498	0.598	0.629	0.681
				(b) Constrained portfolio weights[b]							
$N = 5$											
1	0.023	0.007	0.005	0.069	0.010	0.013	0.014	0.022	0.033	0.037	0.044
12	0.269	0.075	0.068	0.606	0.124	0.157	0.177	0.262	0.369	0.402	0.472
$N = 10$											
1	0.033	0.009	0.013	0.080	0.017	0.021	0.023	0.032	0.044	0.048	0.057
12	0.373	0.079	0.151	0.697	0.124	0.254	0.276	0.368	0.477	0.514	0.577
$N = 11$											
1	0.035	0.009	0.014	0.082	0.019	0.022	0.025	0.034	0.047	0.051	0.060
12	0.391	0.079	0.132	0.751	0.230	0.269	0.292	0.386	0.495	0.529	0.591

[a]For each panel, the simulation consists of 10,000 independent replications of 564 independently and identically distributed Gaussian observations for the monthly horizon ($q = 1$) and 47 observations for the annual horizon ($q = 12$).
[b]Shortsales constrained case with nonnegative weights.

Table 9.8.   *Finite-sample distribution of R^2 of a given portfolio under null hypothesis of no predictability, using six variables as predictors*[a]

q	1%	5%	10%	50%	90%	95%	99%
1	0.002	0.003	0.004	0.010	0.019	0.022	0.030
12	0.021	0.038	0.051	0.120	0.224	0.259	0.330

[a]Distribution is tabulated for 564 independently and identically distributed Gaussian observations for the monthly horizon ($q = 1$) and for 47 observations for the annual horizon ($q = 12$).

assets, the maximal R^2 distribution for the unconstrained case has a mean of 50.0% and a 95% critical value of 62.9% for annual returns. Similar results hold for the constrained case—longer-horizon nonoverlapping returns can yield large R^2's even when there is no predictability.

The effects of data snooping under the null hypothesis can be further quantified by comparing Table 9.7 with Table 9.8, in which the percentiles of the finite-sample distribution of the R^2 for an arbitrary individual asset is reported, also under the null hypothesis of no predictability. For $q = 1$ the differences between the distributions in Table 9.7 and the distributions in Table 9.8 are small—for example, the 95% critical value of an individual asset's R^2 is 2.2%, whereas the corresponding critical value for the unconstrained MPP's R^2 are 3.8%, 5.5%, and 5.7% for 5, 10, and 11 assets, respectively. But again, the effects of data snooping become more pronounced at longer horizons. Using annual returns with 10 assets, the distribution of the unconstrained maximal R^2 has a 95% critical value of 60.6%, whereas Table 9.8 shows that without this maximization, the 95% critical value for the R^2 is only 25.9%. These results emphasize the need to interpret portfolio R^2's with caution, particularly when the construction of the portfolios is determined by the data (see also Lo and MacKinlay, 1990a).

The statistical significance of the empirical results of Section 9.4 can now be assessed by relating the maximum sample R^2's in Table 9.5 to the empirical null distributions in Table 9.7. The result of such an exercise is clear: The statistical significance of predictability decreases as the observation horizon increases. For the monthly horizon the sample R^2's are substantially higher than the 95% critical values, whereas at the annual horizon they are not.

Of course, this finding need not imply the absence of predictability over longer horizons, but may simply be due to the lack of power in detecting predictability via the maximal R^2 for long-horizon returns. After all, since we are using nonoverlapping returns, our sample size for the annual return horizon is only 47 observations, and given the variability of equity returns, it is not surprising that there is little evidence of predictability in annual data.

9.6 Three Out-of-Sample Measures of Predictability

Despite the statistical significance of predictability at monthly, semi-annual, and annual horizons, we are still left with the problem of estimating *genuine* predictability: that portion of the maximal R^2 not due to deliberate data snooping. Although it is virtually impossible to provide such a decomposition without placing strong restrictions on the return- and data-generating processes (see, for example, Lo and MacKinlay, 1990a; Foster et al., 1995), an alternative is to measure the out-of-sample predictability of our MPP. Under the null hypothesis of no predictability, our maximization procedure should not impart any statistical biases out-of-sample, but if there is genuine predictability in the MPP, it should be apparent in out-of-sample forecasts.

We consider three out-of-sample measures of predictability. First, in a regression framework we examine the relation between the forecast error of a naive constant-expected-excess-return model—an unconditional forecast—and a conditional forecast minus the naive forecast, where the conditional forecast is conditioned on the factors of Section 9.4.1. If excess returns are unpredictable, these quantities should be uncorrelated. Second, we employ Merton's (1981) test of market timing to measure how predictable the MPP is in the context of a simple asset allocation rule. Third, we present an illustrative profitability calculation for this simple asset allocation rule to gauge the economic significance of the MPP's predictability.

These three measures yield the same conclusion: Recent U.S. stock returns contain genuine predictability that is both statistically and economically significant.

9.6.1 Naive vs. Conditional Forecasts

Denote by Z_t^* the *excess* return for the MPP in month t (in excess of the one-month risk-free rate):

$$Z_t^* \equiv \hat{\gamma}^{*\prime} \boldsymbol{R}_t - R_{ft}, \qquad (9.6.1)$$

where $\boldsymbol{R}_t$ is the vector of primary asset returns, $\hat{\gamma}^*$ is the estimated MPP weights, and R_{ft} is the one-month Treasury bill rate. A naive one-step-ahead forecast of Z_t^* is the weighted average of the (time series) mean excess return for the past returns of each of the primary assets, an *unconditional* forecast of Z_t^* which we denote by $\hat{Z}_t^a$. Now denote by $\hat{Z}_t^b$ the *conditional* one-step-ahead forecast of Z_t^*, conditioned on the economic variables of Section 9.4.1,

$$\hat{Z}_t^b \equiv \hat{\gamma}^{*\prime} (\tilde{\boldsymbol{Z}}_t + \hat{\boldsymbol{\mu}}) - R_{ft}, \qquad (9.6.2)$$

where we have added back the estimated mean vector $\hat{\boldsymbol{\mu}}$ of the primary assets since $\tilde{\boldsymbol{Z}}_t$ is the conditional forecast of de-meaned returns.

To compare the incremental value of the conditional forecast $\hat{Z}_t^b$ beyond the naive forecast $\hat{Z}_t^a$, we estimate the following regression equation:

$$Z_t^* - \hat{Z}_t^a = \beta_0 + \beta_1(\hat{Z}_t^b - \hat{Z}_t^a) + \epsilon_t. \qquad (9.6.3)$$

If $\hat{Z}_t^b$ has no forecast power beyond the naive forecast $\hat{Z}_t^a$, then the estimated coefficient $\hat{\beta}_1$ should not be statistically different from zero.

To estimate (9.6.3) for each of our three groups of assets, we first estimate the parameters of the conditional factor model (9.4.1) and the MPP weights $\hat{\gamma}^*$ for monthly SBU, SIZE, and SECTOR asset returns using the first 20 years of our sample, from 1947:1 to 1966:12. The one-month-ahead naive and conditional forecasts, $\hat{Z}_t^a$ and $\hat{Z}_t^b$, are then generated month by month beginning in 1967:1 and ending in 1993:12, using a rolling procedure where the earliest observation is dropped as each new observation is added, keeping the rolling sample size fixed at 20 years of monthly observations. Therefore, the conditional-factor model's parameter estimates and the MPP's weights $\hat{\gamma}^*$ are updated monthly.

For the 324-month out-of-sample period from 1967:1 to 1993:12, the ordinary least squares estimates of (9.6.3) for the three groups of assets are reported in Panel (a) of Table 9.9, labeled "monthly:monthly" to emphasize that monthly returns are used to construct the forecast and that monthly returns are being forecasted (see below). For the SBU asset group, the z-statistic of the slope coefficient is 1.47, implying that the power of the one-step-ahead conditional forecast of the MPP return is statistically indistinguishable from that of the naive forecast. However, for both the SIZE and SECTOR groups, the corresponding z-statistics are 3.20 and 3.30, respectively, which suggests that the conditional forecasts do add value in these cases.

To see how the return horizon affects forecast power, we perform a similar analysis for annual returns— we use annual returns to forecast one annual-step ahead. These results are reported in Panel (b) of Table 9.9, labeled "annual:annual." At the annual frequency, conditional forecasts seem to add value for SBU and SIZE assets, but not for SECTOR assets.

Finally, in Panel (c) of Table 9.9, we consider the effect of using annual returns to forecast monthly returns. For example, annual returns are used to forecast one annual-step ahead, but this annual forecast is divided by 12 and is considered the one-month-ahead forecast. This procedure is then repeated in a rolling fashion for each month and the results are reported in Table 9.9's Panel (c) labeled "annual:monthly."[18]

Interestingly, in the mixed return/forecast-horizon case, conditional forecasts add value for all three asset groups, with z-statistics ranging from

---

[18]We have investigated other mixed return/forecast-horizon regressions but, in the interest of brevity, do not report them here.

Table 9.9. *Out-of-sample evaluation of conditional one-step-ahead forecasts of MPP using a regression model with six predictors[a]*

Asset group	Constant	$\hat{Z}^b - \hat{Z}^a$	D.W.[b]	R^2
	(a) Monthly:Monthly[c]			
SBU	−0.01	0.32	1.91	0.013
	(−0.05)	(1.47)		
SIZE	−0.64	0.53	1.83	0.034
	(−1.46)	(3.20)		
SECTOR	−0.35	0.51	1.71	0.035
	(−0.95)	(3.30)		
	(b) Annual:Annual[c]			
SBU	−1.31	0.36	2.13	0.182
	(−0.43)	(2.38)		
SIZE	−1.96	0.25	1.81	0.104
	(−0.46)	(2.39)		
SECTOR	−0.45	0.24	1.62	0.075
	(−0.09)	(1.67)		
	(c) Annual:Monthly[d]			
SBU	−0.35	0.72	1.81	0.052
	(−1.59)	(3.85)		
SIZE	−0.51	0.64	1.75	0.043
	(−1.82)	(3.65)		
SECTOR	−0.22	0.40	1.64	0.013
	(−0.77)	(2.07)		

[a]Conditional forecasts are evaluated by regressing the deviation of the MPP excess return from its unconditional forecast on the deviation of the conditional MPP excess return forecast from the same unconditional forecast (denoted as $\hat{Z}^b - \hat{Z}^a$). Conditional forecasts for the time period 1967:1 to 1993:12 are constructed for three asset groups and for two time horizons. Heteroskedasticity-consistent z-statistics are given in parentheses.
[b]Durbin-Watson test stastic for dependence in the regression residual.
[c]Forecasts are evaluated using a return horizon equal to the forecast horizon.
[d]Annual returns are used to forecast monthly returns.

2.07 (SECTOR assets) to 3.85 (SBU assets). This suggests the possibility that an optimal forecasting procedure may use returns of one frequency to forecast those of another. In particular, we shall see in Section 9.6.3 that within the SBU asset group, the economic significance of predictability is considerably greater when annual returns are used to forecast monthly returns than for the monthly-return-horizon/monthly-forecast-horizon combination.

These out-of-sample forecast regressions suggest that statistically significant forecastability is present in the MPP, but the degree of predictability varies with the asset groups and with the return and forecast horizon.

9.6.2 Merton's Measure of Market Timing

As another measure of the out-of-sample predictability of the MPP, consider the following naive asset-allocation rule: If next month's MPP return is forecasted to exceed the risk-free rate, then invest the entire portfolio in it; otherwise, invest the entire portfolio in Treasury bills. More formally, let θ_t denote the fraction of the portfolio invested in the MPP in month t. Then our naive asset-allocation strategy is given by

$$
\theta_t = \begin{cases} 1 & \text{if } \hat{Z}_t^b > 0 \\ 0 & \text{if } \hat{Z}_t^b \leq 0, \end{cases}
$$

where $\hat{Z}_t^b$, defined in (9.6.2), is the forecasted *excess* return on the MPP, in excess of the risk-free rate.

We can measure the out-of-sample predictability of the MPP by using Merton's (1981) framework for measuring market-timing skills. In particular, if the MPP return Z_t^* were considered the "market," then one could ask whether the asset allocation rule θ_t exhibited positive market-timing performance. Merton (1981) shows that this depends on whether the sum of p_1 and p_2 exceeds unity, where

$$
p_1 = \text{Prob}(\theta_t = 1 \mid Z_t^* > 0), \tag{9.6.4}
$$

$$
p_2 = \text{Prob}(\theta_t = 0 \mid Z_t^* \leq 0). \tag{9.6.5}
$$

These two conditional probabilities are the probabilities that the forecast is correct in "up" and "down" markets, respectively. If $p_1 + p_2$ is greater than 1, then the forecast θ_t has value, i.e., Z_t^* is predictable; otherwise it does not.

To perform the Merton test, we use the same 20-year rolling estimation procedure as in Section 9.6.2 to generate our MPP returns and the one-month-ahead forecast θ_t. From these forecasts and the realized excess returns Z_t^* of the MPP, we construct the following (2×2) contingency table:

$$
\begin{array}{c} \\ \theta_t > 0 \\ \theta_t \leq 0 \end{array} \begin{array}{cc} Z_t^* > 0 & Z_t^* \leq 0 \\ \left[\begin{array}{cc} n_1 & n_2 \\ N_1 - n_1 & N_2 - n_2 \end{array} \right] \end{array}, \tag{9.6.6}
$$

where n_1 is the number of correct forecasts in "up" markets, n_2 is the number of incorrect forecasts in "down" markets, and N_1 and N_2 are the number of up-market and down-market periods, respectively, in the sample. Henriksson and Merton (1981) show that n_1 has a hypergeometric distribution under the null hypothesis of no market-timing ability, which may be

Table 9.10.   Out-of-sample evaluation of conditional one-step-ahead forecasts of MPP using Merton's measure of market timing[a]

Asset group	$Z > 0$ $\hat{Z} > 0$	$Z > 0$ $\hat{Z} \leq 0$	$Z \leq 0$ $\hat{Z} > 0$	$Z \leq 0$ $\hat{Z} \leq 0$	$\hat{p}_1 + \hat{p}_2$	p value
(a) Monthly:Monthly[b]						
SBU	139	92	40	53	1.172	0.001
SIZE	127	107	47	43	1.021	0.349
SECTOR	137	105	43	39	1.042	0.226
(b) Annual:Annual[b]						
SBU	15	4	4	4	1.289	0.048
SIZE	14	5	4	4	1.237	0.092
SECTOR	13	5	6	3	1.056	0.362
(c) Annual:Monthly[c]						
SBU	160	98	29	37	1.181	0.002
SIZE	130	94	49	51	1.090	0.038
SECTOR	144	100	41	39	1.078	0.084

[a]Merton (1981). The number of outcomes are calculated for each of four possible excess return-forecast outcomes: a positive MPP excess return and a positive MPP conditional forecast, a positive excess return and a nonpositive conditional forecast, a nonpositive excess return and a positive conditional forecast, and a nonpositive excess return and a nonpositive conditional forecast. Z denotes the excess return and $\hat{Z}$ denotes the conditional forecast; $\hat{p}_1$ is the sample probability of a positive conditional forecast given a positive excess return and $\hat{p}_2$ is the sample probability of a nonpositive conditional forecast given a nonpositive excess return. The p value is the probability of obtaining at least the number of correct positive conditional forecasts under the null hypothesis of no forecastability. Conditional forecasts for the time period 1967:1 to 1993:12 are constructed for three asset groups and for two time horizons.
[b]Forecasts are evaluated using a return horizon equal to the forecast horizon.
[c]Annual returns are used to forecast monthly returns.

approximated by

$$n_1 \overset{a}{\sim} \mathcal{N}\left(\frac{nN_1}{N}, \ \frac{n_1 N_1 N_2 (N - n)}{N^2 (N - 1)} \right), \tag{9.6.7}$$

where $N \equiv N_1 + N_2$ and $n \equiv n_1 + n_2$.

Using this sampling theory, we perform nonparametric tests for market-timing ability in our one-step-ahead conditional forecasts in Table 9.10 for the same return- and forecast-horizon combinations as in Table 9.9. Table 9.10 reports the number of forecasts in each category of (9.6.6), the estimated sum $\hat{p}_1 + \hat{p}_2$, and the p value based on (9.6.7).

The three panels of Table 9.10 show that predictability is statistically significant for the SBU asset group at both horizons. When annual returns are used to construct monthly forecasts, both SBU and SIZE asset groups have significant predictability. Merton's (1981) market-timing measure also confirms the presence of predictability in the MPP.

9.6.3 The Profitability of Predictability

As a final out-of-sample measure of predictability—one that addresses the economic significance of the MPP's predictability—we compare the total return of a passive or *buy-and-hold* investment in the MPP over the entire sample period with the total return of the active asset allocation strategy described in Section 9.6.2. In particular, for each of the three asset groups, and for the various return and forecast horizons, we calculate the following two quantities:

$$W_T^{\text{Passive}} \equiv \prod_{t=1}^{T}(1 + R_t^*), \tag{9.6.8}$$

$$W_T^{\text{Active}} \equiv \prod_{t=1}^{T}\left[\theta_t(1 + R_t^*) + (1 - \theta_t)(1 + R_{ft})\right], \tag{9.6.9}$$

where θ_t is given in (9.6.4), R_t^* is the simple return of the MPP in month t, and W_T is the end-of-period value of an investment of \$1 over the entire investment period, which we take to be the 324-month period from 1967:1 to 1993:12 to match the empirical results from Sections 9.6.1 and 9.6.2.

Table 9.11 shows that the active asset allocation strategy generally outperforms the passive for each of the three asset groups for all three return/forecast horizon pairs, yielding a higher mean return, a lower standard deviation of return, and a larger total return W_T over the investment period. For example, the monthly passive strategy for the MPP in the SECTOR group of assets has a mean excess return of 0.82% per month and a standard deviation of 6.15% per month, whereas the active strategy has a mean excess return of 1.00% per month and a standard deviation of 5.26% per month. These values imply Sharpe ratios of $\sqrt{12} \times 0.82/6.15 = 0.462$ for the passive SECTOR strategy and $\sqrt{12} \times 1.00/5.26 = 0.659$ for the active SECTOR strategy.

Table 9.11 also shows that the total returns of the active strategy dominate those of the passive for each of the three asset groups and for all return/forecast horizon pairs. A passive \$1 monthly investment in the SECTOR asset group at the beginning of 1967:1 yields a total return of \$46.73 at the end of 1993:12, whereas the corresponding active strategy yields a return of \$99.38.

Of course, the total returns of the active strategy do not include transactions costs, which can be substantial. To determine the importance of such costs, Table 9.11 also reports *break-even* transactions costs, defined as that

Table 9.11. *Out-of-sample evaluation of conditional one-step-ahead forecasts of MPP using a comparison of passive and active investment strategies in the portfolio*[a]

Asset group	Passive strategy			Active strategy				
	Mean excess return (%)	S.D. (%)	Ending value ($)	Mean excess return (%)	S.D. (%)	Ending value ($)[b]	Number of switches[c]	Break-even cost (%)[d]
(a) Monthly:Monthly								
SBU	0.46	3.72	21.21	0.58	3.20	33.15	58	0.77
SIZE	0.76	7.65	28.98	0.96	6.17	75.57	80	1.19
SECTOR	0.82	6.15	46.73	1.00	5.26	99.38	66	1.14
(b) Annual:Annual								
SBU	5.93	17.57	19.44	7.98	14.26	35.70	12	4.94
SIZE	8.77	22.63	30.89	9.72	18.09	48.00	10	4.31
SECTOR	10.33	25.55	40.55	10.99	22.07	58.21	12	2.97
(c) Annual:Monthly								
SBU	0.54	3.93	27.55	0.70	3.53	47.70	30	1.81
SIZE	0.46	5.03	18.01	0.66	4.09	39.14	34	2.26
SECTOR	0.67	4.99	35.01	0.78	4.24	56.30	16	2.93

[a]Conditional forecasts for the time period 1967:1 to 1993:12 are constructed for three asset groups and for two time horizons. The forecasts are evaluated using a return horizon equal to the forecast horizon. For annual forecasts a monthly return horizon is also considered. The active strategies invest 100% in the MPP if the conditional excess return forecast is positive and invest 100% in Treasury bills otherwise.

[b]Terminal value of a $1 investment over entire sample.

[c]Number of times the active strategy shifted into or out of the MPP.

[d]One-way percentage transaction cost that equates the active and passive strategy's ending value.

percentage cost $100 \times s$ of buying or selling the MPP that would equate the active strategy's total return to the passive strategy's. More formally, if the active strategy requires k switches into or out of the MPP over the 324-month investment period, then the one-way break-even transactions cost $100 \times s$ is defined by

$$W_T^{\text{Passive}} = W_T^{\text{Active}} \times (1-s)^k, \tag{9.6.10}$$

$$s = 1 - \left(\frac{W_T^{\text{Passive}}}{W_T^{\text{Active}}} \right)^{1/k}. \tag{9.6.11}$$

For a monthly-return/monthly-forecast horizon, Table 9.11 shows that the number of switches into or out of the MPP ranges from 58 (SBU) to 80 (SIZE), implying two or three switches per year on average. This, in turn, implies that the one-way transactions cost would have to be somewhere between 0.77% (SBU asset group) and 1.19% (SIZE asset group) for the active strategy to yield the same total return as the passive.

At the annual-return/annual-forecast horizon, the number of switches declines by construction, dropping to approximately one switch every 4.5 years, hence the break-even transactions cost increases dramatically. In this case, the one-way transactions cost would have to be somewhere between 2.97% and 4.94% to equate the active and passive strategies' total returns.

Now we cannot conclude from Table 9.11 that the MPP is a market inefficiency that is exploitable by the average investor since we have not formally quantified the (dynamic) risks of the passive and active strategies. Although the active strategy's return has a lower standard deviation and a higher mean, this need not imply that every risk-averse investor would prefer it to the passive strategy. To address this more complex issue, we must specify the investor's preferences and derive his optimal consumption and portfolio rules dynamically, which lies beyond the scope of this chapter. Nevertheless, the three out-of-sample measures do indicate the presence of genuine predictability in the MPP, which is both statistically and economically significant.[19]

9.7 Conclusion

That stock-market prices contain predictable components is now a well-established fact. At issue are the economic sources of predictability in asset returns, since this lies at the heart of several current controversies involving the efficient-markets hypothesis, stock-market rationality, and the existence of "excessively" profitable trading strategies. Our results show that predictable components are indeed present in the stock market, and that

---

[19]See also Breen, Glosten, and Jagannathan (1989, Table IV), who find similar results for monthly equal- and value-weighted NYSE stock index returns.

sophisticated forecasting models based on measures of economic conditions do have predictive power. By studying the MPP, we see that the degree and sources of predictability also vary considerably among assets and over time. Some industries have better predictive power at shorter horizons, whereas others have more power at longer horizons. The changing composition of the MPP points to important differences among groups of securities that warrant further investigation. Nevertheless, predictability is both statistically and economically significant, both in sample and out of sample.

We hasten to emphasize that predictabilities need not be a symptom of market inefficiency. While dynamic investment strategies exploiting predictability have yielded higher returns historically, we have not attempted to adjust for risk or for subtle selection biases that might explain such phenomena. But despite the ambiguity of the economic sources of predictability, our results suggest that ignoring predictability cannot be rational either.

Part III

In Parts I and II we have documented the presence of statistically significant sources of predictability in recent US stock and bond returns. The natural question that follows is whether such predictability is also economically significant, i.e., is it something that investors should consider in formulating their portfolio strategies, or are the effects too small, too short-lived, or too concentrated in illiquid securities to be of any practical value? In other words, is there value left after trading costs have been deducted? This depends, of course, on the magnitude of trading costs, the frequency of trades, and the impact of market conditions on both. These implementation issues naturally revolve around higher-frequency investment horizons—intradaily trading, in contrast to the weekly and monthly horizons of the studies in Parts I and II—and the microstructure of securities markets. This is the focus of Part III.

In Chapter 10 we develop a nonlinear econometric model of transaction price changes—also known as "tick" data—that relates trade-by-trade price changes to trade size, past order flow, bid/offer spreads, elapsed time between trades, and other aspects of market conditions. Using a statistical technique known as *ordered probit*, we are able to accommodate price discreteness (until recently, stock prices moved in minimum increments of 1/8 of a dollar, and currently move in minimum increments of 1/16), an important feature of the data that cannot be ignored, especially for purposes of measuring price impact and trading costs. The ordered probit model allows us to estimate the conditional distribution of price changes, conditional on the regressors, and from this conditional distribution we can develop estimators of market liquidity and price impact while controlling for the effects of order flow, volatility, bid/offer spreads, and general market conditions.

Transaction prices also provide valuable insights into the linkages *between* markets. In particular, in Chapters 11 and 12 we explore the link between the futures market and the cash market for the Standard and Poor's 500 Index. In an efficient market, we would expect the link between the cash and futures

markets to be a strong one. Chapter 11 investigates the properties of the
link by considering both the cash index price and the futures contract price.
We hypothesize that the tightness of the link is maintained by arbitrage
activities, and test this and related hypotheses using transactions data. We
find evidence that futures-price changes are more volatile than spot-price
changes, and this finding is not completely explained by nonsynchronous
trading (see Chapter 4), but is consistent with information being reflected
more quickly in the futures market. Using the cost-of-carry relation, we
examine the time series behavior of the basis, i.e., the difference between
the futures price and the spot price adjusted for the cost of carry. We find
that the basis exhibits greater volatility the longer the time to maturity of
the futures contract and also displays some path dependence. Both of the
findings are consistent with arbitrageurs playing a key role in linking the
spot and futures markets together.

In Chapter 12, we turn to "Black Monday," October 19, 1987. This was
one of the most dramatic trading days in recent stock market history, with
a decline in US stock market prices of more than 20%. During this precipi-
tous decline, demand for trading outstripped the financial system's capacity,
market linkages suffered a breakdown, and pandemonium ensued. This unusual event provides a unique opportunity to study the behavior of prices
in the absence of a tight link between the spot and futures markets, which
can shed considerable light on the importance of such links in general.

In particular, we examine the behavior of individual stocks on October
19 and 20, 1987, and find that on these two days not only was there a
breakdown of the link between the cash index and futures price, but there
was also a breakdown of the link among stocks. Stocks with larger order
imbalances declined more on Monday and rebounded more on Tuesday.
These results suggest that at least part of the decline was not due to economic
factors, but due to the inability of the system to handle the trading volume
and that, with substantially more capacity in place today, the likelihood of a
repeat of October 19, 1987 is reduced.

The studies in Part III underscore the importance of implementation issues in exploiting the research findings of Parts I and II. While predictability
in US stock and bond markets are both statistically and economically significant, an entirely different set of technologies may be required to take
advantage of such predictability, some of which we develop in this last part.

10

An Ordered Probit Analysis
of Transaction Stock Prices

10.1 Introduction

VIRTUALLY ALL EMPIRICAL INVESTIGATIONS of the microstructure of securities markets require a statistical model of asset prices that can capture the
salient features of price movements from one transaction to the next. For
example, because there are several theories of why bid/ask spreads exist,
a stochastic model for prices is a prerequisite to empirically decomposing
observed spreads into components due to order-processing costs, adverse
selection, and specialist market power.[1] The benefits and costs of particular
aspects of a market's microstructure, such as margin requirements, the degree of competition faced by dealers, the frequency that orders are cleared,
and intraday volatility also depend intimately on the particular specification
of price dynamics.[2] Even the event study, a tool that does not explicitly
assume any particular theory of the market microstructure, depends heavily
on price dynamics (see, for example, Barclay and Litzenberger (1988)). In
fact, it is difficult to imagine an economically relevant feature of transaction
prices and the market microstructure that does *not* hinge on such price
dynamics.

Since stock prices are perhaps the most closely watched economic variables to date, they have been modeled by many competing specifications,
beginning with the simple random walk or Brownian motion. However, the
majority of these specifications have been unable to capture at least three
aspects of *transaction* prices. First, on most U.S. stock exchanges, prices
are quoted in increments of eighths of a dollar, a feature not captured by

---

[1] See, for example, Glosten and Harris (1988), Hasbrouck (1988), Roll (1984a), and Stoll
(1989).
[2] See Cohen et al. (1986), Harris, Sofianos, and Shapiro (1994), Hasbrouck (1991a, 1991b),
Madhavan and Smidt (1991), and Stoll and Whaley (1990).

stochastic processes with continuous state spaces. Of course, discreteness is less problematic for coarser-sampled data, which may be well-approximated by a continuous-state process. But discreteness is of paramount importance for intraday price movements, since such finely-sampled price changes may take on only five or six distinct values.[3]

The second distinguishing feature of transaction prices is their timing, which is irregular and random. Therefore, such prices may be modeled by discrete-time processes only if we are prepared to ignore the information contained in waiting times between trades.

Finally, although many studies have computed correlations between transaction price changes and other economic variables, to date none of the existing models of discrete transaction prices have been able to quantify such effects formally. Such models have focused primarily on the *unconditional* distribution of price changes, whereas what is more often of economic interest is the *conditional* distribution, conditioned on quantities such as volume, time between trades, and the *sequence* of past price changes.[4] For example, one of the unresolved empirical issues in this literature is what the total costs of immediate execution are, which many take to be a measure of market liquidity. Indeed, the largest component of these costs may be the price impact of large trades. A floor broker seeking to unload 100,000 shares of stock will generally break up the sale into smaller blocks to minimize the price impact of the trades. How do we measure price impact? Such a question is a question about the conditional distribution of price changes, conditional upon a particular sequence of volume and price changes, i.e., order flow.

In this chapter, we propose a specification of transaction price changes that addresses all three of these issues, and yet is still tractable enough to permit estimation via standard techniques. This specification is known as *ordered probit*, a technique used most frequently in cross-sectional studies of dependent variables that take on only a finite number of values possessing a natural ordering.[5] For example, the dependent variable might be the level of education, as measured by three categories: less than high school, high school, and college education. The dependent variable is discrete, and is naturally ordered since college education always follows high school (see Maddala

---

[3]The implications of discreteness have been considered in many studies, e.g., Cho and Frees (1988), Gottlieb and Kalay (1985), Harris (1989a, 1991), Petersen (1986), and Pritsker (1990).

[4]There is, however, a substantial literature on price/volume relations in which discreteness is ignored because of the return horizons involved (usually daily or longer). See, for example, Campbell, Grossman, and Wang (1991), Gallant, Rossi, and Tauchen (1992), and Karpoff (1987).

[5]The ordered probit model was developed by Aitchison and Silvey (1957) and Ashford (1959), and generalized to nonnormal disturbances by Gurland, Lee, and Dahm (1960). For more recent extensions, see Maddala (1983), McCullagh (1980), and Thisted (1991).

(1983) for further details). Heuristically, ordered probit analysis is a generalization of the linear regression model to cases where the dependent variable is discrete. As such, among the existing models of stock price discreteness (e.g., Ball (1988), Cho and Frees (1988), Gottlieb and Kalay (1985), and Harris (1991)), ordered probit is perhaps the only specification that can easily capture the impact of "explanatory" variables on price changes while also accounting for price discreteness and irregular trade times.

Underlying the analysis is a "virtual" regression model with an unobserved continuous dependent variable Z^* whose conditional mean is a linear function of observed "explanatory" variables. Although Z^* is unobserved, it is related to an observable discrete random variable Z, whose realizations are determined by where Z^* lies in its domain or state space. By partitioning the state space into a finite number of distinct regions, Z may be viewed as an indicator function for Z^* over these regions. For example, a discrete random variable Z taking on the values $\{-\frac{1}{8}, 0, \frac{1}{8}\}$ may be modeled as an indicator variable that takes on the value $-\frac{1}{8}$ whenever $Z^* \le \alpha_1$, the value 0 whenever $\alpha_1 < Z^* \le \alpha_2$, and the value $\frac{1}{8}$ whenever $Z^* > \alpha_2$. Ordered probit analysis consists of estimating α_1, α_2, and the coefficients of the unobserved regression model that determines the conditional mean and variance of Z^*.

Since α_1, α_2, and Z^* may depend on a vector of "regressors" X, ordered probit analysis is considerably more general than its simple structure suggests. In fact, it is well-known that ordered probit can fit any arbitrary multinomial distribution. However, because of the underlying linear regression framework, ordered probit can also capture the price effects of many economic variables in a way that models of the unconditional distribution of price changes cannot.

To motivate our methodology and to focus it on specific market microstructure applications, we consider three questions concerning the behavior of transaction prices. First, how does the particular sequence of trades affect the conditional distribution of price changes, and how do these effects differ across stocks? For example, does a sequence of three consecutive buyer-initiated trades ("buys") generate price pressure, so that the next price change is more likely to be positive than if the sequence were three consecutive seller-initiated trades ("sells"), and how does this pressure change from stock to stock? Second, does trade size affect price changes as some theories suggest, and if so, what is the price impact per unit volume of trade from one transaction to the next? Third, does price discreteness matter? In particular, can the conditional distribution of price changes be modeled as a simple linear regression of price changes on explanatory variables without accounting for discreteness at all? Within the context of the ordered probit framework, we shall obtain sharp answers to each of these questions.

In Section 10.2, we review the ordered probit model and describe its estimation via maximum likelihood. We describe the data in Section 10.3

by presenting detailed summary statistics for an initial sample of six stocks. In Section 10.4, we discuss the empirical specification of the ordered probit model and the selection of conditioning or "explanatory" variables. The maximum likelihood estimates for our initial sample are reported in Section 10.5, along with some diagnostic specification tests. In Section 10.6, we use these maximum likelihood estimates in three specific applications: (1) testing for order-flow dependence, (2) measuring price impact, and (3) comparing ordered probit to simple linear regression. And as a check on the robustness of our findings, in Section 10.7 we present less detailed results for a larger and randomly chosen sample of 100 stocks. We conclude in Section 10.8.

10.2 The Ordered Probit Model

Consider a sequence of transaction prices $P(t_0), P(t_1), P(t_2), \ldots, P(t_n)$ observed at times $t_0, t_1, t_2, \ldots, t_n$, and denote by $Z_1, Z_2, \ldots, Z_n$ the corresponding price changes, where $Z_k \equiv P(t_k) - P(t_{k-1})$ is assumed to be an integer multiple of some divisor called a "tick" (such as an eighth of a dollar). Let Z_k^* denote an unobservable continuous random variable such that

$$Z_k^* = X_k'\beta + \epsilon_k, \quad \mathrm{E}[\epsilon_k \mid X_k] = 0, \quad \epsilon_k \text{ i.n.i.d. } \mathcal{N}(0, \sigma_k^2) \qquad (10.2.1)$$

where "i.n.i.d." indicates that the ϵ_k's are independently but *not* identically distributed, and X_k is a $q \times 1$ vector of predetermined variables that governs the conditional mean of Z_k^*. Note that subscripts are used to denote "transaction" time, whereas time arguments t_k denote calendar or "clock" time, a convention we shall follow throughout the chapter.

The essence of the ordered probit model is the assumption that observed price changes Z_k are related to the continuous variable Z_k^* in the following manner:

$$Z_k = \begin{cases} s_1 & \text{if} \quad Z_k^* \in A_1, \\ s_2 & \text{if} \quad Z_k^* \in A_2, \\ \vdots & \vdots \\ s_m & \text{if} \quad Z_k^* \in A_m, \end{cases} \qquad (10.2.2)$$

where the sets A_j form a *partition* of the state space $\mathcal{S}^*$ of Z_k^*, i.e., $\mathcal{S}^* = \bigcup_{j=1}^m A_j$ and $A_i \cap A_j = \varnothing$ for $i \neq j$, and the s_j's are the discrete values that comprise the state space $\mathcal{S}$ of Z_k.

The motivation for the ordered probit specification is to uncover the mapping between $\mathcal{S}^*$ and $\mathcal{S}$ and relate it to a set of economic variables or "regressors." In our current application, the s_j's are $0, -\frac{1}{8}, +\frac{1}{8}, -\frac{2}{8}, +\frac{2}{8}$, and so on, and for simplicity we define the state-space partition of $\mathcal{S}^*$ to be intervals:

$$A_1 \equiv (-\infty, \alpha_1], \qquad\qquad (10.2.3)$$

$$A_2 \equiv (\alpha_1, \alpha_2], \qquad\qquad (10.2.4)$$

$$\vdots$$

$$A_i \equiv (\alpha_{i-1}, \alpha_i], \qquad\qquad (10.2.5)$$

$$\vdots$$

$$A_m \equiv (\alpha_{m-1}, \infty). \qquad\qquad (10.2.6)$$

Although the observed price change can be any number of ticks, positive or negative, we assume that m in (10.2.2) is finite to keep the number of unknown parameters finite. This poses no problems, since we may always let some states in $\mathcal{S}$ represent a multiple (and possibly countably infinite) number of values for the observed price change. For example, in our empirical application we define s_1 to be a price change of -4 ticks *or less*, s_9 to be a price change of $+4$ ticks *or more*, and s_2 to s_8 to be price changes of -3 ticks to $+3$ ticks respectively. This parsimony is obtained at the cost of losing *price resolution*—under this specification the ordered probit model does not distinguish between price changes of $+4$ and price changes greater than $+4$ (since the $+4$-tick outcome and the greater than $+4$-tick outcome have been grouped together into a common event), and similarly for price changes of -4 ticks versus price changes less than -4. Of course, in principle the resolution may be made arbitrarily finer by simply introducing more states, i.e., by increasing m. Moreover, as long as (10.2.1) is correctly specified, then increasing price resolution will not affect the estimated β's asymptotically (although finite sample properties may differ). However, in practice the data will impose a limit on the fineness of price resolution simply because there will be no observations in the extreme states when m is too large, in which case a subset of the parameters is not identified and cannot be estimated.

Observe that the ϵ_k's in (10.2.1) are assumed to be conditionally independently but *not* identically distributed, conditioned on the X_k's and other economic variables W_k influencing the conditional variance σ_k^2.[6] This allows for clock-time effects, as in the case of an arithmetic Brownian motion where the variance σ_k^2 of price changes is linear in the time between trades. We also allow for more general forms of conditional heteroskedasticity by letting σ_k^2 depend linearly on other economic variables W_k, which differs

---

[6]Unless explicitly stated otherwise, all the probabilities we deal with in this study are conditional probabilities, and all statements concerning these probabilities are conditional statements, conditioned on these variables.

from Engle's (1982) ARCH process only in its application to a discrete dependent variable model requiring an additional identification assumption that we shall discuss below in Section 10.4.

The dependence structure of the observed process Z_k is clearly induced by that of Z_k^* and the definitions of the A_j's, since

$$P(Z_k = s_j \mid Z_{k-1} = s_i) = P(Z_k^* \in A_j \mid Z_{k-1}^* \in A_i). \qquad (10.2.7)$$

As a consequence, if the variables X_k and W_k are temporally independent, the observed process Z_k is also temporally independent. Of course, these are fairly restrictive assumptions and are certainly not necessary for any of the statistical inferences that follow. We require only that the ϵ_k's be *conditionally* independent, so that all serial dependence is captured by the X_k's and the W_k's. Consequently, the independence of the ϵ_k's does not imply that the Z_k^*'s are independently distributed because we have placed no restrictions on the temporal dependence of the X_k's or W_k's.

The conditional distribution of observed price changes Z_k, conditioned on X_k and W_k, is determined by the partition boundaries and the particular distribution of ϵ_k. For Gaussian ϵ_k's, the conditional distribution is

$$P(Z_k = s_i \mid X_k, W_k)$$

$$= P(X_k'\beta + \epsilon_k \in A_i \mid X_k, W_k) \qquad (10.2.8)$$

$$= \begin{cases} P(X_k'\beta + \epsilon_k \leq \alpha_1 \mid X_k, W_k) & \text{if } i = 1, \\ P(\alpha_{i-1} < X_k'\beta + \epsilon_k \leq \alpha_i \mid X_k, W_k) & \text{if } 1 < i < m, \\ P(\alpha_{m-1} < X_k'\beta + \epsilon_k \mid X_k, W_k) & \text{if } i = m, \end{cases} \qquad (10.2.9)$$

$$= \begin{cases} \Phi\left(\frac{\alpha_1 - X_k'\beta}{\sigma_k}\right) & \text{if } i = 1 \\ \Phi\left(\frac{\alpha_i - X_k'\beta}{\sigma_k}\right) - \Phi\left(\frac{\alpha_{i-1} - X_k'\beta}{\sigma_k}\right) & \text{if } 1 < i < m \\ 1 - \Phi\left(\frac{\alpha_{m-1} - X_k'\beta}{\sigma_k}\right) & \text{if } i = m, \end{cases} \qquad (10.2.10)$$

where $\Phi(\cdot)$ is the standard normal cumulative distribution function.

To develop some intuition for the ordered probit model, observe that the probability of any particular observed price change is determined by where the conditional mean lies relative to the partition boundaries. Therefore, for a given conditional mean $X_k'\beta$, shifting the boundaries will alter the probabilities of observing each state (see Figure 10.1). In fact, by shifting the boundaries appropriately, ordered probit can fit any arbitrary multinomial distribution. This implies that the assumption of normality underlying ordered probit plays no special role in determining the probabilities of states; a logistic distribution, for example, could have served equally well.

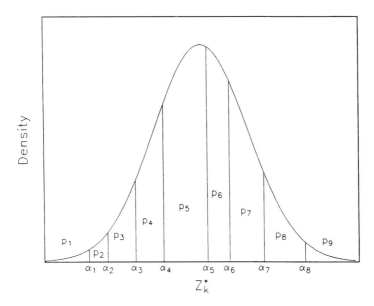

Figure 10.1. *Illustration of ordered probit probabilities p_i of observing a price change of s_i ticks, which are determined by where the unobservable "virtual" price change Z_k^* falls. In particular, if Z_k^* falls in the interval $(\alpha_{i-1}, \alpha_i]$, then the ordered probit model implies that the observed price change Z_k is s_i ticks. More formally, $p_i \equiv \mathrm{Prob}(Z_k = s_i \mid X_k, W_k) = \mathrm{Prob}(\alpha_{i-1} < Z_k^* \leq \alpha_i \mid X_k, W_k)$, $i = 1, \ldots, 9$, where, for notational simplicity, we define $\alpha_0 = -\infty$ and $\alpha_9 \equiv +\infty$. The ordered probit model captures the effect of economic variables X_k, W_k on the virtual price change and places enough structure on the probabilities p_i to permit their estimation by maximum likelihood.*

However, since it is considerably more difficult to capture conditional heteroskedasticity in the ordered logit model, we have chosen the Gaussian specification.

Given the partition boundaries, a higher conditional mean $X_k'\beta$ implies a higher probability of observing a more extreme positive state. Of course, the labeling of states is arbitrary, but the *ordered* probit model makes use of the natural ordering of the states. The regressors allow us to separate the effects of various economic factors that influence the likelihood of one state versus another. For example, suppose that a large positive value of X_1 usually implies a large negative observed price change and vice versa. Then the ordered probit coefficient β_1 will be negative in sign and large in magnitude (relative to σ_k of course).

By allowing the data to determine the partition boundaries α, the coefficients β of the conditional mean, and the conditional variance σ_k^2, the ordered probit model captures the empirical relation between the unobservable continuous state space $\mathcal{S}^*$ and the observed discrete state space $\mathcal{S}$ as a function of the economic variables X_k and W_k.

10.2.1 Other Models of Discreteness

From these observations, it is apparent that the rounding/eighths-barriers models of discreteness in Ball (1988), Cho and Frees (1988), Gottlieb and Kalay (1985) and Harris (1991) may be reparametrized as ordered probit models. Consider first the case of a "true" price process that is an arithmetic Brownian motion, with trades occurring only when this continuous-state process crosses an eighths threshold (see Cho and Frees (1988)). Observed trades from such a process may be generated by an ordered probit model in which the partition boundaries are fixed at multiples of eighths and the single regressor is the time interval (or first-passage time) between crossings, appearing in both the conditional mean and variance of Z_k^*.

To obtain the rounding models of Ball (1988), Gottlieb and Kalay (1985), and Harris (1991), which do not make use of waiting times between trades, define the partition boundaries as the midpoint between eighths, e.g., the observed price change is $\frac{3}{8}$ if the virtual price process lies in the interval $[\frac{5}{16}, \frac{7}{16})$, and omit the waiting time as a regressor in both the conditional mean and variance (see the discussion in Section 10.6.3 below).

The generality of the ordered probit model comes from the fact that the rounding and eighths-barrier models of discreteness are both special cases of ordered probit under appropriate restrictions on the partition boundaries. In fact, since the boundaries may be parametrized to be time- and state-dependent, ordered probit can allow for considerably more general kinds of rounding and eighths barriers. In addition to fitting any arbitrary multinomial distribution, ordered probit may also accommodate finite-state Markov chains and compound Poisson processes.

Of course, other models of discreteness are not necessarily obsolete, since in several cases the parameters of interest may not be simple functions of the ordered probit parameters. For example, a tedious calculation will show that although Harris's (1991) rounding model may be represented as an ordered probit model, the bid/ask spread parameter c is not easily recoverable from the ordered probit parameters. In such cases, other equivalent specifications may allow more direct estimation of the parameters of interest.

10.2.2 The Likelihood Function

Let Y_{ik} be an indicator variable which takes on the value one if the realization of the kth observation Z_k is the ith state s_i, and zero otherwise. Then the log-likelihood function $\mathcal{L}$ for the vector of price changes $Z = [Z_1\, Z_2 \cdots Z_n]'$, conditional on the explanatory variables $X = [X_1 \ X_2 \cdots X_n]'$, is given by

$$
\mathcal{L}(Z \mid X) = \sum_{k=1}^{n} \left\{ Y_{1k} \cdot \log \Phi \left(\frac{\alpha_1 - X_k'\beta}{\sigma_k} \right) \right.
$$

$$
+ \sum_{i=2}^{m-1} Y_{ik} \cdot \log \left[\Phi \left(\frac{\alpha_i - X_k'\beta}{\sigma_k} \right) - \Phi \left(\frac{\alpha_{i-1} - X_k'\beta}{\sigma_k} \right) \right]
$$

$$
\left. + Y_{mk} \cdot \log \left[1 - \Phi \left(\frac{\alpha_{m-1} - X_k'\beta}{\sigma_k} \right) \right] \right\}. \quad (10.2.11)
$$

Recall that σ_k^2 is a conditional variance, conditioned upon X_k. This allows for conditional heteroskedasticity in the Z_k^*'s, as in the rounding model of Cho and Frees (1988) where the Z_k^*'s are increments of arithmetic Brownian motion with variance proportional to $t_k - t_{k-1}$. In fact, arithmetic Brownian motion may be accommodated explicitly by the specification

$$
X_k'\beta = \mu \Delta t_k, \quad (10.2.12)
$$
$$
\sigma_k^2 = \gamma^2 \Delta t_k. \quad (10.2.13)
$$

More generally, we may also let σ_k^2 depend on other economic variables W_k, so that

$$
\sigma_k^2 = \gamma_0^2 + \sum_{i=1}^{K_\sigma} \gamma_i^2 \, W_{ik}. \quad (10.2.14)
$$

There are, however, some constraints that must be placed on these parameters to achieve identification since, for example, doubling the α's, the β's, and σ_k leaves the likelihood unchanged. We shall return to this issue in Section 10.4.

10.3 The Data

The Institute for the Study of Securities Markets (ISSM) transaction database consists of time-stamped trades (to the nearest second), trade size, and bid/ask quotes from the New York and American Stock Exchanges and the consolidated regional exchanges from January 4 to December 30 of 1988. Because of the sheer size of the ISSM database, most empirical studies of the market microstructure have concentrated on more manageable subsets of the database, and we also follow this practice. But because there is so much data, the "pretest" or "data-snooping" biases associated with any non-random selection procedure used to obtain the smaller subsets are likely to be substantial. As a simple example of such a bias, suppose we choose our stocks by the seemingly innocuous requirement that they have a minimum of 100,000 trades in 1988. This rule will impart a substantial downward bias on our measures of price impact because stocks with over 100,000 trades per year are generally more liquid and, almost by definition, have smaller price impact. Therefore, how we choose our subsample of stocks may have important consequences for how our results are to be interpreted, so we shall describe our procedure in some detail here.

We first begin with an initial "test" sample containing five stocks that did not engage in any stock splits or stock dividends greater than 3 : 2 during 1988: Alcoa, Allied Signal, Boeing, DuPont, and General Motors. We restrict splits because the effects of price discreteness to be captured by our model are likely to change in important ways with dramatic shifts in the price level; by eliminating large splits we reduce the problem of large changes in the price level without screening on prices directly. (Of course, if we were interested in explaining stock splits, this procedure would obviously impart important biases in the empirical results.) We also chose these five stocks because they are relatively large and visible companies, each with a large number of trades, and therefore likely to yield accurate parameter estimates. We then performed the standard "specification searches" on these five stocks, adding, deleting, and transforming regressors to obtain a "reasonable" fit. By "reasonable" we mean primarily the convergence of the maximum likelihood estimation procedure, but it must also include Leamer's (1978) kind of informal or *ad hoc* inferences that all empiricists engage in.

Once we obtain a specification that is "reasonable," we estimate it *without further revision* for our primary sample of six new stocks, chosen to yield a representative sample with respect to industries, market value, price levels, and sample sizes. They are International Business Machines Corporation (IBM), Quantum Chemical Corporation (CUE), Foster Wheeler Corporation (FWC), Handy and Harman Company (HNH), Navistar International Corporation (NAV), and American Telephone and Telegraph Incorporated (T). (Our original primary sample consists of eleven stocks but we omitted the results for five of them to conserve space. See Hausman, Lo, and MacKinlay (1991) for the full set of results.) By using the specification derived from the test sample on stocks in this fresh sample, we seek to lessen the impact of any data-snooping biases generated by our specification searches. If, for example, our parameter estimates and subsequent inferences change dramatically in the new sample (in fact, they do not) this might be a sign that our test-sample findings were driven primarily by selection biases.

As a final check on the robustness of our specification, we estimate it for a larger sample of 100 stocks chosen randomly, and these companies are listed in Table 10.5. From this larger sample, it is apparent that our smaller six-stock sample does suffer from at least one selection bias: it is comprised of relatively well-known companies. In contrast, relatively few companies in Table 10.5 are as familiar. Despite this bias, virtually all of our empirical findings are confirmed by the larger sample. To conserve space and to focus attention on our findings, we report the complete set of summary statistics and estimation results only for the smaller sample of six stocks, and present broader and less detailed findings for the extended sample afterwards.

Of course, as long as there is cross-sectional dependence among the two samples it is impossible to eliminate such biases completely. Moreover, samples drawn from a different time period are not necessarily free from selection bias as some have suggested, due to the presence of *temporal* dependence. Unfortunately, nonexperimental inference is always subject to selection biases of one kind or another since specification searches are an unavoidable aspect of genuine progress in empirical research (see, for example, Lo and MacKinlay (1990b)). Even Bayesian inference, which is not as sensitive to the kinds of selection biases discussed in Leamer (1978), can be distorted in subtle ways by specification searches. Therefore, beyond our test-sample procedure, we can only alert readers to the possibility of such biases and allow them to adjust their own inferences accordingly.

10.3.1 Sample Statistics

We take as our basic time series the *intraday* price changes from trade to trade, and discard all overnight price changes. That the statistical properties of overnight price changes differ considerably from those of intraday price changes has been convincingly documented by several authors, most recently by Amihud and Mendelson (1987), Stoll and Whaley (1990), and Wood, McInish, and Ord (1985). Since the three market microstructure applications we are focusing on involve intraday price behavior, and overnight price changes are different enough to warrant a separate specification, we use only intraday price changes. The first and last transaction prices of each day are also discarded, since they differ systematically from other prices due to institutional features (see Amihud and Mendelson (1987) for further details).

Several other screens were imposed to eliminate "problem" trades and quotes, yielding sample sizes ranging from 3,174 trades for HNH to 206,794 trades for IBM. Specifically: (1) all trades flagged with the following ISSM condition codes were eliminated: A, C, D, O, R, and Z (see the ISSM documentation for further details concerning trade condition codes); (2) transactions exceeding 3,276,000 shares [termed "big trades" by ISSM] were also eliminated; (3) because we use three lags of price changes and three lags of five-minute returns on the S&P 500 index futures prices as explanatory variables, we do not use the first three price changes or price changes during the first 15 minutes of each day (whichever occurs later) as observations of the dependent variable; and (4) since S&P 500 futures data were not available on November 10, 11, and the first two trading hours of May 3, trades during these times were also omitted.

For some stocks, a small number of transactions occurred at prices denominated in $\frac{1}{16}$'s, $\frac{1}{32}$'s, or $\frac{1}{64}$'s of a dollar (non-NYSE trades). In these cases, we rounded the price randomly (up or down) to the nearest $\frac{1}{8}$, and if necessary, also rounded the bid/ask quotes in the same direction.

Quotes implying bid/ask spreads greater than 40 ticks or flagged with the following ISSM condition codes were also eliminated: C, D, F, G, I, L, N, P, S, V, X, and Z (essentially all "BBO-ineligible" quotes; see the ISSM documentation for further details concerning the definitions of the particular trade and quote condition codes, and Eikeboom (1992) for a thorough study of the relative frequencies of these condition codes for a small subset of the ISSM database).

Since we also use bid and ask prices in our analysis, some discussion of how we matched quotes to prices is necessary. Bid/ask quotes are reported on the ISSM tape only when they are revised, hence it is natural to match each transaction price to the most recently reported quote *prior* to the transaction. However, Bronfman (1991), Lee and Ready (1991), and others have shown that prices of trades that precipitate quote revisions are sometimes reported with a lag, so that the order of quote revision and transaction price is reversed in official records such as the ISSM tapes. To address this issue, we match transaction prices to quotes that are set *at least five seconds prior* to the transaction; the evidence in Lee and Ready (1991) suggests that this will account for most of the missequencing.

To provide some intuition for this enormous dataset, we report a few summary statistics in Table 10.1. Our sample contains considerable price dispersion, with the low stock price ranging from $3.125 for NAV to $104.250 for IBM, and the high ranging from $7.875 for NAV to $129.500 for IBM. At $219 million, HNH has the smallest market capitalization in our sample, and IBM has the largest with a market value of $69.8 billion.

For our empirical analysis we also require some indicator of whether a transaction was buyer-initiated or seller-initiated. Obviously, this is a difficult task because for every trade there is always a buyer and a seller. What we are attempting to measure is which of the two parties is more anxious to consummate the trade and is therefore willing to pay for it in the form of the bid/ask spread. Perhaps the most obvious indicator is whether the transaction occurs at the ask price or at the bid price; if it is the former then the transaction is most likely a "buy," and if it is the latter then the transaction is most likely a "sell." Unfortunately, a large number of transactions occur at prices strictly *within* the bid/ask spread, so that this method for signing trades will leave the majority of trades indeterminate.

Following Blume, MacKinlay, and Terker (1989) and many others, we classify a transaction as a buy if the transaction price is higher than the mean of the prevailing bid/ask quote (the most recent quote that is set at

Table 10.1. *Summary statistics for transaction prices and corresponding ordered probit explanatory variables of International Business Machines Corporation (IBM – 206,794 trades), Quantum Chemical Corporation (CUE – 26,927 trades), Foster Wheeler Corporation (FWC – 18,199 trades), Handy and Harman Company (HNH – 3,174 trades), Navistar International Corporation (NAV – 96,127 trades), and American Telephone and Telegraph Company (T – 180,726 trades), for the period from January 4, 1988, to December 30, 1988.*

Statistic	IBM	CUE	FWC	HNH	NAV	T
Low Price	104.250	65.500	11.500	14.250	3.125	24.125
High Price	129.500	108.250	17.250	18.500	7.875	30.375
Market Value ($Billions)[1]	69.815	2.167	0.479	0.219	0.998	28.990
% Trades at Prices:						
> Midquote	43.81	43.19	37.13	22.53	40.80	32.37
= Midquote	12.66	18.67	23.58	26.28	18.11	25.92
< Midquote	43.53	38.14	39.29	51.20	41.09	41.71
Price Change, Z_k						
Mean:	−0.0010	0.0016	−0.0017	−0.0028	−0.0002	0.0001
SD:	0.7530	1.2353	0.6390	0.7492	0.6445	0.6540
Time Between Trades, Δt_k						
Mean:	27.21	203.52	296.54	1129.37	58.36	31.00
SD:	34.13	282.16	416.49	1497.44	76.53	34.39
Bid/Ask Spread, AB_k						
Mean:	1.9470	3.2909	2.0830	2.4707	1.4616	1.6564
SD:	1.4625	1.6203	1.1682	0.8994	0.6713	0.7936
SP500 Futures Return, $S\&P500_k$[2]						
Mean:	−0.0000	−0.0004	−0.0017	−0.0064	0.0001	−0.0001
SD:	0.0716	0.1387	0.1475	0.1963	0.1038	0.0765
Buy/Sell Indicator, IBS_k[3]						
Mean:	0.0028	0.0505	−0.0216	−0.2867	−0.0028	−0.0933
SD:	0.9346	0.9005	0.8739	0.8095	0.9049	0.8556
Signed Transformed Volume[4]						
Mean:	0.1059	0.3574	−0.0523	−1.9543	0.0332	−0.4256
SD:	6.1474	5.6643	6.2798	6.0890	6.9705	7.5846
Median Trading Volume ($)	57,375	40,900	6,150	5,363	3,000	7,950

[1] Computed at the beginning of the sample period.

[2] Five-minute continuously compounded returns of the S&P 500 index futures price, for the contract maturing in the closest month beyond the month in which transaction k occurred, where the return corresponding to the kth transaction is computed with the futures price recorded one minute before the nearest round minute *prior* to t_k and the price recorded five minutes before this.

[3] Takes the value 1 if the kth transaction price is greater than the average of the quoted bid and ask prices at time t_k, the value −1 if the kth transaction price is less than the average of the quoted bid and ask prices at time t_k, and 0 otherwise.

[4] Box-Cox transformation of dollar volume multiplied by the buy/sell indicator, where the Box-Cox parameter λ is estimated jointly with the other ordered probit parameters via maximum likelihood. The Box-Cox parameter λ determines the degree of curvature that the transformation $T_\lambda(\cdot)$ exhibits in transforming dollar volume V_k before inclusion as an explanatory variable in the ordered probit specification. If $\lambda = 1$, the transformation $T_\lambda(\cdot)$ is linear, hence dollar volume enters the ordered probit model linearly. If $\lambda = 0$, the transformation is equivalent to $\log(\cdot)$, hence the natural logarithm of dollar volume enters the ordered probit model. When λ is between 0 and 1, the curvature of $T_\lambda(\cdot)$ is between logarithmic and linear.

least five seconds prior to the trade), and classify it as a sell if the price is lower. Should the price equal the mean of the prevailing bid/ask quote, we classify the trade as an "indeterminate" trade. This method yields far fewer indeterminate trades than classifying according to transactions at the bid or at the ask.

Unfortunately, little is known about the relative merits of this method of classification versus others such as the "tick test" (which classifies a transaction as a buy, a sell, or indeterminate if its price is greater than, less than, or equal to the previous transaction's price, respectively), simply because it is virtually impossible to obtain the data necessary to evaluate these alternatives. The only study we have seen is by Robinson (1988, Chapter 4.4.1, Table 19), in which he compared the tick test rule to the bid/ask mean rule for a sample of 196 block trades initiated by two major Canadian life insurance companies, and concluded that the bid/ask mean rule was considerably more accurate.

From Table 10.1 we see that 13–26% of each stock's transactions are indeterminate, and the remaining trades fall almost equally into the two remaining categories. The one exception is the smallest stock, HNH, which has more than twice as many sells as buys.

The means and standard deviations of other variables to be used in our ordered probit analysis are also given in Table 10.1. The precise definitions of these variables will be given below in Section 10.4, but briefly, Z_k is the price change between transactions $k - 1$ and k, Δt_k is the time elapsed between these trades, AB_k is the bid/ask spread prevailing at transaction k, $SP500_k$ is the return on the S&P 500 index futures price over the five-minute period immediately preceding transaction k, IBS_k is the buy/sell indicator described above (1 for a buy, -1 for a sell, and 0 for an indeterminate trade), and $T_\lambda(V_k)$ is a transformation of the dollar volume of transaction k, transformed according to the Box and Cox (1964) specification with parameter λ_i which is estimated for each stock i by maximum likelihood along with the other ordered probit parameters.

From Table 10.1 we see that for the larger stocks, trades tend to occur almost every minute on average. Of course, the smaller stocks trade less frequently, with HNH trading only once every 18 minutes on average. The median dollar volume per trade also varies considerably, ranging from $3,000 for relatively low-priced NAV to $57,375 for higher-priced IBM.

Finally, Figure 10.2 contains histograms for the price change, time-between-trade, and dollar volume variables for the six stocks. The histograms of price changes are constructed so that the most extreme cells also include observations *beyond* them, i.e., the level of the histogram for the -4 tick cell reflects all price changes of -4 ticks *or less*, and similarly for the $+4$ ticks cell. Surprisingly, these price histograms are remarkably symmetric across all stocks. Also, virtually all the mass in each histogram is concentrated in five or seven cells—there are few absolute price changes

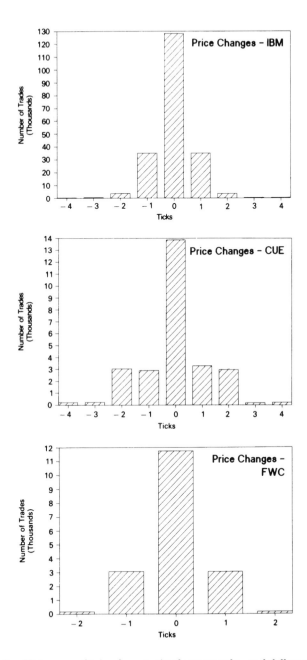

Figure 10.2.   *Histograms of price changes, time-between-trades, and dollar volume of International Business Machines Corporation (IBM – 206,794 trades), Quantum Chemical Corporation (CUE – 26,927 trades), Foster Wheeler Corporation (FWC – 18,199 trades), Handy and Harman Company (HNH – 3,174 trades), Navistar International Corporation (NAV – 96,127 trades), and American Telephone and Telegraph Company (T – 180,726 trades), for the period from January 4, 1988, to December 30, 1988.*

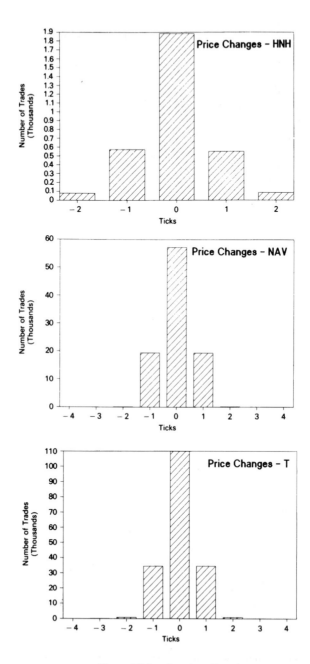

Figure 10.2.   *(continued)*

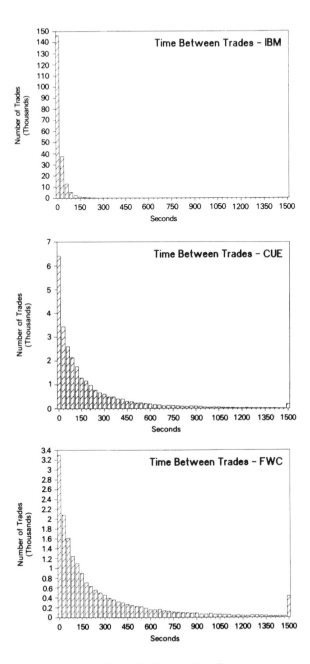

Figure 10.2. *(continued)*

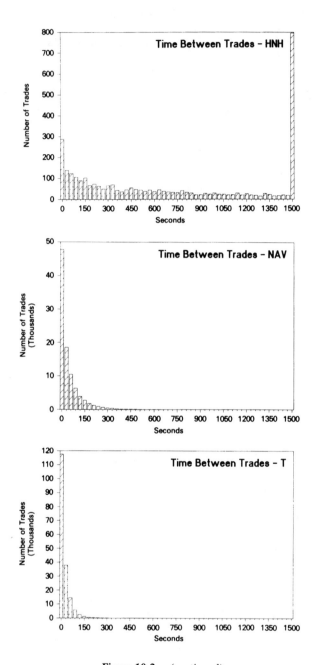

Figure 10.2.   *(continued)*

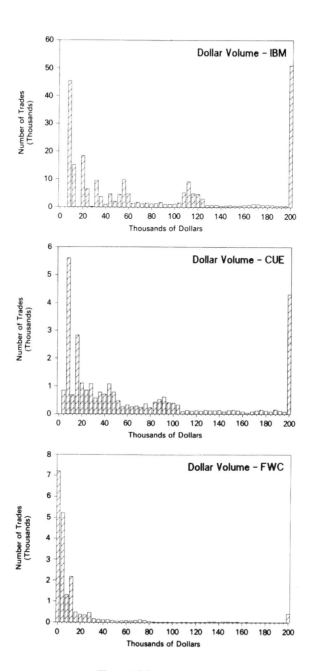

Figure 10.2.   *(continued)*

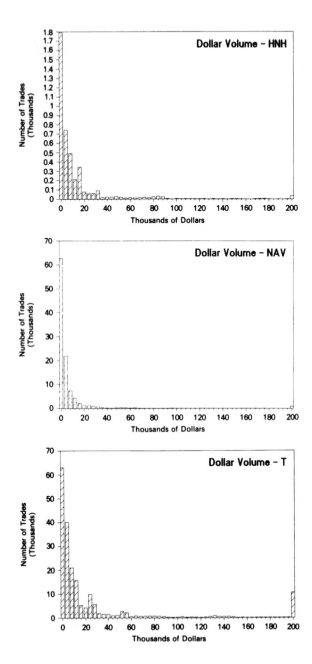

Figure 10.2.   *(continued)*

of four ticks or more, which underscores the importance of discreteness in transaction prices.

For both the time-between-trade and dollar volume variables, the *largest* cell, i.e., 1,500 seconds or $200,000, also includes all trades beyond it. As expected, the histograms for these quantities vary greatly according to market value and price level. For the larger stocks, the time between trades is relatively short, hence most of the mass in those histograms is in the lower-valued cells. But the histograms of smaller, less liquid stocks like HNH have spikes in the largest-valued cell. Histograms for dollar volume are sometimes bimodal, as in the case of IBM, reflecting both round-lot trading at 100 shares ($10,000 on average for IBM's stock price during 1988) and some very large trades, presumably by institutional investors.

10.4 The Empirical Specification

To estimate the parameters of the ordered probit model via maximum likelihood, we must first specify (i) the number of states m, (ii) the explanatory variables X_k, and (iii) the parametrization of the variance σ_k^2.

In choosing m, we must balance price resolution against the practical constraint that too large an m will yield no observations in the extreme states s_1 and s_m. For example, if we set m to 101 and define the states s_1 and s_{101} symmetrically to be price changes of -50 ticks and $+50$ ticks respectively, we would find no Z_k's among our six stocks falling into these two states. Using the histograms in Figure 10.2 as a guide, we set $m = 9$ for the larger stocks, implying extreme states of -4 ticks or less and $+4$ ticks or more. For the two smaller stocks, FWC and HNH, we set $m = 5$, implying extreme states of -2 ticks or less and $+2$ ticks or more. Although the definition of states need not be symmetric (state s_1 can be -6 ticks or less, implying that state s_9 is $+2$ ticks or more), the symmetry of the histogram of price changes in Figure 10.2 suggests a symmetric definition of the s_j's.

In selecting the explanatory variables X_k, we seek to capture several aspects of transaction price changes. First, we would like to allow for clock-time effects, since there is currently some dispute over whether trade-to-trade prices are stable in transaction time versus clock time. Second, we would like to account for the effects of the bid/ask spread on price changes, since many transactions are merely movements from the bid price to the ask price or vice versa. If, for example, in a sequence of three trades the first and third were buyer-initiated while the second was seller-initiated, the sequence of transaction prices would exhibit reversals due solely to the bid/ask "bounce." Third, we would like to measure how the conditional distribution of price changes shifts in response to a trade of a given volume, i.e., the price impact per unit volume of trade. And fourth, we would like to capture the effects of "systematic" or market-wide movements in prices on the conditional distribution of an individual stock's price changes. To address these four issues, we first construct the following variables:

Δt_k = Time elapsed between transactions $k-1$ and k, in seconds.

AB_{k-1} = Bid/ask spread prevailing at time t_{k-1}, in ticks.

Z_{k-l} = Three lags $[l = 1, 2, 3]$ of the dependent variable Z_k. Recall that for $m = 9$, price changes less then -4 ticks are set equal to -4 ticks (state s_1), and price changes greater than $+4$ ticks are set equal to $+4$ ticks (state s_9), and similarly for $m = 5$.

V_{k-l} = Three lags $[l = 1, 2, 3]$ of the dollar volume of the $(k-l)$th transaction, defined as the price of the $(k-l)$th transaction (in dollars, not ticks) times the number of shares traded (denominated in 100's of shares), hence dollar volume is denominated in \$100's of dollars. To reduce the influence of outliers, if the share volume of a trade exceeds the 99.5 percentile of the empirical distribution of share volume for that stock, we set it *equal* to the 99.5 percentile.[7]

$SP500_{k-l}$ = Three lags $[l = 1, 2, 3]$ of five-minute continuously-compounded returns of the Standard and Poor's 500 index futures price, for the contract maturing in the closest month beyond the month in which transaction $k-l$ occurred, where the return is computed with the futures price recorded one minute before the nearest round minute *prior* to t_{k-l} and the price recorded five minutes before this. More formally, we have:

$$SP500_{k-1} \equiv \log(F(t_{k-1}^- - 60)/F(t_{k-1}^- - 360)), \quad (10.4.1)$$
$$SP500_{k-2} \equiv \log(F(t_{k-1}^- - 360)/F(t_{k-1}^- - 660)), (10.4.2)$$
$$SP500_{k-3} \equiv \log(F(t_{k-1}^- - 660)/F(t_{k-1}^- - 960)), (10.4.3)$$

where $F(t^-)$ is the S&P 500 index futures price at time t^- (measured in seconds) for the contract maturing the closest month beyond the month of transaction $k-l$, and t^- is the nearest round minute prior to time t (for example, if t is $10:35:47$, then t^- is $10:35:00$).[8]

---

[7]This rather convoluted timing for computing $SP500_{k-l}$ ensures that there is no temporal overlap between price changes and the returns to the index futures price. In particular, we first construct a minute-by-minute time series for futures prices by assigning to each round minute the nearest futures transaction price occurring *after* that minute but before the next (hence if the first futures transaction after $10:35:00$ occurs at $10:35:15$, the futures price assigned to $10:35:00$ is this one). If no transaction occurs during this minute, the price prevailing at the previous minute is assigned to the current minute. Then for the price change Z_k, we compute $SP500_{k-1}$ using the futures price one minute before the nearest round minute *prior* to t_{k-1}, and the price five minutes before this (hence if t_{k-1} is $10:36:45$, we use the futures price assigned to $10:35:00$ and $10:30:00$ to compute $SP500_{k-1}$).

[8]For example, the 99.5 percentile for IBM's share volume is 16,500 shares, hence all IBM trades exceeding 16,500 shares are set equal to 16,500 shares. By definition, only one-half of one percent of the 206,794 IBM trades (or 1,034 trades) were "censored" in this manner. We chose not to discard these trades because omitting them could affect our estimates of the lag structure, which is extremely sensitive to the *sequence* of trades. For the five remaining stocks, the 99.5 percentiles for share volume are: CUE = 21,300, FWC = 31,700, HNH = 20,000, NAV = 50,000, and T = 44,100.

IBS_{k-l} = Three lags ($l = 1, 2, 3$) of an indicator variable that takes the value 1 if the $(k-l)$th transaction price is greater than the average of the quoted bid and ask prices at time t_{k-l}, the value -1 if the $(k-l)$th transaction price is less than the average of the bid and ask prices at time t_{k-l}, and 0 otherwise, i.e.,

$$
IBS_{k-l} \equiv \begin{cases} 1 & \text{if } P_{k-l} > \frac{1}{2}(P^a_{k-l} + P^b_{k-l}), \\ 0 & \text{if } P_{k-l} = \frac{1}{2}(P^a_{k-l} + P^b_{k-l}), \\ -1 & \text{if } P_{k-l} < \frac{1}{2}(P^a_{k-l} + P^b_{k-l}). \end{cases} \tag{10.4.4}
$$

Whether the $(k-l)$th transaction price is closer to the ask price or the bid price is one measure of whether the transaction was buyer-initiated ($IBS_{k-l} = 1$) or seller-initiated ($IBS_{k-l} = -1$). If the transaction price is at the midpoint of the bid and ask prices, the indicator is indeterminate ($IBS_{k-l} = 0$).

Our specification of $X'_k\beta$ is then given by the following expression:

$$
\begin{aligned}
X'_k\beta = {} & \beta_1 \Delta t_k + \beta_2 Z_{k-1} + \beta_3 Z_{k-2} + \beta_4 Z_{k-3} + \beta_5 SP500_{k-1} + \beta_6 SP500_{k-2} \\
& + \beta_7 SP500_{k-3} + \beta_8 IBS_{k-1} + \beta_9 IBS_{k-2} + \beta_{10} IBS_{k-3} \\
& + \beta_{11}\{T_\lambda(V_{k-1}) \cdot IBS_{k-1}\} + \beta_{12}\{T_\lambda(V_{k-2}) \cdot IBS_{k-2}\} \\
& + \beta_{13}\{T_\lambda(V_{k-3}) \cdot IBS_{k-3}\}.
\end{aligned} \tag{10.4.5}
$$

The variable Δt_k is included in X_k to allow for clock-time effects on the conditional mean of Z^*_k. If prices are stable in transaction time rather than clock time, this coefficient should be zero. Lagged price changes are included to account for serial dependencies, and lagged returns of the S&P 500 index futures price are included to account for market-wide effects on price changes.

To measure the price impact of a trade per unit volume we include the term $T_\lambda(V_{k-l})$, dollar volume transformed according to the Box and Cox (1964) specification $T_\lambda(\cdot)$:

$$
T_\lambda(x) \equiv (x^\lambda - 1/\lambda), \tag{10.4.6}
$$

where $\lambda \in [0, 1]$ is also a parameter to be estimated. The Box-Cox transformation allows dollar volume to enter into the conditional mean nonlinearly, a particularly important innovation since common intuition suggests that price impact may exhibit economies of scale with respect to dollar volume, i.e., although total price impact is likely to increase with volume, the marginal price impact probably does not. The Box-Cox transformation captures the linear specification ($\lambda = 1$) and concave specifications up to and including the logarithmic function ($\lambda = 0$). The estimated curvature of this transformation will play an important role in the measurement of price impact.

The transformed dollar volume variable is interacted with IBS_{k-l}, an indicator of whether the trade was buyer-initiated ($IBS_k = 1$), seller-initiated ($IBS_k = -1$), or indeterminate ($IBS_k = 0$). A positive β_{11} would imply that buyer-initiated trades tend to push prices up and seller-initiated trades tend to drive prices down. Such a relation is predicted by several information-based models of trading, e.g., Easley and O'Hara (1987). Moreover, the magnitude of β_{11} is the per-unit volume impact on the conditional mean of Z_k^*, which may be readily translated into the impact on the conditional probabilities of observed price changes. The sign and magnitudes of β_{12} and β_{13} measure the persistence of price impact.

Finally, to complete our specification we must parametrize the conditional variance $\sigma_k^2 \equiv \gamma_0^2 + \sum \gamma_i^2 W_{ik}$. To allow for clock-time effects we include Δt_k, and since there is some evidence linking bid/ask spreads to the information content and volatility of price changes (see, for example, Glosten (1987), Hasbrouck (1988, 1991a,b), and Petersen and Umlauf (1990)), we also include the lagged spread AB_{k-1}. Also, recall from Section 10.2.2 that the parameters α, β, and γ are unidentified without additional restrictions, hence we make the identification assumption that $\gamma_0^2 = 1$. Our variance parametrization is then:

$$\sigma_k^2 \equiv 1 + \gamma_1^2 \Delta t_k + \gamma_2^2 AB_{k-1}. \tag{10.4.7}$$

In summary, our nine-state specification requires the estimation of 24 parameters: the partition boundaries $\alpha_1, \ldots, \alpha_8$, the variance parameters γ_1 and γ_2, the coefficients of the explanatory variables $\beta_1, \ldots, \beta_{13}$, and the Box-Cox parameter λ. The five-state specification requires the estimation of only 20 parameters.

10.5 The Maximum Likelihood Estimates

We compute the maximum likelihood estimators numerically using the algorithm proposed by Berndt, Hall, Hall, and Hausman (1974), hereafter BHHH. The advantage of BHHH over other search algorithms is its reliance on only first derivatives, an important computational consideration for sample sizes such as ours.

The asymptotic covariance matrix of the parameter estimates was computed as the negative inverse of the matrix of (numerically determined) second derivatives of the log-likelihood function with respect to the parameters, evaluated at the maximum likelihood estimates. We used a tolerance of 0.001 for the convergence criterion suggested by BHHH (the product of the gradient and the direction vector). To check the robustness of our numerical search procedure, we used several different sets of starting values for each stock, and in all instances our algorithm converged to virtually identical parameter estimates.

All computations were performed in double precision in an ULTRIX environment on a DEC 5000/200 workstation with 16 Mb of memory, using our own FORTRAN implementation of the BHHH algorithm with analytical first derivatives. As a rough guide to the computational demands of ordered probit, note that the numerical estimation procedure for the stock with the largest number of trades (IBM, with 206,794 trades) required only 2 hours and 45 minutes of cpu time.

In Table 10.2a, we report the maximum likelihood estimates of the ordered probit model for our six stocks. Entries in each of the columns labeled with ticker symbols are the parameter estimates for that stock, and to the immediate right of each parameter estimate is the corresponding z-statistic, which is asymptotically distributed as a standard normal variate under the null hypothesis that the coefficient is zero, i.e., it is the parameter estimate divided by its asymptotic standard error.

Table 10.2a shows that the partition boundaries are estimated with high precision for all stocks. As expected, the z-statistics are much larger for those stocks with many more observations. The parameters for σ_k^2 are also statistically significant, hence homoskedasticity may be rejected at conventional significance levels; larger bid/ask spreads and longer time intervals increase the conditional volatility of the disturbance.

The conditional means of the Z_k^*'s for all stocks are only marginally affected by Δt_k. Moreover, the z-statistics are minuscule, especially in light of the large sample sizes. However, as mentioned above, Δt does enter into the σ_k^2 expression significantly, hence clock time is important for the conditional variances, but not for the conditional means of Z_k^*. Note that this does not necessarily imply the same for the conditional distribution of the Z_k's, which is *nonlinearly* related to the conditional distribution of the Z_k^*'s. For example, the conditional mean of the Z_k's may well depend on the conditional variance of the Z_k^*'s, so that clock time can still affect the conditional mean of observed price changes even though it does not affect the conditional mean of Z_k^*.

More striking is the significance and sign of the lagged price change coefficients $\hat{\beta}_2$, $\hat{\beta}_3$, and $\hat{\beta}_4$, which are negative for all stocks, implying a tendency towards price reversals. For example, if the past three price changes were each one tick, the conditional mean of Z_k^* changes by $\hat{\beta}_2 + \hat{\beta}_3 + \hat{\beta}_4$. However, if the sequence of price changes was $1/-1/1$, then the effect on the conditional mean is $\hat{\beta}_2 - \hat{\beta}_3 + \hat{\beta}_4$, a quantity closer to zero for each of the security's parameter estimates.[9]

---

[9]In an earlier specification, in place of lagged price changes we included separate indicator variables for eight of the nine states of each lagged price change. But because the coefficients of the indicator variables increased monotonically from the -4 state to the $+4$ state (state 0 was omitted) in almost exact proportion to the tick change, we chose the more parsimonious specification of including the actual lagged price change.

Table 10.2a.   *Maximum likelihood estimates of the ordered probit model for transaction price changes of International Business Machines Corporation (IBM – 206,794 trades), Quantum Chemical Corporation (CUE – 26,927 trades), Foster Wheeler Corporation (FWC – 18,199 trades), Handy and Harman Company (HNH – 3,174 trades), Navistar International Corporation (NAV – 96,127 trades), and American Telephone and Telegraph Company (T – 180,726 trades), for the period from January 4, 1988, to December 30, 1988. Each z-statistic is asymptotically standard normal under the null hypothesis that the corresponding coefficient is zero.*

Parameter	IBM	z	CUE	z	FWC[b]	z	HNH[b]	z	NAV	z	T	z
Partition boundaries[a]												
α_1	-4.670	-145.65	-6.213	-18.92	-4.378	-25.24	-4.456	-5.98	-7.263	-39.23	-8.073	-56.95
α_2	-4.157	-157.75	-5.447	-18.99	-1.712	-25.96	-1.801	-5.92	-7.010	-36.53	-7.270	-62.40
α_3	-3.109	-171.59	-2.795	-19.14	1.679	26.32	1.923	5.97	-6.251	-37.22	-5.472	-63.43
α_4	-1.344	-155.47	-1.764	-18.95	4.334	25.26	4.477	5.85	-1.972	-34.59	-1.850	-61.41
α_5	1.326	154.91	1.605	18.81	—	—	—	—	1.938	34.66	1.977	62.82
α_6	3.126	167.81	2.774	19.11	—	—	—	—	6.301	36.36	5.378	62.43
α_7	4.205	152.17	5.502	19.10	—	—	—	—	7.742	31.63	7.294	57.63
α_8	4.732	138.75	6.150	18.94	—	—	—	—	8.638	30.26	8.156	56.23
γ_1: $\Delta t/100$	0.399	15.57	0.499	11.62	0.275	11.26	0.187	4.07	0.428	10.01	0.387	8.89
γ_2: AB_{-1}	0.515	71.08	1.110	15.39	0.723	14.54	1.109	4.48	0.869	19.93	0.868	38.16
β_1: $\Delta t/100$	-0.115	-11.42	-0.014	-2.14	0.013	-3.50	-0.010	-2.69	-0.032	-3.82	-0.127	-9.51
β_2: Z_{-1}	-1.012	-135.57	-0.333	-13.46	-1.325	-24.49	-0.740	-5.18	-2.609	-36.32	-2.346	-62.74
β_3: Z_{-2}	-0.532	-85.00	-0.000	-0.03	-0.638	-16.45	-0.406	-4.06	-1.521	-34.13	-1.412	-56.52
β_4: Z_{-3}	-0.211	-47.15	-0.020	-1.42	-0.223	-9.23	-0.116	-1.84	-0.536	-31.63	-0.501	-47.91
β_5: $SP500_{-1}$	1.120	54.22	2.292	13.54	1.359	13.49	0.472	1.36	0.419	8.05	0.625	17.12
β_6: $SP500_{-2}$	-0.257	-12.06	1.373	9.61	0.302	2.93	0.448	1.20	0.150	2.87	0.177	4.96
β_7: $SP500_{-3}$	0.006	0.26	0.677	5.15	0.204	1.97	0.388	1.13	0.159	3.02	0.141	3.93

(continued)

Table 10.2a.   (continued)

Parameter	IBM	z	CUE	z	FWC[b]	z	HNH[b]	z	NAV	z	T	z
β_8: IBS_{-1}	-1.137	-63.64	-1.915	-15.36	-0.791	-7.81	-0.803	-2.89	-0.501	-17.38	-0.740	-23.01
β_9: IBS_{-2}	-0.369	-21.55	-0.279	-3.37	-0.184	-3.66	-0.184	-0.75	-0.370	-15.38	-0.340	-18.11
β_{10}: IBS_{-3}	-0.174	-10.29	0.079	0.98	-0.177	-3.64	-0.022	-0.17	-0.301	-15.37	-0.299	-19.78
β_{11}: $T_\lambda(V_{-1})\,IBS_{-1}$ [c]	0.122	47.37	0.217	12.97	0.050	1.80	0.038	0.55	0.013	2.56	0.032	4.51
β_{12}: $T_\lambda(V_{-2})\,IBS_{-2}$	0.047	18.57	0.036	2.83	0.015	1.54	0.036	0.55	0.011	2.54	0.014	4.22
β_{13}: $T_\lambda(V_{-3})\,IBS_{-3}$	0.019	7.70	0.007	0.59	0.015	1.56	-0.006	-0.34	0.005	2.09	0.005	3.02
λ	0	—	0	—	0.165	1.58	0.191	0.55	0.277	3.50	0.182	5.00

[a] According to the ordered probit model, if the "virtual" price change Z_k^* is less than α_1, then the observed price change is -4 ticks or less; if Z_k^* is between α_1 and α_2, then the observed price change is -3 ticks; and so on.

[b] The ordered probit specification for FWC and HNH contains only five states (-2 ticks or less, -1, 0, $+1$, $+2$ ticks or more), hence only four α's were required.

[c] Box-Cox transformation of lagged dollar volume multiplied by the lagged buy/sell indicator, where the Box-Cox parameter λ is estimated jointly with the other ordered probit parameters via maximum likelihood. The Box-Cox parameter λ determines the degree of curvature that the transformation $T_\lambda(\cdot)$ exhibits in transforming dollar volume V_k before inclusion as an explanatory variable in the ordered probit specification. If $\lambda = 1$, the transformation $T_\lambda(\cdot)$ is linear, hence dollar volume enters the ordered probit model linearly. If $\lambda = 0$, the transformation is equivalent to $\log(\cdot)$, hence the natural logarithm of dollar volume enters the ordered probit model. When λ is between 0 and 1, the curvature of $T_\lambda(\cdot)$ is between logarithmic and linear.

Table 10.2b. Cross-autocorrelation coefficients $\hat{v}_j$, $j = 1, \ldots, 12$, of generalized residuals $\{\hat{\epsilon}_k\}$ with lagged generalized fitted price changes $\hat{Z}_{k-j}$ from the ordered probit estimation for transaction price changes of International Business Machines Corporation (IBM – 206,794 trades), Quantum Chemical Corporation (CUE – 26,927 trades), Foster Wheeler Corporation (FWC – 18,199 trades), Handy and Harman Company (HNH – 3,174 trades), Navistar International Corporation (NAV – 96,127 trades), and American Telephone and Telegraph Company (T – 180,726 trades), for the period from January 4, 1988 to December 30, 1988.[a]

Stock	$\hat{v}_1$	$\hat{v}_2$	$\hat{v}_3$	$\hat{v}_4$	$\hat{v}_5$	$\hat{v}_6$	$\hat{v}_7$	$\hat{v}_8$	$\hat{v}_9$	$\hat{v}_{10}$	$\hat{v}_{11}$	$\hat{v}_{12}$
IBM	-0.005	0.002	0.005	-0.043	-0.008	0.001	-0.001	0.001	0.000	-0.001	-0.005	0.000
CUE	-0.008	0.001	-0.006	0.010	0.013	0.003	0.006	0.008	-0.002	0.004	-0.004	0.000
FWC	-0.006	0.000	0.007	-0.032	-0.001	-0.007	-0.004	-0.003	-0.003	-0.003	0.013	-0.004
HNH	-0.012	-0.007	0.007	-0.027	-0.009	0.012	0.019	-0.001	0.009	0.030	-0.018	0.018
NAV	0.005	0.014	0.020	-0.088	-0.011	-0.014	-0.016	-0.011	-0.010	-0.013	-0.009	-0.014
T	0.002	0.013	0.015	-0.080	-0.005	-0.011	-0.006	-0.007	-0.007	-0.006	-0.001	-0.006

[a]If the ordered probit model is correctly specified, these cross-autocorrelations should be close to zero.

Table 10.2c. *Score test statistics $\hat{\xi}_j$, $j = 1, \ldots, 12$, where $\hat{\xi}_j \stackrel{a}{\sim} \chi_1^2$ under the null hypothesis of no serial correlation in the ordered probit disturbances $\{\epsilon_k\}$, using the generalized residuals $\{\hat{\epsilon}_k\}$ from ordered probit estimation for transaction price changes of International Business Machines Corporation (IBM – 206,794 trades), Quantum Chemical Corporation (CUE – 26,927 trades), Foster Wheeler Corporation (FWC – 18,199 trades), Handy and Harman Company (HNH – 3,174 trades), Navistar International Corporation (NAV – 96,127 trades), and American Telephone and Telegraph Company (T – 180,726 trades), for the period from January 4, 1988, to December 30, 1988.[a]*

Stock	$\hat{\xi}_1$ (p-value)	$\hat{\xi}_2$ (p-value)	$\hat{\xi}_3$ (p-value)	$\hat{\xi}_4$ (p-value)	$\hat{\xi}_5$ (p-value)	$\hat{\xi}_6$ (p-value)	$\hat{\xi}_7$ (p-value)	$\hat{\xi}_8$ (p-value)	$\hat{\xi}_9$ (p-value)	$\hat{\xi}_{10}$ (p-value)	$\hat{\xi}_{11}$ (p-value)	$\hat{\xi}_{12}$ (p-value)
IBM	3.29 (0.07)	0.94 (0.33)	3.40 (0.07)	313.2 (0.00)	9.71 (0.00)	0.19 (0.66)	0.28 (0.60)	0.25 (0.62)	0.00 (1.00)	0.21 (0.65)	3.76 (0.05)	0.03 (0.86)
CUE	1.25 (0.26)	0.01 (0.92)	0.72 (0.40)	2.39 (0.12)	4.01 (0.05)	0.24 (0.62)	0.94 (0.33)	1.54 (0.21)	0.11 (0.74)	0.41 (0.52)	0.32 (0.57)	0.00 (1.00)
FWC	0.58 (0.45)	0.00 (1.00)	0.82 (0.37)	17.42 (0.00)	0.02 (0.89)	0.75 (0.39)	0.21 (0.65)	0.14 (0.71)	0.15 (0.70)	0.16 (0.69)	3.01 (0.08)	0.27 (0.60)
HNH	0.35 (0.55)	0.13 (0.72)	0.15 (0.70)	2.10 (0.15)	0.22 (0.64)	0.40 (0.53)	1.06 (0.30)	0.00 (1.00)	0.24 (0.62)	2.60 (0.11)	0.96 (0.33)	1.00 (0.32)
NAV	2.37 (0.12)	17.50 (0.00)	38.00 (0.00)	684.06 (0.00)	11.76 (0.00)	18.20 (0.00)	22.38 (0.00)	11.72 (0.00)	9.95 (0.00)	14.61 (0.00)	7.14 (0.01)	17.02 (0.00)
T	0.94 (0.33)	30.12 (0.00)	40.42 (0.00)	1003.69 (0.00)	3.02 (0.08)	17.87 (0.00)	4.96 (0.03)	6.22 (0.01)	7.29 (0.01)	5.52 (0.02)	0.04 (0.84)	4.89 (0.03)

[a]If the ordered probit model is correctly specified, these test statistics should follow a χ_1^2 statistic which falls in the interval [0.00, 3.84] with 95% probability.

Note that these coefficients measure reversal tendencies beyond that induced by the presence of a constant bid/ask spread as in Roll (1984a). The effect of this "bid/ask bounce" on the conditional mean should be captured by the indicator variables IBS_{k-1}, IBS_{k-2}, and IBS_{k-3}. In the absence of all other information (such as market movements, past price changes, etc.), these variables pick up any price effects that buys and sells might have on the conditional mean. As expected, the estimated coefficients are generally negative, indicating the presence of reversals due to movements from bid to ask or ask to bid prices. In Section 10.6.1 we shall compare their magnitudes explicitly, and conclude that the conditional mean of price changes is *path-dependent* with respect to past price changes.

The lagged S&P 500 returns are also significant, but have a more persistent effect on some securities. For example, the coefficient for the first lag of the S&P 500 is large and significant for IBM, but the coefficient for the third is small and insignificant. However, for the less actively traded stocks such as CUE, all three coefficients are significant and are about the same order of magnitude. As a measure of how quickly market-wide information is impounded into prices, these coefficients confirm the common intuition that smaller stocks react more slowly than larger stocks, which is consistent with the lead/lag effects uncovered by Lo and MacKinlay (1990a).

10.5.1 Diagnostics

A common diagnostic for the specification of an ordinary least squares regression is to examine the properties of the residuals. If, for example, a time series regression is well-specified, the residuals should approximate white noise and exhibit little serial correlation. In the case of ordered probit, we cannot calculate the residuals directly since we cannot observe the latent dependent variable Z_k^* and therefore cannot compute $Z_k^* - X_k'\hat{\beta}$. However, we do have an estimate of the conditional distribution of Z_k^*, conditioned on the X_k's, based on the ordered probit specification and the maximum likelihood parameter estimates. From this we can obtain an estimate of the conditional distribution of the ϵ_k's, from which we can construct *generalized residuals* $\hat{\epsilon}_k$ along the lines suggested by Gourieroux, Monfort, and Trognon (1985):

$$\hat{\epsilon}_k \equiv \mathrm{E}[\epsilon_k \mid Z_k, X_k, W_k; \hat{\theta}_{\mathrm{ml}}], \qquad (10.5.1)$$

where $\hat{\theta}_{\mathrm{ml}}$ is the maximum likelihood estimator of the unknown parameter vector containing $\hat{\alpha}$, $\hat{\gamma}$, $\hat{\beta}$, and $\hat{\lambda}$. In the case of ordered probit, if Z_k is in the jth state, i.e., $Z_k = s_j$, then the generalized residual $\hat{\epsilon}_k$ may be expressed explicitly using the moments of the truncated normal distribution as

$$\begin{aligned} \hat{\epsilon}_k &= \mathrm{E}[\epsilon_k \mid Z_k = s_j, X_k, W_k; \hat{\theta}_{\mathrm{ml}}] \\ &= \hat{\sigma}_k \cdot \frac{\phi(c_1) - \phi(c_2)}{\Phi(c_2) - \Phi(c_1)}, \end{aligned} \qquad (10.5.2)$$

$$c_1 \equiv \frac{1}{\hat{\sigma}_k} \left(\hat{\alpha}_{j-1} - X_k'\hat{\beta} \right), \tag{10.5.3}$$

$$c_2 \equiv \frac{1}{\hat{\sigma}_k} \left(\hat{\alpha}_j - X_k'\hat{\beta} \right), \tag{10.5.4}$$

$$\hat{\sigma}_k \equiv \sqrt{1 + \hat{\gamma}_1^2 \Delta t_k + \hat{\gamma}_2^2 AB_{k-1}}, \tag{10.5.5}$$

where $\phi(\cdot)$ is the standard normal probability density function and for notational convenience, we define $\alpha_0 \equiv -\infty$ and $\alpha_m \equiv +\infty$. Gourieroux, Monfort, and Trognon (1985) show that these generalized residuals may be used to test for misspecification in a variety of ways. However, some care is required in performing such tests. For example, although a natural statistic to calculate is the first-order autocorrelation of the $\hat{\epsilon}_k$'s, Gourieroux et al. observe that the theoretical autocorrelation of the generalized residuals does not in general equal the theoretical autocorrelation of the ϵ_k's. Moreover, if the source of serial correlation is an omitted lagged endogenous variable (if, for example, we included too few lags of Z_k in X_k), then further refinements of the usual specification tests are necessary.

Gourieroux et al. derive valid tests for serial correlation from lagged endogenous variables using the *score statistic*, essentially the derivative of the likelihood function with respect to an autocorrelation parameter, evaluated at the maximum likelihood estimates under the null hypothesis of no serial correlation. More specifically, consider the following model for our Z_k^*:

$$Z_k^* = \varphi Z_{k-1}^* + X_k'\beta + \epsilon_k, \quad |\varphi| < 1. \tag{10.5.6}$$

In this case, the score statistic $\hat{\xi}_1$ is the derivative of the likelihood function with respect to φ evaluated at the maximum likelihood estimates. Under the null hypothesis that $\varphi = 0$, it simplifies to the following expression:

$$\hat{\xi}_1 \equiv \left(\sum_{k=2}^{n} \hat{Z}_{k-1}\hat{\epsilon}_k \right)^2 \bigg/ \sum_{k=2}^{n} \hat{Z}_{k-1}^2 \hat{\epsilon}_k^2 \tag{10.5.7}$$

where

$$\hat{Z}_k \equiv E[Z_k^* \mid Z_k, X_k, W_k; \hat{\theta}_{ml}] \tag{10.5.8}$$

$$= X_k'\hat{\beta} + \hat{\epsilon}_k. \tag{10.5.9}$$

When $\varphi = 0$, $\hat{\xi}_1$ is asymptotically distributed as a χ_1^2 variate. Therefore, using $\hat{\xi}_1$ we can test for the presence of autocorrelation induced by the omitted variable Z_{k-1}^*. More generally, we can test the higher-order specification:

$$Z_k^* = \varphi Z_{k-j}^* + X_k'\beta + \epsilon_k, \quad |\varphi| < 1, \tag{10.5.10}$$

by using the score statistic $\hat{\xi}_j$,

$$\hat{\xi}_j \equiv \left(\sum_{k=j+1}^{n} \hat{Z}_{k-j} \hat{\epsilon}_k \right)^2 / \sum_{k=j+1}^{n} \hat{Z}_{k-j}^2 \hat{\epsilon}_k^2, \qquad (10.5.11)$$

which is also asymptotically χ_1^2 under the null hypothesis that $\varphi = 0$.

For further intuition, we can compute the sample correlation $\hat{v}_j$ of the generalized residual $\hat{\epsilon}_k$ with the lagged generalized fitted values $\hat{Z}_{k-j}$. Under the null hypothesis of no serial correlation in the ϵ_k's, the theoretical value of this correlation is zero, hence the sample correlation will provide one measure of the *economic* impact of misspecification. These are reported in Table 10.2b for our sample of six stocks, and they are all quite small, ranging from -0.088 to 0.030.

Finally, Table 10.2c reports the score statistics $\hat{\xi}_j$, $j = 1, \ldots, 12$. Since we have included three lags of Z_k in our specification of X_k, it is no surprise that none of the score statistics for $j = 1, 2, 3$ are statistically significant at the 5% level. However, at lag 4, the score statistics for all stocks except CUE and HNH are significant, indicating the presence of some serial dependence not accounted for by our specification. But recall that we have very large sample sizes so that virtually any point null hypothesis will be rejected. With this in mind, the score statistics seem to indicate a reasonably good fit for all but one stock, NAV, whose score statistic is significant at every lag, suggesting the need for respecification. Turning back to the cross-autocorrelations reported in Table 10.2b, we see that NAV's residual $\hat{\epsilon}_k$ has a -0.088 correlation with $\hat{Z}_{k-4}$, the largest in Table 10.2b in absolute value. This suggests that adding Z_{k-4} as a regressor might improve the specification for NAV.

There are a number of other specification tests that can check the robustness of the ordered probit specification, but they should be performed with an eye towards particular applications. For example, when studying the impact of information variables on volatility, a more pressing concern would be the specification of the conditional variance σ_k^2. If some of the parameters have important economic interpretations, their stability can be checked by simple likelihood ratio tests on subsamples of the data. If forecasting price changes is of interest, an R^2-like measure can readily be constructed to measure how much variability can be explained by the predictors. The ordered probit model is flexible enough to accommodate virtually any specification test designed for simple regression models, but has many obvious advantages over OLS as we shall see below.

10.5.2 Endogeneity of Δt_k and IBS_k

Our inferences in the preceding sections are based on the implicit assumption that the explanatory variables X_k are all exogenous or predetermined with respect to the dependent variable Z_k. However, the variable Δt_k is contemporaneous to Z_k and deserves further discussion.

Recall that Z_k is the price change between trades at time t_{k-1} and time t_k. Since Δt_k is simply $t_k - t_{k-1}$, it may well be that Δt_k and Z_k are determined simultaneously, in which case our parameter estimates are generally inconsistent. In fact, there are several plausible arguments for the endogeneity of Δt_k (see, for example, Admati and Pfleiderer (1988), 1989) and Easley and O'Hara (1992)). One such argument turns on the tendency of floor brokers to break up large trades into smaller ones, and time the executions carefully during the course of the day or several days. By "working" the order, the floor broker can minimize the price impact of his trades and obtain more favorable execution prices for his clients. But by selecting the times between his trades based on current market conditions, which include information also affecting price changes, the floor broker is creating endogenous trade times.

However, any given sequence of trades in our dataset does not necessarily correspond to consecutive transactions of any single individual (other than the specialist of course), but is the result of many buyers and sellers interacting with the specialist. For example, even if a floor broker were working a large order, in between his orders might be purchases and sales from other floor brokers, market orders, and triggered limit orders. Therefore, the Δt_k's also reflect these trades, which are not necessarily information-motivated.

Another more intriguing reason that Δt_k may be exogenous is that floor brokers have an economic incentive to minimize the correlation between Δt_k and virtually all other exogenous and predetermined variables. To see this, suppose the floor broker timed his trades in response to some exogenous variable also affecting price changes, call it "weather." Suppose that price changes tend to be positive in good weather and negative in bad weather. Knowing this, the floor broker will wait until bad weather prevails before buying, hence trade times and price changes are simultaneously determined by weather. However, if other traders are also aware of these relations, they can garner information about the floor broker's intent by watching his trades and by recording the weather, and trade against him successfully. To prevent this, the floor broker must trade to deliberately minimize the correlation between his trade times and the weather. Therefore, the floor broker has an economic incentive to reduce simultaneous equations bias! Moreover, this argument applies to any other economic variable that can be used to jointly forecast trade times and price changes. For these two reasons, we assume that Δt_k is exogenous.

We have also explored some adjustments for the endogeneity of Δt_k along the lines of Hausman (1978) and Newey (1985), and our preliminary estimates show that although exogeneity of Δt_k may be rejected at conventional significance levels (recall our sample sizes), the estimates do not change much once endogeneity is accounted for by an instrumental variables estimation procedure.

There are, however, other contemporaneous variables that we would like to include as regressors which cannot be deemed exogenous (see the discussion of IBS_k in Section 10.6.2 below), and for these we must wait until the appropriate econometric tools become available.

10.6 Applications

In applying the ordered probit model to particular issues of the market microstructure, we must first consider how to interpret its parameter estimates from an economic perspective. Since ordered probit may be viewed as a generalization of a linear regression model to situations with a discrete dependent variable, interpreting its parameter estimates is much like interpreting coefficients of a linear regression: the particular interpretation depends critically on the underlying economic motivation for including and excluding the specific regressors.

In a very few instances, theoretical paradigms might yield testable implications in the form of linear regression equations, e.g., the CAPM's security market line. In most cases, however, linear regression is used to capture and summarize empirical relations in the data that have not yet been derived from economic first principles. In much the same way, ordered probit may be interpreted as a means of capturing and summarizing relations among price changes and other economic variables such as volume. Such relations have been derived from first principles only in the most simplistic and stylized of contexts, under very specific and, therefore, often counterfactual assumptions about agents' preferences, information sets, alternative investment possibilities, sources of uncertainty and their parametric form (usually Gaussian), and the timing and allowable volume and type of trades.[10] Although such models do yield valuable insights about the economics of the market microstructure, they are too easily rejected by the data because of the many restrictive assumptions needed to obtain readily interpretable closed-form results.

Nevertheless, the broader implications of such models can still be "tested" by checking for simple relations among economic quantities, as we illustrate in Section 10.6.1. However, some care must be taken in interpreting such results, as in the case of a simple linear regression of prices on quantities which cannot be interpreted as an estimated demand curve without imposing additional economic structure.

---

[10]Just a few recent examples of this growing literature are Admati and Pfleiderer (1988), 1989), Amihud and Mendelson (1980), Easley and O'Hara (1987), Garman (1976), Glosten and Milgrom (1985), Grundy and McNichols (1989), Ho and Stoll (1980, 1981), Karpoff (1986), Kyle (1985), Stoll (1989), and Wang (1994).

In particular, although the ordered probit model can shed light on how price changes respond to specific economic variables, it cannot give us economic insights beyond whatever structure we choose to impose *a priori*. For example, since we have placed no specific theoretical structure on how prices are formed, our ordered probit estimates cannot yield sharp implications for the impact of floor brokers "working" an order (executing a large order in smaller bundles to obtain the best average price). The ordered probit estimates will reflect the combined actions and interactions of these floor brokers, the specialists, and individual and institutional investors, all trading with and against each other. Unless we are estimating a fully articulated model of economic equilibrium that contains these kinds of market participants, we cannot separate their individual impact in determining price changes. For example, without additional structure we cannot answer the question: What is the price impact of an order that is *not* "worked"?

However, if we were able to identify those large trades that did benefit from the services of a floor broker, we could certainly compare and contrast their empirical price dynamics with those of "unworked" trades using the ordered probit model. Such comparisons might provide additional guidelines and restrictions for developing new theories of the market microstructure. Interpreted in this way, the ordered probit model can be a valuable tool for uncovering empirical relations even in the absence of a highly parametrized theory of the market microstructure. To illustrate this aspect of ordered probit, in the following section we consider three specific applications of the parameter estimates of Section 10.5: a test for order-flow dependence in price changes, a measure of price impact, and a comparison of ordered probit to ordinary least squares.

10.6.1 Order-Flow Dependence

Several recent theoretical papers in the market microstructure literature have shown the importance of information in determining relations between prices and trade size. For example, Easley and O'Hara (1987) observe that because informed traders prefer to trade larger amounts than uninformed liquidity traders, the size of a trade contains information about who the trader is and, consequently, also contains information about the traders' private information. As a result, prices in their model do not satisfy the Markov property, since the conditional distribution of next period's price depends on the entire history of past prices, i.e., on the order flow. That is, the sequence of price changes of $1/-1/1$ will have a different effect on the conditional mean than the sequence $-1/1/1$, even though both sequences yield the same total price change over the three trades.

One simple implication of such order-flow dependence is that the coefficients of the three lags of Z_k's are not identical. If they are, then only the sum of the most recent three price changes matters in determining the conditional mean, and not the order in which those price changes occurred. Therefore, if we denote by β_p the vector of coefficients $[\beta_2 \; \beta_3 \; \beta_4]'$ of the lagged price changes, the null hypothesis H of order-flow independence is simply:

$$H: \beta_2 = \beta_3 = \beta_4.$$

This may be recast as a linear hypothesis for β_p, namely $A\beta_p = 0$, where

$$A \equiv \begin{pmatrix} 1 & -1 & 0 \\ 0 & 1 & -1 \end{pmatrix}. \tag{10.6.1}$$

Then under H, we obtain the following test statistic:

$$\hat{\beta}_p' A' (A \hat{V}_p A')^{-1} A \hat{\beta}_p \overset{a}{\sim} \chi_2^2, \tag{10.6.2}$$

where $\hat{V}_p$ is the estimated asymptotic covariance matrix of $\hat{\beta}_p$. The values of these test statistics for the six stocks are: IBM = 11,462.43, CUE = 152.05, FWC = 446.01, HNH = 18.62, NAV = 1,184.48, and T = 3,428.92. The null hypothesis of order-flow independence may be rejected at all the usual levels of significance for all six stocks. These findings support Easley and O'Hara's observation that information-based trading can lead to path-dependent price changes, so that the order flow (and the entire history of other variables) may affect the conditional distribution of the next price change.

10.6.2 Measuring Price Impact Per Unit Volume of Trade

By price impact we mean the effect of a current trade of a given size on the conditional distribution of the *subsequent* price change. As such, the coefficients of the variables $T_\lambda(V_{k-j}) \cdot IBS_{k-j}, \; j = 1, 2, 3$, measure the price impact of trades per unit of transformed dollar volume. More precisely, recall that our definition of the volume variable is the Box-Cox transformation of dollar volume divided by 100, hence the coefficient β_{11} for stock i is the contribution to the conditional mean $X_k'\beta$ that results from a trade of $\$100 \cdot (1 + \lambda_i)^{1/\lambda_i}$ (since $T_\lambda((1 + \lambda_i)^{1/\lambda_i}) = 1$). Therefore, the impact of a trade of size $\$M$ at time $k - 1$ on $X_k'\beta$ is simply $\beta_{11} T_\lambda(M/100)$. Now the estimated $\hat{\beta}_{11}$'s in Table 10.2a are generally positive and significant, with the most recent trade having the largest impact. But this is not the impact we seek, since $X_k'\beta$ is the conditional mean of the unobserved variable Z_k^* and not of the observed price change Z_k. In particular, since $X_k'\beta$ is scaled by σ_k in (10.2.10), it is difficult to make meaningful comparisons of the $\hat{\beta}_{11}$'s across stocks.

To obtain a measure of a trade's price impact that we *can* compare across stocks, we must translate the impact on $X_k'\beta$ into an impact on the conditional distribution of the Z_k's, conditioned on the trade size and other quantities. Since we have already established that the conditional distribution of price changes is order-flow-dependent, we must condition on a specific *sequence* of past price changes and trade sizes. We do this by substituting our parameter estimates into (10.2.10), choosing particular values for the explanatory variables X_k, and computing the probabilities explicitly. Specifically, for each stock i we set Δt_k and AB_{k-1} to their sample means for that stock and set the remaining regressors to the following values:

$$V_{k-2} = \tfrac{1}{100} \cdot \text{median dollar volume for stock } i,$$

$$V_{k-3} = \tfrac{1}{100} \cdot \text{median dollar volume for stock } i,$$

$$SP500_{k-1} = 0.001, \quad SP500_{k-2} = 0.001, \quad SP500_{k-3} = 0.001,$$

$$IBS_{k-1} = 1, \quad IBS_{k-2} = 1, \quad IBS_{k-3} = 1.$$

Specifying values for these variables is equivalent to specifying the market conditions under which price impact is to be measured. These particular values correspond to a scenario in which the most recent three trades are buys, where the sizes of the two earlier trades are equal to the stock's median dollar volume, and where the market has been rising during the past 15 minutes. We then evaluate the probabilities in (10.2.10) for different values of V_{k-1}, Z_{k-1}, Z_{k-2}, and Z_{k-3}.

For brevity, we focus only on the means of these conditional distributions, which we report for the six stocks in Table 10.3. The entries in the upper panel of Table 10.3 are computed under the assumption that $Z_{k-1} = Z_{k-2} = Z_{k-3} = +1$, whereas those in the lower panel are computed under the assumption that $Z_{k-1} = Z_{k-2} = Z_{k-3} = 0$. The first entry in the "IBM" column of Table 10.3's upper panel, -1.315, is the expected price change in ticks of the next transaction of IBM following a \$5,000 buy. The seemingly counterintuitive sign of this conditional mean is the result of the "bid/ask bounce"; since the past three trades were assumed to be buys, the parameter estimates reflect the empirical fact that the next transaction can be a sell, in which case the transaction price change will often be negative since the price will go from ask to bid. To account for this effect, we would need to include a *contemporaneous* buy/sell indicator, IBS_k, in X_k' and condition on this variable as well. But such a variable is clearly endogenous to Z_k and our parameter estimates would suffer from the familiar simultaneous-equations biases.

In fact, including the contemporaneous buy/sell indicator IBS_k and contemporaneous transformed volume $T_\lambda(V_k)$ would yield a more natural measure of price impact, since such a specification, when consistently estimated, can be used to quantify the expected total cost of transacting a given volume. Unfortunately, there are few circumstances in which the contemporaneous buy/sell indicator IBS_k may be considered exogenous, since simple

Table 10.3. *Price impact of trades as measured by the change in conditional mean of Z_k, or $\Delta E[Z_k]$, when trade sizes are increased incrementally above the base case of a $5,000 trade. These changes are computed from the ordered probit probabilities for International Business Machines Corporation (IBM – 206,794 trades), Quantum Chemical Corporation (CUE – 26,927 trades), Foster Wheeler Corporation (FWC – 18,199 trades), Handy and Harman Company (HNH – 3,174 trades), Navistar International Corporation (NAV – 96,127 trades), and American Telephone and Telegraph Company (T – 180,726 trades), for the period from January 4, 1988, to December 30, 1988. Price impact measures expressed in percent are percentages of the average of the high and low prices of each security.*

	$Volume	IBM	CUE	FWC	HNH	NAV	T
Increasing Price Sequence, (1/1/1):							
Price Impact in Ticks							
$E[Z_k]$:	5,000	−1.315	−0.629	−0.956	−0.621	−1.670	−1.604
$\Delta E[Z_k]$:	10,000	0.060	0.072	0.025	0.019	0.017	0.022
$\Delta E[Z_k]$:	50,000	0.193	0.239	0.096	0.074	0.070	0.082
$\Delta E[Z_k]$:	100,000	0.248	0.310	0.133	0.103	0.100	0.113
$\Delta E[Z_k]$:	250,000	0.319	0.403	0.189	0.148	0.148	0.159
$\Delta E[Z_k]$:	500,000	0.371	0.473	0.236	0.188	0.191	0.197
Price Impact in Percent							
$E[Z_k]$:	5,000	−0.141	−0.090	−0.831	−0.474	−3.796	−0.736
$\Delta E[Z_k]$:	10,000	0.006	0.010	0.022	0.015	0.038	0.010
$\Delta E[Z_k]$:	50,000	0.021	0.034	0.084	0.057	0.158	0.038
$\Delta E[Z_k]$:	100,000	0.027	0.045	0.116	0.079	0.227	0.052
$\Delta E[Z_k]$:	250,000	0.034	0.058	0.164	0.113	0.336	0.073
$\Delta E[Z_k]$:	500,000	0.040	0.068	0.205	0.143	0.434	0.090
Constant Price Sequence, (0/0/0):							
Price Impact in Ticks							
$E[Z_k]$:	5,000	−0.328	−0.460	−0.214	−0.230	−0.235	−0.294
$\Delta E[Z_k]$:	10,000	0.037	0.071	0.021	0.018	0.007	0.013
$\Delta E[Z_k]$:	50,000	0.120	0.236	0.080	0.070	0.031	0.050
$\Delta E[Z_k]$:	100,000	0.155	0.306	0.111	0.098	0.044	0.069
$\Delta E[Z_k]$:	250,000	0.200	0.398	0.156	0.140	0.066	0.098
$\Delta E[Z_k]$:	500,000	0.234	0.468	0.195	0.177	0.087	0.123
Price Impact in Percent							
$E[Z_k]$:	5,000	−0.035	−0.066	−0.186	−0.175	−0.534	−0.135
$\Delta E[Z_k]$:	10,000	0.004	0.010	0.018	0.014	0.017	0.006
$\Delta E[Z_k]$:	50,000	0.013	0.034	0.070	0.053	0.070	0.023
$\Delta E[Z_k]$:	100,000	0.017	0.044	0.096	0.074	0.100	0.032
$\Delta E[Z_k]$:	250,000	0.021	0.057	0.136	0.107	0.151	0.045
$\Delta E[Z_k]$:	500,000	0.025	0.067	0.169	0.135	0.197	0.056

economic intuition suggests that factors affecting price changes must also enter the decision to buy or sell. Indeed, limit orders are explicit functions of the current price. Therefore, if IBS_k is to be included as an explanatory variable in X_k, its endogeneity must be taken into account. Unfortunately, the standard estimation techniques such as two-stage or three-stage least squares do not apply here because of our discrete dependent variable. Moreover, techniques that allow for discrete dependent variables cannot be applied because the endogenous regressor IBS_k is also discrete. In principle, it may be possible to derive consistent estimators by considering a joint ordered probit model for both variables, but this is beyond the scope of this chapter. For this reason, we restrict our specification to include only lags of IBS_k and V_k.

However, we can "net out" the effect of the bid/ask spread by computing the *change* in the conditional mean for trade sizes larger than our base case $5,000 buy. As long as the bid/ask spread remains relatively stable, the change in the conditional mean induced by larger trades will give us a measure of price impact that is independent of it. In particular, the second entry in the "IBM" column of Table 10.3's upper panel shows that purchasing an additional $5,000 of IBM ($10,000 total) increases the conditional mean by 0.060 ticks. However, purchasing an additional $495,000 of IBM ($500,000 total) increases the conditional mean by 0.371 ticks; as expected, trading a larger quantity always yields a larger price impact.

A comparison across columns in the upper panel of Table 10.3 shows that larger trades have higher price impact for CUE than for the other five stocks. However, such a comparison ignores the fact that these stocks trade at different price levels, hence a price impact of 0.473 ticks for $500,000 of CUE may not be as large a percentage of price as a price impact of 0.191 ticks for $500,000 of NAV. The lower portion of Table 10.3's upper panel reports the price impact as percentages of the average of the high and low prices of each stock, and a trade of $500,000 does have a higher percentage price impact for NAV than for CUE—0.434 percent versus 0.068 percent—even though its impact is considerably smaller when measured in ticks. Interestingly, even as a percentage, price impact increases with dollar volume.

In the lower panel of Table 10.3 where price impact values have been computed under the alternative assumption that $Z_{k-1} = Z_{k-2} = Z_{k-3} = 0$, the conditional means $E[Z_k]$ are closer to zero for the $5,000 buy. For example, the expected price change of NAV is now -0.235 ticks, whereas in the upper panel it is -1.670 ticks. Since we are now conditioning on a different scenario, in which the three most recent transactions are buys that have no impact on prices, the empirical estimates imply more probability in the right tail of the conditional distribution of the subsequent price change.

That the conditional mean is still negative may signal the continued importance of the bid/ask spread, nevertheless the price impact measure

$\Delta E[Z_k]$ does increase with dollar volume in the lower panel. Moreover, these values are similar in magnitude to those in the upper panel—in percentage terms the price impact is virtually the same in both panels of Table 10.3 for most of the six stocks. However, for NAV and T the percentage price impact measures differ considerably between the upper and lower panels of Table 10.3, suggesting that price impact must be measured individually for each security.

Of course, there is no reason to focus solely on the mean of the conditional distribution of Z_k since we have at our disposal an estimate of the entire distribution. Under the scenarios of the upper and lower panels of Table 10.3 we have also computed the standard deviations of conditional distributions, but since they are quite stable across the two scenarios for the sake of brevity we do not report them here.

To get a sense of their sensitivity to the conditioning variables, we have plotted in Figure 10.3 the estimated conditional probabilities for the six stocks under both scenarios. In each graph, the cross-hatched bars represent the conditional distribution for the sequence of three buys with a 0 tick price change at each trade, and a fixed trade size equal to the sample median volume for each. The dark-shaded bars represent the conditional distribution for the same sequence of three buys but with a +1 tick price change for each of the three transactions, also each for a fixed trade size equal to the sample median. The conditional distribution is clearly shifted more to the right under the first scenario than under the second, as the conditional means in Table 10.3 foreshadowed. However, the general shape of the distribution seems rather well-preserved; changing the path of past price changes seems to *translate* the conditional distribution without greatly altering the tail probabilities.

As a final summary of price impact for these securities, we plot "price response" functions in Figure 10.4 for the six stocks. The price response function, which gives the percentage price impact as a function of dollar volume, reveals several features of the market microstructure that are not as apparent from the numbers in Table 10.3. For example, market liquidity is often defined as the ability to trade any volume with little or no price impact, hence in very liquid markets the price response function should be constant at zero—a flat price response function implies that the percentage price impact is not affected by the size of the trade. Therefore a visual measure of liquidity is the curvature of the price response function; it is no surprise that IBM possesses the flattest price response function of the six stocks.

More generally, the shape of the price response function measures whether there are any economies or diseconomies of scale in trading. An upward-sloping curve implies diseconomies of scale, with larger dollar volume trades yielding a higher percentage price impact. As such, the slope may be one measure of "market depth." For example, if the market for a

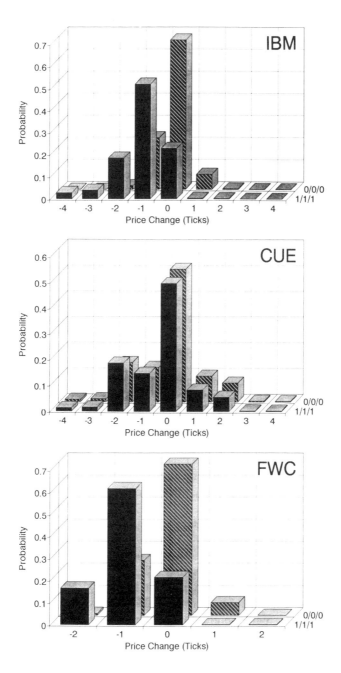

Figure 10.3. *Comparison of estimated ordered probit probabilities of price change, conditioned on a sequence of increasing prices (1/1/1) versus a sequence of constant prices (0/0/0).*

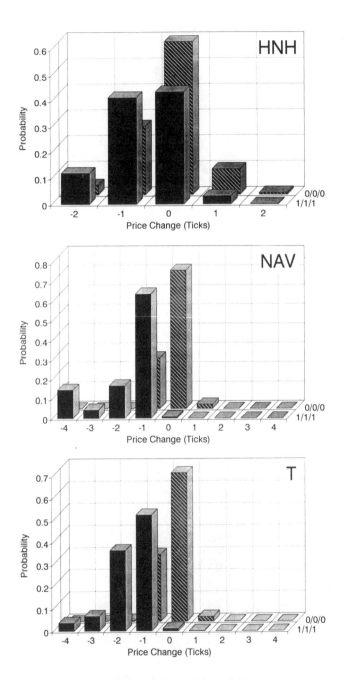

Figure 10.3.   *(continued)*

Table 10.4. *Discreteness cannot be completely captured by simple rounding: χ^2 tests reject the null hypothesis of equally-spaced partition boundaries $\{\alpha_i\}$ of the ordered probit model for International Business Machines Corporation (IBM – 206,794 trades), Quantum Chemical Corporation (CUE – 26,927 trades), Foster Wheeler Corporation (FWC – 18,199 trades), Handy and Harman Company (HNH – 3,174 trades), Navistar International Corporation (NAV – 96,127 trades), and American Telephone and Telegraph Company (T – 180,726 trades), for the period from January 4, 1988, to December 30, 1988.[1] Entries in the column labelled "m" denote the number of states in the ordered probit specification. The 5% and 1% critical values of a χ^2_2 random variate are 5.99 and 9.21, respectively; the 5% and 1% critical values of a χ^2_6 random variate are 12.6 and 16.8, respectively.*

Stock	Sample Size	$\psi \overset{a}{\sim} \chi^2_{m-3}$	m
IBM	206,794	15,682.35	9
CUE	26,927	366.41	9
FWC	18,199	188.28	5
HNH	3,174	30.59	5
NAV	96,127	998.13	9
T	180,726	1,968.39	9

[1] If price discreteness were simply the result of rounding a continuous "virtual" price variable to the nearest eighth of a dollar, the ordered probit partition boundaries $\{\alpha_i\}$ will be equally spaced. If they are, then the statistic ψ should behave as a χ^2_{m-3}-variate where m is the number of states in the ordered probit specification.

security is "deep," this is usually taken to mean that large volumes may be traded before much of a price impact is observed. In such cases the price response function may even be downward-sloping. In Figure 10.4, all six stocks exhibit trading diseconomies of scale since the price response functions are all upward-sloping, although they increase at a decreasing rate. Such diseconomies of scale suggest that it might pay to break up large trades into sequences of smaller ones. However, recall that the values in Figure 10.4 are derived from conditional distributions, conditioned on particular sequences of trades and prices. A comparison of the price impact of, say, one $100,000 trade with two $50,000 trades can be performed only if the conditional distributions are recomputed to account for the different sequences implicit in the two alternatives. Since these two distinct sequences have not been accounted for in Figure 10.4, the benefits of dividing large trades into smaller ones cannot be inferred from it. Nevertheless, with the maximum

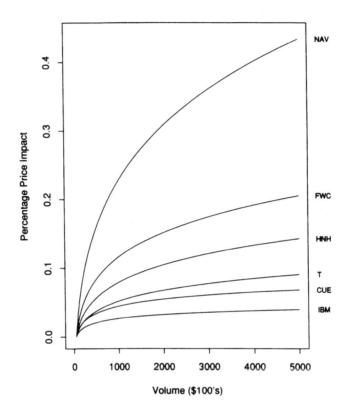

Figure 10.4. *Percentage price impact as a function of dollar volume computed from ordered probit probabilities, conditional on the three most recent trades being buyer-initiated, and the three most recent price changes being +1 tick each, for IBM (206,794 trades), CUE (26,927 trades). FWC (18,199 trades), HNH (3,174 trades), NAV (96,127 trades), and T (180,726 trades), for the period from January 4, 1988, to December 30, 1988. Percentage price impact is measured as a percentage of the average of the high and low prices for each stock.*

likelihood estimates in hand, such comparisons are trivial to calculate on a case-by-case basis.

Since price response functions are defined in terms of percentage price impact, cross-stock comparisons of liquidity can also be made. Figure 10.4 shows that NAV, FWC, and HNH are considerably less liquid than the other stocks, which is partly due to the low price ranges that the three stocks traded in during 1988 (see Table 10.1)—although HNH and NAV have comparable price impacts when measured in ticks (see Table 10.3's upper panel), NAV looks much less liquid when impact is measured as a percentage of price since it traded between \$3.125 and \$7.875, whereas HNH traded between \$14.250 and \$18.500 during 1988. Not surprisingly, since their price ranges are among the highest in the sample, IBM and CUE have the lowest price response functions of the six stocks.

10.6.3 Does Discreteness Matter?

Despite the elegance and generality with which the ordered probit framework accounts for price discreteness, irregular trading intervals, and the influence of explanatory variables, the complexity of the estimation procedure raises the question of whether these features can be satisfactorily addressed by a simpler model. Since ordered probit may be viewed as a generalization of the linear regression model to discrete dependent variables, it is not surprising that the latter may share many of the advantages of the former, price discreteness aside. However, linear regression is considerably easier to implement. Therefore, what is gained by ordered probit?

In particular, suppose we ignore the fact that price changes Z_k are discrete and estimate the following simple regression model via ordinary least squares:

$$Z_k = X_k'\beta + \epsilon_k. \tag{10.6.3}$$

Then, suppose we compute the conditional distribution of Z_k by rounding to the nearest eighth, thus

$$\Pr\left(Z_k = \tfrac{j}{8}\right) = \Pr\left(\tfrac{j}{8} - \tfrac{1}{16} \le X_k'\beta + \epsilon_k < \tfrac{j}{8} + \tfrac{1}{16}\right). \tag{10.6.4}$$

With suitable restrictions on the ϵ_k's, the regression model (10.6.3) is known as the "linear probability" model. The problems associated with applying ordinary least squares to (10.6.3) are well-known (see for example Judge, Griffiths, Hill, Lütkepohl, and Lee (1985, Chapter 18.2.1)), and numerous extensions have been developed to account for such problems. However, implementing such extensions is at least as involved as maximum likelihood estimation of the ordered probit model and therefore the comparison is of less immediate interest. Despite these problems, we may still ask whether the OLS estimates of (10.6.3) and (10.6.4) yield an adequate "approximation" to a more formal model of price discreteness. Specifically, how different are the probabilities in (10.6.4) from those of the ordered probit model? If the differences are small, then the linear regression model (10.6.3) may be an adequate substitute to ordered probit.

Under the assumption of IID Gaussian ϵ_k's, we evaluate the conditional probabilities in (10.6.4) using the OLS parameter estimates and the same values for the X_k's as in Section 10.6.2, and graph them and the corresponding ordered probit probabilities in Figure 10.5. These graphs show that the two models can yield very different conditional probabilities. All of the OLS conditional distributions are unimodal and have little weight in the tails, in sharp contrast to the much more varied conditional distributions generated by ordered probit. For example, the OLS conditional probabilities show no

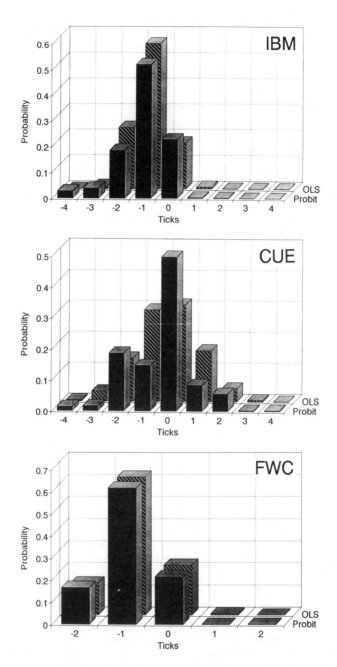

Figure 10.5. *Discreteness matters. A comparison of OLS probabilities versus ordered probit probabilities for price change, conditioned on an increasing price sequence (1/1/1) caused by buyer-initiated trading. Note the nonlinear properties of the CUE and NAV ordered probit probabilities which OLS cannot capture.*

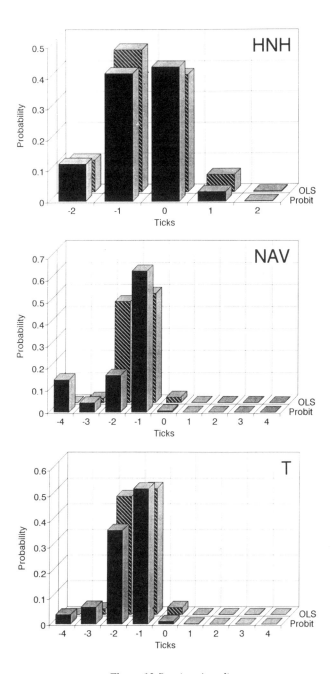

Figure 10.5. *(continued)*

evidence of the nonmonotonicity that is readily apparent from the ordered probit probabilities of CUE and NAV. In particular, for NAV a price change of -3 ticks is clearly less probable than either -2 or -4 ticks, and for CUE, a price change of -1 tick is less probable than of -2 ticks.

Nevertheless, for FWC the OLS and ordered probit probabilities are rather close. However, it is dangerous to conclude from these matches that OLS is generally acceptable, since these conditional distributions depend sensitively on the values of the conditioning variables. For example, if we plot the same probabilities conditioned on much higher values for σ_k^2, there would be strong differences between the OLS and ordered probit distributions for *all* six stocks.

Because the ordered probit partition boundaries $\{\alpha_i\}$ are determined by the data, the tail probabilities of the conditional distribution of price changes may be large or small relative to the probabilities of more central observations, unlike the probabilities implied by (10.6.3) which are dictated by the (Gaussian) distribution function of ϵ_k. Moreover, it is unlikely that using another distribution function will provide as much flexibility as ordered probit, for the simple reason that (10.6.3) constrains the state probabilities to be *linear* in the X_k's (hence the term "linear probability model"), whereas ordered probit allows for *nonlinear* effects by letting the data determine the partition boundaries $\{\alpha_i\}$.

That OLS and ordered probit can differ is not surprising given the extra degrees of freedom that the ordered probit model has to fit the conditional distribution of price changes. In fact, it may be argued that the comparison of OLS and ordered probit is not a fair one because of these extra degrees of freedom (for example, why not allow the OLS residual variance to be heteroskedastic?). But this misses the point of our comparison, which was not meant to be fair but rather to see whether a *simpler* technique can provide approximately the same information that a more complex technique like ordered probit does. It should come as no surprise that OLS can come close to fitting nonlinear phenomena if it is suitably extended (in fact, ordered probit is one such extension). But such an extended OLS analysis is generally as complicated to perform as ordered probit, making the comparison less relevant for our purposes.

A more direct test of the difference between ordered probit and the simple "rounded" linear regression model is to consider the special case of ordered probit in which all the partition boundaries $\{\alpha_i\}$ are equally spaced and fall on sixteenths. That is, let the observed discrete price change Z_k be related to the unobserved continuous random variable Z_k^* in the following manner:

$$Z_k = \begin{cases} -\frac{4}{8} \text{ or less} & \text{if } Z_k^* \in \left(-\infty, -\frac{4}{8}+\frac{1}{16}\right), \\ \frac{j}{8} & \text{if } Z_k^* \in \left[\frac{j}{8}-\frac{1}{16}, \frac{j}{8}+\frac{1}{16}\right), \ j=-3,\ldots,3, \quad (10.6.5) \\ \frac{4}{8} \text{ or more} & \text{if } Z_k^* \in \left[\frac{4}{8}-\frac{1}{16}, \infty\right). \end{cases}$$

This is in the spirit of Ball (1988) in which there exists a "virtual" or "true" price change Z_k^* linked to the observed price change Z_k by rounding Z_k^* to the nearest multiple of eighths of a dollar. A testable implication of (10.6.5) is that the partition boundaries $\{\alpha_i\}$ are equally-spaced, i.e.,

$$\alpha_2 - \alpha_1 = \alpha_3 - \alpha_2 = \cdots = \alpha_{m-1} - \alpha_{m-2}, \tag{10.6.6}$$

where m is the number of states in our ordered probit model. We can rewrite (10.6.6) as a linear hypothesis for the $(m-1) \times 1$-vector of α's in the following way:

$$\text{H:} \quad A\alpha = 0, \tag{10.6.7}$$

where

$$\underset{(m-3)\times(m-1)}{A} \equiv \begin{pmatrix} 1 & -2 & 1 & 0 & 0 & 0 & \cdots & 0 \\ 0 & 1 & -2 & 1 & 0 & 0 & \cdots & 0 \\ 0 & 0 & 1 & -2 & 1 & 0 & \cdots & 0 \\ \vdots & \vdots & & \ddots & \ddots & \ddots & & \vdots \\ 0 & 0 & 0 & 0 & 0 & 1 & -2 & 1 \end{pmatrix}. \tag{10.6.8}$$

Since the asymptotic distribution of the maximum likelihood estimator $\hat{\alpha}$ is given by

$$\sqrt{n}(\hat{\alpha} - \alpha) \overset{a}{\sim} \mathcal{N}(0, \Sigma), \tag{10.6.9}$$

where Σ is the appropriate submatrix of the inverse of the information matrix corresponding to the likelihood function (10.2.11), the "delta method" yields the asymptotic distribution of the following statistic ψ under the null hypothesis H:

$$\text{H:} \quad \psi \equiv n\hat{\alpha}' A' (A\Sigma A')^{-1} A\hat{\alpha} \overset{a}{\sim} \chi^2_{m-3}. \tag{10.6.10}$$

Table 10.4 reports the ψ's for our sample of six stocks, and since the 1% critical values of the χ^2_2 and χ^2_6 are 9.21 and 16.8, respectively, we can easily reject the null hypothesis H for each of the stocks. However, because our sample sizes are so large, large χ^2 statistics need not signal important *economic* departures from the null hypothesis. Nevertheless, the point estimates of the α's in Table 10.2a show that they do differ in economically important ways from the simpler rounding model (10.6.5). With CUE, for example, $\hat{\alpha}_3 - \hat{\alpha}_2$ is 2.652 but $\hat{\alpha}_4 - \hat{\alpha}_3$ is 1.031. Such a difference captures the empirical fact that, conditioned on the X_k's and W_k's, -1-tick changes are less frequent than -2-tick changes, even less frequent than predicted by the simple linear probability model.

Discreteness does matter.

Table 10.5. *Names, ticker symbols, market values, and sample sizes over the period from January 4, 1988, to December 30, 1988 for 100 randomly selected stocks for which the ordered probit model was estimated. The selection procedure involved ranking all companies on the CRSP daily returns file by beginning-of-year market value and randomly choosing 20 companies in each of deciles 6 through 10 (decile 10 containing the largest firms), discarding companies which are clearly identified as equity mutual funds. Asterisks next to ticker symbols indicate those securities for which the maximum likelihood estimation procedure did not converge.*

Ticker Symbol	Company Name	Market Value × $1,000	Sample Size
Decile 6			
ACP	AMERICAN REAL ESTATE PARTNERS L	217,181	2,394
BCL	BIOCRAFT LABS INC	230,835	7,092
CUL	CULLINET SOFTWARE INC	189,680	18,712
DCY	DCNY CORP	149,073	1,567
FCH	FIRST CAPITAL HLDGS CORP	159,088	8,899
GYK	GIANT YELLOWKNIFE MINES LTD	137,337	1,594
ITX	INTERNATIONAL TECHNOLOGY CORP	161,960	14,675
LOM	LOMAS & NETTLETON MTG INVS	219,450	5,471
MCI*	MASSMUTUAL CORPORATE INVS INC	159,390	727
NET*	NORTH EUROPEAN OIL RTY TR	134,848	708
NPK	NATIONAL PRESTO INDS INC	193,489	1,222
OCQ*	ONEIDA LTD	133,665	1,643
OIL	TRITON ENERGY CORP	195,815	3,203
SII	SMITH INTERNATIONAL INC	148,779	5,435
SKY	SKYLINE CORP	145,821	5,804
SPF	STANDARD PACIFIC CORP DE LP	215,360	11,530
TOL	TOLL BROTHERS INC	157,463	5,519
WIC	WICOR INC	228,044	1,331
WJ	WATKINS JOHNSON CO	192,648	1,647
XTR	XTRA CORP	163,465	1,923
Decile 7			
CER	CILCORP INC	400,138	1,756
CKL	CLARK EQUIPMENT CO	408,509	11,580
CTP	CENTRAL MAINE POWER CO	353,648	5,326
DEI	DIVERSIFIED ENERGIES INC DE	395,505	3,411
FDO	FAMILY DOLLAR STORES INC	286,533	8,513
FRM	FIRST MISSISSIPPI CORP	306,931	8,711
FUR	FIRST UNION REAL EST EQ&MG INVTS	329,041	3,213
KOG	KOGER PROPERTIES INC	265,815	3,508
KWD	KELLWOOD COMPANY	236,271	4,138
LOG	RAYONIER TIMBERLANDS LP	302,500	2,670
MGM	MGMUA COMMUNICATIONS	312,669	10,376
NPR*	NEW PLAN RLTY TR	376,332	1,983
OKE	ONEOK INC	234,668	12,788
SFA	SCIENTIFIC ATLANTA INC	263,801	16,853
SIX*	MOTEL 6 LP	396,768	2,020
SJM	SMUCKER JM CO	373,931	762
SPW	SPX CORP	366,163	7,304
SRR	STRIDE RITE CORP	245,213	5,767
TGR	TIGER INTERNATIONAL INC	352,968	21,612
TRN	TRINITY INDUSTRIES INC	457,366	18,219

(continued)

Table 10.5. *(continued)*

Ticker Symbol	Company Name	Market Value × $1,000	Sample Size
Decile 8			
APS	AMERICAN PRESIDENT COS LTD	617,376	21,554
CAW	CAESARS WORLD INC	525,828	17,900
CBT	CABOT CORP	897,905	5,277
DDS	DILLARD DEPARTMENT STORES INC	758,327	7,267
ERB	ERBAMONT NV	796,698	8,007
FSI	FLIGHT SAFETY INTL INC	833,456	4,562
FVB	FIRST VIRGINIA BANKS INC	496,325	2,637
GLK	GREAT LAKES CHEM CORP	938,358	6,982
HD	HOME DEPOT INC	921,506	16,025
HPH	HARNISCHFEGER INDUSTRIES INC	469,921	7,573
KU	KENTUCKY UTILITIES CO	675,997	8,116
LAC	LAC MINERALS LTD NEW	921,456	4,900
NVP	NEVADA POWER CO	504,785	8,159
ODR	OCEAN DRILLING & EXPL CO	849,965	4,694
PA	PRIMERICA CORP NEW	946,507	35,390
PST	PETRIE STORES CORP	730,688	12,291
REN	ROLLINS ENVIRONMENTAL SVCS INC	825,353	44,272
SW *	STONE & WEBSTER INC	499,568	847
TW	T W SERVICES INC	691,852	16,863
USR	UNITED STATES SHOE CORP	618,686	24,991
Decile 9			
ABS	ALBERTSONS INC	1,695,456	14,171
BDX	BECTON DICKINSON & CO	2,029,188	17,499
CCL	CARNIVAL CRUISE LINES INC	1,294,152	7,111
CYR	CRAY RESEARCH INC	2,180,374	26,459
FFC	FUND AMERICAN COS INC	1,608,525	6,884
FG	USF & G CORP	2,163,821	56,848
GOU	GULF CANADA RESOURCES LIMITED	1,866,365	2,071
GWF	GREAT WESTERN FINANCIAL CORP	1,932,755	20,705
MEA	MEAD CORP	2,131,043	35,796
MEG	MEDIA GENERAL INC	1,002,059	6,304
MLL	MACMILLAN INC	1,387,400	22,083
NSP	NORTHERN STATES POWER CO MN	1,852,777	14,482
PDQ	PRIME MOTOR INNS INC	1,006,803	11,470
PKN	PERKIN ELMER CORP	1,088,400	17,181
RYC	RAYCHEM CORP	1,597,194	16,680
SNG	SOUTHERN NEW ENGLAND TELECOM	1,397,070	4,662
SPS	SOUTHWESTERN PUBLIC SERVICE CO	966,688	10,640
TET	TEXAS EASTERN CORP	1,146,380	29,428
WAG	WALGREEN COMPANY	1,891,310	23,684
WAN	WANG LABS INC	1,801,475	36,607

(continued)

Table 10.5. *(continued)*

Ticker Symbol	Company Name	Market Value × $1,000	Sample Size
Decile 10			
AN	AMOCO CORP	7,745,076	39,906
BN	BORDEN INC	3,671,366	22,630
BNI	BURLINGTON NORTHERN INC	4,644,253	33,224
BT	BANKERS TRUST NY CORP	2,426,399	18,502
CAT	CATERPILLAR INC DE	6,137,566	36,379
CBS	CBS INC	3,709,910	18,630
CCB	CAPITAL CITIES ABC INC	5,581,410	14,585
CPC	CPC INTERNATIONAL INC	3,317,679	27,852
DUK	DUKE POWER CO	4,341,008	17,918
GCI	GANNETT INC	6,335,081	33,512
GIS	GENERAL MILLS INC	4,378,513	26,786
MAS	MASCO CORP	2,867,259	25,746
MHP	MCGRAW HILL INC	2,438,169	36,047
NT	NORTHERN TELECOM LTD	4,049,909	10,128
NYN	NYNEX CORP	3,101,539	40,514
PCG	PACIFIC GAS & ELEC CO	5,982,064	93,981
PFE	PFIZER INC	7,693,452	68,035
RAL	RALSTON PURINA CO	4,517,751	24,710
SGP	SCHERING PLOUGH CORP	5,438,652	34,161
UCC	UNION CAMP CORP	2,672,966	14,080

10.7 A Larger Sample

Although our sample of six securities contains several hundred thousand observations, it is still only a small cross-section of the ISSM database, which contains the transactions of over two thousand stocks. It would be impractical for us to estimate our ordered probit model for each one, so we apply our specification to a larger sample of 100 securities chosen randomly, twenty from each of market-value deciles 6 through 10 (decile 10 contains companies with beginning-of-year market values in the top 10% of the CRSP database), also with the restriction that none of these one hundred engaged in stock splits or stock dividends greater than or equal to 3:2. We also discarded (without replacement) randomly chosen stocks that were obviously mutual funds, replacing them with new random draws. Table 10.5 lists the companies' names, ticker symbols, market values, and number of trades included in our final samples.

Securities from deciles 1 through 5 were not selected because many of them are so thinly traded that the small sample sizes would not permit accurate estimation of the ordered probit parameters. For example, even in deciles 6, 7, and 8, containing companies ranging from $133 million to

Table 10.6.   *Summary statistics for the sample of 100 randomly chosen securities for the period from January 4, 1988, to December 30, 1988. Market values are computed at the beginning of the year.*

Statistic	6	7	Deciles 8	9	10
Low Price ($)					
Decile Mean	13.94	17.95	21.47	28.02	59.90
Decile Std. Dev.	9.14	9.75	12.47	12.95	62.27
High Price ($)					
Decile Mean	21.11	27.25	33.61	41.39	77.56
Decile Std. Dev.	11.42	12.16	14.85	21.20	76.93
Market Value $\times$ 10^9					
Decile Mean	0.177	0.333	0.726	1.602	5.553
Decile Std. Dev.	0.033	0.065	0.167	0.414	3.737
% Prices > Midquote					
Decile Mean	40.68	41.47	41.77	42.53	43.55
Decile Std. Dev.	6.36	6.37	3.98	3.71	3.19
% Prices = Midquote					
Decile Mean	17.13	19.08	17.91	18.47	16.85
Decile Std. Dev.	3.99	3.67	4.51	3.93	2.97
% Prices < Midquote					
Decile Mean	42.18	39.45	40.32	39.00	39.60
Decile Std. Dev.	4.03	4.77	4.30	3.80	2.15
Avg. Price Change					
Decile Mean	0.0085	0.0038	0.0058	−0.0006	0.0015
Decile Std. Dev.	0.0200	0.0115	0.0103	0.0054	0.0065
Avg. Time Between Trades					
Decile Mean	1,085.91	873.66	629.35	430.74	222.49
Decile Std. Dev.	512.59	489.01	431.79	330.26	109.14
Avg. Bid/Ask Spread					
Decile Mean	2.1947	2.3316	2.4926	2.5583	2.9938
Decile Std. Dev.	0.5396	0.4657	0.3989	0.6514	1.6637
Avg. S&P 500 Futures Return[1]					
Decile Mean	−0.0048	−0.0037	−0.0026	−0.0020	−0.0009
Decile Std. Dev.	0.0080	0.0035	0.0025	0.0019	0.0006
Avg. Buy/Sell Indicator[2]					
Decile Mean	−0.0150	0.0202	0.0145	0.0353	0.0395
Decile Std. Dev.	0.0987	0.1064	0.0695	0.0640	0.0455
Avg. Signed Transformed Volume [3]					
Decile Mean	3.9822	0.1969	0.0782	0.2287	0.3017
Decile Std. Dev.	17.9222	0.6193	0.3230	0.3661	0.2504

(continued)

Table 10.6.   (continued)

Statistic	Deciles				
	6	7	8	9	10
Median Trading Volume ($)					
Decile Mean	6,002	7,345	12,182	16,483	28,310
Decile Std. Dev.	2,728	3,136	4,985	10,074	13,474
Box-Cox Parameter, $\hat{\lambda}$ [4]					
Decile Mean	0.1347	0.0710	0.0127	0.0230	0.0252
Decile Std. Dev.	0.2579	0.1517	0.0451	0.0679	0.1050

[1] Five-minute continuously-compounded returns of the S&P 500 index futures price, for the contract maturing in the closest month beyond the month in which transaction k occurred, where the return corresponding to the kth transaction of each stock is computed with the futures price recorded one minute before the nearest round minute *prior* to t_k and the price recorded five minutes before this.

[2] Takes the value 1 if the kth transaction price is greater than the average of the quoted bid and ask prices at time t_k, the value -1 if the kth transaction price is less than the average of the quoted bid and ask prices at time t_k, and 0 otherwise.

[3] Box-Cox transformation of dollar volume multiplied by the buy/sell indicator, where the Box-Cox parameter λ is estimated jointly with the other ordered probit parameters via maximum likelihood.

[4] Estimate of Box-Cox parameter λ which determines the degree of curvature that the transformation $T_\lambda(\cdot)$ exhibits in transforming dollar volume V_k before inclusion as an explanatory variable in the ordered probit specification. If $\lambda = 1$, the transformation $T_\lambda(\cdot)$ is linear, hence dollar volume enters the ordered probit model linearly. If $\lambda = 0$, the transformation is equivalent to $\log(\cdot)$, hence the natural logarithm of dollar volume enters the ordered probit model. When λ is between 0 and 1, the curvature of $T_\lambda(\cdot)$ is between logarithmic and linear.

$946 million in market value, there were still six companies for which the maximum likelihood estimation procedure did not converge: MCI, NET, OCQ, NPR, SIX, and SW. In all of these cases, the sample sizes were relatively small, yielding ill-behaved and erratic likelihood functions.

Table 10.6 presents summary statistics for this sample of one hundred securities broken down by deciles. As expected, the larger stocks tend to have higher prices, shorter times between trades, higher bid/ask spreads (in ticks), and larger median dollar volume per trade. Note that the statistics for $T_\lambda(V_k) \cdot IBS_k$ implicitly include estimates $\hat{\lambda}$ of the Box-Cox parameter which differ across stocks. Also, although the mean and standard deviation of $T_\lambda(V_k) \cdot IBS_k$ for decile 6 differ dramatically from those of the other deciles, these differences are driven solely by the outlier XTR. When this security is dropped from decile 6, the mean and standard deviation of $T_\lambda(V_k) \cdot IBS_k$ become -0.0244 and 0.3915, respectively, much more in line with the values of the other deciles.

In Table 10.7 we summarize the price impact measures across deciles, where we now define price impact to be the increase in the conditional expected price change as dollar volume increases from a base case of $1,000 to either the median dollar volume for each individual stock (the first panel of Table 10.7) or a dollar volume of $100,000 (the second panel). The first two rows of both panels report decile means and standard deviations of the *absolute* price impact (measured in ticks), whereas the second two rows of both panels report decile means and standard deviations of *percentage* price impact (measured as percentages of the mean of the high and low prices of each stock). For each stock i, we set Δt_k and AB_{k-1} to their sample means for that stock and condition on the following values for the other regressors:

$$V_{k-2} = \tfrac{1}{100} \cdot \text{median dollar volume for stock } i,$$

$$V_{k-3} = \tfrac{1}{100} \cdot \text{median dollar volume for stock } i,$$

$$SP500_{k-1} = 0.001, \quad SP500_{k-2} = 0.001, \quad SP500_{k-3} = 0.001,$$

$$Z_{k-1} = 1, \quad Z_{k-2} = 1, \quad Z_{k-3} = 1,$$

$$IBS_{k-1} = 1, \quad IBS_{k-2} = 1, \quad IBS_{k-3} = 1,$$

so that we are assuming the three most recent trades are buyer-initiated, accompanied by price increases of one tick each, and the sizes of the two earlier trades are equal to the median dollar volume of the particular stock in question.

From Table 10.7 we see that conditional on a dollar volume equal to the median for the most recent trade, larger capitalization stocks tend to exhibit larger absolute price impact, no doubt due to their higher prices and their larger median dollar volumes per trade. However, as percentages of the average of their high and low prices, the price impact across deciles is relatively constant as shown by the third row in the first panel of Table 10.7: the average price impact for a median trade in decile 6 is 0.0612%, compared to 0.0523% in decile 10. When conditioning on a dollar volume of $100,000, however, the results are quite different: the average absolute price impact is similar across deciles, but the average relative price impact is considerably smaller in decile 10 (0.0778%) than in decile 6 (0.2250%). Not surprisingly, a fixed $100,000 trade will have a greater percentage price impact on smaller capitalization, less liquid stocks than on larger ones.

Further insights on how price impact varies cross-sectionally can be gained from the cross-sectional regressions in Table 10.8, where the four price impact measures and the Box-Cox parameter estimates are each regressed on the following four variables: market value, the initial price level, median dollar volume, and median time-between-trades. Entries in the first row show that the Box-Cox parameters are inversely related to all four vari-

Table 10.7. *Price impact measures, defined as the increase in conditional expected price change given by the ordered probit model as the volume of the most recent trade is increased from a base case of $1,000 to either the median level of volume for each security or a level of $100,000, for the sample of 100 randomly chosen securities for the period from January 4, 1988, to December 30, 1988. Price impact measures expressed in percent are percentages of the average of the high and low prices of each security.*

	Deciles				
Price impact measure	6	7	8	9	10
Price Impact in Ticks					
Lagged volume = Median					
Decile Mean	0.0778	0.0991	0.1342	0.1420	0.2020
Decile Std. Dev.	0.0771	0.0608	0.0358	0.0532	0.0676
Price Impact in Percent					
Lagged volume = Median					
Decile Mean	0.0612	0.0600	0.0703	0.0583	0.0523
Decile Std. Dev.	0.0336	0.0286	0.0207	0.0229	0.0262
Price Impact in Ticks					
Lagged volume = $100,000					
Decile Mean	0.2240	0.2611	0.2620	0.2521	0.2849
Decile Std. Dev.	0.1564	0.1174	0.0499	0.0617	0.0804
Price Impact in Percent					
Lagged volume = $100,000					
Decile Mean	0.2250	0.1660	0.1442	0.1148	0.0778
Decile Std. Dev.	0.1602	0.0745	0.0570	0.0633	0.0383

ables, though none of the coefficient estimates are statistically significant and the adjusted R^2 is negative, a symptom of the imprecision with which the λ_i's are estimated. But the two percentage price impact regressions seem to have higher explanatory power, with adjusted R^2's of 37.6% and 22.1%, respectively. These two regressions have identical sign patterns, implying that percentage price impact is larger for smaller stocks, lower-priced stocks, higher-volume stocks, and stocks that trade less frequently.

Of course, these cross-sectional regressions are merely meant as data summaries, and may not correspond to well-specified regression equations. As a further check on the robustness of these regression-based inferences, in Table 10.9 we report Spearman rank correlations between the dependent and independent variables of Table 10.8, which are nonparametric measures of association and are asymptotically normal with mean 0 and variance $1/(n-1)$ under the null hypothesis of pairwise independence (see,

Table 10.8. *Summary of the cross-sectional dispersion in price impact measures and the nonlinearity of the price-change/volume relation (as measured by the Box-Cox parameters, $\hat{\lambda}_i$), via ordinary least-squares regressions for the sample of 100 randomly chosen securities, using market value, initial price, median volume, and median time-between-trades as explanatory variables, for the period from January 4, 1988, to December 30, 1988. Only 94 stocks are included in each of the regressions since the maximum likelihood estimation procedure did not converge for the omitted six. All the coefficents have been multiplied by a factor of 1,000, and z-statistics are given in parentheses, each of which is asymptotically distributed as $\mathcal{N}(0, 1)$ under the null hypothesis that the corresponding coefficient is zero.*

Dependent Variable	Constant	Market Value	Initial Price	Median Volume	Median Δt_k	$\bar{R}^2$
Box-Cox Parameter, $\hat{\lambda}_i$[1]	118.74	−2.08	−7.42	−8.39	−2.55	−0.008
	(2.11)	(−0.31)	(−1.35)	(−1.04)	(−0.33)	
Price Impact in Ticks	93.82	9.86	1.76	5.25	−2.31	0.184
Lagged Volume = Median	(3.72)	(3.27)	(0.71)	(1.45)	(−0.66)	
Price Impact in Percent	36.07	−1.19	−2.31	6.66	0.67	0.376
Lagged Volume = Median	(4.46)	(−1.23)	(−2.92)	(5.72)	(0.60)	
Price Impact in Ticks	265.34	8.07	−5.64	−3.59	3.25	0.003
Lagged Volume = $100,000	(7.03)	(1.79)	(−1.52)	(−0.66)	(0.62)	
Price Impact in Percent	138.52	−8.53	−9.61	8.53	1.74	0.221
Lagged Volume = $100,000	(4.17)	(−2.15)	(−2.95)	(1.78)	(0.38)	

[1]The Box-Cox parameter λ determines the degree of curvature that the transformation $T_\lambda(\cdot)$ exhibits in transforming dollar volume V_k before inclusion as an explanatory variable in the ordered probit specification. If $\lambda = 1$, the transformation $T_\lambda(\cdot)$ is linear, hence dollar volume enters the ordered probit model linearly. If $\lambda = 0$, the transformation is equivalent to $\log(\cdot)$, hence the natural logarithm of dollar volume enters the ordered probit model. When λ is between 0 and 1, the curvature of $T_\lambda(\cdot)$ is between logarithmic and linear.

for example, Randles and Wolfe (1979)). Since $n = 94$, the two-standard-error confidence interval about zero for each of the correlation coefficients is $[-0.207, 0.207]$. The sign patterns are much the same in Table 10.9 as in Table 10.8, despite the fact that the Spearman rank correlations are not *partial* correlation coefficients.

Such cross-sectional regressions and rank correlations serve only as informal summaries of the data since they are not formally linked to any explicit theories of how price impact should vary across stocks. However, they are consistent with our earlier findings from the six stocks, suggesting that those results are not specific to the behavior of a few possibly peculiar stocks, but may be evidence of a more general and stable mechanism for transaction prices.

Table 10.9. *Robust measure of the cross-sectional dispersion in price impact measures and the nonlinearity of the price-change/volume relation (as measured by the Box-Cox parameters $\hat{\lambda}_i$), via the Spearman rank correlations of $\hat{\lambda}_i$ and price impact measures with market value, initial price, median volume, and median time-between-trades for the sample of 100 randomly chosen securities, of which 94 are used since the maximum likelihood estimation procedure did not converge for the omitted six, over the period from January 4, 1988, to December 30, 1988. Under the null hypothesis of independence, each of the correlation coefficients is asymptotically normal with mean 0 and variance $1/(n-1)$, hence the two-standard-error confidence interval for these correlation coefficients is $[-0.207, 0.207]$.*

	Market Value	Initial Price	Median Volume	Median Δt
Box-Cox Parameter, $\hat{\lambda}_i$ [1]	−0.260	−0.503	−0.032	−0.015
Price Impact in Ticks Lagged Volume = Median	0.604	0.678	0.282	−0.360
Price Impact in Percent Lagged Volume = Median	−0.156	−0.447	0.486	0.082
Price Impact in Ticks Lagged Volume = $100,000	0.273	0.329	−0.020	−0.089
Price Impact in Percent Lagged Volume = $100,000	−0.547	−0.815	0.088	0.316

[1] The Box-Cox parameter λ determines the degree of curvature that the transformation $T_\lambda(\cdot)$ exhibits in transforming dollar volume V_k before inclusion as an explanatory variable in the ordered probit specification. If $\lambda = 1$, the transformation $T_\lambda(\cdot)$ is linear, hence dollar volume enters the ordered probit model linearly. If $\lambda = 0$, the transformation is equivalent to $\log(\cdot)$, hence the natural logarithm of dollar volume enters the ordered probit model. When λ is between 0 and 1, the curvature of $T_\lambda(\cdot)$ is between logarithmic and linear.

10.8 Conclusion

Using 1988 transactions data from the ISSM database, we find that the sequence of trades does affect the conditional distribution for price changes, and the effect is greater for larger capitalization and more actively traded securities. Trade size is also an important factor in the conditional distribution of price changes, with larger trades creating more price pressure, but in a nonlinear fashion. The price impact of a trade depends critically on the *sequence* of past price changes and order flows (buy/sell/buy versus sell/buy/buy). The ordered probit framework allows us to compare the price impact of trading over many different market scenarios, such as trading "with" versus "against" the market, trading in "up" and "down" markets, etc. Finally, we show that discreteness does matter, in the sense that the simpler linear regression analysis of price changes cannot capture all the features of transaction price changes evident in the ordered probit estimates, such as the clustering of price changes on even eighths.

With these applications, we hope to have demonstrated the flexibility and power of the ordered probit model as a tool for investigating the dynamic behavior of transaction prices. Much like the linear regression model for continuous-valued data, the ordered probit model can capture and summarize complex relations between discrete-valued price changes and continuous-valued regressors. Indeed, even in the simple applications considered here, we suffer from an embarrassment of riches in that there are many other empirical implications of our ordered probit estimates that we do not have space to report. For example, we have compared the price impact of only one or two sequences of order flows, price history, and market returns, but there are many other combinations of market conditions, some that might yield considerably different findings. By selecting other scenarios, we may obtain a deeper and broader understanding of how transaction prices react to changing market conditions.

Although we have selected a wide range of regressors to illustrate the flexibility of ordered probit, in practice the specific application will dictate which regressors to include. If, for example, one is interested in testing the implications of Admati and Pfleiderer's (1988) model of intraday patterns in price and volume, natural regressors to include are time-of-day indicators in the conditional mean and variance. If one is interested in measuring how liquidity and price impact vary across markets, an exchange indicator would be appropriate. For intraday event studies, "event" indicators in both the conditional mean and variance are the natural regressors, and in such cases the generalized residuals we calculated as diagnostics can also be used to construct cumulative average (generalized) residuals.

In the few illustrative applications considered here, we have only hinted at the kinds of insights that ordered probit can yield. The possibilities increase exponentially as we consider the many ways our basic specification can be changed to accommodate the growing number of highly parametrized and less stylized theories about the market microstructure, and we expect to see many other applications in the near future.

11

Index-Futures Arbitrage and the Behavior of Stock Index Futures Prices

THE SPECTACULAR GROWTH in the volume of trading in stock index futures contracts reveals the interest in these instruments that is shared by a broad cross section of market participants. It is generally agreed that the linkage in prices between the underlying basket of stocks and the futures is maintained by arbitragcurs. If this link is maintained effectively, then investors who are committed to trade will recognize these markets as perfect substitutes, and their choice between these markets will be dictated by convenience and their transaction costs. However, researchers have reported substantial and sustained deviation in futures prices from their theoretical values; indeed, Rubinstein (1987, p. 84) concludes that "The growth in index futures trading continues to outstrip the amounts of capital that are available for arbitrage."

Considerable attention has been focused on arbitrage strategies involving stock index futures and on their effects on markets, especially on the expiration dates of these contracts. By contrast, there is little work on the stochastic behavior of the deviation of futures prices from fair values. In this chapter, we study transaction data on Standard & Poor's 500 futures contracts in conjunction with minute-by-minute quotes of the S&P 500 index. Our goal is to examine the behavior of these prices in light of the conventional arbitrageur's strategies.

It should be emphasized at the outset that it is extremely difficult to specify a *model* for the deviations of futures prices from "fair values." These deviations are, presumably, affected by the flow of orders as well as by the difference of opinion among participants regarding parameters of the valuation model that provides "fair values." It is well known that the conventional strategies pursued by *arbitrageurs* to take advantage of these deviations are *not* risk-free, and are influenced further by the transaction costs they involve. The purpose of this chapter is to examine the *empirical* behavior of

347

these deviations; in doing so, we examine the validity of certain proposed hypotheses regarding the stochastic behavior of these deviations, given that market participants will attempt to exploit these as profit opportunities.

In Section 11.1 we discuss some considerations of the behavior of futures and index prices after describing the well-known and commonly used pricing model. Section 11.2 provides the empirical results, and we conclude in Section 11.3.

11.1 Arbitrage Strategies and the Behavior of Stock Index Futures Prices

The arguments underlying the valuation of derivative assets exploit the availability of a replicating portfolio of existing assets whose value coincides with the price of the derivative security at its expiration date. In frictionless markets the availability of a perfect substitute for the derivative asset guarantees that a profit opportunity, if one surfaced, would attract "arbitrageurs" who would quickly close the gap between the price of the asset and of its substitute. The presence of transaction costs implies that the price of the derivative asset could fluctuate within a band around its theoretical value without representing a potential profit opportunity. The width of this band would be dictated by the transaction costs of the most favorably situated arbitrageurs. In the context of the daily settlement prices of stock index futures contracts, this has been examined by Modest and Sundaresan (1983). However, the band could also be affected by the fact that the replicating portfolio of existing assets serves only as a close substitute, and that the temporal behavior of the spread between the market price and a model value is further influenced by alternative trading strategies that will be employed by arbitrageurs. We examine these issues in this section.

It is well known, from the work of Black and Scholes (1973), that the replicating portfolio for an option involves a dynamic, self-financing trading rule that depends on the unobservable volatility parameters for the stochastic process of the underlying asset's price. However, for a *forward* contract, the replicating portfolio involves a buy-and-hold strategy that, in the absence of random payouts from the underlying asset, depends only on observable quantities. The differences between forward prices and futures prices have been studied extensively (see, for example, Black (1976); Cox, Ingersoll, and Ross (1981); Richard and Sundaresan (1981); Jarrow and Oldfield (1981); and French (1983)). With nonstochastic interest rates, forward and futures prices will be equal; however, the replicating portfolio for futures contracts will involve a dynamic trading rule even in this case.[1] In

---

[1] See Cox, Ingersoll, and Ross (1981, p. 340). In later discussion (as also in the empirical

practice, it is generally argued that differences in forward and futures prices are small enough to be safely ignored; indeed, many programs that seek to arbitrage the price differences by trading in stock index futures and in the basket of stocks representing the index employ the forward pricing model adjusted for transaction costs. We begin by briefly examining this model for forward prices on stock index portfolios (with and without transaction costs), and we draw implications for the behavior of futures prices over a contract's life.

11.1.1 Forward Contracts on Stock Indexes (No Transaction Costs)

Consider a forward contract on an index of stocks, where the index represents a capitalization-weighted basket of stocks and is a feasible buy-and-hold portfolio. Assume that markets are perfect and frictionless, that any performance bonds necessary to take a position in the forward market can be posted in interest-bearing assets, that borrowing and lending take place at the (constant) continuously compounded rate r, and that the basket of stocks representing the index pays dividends continuously at the rate d. Consider the following portfolio, constructed at date t and held until the forward contract expires at date T:

1. Buy the basket of stocks at the price S_t (the index price at date t) and continuously reinvest the dividends received until date T.
2. Borrow $\$S_t$ at t to finance the acquisition in Equation (11.1.1).
3. Sell a forward contract at the currently quoted forward price $G_{t,T}$.

This portfolio is costless at t; and to avoid certain losses or gains at T, it can be shown that

$$G_{t,T} = S_t e^{(r-d)(T-t)}. \tag{11.1.1}$$

If the forward price at market $G_{t,T}^m$ is greater than $S_t e^{(r-d)(T-t)}$, then a strategy that buys the index and sells forward contracts will earn riskless profits in excess of the risk-free rate r. If $G_{t,T}^m$ is less, then a strategy that sells the index and buys futures contracts will achieve a financing rate below the risk-free rate.[2]

Section 11.2) we use the term *arbitrageur*, consistent with current practice; however, it is clear, as stressed below, that the program trading strategies are not risk-free.

[2] In this case, investors who already own the basket of stocks represented in the index portfolio are in the best position to undertake the arbitrage; investors who are not already in possession of the index basket would be forced to sell stocks short and would be subject to the "uptick" rule for short sales. For a more complete description of these strategies, see Gould (1987); and for analysis of the hedging costs and effectiveness, see Merrick (1988).

11.1.2 The Impact of Transaction Costs

Stoll and Whaley (1986) discuss the impact of transaction costs on the index-futures arbitrage strategy, starting with the forward-contract pricing relation shown above. The impact of transaction costs is to permit the futures price to fluctuate within a band around the formula value in relation (11.1.1). The width of the band derives from round-trip commissions in the stock and futures markets and from the market impact costs of putting on the trade initially. The market impact costs of closing the stock position can be avoided by holding the position until expiration of the futures contract and employing market-on-close orders.[3]

We consider two issues related to this view. First, this line of argument says that the mispricing around the formula value (the band) should not exceed a value (dictated by transaction costs) that is *constant* over the life of the contract. That is, if the transaction costs are independent of the remaining maturity for the contract, then the width of the band should not vary over time.[4] Second, this argument provides no role for the arbitrageurs when futures prices lie within the band; there is no influence on the trajectory of the futures price as long as it does not stray from its transaction-cost-based limits. Consider the commonly defined "mispricing,"[5]

$$x_{t,T} = [F_{t,T} - S_t e^{(r-d)(T-t)}]/S_t, \tag{11.1.2}$$

which is the difference between the market futures price of the stock index futures contract ($F_{t,T}$) and its theoretical price (assuming that it is a forward contract), all normalized by the index value.[6] The transaction-cost limits for $x_{t,T}$ would be given by the sum of the commission costs in the stock and futures markets, plus the market impact cost of trading initially in the stocks and in the futures. Sustained deviations of $x_{t,T}$ outside these limits would be evidence of the lack of arbitrage capital. This view implies that $x_{t,T}$ should be clipped above and below at these limits but provides no guidance with respect to its behavior within the boundaries.

---

[3]Beginning with the June 1987 contract, the expiration has shifted to using the opening index price as the cash settlement price for the futures. Therefore, reversal of stock positions would employ market-on-open orders, and these orders also avoid market impact costs.

[4]Modest and Sundaresan (1983) argue that if arbitrageurs lose the interest earnings on a fraction of the proceeds of the short sale of stocks when their strategy calls for shorting stock, then the band would be asymmetric around the "fair" price and would be wider with more time remaining. However, because of the uptick rule, arbitrageurs rarely use short positions in program-driven strategies; they generally employ the pools of stock they own or control if the futures are underpriced.

[5]We use this term only because we lack a less clumsy alternative—we do not mean to imply that every nonzero level of the "mispricing" is evidence of market inefficiency.

[6]We work with the mispricing in relative terms because the major components of the determinant of the bounds should be proportional to the level of the index.

We argue that larger deviations in $x_{t,T}$ can persist outside these transaction-cost (TC) limits for longer times until expiration $(T - t)$. This may occur for several reasons. First, with longer times until expiration, there is increased risk of unanticipated increases or decreases in dividends. These will erode the anticipated profits from an attempt to arbitrage $x_{t,T}$ when it violates these limits. Put another way, programs that seek riskless profits should account for worst-case dividend policies. Second, the difference between futures and forward prices, which is embedded in the definition in Equation (11.1.2), reflects the unanticipated interest earnings or costs from financing the marking-to-market flows from the futures position. An attempt to replicate the futures-contract payoff will require trading in the stocks, and both of these will contribute to a wider limit for $x_{t,T}$ with greater times to expiration. Finally, attempts at arbitrage-motivated trading that employ less than the full basket of stocks in the index must allow for a greater margin of error with longer times to expiration. This would arise not only because of the possibility that the value of the chosen basket might not track the index accurately, but also because costly adjustments would be necessary prior to expiration. Consequently, wider deviations in $x_{t,T}$ will be required at longer times to maturity in order to induce arbitrageurs to take a position in these markets. These considerations point up the fact that the "arbitrage" strategies are not risk-free.

There are countervailing forces that serve to provide a narrower trading band, and they stem from the fact that arbitrageurs have the option either to reverse their positions prior to the expiration date or to roll forward their futures position into the next available maturity.[7] To see this, suppose that an arbitrageur views the random mispricing $x_{t,T}$ as an arbitrageable sequence whose current level is observable. She knows that the mispricing disappears at date T so that $x_{T,T} = 0$. The arbitrage strategy conventionally considered is to sell $x_{t,T}$ if it is positive at date t and to reverse the position at T, or to buy it if $x_{t,T}$ is negative and to reverse that position at date T, as long as

$$|x_{t,T}| > \text{TC}_1, \qquad (11.1.3)$$

where more TC_1 = round-trip stock commission + round-trip futures commission + market impact in futures + market impact in stocks.[8] However, the arbitrageur knows that at a future date $s < T$ it is possible for her (a) to reverse her position by paying a market impact cost in both the stock and futures markets or (b) to roll her futures position into the next maturity and incur commissions and market impact costs only in the futures mar-

---

[7]Brennan and Schwartz (1986, 1987) make the argument, as we do here, that the arbitrageurs have the option to close out a position prematurely.

[8]This assumes that the transaction costs are the same for long and short positions in futures and for purchases and sales in stocks. It is not crucial to the analysis.

ket. Therefore, the optimal band at which to *undertake* an opening position would be narrower than the optimal band in the absence of strategies (a) and (b). This is because at the current date t, with an arbitrage program trade already in place, the arbitrageur benefits from the option value of closing her position prematurely at perhaps a greater profit than indicated by the current level $x_{t,T}$. Given these two arguments, it is important to examine empirically the behavior of the deviations as a function of time to maturity. We consider this in the next section.

However, this option argument has a further implication. Once an arbitrage trade has been put on, it will be optimal to close that position prior to putting on a new arbitrage program in the reverse direction. Suppose that we had put on an arbitrage at date t (in the past) when $x_{t,T} > 0$ by buying the index basket and selling futures short. Then, to initiate an offsetting trade at the current date, we would incur additional costs TC_2, where TC_2 is simply the sum of the market impact costs in the stock and futures markets. If we were to undertake this as a net new position, we would need to cover the higher costs TC_1. The implication is that the stochastic behavior of the mispricing will display properties, over the next interval, that depend on the history of the mispricing until that point. Suppose that the historical trajectory of the mispricing $x_{t,T}$ has been positive and large. Then arbitrageurs who had undertaken positions long in index stocks and short in futures will undo them when at date $s > T$ the mispricing $x_{s,T}$ has fallen to some negative value. The magnitude of this value will depend, among other things, on the additional transaction costs from closing the position prematurely (TC_2). If the mispricing never "corrects" itself over the life of the contract, then the burden of the reversing trades will fall at the close of the expiration date. In fact, the direction of market-on-close (or, since the June 1987 expiration, market-on-open) orders on expiration days may be predictable only if the history of the mispricing indicates that the arbitrageurs took positions that were all on one side of the market and did not have the opportunity to reverse or roll forward these positions profitably. In Section 11.2 we consider the hypothesis that the behavior of $x_{t,T}$ over time displays non-Markov properties: its distribution over the future is dependent on its path in the past.

11.2 Empirical Evidence

In this section we present evidence using the intraday prices for the Standard & Poor's 500 futures contract and for the underlying index. This evidence deals with the behavior of the futures and index prices and with the hypotheses regarding the behavior of the mispricing series $x_{t,T}$. WE begin first by describing the data employed.

11.2.1 Data

The futures-price database, obtained from the Chicago Mercantile Exchange, consists of time-stamped transaction data for transactions in the S&P 500 futures contracts from April 1982 (the inception of trading) to June 1987. The contracts traded follow the March-June-September-December cycle—although the nearest contract is typically the most heavily traded. Each transaction record contains (in addition to contract identification, time stamp, and price) information which tags that transaction as a sale, a bid, or an offer and which indicates whether it was canceled, corrected, or a designated open or a close. The size (number of contracts) of the transaction is not available.

These transaction data record only transactions with price changes. Because the trading occurs by open outcry in a continuous market, the time stamping of a consummated transaction will lag by a few seconds, and perhaps by more in periods of heavy trading. In these periods particularly, it is possible to have the records stamped out of sequence. We observed several transactions subsequent to 9:00 A.M. (subsequent to 8:30 A.M. after October 1, 1985) occurring before the transaction that was labeled as the open—this signified the end of the opening "round" of transactions. Likewise, we observed transactions after the first designated closing "round" of transactions, occurring after 3:14 P.M. Almost always, these open- and close-designated records are also marked as representing a sale (as opposed to a bid or an offer).

The database of S&P 500 stock index quotes, time-stamped approximately one minute apart, was also provided to us by the Chicago Mercantile Exchange (CME). The index is updated continuously using transaction prices (the most recent prices as reported) of the component 500 stocks. This database captures these quotations approximately 60 seconds apart. While traders on the floor of the CME have access to continuously updated series, the index series available contains stale prices, especially for the thinly traded stocks; and the quoted index fails to use the bid or offer side of the market, so that the price at which one can buy or sell the index basket might be higher or lower than the quoted value. These facts must be kept in mind when working with the mispricing series.

In computing the mispricing series, we use quotes that are approximately 15 minutes apart, and we employ the nearest quotes available *after* the quarter-hour mark. Each contract is followed from the expiration date of the previous contract until its expiration. Because the near futures are heavily traded, and our stock index quotes are clocked one minute apart, this means that our futures price will be stamped almost immediately following the quarter-hour mark, while the index quote will be, on average, 30 seconds after the quarter-hour mark. The mispricing computed from these quotes will be biased, perhaps slightly, in favor of signaling potential profit opportunities. Conversations with market makers suggest that the time taken to put on a simultaneous program in the stock and futures markets depends, among other things, on the size of the trade, on the composition of the stock basket, and on the depth of the market—the estimates range from 60 seconds to several minutes.[9] Usually, the futures leg can be executed very quickly. This means that, because we do not compute a separate series that would represent executable profits after recognizing a profit opportunity, the constructed series may be inappropriate to judge the actual profitability of program trades.

In order to construct the mispricing series $x_{t,T}$, we require dividend forecasts for the 500 stocks in the index, and a measure of the interest rate for loans maturing at the expiration date of the futures. We use the realized daily dividend yield of the value-weighted index of all NYSE stocks supplied by the Center for Research in Security Prices (CRSP) at the university of Chicago as a proxy for the yield of the S&P 500.[10] Given that the S&P 500 is also value-weighted, the CRSP value-weighted dividend yield should be a reasonably proxy. Furthermore, given that the average maturity of our futures contracts is $1\frac{1}{2}$ months, the error in employing this series is likely to be small. The daily interest data for Treasury bills and for certificates of deposit expiring around the expiration date were kindly supplied by Kidder, Peabody. Throughout this chapter we report results using the rates for certificates of deposit; results using the Treasury-bill interest rate were also calculated and are similar to those with the CDs.

The mispricing series so constructed is available for every quarter-hour mark until 4:00 P.M. EST, although the S&P 500 futures contracts continue to trade until 4:15 P.M. This series is constructed starting with the September 1983 contract; we avoided using earlier contracts because prior studies had reported unusual behavior for these.[11] In Section 11.2.2 we report on the behavior of the futures and index series used to construct the mispricing. Section 11.2.3 considers the behavior of the actual mispricing series.

11.2.2 Behavior of Futures and Index Series

In this section we examine the behavior of futures prices and index prices for each of the 16 contracts from September 1983 through June 1987. We

---

[9]This depends on whether the automated order-entry system is employed or not. Toward the end of our sample period, the automated order-entry system became the dominant mode of stock-basket trades. Note also that arbitrageurs, because they have finer information regarding bid and asked prices for the component basket of stocks, would be in a position to exploit this information in constructing their strategies.

[10]For the March and June 1987 contracts, the CRSP data are not available. We used the daily forecasts of dividend yield (remaining until expiration) on the S&P 500 provided to us by Kidder, Peabody.

[11]See, for example, Figlewski (1984).

present evidence on the autocorrelations and on the variability of futures prices and index prices; our focus is on (1) the extent to which nonsynchronous (or state) prices are a problem in available index values and (2) the relative variability of the prices in two markets.[12]

The results reported in this section employ first differences in the logarithm of the futures price and in the logarithm of the index value over the appropriate interval. By varying the interval length (we use 15, 30, 60, and 120 minutes and one trading day), we can assess the importance of stale prices in the index quotes.

Table 11.1 reports the autocorrelation estimates at eight lags for the price changes for both the futures- and the spot-price series using the 15-minute interval. They are computed from intraday intervals only: overnight and weekend intervals are discarded. The autocorrelations of the futures series are close to 0.0 at all eight lags, with only a slight tendency for the first-order autocorrelation coefficient to be negative; it is likely that this is induced by the observed futures prices bouncing between the bid and asked prices. By contrast, the index series is positively autocorrelated at the first lag, with first-order autocorrelations ranging from 0.038 to 0.41 across the 16 contracts. At lags beyond the first, the index series exhibits autocorrelations close to zero. These results are consistent with the presence of stale prices in the available index quotes. It is noteworthy that the problem of stale prices has diminished over time: the first-order autocorrelations for the index series are noticeably smaller in the recent past. This finding may be attributed to increased stock market trading volume in recent years.

The autocorrelations for longer differencing intervals (except for one trading day) are based on estimates that exploit the overlapping nature of the data: these estimators are formed as a function of the estimators for 15-minute intervals. For example, the first-order autocorrelation for the 60-minute differencing interval, $\rho_{60}(1)$, is given by[13]

$$\rho_{60}(1) = \frac{\rho(1) + 2\rho(2) + 3\rho(3) + 4\rho(4) + 3\rho(5) + 2\rho(6) + \rho(7)}{4 + 6\rho(1) + 4\rho(2) + 2\rho(3)},$$

where $\rho(j) = j$th-order correlation for 15-minute intervals. Given that our basic series uses 15-minute intervals, this estimator is efficient in exploiting the degree of overlap. We do not report higher-order autocorrelations for the longer differencing intervals.

---

[12]See Kawaller, Koch, and Koch (1987) and Stoll and Whaley (1990) for an analysis of the lead and lag relationships between the two markets.

[13]This follows from the fact that the price change over an hourly interval is the sum of the four (basic series) price changes over 15-minute intervals. Therefore, the autocorrelation between the lagged price changes at hourly intervals $\rho_{60}(1)$ reflects the autocorrelations from the first lag for 15-minute data to autocorrelations at the *seventh* lag.

Table 11.1.   *Autocorrelations for changes of the logarithm of price in the S&P 500 futures and index by contract, September 1983 to June 1987.*

Contract	Lag								Number of Observations
	1	2	3	4	5	6	7	8	
Panel A: S&P 500 Futures									
Sep 83	0.02	−0.07	−0.05	−0.01	0.03	−0.01	0.06	0.03	1,512
Dec 83	0.00	0.02	0.04	0.00	0.02	0.00	0.02	0.03	1,512
Mar 84	0.00	−0.01	−0.04	0.05	0.01	0.04	−0.02	0.03	1,488
Jun 84	−0.01	0.03	−0.04	0.00	−0.03	−0.03	0.02	0.01	1,440
Sep 84	−0.01	−0.01	0.04	0.00	0.00	−0.04	0.08	−0.04	1,632
Dec 84	−0.05	−0.02	0.05	0.04	0.01	0.03	0.00	−0.05	1,536
Mar 85	−0.08	0.02	0.08	0.00	0.02	−0.01	0.01	0.01	1,368
Jun 85	−0.08	−0.01	0.07	0.04	0.05	0.00	0.02	−0.04	1,632
Sep 85	−0.02	0.05	0.03	0.01	0.05	0.01	0.00	−0.03	1,512
Dec 85	−0.07	0.02	0.06	0.05	−0.02	0.02	−0.02	0.01	1,654
Mar 86	−0.03	0.03	0.01	−0.01	0.01	0.00	0.01	0.00	1,612
Jun 86	0.00	0.00	0.01	0.01	0.03	0.04	0.04	−0.04	1,638
Sep 86	−0.02	0.03	−0.02	−0.01	0.00	0.04	0.01	0.01	1,638
Dec 86	−0.02	−0.01	0.03	−0.02	−0.02	−0.04	0.02	0.01	1,664
Mar 87	−0.14	−0.16	0.22	−0.04	−0.04	0.06	0.01	0.01	1,612
Jun 87	0.05	0.00	0.02	0.00	0.03	−0.02	0.03	−0.02	1,612
Panel B: S&P 500 Index									
Sep 83	0.41	−0.03	−0.09	−0.04	0.02	0.05	0.07	0.06	1,512
Dec 83	0.41	0.03	0.01	0.00	0.00	0.00	0.03	0.03	1,512
Mar 84	0.31	0.03	−0.05	−0.02	−0.01	0.01	0.05	0.03	1,488
Jun 84	0.37	0.04	−0.03	−0.02	0.01	0.03	0.02	0.01	1,440
Sep 84	0.29	−0.02	0.00	0.01	−0.05	−0.03	0.03	0.04	1,632
Dec 84	0.21	−0.03	0.00	0.04	0.04	0.02	0.03	0.02	1,536
Mar 85	0.16	−0.03	0.06	0.03	−0.01	0.00	0.01	0.01	1,368
Jun 85	0.18	−0.03	0.02	0.01	0.02	0.02	0.03	0.04	1,632
Sep 85	0.25	0.03	0.04	0.05	0.04	0.06	0.02	0.01	1,512
Dec 85	0.18	0.02	0.01	−0.03	0.00	0.02	0.01	0.04	1,654
Mar 86	0.14	0.00	0.02	0.02	−0.02	0.03	0.00	0.01	1,612
Jun 86	0.10	−0.02	−0.01	0.06	0.03	0.07	0.03	0.01	1,638
Sep 86	0.04	0.04	0.03	−0.01	−0.02	0.02	0.09	0.02	1,638
Dec 86	0.08	0.00	0.01	0.00	−0.01	−0.02	0.02	0.00	1,664
Mar 87	0.04	−0.07	0.13	0.01	−0.02	−0.02	0.02	0.01	1,612
Jun 87	0.09	0.00	0.00	0.02	0.01	−0.02	−0.04	0.00	1,612

Autocorrelations are based on 15-minute observation intervals.

Panels B, C, D, and E of Table 11.2 present the first-order autocorrelations for the longer differencing intervals of 30, 60, and 120 minutes and one trading day, respectively. Two results emerge from these panels. First, the problem of nonsynchronous data in the index series is mitigated by employing longer differencing intervals: At 30 minutes, the first-order autocorrelation in the index series (panel B) is much smaller than the first-order autocorrelation at 15 minutes (panel A), and the corresponding value at 60 minutes (panel C) is close to zero. Second, whenever the first-order autocorrelation for the index series is high (for any contract, over the longer differencing intervals), the autocorrelation for the futures series also tends to be high. For example, the 120-minute-interval data in panel C provides evidence that, for the September 1984 contract, the index series' autocorrelation was 0.19, but the futures autocorrelation was also high at 0.17. This indicates that nonsynchronous data are *not* the sole source of autocorrelation.

We turn now to the variability of the two data series. If arbitrageurs maintained the link between these markets, then the variability of the two series should be equal: this is in keeping with the "redundant security" view, and it is consistent with the implication from a forward pricing model, as long as interest rates and dividends are nonstochastic. Furthermore, if differences in transaction costs are large between these two markets, it is possible that new information is incorporated with greater speed in one market relative to the other. Therefore, these differences would exhibit themselves when we examine the variability of the two series, especially for the smaller differencing intervals.

Panels A through E of Table 11.2 report the standard deviations for the two series for the five observation intervals. Panel A reports the standard deviation for the basic 15-minute differencing interval as well as the variance ratio for the futures and index series. The standard deviations of the futures series are all higher than those for the index, but this might be due solely to nonsynchronous prices rather than to a structural feature of the markets. The results for longer intervals, in panels B through E, serve to resolve this issue.[14]

If the variability of the two markets is equal, then as the observation interval is lengthened and the stale-price problem is mitigated, the variance ratio of the futures series to the index series should approach 1. However, this is not the case. The ratio in most cases is above 1 for all intervals. Table

---

[14]The standard deviations for longer intervals are efficiently computed using information from the 15-minute interval. For example, the 60-minute-interval standard deviation, σ_{60}, is computed from

$$\sigma_{60} = \sigma_{15}[4 + 6\rho(1) + 4\rho(2) + 2\rho(3)]^{1/2}.$$

This follows from the fact that the hourly return is the sum of four returns over 15-minute intervals, where these are correlated.

Table 11.2.   *Summary statistics for the changes of the logarithm of price in the S&P 500 futures and index by contract, September 1983 to June 1987.*

Contract	Futures		Index		Variance Ratio[2]
	Standard Deviation[1]	First-Order Autocorrelation	Standard Deviation[1]	First-Order Autocorrelation	
Panel A: Data at 15-Minute Intervals					
Sep 83	0.163	0.022	0.128	0.408	1.634
Dec 83	0.125	−0.001	0.095	0.409	1.739
Mar 84	0.147	−0.005	0.119	0.313	1.536
Jun 84	0.150	−0.010	0.114	0.369	1.715
Sep 84	0.176	−0.011	0.149	0.289	1.410
Dec 84	0.155	−0.055	0.114	0.213	1.858
Mar 85	0.145	−0.078	0.112	0.156	1.664
Jun 85	0.115	−0.079	0.093	0.178	1.506
Sep 85	0.108	−0.020	0.083	0.249	1.683
Dec 85	0.128	−0.065	0.102	0.184	1.575
Mar 86	0.172	−0.029	0.137	0.140	1.576
Jun 86	0.171	−0.005	0.142	0.103	1.460
Sep 86	0.202	−0.018	0.173	0.045	1.362
Dec 86	0.182	−0.021	0.147	0.079	1.520
Mar 87	0.219	−0.136	0.168	0.038	1.703
Jun 87	0.219	0.048	0.214	0.086	1.049
Panel B: Data at 30-Minute Intervals					
Sep 83	0.233	−0.085	0.214	0.093	1.186
Dec 83	0.177	0.036	0.159	0.170	1.233
Mar 84	0.208	−0.035	0.193	0.121	1.164
Jun 84	0.210	0.010	0.189	0.152	1.240
Sep 84	0.248	0.007	0.239	0.093	1.081
Dec 84	0.213	−0.027	0.177	0.062	1.448
Mar 85	0.197	0.021	0.171	0.063	1.327
Jun 85	0.156	−0.018	0.143	0.055	1.178
Sep 85	0.151	0.052	0.131	0.137	1.321
Dec 85	0.175	0.013	0.157	0.096	1.244
Mar 86	0.239	0.019	0.207	0.067	1.342
Jun 86	0.242	0.002	0.211	0.020	1.318
Sep 86	0.283	0.014	0.251	0.074	1.280
Dec 86	0.254	−0.004	0.216	0.038	1.380
Mar 87	0.287	−0.143	0.241	0.012	1.417
Jun 87	0.318	0.028	0.316	0.039	1.013
Panel C: Data at 60-Minute Intervals					
Sep 83	0.315	−0.047	0.316	0.029	0.992
Dec 83	0.255	0.051	0.244	0.077	1.092
Mar 84	0.289	0.032	0.289	0.031	1.002
Jun 84	0.299	−0.042	0.287	0.058	1.087
Sep 84	0.352	0.025	0.353	0.019	0.996
Dec 84	0.297	0.083	0.258	0.096	1.326
Mar 85	0.281	0.060	0.249	0.068	1.275
Jun 85	0.218	0.111	0.208	0.075	1.097
Sep 85	0.219	0.089	0.198	0.153	1.223
Dec 85	0.249	0.078	0.232	0.036	1.149
Mar 86	0.342	0.016	0.302	0.054	1.282
Jun 86	0.342	0.064	0.301	0.113	1.294
Sep 86	0.404	0.004	0.367	0.060	1.209
Dec 86	0.359	−0.032	0.312	0.007	1.324
Mar 87	0.376	0.010	0.343	0.060	1.201
Jun 87	0.456	0.041	0.455	0.017	1.001

(continued)

Table 11.2. *(continued)*

Contract	Futures		Index		Variance Ratio[2]
	Standard Deviation[1]	First-Order Autocorrelation	Standard Deviation[1]	First-Order Autocorrelation	
Panel D: Data at 120-Minute Intervals					
Sep 83	0.435	0.069	0.454	0.174	0.919
Dec 83	0.369	0.026	0.358	0.084	1.066
Mar 84	0.415	0.044	0.414	0.107	1.003
Jun 84	0.414	−0.004	0.417	0.082	0.984
Sep 84	0.504	0.174	0.503	0.186	1.002
Dec 84	0.437	0.050	0.382	0.129	1.311
Mar 85	0.410	0.091	0.364	0.133	1.265
Jun 85	0.325	0.021	0.305	0.118	1.134
Sep 85	0.322	0.022	0.300	0.087	1.155
Dec 85	0.365	0.022	0.334	0.076	1.195
Mar 86	0.487	0.038	0.438	0.095	1.236
Jun 86	0.499	0.067	0.449	0.115	1.237
Sep 86	0.572	0.124	0.534	0.183	1.146
Dec 86	0.499	0.031	0.443	0.068	1.273
Mar 87	0.535	0.003	0.500	0.003	1.145
Jun 87	0.658	0.009	0.650	−0.040	1.025
Panel E: Data at One-Trading-Day Intervals[3]					
Sep 83	0.887	−0.062	0.874	0.038	1.032
Dec 83	0.703	0.063	0.709	0.081	0.983
Mar 84	0.845	−0.181	0.839	−0.148	1.013
Jun 84	0.790	−0.074	0.799	−0.015	0.978
Sep 84	0.871	0.060	0.871	0.108	1.001
Dec 84	0.760	−0.133	0.677	−0.003	1.259
Mar 85	0.811	−0.144	0.686	−0.030	1.399
Jun 85	0.595	0.122	0.551	0.194	1.164
Sep 85	0.586	0.027	0.495	0.181	1.400
Dec 85	0.730	0.013	0.667	0.137	1.199
Mar 86	0.840	0.109	0.789	0.059	1.134
Jun 86	1.033	0.156	0.909	0.141	1.292
Sep 86	1.231	0.113	1.120	0.121	1.208
Dec 86	1.017	−0.169	0.884	−0.006	1.324
Mar 87	0.873	0.027	0.781	0.077	1.248
Jun 87	1.278	0.034	1.211	0.031	1.114

[1] The standard deviation is reported in percent.
[2] The variance ratio is the variance of the change of log futures price divided by the variance of the change of log index price.
[3] Results are calculated using prices at 3 p.m. EST.

11.3 reports some aggregated evidence of the higher variability of the futures market. The average variance ratio for the 16 contracts is presented for each interval length. The average drops considerably from the 15-minute-interval average of 1.56 to the 60-minute-interval average of 1.16 but remains flat from the 60-minute interval to the one-trading-day interval. We test the hypothesis that the ratio equals 1 by treating the ratios as being independent across contracts. The z-statistics for this test are reported in Table 11.3. The smallest z-statistic is 4.40 for the 120-minute interval, supporting the hypothesis that the futures market is more variable than the spot market.

Table 11.3.   *Aggregate variance-ratio results (based on 16 contracts, September 1983 to June 1987).*

Observation-time Interval	Average Variance Ratio	Cross-Sectional Standard Deviation	z-statistic[1]
15 minutes	1.56	0.19	11.90
30 minutes	1.26	0.12	8.81
60 minutes	1.16	0.12	5.14
120 minutes	1.13	0.12	4.40
One trading day	1.17	0.14	4.79

[1]The null hypothesis is that the average variance ratio equals 1.

11.2.3 The Behavior of the Mispricing Series

We now examine the behavior of the mispricing series. Data for two contracts, December 1984 and March 1987 (employing data 15 minutes apart), are plotted in Figure 11.1. The graphs display some sharp reversals in the mispricing levels, but the tendency is for the series to stay above or below zero for substantial lengths of time. A single sharp spike that penetrates a transactions bound (placed, say, at ±0.6 percent) is more likely to be symptomatic of a lagging and smoothed index than an arbitrage opportunity. The 100-point-scale interval on the x-axis corresponds to 1500 minutes, or approximately four trading days. These graphs provide a visual description of the typical behavior of the mispricing series.

Table 11.4 reports the means, standard deviations (SDs), and autocorrelations at eight lags for the levels and the first differences in the constructed mispricing series. We report the results for the overall time period, June 1983 through June 1987, as well as for the 16 separate contracts. All statistics are computed using the quarter-hour intervals: overnight and weekend intervals are treated as missing observations and are not included in the computations.

The results for the mispricing levels are in panel A of Table 11.4. Over the 16 contracts, the average mispricing is 0.12 percent. For the December 1986 contract, the average mispricing is the lowest, with a mean of −0.20 percent; it is the highest for the December 1984 contract (0.78 percent). These results are consistent with the hypothesis that the forward pricing model gives a downward-biased estimate for the futures price, but the short time period and the small number of contracts considered prohibit one from drawing strong conclusions. The overall standard deviation of the mispricing levels is 0.44 percent. Panel B of Table 11.4 reports the corresponding

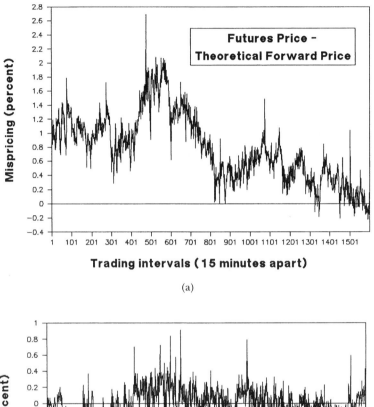

Figure 11.1. Mispricing (percent of index value) for (a) December 1984 and (b) March 1987 S&P 500 futures contracts.

Table 11.4. *Summary statistics on the levels and first differences in mispricing in the S&P 500 futures contracts, by expiration (15-minute-interval transaction data, mispricing in percent of index value).*

Contract	Mean, %	SD, %	1	2	3	4	5	6	7	8	Number of Observations
			\multicolumn{8}{c}{Autocorrelations Lag}								

Panel A: Statistics on the Levels

Contract	Mean, %	SD, %	1	2	3	4	5	6	7	8	Number of Observations
Sep 83	0.01	0.29	0.83	0.73	0.70	0.70	0.70	0.71	0.69	0.67	1,575
Dec 83	0.37	0.29	0.86	0.75	0.65	0.56	0.45	0.33	0.21	0.07	1,575
Mar 84	0.50	0.36	0.85	0.73	0.62	0.52	0.41	0.28	0.12	−0.04	1,550
Jun 84	0.06	0.23	0.81	0.71	0.67	0.66	0.65	0.64	0.63	0.62	1,500
Sep 84	0.11	0.32	0.84	0.79	0.76	0.74	0.73	0.71	0.71	0.68	1,700
Dec 84	0.78	0.48	0.84	0.71	0.58	0.44	0.27	0.10	−0.11	−0.33	1,600
Mar 85	0.64	0.60	0.93	0.87	0.82	0.75	0.69	0.61	0.53	0.44	1,425
Jun 85	0.28	0.34	0.91	0.87	0.83	0.79	0.74	0.69	0.64	0.58	1,700
Sep 85	0.04	0.28	0.94	0.92	0.90	0.89	0.87	0.85	0.84	0.83	1,575
Dec 85	−0.17	0.30	0.91	0.87	0.85	0.83	0.80	0.78	0.76	0.73	1,718
Mar 86	0.01	0.30	0.86	0.82	0.81	0.79	0.78	0.78	0.77	0.77	1,674
Jun 86	−0.03	0.29	0.85	0.81	0.81	0.80	0.78	0.77	0.77	0.76	1,701
Sep 86	−0.16	0.27	0.74	0.66	0.63	0.59	0.56	0.54	0.52	0.48	1,701
Dec 86	−0.20	0.34	0.85	0.82	0.80	0.78	0.76	0.74	0.71	0.67	1,728
Mar 87	−0.02	0.21	0.65	0.58	0.60	0.59	0.56	0.53	0.52	0.51	1,674
Jun 87	−0.11	0.22	0.46	0.34	0.31	0.27	0.25	0.23	0.20	0.17	1,674
Overall	0.12	0.44	0.93	0.91	0.90	0.89	0.88	0.87	0.86	0.85	26,070

Panel B: Statistics on the First Differences

Contract	Mean, %	SD, %	1	2	3	4	5	6	7	8	Number of Observations
Sep 83	0.00	0.15	−0.08	−0.14	−0.12	−0.05	−0.02	0.01	0.05	−0.01	1,512
Dec 83	0.00	0.11	−0.16	−0.14	−0.06	0.00	−0.01	−0.02	0.03	0.01	1,512
Mar 84	0.00	0.14	−0.15	−0.10	−0.11	−0.03	0.00	0.03	−0.06	0.04	1,488
Jun 84	0.00	0.13	−0.17	−0.08	−0.10	−0.02	−0.03	−0.01	0.00	−0.03	1,440
Sep 84	0.00	0.16	−0.19	−0.06	−0.06	−0.05	0.03	−0.04	0.05	−0.06	1,632
Dec 84	0.00	0.13	−0.27	−0.08	0.01	0.04	−0.05	0.04	0.00	−0.06	1,536
Mar 85	0.00	0.12	−0.27	−0.08	0.04	−0.01	−0.04	−0.02	0.00	0.03	1,368
Jun 85	0.00	0.11	−0.25	−0.06	0.00	0.00	0.00	−0.03	0.02	−0.03	1,632
Sep 85	0.00	0.09	−0.26	−0.03	0.00	−0.03	0.02	−0.02	−0.04	0.02	1,512
Dec 85	0.00	0.11	−0.26	−0.09	0.01	0.00	−0.01	0.01	−0.02	0.01	1,654
Mar 86	0.00	0.14	−0.30	−0.01	0.00	−0.02	−0.03	0.03	−0.03	0.02	1,612
Jun 86	0.00	0.14	−0.30	−0.08	0.02	0.01	−0.04	0.01	0.02	−0.06	1,638
Sep 86	0.00	0.16	−0.26	−0.05	−0.01	−0.03	0.01	0.04	−0.01	−0.01	1,638
Dec 86	0.00	0.15	−0.24	−0.06	−0.03	0.01	−0.01	0.02	0.00	0.00	1,664
Mar 87	0.00	0.16	−0.34	−0.10	0.04	0.03	−0.02	0.01	−0.02	0.00	1,612
Jun 87	0.00	0.18	−0.20	−0.05	0.04	−0.03	0.02	−0.01	0.03	−0.04	1,612
Overall	0.00	0.14	−0.23	−0.07	−0.02	−0.01	−0.01	0.01	0.00	−0.02	25,062

Mispricing = futures price − theoretical forward price.

results for the first differences in the mispricing series (the "changes"). The mean of these changes is 0.00 percent for all the contracts—as one might expect, given that the level of the mispricing is constrained by arbitrageurs. The standard deviations are fairly stable across all contracts, that for the overall period being 0.14 percent.

The series of the mispricing levels is highly autocorrelated (Table 11.4, panel A). For the individual contracts, the first-order autocorrelation coefficient ranges from 0.46 to 0.94. For 12 of the 16 contracts, the autocorrelation is quite high for all eight lags reported (a two-hour time interval). This indicates that the series tends to persist above or below zero and not, as one might have conjectured, fluctuate randomly around zero.[15] The autocorrelation behavior of the first differences in the mispricing are close to zero, except for the first two lags for which they are all negative (Table 11.4, panel B). The first-order autocorrelation ranges from -0.34 to -0.08; the second-order autocorrelations are smaller in magnitude and range from -0.14 to -0.01. The negative autocorrelations at low lags are consistent with the implication that when the mispricing deviates from zero it is elastically pulled toward zero by the action of those traders who perceive that transacting in one market is cheaper.[16]

We also examine the relation between the magnitude of the mispricing and the contract's maturity. Because we lack the theoretical framework to suggest a precise functional form, we simply estimate a linear relation between the average absolute mispricing at 15-minute intervals over a given day and the number of days remaining until maturity. The model we estimate is

$$z(t, T) = \beta_0 + \beta_1(T - t) + \epsilon(t, T),$$

$$\text{where} \quad z(t, T) = \text{ABS}\left[\sum_{j=1}^{N_t} \frac{X_{t,T}(j)}{N_t} \right]$$

$$X_{t,T}(j) = \text{mispricing at the } j\text{th quarter-hour mark during day } t,$$
for futures contract maturing at T;

$$N_t = \text{number of observations in day } t.$$

The results indicate that the magnitude of the mispricing is positively related to time until maturity. For the overall time period, the estimates of β_0 and β_1 are 0.014 percent and 4.41, respectively. The z-statistic for the null hypothesis of $\beta_1 = 0$ is 3.83.[17,18] Figure 11.2 is drawn using these estimates from the overall relationship, and it illustrates the cone-shaped boundary that one obtains for the mean mispricing as a function of time

[15]The autocorrelations are actually calculated about the mean of the mispricing for the contract, and not around 0.0.

[16]Negative autocorrelations at low lags can also be induced by stale prices in the index quotes. However, in the recent contracts (September 1986 through June 1987) the negative autocorrelations are present at the low lags, yet the results of Table 11.1 indicate that the stale-price problem (as measured by the autocorrelation of the index changes) is not important.

[17]This z-statistic is corrected for heteroscedasticity and autocorrelation in the regression residual, using the technique of Newey and West (1987). The usual OLS t-statistic for this coefficient is 8.88.

[18]We also ran this regression for each of the 16 contracts individually. For 14 of the 16 contracts the estimate of β_1 is positive (although quite variable), and for 11 of the contracts the z-statistics associated with the β_1 estimates are greater than 2.0. For the two contracts where β_1 estimates are negative (September 1984 and September 1986), the z-statistics associated with the estimates (-1.31 and -0.18) are statistically insignificant.

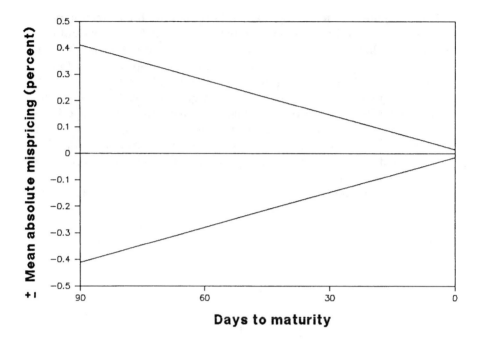

Figure 11.2. *Boundary of mean absolute mispricing as a function of time to maturity.*

until maturity. If these boundaries are strictly determined by round-trip transaction costs alone, then a flat corridor should result. The results indicate that the bounds drawn (as estimated) in Figure 11.2 are consistent with the impact of other factors that are influenced by time to expiration, such as dividend uncertainty, marking-to-market flows, and risk in tracking the stock index with a partial basket of stocks.

11.2.4 Path Dependence of Mispricing

We now investigate the path dependence of the mispricing series. One implication of this hypothesis is that, conditional on the mispricing having crossed one arbitrage bound, it is less likely to cross the opposite bound. This phenomenon is a result of the fact that arbitrageurs will unwind positions established when the mispricing was outside one bound before it reaches the other bound.[19] To investigate this issue, we document for each of the 16 contracts the number of upper-bound and lower-bound mispricing violations

---

[19]We do not consider the possibility that arbitrageurs might roll forward into the next futures contract.

Table 11.5. *Mispricing violations for S&P 500 index futures.*

Contract	Number of Upper-Bound Violations[1]	Number of Upper-Bound Crossings	Average Time above Upper Bound[2]	Number of Lower-Bound Violations[1]	Number of Lower-Bound Crossings	Average Time below Lower Bound[2]	Number of Observations[3]
Sep 83	30	20	23	29	14	31	1,575
Dec 83	371	66	84	0	0	NA	1,575
Mar 84	631	64	148	0	0	NA	1,550
Jun 84	17	9	28	4	4	15	1,500
Sep 84	92	44	31	21	15	21	1,700
Dec 84	974	61	240	0	0	NA	1,600
Mar 85	625	28	335	0	0	NA	1,425
Jun 85	271	29	140	0	0	NA	1,700
Sep 85	64	24	40	0	0	NA	1,575
Dec 85	4	4	15	143	41	52	1,718
Mar 86	7	4	26	36	31	17	1,674
Jun 86	46	23	30	19	17	17	1,701
Sep 86	1	1	15	83	44	28	1,701
Dec 86	2	2	15	233	62	56	1,728
Mar 87	5	5	15	16	9	27	1,674
Jun 87	9	9	15	18	12	23	1,674
Overall	3149	393	120	602	249	36	26,070

[1]The upper bound is set at +0.6 percent and the lower bound at −0.6 percent.
[2]The average time outside the bounds is in trading minutes.
[3]The observations are recorded at 15-minute intervals.

that occur.[20] A tendency for a given contract to have mostly upper-bound violations or mostly lower-bound violations (but not both) is evidence consistent with the mispricing being path-dependent. Indeed, this is the case. Table 11.5 documents the number of upper- and lower-bound violations for each contract. For this table, bounds of ±0.6 percent are selected.[21] With the exception of the September 1983 contract, each contract is dominated by either upper-bound violations or lower-bound violations. For example, the March 1985 contract violated the upper bound 625 times (using 15-minute observations) and did not violate the lower bound for any of the observations. In contrast, the December 1986 contract violated the −0.6 percent mispricing bound 233 times and violated the +0.6 percent bound only two times. Table 11.5 also reports the number of times a given bound was crossed for each contract and the average time (in trading minutes) the mispricing remained outside the bounds. These results indicate that the mispricing remains outside the bounds for a considerable length of time and rules out the possibility that stale prices in the index are a major cause of the observed violations.

We can develop further evidence of the path dependence of the series by examining conditional probabilities. Consider two possibilities:

1. The mispricing is path-independent, following some stochastic process that is pinned to zero at T.
2. The mispricing is path-dependent; conditional on having crossed an upper (lower) bound, the probability of its hitting the lower (upper) bound is smaller.

An implication of argument 1 is that if the mispricing is currently zero, then it is equally likely to hit an upper or a lower bound independent of the past. Argument 2 has a different implication if the mispricing is zero.[22] It implies that if the mispricing has crossed the upper bound in the past, it is more likely to continue to deviate above zero and more likely in the future to hit the upper bound than the lower bound. We address this question empirically by identifying all cases where the mispricing crossed the upper or lower bound, returned to zero, and then *again* crossed the upper or lower bound. For the 16 contracts, there is a total of 142 such cases.

---

[20]Stoll and Whaley (1986) also document violations of these bounds. They use hourly observations and assume a constant dividend yield.

[21]The results are not overly sensitive to the bound selected or to the use of a symmetric bound about zero. We based the selection of 0.6 percent on a round-trip stock commission of 0.70, a round-trip futures commission of 0.08, a market impact cost in futures of 0.05, a market impact in stocks of 0.35, and an index level of 200. We have computed these results with bounds placed at ±0.4 percent and ±0.8 percent, and these show a similar pattern.

[22]We also repeated the calculations using symmetric bounds about 0.14 percent (the overall mispricing mean) in place of zero to account for the possibility that a bias in the forward pricing model may be driving the results. The conclusion remains unaffected.

Eighty-two of these cases are instances where the mispricing hits the upper bound, having previously hit a bound and gone to zero. The path independence argument implies the probability of hitting the upper bound, given that the mispricing is currently at zero, is the same whether it had previously hit the upper or lower bound. The estimates of the conditional probabilities from these 82 cases are:

$$p(x \text{ hitting upper bound} \mid x \text{ has hit lower bound} \\ \text{and has crossed zero}) = 0.36$$

$$p(x \text{ hitting upper bound} \mid x \text{ has hit upper bound} \\ \text{and has crossed zero}) = 0.73.$$

This argument should also hold for violations of the lower bound. For the 60 cases of hitting a bound, crossing zero, and hitting the lower bound, the conditional probability estimates are:

$$p(x \text{ hitting lower bound} \mid x \text{ has hit lower bound} \\ \text{and has crossed zero}) = 0.64$$

$$p(x \text{ hitting lower bound} \mid x \text{ has hit upper bound} \\ \text{and has crossed zero}) = 0.27.$$

These conditional probabilities differ substantially for the two cases.[23] The evidence is consistent with the notion that the arbitrageurs' option to unwind prematurely introduces path dependence into the mispricing series.

The option to unwind prematurely and the path dependence can also be related to the ability to predict expiration-day movements. Even if during the life of the contract there has been substantial positive (negative) mispricing, often there is also some time prior to expiration when the mispricing is negative (positive). (See the September 1984 contract in Figure 11.1 for an example.) Hence, arbitrageurs will often have had the opportunity to unwind at a profit prior to expiration day, making expiration-day predictions based on the identification of mispricing outside the arbitrage bound difficult.

11.3 Conclusion

We have considered the intraday behavior of the S&P 500 futures and index quotes. Comparisons of the autocorrelations of the changes of the log price of these two series indicate that with a 15-minute observation interval, nonsynchronous trading in the stocks in the index poses a problem. As

---

[23]The *p*-value of a chi-square test of the equality of the conditional probabilities is less than 0.001.

the interval length is increased, the autocorrelation disappears, with little evidence of the problem with 60-minute observation intervals. We have also examined the relative variability of the futures and spot markets. The results indicate that the futures market is more variable than the spot market even after controlling for problems caused by nonsynchronous prices in the observed index.

Much of this chapter has focused on the behavior of the mispricing series—the difference between the actual futures price and its theoretical value. We had advanced and examined empirically two hypotheses: (1) that the average magnitude of the mispricing increases with time to maturity and (2) that the mispricing series is path-dependent. Evidence supporting these hypotheses has been provided. The results have implications for the width of the arbitrage bounds, the selection of a stochastic process to "model" mispricing, the valuation of options related to the mispricing series, and the prediction of expiration-day movements of the S&P 500 index.

12

Order Imbalances and Stock Price Movements on October 19 and 20, 1987

THE VARIOUS OFFICIAL REPORTS on the October Crash all point to the breakdown of the linkage between the pricing of the future contract on the S&P 500 and the stocks making up that index.[1] On October 19 and 20, 1987, the future contract often sold at substantial discounts from the cash index, when theoretically it should have been selling at a slight premium. The markets had become "delinked."

On October 19, the S&P 500 dropped by more than twenty percent. On October 20, the S&P 500 initially rose and then fell off for the rest of the day to close with a small increase for the day. These two days provide an ideal laboratory in which to examine the adjustment of prices of individual stocks to major changes in market perceptions. In the turbulent market of these two days, one might reasonably assume that a reevaluation of the overall level of the market, and not information specific to individual firms, caused most of the price changes in individual securities.

If most of the new information arriving on the floor of the NYSE on these two days was related to the overall level of the market and not firm-specific effects, large differences among the returns of large diverse groups of stocks could be attributable to further breakdowns in the linkages within the market.[2] Just as the extreme conditions of these two days resulted in a breakdown of the linkages between the future market and the cash market for stocks, there may well have been other breakdowns.

---

[1] *Black Monday and the Future of Financial Markets* (1989) contains excerpts of these various official reports. It also contains some interesting articles about the crash, separately authored by Robert J. Barro, Eugene F. Fama, Daniel R. Fischel, Allan H. Metzler, Richard W. Roll, and Lester G. Telser.

[2] More technically, if the systematic factors in two large samples of stocks have on average similar factor sensitivities, one would expect the returns to be similar. Some of the statistical analyses will explicitly allow for differences in factor sensitivities.

Since the S&P 500 index plays a crucial role in index-related trading,[3] this study begins with a comparison of the return and volume characteristics of NYSE-listed stocks that are included in the S&P index with those that are not included. This comparison reveals substantial differences in the returns of these two groups. The S&P stocks declined roughly seven percentage points more than non-S&P stocks on October 19 and, in the opening hours of trading on October 20, recovered almost all of this loss. This pattern of returns is consistent with a breakdown in the linkage between the pricing of stocks in the S&P and those not in the S&P.

The study then proposes a measure of order imbalances. Over time, there is a strong relation between this measure and the aggregate returns of both S&P and non-S&P stocks. Cross-sectionally, there is also a significant relation between the order imbalance for an individual security and its concurrent return.

Finally, the analysis shows that those stocks that experienced the greatest losses in the last hour of trading on October 19 experienced the greatest gains in the first hour of trading on October 20. Since those stocks with the greatest losses on October 19 had the greatest order imbalances, this pattern of reversals is consistent with a breakdown of the linkages among the prices of individual securities.

The chapter is organized as follows. Section 12.1 presents a description of the data. Section 12.2 compares the return and volume characteristics of S&P and non-S&P stocks. Section 12.3 contains the analysis of order imbalances. The study concludes with Section 12.4.

12.1 Some Preliminaries

The primary data that this study uses are transaction prices, volume, and quotations for all stocks on the New York Stock Exchange for October 19 and 20. The source of these data is Bridge Data. The data base itself contains only trades and quotations from the NYSE.[4] As such, the data differ somewhat

---

[3]As part of its report (1988), the SEC collected information on specific index-related selling programs. On October 19, these selling programs represented 21.1 percent of the S&P volume. The actual percentage is undoubtedly greater. Moreover, there are some trading strategies involving large baskets of stocks in the S&P that the SEC would not include as index related. Also of interest, the data collected by the SEC indicated that 81.0 percent of the index arbitrage on October 19 involved the December future contract on the S&P Composite Index.

[4]Geewax Terker and Company collected these data on a real time basis from Bridge Data. Bridge Data also provides activity on other Exchanges, but the original collection process did not retain these data.

from the trades reported on the Composite tape that includes activity on regional exchanges.[5]

12.1.1 The Source of the Data

In analyzing these data, it is useful to have an understanding of how Bridge Data obtains its data. For the purposes of this chapter, let us begin with the Market Data System of the NYSE. This system is an automated communication system that collects all new quotations and trading information for all activity on the floor of the NYSE.

One main input to this system is mark-sense cards that exchange employees complete and feed into optical card readers. In this non-automated process, there is always the possibility that some cards are processed out of sequence. We have no direct information on the potential magnitude of this problem; however, individuals familiar with this process have suggested to us that this problem is likely to be more pronounced in periods of heavy volume and particularly with trades that do not directly involve the specialist. Also, when there is a simultaneous change in the quote and a trade based upon the new quote, there is the possibility that the trade will be reported before the new quote.

The Market Data System then transmits the quotation data to the Consolidated Quote System and the transaction data to the Consolidated Tape System, both operated by SIAC (Securities Industry Automation Corporation). These two systems collect all the data from the NYSE and other markets. SIAC then transmits these quotes and transactions to outside vendors and to the floor of the NYSE through IGS (Information Generation System). Except for computer malfunctions, this process is almost instantaneous.

Up to this point, there are no time stamps on the transmitted data. Each vendor and IGS supply their own time stamps. Thus, if there are any delays in the transmission of prices by SIAC to vendors, the time stamps will be incorrect. Two vendors of importance to this study are Bridge Data and ADP. ADP calculates the S&P Composite Index, so that any errors or delays in prices transmitted by SIAC to ADP will affect the Index. Also, the time stamps supplied by Bridge Data may sometimes be incorrect.

According to the studies of the GAO and the SEC, there were on occasion substantial delays in the processing of the mark-sense cards on October 19 and 20. In addition, the SEC reports that SIAC experienced computer

---

[5]On October 19, we found on occasion large differences between the price of the last trade on the NYSE and the last trade as reported in newspapers. For example, the price for the last trade for Texaco on October 19 on the NYSE was 30.875 and was reported at 4:03. In contrast, the closing price in *The Wall Street Journal* was 32.50. Some investigative work disclosed that a clerk on the Midwest Stock Exchange had recorded some early trades in Texaco after the markets had closed but had failed to indicate that the trades were out of sequence.

problems in transmitting transactions to outside vendors, with the result that there were no trades reported from 1:57 p.m. to 2:06 p.m. on October 19 and from 11:47 a.m. to 11:51 a.m. on October 20.[6] According to an official at the NYSE, all trades that should have been transmitted during these two periods were sent to outside vendors as soon as possible after the computer problems were fixed.

There were no reported computer problems associated with the Consolidated Quote System, and outside vendors continued to receive and transmit changes in quotes during these two periods. Since an outside vendor uses the time at which it receives a quote or transaction as its time stamp, the time stamps for the quotes and transactions provided by all outside vendors are out of sequence during and slightly after these two periods. These errors in sequencing may introduce biases in our analyses of buying and selling pressure during these periods, a subject to be discussed below.

An analysis of the data from Bridge discloses that, in addition to these two time intervals, there were no trades reported from 3:41 p.m. to 3:43 p.m. on October 19 and from 3:44 p.m. to 3:45 p.m. on October 20. We do not know the reason for these gaps.

12.1.2 The Published Standard and Poor's Index

The published Standard and Poor's Composite Index is based upon 500 stocks. Of these 500 stocks, 462 have their primary market on the NYSE, eight have their primary market on the American Stock Exchange, and thirty are traded on NASDAQ.

The first step in calculating the index for a specific point in time is to multiply the number of shares of common stock outstanding of each company in the index by its stock price to obtain the stock's market value. The number of shares outstanding comes from a publication of Standard and Poor's (1987).[7] The share price that S&P uses is almost always the price of the last trade on the primary market, not a composite price.[8]

The next step is to sum these 500 market values, and the final step is to divide this sum by a scale factor. This factor is adjusted over time to neutralize the effect on the index of changes either in the composition of

[6] An analysis of the data from Bridge indicates that there were some trades reported during 2:05 p.m. and none during 2:07 p.m. on October 19. We have not been able to determine the reason for this slight discrepancy.

[7] The number of shares outstanding that Standard & Poor's uses in the construction of its indexes sometimes differs from the number reported in other financial publications. These shares outstanding are adjusted for stock dividends and stock splits during the month of October.

[8] In reconstructing the S&P index, it would be ideal to have the NYSE closing prices of NYSE stocks on Friday, October 16. Not having these prices, we utilize for this date the closing prices as reported on the Composite tape.

the index or in the number of shares outstanding for a particular company. S&P set the initial value of this scale factor so that the index value was "10.0 as of 1941–1943."

Since this study had for the most part only access to NYSE prices, the subsequent analyses approximate the S&P index using only the 462 NYSE stocks. The market value of the thirty-eight non-NYSE stocks as of the close on October 16 equals only 0.3 percent of the total market value of the index, so that this approximation might be expected to be quite accurate. Indeed, some direct calculations and some of the subsequent analyses are consistent with this expectation. In one subsequent analysis, the 462 NYSE stocks are partitioned into four size quartiles of roughly an equal number of companies each, based upon market values on October 16. The largest quartile contains 116 companies with market values in excess of 4.6 billion; the second largest quartile contains 115 companies with market values between 2.2 and 4.6 billion; the third contains 116 companies with values between 1.0 billion and 2.2 billion; and the fourth contains 115 companies with market values between 65.4 million and 1.0 billion.

In comparisons of companies included in the S&P with companies not included in the S&P, we exclude the 178 non-S&P companies with market values of less than 65.4 million—the smallest company listed in the S&P.[9] After excluding these 178 companies, there remain 929 non-S&P companies for comparison purposes. These 929 companies are classified into size quartiles by the same break points as the quartiles of the S&P. This classification results in sixteen non-S&P companies with assets in excess of 4.6 billion, twenty-seven companies corresponding to the second largest quartile of S&P stocks, 100 companies for the next S&P quartile, and 786 companies for the smallest S&P quartile.

12.2 The Constructed Indexes

Indexes, such as the S&P 500, utilize the price of the last trade in calculating market values. In a rapidly changing market, some of these past prices may be stale and not reflect current conditions. This problem is particularly acute for stocks that have not yet opened, in which case the index is based upon the closing price of some prior day. As a result of such stale prices, the published S&P index may underestimate losses in a falling market and underestimate gains in a rising market. The Appendix describes an approach to mitigate these biases by constructing indexes that utilize only prices from stocks that have traded in the prior fifteen minutes. After the first hour and a half of trading each day, the analysis in the Appendix indicates that

---

[9]We also excluded foreign companies whose common stocks are traded through ADRs.

this approach virtually eliminates the bias from stale prices. There remains some bias in the first hour and a half of trading.

The comparison of the returns of the NYSE stocks included in the S&P Index with those not included utilizes two indexes—one for S&P stocks and one for non-S&P stocks. To minimize the bias associated with stale prices, both of these indexes utilize only prices of stocks that have traded in the prior fifteen minutes. The index for non-S&P stocks is value weighted in the same way as the constructed index for S&P stocks. Both of these indexes have been standardized to 1.0 as of the close of trading on October 16. To eliminate any confusion, we shall always refer to the index published by S&P as the published index. Without any qualifier, the term "S&P index" will refer to the calculated S&P index as shown in Figure 12.1.

There are substantial differences in the behavior of these two indexes on October 19 and 20. On Monday, October 19, the S&P index dropped 20.5 percent. By the morning of Tuesday, October 20, the S&P index had recaptured a significant portion of this loss. Thereafter, the S&P index fell but closed with a positive gain for the day. In contrast, the return on the non-S&P index was −13.1 on Monday and −5.5 percent on Tuesday.

In addition, the relative trading volume in S&P stocks exceeded the relative trading volume in non-S&P stocks in every fifteen-minute interval on October 19 and 20 (Figure 12.2). The relative trading volume in S&P stocks is defined as the ratio of the total dollar value of trading in all S&P stocks in a fifteen-minute interval to the total market value of all S&P stocks, reexpressed as a percentage. The market values for each fifteen-minute interval are the closing market values on October 16, adjusted for general market movements to the beginning of each fifteen-minute interval.[10] The relative trading volume in non-S&P stocks is similarly defined.

Of particular note, the recovery of the S&P stocks on Tuesday morning brought the S&P index almost in line with the non-S&P index. One possible interpretation of this recovery is that there was considerably greater selling pressure on S&P stocks on October 19 than on non-S&P stocks. This selling pressure pushed prices of S&P stocks down further than warranted, and the recovery in the opening prices of S&P stocks on October 20 corrected this unwarranted decline. The greater relative trading volume on S&P stocks is also consistent with this interpretation.

Before concluding this section, let us consider another explanation for the differences in the returns of the two indexes. The S&P index is weighted more heavily toward larger stocks than the non-S&P index, and it is possible that the differences in the returns on the two indexes may be due solely to a size effect. Although a size effect can explain some of the differences in the returns, it does not explain all of the differences. Results for indexes

[10]The adjustment is made separately for each size quartile.

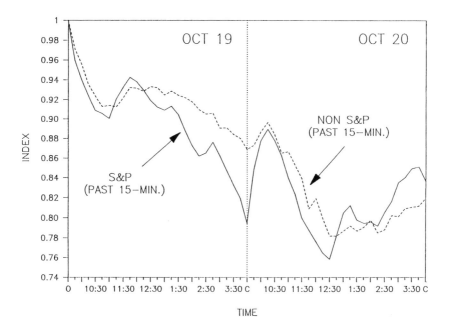

Figure 12.1. *Comparison of price indexes for NYSE stocks included in the S&P 500 Index and not included for October 19 and 20, 1987. On these two dates, the S&P Index included thirty-eight non-NYSE stocks, which are not included in the index. There were 929 non-S&P stocks with market values equal to or greater than the smallest company in the S&P. The indexes themselves are calculated every fifteen minutes. Each value of the index is based upon all stocks that traded in the previous fifteen minutes. The market value of these stocks is estimated at two points in time. The first estimate is based upon the closing prices on October 16. The second estimate is based upon the latest trade price in the previous fifteen minutes. The ratio of the second estimate to the first estimate provides the values of the plotted indexes. The value of the plotted indexes at 9:30 on October 19 is set to one.*

constructed using size quartiles are presented in Table 12.1. From Friday close to Monday close, indexes for any size quartile for S&P stocks declined more than the corresponding indexes for non-S&P stocks.[11] There is no simple relation to size; for S&P stocks, the returns increase slightly with size, and, for non-S&P stocks, they decrease with size.

From Monday close to 10:30 on Tuesday, the returns on S&P stocks for any size quartile exceeded the returns for non-S&P stocks. Yet, unlike the Monday returns, there is a substantial size effect with the larger stocks,

---

[11]These indexes are constructed in exactly the same way as the overall indexes and, thus, are value weighted. However, in view of the control for size, the range of the market values of the companies within each quartile is considerably less than the range for the overall indexes.

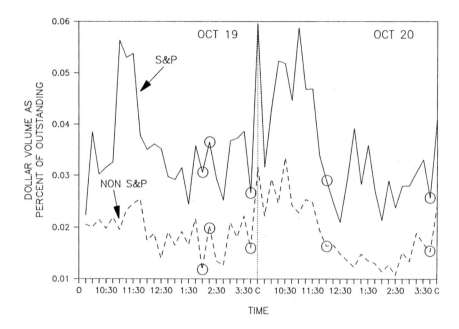

Figure 12.2.   *Plot of dollar volume in each fifteen-minute interval on October 19 and 20, 1987 as a percent of the market value of the stocks outstanding separately for S&P and non-S&P stocks. These plots exclude companies with less than 65.4 million dollars of outstanding stock as of the close on October 16. Market values for each fifteen-minute interval are the closing market values on October 16, adjusted for general market movements to the beginning of each fifteen-minute interval. The adjustment is made separately for each size quartile. The circled points represent time periods in which there were breakdowns in the reporting systems and thus may represent less reliable data.*

particularly those in the S&P index, displaying the greater returns. From Friday close to 10:30 on Tuesday, the losses on S&P stocks for any size quartile exceeded those on non-S&P stocks. There is a size effect with the smaller stocks realizing the greatest losses. Nonetheless, because of the differences in the weightings in the S&P and non-S&P indexes, the difference in the overall returns is only 0.6 percent.[12]

---

[12]The differences in returns for the indexes reported in the text are reasonably accurate measures of what actually happened on October 19 and 20. The S&P index did decline more than the non-S&P index on October 19 and almost eliminated this greater decline by the morning of October 20. The purpose of this footnote is to assess whether the differences between the two indexes are statistically attributable to the inclusion or exclusion from the S&P index, holding constant other factors that might account for the differences. In this exercise, the other factors are the market values of the stocks as of the close on Friday, October 16, and the beta coefficients based upon weekly regressions for the fifty-two weeks ending in September

Table 12.1. *Percentage returns on S&P and non-S&P stocks cross-classified by firm size quartiles for three time intervals on October 19 and 20, 1987. The overall returns from Friday close to Monday close and from Friday close to 10:30 on Tuesday are taken from the index values plotted in Figure 12.1. The overall return from Monday close to 10:30 on Tuesday is derived from these two returns. The breakpoints for the size quartiles are based upon the S&P stocks and are determined so as to include approximately the same number of S&P stocks in each quartile. As a consequence, there are many more non-S&P stocks in the small firm quartile than in the large firm quartile. In a similar way to the overall index, the returns from Friday close for the size quartiles are calculated using only stocks that have traded in the previous fifteen minutes and valued at the last trade in that interval.*

Firm Size Quartile	Friday Close to Monday Close		Monday Close to 10:30 Tuesday		Friday Close to 10:30 Tuesday	
	S&P	Non-S&P	S&P	Non-S&P	S&P	Non-S&P
Large Firms	−20.9	−11.6	12.2	2.0	−11.3	−9.8
2	−20.2	−11.9	8.3	3.3	−13.5	−9.1
3	−18.9	−15.0	6.4	2.2	−13.8	−13.1
Small Firms	−18.8	−14.5	4.4	0.9	−15.2	−13.7
Overall	−20.5	−13.1	10.5	1.7	−12.2	−11.6

1987 on an equally weighted index of all NYSE stocks. (If there were less than fifty-two weeks of available data, betas were still estimated as long as there are at least thirty-seven weeks of data.)

The following regressions are estimated:

$$R\,Mon_i = \begin{matrix} -10.59 \\ (-6.50) \end{matrix} - \begin{matrix} 3.78\ \delta_i \\ (-5.42) \end{matrix} - \begin{matrix} 0.04\ \ln(M_i) \\ (-0.18) \end{matrix} - \begin{matrix} 3.95\ \beta_i, \\ (-6.46) \end{matrix} \quad \overline{R}^2 = 0.13,$$

$$R\,Tues_i = \begin{matrix} -7.89 \\ (-4.11) \end{matrix} + \begin{matrix} 4.07\ \delta_i \\ (5.56) \end{matrix} + \begin{matrix} 1.34\ \ln(M_i) \\ (4.86) \end{matrix} + \begin{matrix} 1.02\ \beta_i, \\ (1.81) \end{matrix} \quad \overline{R}^2 = 0.20,$$

$$R\,Ove_i = \begin{matrix} -17.75 \\ (-12.46) \end{matrix} - \begin{matrix} 0.83\ \delta_i \\ (-1.36) \end{matrix} + \begin{matrix} 1.13\ \ln(M_i) \\ (5.39) \end{matrix} - \begin{matrix} 3.09\ \beta_i, \\ (-5.20) \end{matrix} \quad \overline{R}^2 = 0.06,$$

where $R\,Mon_i$ is the return on stock i from the close on October 16 to the close on October 19; $R\,Tues_i$ is the return, if it can be calculated, from the close on October 19 to the mid-morning price on October 20, defined as the traded price closest to 10:30 in the following fifteen minutes; $R\,Ove_i$ is the return from the close on October 16 to the mid-morning price on October 20; δ_i is a dummy variable assuming a value of one for S&P stocks and zero otherwise; M_i is the October 16 market value of stock i, and β_i is the fifty-two week beta coefficient. The sample for these regressions is the 955 stocks with complete data, of which 420 are S&P stocks. Heteroscedasticity-consistent z-statistics are in parentheses.

12.3 Buying and Selling Pressure

In the last section, a comparison of the indexes for S&P and non-S&P stocks indicates that the prices of S&P stocks declined 7.4 percentage points more than the prices of non-S&P stocks on October 19. By the morning of October 20, the prices of S&P stocks had bounced back nearly to the level of non-S&P stocks.

This greater decline in S&P stocks and subsequent reversal is consistent with the hypothesis that there was greater selling and trading pressure on S&P stocks than on non-S&P stock on Monday afternoon. However, it is also consistent with other hypotheses such as the presence of a specific factor related to S&P stocks alone. Such a factor might be related to index arbitrage.

This section begins with the definition of a statistic to measure buying and selling pressure or, in short, order imbalance. At the aggregate level, there is a strong correlation between this measure of order imbalance and the return on the index. At the security level, there is significant correlation between the order imbalance for individual securities and their returns. Finally, the chapter finds that those stocks that fell the most on October 19 experienced the greatest recovery on October 20. This finding applies to both S&P and non-S&P stocks.

12.3.1 A Measure of Order Imbalance

The measure of order imbalance that this study uses is the dollar volume at the ask price over an interval of time less the dollar volume at the bid price over the same interval. Implicit in this measure is the assumption that trades between the bid and the ask price generate neither buying nor selling pressure. A positive value for this measure indicates net buying pressure, and a negative value indicates net selling pressure.

In estimating this measure of order imbalance, it is important to keep in mind some of the limitations of the data available to this study. As already mentioned, the procedures for recording changes in quotations and for reporting transactions do not always guarantee that the time sequence of these records is correct. Sometimes, when there is a change in the quotes

---

The estimates of the coefficients of these regressions are consistent with the relations presented in the text. The coefficient on the dummy variable is significantly negative on Monday, significantly positive on Tuesday, and nonsignificant over the two periods combined. On Monday, the beta coefficient enters significantly, while, on Tuesday, the market value enters significantly. Over the two periods combined, both the beta coefficient and the market value enter significantly. The behavior of the coefficients in these three regressions suggests that there is some interaction between market value and beta that the linear specification does not capture. The availability of two days of data for this study precludes our pursuing the nature of this interaction.

and an immediate transaction, the transaction is recorded before the change in the offer prices and sometimes after.[13] Although orders matched in the crowd should be recorded immediately, they sometimes are not. Finally, there are outright errors.[14]

To cope with these potential problems, the estimate of the order imbalance uses the following algorithm: let t be the minute in which a transaction occurs.[15] Let t_p be the minute which contains the nearest prior quote. If the transaction price is between the bid and the ask of this prior quote, the transaction is treated as a cross and not included in the estimate of the order imbalance. If the transaction price is at the bid, the dollar value of the transaction is classified as a sale. If the price is at the ask, the dollar value of the transaction is classified as a buy. A quote that passes one of these three tests is termed a "matched" quote.

If the quote is not matched, the transaction price is then compared in reverse chronological order to prior quotations, if any, in t_p to find a matched quote. If a matched quote is found, the quote is used to classify the trade as a buy, cross, or sell. If no matched quote is found, the quotes in minute t following the trade are examined in chronological order to find a matched quote to classify the trade. If no matched quote is found, the minute $(t_p - 1)$ is searched in reverse chronological order. If still no quote is found, the minute $(t + 1)$ is searched. This process is repeated again and again until minutes $(t_p - 4)$ and $(t + 4)$ are searched. If finally there are no matched quotes, the transaction is dropped.

On October 19, 82.8 percent of trades in terms of share volume[16] match with the immediately previous quote, 9.5 percent with a following quote in minute t, and 6.2 percent with quotes in other minutes, leaving 1.5 percent of the trades unmatched. Of the matched trades, 40.7 percent in terms of share volume occurred within the bid and ask prices. The percentages for October 20 are 81.6 percent with the immediately previous quote, 12.3 percent with a following quote in minute t, 4.5 percent with other quotes, and 1.6 percent with no matched quotes. Finally, 42.4 percent of the matched trades occurred within the bid and ask prices.

This estimate of order imbalance obviously contains some measurement error, caused by misclassification.[17] However, given the strong relation between this estimate of order imbalance and concurrent price movements,

---

[13]Changes in offer prices and recording of transactions take place in part in different computers. If these computers at critical times are out of phase, there will be errors in sequences.

[14]As examples, a smudged optical card or failure to code an order out of sequence would introduce errors.

[15]Trades marked out of sequence are discarded.

[16]Trades marked out of sequence are discarded.

[17]An error might occur in the following scenario. Assume that the prior quote was 20 bid and $20\frac{1}{8}$ ask and the next prior quote was $19\frac{7}{8}$ bid and 20 ask. The algorithm would classify a trade at 20 as a sell, even though it might be a buy.

the measurement error does not obscure the relation. Nonetheless, in interpreting the following empirical results, the reader should bear in mind the potential biases that these measurement errors might introduce.

12.3.2 Time-Series Results

The analysis in this section examines the relation between fifteen-minute returns and aggregate order imbalances. As detailed in the Appendix, the estimates of fiteen-minute returns utilize only stocks that trade in two consecutive fifteen-minute periods. The actual estimate of the fifteen-minute return is the ratio of the aggregate market value of these stocks at the end of the fifteen-minute interval to the aggregate market value of these stocks at the end of the prior fifteen-minute interval, reexpressed as a percentage. The price used in calculating the market value is the mean of the bid and ask prices at the time of the last transaction in each interval.[18] The aggregate order imbalance is the sum of the order imbalances of the individual securities within the fifteen-minute interval.

In the aggregate, there is a strong positive relation between the fifteen-minute returns for the S&P stocks and the aggregate net buying and selling pressure (Figures 12.3 and 12.4). For October 19, the sample correlation is 0.81 and, for October 20, 0.86. The relations for non-S&P stocks are slightly weaker, with correlations of 0.81 and 0.72 (Figures 12.5 and 12.6). All four of these correlation coefficients are significant at usual levels.[19]

This positive relation is consistent with an inventory model in which specialists reduce their bid and ask prices when their inventories increase and raise these prices when their inventories decrease. This positive relation is also consistent with a cascade model in which an order imbalance leads to a price change and this price change in turn leads to further order imbalance, and so on. This positive relation by itself does not establish that there is a simple causal relation between order imbalances and price changes.

---

[18]We use the mean of the bid and ask prices instead of transaction prices to guard against a potential bias. For example, during a period of substantial and positive order imbalance, there may be a greater chance that the last transaction would be executed at the ask price. If so, the return would be overstated and the estimated correlation between the return and the order imbalance biased upwards. Likewise, if the order imbalance were negative, the return would be understated, again leading to an upward bias in the estimated correlation. In fact, this potential bias is not substantial. In an earlier version of this chapter, we employed an alternative estimate of the fifteen-minute return, namely the ratio of the value of the constructed index at the end of the interval to the value at the end of the previous interval. This alternative utilizes transaction prices and does not require that a stock trade in two successive fifteen-minute periods. Although not reported here, the empirical results using this alternative measure are similar.

[19]On the basis of Fisher's z-test and twenty-five observations, any correlation greater than 0.49 is significant at the one percent level.

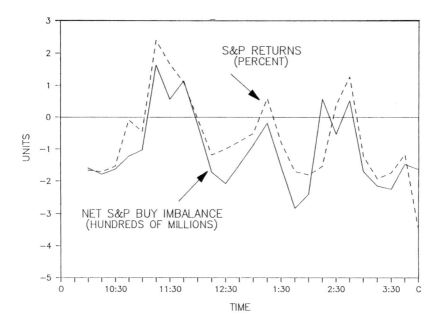

Figure 12.3. *Plot of fifteen-minute returns on S&P stocks versus the order imbalance in S&P stocks in the same fifteen minutes for October 19, 1987. The fifteen-minute returns are derived from stocks that traded in the fifteen-minute interval and traded in the prior fifteen-minute interval. The fifteen-minute return itself is the ratio of the total value of these stocks in the interval to the total value in the prior fifteen-minute interval, reexpressed as a percentage. The price of each stock is taken as the mean of the bid and the ask price at the time of the last transaction in each interval. The first return is for the interval 9:45–10:00. The net S&P buy imbalance is the dollar value of the trades at the ask less the dollar value of the trades at the bid in the fifteen-minute interval. The correlation between the fifteen-minute returns and the order imbalance is 0.81.*

12.3.3 Cross-Sectional Results

The aggregate time series analysis indicates a strong relation between order imbalances and stock returns. This finding, however, provides no guarantee that there will be any relation between the realized returns of individual securities and some measure of their order imbalances in any cross-section. In the extreme, if all trading is due to index-related strategies and these strategies buy or sell all stocks in the index in market proportions, all stocks will be subject to the same buying or selling pressure. As a result, there will be no differential effects in a cross-section.

Let us for a moment continue to assume that all trading is due to index-related strategies, but let us assume that these strategies buy or sell subsets of the stocks in the index and not necessarily in market proportions. Even

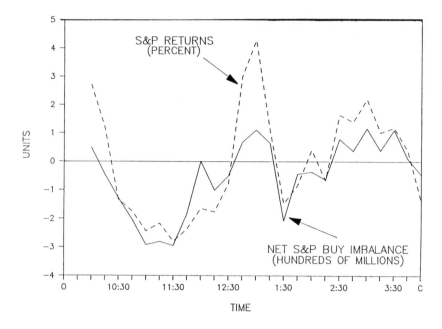

Figure 12.4.   Plot of fifteen-minute returns on S&P stocks versus the order imbalance in the same fifteen minutes for October 20, 1987. The fifteen-minute returns are derived from stocks that traded in the fifteen-minute interval and traded in the prior fifteen-minute interval. The fifteen-minute return itself is the ratio of the total value of these stocks in the interval to the total value in the prior fifteen-minute interval, reexpressed as a percentage. The price of each stock is taken as the mean of the bid and the ask price at the time of the last transaction in each interval. The first return is for the interval 9:45–10:00. The net S&P buy imbalance is the dollar value of the trades at the ask less the dollar value of the trades at the bid in the fifteen-minute interval. The correlation between the fifteen-minute returns and the order imbalance is 0.86.

in this case, it is theoretically possible that there will be no cross-sectional relations if, for instance, all stocks are perfect substitutes at all times.

As a result, finding no relation between realized returns and order imbalances in a cross-section of securities does not preclude a time series relation. Finding a relation in a cross-section indicates that, in addition to any aggregate relation over time, the relative amount of order imbalance is related to individual returns.

With this preamble, let us turn to the cross-sectional analysis. To begin, the trading hours of October 19 and October 20 are divided into half-hour intervals. The sample for a given half hour includes all securities that traded in the fifteen minutes prior to the beginning of the interval and in the fifteen minutes prior to the end of the interval. For each security, the order imbalance includes all trades following the last trade in the prior fifteen

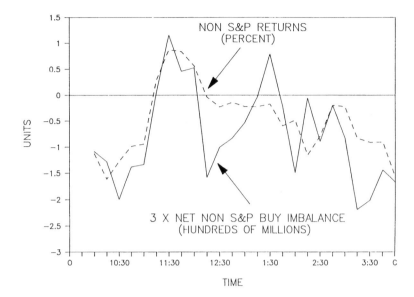

Figure 12.5. *Plot of fifteen-minute returns on non-S&P stocks versus the order imbalance in the same fifteen minutes for October 19, 1987. The fifteen-minute returns are derived from stocks that traded in the fifteen-minute interval and traded in the prior fifteen-minute interval. The fifteen-minute return itself is the ratio of the total value of these stocks in the interval to the total value in the prior fifteen-minute interval, reexpressed as a percentage. The price of each stock is taken as the mean of the bid and the ask price at the time of the last transaction in each interval. The first return is for the interval 9:45–10:00. The net non-S&P buy imbalance is the dollar value of the trades at the ask less the dollar value of the trades at the bid in the fifteen-minute interval. The correlation between the fifteen-minute returns and the order imbalance is 0.81.*

minutes through and including the last trade in the half-hour interval. The return for each security is measured over the same interval as the trading imbalance using the mean of the bid and ask prices. To control for size, the order imbalance for each security is deflated by its market value as of October 16 to yield a normalized order imbalance.

The estimated rank order correlation coefficients for the S&P stock are uniformly positive for the half-hour intervals on Monday and Tuesday (Table 12.2). They range from 0.11 to 0.51 and are statistically significant at the five percent level. The smallest estimate of 0.11 is for the 2:00 to 2:30 interval on Monday afternoon, during part of which the SIAC system was inoperable. All other estimates are above 0.20. The rank order correlation coefficients for the non-S&P stocks are similar to those for the S&P stocks. They range from 0.23 to 0.54, with the exception of the 2:00 to 2:30 interval on Monday. This analysis provides support for the hypothesis that there is

Table 12.2. *Cross-sectional rank correlations of individual security returns and normalized order imbalance by half hour intervals. For a given half hour, a security is included if it trades in the fifteen minutes prior to the beginning of the interval and in the last fifteen minutes of the interval. The return is calculated using the mean of the bid and ask prices after the last transaction prior to the interval and the mean of the bid and ask prices at the end of the interval. Thus, there is a significant relation to order imbalances for S&P stocks, but not to order imbalances as measured here for non-S&P stock. Adding the Monday return to the S&P regression leads to a reduction in the z-statistic on scaled order imbalances to −0.92. As reported in footnote 23, the Monday returns enter significantly for both groups of stocks. This behavior of the regression statistics is consistent with the hypothesis that the scaled order imbalance measures selling pressure for individual securities with substantial measurement error and that the Monday return measures selling pressure with less error.*

Interval	S&P 500 Stocks		Non-S&P Stocks	
	Rank Correlation[a]	No. of Stocks	Rank Correlation[a]	No. of Stocks
Monday, October 19				
10:00–10:30	0.31	278	0.30	427
10:30–11:00	0.30	364	0.32	560
11:00–11:30	0.51	396	0.54	607
11:30–12:00	0.51	417	0.51	565
12:00–12:30	0.47	431	0.42	543
12:30– 1:00	0.31	437	0.45	546
1:00– 1:30	0.33	435	0.42	470
1:30– 2:00	0.33	436	0.44	465
2:00– 2:30	0.11	431	0.00	515
2:30– 3:00	0.36	436	0.44	551
3:00– 3:30	0.22	433	0.40	563
3:30– 4:00	0.27	415	0.23	681
Average	0.34		0.37	
Tuesday, October 20				
10:00–10:30	0.51	323	0.51	462
10:30–11:00	0.52	400	0.44	575
11:00–11:30	0.30	406	0.43	577
11:30–12:00	0.12	365	0.16	583
12:00–12:30	0.32	343	0.35	574
12:30– 1:00	0.47	341	0.47	571
1:00– 1:30	0.35	361	0.39	550
1:30– 2:00	0.40	381	0.46	461
2:00– 2:30	0.47	398	0.37	446
2:30– 3:00	0.43	402	0.50	495
3:00– 3:30	0.43	405	0.40	516
3:30– 4:00	0.31	428	0.34	604
Average	0.39		0.40	

[a]The asymptotic standard error of the rank correlation estimates is $1/\sqrt{\text{no. of stocks}}$ under the null hypothesis of zero correlation.

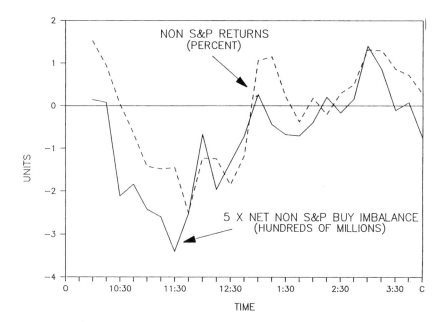

Figure 12.6. *Plot of fifteen-minute returns on non-S&P stocks versus the order imbalance in the same fifteen minutes for October 20, 1987. The fifteen-minute returns are derived from stocks that traded in the fifteen-minute interval and traded in the prior fifteen-minute interval. The fifteen-minute return itself is the ratio of the total value of these stocks in the interval to the total value in the prior fifteen-minute interval, reexpressed as a percentage. The price of each stock is taken as the mean of the bid and the ask price at the time of the last transaction in each interval. The first return is for the interval 9:45–10:00. The net non-S&P buy imbalance is the dollar value of the trades at the ask less the dollar value of the trades at the bid in the fifteen-minute interval. The correlation between the fifteen-minute returns and the order imbalance is 0.72.*

a positive cross-sectional relation between the return and normalized order imbalance.

12.3.4 Return Reversals

The significant relation between order imbalances and realized returns leads to the conjecture that some of the price movement for a given stock during the periods of high order imbalance is temporary in nature. We might expect that, if negative order imbalances are associated with greater negative stock returns, the price will rebound once the imbalance is eliminated. If on Monday afternoon those securities exhibiting the greatest losses were subject to the greatest order imbalances, these securities should have the greatest rebounds on Tuesday if the imbalance is no longer there. This cross-sectional conjecture is the subject of this section.

The last hour of trading on October 19 and the first hour of trading on October 20 are considered in the analysis. For a stock to be included in the analysis, it had to trade on Monday between 2:45 and 3:00 and between 3:45 and the close of the market and had to open on Tuesday prior to 10:30.[20] The Monday return is calculated using the mean of the bid and ask prices for the last quote prior to 3:00 and the mean of the bid and ask prices for the closing quote. The Tuesday return is calculated using the mean of the bid and ask prices for Monday's closing quote and the mean of the bid and ask prices for the opening quote Tuesday.[21]

There are 795 stocks with both Monday and Tuesday returns as well as beta coefficients that will be used below. The cross-sectional regression of $Tues_i$, the Tuesday return for stock i, on the Mon_i, the Monday return, and δ_i, a dummy variable with the value of one for a stock in the S&P 500 and zero otherwise, is

$$Tues_i = \begin{matrix} -3.33 \\ (-9.20) \end{matrix} + \begin{matrix} 3.91 \ \delta_i \\ (8.49) \end{matrix} - \begin{matrix} 0.54 \ Mon_i, \\ (-7.93) \end{matrix} \quad \overline{R}^2 = 0.26,$$

where the numbers in parentheses are the associated heteroscedasticity-consistent z-statistics.[22] The positive estimated coefficient for the dummy variable reflects the previously observed greater aggregate drop and subsequent recovery in S&P stocks. The significantly negative coefficient on the Monday return is consistent with the conjecture of a reversal effect.[23]

Another explanation of this reversal pertains to a beta effect.[24] If those stocks that fell the most on Monday had the greatest betas, these same stocks might exhibit the greatest returns on Tuesday, regardless of the level of order imbalances. Further, it is always possible that the reversal might be just a size effect. The following regression allows for the effects of these other two variables:

$$Tues_i = \begin{matrix} -13.50 \\ (-8.87) \end{matrix} + \begin{matrix} 0.76 \ \delta_i \\ (1.43) \end{matrix} - \begin{matrix} 0.54 \ Mon_i \\ (-7.62) \end{matrix} + \begin{matrix} 1.90 \ \ln(M_i) \\ (8.03) \end{matrix} - \begin{matrix} 1.02 \ \beta_i, \\ (-1.93) \end{matrix} \quad \overline{R}^2 = 0.34,$$

---

[20]The selection of these particular intervals is based on an examination of the indexes in Figure 12.1. Other time periods considered lead to similar results.

[21]The following analysis was repeated using transaction prices. The results did not change materially.

[22]The usual t-values are, respectively, -8.84, 8.22, and -12.30.

[23]We also regressed the Tuesday returns on the Monday returns separately for the 366 S&P stocks and for the 429 non-S&P stocks. The slope coefficient for the S&P regression is -0.68 with a z-statistic of -6.19, and the slope coefficient for the non-S&P regression is -0.42 with a z-statistic of -4.73. The respective $\overline{R}^2$'s are 0.19 and 0.13.

[24]Kleidon (1992) provides an analysis of this explanation.

where M_i is the market value of stock i as of the close on October 16 and β_i is a beta coefficient estimated from the fifty-two weekly returns ending in September 1987 as described in footnote 12.[25] The estimated coefficient on Monday's return is virtually unchanged. The estimated coefficient on the dummy variable is no longer significant at the five percent level. Thus, in explaining the return during the first hour of trading on Tuesday, the distinction between S&P and non-S&P stocks becomes less important once one holds constant a stock's market value and beta in addition to its return during the last hour on Monday.

These results are consistent with a price pressure hypothesis and lead to the conclusion that some of the largest declines for individual stocks on Monday afternoon were temporary in nature and can partially be attributed to the inability of the market structure to handle the large amount of selling volume.

12.4 Conclusion

The primary purpose of this chapter was to examine order imbalances and the returns of NYSE stocks on October 19 and 20, 1987. The evidence shows that there are substantial differences in the returns realized by stocks that are included in the S&P Composite Index and those that are not. In the aggregate, the losses on S&P stocks on October 19 are much greater than the losses on non-S&P stocks. Importantly, by mid morning of October 20, the S&P stocks had recovered nearly to the level of the non-S&P stocks. Not surprisingly, the volume of trading in S&P stocks with size held constant exceeds the volume of trading in non-S&P stocks.

In the aggregate, there is a significant relation between the realized returns on S&P stocks in each fifteen-minute interval and a concurrent measure of buying and selling imbalance. Non-S&P stocks display a similar

---

[25] A more direct test of the price pressure hypothesis suggested by the referee is to regress Tuesday returns on some scaled measure of order imbalance for the last hour on Monday rather than on the return for this hour. To accommodate differences between S&P and non-S&P stocks, we report the regression separately for these two groups. The regression for the S&P stocks is

$$Tues_i = -21.48 \quad - \quad 0.14 \; OrdImb_i \quad + \quad 3.39 \; \ln(M_i) \quad - \quad 0.99 \; \beta_i, \qquad \overline{R}^2 = 0.25.$$
$$ (-7.80) \qquad (-2.52) \qquad\qquad (10.43) \qquad\qquad (-0.97)$$

The regression for non-S&P stocks is

$$Tues_i = \quad -5.35 \quad - \quad 0.002 \; OrdImb_i \quad + \quad 0.77 \; \ln(M_i) \quad - \quad 0.33 \; \beta_i, \qquad \overline{R}^2 = 0.02.$$
$$ (-2.89) \qquad (-1.09) \qquad\qquad (2.74) \qquad\qquad (-0.59)$$

$OrdImb_i$ is the appropriately scaled order imbalance, and the numbers in parentheses are z-statistics.

but weaker relation. Quite apart from this aggregate relation, the study finds a relation within half-hour intervals between the returns and the relative buying and selling imbalances of individual stocks. Finally, those stocks with the greatest losses in the afternoon of October 19 tended to realize the greatest gains in the morning of October 20.

These results are consistent with, but do not prove, the hypothesis that S&P stocks fell more than warranted on October 19 because the market was unable to absorb the extreme selling pressure on those stocks.[26] If this hypothesis is correct, a portion of the losses on S&P stocks on October 19 is related to the magnitude of the trading volume and not real economic factors. A question of obvious policy relevance that this chapter has not addressed is whether buying and selling imbalances induced by index-related strategies have a differential relation to price movements from order imbalances induced by other strategies.

---

[26]An alternative hypothesis consistent with the data is that S&P stocks adjust more rapidly to new information than non-S&P stocks, and, between the close on October 19 and the opening on October 20, there was a release of some favorable information. Under this hpothesis, the losses on non-S&P stocks on October 19 were not as great as they should have been.

Appendix A12

THIS APPENDIX DESCRIBES the procedures used in this chapter to construct both the levels and returns of various indexes. The evidence indicates that after the first hour and a half of trading on either October 19 or 20, 1987, the biases from stale prices are minimal. To conserve space, we present detailed statistics only for the S&P index for October 19. The full analysis is available from the authors.

A12.1 Index Levels

To estimate index levels,[27] we consider four alternative approaches. The first utilizes priccs only of stocks that have traded in the past fifteen minutes. Every fifteen minutes, we estimate the return on the index as follows. To take a specific case, say 10:00 on October 19, we identify all stocks that have traded in the past fifteen minutes, ensuring that no price is more than fifteen minutes old. Using the closest transaction price in the past fifteen minutes to 10:00, we calculate the market value of these stocks and also the value of these same stocks using the closing prices on October 16. The ratio of the 10:00 market value to the closing market value on October 16 gives an estimate of one plus the return on the index from Friday close to 10:00.

Applying this return to the actual closing value of the index on October 16 of 282.70 provides an estimate of the index at 10:00. Alternatively, since the level of the index is arbitrary, one could set the index to one at the close of October 16 and interpret this ratio as an index itself.

The second approach is identical to the first in that it is based only upon stocks that have traded in the previous fifteen minutes. The difference is

---

[27]The reader is referred to Harris (1989a) for another approach to mitigate biases associated with stale prices.

that, instead of the transaction price, this index utilizes the mean of the bid and ask prices at the time of the transaction.

The third approach utilizes only stocks that have traded in the next fifteen minutes and for these stocks using the nearest price in the next fifteen minutes to calculate the market value. The set of stocks using the past fifteen minutes will usually differ somewhat from the set of stocks using the next fifteen minutes.

One criticism of this approach is that, in the falling market of October 19, there may be some stocks that did not trade in either the past fifteen minutes or the next fifteen minutes because there was no one willing to buy. The argument goes that the returns on these stocks if they could have been observed would be less than the returns on those that traded. Excluding these stocks would then cause the index as calculated here to overstate the true index.

One way to assess this potential bias is to estimate a fourth index using the first available next trade price, whenever it occurs. This index corresponds to a strategy of placing market orders for each of the stocks in the index. In some cases, this price would be the opening price of the following day. However, if the next trade price is too far distant, the market could have fallen and recovered, so that the next trade price might even overstate the true unopened price at the time.

For October 19, the four indexes for the S&P stocks are very similar except for the first hour and a half of trading (Figure A12.1). This similarity stems from the fact that the bulk of the S&P stocks had opened and then continued to trade. By 11:00 on October 19, stocks representing 87.1 percent of the market value of the 462 NYSE stocks in the S&P Composite had opened and had traded in the prior fifteen minutes (Table A12.1). There was a tendency for the larger stocks to open later than the smaller stocks (Table A12.2). Thereafter, a substantial number of stocks traded in every fifteen-minute interval.

The differences in the indexes in the first hour and a half of trading are partly related to the delays in opening and to the rapid drop in the market. If the prices of stocks that have not opened move in alignment with the stocks that have opened, the true level of the market would be expected to fall within the index values calculated with the last fifteen-minute price and the next fifteen-minute price.

If, in the falling market of October 19, the true losses on stocks that had not opened exceeded the losses on stocks that had opened, the true market index might even be less than the index calculated with the next fifteen-minute price. This argument may have some merit. For any specific fifteen-minute interval from 9:45 to 11:00, there is a strong negative relation between the returns realized from Friday close and the time of opening (Table A12.1).

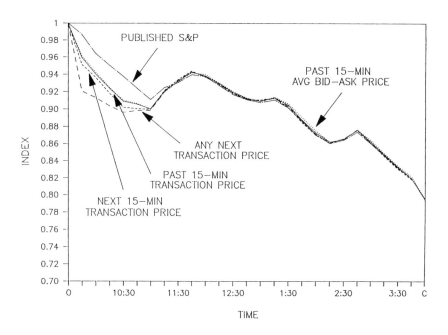

Figure A12.1.   *Comparison of various constructed indexes measuring the S&P Composite Index with the published S&P Index on October 19, 1987. There are four types of constructed indexes, and they are calculated every fifteen minutes. The four constructed indexes differ in the estimate of the market value at each fifteen-minute interval. The first index (used in the body of the chapter) is based on all S&P stocks that traded in the previous or past fifteen minutes and utilizes the last transaction price in the interval to estimate the total market value of these stocks. The ratio of this market value to the market value of these same stocks as of the close on Friday, October 16, 1987, provides the index value that is plotted. The second index is the same as the first except that the estimate of the market values of the stocks at the end of the fifteen-minute interval utilizes as the price of each stock the mean of the last bid and ask price in the minute of the last transaction. The third is based upon S&P stocks that trade in the next fifteen-minute interval and estimates the market value by the earliest transaction price in the interval. The fourth is based upon S&P stocks that trade in any future interval on October 19 and estimates the market value by the earliest transaction price. The published index is the actual index rescaled to have a value of 1.0 as of the close on October 16. The indexes using future prices are only calculated through 3:45.*

The behavior of these four indexes for S&P stocks for October 20 is similar to that of October 19 in that the four indexes approximate each other quite closely after the first hour and a half of trading. The major difference is that the market initially rose on October 20, and there is some evidence that the returns on stocks that opened later in the morning exceeded the returns of those that had already opened.

Table A12.1. *Realized returns from Friday close cross-classified by opening time and trading interval for S&P stocks during the first hour and a half of trading on October 19, 1987.*

Trading Interval	Variable	Opening Time						Overall
		9:30–9:45	9:45–10:00	10:00–10:15	10:15–10:30	10:30–10:45	10:45–11:00	
9:30– 9:45	Return[a]	−4.0						−4.0
	Number[b]	201						201
	% of Value[c]	29.7						29.7
9:45–10:00	Return	−5.8	−6.2					−6.0
	Number	198	130					328
	% of Value	29.5	28.3					57.8
10:00–10:15	Return	−7.4	−7.6	−8.7				−7.6
	Number	197	129	36				362
	% of Value	29.4	28.2	4.8				62.5
10:15–10:30	Return	−8.6	−9.0	−10.1	−13.0			−9.1
	Number	194	128	35	19			376
	% of Value	29.3	28.2	4.8	3.8			66.1
10:30–10:45	Return	−8.7	−9.0	−10.4	−11.6	−11.1		−9.4
	Number	192	128	35	18	19		392
	% of Value	29.4	28.1	4.8	3.7	12.4		78.4
10:45–11:00	Return	−9.2	−9.5	−11.0	−12.3	−9.9	−12.3	−10.0
	Number	194	128	34	18	18	19	411
	% of Value	29.3	28.1	4.7	3.7	12.3	9.0	87.1

[a]Ratio of total market value of stocks using last prices in trading interval to total market value of same stocks using Friday closing prices, expressed as a percentage. The overall return is calculated in a similar fashion and is not a simple average of the returns in the cells.
[b]Number of stocks that opened at the designated time and traded in the trading interval.
[c]Ratio of total market value of stocks in cell to the total market value of all 462 stocks; both market values are based upon Friday closing prices.

Similarly, the four indexes for non-S&P stocks track each other closely after the first hour and a half of trading, but not quite as closely as the S&P indexes. Likewise, there is evidence that, in the falling market of October 19, the later opening non-S&P stocks experienced greater losses than those that opened earlier, and the reverse in the rising market of October 20.

In view of these results, the analyses of levels of the market will be based upon the indexes using only stocks that have traded in the past fifteen minutes. Further, since the S&P Composite Index utilizes transaction prices, we shall conform to the same convention. Utilizing the mean of the bid and ask prices leads to virtually identical results.

Table A12.2. *Percentage of S&P stocks traded by firm size quartile in each fifteen-minute interval during the opening hour of October 19, 1987. The partitions for the quartiles are constructed to have approximately an equal number of stocks in each quartile. The numbers reported are the percentage of stocks that traded in the indicated interval out of the total number of stocks in the size category.*

Time Interval	9:30–9:45	9:45–10:00	10:00–10:15	10:15–10:30
Large Quartile	31.9	61.2	65.5	69.8
2	36.5	67.8	74.8	81.7
3	44.8	70.7	82.8	85.3
Small Quartile	60.9	84.3	90.4	88.7
Overall	43.5	71.0	78.4	81.4

A12.2 Fifteen-Minute Index Returns

The analysis of aggregate order imbalances employs returns on the indexes over a fifteen-minute interval. One way to calculate such a return is to divide the index level at the end of one fifteen-minute interval by the index level at the end of the previous interval and express this ratio as a percentage return.

Another way is to use only stocks that have traded in consecutive fifteen-minute intervals. The fifteen-minute return is then defined as the ratio of the market value of these stocks in one fifteen-minute interval divided by the market value of these same stocks in the previous interval and reexpressed as a percentage return.

In the first approach, the set of stocks in one fifteen-minute interval differs slightly from the set in the previous fifteen-minute interval, and this difference may introduce some noise into the return series. However, in comparison to the first approach, estimates based upon this second method employ a lesser number of securities which may introduce some noise. As a result, neither method clearly dominates the other.[28]

---

[28] Another method to construct the levels of the index is to link the fifteen-minute returns derived from stocks that trade in consecutive intervals. This alternative is dominated by that given in the text of the Appendix. Relating market values at any point in time to the market values as of the close on Friday, October 16, assures that an error introduced into the index at one point in time would not propagate itself into future values of the index. Linking fifteen-minute returns would propagate such errors. Moreover, the method in the text utilizes as many stocks as available.

Since there is a theoretical possibility that the use of transaction prices might induce a positive correlation between the measure of order imbalance described in the body of the chapter and the estimated fifteen-minute returns, the results reported in the text will use the mean of the bid and the ask prices to measure market values. To conserve space, the principal empirical results reported in the text utilize the fifteen-minute returns based upon stocks that trade in consecutive fifteen-minute intervals. The results based upon other methods of estimating the fifteen-minute returns are similar.

References

Admati, A., and P. Pfleiderer, 1988, "A Theory of Intraday Patterns: Volume and Price Variability," *Review of Financial Studies*, 1, 3–40.

Admati, A., and P. Pfleiderer, 1989, "Divide and Conquer: A Theory of Intraday and Day-of-the-Week Mean Effects," *Review of Financial Studies*, 2, 189–224.

Aitchison, J., and S. Silvey, 1957, "The Generalization of Probit Analysis to the Case of Multiple Responses," *Biometrika*, 44, 131–140.

Aldous, D., 1989, *Probability Approximations via the Poisson Clumping Heuristic*, Springer-Verlag, New York.

Alexander, S., 1961, "Price Movements in Speculative Markets: Trends or Random Walks," *Industrial Management Review*, 2, 7–26.

Alexander, S., 1964, "Price Movements in Speculative Markets: Trends or Random Walks, No. 2," in P. Cootner (ed.), *The Random Character of Stock Market Prices*, MIT Press, Cambridge, MA.

Amihud, Y., and H. Mendelson, 1986, "Asset Pricing and the Bid-Ask Spread," *Journal of Financial Economics*, 17, 223–250.

Amihud, Y., and H. Mendelson, 1987, "Trading Mechanisms and Stock Returns: An Empirical Investigation," *Journal of Finance*, 42, 533–553.

Andrews, D., 1984, "Non-Strong Mixing Autoregressive Processes," *Journal of Applied Probability*, 21, 930–934.

Andrews, D., 1991, "Heteroskedasticity and Autocorrelation Consistent Covariance Matrix Estimation," *Econometrica*, 59, 817–858.

Arnott, R., Kelso, C., Kiscadden, S., and R. Macedo, 1989, "Forecasting Factor Returns: An Intriguing Possibility," *Journal of Portfolio Management*, 16, 28–35.

Atchison, M., K. Butler, and R. Simonds, 1987, "Nonsynchronous Security Trading and Market Index Autocorrelation," *Journal of Finance*, 42, 111–118.

Bachelier, L., 1900, "Theory of Speculation," reprinted in P. Cootner (ed.), *The Random Character of Stock Market Prices*, MIT Press, Cambridge, 1964.

Ball, C., 1988, "Estimation Bias Induced by Discrete Security Prices," *Journal of Finance*, 43, 841–865.

Ball, R., and P. Brown, 1968, "An Empirical Evaluation of Accounting Income Numbers," *Journal of Accounting Reszearch*, 5, 159–178.

Banz, R. W., 1978, "Limited Diversification and Market Equilibrium: An Empirical Analysis," Unpublished Ph.D. dissertation, University of Chicago, Chicago, IL.

Banz, R. W., 1981, "The Relationship between Return and Market Value of Common Stocks," *Journal of Financial Economics*, 9, 3–18.

Barclay, M., and R. Litzenberger, 1988, "Announcement Effects of New Equity Issues and the Use of Intraday Price Data," *Journal of Financial Economics*, 21, 71–100.

Basu, Sanjoy, 1977, "Investment Performance of Common Stocks Relative to their Price-Earnings Ratio: A Test of the Efficient Market Hypothesis," *Journal of Finance*, 32, 663–682.

Berger, J., and R. Wolpert, 1984, *The Likelihood Principle*, Lecture Notes—Monograph Series, Vol. 6, Institute of Mathematical Statistics, Hayward.

Bernard, V., and J. Thomas, 1990, "Evidence that Stock Prices Do Not Fully Reflect the Implications of Current Earnings for Future Earnings," *Journal of Accounting and Economics*, 13, 305–340.

Berndt, E., B. Hall, R. Hall, and J. Hausman, 1974, "Estimation and Inference in Nonlinear Structural Models," *Annals of Economic and Social Measurement*, 3, 653–665.

Bessembinder, H., and K. Chan, 1992, "Time-Varying Risk Premia and Forecastable Returns in Futures Markets," *Journal of Financial Economics*, 32, 169–194.

Beveridge, S., and C. Nelson, 1981, "A New Approach to Decomposition of Economic Time Series into Permanent and Transitory Components with Particular Attention to Measurement of the 'Business Cycle'," *Journal of Monetary Economics*, 7, 151–174.

Bhattacharya, P. K., 1974, "Convergence of Sample Paths of Normalized Sums of Induced Order Statistics," *Annals of Statistics*, 2, 1034–1039.

Bhattacharya, P. K., 1984, "Induced Order Statistics: Theory and Applications," in P. R. Krishnaiah and P. K. Sen (eds.), *Handbook of Statistics 4: Nonparametric Methods*, North-Holland, Amsterdam.

Billingsley, P., 1968, *Convergence of Probability Measures*, John Wiley and Sons, New York.

Black, F., 1976, "The Pricing of Commodity Contracts," *Journal of Financial Economics*, 3, 167–179.

Black, F., 1986, "Noise," *Journal of Finance*, 41, 529–544.

Black, F., and M. S. Scholes, 1973, "The Pricing of Options and Corporate Liabilities," *Journal of Political Economy*, May–June, 637–659.

Black, F., M. Jensen, and M. Scholes, 1972, "The Capital Asset Pricing Model: Some Empirical Tests," in M. Jensen (ed.), *Studies in the Theory of Capital Markets*, Praeger, New York.

Blume, M., and I. Friend, 1978, *The Changing Role of the Individual Investor*, John Wiley and Sons, New York.

Blume, M., C. MacKinlay, and B. Terker, 1989, "Order Imbalances and Stock Price Movements on October 19 and 20, 1987," *Journal of Finance*, 44, 827–848.

Blume, M., and R. Stambaugh, 1983, "Biases in computed returns: An application to the size effect, *Journal of Financial Economics*, 12, 387–404.

Boes, D., R. Davis, and S. Gupta, 1989, "Parameter Estimation in Low Order Fractionally Differenced ARMA Processes," working paper, Department of Statistics, Colorado State University.

Bollerslev, T., R. Chou, and K. Kroner, 1992, "ARCH Modeling in Finance: Review of the Theory and Empirical Evidence," *Journal of Econometrics*, 52, 5–59.

Bollerslev, T., R. Engle, and J. Wooldridge, 1988, "A Capital Asset Pricing Model With Time-Varying Covariances," *Journal of Political Economy*, 96, 116–131.

Booth, G., and F. Kaen, 1979, "Gold and Silver Spot Prices and Market Information Efficiency," *Financial Review*, 14, 21–26.

Booth, G., F. Kaen, and P. Koveos, 1982, "R/S Analysis of Foreign Exchange Rates under Two International Monetary Regimes," *Journal of Monetary Economics*, 10, 407–415.

Bossaerts, P., and R. Green, 1989, "A General Equilibrium Model of Changing Risk Premia: Theory and Tests," *Review of Financial Studies*, 2, 467–493.

Box, G., and D. Cox, 1964, "An Analysis of Transformations," *Journal of the Royal Statistical Society, Series B*, 26, 211–243.

Box, G., and D. Pierce, 1970, "Distribution of Residual Autocorrelations in Autoregressive-Integrated Moving Average Time Series Models," *Journal of the American Statistical Association*, 65, 1509–1526.

Box, G., and G. Tiao, 1977, "A Canonical Analysis of Multiple Time Series," *Biometrika*, 64, 355–365.

Breen, W., and R. Korajczyk, 1993, "On Selection Biases in Book-to-Market Based Tests of Asset Pricing Models," Working Paper 167, Northwestern University, Evanston, IL.

Breen, W., L. Glosten, and R. Jagannathan, 1989, "Economic Significance of Predictable Variations in Stock Index Returns," *Journal of Finance*, 44, 1177–1189.

Brennan, M. J., and E. S. Schwartz, 1986, "Optimal Arbitrage Strategies under Basis Variability," Working Paper 21-86, Graduate School of Management, UCLA.

Brennan, M. J., and E. S. Schwartz, 1990, "Arbitrage in Stock Index Futures," *Journal of Business*, 63, 7–31.

Bronfman, C., 1991, "From Trades to Orders on the NYSE: Pitfalls in Inference Using Transactions Data," working paper, Department of Finance and Real Estate, College of Business and Public Administration, University of Arizona, Tucson, AZ.

Brown, P., A. Kleidon, and T. Marsh, 1983, "New Evidence on the Nature of Size Related Anomalies in Stock Prices," *Journal of Financial Economics*, 12, 33–56.

Brown, S., and M. Weinstein, 1983, "A New Approach to Testing Arbitrage Pricing Models: The Bilinear Paradigm," *Journal of Finance*, 38, 711–743.

Buck, R., 1978, *Advanced Calculus*, McGraw-Hill, New York.

Campbell, J. Y., 1987, "Stock Returns and the Term Structure," *Journal of Financial Economics*, 18, 373–400.

Campbell, J. Y., and N. G. Mankiw, 1987, "Are Output Fluctuations Transitory?," *Quarterly Journal of Economics*, 102, 857–880.

Campbell, J., S. Grossman, and J. Wang, 1991, "Trading Volume and Serial Correlation in Stock Returns," working paper, Princeton University, Princeton, NJ.

Capaul, C., I. Rowley, and W. Sharpe, 1993, "International value and growth stock returns," *Financial Analysts Journal*, 49, 27–36.

Cecchetti, S., and N. Mark, 1990, "Evaluating empirical tests of asset pricing models," *American Economic Review*, 80, 48–51.

Chamberlain, G., 1983, "Funds, Factors, and Diversification in Arbitrage Pricing Models," *Econometrica*, 51, 1305–1323.

Chamberlain, G., and M. Rothschild, 1983, "Arbitrage, Factor Structure, and Mean-Variance Analysis on Large Asset Markets," *Econometrica*, 51, 1281–1304.

Chan, L. K. C. and J. Lakonishok, 1993, "Are Reports of Beta's Death Premature?," *Journal of Portfolio Management*, 19, 51–62.

Chan, N., and C. Wei, 1988, "Limiting Distributions of Least Squares Estimates of Unstable Autoregressive Processes," *Annals of Statistics*, 16, 367–401.

Chan, K., N. Chen, and D. Hsieh, 1985, "An Exploratory Investigation of the Firm Size Effect," *Journal of Financial Economics*, 14, 451–471.

Chen, N., 1991, "Financial Investment Opportunities and the Macroeconomy," *Journal of Finance*, 46, 529–554.

Chen, N., R. Roll, and S. Ross, 1986, "Economic Forces and the Stock Market," *Journal of Business*, 59, 383–403.

Cho, D., and E. Frees, 1988, "Estimating the Volatility of Discrete Stock Prices," *Journal of Finance*, 43, 451–466.

Chopra, N., J. Lakonishok, and J. Ritter, 1992, "Measuring Abnormal Performance: Do Stocks Overreact?," *Journal of Financial Economics*, 31, 235–268.

Clarke, R., M. FitzGerald, P. Berent, and M. Statman, 1989, "Market Timing with Imperfect Information," *Financial Analysts Journal*, 45, 27–36.

Cochrane, J. H., 1987c, "Spectral Density Estimates of Unit Roots," working paper, University of Chicago, Chicago, IL.

Cochrane, J., 1988, "How Big Is the Random Walk in GNP?," *Journal of Political Economy*, 96, 893–920.

Cochrane, J., 1991, "A Critique of the Application of Unit Root Tests," *Journal of Economic Dynamics and Control*, 15, 275–284.

Cohen, K., G. Hawawini, S. Maier, R. Schwartz, and D. Whitcomb, 1983a, "Friction in the Trading Process and the Estimation of Systematic Risk," *Journal of Financial Economics*, 12, 263–278.

Cohen, K., G. Hawawini, S. Maier, R. Schwartz, and D. Whitcomb, 1983b, "Estimating and Adjusting for the Intervalling-Effect Bias in Beta," *Management Science*, 29, 135–148.

Cohen, K., S. Maier, R. Schwartz, and D. Whitcomb, 1978, "The Returns Generation Process, Returns Variance, and the Effect of Thinness in Securities Markets," *Journal of Finance*, 33, 149–167.

Cohen, K., S. Maier, R. Schwartz, and D. Whitcomb, 1979, "On the Existence of Serial Correlation in an Efficient Securities Market," *TIMS Studies in the Management Sciences*, 11, 151–168.

Cohen, K., S. Maier, R. Schwartz, and D. Whitcomb, 1986, *The Microstructure of Securities Markets*, Prentice-Hall, Englewood Cliffs, NJ.

Connor, G., and R. Korajczyk, 1986, "Performance Measurement with the Arbitrage Pricing Theory: A New Framework For Analysis," *Journal of Financial Economics*, 15, 373–394.

Connor, G., and R. Korajczyk, 1988, "Risk and Return in an Equilibrium APT: Application of a New Test Methodology," *Journal of Financial Economics*, 21, 255–290.

Conrad, J., and G. Kaul, 1993, "Long-Term Market Overreaction or Biases in Computed Returns?," *Journal of Finance*, 48, 39–63.

Conrad, J., G. Kaul, and M. Nimalendran, 1988, "Components of Short-Horizon Individual Security Returns," *Journal of Financial Economics*, 29, 365–384.

Constantinides, G., 1980, "Admissible Uncertainty in the Intertemporal Asset Pricing Model," *Journal of Financial Economics*, 8, 71–86.

Cootner, P., 1962, "Stock Prices: Random vs. Systematic Changes," *Industrial Management Review*, 3, 24–45.

Cootner, P. (ed.), 1964, *The Random Character of Stock Market Prices*, MIT Press, Cambridge.

Copeland, T. and D. Mayers, 1982, "The Value Line Enigma (1965–1978): A Case Study of Performance Evaluation Issues," *Journal of Financial Economics*, 10, 289–322.

Cowles, A., 1960, "A Revision of Previous Conclusions Regarding Stock Price Behavior," *Econometrica*, 28, 909–915.

Cowles, A., and H. Jones, 1937, "Some A Posteriori Probabilities in Stock Market Action," *Econometrica*, 5, 280–294.

Cox, J. C., J. E. Ingersoll, and S. A. Ross, 1981, "The Relation between Forward Prices and Futures Prices," *Journal of Financial Economics*, 9, 321–346.

David, H. A., 1973, "Concomitants of Order Statistics," *Bulletin of the International Statistical Institute*, 45, 295–300.

David, H. A., 1981, *Order Statistics* (2d ed.), John Wiley and Sons, New York.

David, H. A., and J. Galambos, 1974, "The Asymptotic Theory of Concomitants of Order Statistics," *Journal of Applied Probability*, 11, 762–770.

Davies, R., and D. Harte, 1987, "Tests for Hurst Effect," *Biometrika*, 74, 95–101.

Davydov, Y., 1970, "The Invariance Principle for Stationary Processes," *Theory of Probability and Its Applications*, 15, 487–489.

DeBondt, W., and R. Thaler, 1985, "Does the Stock Market Overreact?," *Journal of Finance*, 40, 793–805.

DeBondt, W., and R. Thaler, 1987, "Further Evidence on Investor Overreaction and Stock Market Seasonality," *Journal of Finance*, 42, 557–582.

DeLong, B., A. Shleifer, L. Summers, and R. Waldmann, 1989, "Positive Feedback Investment Strategies and Destabilizing Rational Speculation," Working Paper 2880, NBER.

Dickey, D. A., 1976, "Estimation and Hypothesis Testing for Nonstationary Time Series," Unpublished Ph.D. dissertation, Iowa State University, Ames, IA.

Dickey, D. A., and W. A. Fuller, 1979, "Distribution of the Estimators for Autoregressive Time Series with a Unit Root," *Journal of the American Statistical Association*, 74, 427–431.

Dickey, D. A., and W. A. Fuller, 1981, "Likelihood Ratio Statistics for Autoregressive Time Series with a Unit Root," *Econometrica*, 49, 1057–1072.

Diebold, F., 1987, "Deviations from Random-Walk Behavior: Tests Based on the Variance-Time Function," Special Studies Paper 224, Federal Reserve Board, Washington, DC.

Diebold, F., and G. Rudebusch, 1989, "Long Memory and Persistence in Aggregate Output," *Journal of Monetary Economics*, 24, 189–209.

Dimson, E., 1979, "Risk Measurement When Shares Are Subject to Infrequent Trading," *Journal of Financial Economics*, 7, 197–226.

Droms, W., 1989, "Market Timing as an Investment Policy," *Financial Analysts Journal*, January/February, 73.

Dufour, J. M., 1981, "Rank Tests for Serial Dependence," *Journal of Time Series Analysis*, 2, 117–128.

Dufour, J. M., and R. Roy, 1985, "Some Robust Exact Results on Sample Autocorrelations and Tests of Randomness," *Journal of Econometrics*, 29, 257–273.

Easley, D., and M. O'Hara, 1987, "Price, Trade Size, and Information in Securities Markets," *Journal of Financial Economics*, 19, 69–90.

Easley, D., and M. O'Hara, 1992, "Time and the Process of Security Price Adjustment," *Journal of Finance*, 47, 576–605.

Eberlein, E., and M. Taqqu, 1986, *Dependence in Probability and Statistics: A Survey of Recent Result*, Birkhäuser, Boston.

Eikeboom, A., 1992, "The Dynamics of the Bid-Ask Spread," working paper, Sloan School of Management, Massachusetts Institute of Technology, Cambridge, MA.

Engle, R., 1982, "Autoregressive Conditional Heteroscedasticity with Estimates of the Variance of United Kingdom Inflation," *Econometrica*, 50, 987–1007.

Engle, R., D. Lilien, and R. Robbins, 1987, "Estimating Time Varying Risk Premia in the Term Structure: The ARCH-M Model," *Econometrica*, 55, 391–407.

Estrella, A., and G. Hardouvelis, 1991, "The Term Structure as a Predictor of Real Economic Activity," *Journal of Finance*, 46, 555–576.

Evans, G. B. A., and N. E. Savin, 1981a, "The Calculation of the Limiting Distribution of the Least Squares Estimator of the Parameter in a Random Walk Model," *Annals of Statistics*, 9, 1114–1118.

Evans, G. B. A., and N. E. Savin, 1981b, "Testing for Unit Roots: 1," *Econometrica*, 49, 753–779.

Evans, G. B. A., and N. E. Savin, 1984, "Testing for Unit Roots: 2," *Econometrica*, 52, 1241–1269.

Eytan, T., and G. Harpaz, 1986, "The Pricing of Futures and Options Contracts on the Value Line Index," *Journal of Finance*, 41, 843–856.

Fama, E., 1965, "The Behavior of Stock Market Prices," *Journal of Business*, 38, 34–105.

Fama, E., 1970, "Efficient Capital Markets: A Review of Theory and Empirical Work," *Journal of Finance*, 25, 383–417.

Fama, E., 1996, "Multifactor Portfolio Efficiency and Multifactor Asset Pricing," *Journal of Financial and Quantitative Analysis*, 31, 441–465.

Fama, E., and M. Blume, 1966, "Filter Rules and Stock Market Trading Profits," *Journal of Business*, 39, 226–241.

Fama, E., and K. French, 1988, "Permanent and Temporary Components of Stock Prices," *Journal of Political Economy*, 96, 246–273.

Fama, E., and K. French, 1990, "Business Conditions and Expected Returns on Stocks and Bonds," *Journal of Financial Economics*, 25, 23–49.

Fama, E., and K. French, 1992, "The Cross-section of Expected Stock Returns," *Journal of Finance*, 47, 427-465.

Fama, E., and K. French, 1993, "Common Risk Factors in the Returns on Stocks and Bonds," *Journal of Financial Economics*, 33, 3–56.

Fama, E., and J. MacBeth, 1973, "Risk, Return, and Equilibrium: Empirical Tests," *Journal of Political Economy*, 71, 607–636.

Feller, W., 1951, "The Asymptotic Distribution of the Range of Sums of Independent Random Variables," *Annals of Mathematical Statistics*, 22, 427–432.

Ferson, W., 1989, "Changes in Expected Security Returns, Risk, and the Level of Interest Rates," *Journal of Finance*, 44, 1191–1217.

Ferson, W., 1990, "Are the Latent Variables in Time-Varying Expected Returns Compensation for Consumption Risk?," *Journal of Finance*, 45, 397–430.

Ferson, W., and C. Harvey, 1991a, "Sources of Predictability in Portfolio Returns," *Financial Analysts Journal*, May–June, 49–56.

Ferson, W., and C. Harvey, 1991b, "The Variation of Economic Risk Premiums," *Journal of Political Economy*, 99, 385–415.

Ferson, W., and C. Harvey, 1993, "The Risk and Predictability of International Equity Returns," *Review of Financial Studies*, 6, 527–566.

Ferson, W., S. Kandel, and R. Stambaugh, 1987, "Tests of Asset Pricing with Time-Varying Expected Risk Premiums and Market Betas," *Journal of Finance*, 42, 201–220.

Ferson, W., and R. Korajczyk, 1995, "Do Arbitrage Pricing Models Explain the Predictability of Stock Returns?," *Journal of Business*, 68, 309–349.

Figlewski, S., 1984, "Hedging Performance and Basis Risk in Stock Index Futures," *Journal of Finance*, 39, 657–669.

Fisher, L., 1966, "Some New Stock Market Indexes," *Journal of Business*, 39, 191–225.

Foerster, S., and D. Keim, 1989, "Direct Evidence of Non-Trading of NYSE and AMEX Securities," working paper, Wharton School, University of Pennsylvania.

Foster, D., T. Smith, and R. Whaley, 1997, "Assessing Goodness-of-Fit of Asset Pricing Models: The Distribution of the Maximal R^2," *Journal of Finance*, 52, 591–607.

Fox, R., and M. Taqqu, 1986, "Large-Sample Properties of Parameter Estimates for Strongly Dependent Stationary Gaussian Time Series," *Annals of Statistics*, 14, 517–532.

French, K., 1983, "A Comparison of Futures and Forward Prices," *Journal of Financial Economics*, 12, 311–342.

French, K., and R. Roll, 1986, "Stock Return Variances: The Arrival of Information and the Reaction of Traders," *Journal of Financial Economics*, 17, 5–26.

French, K., G. W. Schwert, and R. F. Stambaugh, 1987, "Expected Stock Returns and Volatility," *Journal of Financial Economics*, 19, 3–30.

Fuller, W., 1976, *Introduction to Statistical Time Series*, Wiley, New York.

Gallant, R., 1987, *Nonlinear Statistical Models*, John Wiley and Sons, New York.

Gallant, A., and G. Tauchen, 1989, "Semi-Nonparametric Estimation of Conditionally Constrained Heterogeneous Processes: Asset-Pricing Applications," *Econometrica*, 57, 1091–1120.

Gallant, R., P. Rossi, and G. Tauchen, 1992, "Stock Prices and Volume," *Review of Financial Studies*, 5, 199–242.

Gantmacher, F., 1959, *The Theory of Matrices*, Volume I, Chelsea Publishing Company, New York.

Garman, M., 1976, "Market Microstructure," *Journal of Financial Economics*, 3, 257–275.

Geweke, J., and S. Porter-Hudak, 1983, "The Estimation and Application of Long Memory Time Series Models," *Journal of Time Series Analysis*, 4, 221–238.

Gibbons, M. R., 1982, "Multivariate Tests of Financial Models: A New Approach," *Journal of Financial Economics*, 10, 3–27.

Gibbons, M. R., and W. Ferson, 1985, "Testing Asset Pricing Models with Changing Expectations and an Unobservable Market Portfolio," *Journal of Financial Economics*, 14, 217–236.

Gibbons, M. R., S. A. Ross, and J. Shanken, 1989, "A Test of the Efficiency of a Given Portfolio," *Econometrica*, 57, 1121–1152.

Glosten, L., 1987, "Components of the Bid-Ask Spread and the Statistical Properties of Transaction Prices," *Journal of Finance*, 42, 1293–1307.

Glosten, L., and L. Harris, 1988, "Estimating the Components of the Bid/Ask Spread," *Journal of Financial Economics*, 21, 123–142.

Glosten, L., and P. Milgrom, 1985, "Bid, Ask and Transaction Prices in a Specialist Market with Heterogeneously Informed Traders," *Journal of Financial Economics*, 14, 71–100.

Goldfeld, S., and R. Quandt, 1973, "A Markov Model for Switching Regressions," *Journal of Econometrics*, 1, 3–16.

Gottlieb, G., and A. Kalay, 1985, "Implications of the Discreteness of Observed Stock Prices," *Journal of Finance*, 40, 135–154.

Gould, F. J., 1987, "Stock Index Futures: The Arbitrage Cycle and Portfolio Insurance," mimeo, Graduate School of Business, University of Chicago.

Gould, J., and C. Nelson, 1974, "The Stochastic Structure of the Velocity of Money," *American Economic Review*, 64, 405–417.

Gourieroux, C., A. Monfort, and A. Trognon, 1985, "A General Approach to Serial Correlation," *Econometric Theory*, 1, 315–340.

Granger, C., 1966, "The Typical Spectral Shape of an Economic Variable," *Econometrica*, 34, 150–161.

Granger, C., 1980, "Long Memory Relationships and the Aggregation of Dynamic Models," *Journal of Econometrics*, 14, 227–238.

Granger, C., and R. Joyeux, 1980, "An Introduction to Long-Memory Time Series Models and Fractional Differencing," *Journal of Time Series Analysis*, 1, 15–29.

Granger, C., and O. Morgenstern, 1963, "Spectral Analysis of New York Stock Market Prices," *Kyklos*, 16, 1–27.

Greene, M., and B. Fielitz, 1977, "Long-Term Dependence in Common Stock Returns," *Journal of Financial Economics*, 4, 339–349.

Grossman, S., 1976, "On the Efficiency of Competitive Stock Markets where Trades have Diverse Information," *Journal of Finance*, 31, 573–585.

Grossman, S., and J. Stiglitz, 1980, "On the Impossibility of Informationally Efficient Markets," *American Economic Review*, 70, 393–408.

Grundy, B., and M. McNichols, 1989, "Trade and Revelation of Information through Prices and Direct Disclosure," *Review of Financial Studies*, 2, 495–526.

Gurland, J., T. Lee, and P. Dahm, 1960, "Polychotomous Quantal Response in Biological Assay," *Biometrics*, 16, 382–398.

Hald, A., 1990, *A History of Probability and Statistics and Their Applications Before 1750*, John Wiley and Sons, New York.

Hall, R., 1978, "Stochastic Implications of the Life Cycle-Permanent Income Hypothesis: Theory and Evidence," *Journal of Political Economy*, 86, 971–987.

Hall, P., and C. Heyde, 1980, *Martingale Limit Theory and Its Application*, Academic Press, New York.

Hamilton, J., 1989, "A New Approach to the Economic Analysis of Nonstationary Time Series and the Business Cycle," *Econometrica*, 57, 357–384.

Hannan, E., 1970, *Multiple Time Series*, John Wiley and Sons, New York.

Hansen, L., 1982, "Large Sample Properties of Generalized Method of Moments Estimators," *Econometrica*, 50, 1029–1054.

Hansen, L., and R. Jagannathan, 1991, "Implications of Security Market Data for Models of Dynamic Economies," *Journal of Political Economy*, 99, 225–262.

Hansen, L., and R. Jagannathan, 1997, "Assessing Specification Errors in Stochastic Discount Factor Models," *Journal of Finance*, 52, 557–590.

Hardy, D., 1990, "Market Timing and International Diversification," *Journal of Portfolio Management*, 16, 23–27.

Harris, L., 1989b, "The October 1987 S&P 500 Stock Futures Basis," *Journal of Finance*, 44, 77–100.

Harris, L., 1989c, "Stock Price Clustering, Discreteness Regulation and Bid/Ask Spreads," Working Paper 89-01, New York Stock Exchange, New York.

Harris, L., 1990, "Estimation of Stock Price Variances and Serial Covariances from Discrete Observations," *Journal of Financial and Quantitative Analysis*, 25, 291–306.

Harris, L., 1991, "Stock Price Clustering and Discreteness," *Review of Financial Studies*, 4, 389–415.

Harris, L., G. Sofianos, and J. Shapiro, 1994, "Program Trading and Intraday Volatility," *Review of Financial Studies*, 7, 653–685.

Harvey, C., 1989, "Time-Varying Conditional Covariances in Tests of Asset Pricing Models," *Journal of Financial Economics*, 24, 289–317.

Hasbrouck, J., 1988, "Trades, Quotes, Inventories, and Information," *Journal of Financial Economics*, 22, 229–252.

Hasbrouck, J., 1991a, "Measuring the Information Content of Stock Trades," *Journal of Finance*, 46, 179–208.

Hasbrouck, J., 1991b, "The Summary Informativeness of Stock Trades: An Econometric Analysis," *Review of Financial Studies, Review of Financial Studies*, 4, 571–595.

Hasbrouck, J., and T. Ho, 1987, "Order Arrival, Quote Behavior, and the Return-Generating Process," *Journal of Finance*, 42, 1035–1048.

Haubrich, J., 1993, "Consumption and Fractional Differencing: Old and New Anomalies," *Review of Economics and Statistics*, 75, 767–772.

Haubrich, J., and A. Lo, 1989, "The Sources and Nature of Long-Term Dependence in the Business Cycle," Working Paper 2951, NBER.

Hausman, J., 1978, "Specification Tests in Econometrics," *Econometrica*, 46, 1251–1272.

Hausman, J., 1988, "The Optimality of Autocorrelation-Based Tests of the Random Walk Hypothesis," working paper, Department of Economics, Massachusetts Institute of Technology, Cambridge, MA.

Hausman, J., A. Lo, and C. MacKinlay, 1991, "An Ordered Probit Analysis of Transaction Stock Prices," Working Paper 3888, NBER, Cambridge, MA.

Helms, B., F. Kaen, and R. Rosenman, 1984, "Memory in Commodity Futures Contracts," *Journal of Futures Markets*, 4, 559–567.

Helson, H., and D. Sarason, 1967, "Past and Future," *Mathematica Scandinavia*, 21, 5–16.

Henriksson, R., and R. Merton, 1981, "On Market Timing and Investment Performance II: Statistical Procedures for Evaluating Forecasting Skills," *Journal of Business*, 54, 513–533.

Herrndorf, N., 1984, "A Functional Central Limit Theorem for Weakly Dependent Sequences of Random Variables," *Annals of Probability*, 12, 141–153.

Herrndorf, N., 1985, "A Functional Central Limit Theorem for Strongly Mixing Sequences of Random Variables," *Z. Wahrscheinlichkeitstheorie verw. Gebiete*, 541–550.

Ho, T., and H. Stoll, 1980, "On Dealership Markets under Competition," *Journal of Finance*, 35, 259–267.

Ho, T., and H. Stoll, 1981, "Optimal Dealer Pricing under Transactions and Return Uncertainty," *Journal of Financial Economics*, 9, 47–73.

Hosking, J., 1981, "Fractional Differencing," *Biometrika*, 68, 165–176.

Hosking, J., 1996, "Asymptotic Distributions of the Sample Mean, Autocovariances, and Autocorrelations of Long-Memory Time Series," *Journal of Econometrics*, 73, 261–284.

Huberman, G., and S. Kandel, 1987, "Mean Variance Spanning," *Journal of Finance*, 42, 873–888.

Huberman, G., S. Kandel, and R. Stambaugh, 1987, "Mimicking Portfolios and Exact Arbitrage Pricing," *Journal of Finance*, 42, 1–10.

Huizinga, J., 1987, "An Empirical Investigation of the Long-Run Behavior of Real Exchange Rates," in *Carnegie-Rochester Conference Series on Public Policy*.

Hurst, H., 1951, "Long Term Storage Capacity of Reservoirs," *Transactions of the American Society of Civil Engineers*, 116, 770–799.

Ibragimov, I., and Y. Rozanov, 1978, *Gaussian Random Processes*, Springer-Verlag, New York.

Ingersoll, J., 1984, "Some Results in the Theory of Arbitrage Pricing," *Journal of Finance*, 39, 1021–1039.

Iyengar, S., and J. Greenhouse, 1988, "Selection Models and the File Drawer Problem," *Statistical Science*, 3, 109–135.

Jarrow, R. A., and G. S. Oldfield, 1981, "Forward Contracts and Futures Contracts," *Journal of Financial Economics*, 9, 373–382.

Jegadeesh, N., 1990, "Evidence of Predictable Behavior of Security Returns," *Journal of Finance*, 45, 881–898.

Jegadeesh, N., 1989, "On Testing for Slowly Decaying Components in Stock Prices," working paper, Anderson Graduate School of Management, U.C.L.A.

Jegadeesh, N., 1990, "Evidence of Predictable Behavior of Security Returns," *Journal of Finance*, 45, 881–898.

Jegadeesh, N., 1991, "Seasonality in Stock Price Mean Reversion: Evidence from the U.S. and the U.K.," *Journal of Finance*, 46, 1427–1444.

Jensen, M., 1978a, "Some Anomalous Evidence Regarding Market Efficiency," *Journal of Financial Economics*, 6, 95–102.

M. Jensen (ed.), 1978b, *Symposium on Some Anomalous Evidence Regarding Market Efficiency* (issue title), *Journal of Financial Economics*.

Jobson, J. D., and B. Korkie, 1980, "Estimation for Markowitz Efficient Portfolios," *Journal of the American Statistical Association*, 75, 544–554.

Jobson, J. D., and B. Korkie, 1982, "Potential Performance and Tests of Portfolio Efficiency," *Journal of Financial Economics*, 10, 433–466.

Jonas, A., 1983, "Persistent Memory Random Processes," Unpublished Ph.D. dissertation, Department of Statistics, Harvard University.

Judge, G., W. Griffiths, C. Hill, H. Lĭkepohl, and T.-C. Lee, 1985, *The Theory and Practice of Econometrics*, John Wiley and Sons, New York.

Kale, J., N. Hakansson, and G. Platt, 1991, "Industry vs. Other Factors in Risk Prediction," Finance Working Paper No. 201, Walter A. Haas School of Business, University of California at Berkeley.

R. W. Kamphuis, R. C. Kormendi, and J. W. H. Watson (eds.), 1989, *Black Monday and the Future of the Financial Markets*, Dow Jones-Irwin, Inc., Homewood, IL.

Kandel, S., and R. Stambaugh, 1987, "On Correlations and Inferences about Mean-Variance Efficiency," *Journal of Financial Economics*, 18, 61–90.

Kandel, S., and R. Stambaugh, 1988, "Modeling Expected Stock Returns for Long and Short Horizons," Rodney L. White Center Working Paper No. 42-88, Wharton School, University of Pennsylvania.

Kandel, S., and R. Stambaugh, 1989, "Modelling Expected Stock Returns for Long and Short Horizons," Working Paper 42-88, Rodney L. White Center, Wharton School, University of Pennsylvania.

Kandel, S., and R. Stambaugh, 1990, "A Mean-Variance Framework for Tests of Asset Pricing Models," *Review of Financial Studies*, 2, 125–156.

Kandel, S., and R. Stambaugh, 1990, 1991, "Asset Returns and Intertemporal Preferences," *Journal of Monetary Economics*, 27, 39–71.

Kandel, S., and R. Stambaugh, 1995, "Portfolio Inefficiency and the Cross-section of Mean Returns," *Journal of Finance*, 50, 157–184.

Karpoff, J., 1986, "A Theory of Trading Volume," *Journal of Finance*, 41, 1069–1088.

Karpoff, J., 1987, "The Relation between Price Changes and Trading Volume: A Survey," *Journal of Financial and Quantitative Analysis*, 22, 109–126.

Kawaller, I. G., P. D. Koch, and T. W. Koch, 1987, "The Temporal Price Relationship between S&P 500 Futures and the S&P 500 Index," *Journal of Finance*, 42, 1309–1330.

Keim, D., 1983, "Size-Related Anomalies and Stock Return Seasonality: Further Empirical Evidence," *Journal of Financial Economics*, 12, 13–32.

Keim, D., and R. Stambaugh, 1986, "Predicting Returns in Stock and Bond Markets," *Journal of Financial Economics*, 17, 357–390.

Kendall, M., 1953, "The Analysis of Economic Time Series—Part I: Prices," *Journal of the Royal Statistical Society*, 96, 11–25.

Kennedy, D., 1976, "The Distribution of the Maximum Brownian Excursion," *Journal of Applied Probability*, 13, 371–376.

Kester, G., 1990, "Market Timing with Small-Firm Stocks," *Financial Analysts Journal*, 46, 63–69.

Keynes, J. M., 1936, *The General Theory of Employment, Interest, and Money*, Harcourt, Brace, New York, chap. 12.

Kim, M., C. Nelson, and R. Startz, 1991, "Mean Reversion in Stock Prices? A Reappraisal of the Empirical Evidence," *Review of Economic Studies*, 58, 515–528.

King, B., 1966, "Market and Industry Factors in Stock Price Behavior," *Journal of Business*, 39, 139–190.

Kleidon, A. W., 1986, "Variance Bounds Tests and Stock Price Valuation Models," *Journal of Political Economy*, 94, 953–1001.

Kleidon, A., 1992, "Arbitrage, Nontrading, and Stale Prices: October 1987," *Journal of Business*, 65, 483–507.

Kothari, S. P., J. Shanken, and R. Sloan, 1995, "Another Look at the Cross-section of Expected Returns," *Journal of Finance*, 50, 185–224.

Kyle, A., 1985, "Continuous Auctions and Insider Trading," *Econometrica*, 53, 1315–1335.

Lakonishok, J., and S. Smidt, 1988, "Are Seasonal Anomalies Real? A Ninety-Year Perspective," *Review of Financial Studies*, 1, 403–426.

Lakonishok, J., A. Shleifer, and R. Vishny, 1994, "Contrarian Investment, Extrapolation, and Risk," *Journal of Finance*, 49, 1541–1578.

Larson, A., 1960, "Measurement of a Random Process in Futures Prices," *Food Research Institute*, 1, 313–324.

Leamer, E., 1978, *Specification Searches*, John Wiley and Sons, New York.

Lee, C., and S. Rahman, 1990, "Market Timing, Selectivity and Mutual Fund Performance: An Empirical Investigation," *Journal of Business*, 63, 261–278.

Lee, C., and S. Rahman, 1991, "New Evidence on Market Timing and Security Selection Skill of Mutual Fund Managers," *Journal of Portfolio Management*, 17, 80–83.

Lee, C., and M. Ready, 1991, "Inferring Trade Direction from Intraday Data," *Journal of Finance*, 46, 733–746.

Lehmann, B., 1987, "Orthogonal Frontiers and Alternative Mean Variance Efficiency Tests," *Journal of Finance*, 42, 601–619.

Lehmann, B., 1990, "Fads, Martingales, and Market Efficiency," *Quarterly Journal of Economics*, 105, 1–28.

Lehmann, B., 1992, "Empirical Testing of Asset Pricing Models," in Peter Newman, Murray Milgate, and John Eatwell (eds.), *The New Palgrave Dictionary of Money and Finance*, Stockton Press, New York, pp. 749–759.

Lehmann, B. N., and D. Modest, 1988, "The Empirical Foundations of the Arbitrage Pricing Theory," *Journal of Financial Economics*, 21, 213–254.

Leroy, S. F., 1973, "Risk Aversion and the Martingale Property of Stock Returns," *International Economic Review*, 14, 436–446.

LeRoy, S., 1989, "Efficient Capital Markets and Martingales," *Journal of Economic Literature*, 27, 1583–1621.

Lintner, John, 1965, "The Valuation of Risky Assets and the Selection of Risky Investments in Stock Portfolios and Capital Budgets," *Review of Economics and Statistics*, 47, 13–37.

Ljung, G., and G. Box, 1978, "On a Measure of Lack of Fit in Time Series Models," *Biometrika*, 66, 67–72.

Lo, A. W., and A. C. MacKinlay, 1987b, "Stock Market Prices Do Not Follow Random Walks: Evidence from a Simple Specification Test," Working Paper 5-87, Rodney L. White Center, Wharton School, University of Pennsylvania.

Lo, A. W., and A. C. MacKinlay, 1988a, "Notes on a Markov Model of Nonsynchronous Trading," working paper, Sloan School of Management, Massachusetts Institute of Technology.

Lo, A. W., and A. C. MacKinlay, 1988b, "Stock Market Prices Do Not Follow Random Walks: Evidence from a Simple Specification Test," *Review of Financial Studies*, 1, 41–66.

Lo, A., and C. MacKinlay, 1989a, "The Size and Power of the Variance Ratio Test in Finite Samples: A Monte Carlo Investigation," *Journal of Econometrics*, 40, 203–238.

Lo, A., and C. MacKinlay, 1990a, "Data-Snooping Biases in Tests of Financial Asset Pricing Models," *Review of Financial Studies*, 3, 431–468.

Lo, A., and C. MacKinlay, 1990b, "When Are Contrarian Profits Due to Stock Market Overreaction?," *Review of Financial Studies*, 3, 175–208.

Lo, A., and C. MacKinlay, 1990c, "An Econometric Analysis of Nonsynchronous Trading," *Journal of Econometrics*, 45, 181–211.

Lo, A., and C. MacKinlay, 1992, "Maximizing Predictability in the Stock and Bond Markets," Working Paper No. 3450–92–EFA, Sloan School of Management, MIT.

Lo, A., and C. MacKinlay, 1998, "Stumbling Block for the Random Walk," in G. Bickerstaffe (ed.), *The Complete Finance Companion*, Pitman Publishing, London, UK.

Lucas, R. E., 1978, "Asset Prices in an Exchange Economy," *Econometrica*, 46, 1429–1446.

MacKinlay, A. C., 1987, "On Multivariate Tests of the CAPM," *Journal of Financial Economics*, 18, 341–372.

MacKinlay, A. C., and M. Richardson, 1991, "Using Generalized Methods of Moments to Test Mean-Variance Efficiency," *Journal of Finance*, 46, 511–527.

Maddala, G., 1983, *Limited-Dependent and Qualitative Variables in Econometrics*, Cambridge University Press, Cambridge, UK.

Madhavan, A., and S. Smidt, 1991, "A Bayesian Model of Intraday Specialist Pricing," *Journal of Financial Economics*, 30, 99–134.

Maheswaran, S., 1990, "Predictable Short-Term Variation in Asset Prices: Theory and Evidence," unpublished working paper, Carlson School of Management, University of Minnesota.

Magnus, J., and H. Neudecker, 1980, "The Elimination Matrix: Some Lemmas and Applications," *SIAM Journal on Algebraic and Discrete Methods*, 1, 422–449.

Maheswaran, S., and C. Sims, 1990, "Empirical Implications of Arbitrage Free Asset Markets," Discussion Paper, Department of Economics, University of Minnesota.

Mandelbrot, B., 1963, "The Variation of Certain Speculative Prices," *Journal of Business*, 36, 394–419.

Mandelbrot, B., 1971, "When Can Price Be Arbitraged Efficiently? A Limit to the Validity of the Random Walk and Martingale Models," *Review of Economics and Statistics*, 53, 225–236.

Mandelbrot, B., 1972, "Statistical Methodology for Non-Periodic Cycles: From the Covariance to R/S Analysis," *Annals of Economic and Social Measurement*, 1, 259–290.

Mandelbrot, B., 1975, "Limit Theorems on the Self-Normalized Range for Weakly and Strongly Dependent Processes," *Z. Wahrscheinlichkeitstheorie verw.*, Gebiete 31, 271–285.

Mandelbrot, B., and M. Taqqu, 1979, "Robust R/S Analysis of Long-Run Serial Correlation," *Bulletin of the International Statistical Institute*, 48(Book 2), 59–104.

Mandelbrot, B., and J. Van Ness, 1968, "Fractional Brownian Motion, Fractional Noises and Applications," *S.I.A.M. Review*, 10, 422–437.

Mandelbrot, B., and J. Wallis, 1968, "Noah, Joseph and Operational Hydrology," *Water Resources Research*, 4, 909–918.

Mandelbrot, B., and J. Wallis, 1969a, "Computer Experiments with Fractional Gaussian Noises. Parts 1, 2, 3," *Water Resources Research*, 5, 228–267.

Mandelbrot, B., and J. Wallis, 1969b, "Robustness of the Rescaled Range R/S in the Measurement of Noncyclic Long Run Statistical Dependence," *Water Resources Research*, 5, 967–988.

Mandelbrot, B., and J. Wallis, 1969c, "Some Long Run Properties of Geophysical Records," *Water Resources Research*, 5, 321–340.

Marsh, T., and R. Merton, 1986, "Dividend Variability and Variance Bounds Tests for the Rationality of Stock Market Prices," *American Economic Review*, 76, 483–498.

McCullagh, P., 1980, "Regression Models for Ordinal Data," *Journal of the Royal Statistical Society Series B*, 42, 109–142.

McLeish, D., 1977, "On the Invariance Principle for Nonstationary Mixingales," *Annals of Probability*, 5, 616–621.

Mehra, R., and E. Prescott, 1985, "The Equity Premium: A Puzzle," *Journal of Monetary Economics*, 15, 145–162.

Merrick, J., 1988, "Hedging with Mispriced Futures," *Journal of Financial and Quantitative Analysis*, 23, 451–464.

Merton, R. C., 1973, "An Intertemporal Capital Asset Pricing Model," *Econometrica*, 41, 867–887.

Merton, R. C., 1980, "On Estimating the Expected Return on the Market: An Exploratory Investigation," *Journal of Financial Economics*, 8, 323–361.

Merton, R. C., 1981, "On Market Timing and Investment Performance I: An Equilibrium Theory of Value for Market Forecasts," *Journal of Business*, 54, 363–406.

Merton, R., 1987, "On the Current State of the Stock Market Rationality Hypothesis," in R. Dornbusch, S. Fischer, and J. Bossons (eds.), *Macroeconomics and Finance: Essays in Honor of Franco Modigliani*, MIT Press, Cambridge.

Modest, D., and M. Sundaresan, 1983, "The Relationship between Spot and Futures Prices in Stock Index Futures Markets: Some Preliminary Evidence," *Journal of Futures Markets*, 3, 15–42.

Muirhead, R., 1982, *Aspects of Multivariate Statistical Theory*, John Wiley and Sons, New York.

Muth, J., 1960, "Optimal Properties of Exponentially Weighted Forecasts," *Journal of the American Statistical Association*, 55, 299–306.

Muthuswamy, J., 1988, "Asynchronous Closing Prices and Spurious Autocorrelations in Portfolio Returns," working paper, Graduate School of Business, University of Chicago.

Nagaraja, H. N., 1982a, "Some Asymptotic Results for the Induced Selection Differential," *Journal of Applied Probability*, 19, 233–239.

Nagaraja, H. N., 1982b, "Some Nondegenerate Limit Laws for the Selection Differential," *Annals of Statistics*, 10, 1306–1310.

Nagaraja, H. N., 1984, "Some Nondegenerate Limit Laws for Sample Selection Differential and Selection Differential," *Sankhyā*, 46 (Series A), 355–369.

Nankervis, J. C., and N. E. Savin, 1985, "Testing the Autoregressive Parameter with the *t* Statistic," *Journal of Econometrics*, 27, 143–161.

Newey, W., 1985, "Semiparametric Estimation of Limited Dependent Variable Models with Endogenous Explanatory Variables," *Annales de L'Insee*, 59/60, 219–237.

Newey, W. K., and K. D. West, 1987, "A Simple Positive Definite, Heteroscedasticity and Autocorrelation Consistent Covariance Matrix," *Econometrica*, 55, 703–708.

Niederhoffer, V., 1997, *Education of a Speculator*, John Wiley and Sons, New York.

Niederhoffer, V., and M. Osborne, 1966, "Market Making and Reversal on the Stock Exchange," *Journal of the American Statistical Association*, 61, 897–916.

Osborne, M., 1959, "Brownian Motion in the Stock Market," *Operations Research*, 7, 145–173.

Osborne, M., 1962, "Periodic Structure in the Brownian Motion of Stock Prices," *Operations Research*, 10, 345–379.

Perron, P., 1986, "Tests of Joint Hypotheses for Time Series Regression with a Unit Root," in Fomby and Rhodes (eds.), *Advances in Econometrics: Spurious Regressions, Cointegration and Unit Roots*, JAI Press, Greenwich, CT.

Petersen, M., 1986, "Testing the Efficient Market Hypothesis: Information Lags, the Spread, and the Role of the Market Makers," Undergraduate thesis, Princeton University, Princeton, NJ.

Petersen, M., and S. Umlauf, 1990, "An Empirical Examination of the Intraday Behavior of the NYSE Specialist," working paper, Massachusetts Institute of Technology, Cambridge, MA.

Phillips, P. C. B., 1986, "Understanding Spurious Regressions in Econometrics," *Journal of Econometrics*, 33, 311–40.

Phillips, P. C. B., 1988, "Regression Theory for Near-Integrated Time Series," *Econometrica*, 56, 1021–1043.

Phillips, P. C. B., 1987, "Time Series Regression with a Unit Root," *Econometrica*, 55, 277–302.

Phillips, P. C. B., and P. Perron, 1988, "Testing for a Unit Root in Time Series Regression," *Biometrika*, 75, 335–346.

Porter-Hudak, S., 1990, "An Application of the Seasonal Fractionally Differenced Model to the Monetary Aggregates," *Journal of the American Statistical Association*, 85, 338–344.

Poterba, J., and L. Summers, 1986, "The Persistence of Volatility and Stock Market Fluctuations," *American Economic Review*, 76, 1142–1151.

Poterba, J., and L. Summers, 1988, "Mean Reversion in Stock Returns: Evidence and Implications," *Journal of Financial Economics*, 22, 27–60.

Presidential Task Force on Market Mechanisms, 1988, *Report of The Presidential Task Force on Market Mechanisms*, U.S. Government Printing Office, Washington, DC.

Priestley, M., 1981, *Spectral Analysis and Time Series*, Academic Press, London.

Pritsker, M., 1990, "Market Microstructure, Market Efficiency, and the Information Revealed through Trade," working paper, Princeton University, Princeton, NJ.

Randles, R., and D. Wolfe, 1979, *Introduction to the Theory of Nonparametric Statistics*, John Wiley and Sons, New York.

Reinsel, G., 1983, "Some Results on Multivariate Autoregressive Index Models," *Biometrika*, 70, 145–156.

Resnick, S., 1987, *Extreme Values, Regular Variation, and Point Processes*, Springer-Verlag, New York.

Richardson, M., and J. Stock, 1990, "Drawing Inferences From Statistics Based on Multiyear Asset Returns," *Journal of Financial Economics*, 25, 323–348.

Richard, S. F., and M. Sundaresan, 1981, "A Continuous Time Equilibrium Model of Forward Prices and Futures Prices in a Multigood Economy," *Journal of Financial Economics*, 9, 347–372.

Richardson, M., 1993, "Temporary Components of Stock Prices: A Skeptic's View," *Journal of Business and Economic Statistics*, 11, 199–207.

Richardson, M., and J. Stock, 1990, "Drawing Inferences from Statistics Based on Multiyear Asset Returns," *Journal of Financial Economics*, 25, 323–348.

Roberts, H., 1959, "Stock-Market 'Patterns' and Financial Analysis: Methodological Suggestions," *Journal of Finance*, 14, 1–10.

Roberts, H., 1967, "Statistical versus Clinical Prediction of the Stock Market," unpublished manuscript, Center for Research in Security Prices, University of Chicago, May.

Robinson, M., 1988, "Block Trades on the Major Canadian and U.S. Stock Exchanges: A Study of Pricing Behavior and Market Efficiency," Unpublished Ph.D. dissertation, School of Business Administration, University of Western Ontario, Ontario, Canada.

Roll, R., 1977, "A Critique of the Asset Pricing Theory's Tests: Part I," *Journal of Financial Economics*, 4, 129–176.

Roll, R., 1980, "Orthogonal Portfolios," *Journal of Financial and Quantitative Analysis*, 15, 1005–1023.

Roll, R., 1983, "Vas Is Das? The Turn-of-the-Year Effect and the Return Premia of Small Firms," *Journal of Portfolio Management*, 9, 18–28.

Roll, R., 1984a, "A Simple Implicit Measure of the Effective Bid-Ask Spread in an Efficient Market," *Journal of Finance*, 39, 1127–1140.

Roll, R., 1984b, "Orange Juice and Weather," *American Economic Review*, 74, 861–880.

Roll, R., 1988, "R^2," *Journal of Finance*, 43, 541–566.

Roll, R., and S. Ross, 1980, "An Empirical Investigation of the Arbitrage Pricing Theory," *Journal of Finance*, 35, 1073–1103.

Roll, R., and S. Ross, 1994, "On the Cross-Sectional Relation between Expected Returns and Betas," *Journal of Finance*, 49, 101–122.

Rosenberg, B., K. Reid, and R. Lanstein, 1985, "Persuasive Evidence of Market Inefficiency," *Journal of Portfolio Management*, 11, 9–17.

Rosenblatt, M., 1956, "A Central Limit Theorem and a Strong Mixing Condition," *Proceedings of the National Academy of Sciences*, 42, 43–47.

Ross, S., 1976, "The Arbitrage Theory of Capital Asset Pricing," *Journal of Economic Theory*, 13, 341–360.

Ross, S., 1987, "Regression to the Max," working paper, Yale School of Organization and Management.

Rozeff, M., 1984, "Dividend Yields and Equity Risk Premiums," *Journal of Portfolio Management*, 11, 68–75.

Rozeff, M., and W. Kinney Jr., 1976, "Capital Market Seasonality: The Case of Stock Returns," *Journal of Financial Economics*, 3, 379–402.

Rubinstein, M., 1987, "Derivative Assets Analysis," *Economic Perspectives*, 1(2), 73–93.

Samuelson, P., 1965, "Proof that Properly Anticipated Prices Fluctuate Randomly," *Industrial Management Review*, 6, 41–49.

Samuelson, P., 1989, "The Judgment of Economic Science on Rational Portfolio Management: Indexing, Timing, and Long-Horizon Effects," *Journal of Portfolio Management*, 16, 4–12.

Samuelson, P., 1990, "Asset Allocation Could Be Dangerous to Your Health," *Journal of Portfolio Management*, 16, 5–8.

Sandström, A., 1987, "Asymptotic Normality of Linear Functions of Concomitants of Order Statistics," *Metrika*, 34, 129–142.

Scholes, M., and J. Williams, 1976, "Estimating Betas from Daily Data," working paper, University of Chicago.

Scholes, M., and J. Williams, 1977, "Estimating Beta from Nonsynchronous Data," *Journal of Financial Economics*, 5, 309–328.

Schwartz, R., and D. Whitcomb, 1977, "The Time-Variance Relationship: Evidence on Autocorrelation in Common Stock Returns," *Journal of Finance*, 32, 41–55.

Schwert, G., 1987a, "Effects of Model Specification on Tests for Unit Roots in Macroeconomic Data," *Journal of Monetary Economics*, 20, 73–104.

Schwert, W., 1989, "Tests for Unit Roots: A Monte Carlo Investigation," *Journal of Business and Economic Statistics*, 7, 147–159.

Sclove, S., 1983, "Time-Series Segmentation: A Model and a Method," *Information Sciences*, 29, 7–25.

Sen, P. K., 1976, "A Note on Invariance Principles for Induced Order Statistics," *Annals of Probability*, 4, 474–479.

Sen, P. K., 1981, "Some Invariance Principles for Mixed Rank Statistics and Induced Order Statistics and Some Applications," *Communications in Statistics*, A10, 1691–1718.

Shanken, J., 1985, "Multivariate Tests of the Zero-Beta CAPM," *Journal of Financial Economics*, 14, 327–348.

Shanken, J., 1987a, "Nonsynchronous Data and the Covariance-Factor Structure of Returns," *Journal of Finance*, 42, 221–232.

Shanken, J., 1987b, "Multivariate Proxies and Asset Pricing Relations: Living with the Roll Critique," *Journal of Financial Economics*, 18, 91–110.

Shanken, J., 1992, "The Current State of the Arbitrage Pricing Theory," *Journal of Finance*, 47, 1569–1574.

Sharpe, W., 1964, "Capital Asset Prices: A Theory of Market Equilibrium Under Conditions of Risk," *Journal of Finance*, 19, 425–442.

Shefrin, H., and M. Statman, 1985, "The Disposition to Ride Winners Too Long and Sell Lowers Too Soon: Theory and Evidence," *Journal of Finance*, 41, 774–790.

Shiller, R. J., 1981, "The Use of Volatility Measures in Assessing Market Efficiency," *Journal of Finance*, 36, 291–304.

Shiller, R. J., 1984, "Stock Prices and Social Dynamics," *Brookings Papers on Economic Activity*, 2, 457–498.

Shiller, R. J., and P. Perron, 1985, "Testing the Random Walk Hypothesis: Power Versus Frequency of Observation," *Economics Letters*, 18, 381–386.

Shilling, G., 1992, "Market Timing: Better Than a Buy-and-Hold Strategy," *Financial Analysts Journal*, 48, 46–50.

Siddiqui, M., 1976, "The Asymptotic Distribution of the Range and Other Functions of Partial Sums of Stationary Processes," *Water Resources Research*, 12, 1271–1276.

Sims, C., 1974, "Output and Labor Input in Manufacturing," *Brookings Papers on Economic Activity*, 3, 695–728.

Sims, C., 1977, "Exogeneity and Causal Ordering in Macroeconomic Models," in *New Methods in Business Cycle Research: Proceedings from a Conference*, Federal Reserve Bank of Minneapolis.

Sims, C., 1984, "Martingale-Like Behavior of Asset Prices and Interest Rates," Discussion Paper 205, Center for Economic Research, Department of Economics, University of Minnesota.

Sowell, F., 1992, "Maximum Likelihood Estimation of Stationary Univariate Fractionally Integrated Time Series Models," *Journal of Econometrics*, 53, 165–188.

Sowell, F., 1990, "The Fractional Unit Root Distribution," *Econometrica*, 58, 495–506.

Stambaugh, R. F., 1982, "On the Exclusion of Assets from Tests of the Two Parameter Model," *Journal of Financial Economics*, 10, 235–268.

Standard & Poor's Corp., 1987, *Stocks in the Standard & Poor's 500 as of: September 30, 1987*, New York.

Steiger, W., 1964, "A Test of Nonrandomness in Stock Price Changes," in P. Cootner (ed.), *The Random Character of Stock Market Prices*, MIT Press, Cambridge, MA.

Stoll, H., 1989, "Inferring the Components of the Bid-Ask Spread: Theory and Empirical Tests," *Journal of Finance*, 44, 115–134.

Stoll, H. R., and R. E. Whaley, 1986, "Expiration Day Effects of Index Options and Futures," Monograph 1986-3, Salomon Brothers Center for the Study of Financial Institutions, Graduate School of Business Administration, New York University.

Stoll, H. R., and R. E. Whaley, 1990, "The Dynamics of Stock Index and Stock Index Futures Returns," *Journal of Financial and Quantitative Analysis*, 25, 441–468.

Stoll, H., and R. Whaley, 1990, "Stock Market Structure and Volatility," *Review of Financial Studies*, 3, 37–71.

Stuart, A., and J. Ord, 1987, *Kendall's Advanced Theory of Statistics*, Oxford University Press, New York.

Summers, L. H., 1986, "Does the Stock Market Rationally Reflect Fundamental Values?," *Journal of Finance*, 41, 591–600.

Sy, W., 1990, "Market Timing: Is It a Folly?," *Journal of Portfolio Management*, 16, 11–16.

Taqqu, M., 1975, "Weak Convergence to Fractional Brownian Motion and to the Rosenblatt Process," *Z. Wahrscheinlichkeitstheorie verw.*, Gebiete 31, 287–302.

Taylor, S., 1984, "Estimating the Variances of Autocorrelations Calculated from Financial Time Series," *Applied Statistics*, 33, 300–308.

Thisted, R., 1991, "Assessing the Effect of Allergy Medications: Models for Paired Comparisons on Ordered Categories," *Statistics of Medicine*, forthcoming.

U.S. General Accounting Office, 1988, *Financial Markets: Preliminary Observations on the October 1987 Crash*, Washington, DC.

U.S. Securities and Exchange Commission, 1988, *The October 1987 Market Break: A Report by the Division of Market Regulation U.S. Securities and Exchange Commission*, U.S. Government Printing Office, Washington, DC.

Vandell, R., and J. Stevens, 1989, "Evidence of Superior Performance from Timing," *Journal of Portfolio Management*, 15, 38–42.

Velu, R., G. Reinsel, and D. Wichern, 1986, "Reduced Rank Models for Multiple Time Series," *Biometrika*, 73, 105–118.

Wagner, J., S. Shellans, and R. Paul, 1992, "Market Timing Works Where It Matters Most . . . In the Real World," *Journal of Portfolio Management*, 18, 86–90.

Wang, T., 1988, "Essays on the Theory of Arbitrage Pricing," Unpublished Ph.D. dissertation, Wharton School, University of Pennsylvania.

Wang, J., 1994, "A Model of Competitive Stock Trading Volume," *Journal of Political Economy*, 102, 127–168.

Watterson, G. A., 1959, "Linear Estimation in Censored Samples from Multivariate Normal Populations," *Annals of Mathematical Statistics*, 30, 814–824.

Weigel, E., 1991, "The Performance of Tactical Asset Allocation," *Financial Analysts Journal*, 47, 63–70.

White, H., 1980, "A Heteroscedasticity-Consistent Covariance Matrix Estimator and a Direct Test for Heteroscedasticity," *Econometrica*, 48, 817–838.

White, H., 1984, *Asymptotic Theory for Econometricians*, Academic Press, New York.

White, H., and I. Domowitz, 1984, "Nonlinear Regression with Dependent Observations," *Econometrica*, 52, 143–162.

Wood, R., T. McInish, and K. Ord, 1985, "An Investigation of Transactions Data for NYSE Stocks," *Journal of Finance*, 40, 723–738.

Wooldridge, J., and H. White, 1988, "Some Invariance Principles and Central Limit Theorems for Dependent Heterogeneous Processes," *Econometric Theory*, 4, 210–230.

Working, H., 1960, "Note on the Correlation of First Differences of Averages in a Random Chain," *Econometrica*, 28, 916–918.

Yajima, Y., 1985, "On Estimation of Long-Memory Time Series Models," *Australian Journal of Statistics*, 303–320.

Yajima, Y., 1988, "On Estimation of a Regression Model with Long-Memory Stationary Errors," *Annals of Statistics*, 16, 791–807.

Yang, S. S., 1977, "General Distribution Theory of the Concomitants of Order Statistics," *Annals of Statistics*, 5, 996–1002.

Yang, S. S., 1981a, "Linear Combinations of Concomitants of Order Statistics with Application to Testing and Estimation," *Annals of the Institute of Statistical Mathematics*, 33 (Part A), 463–470.

Yang, S. S., 1981b, "Linear Functions of Concomitants of Order Statistics with Application to Nonparametric Estimation of a Regression Function," *Journal of the American Statistical Association*, 76, 658–662.

Zarowin, P., 1990, "Size, Seasonality, and Stock Market Overreaction," *Journal of Financial and Quantitative Analysis*, 25, 113–125.

Index

absolute price impact, 341
active asset-allocation strategy, 281
active investment management, 8–10
ADP, 371
aggregation value, 50
animal spirits. *See* fads
arbitrage, asymptotic, in finite
  economies, 208–212
arbitrage strategies, 351
  behavior of stock index futures prices
  and, 348–352
ARCH process, 25, 52, 62, 292
ARIMA(1,1,0) alternative, 79, 82–83
ARIMA(1,1,1) alternative, 75–81
ask price, 298
asset-allocation strategy, active and
  passive, 281
asset prices, statistical model of, 287
asset-pricing model tests, 196
asset-pricing models
  data-snooping biases in tests of,
  213–247
  equilibrium, 186
  one-factor, 199
assets, derivative, valuation of, 348
asymptotic approximation, 231
asymptotic arbitrage in finite economies,
  208–212
asymptotic covariance matrix, 310
asymptotic properties of induced order
  statistics, 216–219
asymptotic variance, 21
autocorrelation properties of weekly
  returns, 118–121
autocorrelations
  cross-. *See* cross-autocorrelations
  daily nontrading probabilities implicit
  in, 101–104

index, nontrading and, 104–105
nontrading induced, 91–92
spurious, induced by nontrading,
  34–38
of time-aggregated returns, 97–98
variance ratios and, 54
autocorrelograms, fractionally-
  differenced, 170
autocovariance function, 19n
autocovariance matrix, 93

Bernoulli random variables, 89
Bernoulli trials, 35
beta coefficients, 104–105
  sorting by, 238–240
beta effect, 386–387
beta estimation error, 239
BHHH (Berndt, Hall, Hall, and
  Hausman) algorithm, 310–311
biases
  data-snooping. *See* data-snooping
  biases
  induced by bid-ask spread, 205
  pretest, 213–214, 262
  survivorship, 135
  of tests based on individual securities,
  219–224
  of tests based on portfolios, 224–228
bid/ask bounce, 132, 316
bid/ask quotes, 298
bid/ask spread, 287, 308
  bias induced by, 205
  common factor and, 130–132
  model of, 131
bid price, 298
"Black Monday" (October Crash), 286,
  369–394

Black-Scholes pricing formula, 40
book-value/market-value ratios, expected
    returns and, 186
Box-Cox transformation, 309
Box-Pierce Q-statistic, 24n, 54
Box-Pierce Q-test, 48–49
    heteroskedasticity-robust, 60
break-even transaction costs, 281, 283
Bridge Data, 370–372
Brownian bridge, 160–161
Brownian motion, fractional, 163
buy-and-hold investment, 281
buy-and-hold strategy, 348
buy/sell indicator, contemporaneous,
    323
buyer-initiated trade, 310
buying pressure, 378
"buys," 289

calendar effects, 186
Capital Asset Pricing Model (CAPM),
    186, 189, 216
    deviations from, multifactor models
        and, 189–212
    Intertemporal, 186
    violations of, 189
CAPM. *See* Capital Asset Pricing Model
Center for Research in Security Prices
    (CRSP), 354
Chicago Mercantile Exchange (CME),
    353
classical rescaled range (R/S) statistic,
    155
closing prices, 85
CME (Chicago Mercantile Exchange),
    353
common factor, bid-ask spread and,
    130–132
computation-intensive strategies, 10
concomitant, term, 218n
conditional distribution, 292
conditional-factor model, estimating,
    262–269
conditional factors, 259n, 261–262
conditional forecasts, naive forecasts
    versus, 276–278
conditional heteroskedasticity, 152
conditional probabilities, estimated,
    326–328
Consolidated Quote System, 371–372
Consolidated Tape System, 371
constrained maximally predictable
    portfolio, 269
consumer education, 9

contemporaneous buy/sell indicator, 323
continuous-state process, 288
continuous-time process, 20
contrarian portfolio strategy, 116–117
contrarian profitability, analysis of,
    121–132
cross-autocorrelations, importance of,
    121
cross-autocovariances, 121
    positive, 116
cross effects, importance of, 127
cross-sectional dependence, F-tests with,
    236–238
cross-sectional independence, 236
cross-stock comparisons of liquidity, 330
CRSP (Center for Research in Security
    Prices), 354
cumulative distribution function,
    standard normal, 220

daily sampling, 26–27
data mining, 251
data snooping, 251
    term, 214
data-snooping biases, 186–187, 190
    interpreting, as power, 228–229
    Monte Carlo results and, 230–238
    quantifying, with induced order
        statistics, 215–229
    in tests of financial asset pricing
        models, 213–247
data-snooping statistics, 214
DEF (default spread), 261
default spread (DEF), 261
delta method, 335
derivative assets, valuation of, 348
Dickey-Fuller t-test, 48–49, 54, 68
discrete-time process, 20, 288
discreteness, 288, 331–335
    models of, 294
dispersion, 222
distribution, conditional, 292
dividend yield (DY), 261
dollar volume, 309
    on Standard and Poor's Composite 500
        Index, 376
drift parameter, 19
duration of nontrading, 89–90, 128
DY (dividend yield), 261

econometric analysis of nonsynchronous
    trading, 85–113
economic science, 213

economic time series, 147
  sampling of, 85
economics, experimentation in, 213
economies, finite, asymptotic arbitrage
  in, 208–212
education, consumer, 9
efficient markets hypothesis, 4–7, 14, 17
  current state of, 6–8
  tests of, 7
endogenous trade times, 319
equilibrium asset-pricing model, 186
estimated conditional probabilities,
  326–328
estimation approach, 206–208
estimators, 21
  unbiased, 23
  variance, 22
event study, 287
expectations operator, 20
expected returns
  book-value/market-value ratios and,
    186
  price/earnings ratios and, 186
  risk and, 185
experimentation in economics, 213
explanatory variables, 307
extended continuous mapping theorem,
  181
extracted factors, 253

F-tests
  with cross-sectional dependence,
    236–238
  effects of induced ordering on,
    231–236
factor loadings, 259n
fads, 125
  stock market overreaction and,
    124–126
"fair values," futures prices and, 347
fifteen-minute index returns, 393–394
financial asset-pricing models. *See*
  asset-pricing models
financial markets. *See* markets
finite economies, asymptotic arbitrage in,
  208–212
first principal-component portfolio
  (PC1), 254–256
Fisher effect. *See* nonsynchronous trading
5 percent test, 221
floor brokers, 319
forecastability, 115–116
forecasts, naive versus conditional,
  276–278

forward contracts on stock indexes, 349
fractional Brownian motion, 163
fractionally-differenced alternatives,
  power against, 174–179
fractionally-differenced
  autocorrelograms, 170
fractionally-integrated time series
  models, 152–153
frictions, market, 191
futures-price database, 353
futures prices
  behavior of, index price and, 354–359
  "fair values" and, 347

generalized residuals, 316
genuine predictability, 276
grouping securities, 225
growth index, 201

Hausman specification test. *See*
  specification tests
heteroskedastic increments, 24–26
heteroskedastic null hypothesis, 52–53,
  61–68
heteroskcdasticity, conditional, 152
heteroskedasticity-robust Box-Pierce test
  Q, 60
histograms of price changes, 300–307
historical Sharpe measure, 201
holiday seasonalities, 186
homoskedastic increments, 20–24
Hurst coefficient, 158
Hurst-Mandelbrot rescaled range, 167

IGS (Information Generation System),
  371
independently and identically distributed
  (IID) benchmark, 124
independently and identically distributed
  (IID) Gaussian null hypothesis,
  49–51, 55–61
independently but not identically
  distributed, term, 290
indeterminate trade, 310
index autocorrelations, nontrading and,
  104–105
index-futures arbitrage, behavior of stock
  index futures prices and, 347–368
index levels, constructing, 389–393
index price, behavior of futures prices
  and, 354–359
index returns, fifteen-minute, 393–394
indicator variables, 89, 316
individual returns, nontrading
  implications for, 90–93

individual securities
    biases of tests based on, 219–224
    results for, 32–33
induced order statistic, ith, 217–218
induced order statistics, 216
    asymptotic properties of, 216–219
    quantifying data-snooping biases with,
        215–229
    represented, 221
induced ordering, 218
    effects of, on F-tests, 231–236
inefficiency, market, 5, 8
inference, statistical, 213
Information Generation System (IGS),
    371
Institute for the Study of Securities
    Markets (ISSM) transaction database,
    295
integrated AR(1) process, 68, 79–81
interest-rate trend (IRT), 261
Intertemporal Capital Asset Pricing
    Model, 186
intertemporal substitution parameter,
    200
interval length, varying, 355
intraday price changes, 297
intraday volatility, 287
investment management, active, 8–10
investment rule, contrarian, 116–117
investments, passive or buy-and-hold, 281
irrational behavior by market
    participants, 191
IRT (interest-rate trend), 261
ISSM (Institute for the Study of Securities
    Markets) transaction database, 295

Joseph effect, 147

lagged price change coefficients, 311, 316
lead-lag effects, nonsynchronous trading
    and, 127–130
lead-lag relations, trading on white noise
    and, 126–127
lead-lag structure, 117
likelihood analysis, 203–204
likelihood function, 294–295
linear pricing models, 192–193
linear probability model, 331
liquidity
    cross-stock comparisons of, 330
    market, 326
liquidity effects, 191
log-likelihood function, 294–295
log-price process, 19

long horizons, short horizons versus,
    140–142
long-range dependence, short-range
    dependence versus, 149–155
long-range dependent alternatives,
    152–155
long-term memory, 147–148
    in stock market prices, 147–184

mapping theorem, extended continuous,
    181
margin requirements, 287
mark-sense cards, 371
Market Data System, 371
market depth, 326, 329
market frictions, 191
market indexes, results for, 27–30
market inefficiency, 5, 8
market liquidity, 326
market participants, irrational behavior
    by, 191
market perceptions, stock prices and, 369
market timing, Merton's measure of,
    279–281
markets. *See also* stock market *entries*
    financial, 4
    securities, microstructure of, 287
martingale sequence, 18
MAT (maturity spread), 261
maturity, mispricing and, 363–364
maturity spread (MAT), 261
maximally predictable portfolio (MMP),
    250–252
    constrained, 269
    portfolio weights of, 271–272
maximization
    of predictability, 188, 249–284
    of variance, 255
maximum likelihood estimates for
    ordered probit model, 310–320
mean-reverting alternative to random
    walk hypothesis, 38–39
mean-variance analysis, 193
Merton's measure of market timing,
    279–281
microstructure of securities markets, 287
"mimicking portfolios," 233
mispricing
    defined, 350
    maturity and, 363–364
    path dependence of, 364–367
mispricing series, 353–354
    behavior of, 360–364
missing risk factors, 191

MMP. *See* maximally predictable portfolio
Monte Carlo results, data-snooping biases and, 230–238
monthly returns, evidence for, 166–171
multifactor alternative, risk-based, 198
multifactor models, deviations from Capital Asset Pricing Model and, 189–212

naive forecasts, conditional forecasts versus, 276–278
naive strategies, 191
negative own-autocorrelations, 121
New York Stock Exchange (NYSE), 373
noise traders, 6
noncentrality parameter, 198
nonperiodic cycles, 152, 156
nonrisk-based alternatives, risk-based alternatives versus, 196–208
nonrisk-based category, 189
nonsynchronicity, 85
nonsynchronous trading, 86–87, 117
  econometric analysis of, 85–113
  effects of, 99–100
  extensions and generalizations of model of, 105–107
  lead-lag effects and, 127–130
  model of, 88–95
  specification tests for, 87
  time aggregation in, 95–99
nontrading, 86
  duration of, 89–90, 128
  empirical analysis of, 99–105
  implications for individual returns, 90–93
  implications for portfolio returns, 93–95
  index autocorrelations and, 104–105
  model of, 34–35
  spurious autocorrelation induced by, 34–38
nontrading induced autocorrelation, 91–92
nontrading probabilities, 128–129
  daily, implicit in autocorrelations, 101–104
normal cumulative distribution function, standard, 220
null hypotheses, 47–48
  properties of test statistic under, 55–68
null hypothesis, 217
  heteroskedastic, 52–53, 61–68

independently and identically distributed (IID) Gaussian, 49–51, 55–61
NYSE (New York Stock Exchange), 373

observed portfolio returns, 129–130
October Crash ("Black Monday"), 286, 369–394
OLS parameter estimates, 331
one-factor asset-pricing model, 199, 259–260
optimal orthogonal portfolio, 193
order flow, 288
order-flow dependence, ordered probit model and, 321–322
order imbalances
  measure of, 370, 378–380
  stock price movements and, 369–394
ordered probit analysis, 288–289
  of transaction stock prices, 287–345
ordered probit model, 285, 290–295
  applications of, 320–338
  data for, 295–307
  empirical specification of, 307–310
  generality of, 294
  larger sample for, 338–344
  maximum likelihood estimates for, 310–320
  names, ticker symbols, market values, and sizes for stocks for, 336–338
  order-flow dependence and, 321–322
  sample statistics for, 297–307
overreaction, stock market. *See* stock market overreaction
own-autocorrelations, negative, 121

partition of state space, 290
passive asset-allocation strategy, 281
passive investment, 281
path-dependent price changes, 316
PC1 (first principal-component portfolio), 254–256
percentage price impact, 341
portfolio, 214
  biases of tests based on, 224–228
  maximally predictable. *See* maximally predictable portfolio
  "mimicking," 233
  optimal orthogonal, 193
  predictability of, defining, 257–258
  principal-component, first (PC1), 254–256
  replicating, 348

size-based, results for, 30–32
size-sorted. *See* size-sorted portfolios
    tangency, 193
portfolio aggregation, 225
portfolio returns
    nontrading implications for, 93–95
    observed, 129–130
portfolio strategy, contrarian, 116–117
portfolio theory, 11
portfolio weights of maximally
    predictable portfolio, 271–272
positive cross-autocovariances, 116
post-earnings announcement drift, 186
power, interpreting data-snooping biases
    as, 228–229
predictability in stock prices, 17–18, 284
    genuine, 276
    maximization of, 188, 249–284
    out-of-sample measures of, 276–283
    of portfolio, defining, 257–258
    search for, 249
pretest biases, 213–214, 262
price change coefficients, lagged, 311,
    316
price changes, 3
    histograms of, 300–307
    intraday, 297
    path-dependent, 316
    sequence of, 288
    "virtual," 293
price/earnings ratios, expected returns
    and, 186
price impact, 288, 322
    measuring, per unit volume of trade,
    322–331
price impact measures, 341, 342
price movements, 287
price resolution, 291
price response functions, 326, 330
pricing formula, Black-Scholes, 40
pricing models, linear, 192–193
primary assets, 257
principal-component portfolio, first
    (PC1), 254–256
principal components, 253
probability theory, 3
profitability
    contrarian, analysis of, 121–132
    of return-reversal strategies, 185
profitability index, 123

quantifying data-snooping biases with
    induced order statistics, 215–229

R/S statistic. *See* rescaled range (R/S)
    statistic
random walk hypothesis, 3–5, 47
    mean-reverting alternative to, 38–39
    rejection of, 4, 39
    testing, 13–15
    for weekly returns, 26–33
random walk increments, 48
range over standard deviation statistic.
    See rescaled range (R/S) statistic
"reasonable" fit, 296
"redundant security" view, 357
regression model, "virtual," 289
"regressors," 290
replicating portfolio, 348
rescaled range, Hurst-Mandelbrot, 167
rescaled range (R/S) statistic, 148,
    155–165
analysis for stock market returns, 165–171
    classical, 155
    modified, 158–160
    sample sizes for, 171–174
return-generating process, 116
return-reversal strategies, 135
    profitability of, 185
return reversals, Standard and Poor's
    Composite 500 Index and, 385–387
returns
    expected. *See* expected returns
    fifteen-minute index, 393–394
    individual, nontrading implications
    for, 90–93
    monthly, evidence for, 166–171
    observed portfolio, 129–130
    portfolio. *See* portfolio returns
    serially independent, 124
    stock market, rescaled range (R/S)
    statistic analysis for, 165–171
    time-aggregated, autocorrelation of,
    97–98
    virtual, 86
    weekly. *See* weekly returns
risk, expected returns and, 185
risk aversion coefficient, 200
risk-based alternatives, nonrisk-based
    alternatives versus, 196–208
risk-based multifactor alternative, 198
risk factors, 191
    missing, 191
risk-free rate, 349
risk tolerance, 9

sampling theory, 144–146

SBU (stocks, bonds, and utilities) vector, 262
scientific discoveries, 214
score statistics, 317–318
seasonalities, 186
sector portfolio vector (SECTOR), 262
securities
  grouping, 225
  individual. *See* individual securities
  portfolio of. *See* portfolio
Securities Industry Automation
  Corporation (SIAC), 371
securities markets, microstructure of, 287
seller-initiated trade, 310
selling pressure, 378
"sells," 289
sequence of price changes, 288
serially independent returns, 124
Sharpe-Lintner capital asset pricing
  model. *See* Capital Asset Pricing
  Model
Sharpe measure, 192
  historical, 201
  squared, 195–196
short horizons, long horizons versus,
  140–142
short-range dependence, long-range
  dependence versus, 149–155
shortsales constraint, 271
SIAC (Securities Industry Automation
  Corporation), 371
SIC code classifications, 260
signal-to-noise ratio, 260
size, sorting by, 240–243
size-based portfolios, results for, 30–32
size deciles vector (SIZE), 262
size effect, 185
size-sorted portfolios, 214
  prevalence of, 215–216
sorting
  by beta coefficients, 238–240
  by size, 240–243
S&P 500 Index return (SPR), 261
SPDY interaction term, 261
specification searches, 217, 249
specification tests, 14, 19–26
  for nonsynchronous trading, 87
spectral density function, 151
splits, restricting, 296
SPR (S&P 500 Index return), 261
squared Sharpe measure, 195–196
Standard and Poor's Composite 500
  Index, 370

buying and selling pressure and,
  378–387
comparison of price indexes on, 375
constructing, 373–377
cross-sectional results with, 381–385
crucial role of, 370
dollar volume on, 376
percentage returns on, 377
published, 372–373
return reversals and, 385–387
term, 374
time-series results with, 380–381
standard normal cumulative distribution
  function, 220
state-space partition, 290, 291
stationary AR(1) process, 68, 70–73
statistical arbitrage, 16
statistical inference, 213
statistical model of asset prices, 287
statistics
  data-snooping, 214
  induced order. *See* induced order
    statistics
stochastic behavior of weekly returns, 18
stochastic process, 49
stock index futures, 347
stock index futures prices,
  behavior of arbitrage strategies and,
    348–352
  index-futures arbitrage and, 347–368
stock indexes, forward contracts on, 349
stock market. *See also* market *entries*
stock market overreaction, 116
  consequence of, 116
  empirical appraisal of, 132–140
  equilibrium theory of, 116
  fads and, 124–126
stock market prices. *See also* stock prices
  long-term memory in, 147–184
stock market returns, rescaled range
  (R/S) statistic analysis for, 165–171
stock-price changes, unpredictability of,
  115
stock price movements, order imbalances
  and, 369–394
stock prices, 287. *See also* stock market
  prices
  market perceptions and, 369
  predictability in. *See* predictability in
    stock prices
stocks, bonds, and utilities (SBU) vector,
  262
strong-mixing time series, 149
survivorship bias, 135

tangency portfolio, 193
temporal aggregation biases, 85
thin trading. *See* nonsynchronous trading
tick test, 299
time-aggregated returns, autocorrelation
    of, 97–98
time aggregation in nonsynchronous
    trading, 95–99
time-averages, 85
time elapsed between transactions, 308
time series, 147
    strong-mixing, 149
time series models,
    fractionally-integrated, 152–153
trace operator, 122
trade, measuring price impact per unit
    volume of, 322–331
trade times, endogenous, 319
transaction costs, 348
    break-even, 281, 283
    impact of, 350–352
transaction database, ISSM, 295
transaction prices, 285–286, 287
transaction stock prices, ordered probit
    analysis of, 287–345
"transaction" time, 290
transactions, time elapsed between, 308
transactions costs, 10
transformed dollar volume variable, 310
truncation lags, 167
turn-of-the-month seasonalities, 186

unbiased estimators, 23
unit root process, 48
unpredictability of stock-price changes,
    115

valuation of derivative assets, 348
value index, 201
Value Line enigma, 185
variance
    asymptotic, 21
    maximization of, 255
variance estimator, 22
variance ratio test, 14–16, 49–54
    in finite samples, 47–83
    for large q, 69
    limitation of, 68–69
    power of, 68–81
    two-sided, 68, 73–74
variance ratios, 18–19n
    autocorrelations and, 54
"virtual" price change, 293
"virtual" regression model, 289
virtual returns, 86

weekend seasonalities, 186
weekly returns
    autocorrelation properties of, 118–
        121
    evidence for, 166–171
    random walk hypothesis for, 26–33
    stochastic behavior of, 18
weekly sampling interval, 14
white noise and lead-lag relations,
    trading on, 126–127
white-noise component, 38
white-noise process, 253
Wiener differential, 20

Z random variable, 289
zero-intercept F-test, 192, 197–198